Analyzing Multidimensional Well-Being

Analyzing Multidimensional Well-Being

A Quantitative Approach

Satya R. Chakravarty

WILEY

This edition first published 2018

Registered Offices
John Wiley & Sons, Inc., 111 River Street, Hoboken, NJ 07030, USA

Editorial Office
111 River Street, Hoboken, NJ 07030, USA

For details of our global editorial offices, customer services, and more information about Wiley products visit us at www.wiley.com.

Wiley also publishes its books in a variety of electronic formats and by print-on-demand. Some content that appears in standard print versions of this book may not be available in other formats.

Library of Congress Cataloging-in-Publication Data

Names: Chakravarty, Satya R., author.
Title: Analyzing multidimensional well-being : a quantitative approach / by Satya R. Chakravarty.
Description: Hoboken, NJ : John Wiley & Sons, Inc., 2018. | Includes bibliographical references and index.
Identifiers: LCCN 2017033909 (print) | LCCN 2017019107 (ebook) | ISBN 9781119256908 (cloth) | ISBN 9781119256946 (pdf) | ISBN 9781119256953 (epub)
Subjects: LCSH: Social indicators. | Economic indicators. | Quality of life–Statistical methods. | Well-being–Statistical methods.
Classification: LCC HN25.C449 2017 (ebook) | LCC HN25 (print) | DDC 306–dc23 LC record available at https://lccn.loc.gov/2017033909

Cover design by Wiley
Cover image: © Wasant/Shutterstock

Set in 10/12pt WarnockPro by SPi Global, Chennai, India

Printed in the United States of America

10 9 8 7 6 5 4 3 2 1

In loving memory of my eldest brother Dr. Keshab R. Chakravarty, whose honesty and dedication towards profession have always been an inspiration to me.

Contents

Preface

Since often an income distribution of a society fails to include heterogeneity in the distributions of one or more other dimensions of well-being of a population such as health, education, and housing etc.; income's unsuitability as the solitary attribute of well-being is clearly understandable. In fact, it has now become well-recognized that human prosperity should be treated as a multidimensional aspect. Consequently, there has been a spur among researchers to work on multidimensional economic well-being.

There has been significant development in the areas of multivariate welfare, inequality, and poverty in the recent past, and hence, I felt the need to take the opportunity to delve deeper into the core values of the stated concepts. What is presented in this book is a theory of multidimensional welfare, inequality, and poverty in an axiomatic architecture. The aim is to clarify how we can proceed to the evaluation of the three issues and address the questions of enhancing welfare and reducing inequality and poverty.

The monograph casts ample light on the concepts, and I believe such an elusive discussion will intrigue students, teachers, researchers, and practitioners in the area. Substantive coverage of ongoing and advanced topics and their inquisitive, eloquent, accurate bestowal make the treatise theoretically and methodologically quite concurrent and comprehensive and highly susceptible to the practical problems of recent concern.

Since the use of simple one-dimensional indices for reckoning welfare and inequality of a population or the comparison of similar measurements pertaining to another population is an improper analysis, Chapter 1 looks to assess how well off a society can be in terms of individual achievements in different dimensions. The purpose of Chapter 2 is to review the alternative approaches to the evaluation of multidimensional inequality. Picking up from the note that welfare of a population needs an appraisal from a multivariate perspective, poverty can be regarded as a demonstration of inadequacy of achievements in different dimensions of wellbeing. Hence, Chapters 3 attempts to present an analytical discussion on the axiomatic approach to the measurement of multidimensional poverty.

There might arise a problem of gathering sufficient information on achievements in different dimensions of well-being, thereby raising questions at the poverty status of an individual. To tackle this ambiguity, fuzzy set theory can be employed to handle the vagueness resulting from obscurity. This fuzzy set approach to multidimensional poverty judgment has been addressed in Chapter 4.

In the persuasive investigations made in Chapters 3 and 4, which are based on the individual multidimensional achievements as inputs in a single period, time span of poverty is ignored. Nevertheless, there are plentiful reasons to believe that poverty is not a timeless concept. It can be regarded as a concept that endures changes over time. Furthermore, it would be wrong to expect that the transformations of income and nonincome dimensions of life will be the same across time. In view of this, Chapter 5 throws light on the different approaches that scrutinize lifetime poverty in a multidimensional framework.

Vulnerability and security risks always go hand in hand. In a wide sense, we can define vulnerability in terms of a system's disclosure and capability to cope sufficiently with discomfort. The study of vulnerability is hence quite significant because of the highly important follow-ups that may be generated as its implications for economic efficiency and long-term individual welfare. The purpose of Chapter 6 is deliberation of vulnerability as a multidimensional issue.

Finally, Chapter 7 reflects on the practicality of some composite and individualistic indices. A composite index is a summary measure, giving an all-inclusive picture of dimensional indices, associated with a dashboard. In the individualistic approach, individualwise indicators are derived initially by combining respective dimensional achievements and then by amalgamating the individual-level indicators.

At Paris School of Economics, I have had the excellent opportunity of working together with François Bourguignon, and I learned a great deal from talking with him. His influence has come not only through extensive discussions during the period but also through the use I made of the analytical framework in my later works that we developed. It is difficult for me to express my gratitude to him in words.

I have also worked jointly in this expanding area with Sabina Alkire, Mauricio Apablaza, Walter Bossert, Lidia Ceriani, Nachiketa Chattopadhyay, Conchita D'Ambrosio, Joseph Deutsch, Maria Ana Lugo, Diganta Mukherjee, Zoya Nissanov, Liu Qingbin, Ravi Ranade, Jacques Silber, Guanghua Wan, Gaston Yalonetzky, and Claudio Zoli. I have been very fortunate in having them as coauthors with whom I have had very illuminating conversations. I must acknowledge my extensive debt to them.

During the years, I have been privileged to receive comments and suggestions from Rolf Aaberge, Matthew D. Adler, Tony Atkinson, Valérie Berenger, Charles Blackorby, Kristof Bosmans, Florent Bresson, Koen Decancq, Stefan Dercon, David Donaldson, Jean-Yves Duclos, Indranil Dutta, Marc Fleurbaey,

James E. Foster, Mridu P. Goswami, Carlos Gradin, Nanak C. Kakwani, Serge-Christophe Kolm, Casilda Lasso de la Vega, François Maniquet, Ajit Mishra, Patrick Moyes, Conan Mukherjee, Erwin Ooghe, Rupayan Pal, Eugenio Peluso, Iñaki Permanyer, Krishna Pendakur, Martin Ravallion, Ernesto Savaglio, Amartya K. Sen, John A. Weymark, and Buhong Zheng. I would like to acknowledge the benefit I received from the interactions with them.

I benefitted a lot from the critiques of my students at the Bocconi University, Milan, Italy; Indian Statistical Institute, Kolkata, India; and Indira Gandhi Institute of Development Research, Mumbai, India. I am grateful to them for the joys and benefits that I derived from interactive teaching. The figure files were generated by Nandish Chattopadhyay and Snigdha Chatterjee sat through some sessions of proof corrections. It is a pleasure for me to acknowledge the help I received from them.

I must note the help and advice I have received from my wife Sumita and son Ananyo, whose influence is reflected throughout the book.

The book has been dedicated to the memory of my eldest brother Keshab R. Chakravarty, a renowned cardiologist, who has started his after-life journey on 1 August 2016 at 7.43 pm.

Kolkata *Satya R. Chakravarty*

Endorsements

1) "Analyzing Multidimensional Well-Being" by Satya Chakravarty provides a comprehensive review of a burgeoning new area of welfare economics and elaborates further on the way key unidimensional welfare concepts can be extended to the multidimensional case. An indispensable reference for all researchers interested in the measurement of social welfare and who feel the monetary focus is unduly restrictive.
   François Bourguignon, Emeritus Professor at Paris School of Economics, Former Chief Economist of the World Bank.
2) It has become the norm in the profession to define and measure well-being as a multidimensional concept instead of relying on income only. In his monograph, Satya Chakravarty provides us with a detailed, insightful, and pedagogical presentation of the theoretical grounds of multidimensional well-being, inequality, and poverty measurement. Any student, researcher, and practitioner interested in the multidimensional approach should begin their journey into such a fascinating theme with this wonderful book.
   François Maniquet, Professor, Catholic University of Louvain, Belgium.
3) This book starts from the premise that income cannot be the only indicator on which the measurement of well-being should be based. Other dimensions of well-being need to be taken into account, such as health, education, and housing. The implication of such a "Weltanschauung" is that well-being is a multidimensional phenomenon. But how should we then measure it? Satya Chakravarty, who has made fundamental contributions to this domain, gives us here a systematic presentation of the issues related to the measurement of multidimensional inequality, multidimensional poverty (with separate chapters on the fuzzy approach to poverty and poverty and time), multidimensional vulnerability, and composite indices such as the Human Development Index. In each chapter, the axioms underlying the various indices are clearly explained and the indices derived are well interpreted. In short, this is a remarkably rigorous and enlightening book

that should be required reading for anyone, researcher or graduate student, desiring to learn more about multidimensional well-being.
Jacques Silber, Emeritus Professor, Bar-Ilan University, Israel.

4) In response to the limitations of GDP as a measure of societal well-being, new indices such as the UN's Human Development Index and the OECD's Better Life Index have been developed to better capture the multidimensional nature of well-being. Chakravarty provides an accessible and lucid introduction to the theoretical literature on the multidimensional measurement of inequality, poverty, and well-being, with a particular focus on the indices that have been proposed and their axiomatic foundations. This volume is recommended to both academics and practitioners who want a state-of-the art survey of these measurement issues.
John A. Weymark, Gertrude Conaway Vanderbilt Professor of Economics and Professor of Philosophy, Vanderbilt University.

1

Well-Being as a Multidimensional Phenomenon

1.1 Introduction

The choice of income as the only attribute or dimension of well-being of a population is inappropriate since it ignores heterogeneity across individuals in many other dimensions of living conditions. Each dimension represents a particular aspect of life about which people care. Examples of such dimensions include health, literacy, and housing. A person's achievement in a dimension indicates the extent of his performance in the dimension, for instance, how healthy he is, how friendly he is, how much is his monthly income, and so on.

Only income-dependent well-being quantifiers assume that individuals with the same level of income are regarded as equally well-off irrespective of their positions in such nonincome dimensions. In their report, prepared for the Commission on the Measurement of Economic Performance and Social Progress, constituted under a French Government initiative, Stiglitz et al. (2009, p. 14) wrote "To define what wellbeing means, a multidimensional definition has to be used. Based on academic research and a number of concrete initiatives developed around the world, the Commission has identified the following key dimensions that should be taken into account. At least in principle, these dimensions should be considered simultaneously: (i) Material living standards (income, consumption and wealth); (ii) Health; (iii) Education; (iv) Personal activities including work; (v) Political voice and governance; (vi) Social connections and relationships; (vii) Environment (present and future conditions); (viii) Insecurity, of an economic as well as a physical nature. All these dimensions shape people's wellbeing, and yet many of them are missed by conventional income measures."

The need for analysis of well-being from multidimensional perspectives has also been argued in many contributions to the literature, including those of Rawls (1971); Kolm (1977); Townsend (1979); Streeten (1981); Atkinson and Bourguignon (1982); Sen (1985); Stewart (1985); Doyal and Gough (1991); Ramsay (1992); Tsui (1995); Cummins (1996); Ravallion (1996); Brandolini and D'Alessio (1998); Narayan (2000); Nussbaum (2000); Osberg and Sharpe

Analyzing Multidimensional Well-Being: A Quantitative Approach, First Edition. Satya R. Chakravarty.

(2002); Atkinson (2003); Bourguignon and Chakravarty (2003); Savaglio (2006a,b); Weymark (2006); Thorbecke (2008), Lasso de la Vega et al. (2009), Fleurbaey and Blanchet (2013); Aaberge and Brandolini (2015), Alkire et al. (2015); Duclos and Tiberti (2016).[1]

Nonmonetary dimensions of well-being are not unambiguously perfectly correlated with income. Consider a situation where, in some municipality of a developing country, there is a suboptimal supply of a local public good, say, mosquito control program. A person with a high income may not be able to trade off his income to improve his position in this nonmarketed, nonincome dimension of well-being (see Chakravarty and Lugo, 2016 and Decancq and Schokkaert, 2016).

In the capability-functioning approach, the notion of human well-being is intrinsically multidimensional (Sen, 1985, 1992; Sen and Nussbaum, 1993; Nussbaum, 2000; Pogge, 2002; Robeyns, 2009). Following John Stuart Mill, Adam Smith, and Aristotle, in the last 30 years or so, it has been reinterpreted and popularized by Sen in a series of contributions. In this approach, the traditional notions of commodity and utility are replaced respectively with functioning and capability.

Any kind of activity done or a state acquired by a person and a characteristic related to full description of the person can be regarded as a functioning. Examples include being well nourished, being healthy, being educated, and interaction with friends. Such a list can be formally represented by a vector of functionings. Capability may be defined as a set of functioning vectors that the person could have achieved.

It is possible to make a distinction between a good and functioning on the basis of operational difference. Of two persons, each owning a bicycle, the one who is physically handicapped cannot use the bike to go to the workplace as fast as the other person can. The bicycle is a good, but possessing the skill to ride it as per convenience is a functioning. This indicates that a functioning can be enacted by a good, but they are distinct concepts. Consequently, these two persons, each owning a bicycle, are not able to attain the same functioning (see Basu and López-Calva, 2011). Since the physically handicapped person, who lacks sufficient freedom to ride the bike as per desire, has a smaller capability set than the other person.

As Sen argued in several contributions, there is a clear distinction between starvation and fasting. Two persons may be in the same nutritional state, but one person fasting on some religious ground, say, is better off than the other person who is starving because he is poor. Since the former person has the freedom not to starve, his capability set is larger than that of the poor person

---

1 See also Clark (2016), Decancq and Neumann (2016), and Graham (2016). A recent overview of some of the related issues is available in Decancq et al. (2015).

(see also Fleurbaey, 2006a). Consequently, capabilities become closely related to freedom, opportunity, and favorable circumstances.[2]

Once the identification step, the selection of dimensions for determining human well-being, is over, at the next stage, we face the aggregation problem. The second step involves the construction of a comprehensive measure of well-being by aggregating the dimensional attainments of all individuals in the society. One simple approach can be dimension-by-dimension evaluation, resulting in a dashboard of dimensional metrics. A dashboard is a portfolio of dimension-wise well-being indictors (see Atkinson et al., 2002).[3] A dashboard can be employed to monitor each dimension in separation. But the dashboard approach has some disadvantages as well. In the words of Stiglitz et al. (2009, p. 63), "dashboards suffer because of their heterogeneity, at least in the case of very large and eclectic ones, and most lack indications about...hierarchies among the indicators used. Furthermore, as communications instruments, one frequent criticism is that they lack what has made GDP a success: the powerful attraction of a single headline figure that allows simple comparisons of socio-economic performance over time or across countries." The problem of heterogeneity across dimensional metrics can be taken care of by aggregating the dashboard-based measures into a composite index. The main disadvantage of this aggregation criterion is that it completely ignores relationships across dimensions. An alternative way to proceed toward building an all-inclusive measure of well-being is by clustering dimensional achievements across persons in terms of a real number. (See Ravallion, 2011, 2012, for a systematic comparison.)

The objective of this chapter is to evaluate how well a society is doing with respect to achievements of all the individuals in different dimensions. This is done using a social welfare function, which informs how well the society is doing when the distributions of dimensional achievements across different persons are considered. A social welfare function is regarded as a fundamental instrument in theoretical welfare economics. It has many policy-related applications. Examples include targeted equitable redistribution of income, assessment of environmental change, evaluation of health policy, cost–benefit analysis of a desired change, optimal provision of a public good, promoting goodness for future generations, assessment of legal affairs, and targeted poverty evaluation (see, among others, Balckorby et al., 2005; Adler, 2012, 2016; Boadway, 2016; Broome, 2016, and Weymark, 2016).

In order to make the chapter self-contained, in the next section, there will be a brief survey of univariate welfare measurement. Section 1.3 addresses the measurability problem of dimensional achievements. In other words, this

2 See also Qizilbash et al. (2006), Elson et al. (2011), Alkire (2016), and Krishnakumar (2007).

3 See also Slottje et al. (1991), Hicks (1997), Easterlin (2000), Hobijn and Franses (2001), Neumayer (2003), World Bank (2006), and United Nations Development Program (2005, 2010).

section clearly investigates how achievements in different dimensions can be measured. Some basics for multivariate analysis of welfare are presented in Section 1.4. The concern of Section 1.5 is the dashboard approach to the evaluation of well-being. There will be a detailed scrutiny of alternative techniques for setting weights to individual dimensional metrics. In Section 1.6, there will be an analytical discussion on axioms for a multivariate welfare function. Each axiom is a representation of a property of a welfare measure that can be defended on its own merits. Often, axioms become helpful in narrowing down the choice of welfare measures. Section 1.7 studies welfare functions, including their information requirements, which have been proposed in the literature to assess multivariate distributions of well-being. Finally, Section 1.8 concludes the discussion.

1.2 Income as a Dimension of Well-Being and Some Related Aggregations

The measurement of multidimensional welfare originates from its univariate counterpart. In consequence, a short analytical treatment of one-dimensional welfare measurement at the outset will prepare the stage for our expositions in the following sections.

It is assumed before all else that no ambiguity arises with respect to definitions and related issues of the primary elements of the analysis. For instance, should the variable on which the analysis relies be income or expenditure? How is expenditure defined? What should be the reference period of observation of incomes/expenditure? How is the threshold income that represents a minimal standard of living determined (see Chapter 2)[4]? Generally, income data are collected at the household level. Income at the individual level can be obtained from the household income by employing an appropriate equivalence scale. (See Lewbel and Pendakur, 2008, for an excellent discussion on equivalence scale.) For simplicity of exposition, we assume that the unit of analysis is "individual." If necessary, the study can be carried out at the household level.

For a population of size n, we denote an income distribution by a vector $u = (u_1, u_2, \dots, u_n) \in \mathfrak{R}^n_{++}$, where $\mathfrak{R}^n_{++}$ is the nonnegative part $\mathfrak{R}^n_{+}$ of the n-dimensional Euclidean space $\mathfrak{R}^n$ with the origin deleted. More precisely, $\mathfrak{R}^n_{++} = \mathfrak{R}^n_{+}/\{0.1^n\}$, where 1^n is the n-coordinated vector of 1s. Here u_i stands for the income of individual i in the population. Let D^n be the positive part of $\mathfrak{R}^n_{++}$ so that $D^n = \{u \in \mathfrak{R}^n_{++} | u_i > 0 \text{ for all } i \in \{1, 2, \dots, n\}\}$. In consequence,

4 For discussion, see, among others, Anand (1983), Deaton (1992, 1997), Ravallion (1994, 1996, 2008), Deaton and Grosh (2000), World Bank (2000), Hentschel and Lanjouw (2000), Klugman (2002), Grusky and Kanbur (2006), Jenkins and Micklewright (2007), Haughton and Khandker (2009), Banerjee and Duflo (2011), Foster et al. (2013a,b), and Alkire et al. (2015).

the sets of all possible income distributions associated with $\Re^n_{++}$ and D^n become respectively $\Re_{++} = \underset{n \in N}{\cup} \Re^n_{++}$ and $D = \underset{n \in N}{\cup} D^n$, where N is a set of positive integers.

Unless stated, it will be assumed that $\Re_{++}$ represents the set of all possible income distributions. For the purpose at hand, we need to introduce some more notation. For all $n \in N$, for all $u \in \Re^n_{++}$, $\lambda(u)$ (or, simply λ) is the mean of u, $\frac{1}{n}\sum_{i=1}^{n} u_i$. For all $n \in N$, $u \in \Re^n_{++}$, let u^0 denote the nonincreasingly ordered permutation of u, that is, $u_1^0 \geq u_2^0 \geq \cdots \geq u_n^0$. Similarly, we write $\tilde{u}$ for the nondecreasingly ordered permutation of u, that is, $\tilde{u}_1 \leq \tilde{u}_2 \leq \cdots \leq \tilde{u}_n$. For all $n \in N$, for all $u, u' \in \Re^n_{++}$, we write $u \geq u'$ to mean that $u_i \geq u_i'$ for all $i \in \{1, 2, \ldots, n\}$ and $u \neq u'$. Hence, $u \geq u'$ means that at least one income in u is greater than the corresponding income in u' and no income in u is less than that in u'. The notation $u > u'$ will be used to mean that $u_i > u_i'$ for all $i \in \{1, 2, \ldots, n\}$.

An income-distribution-based social welfare function is a summary measure of the extent of well-being enjoyed by the individuals in a society, resulting from the spread of a given size of income among the individuals of the society. We denote this function by W. Formally, $W : \Re_{++} \to \Re^1_+$. For any $n \in N$, $u \in \Re^n_{++}$, $W(u)$ signifies the extent of welfare manifested by u. It is assumed beforehand that W is continuous so that small changes in incomes will change welfare only marginally. Since it determines the standard of welfare, we can also refer to as a welfare standard.

Next, we state certain desirable axioms for W. The terms "axiom" and "postulate" will be used interchangeably because they are assumed without proof. Each axiom represents a particular value judgment, and it may not be verifiable by factual evidence. We will as well use the terms "property" and "principle" in place of axiom. Implicit under the choice of a welfare function W is also acceptance of the axioms that are verified by W. Rawls (1971, p. 80) refers to the choice of a form W as the index problem. Since our study of their multidimensional dittos will be extensive, here our discussion will be brief.

Symmetry: For all $n \in N$, $u \in \Re^n_{++}$, $W(u) = W(\overline{u})$, where $\overline{u}$ is any reordering of u.

According to this postulate, welfare evaluation of the society remains unaffected if any two individuals swap their positions in the distribution. Equivalently, any feature other than income has no role in welfare assessment.

Symmetry Axiom for Population: For all $n \in N$, $u \in \Re^n_{++}$, $W(u) = W(u^k)$, where $u^k \in \Re^{nk}_{++}$ is the income vector in which each u_i is repeated k times, $k \geq 2$ being any positive integer.

This property, introduced by Dalton (1920), requires W to be expressed in terms of an average of the population size so that welfare judgment remains unchanged when the same population is pooled several times. It demonstrates neutrality property of the welfare standard W with respect to population size, indicating invariance of the standard under replications of the population. Consequently, the postulate becomes useful in performing comparisons of welfare across societies and of the same society over time, where the underlying population sizes are likely to differ.[5]

Increasingness: For all $n \in N$, for all $u, u' \in \Re^n_{++}$, if $u \geq u'$, then $W(u) > W(u')$.

This property claims that if at least one person's income registers an increase, then the society moves to a better welfare position. An increasing welfare function indicates preferences for higher incomes; more income is preferred to less.

The final property we wish to introduce represents equity biasness of the welfare standard. Equity orientation in welfare evaluation can be materialized through a progressive transfer, an equitable redistribution of income. Formally, for all $n \in N/\{1\}, u, u' \in \Re^n_{++,}$ we say that u is obtained from u' by a progressive transfer if for some i, j and $c > 0$ $u_i = u'_i + c \leq u_j$, $u_j = u'_j - c$, and $u_k = u'_k$ for all $k \neq i, j$. That is, u is obtained from u' by a transfer of c units of income from a person j to a person i who has lower income than j such that the transfer does not make j poorer than i and incomes of all other persons remain unaffected. Equivalently, we say that u' is obtained from u by a regressive transfer.

Pigou–Dalton Transfer: For all $n \in N/\{1\}$, for all $u, u' \in \Re^n_{++}$, if, u is obtained from u' by a progressive transfer, then $W(u) > W(u)$.

In words, welfare should increase under a progressive transfer.[6] The Pigou–Dalton transfer principle, despite its limitations, is easy to understand and becomes equivalent to several seemingly unrelated conditions. Our multidimensional dominance properties that require welfare to rise when equitable redistributions occur bear similarities with these conditions. Consequently, a discussion on these conditions becomes justifiable.

Use of a numerical example will probably make the situation clearer. Consider the ordered income vectors $u^2 = (2, 3, 4)$ and $u^1 = (1, 3, 5)$. Of these two ordered profiles, the former is obtained from the latter by a progressive

---

5 The term Symmetry Axiom for Population was suggested in Dasgupta et al. (1973), where overall welfare has been defined as a total concept, and replication invariance of the average welfare, overall welfare divided by the population size, was sought. Evidently, the two formulations convey the same information.

6 A limitation of a Pigou–Dalton transfer is that its size is independent of the incomes of the two affected persons. Fleurbaey and Michel (2001) suggested a proportional transfer principle where the transfer size is proportional to the incomes of the affected persons (see also Fleurbaey, 2006a). In this "leaky-bucket" transfer, the recipient receives less than what the donor transfers. A progressive transfer also disregards incomes of the persons who are richer and poorer than the donor and the recipient, respectively. For discussions on other limitations and variants of the Pigou–Dalton transfer principle, see Châteauneuf and Moyes (2006) and Chakravarty (2009, Chapter 3).

transfer of 1 unit of income from the richest person to the poorest person. This transfer does not alter the rank orders of the individuals. That is why it is a rank-preserving progressive transfer. Equivalently, we can generate u^2 by postmultiplying u^1 by some 3×3 bistochastic matrix.[7] If we denote this bistochastic matrix by B, then

$$(2,3,4) = (1,3,5)\ B = (1,3,5)\begin{pmatrix} \frac{3}{4} & 0 & \frac{1}{4} \\ 0 & 1 & 0 \\ \frac{1}{4} & 0 & \frac{3}{4} \end{pmatrix}. \tag{1.1}$$

An alternative equivalent condition for executing the redistributive operation that takes us from u^1 to u^2 is to postmultiply the former by some $n \times n$ Pigou–Dalton matrix.[8] To see this more concretely, denote the underlying Pigou–Dalton matrix by T. Then

$$(2,3,4) = (1,3,5)\ T = (1,3,5)\left[\frac{3}{4}\begin{pmatrix} 1 & 0 & 0 \\ 0 & 1 & 0 \\ 0 & 0 & 1 \end{pmatrix} + \frac{1}{4}\begin{pmatrix} 0 & 0 & 1 \\ 0 & 1 & 0 \\ 1 & 0 & 0 \end{pmatrix}\right]. \tag{1.2}$$

The particular Pigou–Dalton matrix T in (1.2) is the sum of $\frac{3}{4}$ times the 3×3 identity matrix and $\frac{1}{4}$ times a 3×3 permutation matrix obtained by swapping the first and third entries in the first and third rows, respectively, of the identity matrix.

A graphical equivalence of the aforementioned three interchangeable statements is that u^2 Lorenz dominates u^1, which means that the Lorenz curve of the former in no place lies below that of the latter and lies above in some places (at least).[9] In terms of welfare ranking, this is the same as the requirement that $W(u^2) > W(u^1)$, where W is any arbitrary strictly S-concave social welfare function.[10]

---

7 An $n \times n$ nonnegative matrix is called a bistochastic matrix of order n if the entries in each of its rows and columns add up to 1. An $n \times n$ bistochastic matrix is called a permutation matrix if it has exactly one positive entry in each row and column.

8 A Pigou–Dalton matrix is known as a strict T-transformation in the literature. A strict T-transformation, a linear transformation defined by an $n \times n$ matrix T, is a weighted average of the $n \times n$ identity matrix and an $n \times n$ permutation matrix that just interchanges two coordinates, where the positive weights add up to 1. An $n \times n$ identity matrix is an $n \times n$ matrix whose diagonal entries are 1 and off-diagonal entries are 0 (see Marshall et al., 2011, p. 32).

9 The Lorenz curve of a nondecreasingly ordered income distribution is the graph of the cumulative proportion of the total income possessed by the bottom t proportion of the population, where t varies from 0 to 1 so that 0% of the population owns 0% of the total income and 100% of the population obtains the entire income. For an unordered or nonincreasingly ordered distribution, incomes have to be ordered nondecreasingly, and then the curve can be drawn. Upon multiplication by the mean income, the Lorenz curve of an income distribution becomes its generalized Lorenz curve.

10 A social welfare function $W: \Re_{++} \to \Re^1_+$ is called S-concave if for all $n \in N$, $u \in \Re^n_{++}$, and all $n \times n$ bistochastic matrices B, $W(uB) \geq W(u)$. W is called strictly S-concave, if the weak

We now review three well-known examples of univariate social welfare functions. Since multidimensional translations of these functions will be explored in detail in one of the following sections, this brief study becomes rewarding. The first example we wish to scrutinize is the symmetric mean of order $\theta(< 1)$, which for any $x \in D^n$ and $n \in N$ is defined as

$$W_A^\theta(u) = \begin{cases} \left(\frac{1}{n}\sum_{i=1}^{n} u_i^\theta\right)^{\frac{1}{\theta}}, & \theta < 1, \ \theta \neq 0, \\ \prod_{i=1}^{n} (u_i)^{\frac{1}{n}}, & \theta = 0. \end{cases} \tag{1.3}$$

Since W_A^θ is undefined for $\theta < 0$ if at least one income is nonpositive, D^n is chosen as its domain. The superscript θ in W_A^θ signifies sensitivity of the parameter θ to $W_{A,}^\theta$ and the subscript A is used to indicate that it corresponds to the Atkinson (1970) inequality index (see Chapter 2). For any $\theta \neq 0$, the aggregation process invoked in W_A^θ is as follows. First, all incomes are transformed by taking their θth power. The transformation, defined by $\left(\frac{1}{\theta}\right)$ th power of a positive real number, employed on the average $\left(\frac{1}{n}\sum_{i=1}^{n} u_i^\theta\right)$ gives us W_A^θ. This continuous, increasing, symmetric, and population-size-invariant welfare function demonstrates equity orientation (satisfaction of strict S-concavity) if and only if $\theta < 1$. Adler (2012) suggested the use of this welfare standard for moral assessment of decisions that have significant social implications.

For any income profile, an increase in the value of θ increases welfare. The reason behind this is that as the value of θ decreases, higher weights are assigned to lower incomes in the aggregation. Since the assignment of higher weights to lower income holds for all $\theta < 1$, a progressive income transfer will increase welfare by a larger amount, the lower the income of the recipient is. For $\theta = -1$, W_A^θ becomes the harmonic mean. It reduces to the geometric mean if $\theta = 0$. As $\theta \to -\infty$, W_A^θ approaches $\min_i\{u_i\}$, the maximin welfare function (Rawls, 1971), a welfare standard that prioritize the worst-off individual. In other words, in this case, welfare ranking is decided by the income of the worst-off individual.

The second welfare function we choose is the Donaldson and Weymark (1980) well-known S-Gini welfare function, which for any $u \in \mathfrak{R}_{++}^n$ and $n \in N$ is defined as

$$W_{DW}^\rho(u) = \frac{1}{n^\rho}\sum_{i=-1}^{n} [i^\rho - (i-1)^\rho]u_i^0. \tag{1.4}$$

inequality is replaced by a strict inequality whenever uB is not a reordering of u. For formal statements on equivalence between these conditions, see Dasgupta et al. (1973) and Marshall et al. (2011, p. 35). All S-concave functions are symmetric.

Given that incomes are nonincreasingly arranged, increasingness of the weight sequence $\{i^\rho - (i-1)^\rho\}$, where $\rho > 1$, ensures strict S-concavity (hence symmetry) of W^ρ_{DW}. This continuous, increasing, and population-size-invariant welfare function possesses a simple disaggregation property. If each income is broken down into two components, say, salary income and interest income, and the ranks of the individuals in the two distributions are the same, then overall welfare is simply the sum of welfares from two component distributions (see Weymark, 1981). A higher value of ρ makes welfare standard more sensitive to lower incomes within a distribution. When the single parameter ρ increases unboundedly, W^ρ_{DW} converges toward the maximin function. For $\rho = 2$, W^ρ_{DW} becomes the one-dimensional Gini welfare function $W_G(u) = \frac{1}{n^2}\sum_{i=-1}^{n}[i^2 - (i-1)^2]\,u_i^0$, a weighted average of rank-ordered incomes, where the weights themselves are rank-dependent. It is also popularly known as the Gini mean (Fleurbaey and Maniquet, 2011). Foster et al. (2013a,b) refer to this as the Sen mean.[11] It can alternatively be written as the expected value of the minimum of two randomly drawn incomes, where the random drawing is done with replacement. More precisely, $W_G(u) = \frac{1}{n^2}\sum_{i=1}^{n}\sum_{j=1}^{n}\min(u_i, u_j)$. From this formulation of the Gini mean, it is evident that for any unequal $u \in \Re^n_{++}$, it is less than the ordinary mean $\lambda(u)$.

Pollak (1971) analyzed the family of exponential additive welfare functions, of which a simple symmetric representation is $W^\nu_P(u) = -\sum_{i=-1}^{n}\exp(-\nu u_i)$, where $u \in \Re^n_+$ and $n \in N$ are arbitrary; $\nu > 0$ is a parameter; and "exp" stands for the exponential function. This sign restriction on $\nu > 0$ ensures that W^ν_P is increasing and strictly S-concave. It indicates sensitivity to lower incomes in the population. This welfare standard fails to satisfy a common property of W^θ_A and W^ρ_{DW}; if incomes are equal across individuals, welfare is judged by the equal income itself. However, the following function

$$W^\nu_{KP}(u) = -\frac{1}{\nu}\log\left(\frac{1}{n}\sum_{i=1}^{n}\exp(-\nu u_i)\right), \tag{1.5}$$

analyzed by Kolm (1976), which is related to W^ν_P via the continuous, increasing transformation $W^\nu_{KP}(u) = -\frac{1}{\nu}\log\left(-\frac{1}{n}W^\nu_P(u)\right)$, fulfills this criterion. Consequently, they will rank two income vectors over the same population in the same way. This transformation also makes W^ν_{KP} fulfill the symmetry postulate for population and preserves strict S-concavity (hence, symmetry) of W^ν_P.

11 Its first welfare theoretic axiomatic characterization was developed by Sen (1974). The characterization specifies a set of axioms for a social welfare function, which hold simultaneously if and only if the welfare function is the Sen mean. In other words, the axioms uniquely identify the Sen mean in a specific framework.

As v is increased limitlessly, W_{KP}^{v} becomes closer and closer to the maximin function.

We conclude this section by noting that while W_{A}^{θ} is linear homogeneous, W_{KP}^{v} is unit translatable. According to linear homogeneity, an equiproportionate variation in all incomes will change welfare by the same proportion. In contrast, unit translatability claims that an equal absolute change in all incomes will change welfare by the absolute amount itself.[12] An example of a linear homogeneous and unit translatable welfare function is W_{DW}^{ρ}.

1.3 Scales of Measurement: A Brief Exposition

Measurement scales specify the ways in which we can classify the variables. For each class of variables, some relevant operations can be executed so that the transmissions do not generate any loss of information (Stevens, 1946).

To grasp the issue in greater detail, suppose that w, a person's weight, is measured in kilograms. By multiplying w by 1000, we can alternatively express this weight as $w' = 1000w$ grams. This process of conversion of weight from kilograms to grams, by multiplying by the ratio $\frac{w'}{w}$, which does not lead to any loss of information on the person's weight, is admitted by indicators of ratio scale. Formally, an indicator l is said to measurable on ratio scale if there is perfect substitutability between its value v_l and cv_l, where $c > 0$ is a constant. For ratio-scale indicators, there is a natural "zero"; 0 weight means "no weight," whether it is expressed in kilograms or grams. A second example of a ratio-scale dimension is height.

An interval scale refers to a measurement in which the difference between two values can be meaningfully compared. To understand this, consider the vector of temperatures $t_C = (10, 20, 30, 40)$ expressed in degree centigrade. These temperatures can equivalently be specified in degree Fahrenheit as $t_F = (50, 68, 86, 104)$. The difference between the temperatures 20 and 10 degrees is the same as that between 40 and 30 in t_C. Similarly, there is a common difference between 68 and 50 and between 104 and 86 in t_F. The two common differences are different because the temperatures in Centigrade (C) and Fahrenheit scales (F) are connected by the one-to-one transformation $\frac{C}{5} = \frac{(F-32)}{9}$. But a temperature of 30 °C cannot be regarded as thrice as that of 10 °C. However, for a ratio-scale variable, this is meaningful. Further, there is no natural "zero" in interval scale. A 0 degree temperature does not indicate absence of heat, irrespective of whether it is stated in Centigrade or in Fahrenheit. More generally, an indicator l is said to be measurable on interval scale if its value v_l can be perfectly substituted by $a + bv_l$, where $b > 0$ and a

12 Formally, $W : \mathfrak{R}_{++} \to \mathfrak{R}_{+}^{1}$ is called linear homogeneous if for all $n \in N$, $u \in \mathfrak{R}_{++}^{n}$, $W(cu) = cW(u)$ for all scalars $c > 0$. Unit translatability of W requires that $W(u + c1^n) = W(u) + c$, where c is a scalar such that $(u + c1^n) \in \mathfrak{R}_{++}^{n}$.

are constants. A transformation of this type is called an affine transformation. A second example of an interval-scale indicator is intelligent quotient score. Variables measurable on ratio and interval scales exhaust the class of cardinally measurable variables.

A variable representing two or more mutually exclusive but not ranked categories is known as a categorical or a nominal variable. For example, we can identify female and male workers in an organization as type I and type II categories of workers. But we can as well label male workers as type I and female workers as type II workers. More precisely, there is well-defined division of the categories. Another example of a categorical variable can be labeling of subgroups of population formed by some socioeconomic characteristic, say, race, region, and religion. In contrast, for an ordinally significant variable, there is a well-defined ordering rule of the categories. For instance, we can classify individuals in a society with respect to their educational attainments into five categories: illiterate, having knowledge just to read and write in some language, elementary school graduate, high school graduate, and college graduate. We can assign the numbers 0, 1, 2, 3, and 4 to these levels of educational attainments to rank them in increasing order. Here the difference between 1 and 0 is not the same as that between 3 and 2. We can alternatively rank these categories using the numbers 0, 1, 4, 9, and 16. These numbers are obtained by squaring the previously assigned numbers 0, 1, 2, 3, and 4. Consequently, accreditation of numbers is arbitrary; the only restriction is that a higher number should be attributed to a higher category so that ranking remains preserved. Hence, the category "college graduate" should always be assigned a higher number compared to the category "high school graduate." More generally, a transformation of the type $v_l' = f(v_l)$, where f is increasing, will keep ordering of transformed values v_l's of initial numbers v_ls of the variable l unaltered. Hence, any increasing function f can be regarded as an admissible transformation here. A second example of a variable with ordinal significance is "self-reported health condition," judged in terms of some health level categories, ranked in increasing order of better conditions. (See, for example, Allison and Foster (2004).) Such variables are also known as qualitative variables.[13]

1.4 Preliminaries for Multidimensional Welfare Analysis

Before we discuss the relevance of our presentation in the earlier section in the present context, let us introduce some preliminaries. We consider a

13 See, among others, Chakravarty and D'Ambrosio (2006), Jayraj and Subramanian (2009), Lasso de la Vega (2010), Aaberge and Peluso (2011), Chakravarty and Zoli (2012), Bossert et al. (2013), Aaberge and Brandolini (2014), and Alkire et al. (2015) for discussions on measurability of some socioeconomic variables that are relevant for our purpose.

society consisting of $n \in N$ individuals. Assume that there are d dimensions of well-being. The set of well-being dimensions $\{1, 2, \ldots, d\}$ is denoted by Q. The number of dimensions d is assumed to be exogenously given. Let $x_{ij} \geq 0$ stand for person i's achievement in dimension j. It is assumed at the beginning that we have complete information on these primary elements of analysis. (For social evaluations based on individuals' consumption patterns, see Jorgenson and Slesnick, 1984.)

Since $i \in \{1, 2, \ldots, n\}$ and $j \in Q$ are arbitrary, distribution of dimensional achievements in the population is represented by an $n \times d$ achievement matrix X whose (i, j)th entry is x_{ij}. The jth column of X, denoted by $x_{.j}$, shows the distribution of the total achievement $\sum_{i=1}^{n} x_{ij}$ in dimension j across n individuals. For any $j \in Q$, $\lambda(x_{.j})$ stands for the mean of the distribution $x_{.j}$. The ith row of X, denoted by $x_{i.}$, is an array of person i's achievements in different dimensions. We say that $x_{i.}$ represents person i's achievement profile in X. We will often use the terms "social matrix," "distribution matrix," and "social distribution" for an achievement matrix.

The matrix X is an arbitrary element of the set M_1^n, the set of all $n \times d$ achievement matrices with nonnegative achievements in each dimension. Let $M_2^n = \{X \in M_1^n | \lambda(x_{.j}) > 0 \quad \text{for all } j \in Q\}$. In words, M_2^n is a set of achievement matrices over the population consisting of n individuals, and the mean of achievements in each dimension is positive. Finally, define M_3^n as a set of achievement matrices over the population with size n such that for each individual, all dimensional achievements are positive. Formally, $M_3^n = \{X \in M_1^n | x_{ij} > 0 \text{for all } i \in \{1, 2, \ldots, n\} \text{and} j \in Q\}$. Evidently, M_1^n, M_2^n, and M_3^n can be regarded as multidimensional analogs of $\Re_+^n$, $\Re_{++}^n$, and D^n, respectively. Let M_1 stand for the set of all possible achievement matrices corresponding to M_1^n, that is, $M_1 = \bigcup_{n \in N} M_1^n$. The corresponding sets of all achievement matrices associated with M_2^n and M_3^n that parallel to M_1 are denoted respectively by M_2 and M_3. Barring anything specified, our presentation in the following sections will be made in terms of an arbitrary $M \in \{M_1, M_2, M_3\}$.

For illustrative purpose, let us assume that there are three dimensions of well-being, namely daily energy consumption in calories by an adult male,[14] per capita income, and life expectancy, measured respectively in dollars and years. With these three dimensions of well-being, we consider the following matrix X_1 as an example of an achievement matrix in a four-person economy:

$$X_1 = \begin{bmatrix} 2700 & 59.6 & 490 \\ 2500 & 65 & 900 \\ 1900 & 59.5 & 400 \\ 2700 & 62 & 600 \end{bmatrix}.$$

14 According to the US Government, an adult male requires 2700 calories per day (Public Health News, Medical News Today, 26 September 2014).

The first entry in row i of X_1 indicates person i's daily calorie intake. On the other hand, the second and third entries of the row specify respectively the person's life expectancy and income.

All our axioms in this chapter will be stated using a social welfare function W, a real-valued function defined on the set of achievement matrices. Formally, $W: M \rightarrow \mathfrak{R}^1$, where for any $n \in N$, $X \in M^n$, $W(X)$ indicates the level of well-being associated with the distributions of totals of achievements in different dimensions among the individuals, as displayed by the achievement matrix X. Consequently, a social welfare standard W involves aggregations across dimensions and across individuals. Since for any $n \in N$, $X \in M^n$ is a social alternative, a welfare function can be applied to determine social ranking of the alternatives. It is a grand mapping that establishes unambiguous ranking of all social distributions.

One way to proceed to welfare-based social evaluation is to adopt welfarism. Under welfarism, individual well-being measures, utilities, can be determined by treating welfare as an independent normative issue. For overall ethical valuations, only these well-being standards are of relevance. In other words, a social welfare function unquestionably falls under the category welfarism if it incorporates only individual utilities associated with different alternatives. In concrete sense, here social evaluation is performed in terms of vectors of utilities, obtained by the individuals in the society. As a consequence, under welfarism, all nonutility features are ignored in welfare evaluation of the society (see, among others, d'Aspremont and Gevers, 2002; Bossert and Weymark, 2004 and Weymark, 2016, for detailed surveys).

Let $U: \Sigma \rightarrow \mathfrak{R}^1$ denote individual i's utility function, where $\Sigma = \mathfrak{R}^d_+$ (respectively $\mathfrak{R}^d_{++}$, D^d) if $M = M_1$ (respectively M_2, M_3). Then the real number $U(x_{i.})$ quantifies the extent of well-being enjoyed by the person when his achievement profile is given by $x_{i.}$. Since $i \in \{1, 2, \ldots, n\}$ is arbitrary, the utility function is assumed to be the same across individuals. For any $n \in N$, $X \in M^n$, $(U(x_{1.}), U(x_{2.}), \ldots, U(x_{n.}))$ is the vector of individual utilities. Assume that social evaluation is done using the utilitarian welfare function, with an identical utility function U. It is formally defined as

$$W(X) = \sum_{i=1}^{n} U(x_{i.}), \tag{1.6}$$

where $X \in M^n$ and $n \in N$ are arbitrary (see Blackorby et al., 1984). Implicit under this are some assumptions on measurability and comparability of utilities. A measurability assumption here states the transformations that can be applied to an individual's utility function without altering any available information. A comparability assumption specifies the extents to which they are comparable across persons, that is, whether they are identical, or nonidentical, and so on.[15] The application of a welfare function with the objective of

15 A taxonomy of alternative notions of measurability and comparability is available in Sen (1977). See also, among others, Hammond (1976, 1991), D'Aspremont and Gevers (1977),

ranking social distributions does not necessarily presume that alternatives are ranked only on the basis of individual utilities. If the welfare function is directly defined on dimensional achievements, a person's achievement in a dimension can be assumed to reflect his well-being from the achievement. In consequence, any two individuals with the same level of achievement can be assumed to be associated with the same extent of well-being.

1.5 The Dashboard Approach and Weights on Dimensional Metrics in a Composite Index

A dashboard in multivariate welfare analysis is a portfolio of individual dimensional quantifiers of welfare. Formally, if $W_j : \Sigma \to \Re^1_+$ denotes the well-being metric for dimension j, the corresponding dashboard may be represented by the $1 \times d$ dimensional matrix $(W_1, W_2, \ldots, W_d)$, where $\Gamma = \Re^d_+$ (respectively $\Re^d_{++}$, D^d) if $M = M_1$ (respectively M_2, M_3). For any $n \in N, X \in M^n$, $W_j(x_{.j})$ quantifies the extent of well-being associated with $x_{.j}$, the distribution of achievements in dimension j. This formulation of the dashboard is quite general; functional forms of W_j's need not be the same across dimensions. Consequently, while for income dimension, the ordinary mean can be taken as the metric, for life expectancy, it can be the harmonic mean. "The best indicator for each basic need" (Hicks and Streteen, 1979, p. 577) can be considered to design a dashboard in the basic needs.

There are several advantages of the dashboard approach. It is very simple and easy to understand. Presentation of dimension-by-dimension indices makes it quite rich informationally. Progress in any given dimension may be required for some policy purpose. Inquiries such as whether the society's progress in educational attainments has been at the desired level can be addressed.

However, the dashboard approach has some serious drawbacks as well. It fails to take into account the interdimensional association, an intrinsic characteristic of the notion of multivariate analysis. In other words, by concentrating on dimension-by-dimension analysis, it ignores a key factor of multidimensional evaluation, the joint distribution of dimensional achievements. For two different matrices, the distributions of dimensional totals may be the same but the joint distributions may differ. It does not produce a complete ordering of achievement matrices. Of two achievement matrices over the same population size, while some of the metrics may regard the former better than the latter, the reverse ordering may hold for the remaining metrics. A case in point may be a situation where the society has made progress in life expectancy over a certain period; however, its performance in educational status has

---

Basu (1980, ch. 6), Roberts (1980), Blackorby et al. (1984), Fleurbaey and Hammond (2004), Fleurbaey and Maniquet (2011), and Weymark (2016).

indicated a decreasing trend over the period. Furthermore, there is a problem of heterogeneity across dimensional welfare standards.

The problem of heterogeneity and incomplete ordering generated by the dashboard approach can be avoided if we combine the information contained in a dashboard into a single statistic, a composite index. More precisely, a composite index is a nonnegative real-valued function of individual dimensional measures. In other words, the dimensional indices are aggregated by employing some well-defined aggregation function. Analytically, a composite index CI aggregates the components of the vector $(W_1, W_2, \dots, W_d)$ using an aggregator f^d. More accurately, for any $n \in N$, $X \in M^n$, $CI(X) = f^d(W_1(x_{.1}), W_2(x_{.2}), \dots, W_d(x_{.d}))$. Since for each $j \in Q$, $W_j : \Sigma \to \Re^1_+$, $CI: \Re^d_+ \to \Re^1_+$. Equivalently, we can say that the aggregator f^d is a nonnegative real-valued function defined on the nonnegative orthant of the d dimensional Euclidean space. By construction, a composite index provides a complete ordering of achievement matrices. But it also ignores the joint distribution of dimensional achievements. Nevertheless, a composite index has a very high advantage of being "a single headline figure" (Stiglitz et al., 2009, p. 63). It has the convenient property of presenting a single picture to easily obtain overall well-being of a society. (Examples of composite welfare standards will be provided in Section 1.7.)

However, aggregation of dimension-wise metrics involves setting of weights to different metrics. These weights govern the trade-offs between indices. More precisely, we can use them to address questions such as: how much more of one index one has to give up, say, following a reduction in an achievement, to get an extra unit of a second index so that the level of well-being, as indicated by the value of CI, remains fixed?

Decancq and Lugo (2012) partitioned the sets of these weights into three important sets, representing the following categories: data-driven, normative, and hybrid. While normative weights rely on value judgments about trade-offs, data-driven weights do not involve any such value judgment. Instead, they depend on dimensional achievements. The hybrid approach aggregates information on value judgments and distributions of achievements. Next, we briefly discuss alternative categorizations of the weights proposed by these authors.

For each category, several subgroups of weights were identified. The first subgroup of data-driven class includes the weights that depend on the frequency distributions of achievements in different dimensions (Desai and Shah, 1988; Cerioli and Zani, 1990; Cheli and Lemmi, 1995; Deutsch and Silber, 2005; Chakravarty and D'Ambrosio, 2006; Brandolini, 2009). The second subgroup contains weights that rely on the principal component analysis (Noorbakhsh, 1998; Klasen, 2000; Boelhouwer, 2002) and factor analysis (Kuklys, 2005; Di Tommaso, 2006; Noble et al., 2006; Krishnakumar and Ballon, 2008; Krishnakumar and Nadar, 2008). While the former involves a statistical tool with the objective of reducing a larger number of possibly correlated variables to a smaller number of uncorrelated variables, referred to as "principal components," the latter is a statistical tool employed to explain variability between observed and correlated variables with respect to a reduced number of unobserved variables. In the third subgroup, we include weights that depend on a particular case of data envelope analysis, a linear programming technique used for judging the relative importance of variables (Mahlberg and Obersteiner, 2001; Zaim et al., 2001; Despotis, 2005a,b; Cherchye et al., 2007a,b).

The second set that we identify under the category "normative" can be further divided into three subsets, of which the first is the family of equal and arbitrary weights (Mayer and Jencks, 1989; Ravallion, 1997; Chowdhury and Squire, 2006; Fleurbaey, 2009; Chakravarty, 2010). The second family contains weights that are based on expert opinions (Moldan and Billharz, 1997; Mascherini and Hoskins, 2008) and weights that rely on a process originating from multivariate decision-making (Saaty, 1987 and Nardo et al., 2005). Finally, the third subset identified under the category encompasses price-based weights and their extensions (Srinivasan, 1994; Card, 1999; Becker et al., 2005; Murphy and Topel, 2006 and Fleurbaey and Gaulier, 2009).

The set that comprises weights falling under the category "hybrid" can be partitioned into two subfamilies. The first subfamily contains weights that combine data-driven approach and valuation of the persons concerned (Mack and Lansley, 1985; Halleröd, 1995, 1996; and Bossert et al., 2013). The second subfamily incorporates weights that can be obtained from regression of life satisfaction on a set of relevant dimensions and related variants (Ferrer-i Carbonell and Frijters, 2004, Nardo et al., 2005; Schokkaert, 2007; Schokkaert et al., 2009; Fleurbaey et al., 2015).

As Foster and Sen (1997, p. 206) argued, reaching a consensus on allocation of weights is unlikely. Necessity of democratic opinion with respect to setting of weights was mentioned by Wolff and De-Shalit (2007) (see also, Sen, 2009). In a normative framework, Decancq and Ooghe (2010) performed sensitivity analysis to identify the range of weighting schemes that leads to robust results. Zhou et al. (2010) made a systematic comparison between different rankings of countries generated due to the choice of a set of randomly chosen weighting schemes. Weighting sensitivity of social ordering has also been explored in Wolff and De-Shalit (2007).[16]

16 Further discussion on techniques for setting weights can be found in Sen (1992), Brandolini and D'Alessio (1998), Atkinson et al. (2002), Foster et al. (2013a), and Aaberge and Brandolini (2015). Some limitations of different approaches have been discussed, among others, by Srinivasan (1994), Foster and Sen (1997), Ravallion (1997), de Kruijk and Rutten (2007), Nardo et al. (2008), Brandolini (2009), and Somarriba and Pena (2009). See also Saisana et al. (2005), Cherchye et al. (2007a,b), Cherchye et al. (2008), Permanyer (2011, 2012), Wolff et al. (2011), and Høyland et al. (2012) for related issues.

1.6 Multidimensional Welfare Function Axioms

In this section, we introduce the axioms that are used to analyze the welfare functions surveyed in the next section. Since our discussion on the univariate axioms in Section 1.3 was rather brief, here our study on their multidimensional sisters will be elaborative. Further, as we will see, sometimes straightforward multidimensional translations may lead to unintuitive conclusions. It is also necessary to look at the interrelationship between dimensions, which has no relevance in one-dimensional context.

Following Chakravarty and Lugo (2016), we will subdivide the section into several subsections, where the axioms comprising a subsection will share at least one characteristic.

1.6.1 Invariance Axioms

An invariance axiom stipulates that the level of welfare should remain unchanged under certain structural conditions related to a welfare standard. The first invariance axiom we consider is symmetry. As we have seen in the univariate case, symmetry requires no alteration of welfare when two persons trade their positions. In the multivariate setup, an interchange of two individuals' positions can be obtained if the two rows representing their achievement profiles are exchanged. To perceive this, we consider the following achievement matrix with four individuals and three dimensions of well-being:

$$X_1 = \begin{bmatrix} 100 & 62 & 600 \\ 800 & 65 & 900 \\ 200 & 50 & 440 \\ 700 & 59 & 400 \end{bmatrix}.$$

If we interchange the first and the fourth rows of X_1, then the resulting distribution matrix turns out to be

$$Y_1 = \begin{bmatrix} 700 & 59 & 400 \\ 800 & 65 & 900 \\ 200 & 50 & 440 \\ 100 & 62 & 600 \end{bmatrix}.$$

This rearrangement of positions of persons 1 and 4 should not influence the quantification of welfare as long as we assume that welfare should depend only on individual dimensional attainments. In the standard practice for calculation of welfare value, for $X_{1,}$ the dimensional acquisitions of person 1 come first and those of person 4 come at the last stage of aggregation, whereas the reverse order is followed for Y_1. This switch in the order of aggregation does not lead to any information loss in the sense that both X_1 and Y_1 convey us the same information on individual achievements, the only difference is that locations of persons 1 and 4 have been reciprocated. Thus, the occupancy of positions is a characteristic that becomes immaterial to the measurement of welfare. More precisely, welfare needs anonymous treatment of individuals.

This positional trading can be implemented by premultiplying X_1 with a 4×4 permutation matrix whose only positive entry of the first row occurs at column 4 and its only positive entry in the fourth row appears at column 1. For each of the remaining two rows, the diagonal entry is the only positive number. More precisely,

$$Y_1 = \begin{bmatrix} 0 & 0 & 0 & 1 \\ 0 & 1 & 0 & 0 \\ 0 & 0 & 1 & 0 \\ 1 & 0 & 0 & 0 \end{bmatrix} \begin{bmatrix} 100 & 62 & 600 \\ 800 & 65 & 900 \\ 200 & 50 & 440 \\ 700 & 59 & 400 \end{bmatrix}.$$

Evidently, the selection of rows 1 and 4 for positional swap (and hence of the particular 4×4 permutation matrix) was arbitrary, and the choice of X_1 for illustrative purpose was also ad hoc. This invariance postulate, which we refer to as symmetry because it treats individuals symmetrically, can be stated in the general case as follows:

Symmetry: For all $n \in N$, $X, Y \in M^n$, if $Y = \Gamma X$, where Γ is any permutation matrix of order n, then $W(X) = W(Y)$.

This axiom demands that any characteristic other than dimensional realizations of the individuals, such as, their names and marital statuses, should be treated as irrelevant to the measurement of welfare.

Next, we extend the symmetry axiom for population to the multivariate setup. As we know, often it becomes necessary to make cross-population comparisons of welfare. Such a situation arises if we have to compare welfare across two different societies or of the same society intertemporally since population size is likely to vary over time. To understand the issue more explicitly, let us consider two different societies with population sizes 2 and 3, respectively. The dimensions are identical across the populations. Any variation in the dimensions does not make the comparison valid. The two achievement matrices with the same three dimensions considered earlier are respectively

$$X_2 = \begin{bmatrix} 700 & 59 & 800 \\ 200 & 60 & 450 \end{bmatrix} \text{ and } X_3 = \begin{bmatrix} 600 & 65 & 800 \\ 500 & 59 & 700 \\ 700 & 62 & 400 \end{bmatrix}.$$

If we replicate X_2 thrice and X_3 twice, then the replicated matrices become respectively

$$Y_2 = \begin{bmatrix} 700 & 59 & 800 \\ 200 & 60 & 450 \\ 700 & 59 & 800 \\ 200 & 60 & 450 \\ 700 & 59 & 800 \\ 200 & 60 & 450 \end{bmatrix} \text{ and } Y_3 = \begin{bmatrix} 600 & 65 & 800 \\ 500 & 59 & 700 \\ 700 & 62 & 400 \\ 600 & 65 & 800 \\ 500 & 59 & 700 \\ 700 & 62 & 400 \end{bmatrix}.$$

The matrices Y_2 and Y_3 have a common population size, 6. A comparison between their welfare levels is possible now. If X_2 is welfare equivalent to Y_2 and X_3 is welfare equivalent to Y_3, then welfare comparisons between Y_2 and Y_3 will be the same as that between X_2 and X_3. But welfare equality between X_2 and Y_2 and between X_3 and Y_3 is a consequence of satisfaction of the population replication invariance postulate by the welfare function. Formally,

Population Replication Invariance: For all $n \in N, X \in M^n$, $W(X) = W(X^{(k)})$, where $X^{(k)}$ is the k-fold replication X, that is, the $nk \times d$ achievement matrix $X^{(k)}$ is obtained by placing X sequentially from top to below k times, $k \geq 2$ being any integer.

In words, this axiom stipulates that achievement-by-achievement replication of the population keeps welfare unchanged.

1.6.2 Distributional Axioms

A distributional axiom indicates the direction of change in welfare under certain acceptable changes in dimensional achievements. The first two of the axioms under this heading are two versions of the Pareto principle. According to the strong Pareto principle, if at least one person is made better off in some dimensions without at the same affecting all other dimensional achievements, then the society's welfare improves. This postulate is a natural generalization of the monotonicity property stipulated in Section 1.2. Formally,

Strong Pareto Principle: For all $n \in N$, $X, Y \in M^n$, if $x_{ij} = y_{ij} + c_{ij}$, $c_{ij} \geq 0$, for all pairs $(i,j) \in \{1, 2, \dots, n\} \times \{1, 2, \dots, d\}$, with > 0 for at least one pair $(i,j) \in \{1, 2, \dots, n\} \times \{1, 2, \dots, d\}$, then $W(X) > W(Y)$.

We can as well say that X (respectively, Y) is strongly Pareto superior (respectively, inferior) to Y (respectively, X). Equivalently, X is strongly Pareto dominant over Y. However, this strong Pareto dominance relation involving the individual achievement profiles may lead to inconclusive ordering of underlying matrices. For instance, suppose that $x_{ij} = y_{ij} + c_{ij}$, $c_{ij} > 0$, for exactly one pair $(i,j) \in \{1, 2, \dots, n\} \times \{1, 2, \dots, d\}$, and $x_{hk} = y_{hk}$ for all $(h,k) \neq (i,j)$. Then $W(X) > W(Y)$. Now, if we obtain $\overline{X}$ from X by reducing x_{hk} for some $(h,k) \in \{1, 2, \dots, n\} \times \{1, 2, \dots, d\}/\{(i,j)\}$, then $\overline{X}$ is strongly Pareto inferior to X. But no comparison between $\overline{X}$ and Y in terms strong Pareto dominance is possible. In contrast, since to each X, W assigns a unique real number, a complete ordering of social matrices over a given population size is provided by W. In consequence, it will be possible to claim whether $\overline{X}$ welfare is superior or inferior to Y.

For explanatory purpose, let us generate X_4 from Y_1 by increasing only person 3's achievement in dimension 3 and at the same time keeping all other entries of Y_1 unchanged. We then obtain X_5 from X_4 by reducing only person 4's achievement in dimension 2. More precisely,

$$X_4 = \begin{bmatrix} 700 & 59 & 400 \\ 800 & 65 & 900 \\ 200 & 50 & 445 \\ 100 & 62 & 600 \end{bmatrix} \text{ and } X_5 = \begin{bmatrix} 700 & 59 & 400 \\ 800 & 65 & 900 \\ 200 & 50 & 445 \\ 100 & 53 & 600 \end{bmatrix}.$$

Then X_4 strongly Pareto dominates both X_5 and Y_1 so that $W(X_4) > W(Y_1)$ and $W(X_4) > W(X_5)$. But no unambiguous conclusion can be drawn about ranking between X_5 and Y_1 in terms of strong Pareto superiority. Given a functional form of W, it will be possible to order the welfare levels $W(X_4)$, $W(Y_1)$ and $W(X_5)$.

The strong Pareto principle implies the following weaker form of the criterion.

Weak Pareto Principle: For all $n \in N$, $X, Y \in M^n$, if $x_{ij} = y_{ij} + c_{ij}$, $c_{ij} > 0$, for all pairs $(i,j) \in \{1, 2, \dots, n\} \times \{1, 2, \dots, d\}$, then $W(X) > W(Y)$.

Here we say that X weakly Pareto dominates Y. For instance, $X_6 = \begin{bmatrix} 706 & 61 & 410 \\ 808 & 68 & 903 \\ 211 & 56 & 449 \\ 108 & 67 & 603 \end{bmatrix}$ is weakly Pareto superior to X_4. Evidently, the weak Pareto principle shares one characteristic of the strong principle; the inability to order social distributions but any welfare standard obeying it can do the job successfully.

"Pareto optimality only guarantees that no change is possible such that someone would become better off without making anyone worse off. If the lot of the poor cannot be made any better without cutting into the affluence of the rich, the situation would be Pareto optimal despite the disparity between the rich and the poor" (Sen, 1973, p. 7). For example, an increase in person 2's achievement in X_4 in any dimension will make the resulting achievement matrix strongly Pareto superior over X_4. But this Pareto improving reformation is accompanied by an increase in the dispersion in the distribution of achievement. One way to cut back the level of dispersion is through progressive transfer of achievements from the rich to the poor. For the purpose of clarification, note that in X_6, a transfer of 20 units of person 2's achievement in dimension 1 to the corresponding achievement of person 3 will lessen intradimensional dispersion. However, since we are dealing with a multivariate situation, a natural requirement is to involve all the dimensions simultaneously. Multidimensional transfer principles are indicative of equity consciousness of the social welfare functions. They play highly significant role in the welfare assessment of achievement matrices.

Taking cue from Section 1.2, the first transfer principle, we consider, requires progressive transfers in each dimension. This is achieved by multiplying an achievement matrix by a nonpermutation bistochastic matrix (Kolm, 1977). Multiplication by a bistochastic matrix establishes that, for each dimension, each person receives a convex mixture of achievement streams in the society (Bourguignon and Chakravarty, 2003, pp. 30–31). Formally,

Uniform Majorization Principle: For all $n \in N$, $n > 1$, $X, Y \in M^n$, if $X = BY$ for some $n \times n$ bistochastic matrix B that is not a permutation matrix, then $W(X) > W(Y)$.

Equivalently, X uniformly majorizes Y, and this transformation raises society's position on the welfare scale. We also say that X is obtained from Y by a uniform majorization operation, which in turn leads to welfare improvement.

From our discussion in Section 1.2, it should be evident that an alternative way to incorporate egalitarian bias into distributional judgments is through multiplication by Pigou–Dalton matrices. Formally,

Uniform Pigou–Dalton Majorization Principle: For all $n \in N$, $n > 1$, $X, Y \in M^n$, if $X = \overline{B}Y$, where $\overline{B}$ is the product of a finite number of $n \times n$ Pigou–Dalton matrices, then $W(X) > W(Y)$.

Equivalently, X uniformly Pigou–Dalton majorizes Y, and this movement makes X better than Y in terms of welfare. A welfare standard satisfying this postulate is symmetric.

The product of Pigou–Dalton matrices is a nonpermutation bistochastic matrix. The converse is true as well if either the number of dimensions is 1 or there are only two persons in the society. However, for $d \geq 2$ and $n \geq 3$, it is possible to obtain nonpermutation bistochastic matrices that are not products of Pigou–Dalton matrices (Marshall et al., 2011, pp. 53–54). Consequently, except in some special circumstances, the uniform Pigou–Dalton majorization principle is more general than the uniform majorization principle.

However, the two majorization criteria impose strong restrictions on the transfer sequence. Transfer across persons in the same proportion in each dimension is highly demanding. This is a consequence of premultiplication of the achievement matrix by a bistochastic matrix. In addition, a transfer that appears to be quite appealing from egalitarian perspective may not be characterized by either of the two principles. For instance, in X_6, a transfer of 20 units of persons 2's achievement in dimension 1 to the corresponding achievement of person 4 will increase welfare. But this transfer process cannot be captured by premultiplication of X_6 by a bistochastic matrix. For transfers between two persons when one is not unambiguously richer than the other in all dimensions, motivation for unambiguous conclusions about the change of direction in welfare is not evident (see Diez et al., 2007, p. 5 and Lasso de la Vega et al., 2010, p. 320).

There are dimensions of well-being that are nonexclusive and nonrival. Examples include national defense and state-financed inoculation programs against some diseases. Once the defence system is instituted, everyone in the society benefits. These goods that are public in nature are nontradable. Another example that belongs to the nonredistributable category is self-reported health status of a person. This is an ordinally measurable dimension of well-being. A transfer of health condition of a person to another person is not defined. Consequently, welfare treatments of such dimensions have to be dealt with separately. (See Bosmans et al., 2009.) We take up this matter in Chapter 3.

The Pigou–Dalton bundle transfer principle, an intuitive multidimensional generalization of the univariate Pigou–Dalton transfer principle, proposed by Fleurbaey and Trannoy (2003), avoids the aforementioned problems (see also Fleurbaey, 2006b and Fleurbaey and Maniquet, 2011). Assume that achievements in all the dimensions are redistributable. Then for any $n \in N$, $X, Y \in M^n$, $n \in N$, X is said to be obtained from Y by a Pigou–Dalton bundle of progressive transfers if there exist two individuals $i, h \in \{1, 2, \dots, n\}$ such that (i) $y_{i.} < y_{h.}$, that is, $y_{ij} < y_{hj}$ for all $j \in Q$, (ii) $x_{i.} = y_{i.} + \delta, x_{h.} = y_{h.} - \delta$, where $\delta = (\delta_1, \delta_j, \dots, \delta_d) \in \Re^d_{++}$, (iii) $x_{i.} \leq x_{h.}$, that is, $x_{ij} \leq x_{hj}$ for all $j \in Q$, (iv) $y_{l.} = x_{l.}$ for all $l \in \{1, 2, \dots, n\}/\{i, h\}$.

According to condition (i), in Y, person h is richer than person i in all dimensions. Condition (ii) says that in Y, dimension-wise transfers from the achievement profile of person h to that of person i generate the achievement profiles of these two persons in X. Here the d dimensional vector δ stands for the bundle of progressive transfers. Since $\delta \in \Re^d_{++}$, the size of transfer is positive for at least one dimension. Condition (iii) ensures that the transfer size in each dimension is such that achievement of the recipient (person i) in the dimension does not exceed the corresponding dimensional achievement of the donor (person h). Finally, condition (iv) claims that achievements of all other persons in all the dimensions remain unchanged.[17] Equivalently, we can say that Y is obtained from X by a Pigou–Dalton bundle of regressive transfers.

To illustrate the Pigou–Dalton bundle of regressive and progressive transfers graphically, consider individuals 1 and 2 with respective achievement profiles (x_{11}, x_{12}) and (x_{21}, x_{22}). Assume also that $x_{11} > x_{21}$ and $x_{12} > x_{22}$, so that person 1 has higher achievement compared to person 2 in each dimension. These profiles, denoted by the symbols A and B, respectively, are shown in Figure 1.1a. Then the symbols C and D, shown in Figure 1.1a, indicating profiles of individuals 1 and 2, respectively, represent the two individuals' positions in

17 An innovative application of this transfer principle to derive multidimensional inequality indices was made in Lasso de la Vega, Urrutia and Sarachu (2010). Banerjee (2014) formulated a definition of multidimensional Lorenz domination by incorporating this notion of transfer. Earlier, a variant of the uniform majorization principle was suggested by Savaglio (2006a). Trannoy (2006) questioned ethical appropriateness of "price" or "budget majorization." According to budget majorization, a person's dimensional achievement is regarded as more equal than that of another person, if the distribution of dimensional budgets of the former person Lorenz dominates that of the latter person.

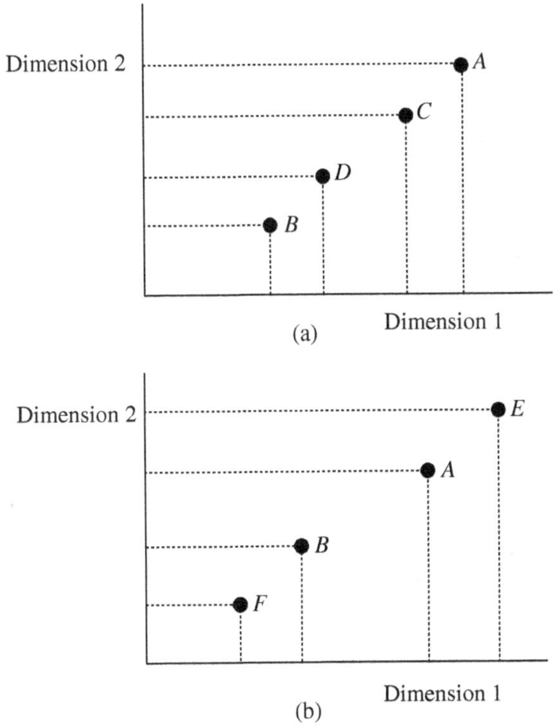

Figure 1.1 (a) Pigou–Dalton bundle of progressive transfers. (b) Pigou–Dalton bundle of regressive transfers.

postprogressive transfer situation. Similarly, the symbols E and F in Figure 1.1b show the individual profiles after a Pigou–Dalton bundle of regressive transfers has been operated between the profiles A and B.

Since an egalitarian redistribution should increase welfare, the following reasonable postulate for a multidimensional welfare function can now be stated.

Multidimensional Transfer: For all $n \in N$, $n > 1$, $Y \in M^n$, if $X \in M^n$ is obtained from Y by a Pigou–Dalton bundle of progressive transfers, then $W(X) > W(Y)$.

Analogously, welfare should reduce under a bundle of regressive transfers.

In X_6, person 2 is richer than person 3 in all the three dimensions. Consequently, the matrix X_7 derived from X_6 by a transfer of the bundle $(50, 3, 40)$ from person 2 to person 3 should increase welfare, that is, $W(X_7) > W(X_6)$,

where $X_7 = \begin{bmatrix} 706 & 61 & 410 \\ 758 & 65 & 863 \\ 261 & 59 & 489 \\ 108 & 67 & 603 \end{bmatrix}$.

Note that the bundle of progressive transfers does not reverse the ranks of the donor and the recipient in X_6.

The axioms presented so far are multidimensional adaptions of their univariate sisters. Our next axiom has significance only in multidimensional situations; it has no univariate counterpart. It represents dependence between dimensions, a concept intrinsic to the notion of multidimensional analysis of well-being. To understand the need for this, consider the following two 3×2 achievement matrices:

$$X_8 = \begin{bmatrix} 800 & 800 \\ 700 & 700 \\ 200 & 200 \end{bmatrix} \text{ and } X_9 = \begin{bmatrix} 800 & 700 \\ 700 & 800 \\ 200 & 200 \end{bmatrix}.$$

In X_8, of the three persons, the first person is top ranked in each of the two dimensions, the second person is ranked second best, and so on. In X_9, the dimensional attainments remain the same but their distributions across persons differ. There is an interchange of achievements in dimension 2 between the best-off and the second best-off persons. The dashboard for the two matrices is the same since each of the four-dimensional welfare standards yielded by X_8 and X_9 is the same. Consequently, a composite index based on the common dashboard associated with the two matrices will generate the identical value. The reason behind this is that four dimension-by-dimension distributions are the same, and hence, aggregation across individuals should yield the same value for dimensional welfare standards (see Decancq et al., 2015). The direction of change in welfare for this barter involving X_8 and X_9 ignores the dependence between the positions of the individuals in the two dimensions. The change should depend on the nature of relationship between the two dimensions, that is, whether they are substitutes, complements, or independents.

Although aggregation of dashboard-based dimensional indices gives us a simple way of arriving at an overall measure, because of its lack of concern for interdimensional association, more precisely, for correlation between dimensions, it does not give us a true picture of the analysis. Consequently, a proper analysis of multidimensional welfare in a society should be sensitive to the correlation between dimensional achievements. Although correlation is a simple indicator of linear association between achievements in two dimensions, here we will use the terms "association" and "correlation" synonymously.

Taking cue from Epstein and Tanny (1980) and Tchen (1980), in their pioneering contribution, Atkinson and Bourguignon (1982) contended that a multidimensional metric of welfare should incorporate correlation between distributions of dimensional achievements.[18] The axiom requires a welfare standard to be responsive to a particular type of movement of achievements across individuals. To illustrate the idea, note that X_8 is obtained from X_9 by interchanging achievements in dimension 2 between persons 1 and 2. This reciprocation of achievements between the two persons increases the interdimensional correlation. The reason behind this is that after the interchange,

18 See also Tsui (1995). An overview of alternative notions of interdimensional association is available in a fine paper by Decancq (2013).

person 1, who was richer than person 2 only in dimension 1, has become richer in both the dimensions. Consequently, this trade-off may be termed as a correlation-increasing switch.

In the general situation, switch between two achievements can take place in one or more dimensions but not in all dimensions. The initial requirement is that one person should be richer than the other in at least one dimension, poorer in at least one dimension, and not poorer in all the remaining dimensions. After one or more barters, the former should not be poorer than the latter in all the dimensions and be richer in at least one dimension. Formally,

Definition 1.1 For all $n \in N$, $n > 1$, $X \in M^n$, suppose that there exist individuals $i, h \in \{1, 2, \ldots, n\}$ and dimensions $j, q \in Q$ such that (i) $x_{ij} < x_{hj}$, (ii) $x_{hq} < x_{iq}$, (iii) $x_{ik} \leq x_{hk}$ for all $k \in Q/\{j, q\}$. Next, suppose that $Y \in M^n$ is obtained from X as follows: (iv) $y_{hj} = x_{hj}, y_{ij} = x_{ij}$, (v) $y_{hq} = x_{iq}, y_{iq} = x_{hq}$, (vi) $y_{hk} = x_{hk}, y_{ik} = x_{ik}$ for all $k \in Q/\{j, q\}$, and (vii) $y_{l.} = x_{l.}$ for all $l \in \{1, 2, \ldots, n\}/\{i, h\}$, where $y_{l.}$ and $x_{l.}$ are respectively the lth rows of Y and X. Then we say that Y is obtained from X by a correlation-increasing switch between two persons. Conversely, it can be said that X is derived from Y by a correlation-decreasing switch between two persons.

According to conditions (i) and (ii) of Definition 1.1, person i is poorer in dimension j but richer in dimension q compared to person h in X. Condition (iii) means that person h is not poorer than person i in all other dimensions. In condition (iv), it is stated precisely that a switch between achievements of persons i and h in dimension j has been implemented. Finally, conditions (iv) and (v), when considered simultaneously, establish that in the postexchange setting, person h is richer than person i in both the dimensions j and q. Person h, who had originally higher achievement compared to person i in dimension q, is getting higher achievement in dimension j as well after the switch. On the other hand, person i has lower achievements in both the dimensions in the postswitch situation. Their achievements in all other dimensions remain unaffected. Consequently, this barter of achievements in dimension j between persons i and h will augment the correlation between the dimensions. Observe that the switch does not affect the achievements of the remaining persons. It may also be worthwhile to note that the switch does not modify the total of achievements in any dimension.

Consider two individuals 1 and 2 with achievement profiles (x_{11}, x_{12}) and (x_{21}, x_{22}), respectively. Assume further that $x_{11} > x_{21}$ and $x_{12} < x_{22}$, so that person 1 has higher achievement compared to person 2 in dimension 1, and the opposite happens in dimension 2. Let us denote these profiles by the symbols A and B, respectively (see Figure 1.2). After a correlation-increasing swap between achievements of the persons in dimension 2, the profiles get transformed into (x_{11}, x_{22}) and (x_{21}, x_{12}), which are indicated by the symbols C and D, respectively. After the switch, person 1, who had more achievement in dimension 1 only, has more achievement in dimension 2 as well.

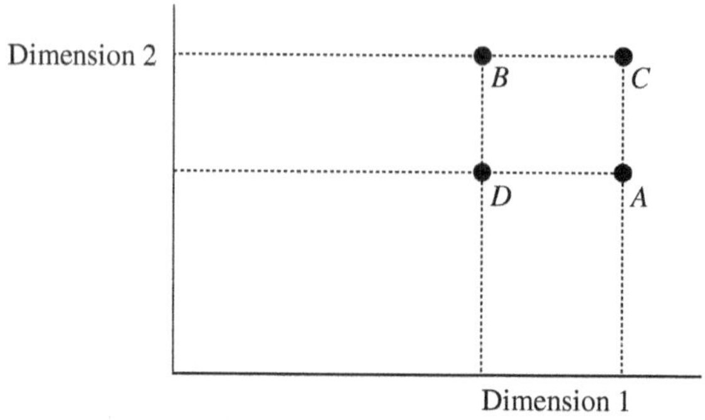

Figure 1.2 Correlation-increasing switch.

If the two dimensions involved in a switch are substitutes, then one counterbalances the deficiency of the other. Since the two dimensions represent similar aspect of well-being because of their closeness in terms of substitutability, the switch makes a poor person poorer and a rich person richer in the concerned dimensions. Consequently, overall welfare position of the society goes down. Similarly, level of welfare should go up under the switch if the dimensions are complements. If the two dimensions are independents, then the welfare function is insensitive to such a switch. A composite index that relies on a dashboard treats the underlying dimensions as independents.

In view of the aforementioned arguments, following Atkinson and Bourguignon (1982) and Bourguignon and Chakravarty (2003), our next axiom can be formally stated as:

Decreasing Welfare under Correlation Increasing Switch: For all $n \in N$, $n > 1$, $X \in M^n$, if $Y \in M^n$ is obtained from X by a correlation-increasing switch, then $W(X) > W(Y)$, whenever the dimensions underlying the switch are substitutes.

The axiom clearly indicates under what type of association between dimensions, unambiguous conclusion about direction of welfare change resulting from a correlation-increasing swap can be made. Variants of this axiom when the dimensions are complements and independents can be stated analogously.[19,20]

19 The value of a symmetric utilitarian welfare function $\sum_{i=1}^{n} U(x_{i.})$ decreases under a correlation-increasing switch if $U:\Sigma \rightarrow \Re^1$, where $\Sigma \in \{\Re^d_+, \Re^d_{++}, D^d\}$ is increasing and strictly L-subadditive. Under required differentiability assumptions of U, strict L-subadditivity means that $\frac{\partial U}{\partial x_{ij}\partial x_{ik}} < 0$ for all $x_{i.} \in \Gamma$ and distinct $j, k \in Q$ (see Weymark, 2006 and Marshall et al., 2011, p. 218). Atkinson and Bourguignon (1982) showed that in a two-dimensional setup, dimensions are complements or substitutes, depending on whether U is strictly L-superadditive ($\frac{\partial U}{\partial x_{ij}\partial x_{ik}} > 0$ for all $x_{i.} \in \Gamma$, where j and k are the dimensions) or L-subadditive.

20 "This corresponds to the Auspitz-Lieben-Edgeworth-Pareto (ALEP) definition and differs from Hick's definition, traditionally used in demand theory (which relates to the properties of the

Dardanoni (1996) proposed and analyzed a weaker form of the correlation-increasing switch axiom. To get an idea of this, suppose that the achievement matrix $X_{10} = \begin{bmatrix} 211 & 61 \\ 808 & 60 \\ 701 & 68 \end{bmatrix}$ is transformed into a new matrix $X_{11} = \begin{bmatrix} 211 & 60 \\ 701 & 61 \\ 808 & 68 \end{bmatrix}$, which clearly indicates the ranks of individuals with respect to their achievements in both the dimensions simultaneously. In fact, we derive X_{11} from X_{10} by employing a sequence of correlation-increasing switches so that one person gets top position in all the dimensions, another person gets the second position in all the dimensions, and so on. More precisely, in X_{11} across all dimensions, the first person is third ranked, the second person is second ranked, and third person is first ranked. Dardanoni (1996) referred to this sequence as unfair rearrangement of dimensional attainments and argued that the transformed social matrix should indicate a lower level of welfare compared to the original one. Analytically,

Decreasing Welfare under Unfair Rearrangement: For all $n \in N$, $n > 1$, $X \in M^n$, if $Y \in M^n$ is obtained from X by a sequence of correlation-increasing switches such that across the dimensions, one individual becomes top ranked, another individual is second ranked, and so on. Then $W(X) > W(Y)$.

If all the dimensions in an achievement matrix are of the same type, say, substitutes or complements, then the changes in welfare associated with all the switches are unidirectional. But when dimensions are mixed in nature, the directions of change in welfare, as judged by the AELP condition, are as well of mixed type (see footnote 20). Consequently, no unambiguous conclusion about the overall directional change of welfare can be drawn.

1.7 Multidimensional Welfare Functions

A multidimensional social welfare function indicates the level of well-being of a population when achievements of all the individuals in the population, in different dimensions of living, are taken into consideration. Since there may be absence of consensus regarding the choice of a welfare function, the measurement of social welfare is a difficult task. A policy analyst may be forced to present a range of evaluations based on alternative social welfare functions. Each of them is a grand mapping that establishes unambiguous ranking of social alternatives.

indifference contours) (Atkinson, 2003:55)" (Alkire et al., 2015, p. 62). See Chipman (1977) for a formal treatment of the notion. Kannai (1980) proposed a refinement of the concept. For further discussions, see Fleurbaey and Trannoy (2003) and Lasso de la Vega, Urrutia and Sarachu (2010). For discussion on the Bourguignon–Chakravarty axiom, see Decancq (2012) and Bosmans et al. (2015).

In this section, we analyze some of the frequently used multivariate social welfare functions. We begin by reviewing two specific forms of the symmetric utilitarian function $W(X) = \sum_{i=1}^{n} U(x_{i.})$, characterized by Tsui (1995). For the first characterization, in addition to continuity, symmetry, and the strong Pareto principle, Tsui assumed strict quasiconcavity,[21] minimal individual separability, introduced by Blackorby et al. (1981), and a strong homotheticity axioms for a general welfare function W defined on M. We state the axioms on the general domain M, and if necessary, a restricted domain will be assumed.

Often from the policy point of view, it becomes necessary to partition a population into two or more subgroups, say, rich and poor subgroups, regional subgroups (see Chapter 2). Then the minimal individual separability axiom enumerates how we can calculate overall welfare in terms of welfare levels of the subgroups. Formally, for all $n \geq 3$, for all $X \in M^n$, $W(X) = W\begin{pmatrix} h(X^1) \\ X^2 \end{pmatrix}$, where h is some continuous function, X^1 is the submatrix of X that contains the achievements of persons in the nonsingleton subgroup S containing, some, say, $n_1 > 1$, persons, and X^2 is the complement of X^1 in X, that is, X^2 includes the achievements of the persons in $\{1, 2, \dots, n\}/S$.

For illustrative purpose, consider the 4×3 achievement matrix $X_{12} = \begin{bmatrix} 200 & 51 & 310 \\ 650 & 72 & 400 \\ 151 & 50 & 788 \\ 98 & 66 & 207 \end{bmatrix}$.

Suppose that we split the population into two subgroups, say, male and female, whose achievement submatrices are given respectively by $X_{12}^1 = \begin{bmatrix} 200 & 51 & 310 \\ 650 & 72 & 400 \end{bmatrix}$ and $X_{12}^2 = \begin{bmatrix} 151 & 50 & 788 \\ 98 & 66 & 207 \end{bmatrix}$. Then the separability axiom states that $W(X_{12}) = W\begin{pmatrix} h(X_{11}^1) \\ X_{11}^2 \end{pmatrix}$.

In order to state the next axiom rigorously, we need to consider a positive diagonal matrix: a square matrix whose diagonal elements are positive and off-diagonal elements are zero. A typical $d \times d$ positive diagonal matrix Ω can be written as $\Omega = \text{diag}(\eta_1, \eta_2, \dots, \eta_d)$, where $\eta_j > 0$ is the jth diagonal element and $j \in Q$.

The strong homotheticity postulate requires that for all $n \in N$, for all $X, Y \in M^n$, $W(X) \geq W(Y) \Leftrightarrow W(X\Omega) \geq W(Y\Omega)$, where Ω is any $d \times d$ positive diagonal matrix. This condition stipulates that welfare inequality between two social distributions X and Y can be equivalently expressed as that between

21 A function $f: M \to \mathfrak{R}^1$ is called strictly quasiconcave if for all $n \in N$; and all non-identical $X, Y \in M^n, f(cX + (1-c)Y) > \min(f(X), f(Y))$, where $0 < c < 1$ and $M \in \{M_1, M_2, M_3\}$ are arbitrary. If in the above inequality we replace $\min(f(X), f(Y))$ by $cf(X) + (1-c)f(Y)$, then f is called strictly concave. Strict concavity implies strict quasiconcavity but the converse is not true.

$X\Omega$ and $Y\Omega$. In other words, the axiom requires invariance of welfare ranking between two distributions under equiproportionate changes in achievements in different dimensions in both the distributions. Note that the proportionality factors need not be the same across dimensions.

To clarify the postulate, observe that under the strong Pareto principle, the achievement matrix $X_{13} = \begin{bmatrix} 35 & 40 \\ 20 & 10 \\ 10 & 10 \end{bmatrix}$ becomes welfare superior to $X_{14} = \begin{bmatrix} 30 & 40 \\ 20 & 10 \\ 10 & 10 \end{bmatrix}$, that is, $W(X_{13}) > W(X_{14})$. This is because we derive X_{14} from X_{13} by decreasing person 1's achievements in dimension 1 by 5 units.

For the 2×2 diagonal matrix $\Omega' = \begin{bmatrix} 2 & 0 \\ 0 & 1 \end{bmatrix}$, strong homotheticity demands that $W\left(\begin{bmatrix} 35 & 40 \\ 20 & 10 \\ 10 & 10 \end{bmatrix}\begin{bmatrix} 2 & 0 \\ 0 & 1 \end{bmatrix}\right) > W\left(\begin{bmatrix} 30 & 40 \\ 20 & 10 \\ 10 & 10 \end{bmatrix}\begin{bmatrix} 2 & 0 \\ 0 & 1 \end{bmatrix}\right)$, which on simplification becomes $W\left(\begin{bmatrix} 70 & 40 \\ 40 & 10 \\ 20 & 10 \end{bmatrix}\right) > W\left(\begin{bmatrix} 60 & 40 \\ 40 & 10 \\ 20 & 10 \end{bmatrix}\right)$. Thus, when each person's achievement in dimension 1 gets doubled and achievement of each of them in the other dimension remains unchanged, the welfare inequality $W(X_{13}) > W(X_{14})$ remains unchanged for the transformed situations as well, that is, $W(X_{13}\Omega') > W(X_{14}\Omega')$ holds. Since we can go back to the original inequality $W(X_{13}) > W(X_{14})$ by postmultiplying each of the two distributions $X_{13}\Omega'$ and $X_{14}\Omega'$ in the inequality $W(X_{13}\Omega') > W(X_{14}\Omega')$ by the 2×2 diagonal matrix whose first and second diagonal elements are respectively $\frac{1}{2}$ and 1, the converse follows immediately.[22]

For $n \geq 3$, $W: M_3 \to \Re^1$ becomes ordinally equivalent to $\sum_{i=1}^{n} U(x_{i.})$ if and only if the six postulates considered earlier hold simultaneously, where $U: D^d \to \Re^1$ is defined as

$$U(x_{i.}) = a + b\prod_{j=1}^{d} x_{ij}^{\theta_j}, \tag{1.7}$$

or

$$U(x_{i.}) = a + \sum_{j=1}^{d} c_j \log x_{ij}, \tag{1.8}$$

$c_j > 0$ for all $j \in Q$, a is a real number and the real numbers b and θ_j, $j \in Q$, are chosen such that U in (1.7) is increasing and strictly concave (see Theorem 1 of Tsui, 1995).

---

22 In this and in several other illustrations, for welfare comparisons, we have strict inequality originally and hence maintain strict inequality in the transformed situations as well. Replacement of the weak inequality by the strict inequality does not miss the essence of the underlying axioms.

The second characterization theorem of Tsui (1995) relies on strong translatability, which requires that for all $n \in N$, for all $X, Y \in M^n$, $W(X) \geq W(Y) \Leftrightarrow W(X+A) \geq W(Y+A)$, where A is a $n \times d$ matrix with identical rows such that $(X+A), (Y+A) \in M^n$. This condition claims that welfare inequality between two social matrices can as well be specified in terms of that between the matrices when the achievements of all the persons in a dimension increase/decrease by the same quantity. We refer to the matrix A in the statement of the postulate as a translation matrix.

For the purpose of clarification, let $A' = \begin{bmatrix} 5 & -4 \\ 5 & -4 \\ 5 & -4 \end{bmatrix}$ be a 3×2 matrix with identical rows. Thus, each person's achievement in dimension 1 increases by 5 units, and there is a reduction in everybody's achievement in dimension 2 by 4 units. Then given that $W(X_{13}) > W(X_{14})$, the axiom requires that $W(X_{13}+A') > W(X_{14}+A')$. That is, $W\left(\begin{bmatrix} 35 & 40 \\ 20 & 10 \\ 10 & 10 \end{bmatrix} + \begin{bmatrix} 5 & -4 \\ 5 & -4 \\ 5 & -4 \end{bmatrix}\right) > W\left(\begin{bmatrix} 30 & 40 \\ 20 & 10 \\ 10 & 10 \end{bmatrix} + \begin{bmatrix} 5 & -4 \\ 5 & -4 \\ 5 & -4 \end{bmatrix}\right)$, which reduces to $W\left(\begin{bmatrix} 40 & 36 \\ 25 & 6 \\ 15 & 6 \end{bmatrix}\right) > W\left(\begin{bmatrix} 35 & 36 \\ 25 & 6 \\ 15 & 6 \end{bmatrix}\right)$. The axiom also demands that this last inequality should imply the original inequality $W(X_{13}) > W(X_{14})$.

Tsui (1995) demonstrated that if in the aforementioned theorem, strong homotheticity is replaced by strong translatability and all other postulates are kept unchanged, then given that $n \geq 3$, all the axioms hold simultaneously if and only if $W: M_1 \to \Re^1$ turns out to be ordinally equivalent to $\sum_{i=1}^{n} U(x_{i.})$, where $U: \Re_+^d \to \Re^1$ is defined as

$$U(x_{i.}) = a + b\prod_{j=1}^{d} \exp(v_j x_{ij}), \tag{1.9}$$

a is an arbitrary real number, the parameters b and v_j, $j \in Q$, are chosen such that U is increasing and strictly concave (see Theorem 2 of Tsui, 1995). The welfare functions $W(X) = \sum_{i=1}^{n} U(x_{i.})$, where the utility functions are of the form (1.7)–(1.9), are symmetric and increasing under a uniform majorization operation.

As we have argued in Section 1.4, a social welfare function can be directly defined on social distributions, represented by achievement matrices. Examples of such welfare standards are the Gajdos–Weymark multidimensional generalized Gini welfare functions (Gajdos and Weymark, 2005). Their characterizations of these welfare functions involve multidimensional twins of the axioms employed by Weymark (1981) to axiomatize the univariate generalized Gini welfare functions.

Of these, homotheticity requires that welfare ranking of two social distributions remains unchanged under common proportional change in dimensional achievements. Formally, for all $n \in N$, $X, Y \in M^n$, $W(X) \geq W(Y)$ if and only if $W(cX) \geq W(cY)$, where $W: M \to \Re^1$ and $c > 0$ is any scalar. To understand this, recall the society's welfare ranking between X_{13} and X_{14}, which is, $W(X_{13}) > W(X_{14})$. Then homotheticity claims that for any $c > 0$, welfare dispreference of cX_{14} over cX_{13} is maintained, that is, $W(X_{13}) > W(X_{14})$ should imply $W(cX_{13}) > W(cX_{14})$. The converse should be true as well. Consequently, if $c = 2$, then $W\left(\begin{bmatrix} 35 & 40 \\ 20 & 10 \\ 10 & 10 \end{bmatrix}\right) > W\left(\begin{bmatrix} 30 & 40 \\ 20 & 10 \\ 10 & 10 \end{bmatrix}\right)$ should imply $W\left(\begin{bmatrix} 70 & 80 \\ 40 & 20 \\ 20 & 20 \end{bmatrix}\right) > W\left(\begin{bmatrix} 60 & 80 \\ 40 & 20 \\ 20 & 20 \end{bmatrix}\right)$. The reverse implication can be deduced by multiplying the entries of $2X_{14}$ and $2X_{13}$ by $\frac{1}{2}$.

Two new axioms, strong attribute separability and weak comonotonic additivity, were invoked as well. To state the first of these two axioms, strong attribute separability, for any nonempty $S \subset Q$, let X^S be the submatrix showing achievements of all the individuals with respect to dimensions in S. Then the axiom demands that the conditional social ranking between two submatrices X^S and Y^S does not depend on the submatrix associated with the dimensions in Q/S, where $n \in N$ and $X \in M^n$ are arbitrary.

To understand the strong attribute separability postulate, let us derive $X_{15} = \begin{bmatrix} 210 & 51 & 310 \\ 650 & 72 & 400 \\ 151 & 50 & 788 \\ 98 & 66 & 207 \end{bmatrix}$ from X_{12} by increasing person 1's achievement in dimension 1 by 10 units. By the strong Pareto principle, $W(X_{15}^S) > W(X_{12}^S)$, where X_{15}^S and X_{12}^S are respectively the submatrices of X_{15} and X_{12} associated with the subset $S = \{1, 2\}$ of $Q = \{1, 2, 3\}$. Note that here $Q/S = \{3\}$ and $X_{12}^{Q/S} = \begin{bmatrix} 310 \\ 400 \\ 788 \\ 207 \end{bmatrix}$, which is the same as $X_{15}^{Q/S}$.

Now, consider a third social distribution $\tilde{X} = \begin{bmatrix} 213 & 50 & 312 \\ 647 & 73 & 400 \\ 155 & 51 & 787 \\ 99 & 67 & 207 \end{bmatrix}$ so that $\tilde{X}^{Q/S} = \begin{bmatrix} 312 \\ 400 \\ 787 \\ 207 \end{bmatrix}$. Then the strong attribute separability axiom demands that the inequality $W(X_{15}^S, X_{15}^{Q/S}) > W(X_{12}^S, X_{12}^{Q/S})$ holds if and only if the inequality $W(X_{15}^S, \tilde{X}^{Q/S}) > W(X_{12}^S, \tilde{X}^{Q/S})$ holds.

An achievement matrix $X \in M^n$ is called nonincreasing comonotonic if for any $j \in Q$, $x_{.j}$, the distribution of achievements in dimension j is nonincreasingly ordered, that is, $x_{1j} \geq x_{2j} \geq \cdots \geq x_{nj}$. That is, the ith person's achievement in any dimension cannot be higher than that of the $(i-1)$th person, where $(i-1) \geq 1$. We denote the set of all of nonincreasing comonotonic matrices associated with M by M^{CM}. Then weak comonotonic additivity demands that for all $X, Y \in M^{CM}$ and $X' \in M_1^{CM}$ for which there exists a $k \in Q$, such that (i) $x_{.j} = y_{.j}$ for all $j \in Q/\{k\}$, (ii) $x'_{ij} = 0$ for all $i \in \{1, 2, \ldots, n\}$ and all $j \in Q/\{k\}$, and (iii) $X + X' \in M^{CM}, Y + X' \in M^{CM}$, $W(X) \geq W(Y)$ if and only if $W(X + X') \geq W(Y + X')$.

We deduce the matrices $X + X'$ and $Y + X'$ from X and Y by adding a common distribution of dimension k to $x_{.k}$ and $y_{.k}$, respectively. The defining conditions $X, Y \in M^{CM}, X + X' \in M^{CM}$, and $Y + X' \in M^{CM}$ ensure that all the matrices $X, Y, X + X'$ and $Y + X'$ are nonincreasing comonotonic. Further, they all have identical achievement distributions in all the dimensions except k (conditions (i) and (ii)). Then the axiom requires that social ranking between the comonotonic achievement matrices X and Y and that between $X + X'$ and $Y + X'$ coincide.

To explain this postulate, note that the matrices X_{13} and X_{14} are nonincreasing comonotonic. In the statement of weak comonotonic additivity, choose $k = 1$ and $X' = \begin{bmatrix} 4 & 0 \\ 3 & 0 \\ 2 & 0 \end{bmatrix}$. Consequently, $X_{13} + X' = \begin{bmatrix} 39 & 40 \\ 23 & 10 \\ 12 & 10 \end{bmatrix}$ and $X_{14} + X' = \begin{bmatrix} 34 & 40 \\ 23 & 10 \\ 12 & 10 \end{bmatrix}$. Evidently, X', $X_{13} + X'$, and $X_{14} + X'$ are nonincreasing comonotonic, which ensure satisfaction of condition (iii). Conditions (i) and (ii) are verified as well. Then the axiom demands that $W(X_{13}) > W(X_{14})$ implies and is implied by $W(X_{13} + X') > W(X_{14} + X')$.

Assuming that $M = M_2$ and $d \geq 3$, Gajdos and Weymark (2005) demonstrated that a social welfare function $W_{GWM} : M_2 \to \Re^1$ satisfies continuity, the strong Pareto principle, symmetry, the uniform Pigou–Dalton majorization principle, strong attribute separability, weak comonotonic additivity, and homotheticity if and only if there exist an $n \times d$ matrix C possessing positive entries c_{ij}, where $c_{.j}$ is increasing and $\sum_{i=1}^{n} c_{ij} = 1$ for all $j \in Q$; a (positive) vector $\gamma \in D^d$ with $\sum_{j=1}^{d} \gamma_j = 1$; and a scalar k such that

$$W_{GWM}(X) = \left[\sum_{j=1}^{d} \gamma_j \left(\sum_{i=1}^{n} c_{ij} x_{ij}^0 \right)^k \right]^{\frac{1}{k}}, \tag{1.10}$$

if $k \neq 0$ and

$$W_{GWM}(X) = \prod_{j=1}^{d} \left(\sum_{i=1}^{n} c_{ij} x_{ij}^0 \right)^{\gamma_j}, \tag{1.11}$$

if $k = 0$; $n \in N$ and $X \in M_2^n$ being arbitrary; and for any $j \in Q$, $x_{.j}^0$ is the nonincreasingly ordered permutation of $x_{.j}$, that is, $x_{1j}^0 \geq x_{2j}^0 \geq \cdots \geq x_{nj}^0$.

In (1.10), given any dimension j, W_{GWM} first takes a weighted average of the nonincreasingly ordered dimensional quantities possessed by different persons using increasingly ordered positive weights. Since $X \in M_2^n$, these averages are positive for all dimensions $j \in Q$. These positive averages are then averaged, using positive weights, over dimensions by raising each of them to the power k, with k being a nonzero real number. Finally, $\left(\frac{1}{k}\right)$ th power of the (positive) average obtained at the second stage is taken to arrive at W_{GWM}. In (1.11), geometric average of the positive numbers $\left(\sum_{i=1}^{n} c_{ij} x_{ij}^0\right)$ across dimensions is taken to arrive at the expression for W_{GWM}. The two welfare functions (1.10) and (1.11) are linear homogeneous; multiplication of all the achievements across dimensions with a positive scalar will multiply their values by the scalar itself. We refer to these two functions as the Gajdos–Weymark multidimensional generalized Gini homothetic welfare functions, since they apply one-dimensional Gini, more precisely, generalized Gini-type aggregation (see Weymark, 1981).

Gajdos and Weymark (2005) characterized translatable variants of (1.10) and (1.11). A social welfare function $W: M \to \mathfrak{R}^1$ is called translatable if for all $n \in N, X, Y \in M^n$, $W(X) \geq W(Y)$ if and only if $W(X + c\mathbf{1}_{\mathbf{n \times d}}) \geq W(Y + c\mathbf{1}_{\mathbf{n \times d}})$, where $\mathbf{1}_{\mathbf{n \times d}}$ is the $n \times d$ matrix all of whose entries are 1, and c is any real number such that $(X + c\mathbf{1}_{\mathbf{n \times d}}), (Y + c\mathbf{1}_{\mathbf{n \times d}}) \in M^n$. Translatability means that welfare ranking of two social distributions does not change when achievements of all the individuals in all the dimensions are reduced or augmented by the same quantity.

To illustrate this, consider again the social distribution matrices X_{13} and X_{14} so that $W(X_{13}) > W(X_{14})$. Suppose that each person's achievements in all the dimensions in matrices X_{13} and X_{14} increase by the same amount 2. Denote the resulting matrices by X_{16} and $X_{17,}$ respectively. Thus, $X_{16} = \begin{bmatrix} 37 & 42 \\ 22 & 12 \\ 12 & 12 \end{bmatrix}$ and $X_{17} = \begin{bmatrix} 32 & 42 \\ 22 & 12 \\ 12 & 12 \end{bmatrix}$. Then translatability claims that $W(X_{13}) > W(X_{14})$ should imply and is implied by $W(X_{16}) > W(X_{17})$.

If in the characterization of (1.10) and (1.11) we replace homotheticity by translatability and maintain all other axioms, then, given $d \geq 3$, Gajdos and Weymark (2005) showed that the only social welfare function $W_{GWA}: M_1 \to \mathfrak{R}^1$ for which these axioms hold together are given by

$$W_{GWA}(X) = \frac{1}{k} \log \left[\sum_{j=1}^{d} \gamma_j' \exp\left(k \sum_{i=1}^{n} c_{ij} x_{ij}^0 \right) \right], \tag{1.12}$$

if the scalar k is nonzero and

$$W_{GWA}(X) = \left[\sum_{j=1}^{d} \gamma'_j \left(\sum_{i=1}^{n} c_{ij} x^0_{ij}\right)\right], \tag{1.13}$$

if $k = 0$, where $\gamma' \in D^d$ is a (positive) vector, $c_{ij}s$ are the same as in (1.10) and (1.11); $n \in N$ and $X \in M_1^n$ are arbitrary; and for any $j \in Q$, $x^0_{.j}$ is the nonincreasingly ordered permutation of $x_{.j}$. While in (1.12) a Kolm–Pollak type aggregation is employed, (1.13) uses a generalized Gini-type aggregation.

So, if $k \neq 0$, first an exponential-type aggregation is employed over individuals and then a logarithmic aggregation is used over the dimensions. Note that if $k = 0$, we have linear aggregation at each stage. The two standards in (1.12) and (1.13) are translatable. An equal absolute increase in all the dimensional achievements will increase the welfare values in terms of the absolute amount itself. These two standards can be called the Gajdos–Weymark multidimensional generalized Gini translatable welfare functions. It should be clear that strong attribute separability makes the welfare standards (1.10)–(1.13) insensitive to a correlation-increasing switch.

Decancq and Lugo (2012) proposed two social welfare functions that involve two-stage aggregations. For the first, a specific procedure following Kolm (1977) is adopted. More precisely, a dashboard of individual dimensional welfare functions is constructed. These dashboard-based welfare metrics are then aggregated to arrive at an overall quantifier of welfare. In the second, which following Kolm (1977), referred to as the individualistic approach, the aforementioned procedure is reversed. In other words, for each individual, a well-being index, defined on the person's dimensional attainments, is designed. These individual metrics are combined to compose a well-being quantifier for the population as a whole (see also Dutta et al., 2003 and Chakravarty and Lugo, 2016).

Formally, for all $n \in N$ and $X \in M_3^n$:

$$W^1(X) = W^d(W^n(x_{.1}), W^n(x_{.2}), \ldots, W^n(x_{.d})), \tag{1.14}$$

$$W^2(X) = W^n(W^d(x_{1.}), W^d(x_{2.}), \ldots, W^d(x_{n.})). \tag{1.15}$$

Here $W^n : D^d \to D^1$ is the common functional form of welfare statistic of achievements in a dimension, and the argument $x_{.j}$ of $W^n(x_{.j})$ shows that the index value is calculated for each dimension $j \in Q$ separately. Similarly, $W^d : D^n \to D^1$ is the common metric of individual well-being. Its value is determined for each of the n persons separately.

The following forms of the dimensional and individual indices were considered by Decancq and Lugo (2012):

$$W^n_\rho(x_{.j}) = \left(\sum_{i=1}^{n} \left[\left(\frac{r^i_j}{n}\right)^\rho - \left(\frac{r^i_j - 1}{n}\right)^\rho\right] x^0_{ij}\right), \tag{1.16}$$

$$W^d(x_{i.}) = \begin{cases} \left(\sum_{j=1}^{d} w_j x_{ij}^{\beta}\right)^{\frac{1}{\beta}}, & \beta < 1, \ \beta \neq 0, \\ \prod_{j=1}^{d} x_{ij}^{w_j}, & \beta = 0, \end{cases} \tag{1.17}$$

where $n \in N$ and $X \in M_3^n$ are arbitrary; r_j^i is the rank of individual i with respect to his achievement in dimension j; $w_j > 0$ is the weight assigned to his achievement in dimension j, $\sum_{j=1}^{d} w_j = 1$, and $\rho > 1$ is a parameter. The restriction $\rho > 1$ is necessary to seize bottom awareness of aggregator.[23] The positive-valued individual well-being standard W^d is continuous, linear homogenous, and strictly concave.

The $1 \times d$ dimensional dashboard of well-being corresponding to (1.16) is given by $(W_\rho^n(x_{.1}), W_\rho^n(x_{.2}), \dots, W_\rho^n(x_{.d}))$. For $\rho = 2$, $W_\rho^n(x_{.j})$ becomes the Gini welfare function, also known as the Gini mean or the Sen mean, of achievements in dimension $j \in Q$. Consequently, in this particular case, the dashboard may be referred to as the Gini welfare dashboard of well-being dimensions.

The parameter β in (1.17) has a one-to-one correspondence with the elasticity of substitution between dimensions. In fact, the constant elasticity of substitution (CES) between any two dimensions is given by $\frac{1}{(1-\beta)}$. For $\beta = 1$, the well-being standard is linear, and substitutability between any two dimensions is perfect. On the other hand, as $\beta \to -\infty$, elasticity tends to zero, and there is no possibility for substitution. The scope for substitution decreases as the value of β decreases. For $\beta = 0$, the constant elasticity is 1. The associated Cobb–Douglas well-being function rules out the possibility of other elasticity values. Flexibility of functional forms of W^d cannot be accommodated once $\beta = 0$ is assumed. In our future discussion, we will not consider this case. The constancy of the elasticity of substitution between any pair of dimensions is chosen for simplicity. There is no reason for the elasticity of substitution between health and income to be the same as that between income and education. Bourguignon and Chakravarty (2003) argued that the elasticity should depend on dimensional achievements. They also argued that when we have many dimensions, the constancy of the elasticity of substitution between any two dimensions is not realistic. In subsequent discussion here, for simplicity of exposition, we will maintain the constancy assumption.

If the one-dimensional aggregations given by (1.16) and (1.17) are substituted into two initial two-step procedures, the following forms of multidimensional

23 Characterizations of W_ρ^n and W^d were developed respectively by Ebert (1988), and Blackorby and Donaldson (1982) and Tsui and Weymark (1997).

social welfare functions are obtained:

$$W_{DL}^{1}(X) = \left[\sum_{j=1}^{d} w_j \left(\sum_{i=1}^{n} \left[\left(\frac{r_j^i}{n} \right)^{\rho} - \left(\frac{r_j^i - 1}{n} \right)^{\rho} \right] x_{ij}^{0} \right)^{\beta} \right]^{\frac{1}{\beta}}, \tag{1.18}$$

$$W_{DL}^{2}(X) = \sum_{i=1}^{n} \left[\left(\frac{r^i}{n} \right)^{\rho} - \left(\frac{r^i - 1}{n} \right)^{\rho} \right] \left(\sum_{j=1}^{d} w_j (x_{ij})^{\beta} \right)^{\frac{1}{\beta}}. \tag{1.19}$$

In (1.19), r^i is the rank of person i on the basis of $\underline{W^d}$, the vector of non-increasingly ordered individual well-being levels with $W^d(x_{i.}) = \left(\sum_{j=1}^{d} w_j x_{ij}^{\beta} \right)^{\frac{1}{\beta}}$. While, the specific-procedure based on the social welfare function W_{DL}^{1} may be regarded as a special case of the Gajdos–Weymark multidimensional generalized Gini social welfare function given by (1.10), the individualistic function W_{DL}^{2} was introduced to the literature by Decancq and Lugo (2012).

In W_{DL}^{2}, at the first stage, an individual's well-being measure is determined by considering weighted average of the βth power of his accomplishments across dimensions and then taking $\left(\frac{1}{\beta} \right)$th power of the average itself. At the second stage, a weighted average of these well-being quantities, where the weights are dependent on the distribution of well-being levels across persons, generates the final value of the welfare standard. The function (1.19) is an example of an individualistic index of multidimensional welfare. For $\rho = 2$, we may refer to it as the Gini individualistic multidimensional welfare function.

The restrictions $\beta < 1$ and $\rho > 1$ ensure that both W_{DL}^{1} and W_{DL}^{2} increase under a uniform majorization transformation. On the other hand, while W_{DL}^{1} is insensitive to a correlation-increasing switch, W_{DL}^{2} increases under such a switch if the value of ρ exceeds a lower bound that depends on the weight vector, β, and dimensional achievements.

Bosmans et al. (2015) considered the double-CES class social welfare function and analyzed its properties. Using a suggestion put forward by Graaff (1977), they considered a decomposition of its associated inequality measure into inequity and efficiency components (see Chapter 2). The welfare function is formally defined as

$$W(X) = \begin{cases} \left(\frac{1}{n} \sum_{i=1}^{n} (W^d(x_{i.}))^{\alpha} \right)^{\frac{1}{\alpha}}, & \alpha < 1, \ \alpha \neq 0, \\ \prod_{i=1}^{n} (W^d(x_{i.}))^{\frac{1}{n}}, & \alpha = 0, \end{cases} \tag{1.20}$$

where $n \in N$ and $X \in M_3^n$ are arbitrary. Substitution of the explicit form of W^d into (1.20) generates the following explicit form of the welfare function (ignoring the cases $\alpha = 0$ and $\beta = 0$):

$$W_{BDO}(X) = \left(\frac{1}{n} \sum_{i=1}^{n} \left(\left(\sum_{j=1}^{d} w_j x_{ij}^{\beta} \right)^{\frac{1}{\beta}} \right)^{\alpha} \right)^{\frac{1}{\alpha}}. \tag{1.21}$$

There is an important difference between the standards W_{BDO} and W_{DL}^2. While in the former, at the second stage, another constant elasticity-type aggregator is invoked on the individual well-being quantities; in the latter, a rank-dependent weighted average of these quantities is considered.[24] The two-parameter family increases under a uniform majorization transformation and decreases under a correlation-increasing switch if and only if $\alpha < \beta < 1$. Increasingness under both a correlation-increasing switch and a uniform majorization transformation occurs if and only if $\beta < \alpha < 1$ (Seth, 2013).

1.8 Concluding Remarks

Our presentation in this chapter relies directly on dimensional achievements of individuals in a society and ignores the role of their preferences. The transfer principles analyzed in the chapter are nonwelfarist conditions since they recommend transfers of resources without involving individual preferences. The conditions of this kind may come into direct conflict with the Pareto principle (see Gibbard, 1979; Fleurbaey and Trannoy, 2003 and Brun and Tungodden, 2004). However, Roemer (1966) turned down the idea that welfarism is bound to occur when the index obeys individual preferences, although he did not "propose a concrete method in order to define a non-welfarist Paretian index" (Fleurbaey, 2006b, p. 233).

Another important unaddressed issue is inclusion of needs in the analysis. In a recent contribution, building on Atkinson and Bourguignon (1987); Moyes (2012) employed the utilitarian rule to develop dominance conditions for comparing household well-beings, where well-being is assumed to depend on income and needs. Consequently, while advocating redistribution of resources across households, needs have to be taken into account (see also Lambert and Ramos, 2002; Ebert, 2004; Shorrocks, 2004). In our context, it will be admirable to investigate the impact of such a notion of transfer under appropriate formulation, say, by considering a necessary variant of the Pigou–Dalton bundle of progressive transfer principle.

---

24 For alternative characterizations of the double-CES class welfare function, see Lasso de la Vega et al. (2009), Decancq and Ooghe (2010), Lasso de la Vega and Urrutia (2011), and Seth (2013). Discussions on the class are available in Atkinson (2003) and Bourguignon (2009).

References

Aaberge, R. and A. Brandolini. 2014. Social Evaluation of Multidimensional Count Distributions. *ECINEQ Working Paper No. 2014–342.*

Aaberge, R. and A. Brandolini. 2015. Multidimensional Poverty and Inequality. In A.B. Atkinson and F. Bourguignon (eds.), 141–216.

Aaberge, R. and E. Peluso. 2011. A Counting Approach to Measuring Multidimensional Deprivations. *Working Paper No. 07/2011*. Universitá Di Verona.

Adler, M.D. 2012. *Well-Being and Fair Distribution: Beyond Cost-Benefit Analysis.* Oxford: Oxford University Press.

Adler, M.D. 2016. Extended Preferences. In M.D. Adler and M. Fleurbaey (eds.), 476–517.

Adler, M.D. and M. Fleurbaey (eds.) 2016. *Oxford Handbook of Well-Being and Public Policy*. New York: Oxford University Press.

Alkire, S. 2016. The Capability Approach and Well-Being Measurement for Public Policy. In M.D. Adler and M. Fleurbaey (eds.), 615–644.

Alkire, S., J.E. Foster, S. Seth, M.E. Santos, J.M. Roche, and P. Ballón. 2015. *Multidimensional Poverty Measurement and Analysis*. New York: Oxford University Press.

Allison, R.A. and J.E. Foster. 2004. Measuring Health Inequality using Qualitative Data. *Journal of Health Economics* 23: 505–524.

Anand, S. 1983. *Inequality and Poverty in Malaysia: Measurement and Decomposition*. New York: Oxford University Press.

Atkinson, A.B. 1970. On the Measurement of Inequality. *Journal of Economic Theory* 2: 244–263.

Atkinson, A.B. 2003. Multidimensional Deprivation: Contrasting Social Welfare and Counting Approaches. *Journal of Economic Inequality* 1: 51–65.

Atkinson, A.B. and F. Bourguignon. 1982. The Comparison of Multidimensioned Distributions of Economic Status. *Review of Economic Studies* 49: 183–201.

Atkinson, A.B. and F. Bourguignon. 1987. Income Distributions and Differences in Needs. In G. Feiwel (ed.) *Arrow and the Foundations of the Theory of Economic Policy.* New York: MacMillan, 350–370.

Atkinson, A.B. and F. Bourguignon (eds.). 2015. *Handbook of Income Distribution*, Vol. 2A. Amsterdam: North Holland.

Atkinson, A.B., B. Cantillon, E. Marlier, and B. Nolan. 2002. *Social Indicators: The EU and Social Exclusion*. Oxford: Oxford University Press.

Balckorby, C., W. Bossert, and D. Donaldson. 2005. *Population Issues in Social Choice Theory, Welfare Economics and Ethics.* New York: Cambridge University Press.

Banerjee, A.K. 2014. A Multidimensional Lorenz Domination Relation. *Social Choice and Welfare* 42: 171–191.

Banerjee, A.V. and E. Duflo. 2011. *Poor Economics: A Radical Rethinking of the Way to Fight Global Poverty*. New York: Public Affairs.

Barbera, S., P.J. Hammond, and C. Seidl. (eds.). 2004. *Handbook of Utility Theory, Vol. 2: Extensions*. Boston: Kluwer Academic.

Basu, K. 1980. *Revealed Preference of Government*. Cambridge: Cambridge University Press.

Basu, K. and L.F. López-Calva. 2011. Functionings and Capabilities. In K.J. Arrow, A.K. Sen, and K. Suzumura (eds.) *Handbook of Social Choice and Welfare*, Vol. II. Amsterdam: North Holland, 153–187.

Becker, G.S., T.J. Philipson, and R.R. Soares. 2005. The Quantity and Quality of Life and the Evolution of World Inequality. *American Economic Review* 95: 277–291.

Blackorby, C. and D. Donaldson. 1982 Ratio-scale and Translation-scale Full Interpersonal Comparisons without Domain Restrictions: Admissible Social-evaluation Functions. *International Economic Review* 23: 249–268.

Blackorby, C, D. Donaldson, and M. Auersperg. 1981. A New Procedure for the Measurement of Inequality within and among Population Subgroups. *Canadian Journal of Economics* 14: 665–685.

Blackorby, C., D. Donaldson, and J.A. Weymark: 1984. Social Choice Theory with Interpersonal Utility Comparisons: A Diagrammatic Introduction. *International Economic Review* 25: 2–31.

Boadway, R. 2016. Cost-Benefit Analysis. In M.D. Adler and M. Fleurbaey (eds.), 47–81.

Boelhouwer, J. 2002. Quality of Life and Living Conditions in the Netherlands. *Social Indicators Research* 60: 89–113.

Bosmans, K., K. Decancq, and E. Ooghe. 2015. What do Normative Indices of Multidimensional Inequality Really Measure? *Journal of Public Economics* 130: 94–104.

Bosmans, K., L. Lauwers, and E. Ooghe. 2009. A Consistent Multidimensional Pigou–Dalton Transfer Principle. *Journal of Economic Theory* 144: 1358–1371.

Bossert, W., S.R. Chakravarty, and C. D'Ambrosio. 2013. Multidimensional Poverty and Material Deprivation with Discrete Data. *Review of Income and Wealth* 59: 29–43.

Bossert, W. and J.A. Weymark. 2004. Utility in Social Choice. In S. Barbera, P. Hammond, and C. Seidl (eds.), 1099–1177.

Bourguignon, F. 1999. Comment on Multidimensioned Approaches to Welfare Analysis by E. Maasoumi. In J. Silber (ed.) *Handbook of Income Inequality Measurement*. London: Kluwer Academic, 477–484.

Bourguignon, F. and S.R. Chakravarty. 2003. The Measurement of Multidimensional Poverty. *Journal of Economic Inequality* 1: 25–49.

Brandolini, A. 2009. On Synthetic Indices of Multidimensional Well-being: Health and Income Inequalities in France, Germany, Italy and the United Kingdom. In R. Gotoh, P. Dumouchel (eds.) *Against Injustice: The New Economics of Amartya Sen*. Cambridge: Cambridge University Press, 221–251.

Brandolini, A. and D'Alessio. 1998. *Measuring Well-Being in the Functioning Space*. Bank of Italy: Rome.

Broome, J. 2016. The Well-Being of Future Generations. In M.D. Adler and M. Fleurbaey (eds.), 901–927.

Brun, B.C. and B. Tungodden. 2004. Non-welfaristic Theories of Justice: Is "the Intersection Approach" a Solution to the Indexing Impasse? *Social Choice and Welfare* 22: 49–60.

Card, D. 1999. The causal Effect of Education on Earnings. In O. Ashenfelter and D. Card (eds.) *Handbook of Labor Economics.* Vol. III. Amsterdam: North Holland, 1801–1863.

Cerioli, A. and Zani, S. 1990. A Fuzzy Approach to the Measurement of Poverty. In C. Dagum and M. Zenga (eds.) *Income and Wealth Distribution, Inequality and Poverty.* New York: Springer, 272–284.

Chakravarty, S.R. 2009. *Inequality, Polarization and Poverty: Advances in Distributional Analysis.* New York: Springer.

Chakravarty, S.R. 2010. Metodología de la Medición Multidimensional de la Pobreza Para México. In N.M. Martini (ed.) *Medición Multidimensional de la Poberza en México.* Coneval: el Colegio de México, 281–322.

Chakravarty, S.R. and C. D'Ambrosio. 2006. The Measurement of Social Exclusion. *Review of Income and Wealth* 52: 377–398.

Chakravarty, S.R. and M.A. Lugo. 2016. Multidimensional Indicators of Inequality and Poverty. In M.D. Adler and M. Fleurbaey (eds.), 246–285.

Chakravarty, S.R. and C. Zoli. 2012. Stochastic Dominance Relations for Integer Variables. *Journal of Economic Theory* 147: 1331–1341.

Châteauneuf, A. and P. Moyes. 2006. A Non-welfarist Approach to Inequality Measurement. In M. McGillivray (ed.) *Inequality, Poverty and Well-being.* London: Palgrave Macmillan, 22–65.

Cheli, B. and A. Lemmi. 1995. A "Totally" Fuzzy and Relative Approach to the Multidimensional Analysis of Poverty. *Economic Notes* 24: 115–133.

Cherchye, L., W. Moesen, N. Rogge and T. van Puyenbroeck. 2007a. An Introduction to 'Benefit of the Doubt' Composite Indicators. *Social Indicators Research* 82: 111–145.

Cherchye, L., W. Moesen, N. Rogge, T. van Puyenbroeck , M. Saisana, A. Saltelli, R. Liska, and S. Tarantola. 2007b. Creating Composite Indicators with DEA and Robustness Analysis: The Case of Technology Achievement Index. *Journal of the Operations Research Society* 59: 231–251.

Cherchye, L., E. Ooghe, and T. van Puyenbroeck. 2008. Robust Human Development Ranking. *Journal of Economic Inequality* 6: 287–321.

Chipman, J.S. 1977. An Empirical Implication of Auspitz-Edgeworth-Lieben-Pareto Complementarity. *Journal of Economic Theory* 14: 228–231.

Chowdhury, S. and L. Squire. 2006. Setting Weights to Aggregate Indices: An Application to the Commitment to Development Index and Human Development Index. *Journal of Development Studies* 42: 761–771.

Clark, A.E. 2016. SWB as a Measure of Individual Well-Being. In M.D. Adler and M. Fleurbaey (eds.), 518–552.

Cummins, R.A. 1996. Domains of Life Satisfaction: An Attempt to Order Chaos. *Social Indicators Research* 38: 303–328.
d'Aspremont, C. and L. Gevers. 1977. Equity and Informational Basis of Collective Choice. *Review of Economic Studies* 44: 199–209.
d'Aspremont, C. and L. Gevers. 2002. Social Welfare Functionals and Interpersonal Comparability. In K.J. Arrow, A.K. Sen, and K. Suzumura (eds.) *Handbook of Social Choice and Welfare*, Vol. 1. Amsterdam: North-Holland, 459–541.
Dalton, H. 1920. *The Inequality of Incomes.* London: Routledge.
Dardanoni, V. 1996. On Multidimensional Inequality Measurement. *Research on Economic Inequality* 6: 201–205.
Dasgupta, P., A.K. Sen, and D. Starrett. 1973. Notes on the Measurement of Inequality. *Journal of Economic Theory* 6: 180–187.
de Kruijk, H. and M. Rutten. 2007. *Weighting Dimensions of Poverty based on People's Priorities: Constructing a Composite Poverty Index for the Maldives.* Centre for International Studies. University of Toronto.
Deaton, A. 1992. *Understanding Consumption.* New York: Oxford University Press.
Deaton, A. 1997. *The Analysis of Household Surveys: A Microeconometric Approach to Development Policy.* Baltimore, MD: Johns Hopkins University Press.
Deaton, A. and M. Grosh. 2000. Consumption. In M. Grosh and P. Glewwe (eds.) *Designing Household Survey Questionnaire for Developing Countries: Lessons from 15 Years of Living Standard Measurement Study.* Washington, DC: World Bank, 91–133.
Decancq, K. 2012. Elementary Multivariate Rearrangements and Stochastic Dominance on a Frechét Class. *Journal of Economic Theory* 147: 1450–1459.
Decancq, K. 2013. Copula-based Measurement of Dependence between Dimensions of Well-being. *Oxford Economic Papers* 66: 681–701.
Decancq, K., M. Fleurbaey, and E. Schokkaert (2015). Inequality, Income and Well-Being. In A.B. Atkinson and F. Bourguignon (eds.), 67–140.
Decancq, K. and M.A. Lugo. 2012. Inequality of Well-Being: A Multidimensional Approach. *Economica* 79: 721–746.
Decancq, K. and D. Neumann. 2016. Does the Choice of Well-Being Measure Matter Empirically? In M.D. Adler and M. Fleurbaey (eds.), 553–587.
Decancq, K. and E. Ooghe. 2010. Has the World Moved Forward? A Robust Multidimensional. Evaluation. *Economics Letters* 107: 266–269. 81–701.
Decancq, K. and E. Schokkaert. 2016. Beyond GDP: Using Equivalent Incomes to Measure Well-being in Europe. *Social Indicators Research* 126: 21–55.
Desai, M. and A. Shah. 1988. An Econometric Approach to the Measurement Poverty. *Oxford Economic Papers* 40: 505–522.
Despotis, D.K. 2005a. Measuring Human Development via Data Envelopment Analysis: The Case of Asia and the Pacific. *Omega* 33: 385–390.

Despotis, D.K. 2005b. A Reassessment of the Human Development via Data Envelopment Analysis. *Journal of the Operational Research Society* 56: 969–980.

Deutsch, J. and J. Silber. 2005. Measuring Multidimensional Poverty: An Empirical Comparison of Various Approaches. *Review of Income and Wealth* 51: 145–174.

Di Tommaso, M.L. 2006. Measuring the Well-being of Children using a Capability Approach An Application to Indian Data. *Working Paper 05-06,* Centre for Household, Income, Labour and Demographic Economics.

Diez, H., M.C. Lasso de la Vega, A. de Sarachu, and A. Urrutia. 2007. A Consistent Multidimensional Generalization of the Pigou-Dalton Transfer Principle: An Analysis. *B.E. Journal of Theoretical Economics* 7. Available at: http:/www.bepress.com/bejte/vol7/iss1/art45.

Donaldson D. and J.A. Weymark. 1980. A Single Parameter Generalization of the Gini indices of inequality. *Journal of Economic Theory* 22: 67–86.

Doyal, L. and I. Gough. 1991. *A Theory of Human Need*. Basinkstoke: Macmillan.

Duclos, J.-Y. and L. Tiberti. 2016. Multidimensional Poverty Indices: A Critical Assessment. In M.D. Adler and M. Fleurbaey (eds.), 677–710.

Dutta, I. , P.K. Pattanaik, and Y. Xu. 2003. On Measuring Deprivation and the Standard of Living in a Multidimensional Framework on the Basis of Aggregate Data. *Economica* 70: 197–221.

Easterlin, R. 2000. The Worldwide Standard of Living since 1800. *Journal of Economic Perspectives* 14: 7–26.

Ebert, U. 1988. Measurement of Inequality: An Attempt at Unification and Generalization. *Social Choice and Welfare* 5: 147–169.

Ebert, U. 2004. Social Welfare, Inequality and Poverty when Needs Differ. *Social Choice and Welfare* 23: 415–448.

Elson, D., S. Fukuda-Parr, and P. Vizard (eds.) 2011. *Journal of Human Development and Capabilities* 12: Special Issue on Human Rights and Capabilities.

Epstein, L.G. and S.M. Tanny. 1980. Increasing Generalized Correlation: A Dentition and Some Economic Consequences. *Canadian Journal of Economics* 13: 16–34.

Farina, F. and E. Savaglio (eds.) 2006. *Inequality and Economic Integration.* London: Routledge.

Ferrer-i Carbonell, A. and P. Frijters. 2004. How Important is Methodology for the Estimates of the Determinants of Happiness? *Economic Journal* 114: 641–659.

Fleurbaey, F. 2006a. Capabilities, Functionings and Refined Functionings. *Journal of Human Development* 7: 299–310.

Fleurbaey, F. 2006b. Social Welfare, Priority to the Worst-off and the Dimensions of Individual Well-being. In F. Farina and E. Savaglio (eds.), 222–263.

Fleurbaey, F. 2009. Beyond the GDP: The Quest for a Measure of Social Welfare. *Journal of Economic Literature* 47: 1029–1075.

Fleurbaey, F. and D. Blanchet. 2013. *Beyond GDP: Measuring Welfare and Assessing Sustainability.* Oxford: Oxford University Press.

Fleurbaey, F. and G. Gaulier. 2009. International Comparisons of Living Standards by Equivalent Incomes. *Scandinavian Journal of Economics* 111: 597–624.

Fleurbaey, M. and P.J. Hammond. 2004. Interpersonally Comparable Utility. In S. Barbera, P.J. Hammond, and C. Seidl (eds.), 1179–1285.

Fleurbaey, F. and F. Maniquet. 2011. *A Theory of Fairness and Social Welfare.* New York: Cambridge University Press.

Fleurbaey M. and Ph. Michel. 2001. Transfer Principles and Inequality Aversion, with an Application to Optimal Growth. *Mathematical Social Sciences* 42: 1–11.

Fleurbaey, F., E. Schokkaert, and K. Decancq. 2015. Happiness, Equivalent Income and Respect for Individual Preferences. *Economica* 82: 1082–1106.

Fleurbaey M. and A. Trannoy. 2003. The Impossibility of a Paretian Egalitarian. *Social Choice Welfare* 21: 319–329.

Foster, J.E., M. McGillivray, and S. Seth. 2013a. Composite Indices: Rank Robustness, Statistical Association and Redundancy. *Econometric Reviews* 22: 35–56.

Foster, J.E. and A.K. Sen. 1997. *On Economic Inequality: After a Quarter Century, Annex to Enlarged Edition of On Economic Inequality by A.K. Sen.* Oxford: Clarendon Press.

Foster, J.A., S. Seth, M. Lokshin, and Z. Sajaia. 2013b. *A Unified Approach to Measuring Poverty and Inequality: Theory and Practice.* Washington, DC: World Bank.

Gajdos, T. and J.A. Weymark. 2005. Multidimensional Generalized Gini Indices. *Economic Theory* 26: 471–496.

Gibbard, A. 1979. Disparate Goods and Rawls' s Difference Principle: A Social Choice Theoretic Treatment. *Theory and Decision* 11: 267–288.

Graaff, J. de V. 1977. Equity and Efficiency as Components of the General Welfare. *South African Journal of Economics* 45: 362–375.

Graham, C. 2016. Subjective Well-Being in Economics. In M.D. Adler and M. Fleurbaey (eds.), 424–450.

Grusky, D.B. and R. Kanbur.(eds.) 2006. *Poverty and Inequality.* Stanford University Press: Stanford, CA.

Halleröd, B. 1995. The Truly Poor: Direct and Indirect Consensual Measurement of Poverty in Sweden. *Journal of European Social Policy* 5: 111–129.

Halleröd, B. 1996. Deprivation and Poverty: A Comparative Analysis of Sweden and Great Britain. *Acta Sociologica* 39: 141–168.

Hammond, P.J. 1976. Why Ethical Measures of Inequality Need Interpersonal Comparisons? *Theory and Decision* 7: 263–274.

Hammond, P.J. 1991. Interpersonal Comparisons of Utility : Why they are and how they should be made ? In J. Elster and J.E. Roemer (eds.) *Interpersonal Comparisons of Well-Being.* Cambridge: Cambridge University Press, 200–254.

Haughton, J.H. and S.R. Khandker. 2009. *Handbook on Poverty and Inequality*. Washington, DC: World Bank.

Hentschel, J. and P. Lanjouw. 2000. Household Welfare Measurement and the Pricing of Basic Services. *Journal of International Development* 12: 13–27.

Hicks, D. 1997. The Inequality-Adjusted Human Development Index: A constructive Proposal. *World Development* 25: 1283–1298.

Hicks, N. and P. Streeten. 1979. Indicators of Development: The Search for a Basic Needs Yardstick. *World Development* 7: 567–580.

Hobijn, B. and P.H. Franses. 2001. Are Living Standards Converging? *Structural Change and Economic Dynamics* 12: 171–200.

Høyland, B., K. Moene, and F. Willumsen. 2012. The Tranny of International Index Ranking. *Journal of Development Economics* 97: 1–14.

Jayraj, D. and S. Subramanian. 2009. A Chakravarty-D'Ambrosio Approach View of Multidimensional Deprivation: Some Estimates for India. *Economic and Political Weekly* 45: 53–65.

Jenkins, S. and J. Micklewright.(eds.) 2007. *Inequality and Poverty Reexamined*. Oxford: Oxford University Press.

Jorgenson, D.W. and D.T. Slesnick. 1984. Aggregate Consumer Behavior and the Measurement of Inequality. *Review of Economic Studies* 51: 369–392.

Kannai, Y. 1980. The ALEP Definition of Complementarity and Least Concave Utility Functions. *Journal of Economic Theory* 22: 115–117.

Klasen, S. 2000. Measuring Poverty and Deprivation in South Africa. *Review of Income and Wealth* 46: 33–58.

Klugman, J. 2002. *A Sourcebook of Poverty Reduction Strategies*. Washington, DC: World Bank.

Kolm, S.C. 1976. Unequal inequalities I. *Journal of Economic Theory* 12: 416–442.

Kolm, S.C. 1977. Multidimensional Egalitarianism. *Quarterly Journal of Economics* 91: 1–13.

Krishnakumar, J. 2007. Going Beyond Functionings to Capabilities: An Econometric Model to Explain and Estimate Capabilities. *Journal of Human Development* 7: 39–63.

Krishnakumar, J. and P. Ballon. 2008. Estimating Basic Capabilities: A Structural Equation Model Approach Applied to Bolivian Data. *World Development* 36: 992–1010.

Krishnakumar, J. and A. Nadar. 2008. On Exact Statistical Properties of Multidimensional Indices based on Principal Components, Factor Analysis, MIMIC and Structural Equation Models. *Social Indicators Research* 86: 481–496.

Kuklys, W. 2005. *Amartya Sen's Capability Approach: Theoretical Insights and Empirical Applications*. Berlin: Springer.

Lambert, P.J. and X. Ramos. 2002. Welfare Comparisons: Sequential Procedures for Heterogeneous Populations. *Economica* 69: 549–562.

Lasso de la Vega, M.C. 2010. Counting Poverty Orderings and Deprivation Curves. *Research on Economic Inequality* 18: 153–172.

Lasso de la Vega, M.C. and A. Urrutia. 2011. Characterizing How to Aggregate Individuals Deprivations in a Multidimensional Framework. *Journal of Economic Inequality* 9: 183–194.

Lasso de la Vega, M.C., A. Urrutia, and A. Sarachu. 2009. The Bourguignon and Chakravarty Multidimensional Poverty Family: A Characterization. *ECINEQ WP 2009–109*.

Lasso de la Vega, M.C., A. Urrutia, and A. Sarachu. 2010. Characterizations of Multidimensional Inequality Measures which fulfil the Pigou-Dalton Bundle Principle. *Social Choice and Welfare* 35: 319–329.

Lewbel, A. and K. Pendakur. 2008. Equivalence Scales. In S. Durlauf and L.E. Blume (eds.) *The New Palgrave Dictionary of Economics*, Vol. 3, Second Edition. Basingstoke: Palgrave Macmillan, 26–29.

Mack, J., S. Lansley. 1985. *Poor Britain.* London: Allen and Unwin.

Mahlberg, B. and M. Obersteiner. 2001. Remeasuring the HDI by Data Envelopment Analysis. *Interim Report* IR-01-069. International Institute for Applied System Analysis.

Marshall, A.W., I. Olkin, and B.C. Arnold. 2011. *Inequalities: Theory of Majorization and Its Applications.* New York: Springer.

Mascherini, M. and B. Hoskins. 2008. *Retrieving the Expert Opinion on Weights for the Active Citizenship Composite Indicator*. European Commission.

Mayer, S.E. and C. Jencks. 1989. *Poverty* and Distribution of Material Hardship. *Journal of Human Resources* 24: 88–114.

Moldan, B. and S. Billharz. 1997. *Indicators of Sustainable Development.* Chichester: John Wiley.

Moyes, P. 2012. Comparisons of Heterogeneous Distributions and Dominance Criteria. *Journal of Economic Theory* 147: 1351–1383.

Murphy, K.M. and R.H. Topel. 2006. The value of Health and Longevity. *Journal of Political Economy* 114: 871–904.

Narayan, D. 2000. *Voices of the Poor: Can Anyone Hear Us?* Washington, DC: World Bank.

Nardo, M. , M. Saisana, A. Saltelli, S. Tarantola, A. Hoffman, and E. Giovannini. 2005. *Handbook on Constructing Composite Indicators: Methodology and User Guide.* OECD Publishing.

Neumayer, E. 2003. Beyond Income: Convergence in Living Standards, Big Time. *Structural Change and Economic Dynamics* 14: 275–296.

Noble, M, G. Wright, G. Smith, and C. Dibben. 2006. Measuring Multiple Deprivation at the Small Area Level. *Environment and Planning* 38: 169–185.

Noorbakhsh, F. 1998. The Human Development Index: Some Technical Issues and Alternative Indices. *Journal of International Development* 10: 589–605.

Nussbaum, M.C. 2000. *Women and Human Development: The Capabilities Approach.* Cambridge: Cambridge University Press.

Osberg, L. and A. Sharpe. 2002. An Index of Economic Well-being for Selected Countries. *Review of Income and Wealth* 48: 291–316.

Permanyer, I. 2011. Assessing the Robustness of Composite Indices Rankings. *Review of Income and Wealth* 57: 306–326.

Permanyer, I. 2012. Uncertainty and Robustness in Composite Indices Rankings. *Oxford Economic Papers* 64: 57–79.

Pogge, T. 2002. Can the Capability Approach be justified? *Philosophical Topics* 30: 167–228

Pollak, R.A. 1971. Additive Utility Functions and Linear Engel Curves. *Review of Economic Studies* 38: 401–413.

Qizilbash, M., S. Fukuda-Parr, and S. Subramanian (eds.) 2006. Journal of Human Development 7, Number 3: Special Issue: Selected Papers from the 5th International Conference on the Capability Approach and 2005 International Conference of the Human Development and Capability Association.

Ramsay, M. 1992. *Human Needs and the Market,* Aldershot: Avebury

Ravallion, M. 1994. *Poverty Comparisons*. Chur, Switzerland: Harwood.

Ravallion, M. 1996. Issues in Measuring and Modelling Poverty. *Economic Journal* 106: 1328–1343.

Ravallion, M. 1997. Good and Bad Growths: The Human Development Reports. *World Development* 25: 631–638.

Ravallion, M. 2008. Poverty Lines. In S.N. Durlauf and L.E. Blume (eds.) *The New Palgrave Dictionary of Economics,* Vol. 3, Second Edition. Basingstoke: Palgrave Macmillan.

Ravallion, M. 2011. On Multidimensional Indices of Poverty. *Journal of Economic Inequality* 9: 235–248.

Ravallion, M. 2012. Troubling Tradeoffs in the Human Development Index. *Journal of Development Economics* 99: 201–209.

Rawls, J. 1971. *A Theory of Justice.* Cambridge: Harvard University Press.

Roberts, K.W.S. 1980. Interpersonal Comparability and Social Choice Theory. *Review of Economic Studies* 47: 421–439.

Robeyns, I. 2009. Justice as Fairness and the Capability Approach. In K. Basu and R. Kanbur (eds.) *Arguments for a Better World: Essays in Honor of Amartya Sen.* New York: Oxford University Press, 397–413.

Roemer, J.E. 1966. *Theories of Distributive Justice.* Cambridge, MA: Harvard University Press.

Saaty, R.W. 1987. The Analytic Hierarchy Process: What it is and How it is used. *Mathematical Modelling* 9: 161–176.

Saisana, M., A. Saltelli and S. Tarantola. 2005. Uncertainty and Sensitivity Analysis as Tools for the Quality Assessment of Composite Indicators. *Journal of the Royal Statistical Society: Series A* 168: 307–323.

Savaglio, E. 2006a. *Three Approaches to the Analysis of Multidimensional Inequality*. In F. Farina and E. Savaglio (eds.), 264–277.

Savaglio, E. 2006b. Multidimensional Inequality with Variable Population Size. *Economic Theory* 28: 85–94.

Schokkaert, E. 2007. Capabilities and Satisfaction with Life. *Journal of Human development* 8: 415–430.
Schokkaert, E., L. Van Ootegem, and E. Verhofstadt. 2009. Measuring job Quality and Job Satisfaction. FEB Working Article 2009/620.
Sen, A.K. 1973. *On Economic Inequality*. New York: Norton.
Sen, A.K. 1974. Informational Bases of Alternative Welfare Approaches: Aggregation and Income Distribution. *Journal of Public Economics* 3: 387–403.
Sen, A.K. 1977. On Weights and Measures: Informational Constraints in Social Welfare Analysis. *Econometrica* 45: 1539–1572.
Sen, A.K. 1985. Commodities and Capabilities. Amsterdam: North-Holland.
Sen, A.K. 1992. *Inequality Re-examined*. Cambridge, MA: Harvard University Press.
Sen, A.K. 2009. *The Idea of Justice*. Cambridge, MA: Harvard University Press.
Sen, A.K. and M.C. Nussbaum(eds.). 1993. *The Quality of Life*. Oxford: Clarendon Press.
Seth, S. 2013. A Class of Distribution and Association Sensitive multidimensional Welfare Indices. *Journal of Economic Inequality* 11: 133–162.
Shorrocks, A.F. 2004. Inquality and Welfare Evaluation of Heterogenous Income Distribution. *Journal of Economic Inequality* 2: 193–218.
Slottje, D., G. Scully, J.G. Hirschberg, and K. Hayes. 1991. *Measuring the Quality of Life across Countries*. Berkeley, CA: Westview Press.
Somarriba, N. and B. Pena. 2009. Synthetic Indicators of Quality of Life in Europe. *Social Indicators Research* 94: 115–133.
Srinivasan, T.N. 1994. Human Development: A New Paradigm or Reinvention of the Wheel? *American Economic Review Papers and Proceedings* 84: 238–243.
Stevens, S.S. 1946. On the Theory of Scales of Measurement. *Science NS* 103: 677–680.
Stewart, F. 1985. *Basic Needs in Developing Countries*. Baltimore, MD: Johns Hopkins University Press.
Stiglitz, J.E., A. Sen, and J.-P. Fitoussi. 2009. *Report by the Commission on the Measurement of Economic Performance and Social Progress*, www.stiglitz-sen-fitoussi.fr.
Streeten, P. 1981. *First Things First: Meeting Basic Human Needs in Developing Countries*. New York: Oxford University Press.
Tchen, A. 1980. Inequalities for Distributions with Given Margins. *The Annals of Probability* 8: 814–827.
Thorbecke, E. 2008. Multidimensional Poverty: Conceptual and Measurement Issues. In N. Kakwani and J. Silber (eds.) *The Many Dimensions of Poverty*. New York: Palgrave, 3–19.
Townsend, P. 1979. *Poverty in the United Kingdom: A Survey of Household Resources and Standards of Living*. London: Peregrine Books.
Trannoy, A. 2006. Multidimensional Egalitarianism and the Dominance Approach: A Lost Paradise? In F. Farina and E. Savaglio (eds.), 284–302.

Tsui, K.-Y. 1995. Multidimensional Generalizations of the Relative and Absolute Indices: The Atkinson-Kolm-Sen Approach. *Journal of Economic Theory* 67: 251–265.

Tsui, K.-Y. and J.A. Weymark. 1997. Social Welfare Orderings for Ratio-scale Measurable Utilities. *Economic Theory* 10: 241–256.

United Nations Development Program. 2005. *Human Development Report 2005.* New York: Oxford University Press.

Weymark, J.A. 1981. Generalized Gini Inequality Indices. *Mathematical Social Sciences* 1: 409–430.

Weymark, J.A. 2006. The Normative Approach to the Measurement of Multidimensional Inequality. In F. Farina and E. Savaglio (eds.), 303–328.

Weymark, J.A. 2016. Social Welfare Functions. In M.D. Adler and M. Fleurbaey (eds.), 126–159.

Wolff, H., H. Chong, and M. Auffhammer. 2011. Classification, Detection and Consequences of Data Error: Evidence from the Human Development Index. *Economic Journal* 121: 843–870.

Wolff, J. and De-Shalit, A. 2007. *Disadvantage.* New York: Oxford University Press.

World Bank. 2000. *World Development Report 2000/2001.* Washington, DC: World Bank.

World Bank. 2006. *World Development Report 2006: Equity and Development.* Washington, DC: World Bank.

Zaim, O., R. Fare, and S. Grosskopf. 2001. An Economic Approach to Achievement and Improvement Indexes. *Social Indicators Research* 56: 91–118.

Zhou, P., B.W. Ang, and D.Q. Zhou. 2010. Weighting and Aggregation in Composite Indicator Construction: A Multiplicative Optimization Approach. *Social Indicators Research* 96: 169–181.

2

An Overview of Multidimensional Economic Inequality

2.1 Introduction

Use of one-dimensional indices of inequality for looking at inequality of well-being of a population or comparing it with that of another population is highly inappropriate. As we have argued in Chapter 1, well-being of a population is a multidimensional phenomenon. Even then most analyses of inequality have restricted themselves to the analyses of only one dimension of individual well-being, mainly income. Realization of this fact has recently motivated researchers to work on multidimensional economic inequality.

One simple approach to the measurement of multidimensional inequality is to examine dimension-by-dimension inequality levels (see, e.g., Atkinson et al., 2002; Fahey et al., 2005 and World Bank, 2005). For instance, if there are two dimensions of well-being, say income and health, we inspect inequality within each dimension. In consequence, by health inequality, we mean a summary measure of differences between people with respect to their health categories. It does not summarize the differences between income gradients of health, the effects of health on income (see Wagstaff et al., 1991; Wilkinson, 1996; Wagstaff, 2002; Lokshin and Ravallion, 2008; and Decancq and Lugo, 2012). (See also O'Donnell et al., 2015.)

But this extremely simple dimension-by-dimension dashboard approach ignores one noteworthy issue of multivariate analysis of inequality, possible correlation, a measure of association, between dimensions (Atkinson and Bourguignon, 1982). Consequently, such an approach leads to an inadequate picture of multidimensional inequality. An example using intertemporal inequality may justify the situation better. In transitional Russia, over a particular reference period, income inequality started increasing initially, reached the peak in 1998, and then showed a decreasing trend (Gorodnichenko et al., 2008). Over the same reference period, inequality levels of health and education demonstrated a considerable increasing trend (Blam and Kovalev, 2006 and Smolentseva, 2007). Of two multidimensional situations (say, two

Analyzing Multidimensional Well-Being: A Quantitative Approach, First Edition. Satya R. Chakravarty.

countries or two intertemporal positions of the same country), if for each dimension, one is characterized by at least as high inequality as the other, with strict inequality for at least one dimension, then it can be reasonably argued that the latter is less unequal than the former. But the diverging trends we have noted for Russia do not lead to an overall conclusion on the movement in multidimensional inequality over the period. In fact, with the changeover to a market economy in Russia, there has been an increase in correlation between income, health, and education (Blam and Kovalev, 2006; Smolentseva, 2007; Lokshin and Ravallion, 2008; Decancq and Lugo, 2012). The dashboard-based indices can certainly be combined by some aggregation function to generate a composite index. But such a composite index also fails to take into account interdimensional correlation.

In contrast to the dashboard and the composite index approaches, at the outset, we can arrive at a well-being index for each individual as a function of the individual's achievements in all the dimensions. At the second stage, these individual indices are aggregated across individuals to arrive at an overall welfare (and hence inequality) evaluation. Kolm (1977) refers to this as the individualistic approach. (See also Dutta et al., 2003.) Chakravarty and Lugo (2016) refer to this procedure as the inclusive measure of well-being approach.[1]

Another remarkable characteristic of multidimensional inequality analysis is that inequality indices should be consistent with some dominance criteria in the sense of identification of conditions that capacitate us to unambiguously conclude whether one distribution matrix has higher inequality than another. As a result, it becomes necessary to pay some attention to this matter.

The purpose of this chapter is to confer a review of alternative approaches to the evaluation of multidimensional inequality. The indices we scrutinize in this chapter are axiomatic and mostly normatively based. In view of this, we critically evaluate alternative indices with respect to the intuitively reasonable axioms proposed for an index of multidimensional inequality. This, however, should not convey the message that nonnormative indices are insignificant, and the normative indices are meant to supplant them. (See Chakravarty and Lugo, 2016, for a recent discussion on this subject.)

For the sake of completeness, we begin the chapter with a brief survey of univariate inequality indices. This is done in Section 2.2. Section 2.3 is concerned with alternative views on multidimensional inequality. Indices that belong to two general categories, the direct and the inclusive measure of well-being approaches, are analyzed in details. (Lugo (2007) provided a systematic comparison among some of these indices.) Section 2.4 makes some concluding remarks.

---

1 For implications of changes in the sequence of aggregations, see Dutta et al. (2003) and Pattanaik et al. (2012).

2.2 A Review of One-Dimensional Measurement

As a background material for the following sections, in this section, we briefly present a survey of some one-dimensional indices of inequality.[2] We will follow the notation adopted in Section 1.2.

2.2.1 Normative One-Dimensional Inequality Indices

The set of income distributions in an n person society is denoted by $\mathfrak{R}^n_{++}$, the nonnegative part $\mathfrak{R}^n_+$ of the n-dimensional Euclidean space $\mathfrak{R}^n$ with the origin deleted. We write D^n for the positive part of $\mathfrak{R}^n_{++}$. The corresponding sets for all possible population sizes are designated by $\mathfrak{R}_{++}$ and D, respectively. A typical income distribution in an n person society is represented by a vector $u = (u_1, u_2, \dots u_n)$, where u_i indicates person i's income. Since inequality is undefined for a one-person economy, it is assumed throughout the chapter that $n > 1$. More precisely, we assume that $n \in \hat{N}$, where $\hat{N} = N/\{1\}$.

In the remainder of this section, unless stated explicitly, by the domain of an n person income distribution u, we will mean either $\mathfrak{R}^n_{++}$ or D^n. As in Chapter 1, the mean u is symbolized by $\lambda(u)$ (or, simply λ), and u^0 will be used to indicate the nonincreasingly ordered permutation of u.

A normative inequality index is related to a particular social welfare function in a negative monotonic way. For a fixed mean income, an increase in inequality is equivalent to a reduction in social welfare and vice versa. The normative approach to income inequality measurement was initiated in the pioneering contributions of Atkinson (1970) and Kolm (1969) and later on popularized by Sen (1973). Given a social welfare function $W : \mathfrak{R}_{++} \to \mathfrak{R}^1$, the Atkinson–Kolm–Sen "equally distributed equivalent" (ede) income u_e associated $u \in \mathfrak{R}^n_{++}$, where $n \in \hat{N}$ is arbitrary, is defined as that level of income that, if enjoyed by everybody, will make the existing distribution socially indifferent. More precisely,

$$W(u_e.1^n) = W(u). \tag{2.1}$$

Given that W is continuous and increasing, (2.1) can be solved uniquely for u_e and be expressed as $u_e = \mathrm{K}(u)$, where K, being a particular cardinalization of W, possesses all its properties. Contours of K are numbered so that for any $c > 0$, $\mathrm{K}(c.1^n) = c$.

The Atkinson–Kolm–Sen inequality index associated with W is then defined as

$$I_{AKS}(u) = 1 - \frac{\mathrm{K}(u)}{\lambda(u)}, \tag{2.2}$$

2 See Cowell's (2016) recent survey for a more detailed analysis. See also Ebert (1988) for an earlier literature.

where $u \in \mathfrak{R}^n_{++}$ and $n \in \hat{N}$ are arbitrary. It is bounded between 0 and 1, where the lower bound is attained if incomes are equally distributed. It determines the proportion of total income that could be saved if the society arranged to distribute incomes equally across individuals without any loss of welfare. It can as well be interpreted as the fraction of welfare loss emerging from existence of inequality. The relation $\mathrm{K}(u) = \lambda(u)(1 - I_{AKS}(u))$ shows how we can retrieve welfare from (2.2). It also clearly indicates that the monotonic relationship of welfare with inequality and the mean are decreasing and increasing, respectively.

The index I_{AKS} is a relative index, that is, it is invariant under any proportional positive scaling of incomes, if and only if K is linear homogeneous (Blackorby and Donaldson, 1978). We will now illustrate (2.2) by providing two examples, under linear homogeneity of K. Multidimensional extensions of these indices will be analyzed in the next section. The first illustrative example of (2.2) is the Atkinson index, whose associated welfare function is the symmetric mean of order $\theta(< 1)$. For any $x \in D^n$ and $n \in \hat{N}$, it is defined as

$$I_A^\theta(u) = \begin{cases} 1 - \dfrac{\left(\dfrac{1}{n}\displaystyle\sum_{i=1}^{n} u_i^\theta\right)^{\frac{1}{\theta}}}{\lambda(u)}, & \theta < 1,\ \theta \neq 0, \\ 1 - \dfrac{\displaystyle\prod_{i=1}^{n}(u_i)^{\frac{1}{n}}}{\lambda(u)}, & \theta = 0. \end{cases} \tag{2.3}$$

A progressive transfer of income will reduce I_A^θ by a higher amount, the lower is the value of θ. In the extreme case when $\theta \to -\infty$, I_A^θ approaches $1 - \frac{\min\{u_i\}_i}{\lambda(u)}$, the relative Rawlsian maximin index of inequality.

The second illustrative example, we choose, is the Donaldson and Weymark (1980) S-Gini index, which corresponds to the S-Gini welfare function. It is formally defined as

$$I_{DW}^\rho(u) = 1 - \frac{1}{\lambda(u)n^\rho} \sum_{i=-1}^{n} [i^\rho - (i-1)^\rho]\, u_i^0, \tag{2.4}$$

where $u \in \mathfrak{R}^n_{++}$ and $n \in \hat{N}$ are arbitrary. The parametric restriction $\rho > 1$ is necessitated by the Pigou–Dalton transfer principle (see Section 1.3). For $\rho = 2$, I_{DW}^ρ becomes the relative Gini index $I_G(u) = 1 - \frac{1}{\lambda(u)n^2} \sum_{i=-1}^{n} [i^2 - (i-1)^2]u_i^0$, which can as well be written as $\frac{1}{2n^2\lambda(u)} \sum_{i=1}^{n}\sum_{j=1}^{n} |u_i - u_j|$. Thus, I_G is a normalized average of absolute values of all pairwise income differences in a population.[3] In the extreme situation when $\rho \to \infty$, I^{ρ}_{DW} approaches the relative maximin index of inequality.

For any $u \in \Re^n_{++}$ and $n \in \hat{N}$, Kolm's (1976) alternative to I_{AKS}, is analytically defined as

$$I_K(u) = \lambda(u) - \mathrm{K}(u). \tag{2.5}$$

This index achieves its lower bound 0 for the egalitarian income distribution. It is a per capita index in the sense that it determines the per capita income that could be saved if the society redistributed incomes equally without any welfare loss. Since $\mathrm{K}(u) = \lambda(u) - I_K(u)$, welfare is related increasingly to the mean and decreasingly to inequality.

The index I_K is an absolute index, that is, it remains invariant under equal absolute changes in all incomes if and only if K is unit translatable (Blackorby and Donaldson, 1980). An example of this general formula is the Kolm (1976) index, whose related welfare function is the Kolm–Pollak welfare function (see Chapter 1). For any $u \in \Re^n_{++}$ and $n \in \hat{N}$, this inequality standard is defined as

$$I^{\nu}_K(u) = \frac{1}{\nu}\log\left(\frac{1}{n}\sum_{i=1}^{n} e^{\nu(\lambda(u)-u_i)}\right), \tag{2.6}$$

where the positive parameter ν attaches higher weight to a progressive income transfer as the income of the transfer recipient decreases. In the polar case, as ν approaches ∞, $I^{\nu}_K(u)$ approaches $\lambda(u) - \min_i\{u_i\}$, absolute maximin index of inequality.

The index I^{ρ}_{DW} given by (2.4) is a compromise relative index – when multiplied by the mean income, it becomes the Donaldson–Weymark absolute S-Gini index $\lambda(u)I^{\rho}_{DW}(u)$. Hence, $\lambda(u)I_G(u)$ becomes the absolute Gini index $A_G(u) = \lambda(u) - \frac{1}{n^2}\sum_{i=-1}^{n}[i^2 - (i-1)^2]u^0_i$. Evidently, upon dividing the general absolute index $\lambda(u)I^{\rho}_{DW}(u)$ by the mean income, we can generate its relative sister (2.4).

2.2.2 Subgroup-Decomposable Indices of Inequality

Sometimes from policy point of view, it may be necessary to move from aggregate inequality to population subgroup-based inequality, where the separation of the population into subgroups is done with respect to a characteristic

3 Graphically, it is the shortfall of twice the area under the Lorenz curve from unity. Consequently, the relative Gini equality index is determined by twice the area under the Lorenz curve.

such as race, religion, sex, ethnic groups, and age. The relevant policy issue here is determination of contribution of inequality within the subgroups to total inequality. The connected assignment can as well be isolation of the subgroups that are more responsible for existing income differences in the country. A related policy matter is investigation of impact of inequality across subgroups on total inequality.

All such policy affairs can be properly addressed by employing a subgroup-decomposable index of inequality. A subgroup decomposable, also popularly known as additively decomposable index of inequality, is one that can be explicitly disintegrated into within-group and between-group terms. The within-group denomination is obtained by aggregating inequality levels of different subgroups. The between-group part is the level of inequality that arises due to variations in mean incomes across subgroups.

An inequality index $I : D \to \Re^1_+$ is said to satisfy subgroup decomposability, more precisely, population subgroup decomposability, if for all $x^i \in D^{n_i}$, $i = 1,2,\dots,J \geq 2$,

$$I(x) = \sum_{i=1}^{J} w_i(\underline{\lambda}, \underline{n}) I(x^i) + I(\lambda_1 1^{n_1}, \lambda_2 1^{n_2}, \dots, \lambda_J 1^{n_J}), \tag{2.7}$$

where $x = (x^1, x^2, \dots, x^J)$, $n_i \in \hat{N}$ is the population size corresponding to the distribution x^i, $n = \sum_{i=1}^{J} n_i$, $\underline{\lambda} = (\lambda_1, \lambda_2, \dots, \lambda_J)$, $\lambda_i = \lambda(x^i) =$ mean of x^i, $\underline{n} = (n_1, n_2, \dots, n_J)$, $w_i(\underline{\lambda}, \underline{n})$ is the positive weight attached to the inequality in x^i, assumed to depend on the vectors $\underline{n}$ and $\underline{\lambda}$. Equation (2.7) indicates that the population has been segregated into J subgroups, and overall inequality has been expressed as the sum of the within-group and between-group components, given respectively by $\sum_{i=1}^{J} w_i(\underline{\lambda}, \underline{n}) I(x^i)$ and $I(\lambda_1 1^{n_1}, \lambda_2 1^{n_2}, \dots, \lambda_J 1^{n_J})$, where $J \geq 2$ is arbitrary. The within-group part is the weighted sum of subgroup inequalities. On the other hand, between-group part is the level of inequality that arises if everybody in a subgroup enjoys the subgroup mean income. Clearly, the numbering of subgroups and hence arrangement of x^is in x are arbitrary. For instance, if we use the notation x^1 and x^2 to denote, respectively, the income distributions of the males and females in a population, we can alternatively write x^2 and x^1 for male and female income distributions, respectively. This is a simple matter of notation change.

It may be worthy to mention that the aforementioned policy recommendations that are contingent on subgroup decomposability should be employed under certain restrictions. It is frequently noted that in subgroup decomposition analyses, the between-group term is quite low in comparison with the within-group component. Consequently, policy may be administered toward reduction of within-group inequality. But the impact of the between-group factor may be of high concern for a society. Further, the size of the between-group component is likely to increase with the number of subgroups. The significance of the terms of decomposition may change with the nature of the characteristic partitioning the population. However, for a particular characteristic, if the number of subgroups remains fixed, the analysis of trends of percentage contributions made by the two factors of decomposition may be significant from policy perspective. A high between-group inequality may lead to social conflicts and political unrest.[4]

Shorrocks (1980, 1984) established rigorously that the only parametric family of relative subgroup-decomposable inequality indices is the generalized entropy family given by

$$I_S^c(x) = \begin{cases} \dfrac{1}{nc(c-1)}\sum_{i=1}^{n}\left[\left(\dfrac{u_i}{\lambda(u)}\right)^c - 1\right], & c \neq 0,1, \\ \dfrac{1}{n}\sum_{i=1}^{n}\left[\log\left(\dfrac{\lambda(u)}{u_i}\right)\right], & c = 0, \\ \dfrac{1}{n}\sum_{i=1}^{n}\left[\left(\dfrac{u_i}{\lambda(u)}\right)\log\left(\dfrac{u_i}{\lambda(u)}\right)\right], & c = 1. \end{cases} \tag{2.8}$$

For all real values of c, this population replication invariant, symmetric index satisfies the Pigou–Dalton transfer principle. It takes on the minimum value 0 if and only if incomes are equally distributed across individuals. For $c < 1$, it is increasingly related to the Atkinson index. In consequence, for all such values of c, the two indices evaluate inequality in the same way. For $c = 2$, it becomes half the squared coefficient of variation, where the coefficient of variation is defined as the ratio between the standard deviation $\sqrt{\frac{1}{n}\sum_{i=1}^{n}(u_i - \lambda(u))^2}$, the positive square root of the variance $\frac{1}{n}\sum_{i=1}^{n}(u_i - \lambda(u))^2$, and the ordinary mean $\lambda(u)$. For $c = 1$, I_S^c becomes Theil's (1967) first index, the entropy index of inequality. On the other hand, for $c = 0$, it coincides with Theil's (1972) second index, also known as the mean logarithmic deviation, the logarithm of the ratio between the ordinary mean and the geometric mean $\prod_{i=1}^{n}(u_i)^{\frac{1}{n}}$ of incomes.[5]

Other notions of population subgroup decomposability have been suggested by many authors, including Bhattacharya and Mahalanobis (1967); Cowell (1980); Blackorby et al. (1981); Foster and Shneyerov (1999); Zheng (2007a);

4 Kanbur (2006) provides further discussion on this matter.

5 Alternative characterizations of these particular cases of I_S^c were developed respectively by Bourguignon (1979) and Foster (1983).

Chakravarty and Tyagarupananda (2009); Ebert (2010); Bosmans and Cowell (2010).[6]

2.3 Multidimensional Inequality Indices

As in Chapter 1, in a society consisting of $n \in \hat{N}$ individuals, achievement of person $i \in \{1, 2, \dots, n\}$ in dimension $j \in Q$ is denoted by $x_{ij} \geq 0$, where $Q = \{1, 2, \dots, d\}$ stands for the set of d dimensions of well-being. The $1 \times d$ dimensional matrix $x_{i.} = (x_{i1}, x_{i2}, \dots, x_{id})$, person i's achievement profile, represents a listing of person i's achievements in different dimensions of well-being.

Recall from the notation introduced in Chapter 1 that $x_{i.}$ stands for the ith row of an $n \times d$ distribution matrix X, whose jth column $x_{.j}$ indicates the distribution of achievements in dimension j among n individuals, where $(i, j) \in \{1, 2, \dots, n\} \times \{1, 2, \dots, d\}$ is arbitrary. Throughout the chapter, we assume that $\lambda(x_{.j})$, the mean of $x_{.j}$, is positive. Since M_2^n and M_3^n stand, respectively, for the sets of $n \times d$ achievement matrices with nonnegative entries along with the restriction of positive dimensionwise means and positive entries, it is implicit that either $X \in M_2^n$ or $X \in M_3^n$. Consequently, the set M of all achievement matrices with d dimensions will now be an element of the set of sets $\{M_2, M_3\}$ (see Chapter 1). Unless specified, all axioms and inequality indices will be stated in terms of the arbitrary set M, whose restriction when the population size is n is given by M^n.

By a multidimensional inequality index I, we mean a nonconstant, nonnegative valued function defined on M. Technically, $I : M \to \mathfrak{R}^1_+$, where for all $n \in \hat{N}, X \in M^n$, the nonnegative real number $I(X)$ indicates the level of multidimensional inequality existing in the achievement matrix $X \in M^n$. Nonconstancy is a vital requirement since it ensures that multidimensional inequality need not be the same across achievement matrices.

It will be clearly established that while some of the indices correspond to the inclusive measure of well-being approach, some others do not. In view of this, following Chakravarty and Lugo (2016), we divide our presentation of the section into two subsections.

2.3.1 The Direct Approach

In the direct approach, the indices are typically axiomatized, where the axioms specify their properties with regard to the individual dimensional achievements. In view of this, at the outset, it is necessary to state the axioms formally and discuss them.

2.3.1.1 Axioms for a Multidimensional Inequality Index

Since each postulate represents a particular notion of value judgment, it is logical to partition the subsection on axioms into several segments.

6 A recent review of this literature is available in Chakravarty (2015).

Invariance Axioms An invariance axiom depicts a characteristic of the inequality index that keeps its values unchanged under some permissible changes related to inequality.

Following Tsui (1995), our first invariance property can be formally stated as:

Strong Ratio-Scale Invariance: For all $n \in \hat{N}, X \in M^n, I(X\Omega) = I(X)$, where $\Omega = \text{diag}\,(\eta_1, \eta_2, \ldots, \eta_d), \eta_j > 0$ for all $j \in Q$.

The strong ratio-scale invariance condition demands that postmultiplication of the social matrix by a positive diagonal matrix does not change multidimensional inequality. Consequently, inequality remains invariant under any change in the units of measurements of achievements in different dimensions.

To explain this postulate, as in Chapter 1, we consider three dimensions of well-being, daily adult energy consumption, life expectancy, and income, measured respectively in calories, years, and dollars. Given these dimensions, consider the following social distribution for a three-person society:

$$\tilde{X} = \begin{bmatrix} 2500 & 50 & 900 \\ 2600 & 70 & 800 \\ 2500 & 60 & 500 \\ 2700 & 60 & 600 \end{bmatrix}$$

The entries in row i of $\tilde{X}$ shows person i's achievements in the dimensions energy consumption, life expectancy, and income, respectively, where $i = 1,2,3,4$. Now, we can express energy consumption in joules instead of in calories, where 1 cal = 4.18 J. As a result, when expressed in joules, the entries in the first column of $\tilde{X}$, starting from above to below, get transformed into 10 450, 10 868, 10 450, and 11 286, respectively. Next, suppose that we decide to measure life expectancy in months instead of in years, which means that all entries in the second columns of $\tilde{X}$ are multiplied by 12. Finally, suppose that incomes earned in dollars are converted into cents, which are obtained by multiplying all entries in the third column of $\tilde{X}$ by 100. Evidently, under these scale transformations of the achievements in the dimensions, inequality should remain unaffected. This whole transformation process can be generated by postmultiplying $\tilde{X}$ by the diagonal matrix $\Omega = \text{diag}(4.18, 12, 100)$. Our new social distribution $\tilde{Y}$, which is inequality equivalent to $\tilde{X}$, is given by

$$\tilde{Y} = \tilde{X}\,\text{diag}(4.18, 12, 100) = \begin{bmatrix} 2500 & 50 & 900 \\ 2600 & 70 & 800 \\ 2500 & 60 & 500 \\ 2700 & 60 & 600 \end{bmatrix}$$

$$\text{diag}(4.18, 12, 100) = \begin{bmatrix} 10\,450 & 600 & 90\,000 \\ 10\,868 & 840 & 80\,000 \\ 10\,450 & 720 & 50\,000 \\ 11\,286 & 720 & 60\,000 \end{bmatrix}.$$

More precisely, $I(\tilde{X}) = I(\tilde{Y})$.

A weaker form of this postulate, ratio-scale invariance, requires invariance of inequality when the proportionality factors (η_j values) are the same across dimensions. Under variability of units of measurement of achievements across dimensions, this reasoning claims that independent changes in the units do not affect multidimensional inequality. When units of measurement of some of the dimensional achievements are the same, say, those of "incomes in different states of the world," then independent variability of the proportionality factors is not appropriate (Weymark, 2006). However, generally dimensional achievements are measured in different units. Consequently, if we require inequality to remain unchanged under changes in the units of measurements of achievements in different dimensions, then the strong form is the appropriate postulate.

Strong Translation-Scale Invariance: For all $n \in \hat{N}, X \in M^n, I(X + A) = I(X)$, where A is any $n \times d$ dimensional matrix with identical rows such that $X + A \in M^n$.

While the strong ratio-scale invariance axiom requires invariability of inequality under proportionate changes in achievements in different dimensions of well-being, the strong translation-scale invariance axiom claims that inequality stays fixed under equal absolute changes in the achievements in the dimensions. The matrix A in the statement of the axiom is a translation matrix. A weaker form of this axiom, translation-scale invariance, demands invariance of inequality when the absolute change is the same for all achievements across dimensions. An inequality index is called relative (respectively, absolute) if it satisfies the ratio-scale invariance axiom (respectively, the translation-scale invariance axiom). These axioms represent two extreme views concerning inequality invariance in the sense that because of nonconstancy assumption, an inequality index cannot satisfy them simultaneously. Suppose that in $\tilde{X}$, while calorie consumption decreases by 10, income and life expectancy increase respectively by 50 dollars and 5 years. Then the 4×3 dimensional matrix $\tilde{A}$ with identical rows is given by

$$\tilde{A} = \begin{bmatrix} -10 & 5 & 50 \\ -10 & 5 & 50 \\ -10 & 5 & 50 \\ -10 & 5 & 50 \end{bmatrix}.$$

Then according to this second invariance axiom, $I(\tilde{X}) = I(\overline{Y})$, where

$$\overline{Y} = \tilde{X} + \tilde{A} = \begin{bmatrix} 2500 & 50 & 900 \\ 2600 & 70 & 800 \\ 2500 & 60 & 500 \\ 2700 & 60 & 600 \end{bmatrix} + \begin{bmatrix} -10 & 5 & 50 \\ -10 & 5 & 50 \\ -10 & 5 & 50 \\ -10 & 5 & 50 \end{bmatrix} = \begin{bmatrix} 2490 & 55 & 950 \\ 2590 & 75 & 850 \\ 2490 & 65 & 550 \\ 2690 & 65 & 650 \end{bmatrix}.$$

Next, suppose that with these three dimensions of well-being, of two achievement matrices X^1 and X^2, the former is regarded as less unequal than the latter. Now, assume that the units of energy consumption, income, and life expectancy are converted, respectively, from calorie to joules, dollars to cents, and years to months. Then it is natural that inequality ranking between the two matrices remains unchanged. The third invariance axiom, which was suggested by Zheng (2007a,b) in the univariate context and extended by Diez et al. (2008) and Chakravarty and D'Ambrosio (2013) to the multidimensional context, demands this.

Strong Unit Consistency (UCO): For any $n \in \hat{N}, X^1, X^2 \in M^n, I(X^1) < I(X^2)$ implies that $I(X^1\Omega) < I(X^2\Omega)$ for all $\Omega = \text{diag}(\eta_1, \eta_2, \dots, \eta_d)$, $\eta_j > 0$ for all $j \in Q$.

A ratio-scale invariant index is unit consistent, but the converse is not true (see Zheng, 2007a).

The next two invariance axioms, formally stated next without elaborations, are inequality counterparts of the corresponding properties of a social welfare function (see Chapter 1).

Symmetry: For all $n \in \hat{N}, X \in M^n, I(\Pi X) = I(X)$, where Π is any permutation matrix of order n.

Population Replication Invariance: For all $n \in \hat{N}, X \in M^n, I(X) = I(X^{(l)})$, where $X^{(l)}$ is the l-fold replication X, that is, the $nl \times d$ achievement matrix $X^{(l)}$ is obtained by placing X sequentially from top to below l times, $l \geq 2$ being any integer.

Distributional Axioms A welfare function is a summary statistic of the levels of satisfaction enjoyed by the individuals in a society from their achievements in different dimensions. In contrast, an inequality index quantifies interpersonal differences existing in the distribution of dimensional achievements. Taking cue from one-dimensional case, we can say that, under ceteris paribus assumptions, multidimensional inequality should have a negative monotonic association with multidimensional welfare. Consequently, the following two distributional axioms, whose welfare twins have been stated in the earlier chapter, seem quite sensible.

Multidimensional Transfer: For all $n \in \hat{N}, Y \in M^n$, if $X \in M^n$ is obtained from Y by Pigou–Dalton bundle of progressive transfers, then $I(X) < I(Y)$.

Since progressive transfers make the achievement distributions more equitable, inequality should go down under such transfers. The multidimensional transfer axiom states this analytically. Similarly, if the value of an inequality index reduces under a uniform Pigou–Dalton majorization operation, we say that it fulfills the uniform majorization principle.

Increasing Inequality under Correlation-Increasing Switch: For all $n \in \hat{N}$, $X \in M^n$, if $Y \in M^n$ is obtained from X by a correlation-increasing switch, then $I(X) < I(Y)$ if the dimensions underlying the switch are substitutes.

If the two dimensions involving the switch are substitutes, then one counterbalances the deficiency of the other. Now, one of the two persons affected by the switch has at least high achievements as the other in all dimensions, with strict inequality for at least one dimension. Consequently, interdimensional correlation goes up, since before the switch, the former person had lower achievement in one dimension. As a result, inequality should go up if the dimensions underlying the switch are substitutes. In contrast, inequality decreases or remains unchanged, if the two dimensions that are primitive to the switch are complements or independents (see Bourguignon and Chakravarty, 2003).

Technical Axioms There is no inequality in the distribution of dimensional achievements across individuals if everybody possesses the average level of achievements in each dimension. Formally, for any $X \in M^n$, let $X_\lambda \in M^n$ denote the achievement matrix, showing equal distribution of achievements in different dimensions across persons. In other words, each row of X_λ is given by the d coordinated vector $(\lambda(x_{.1}), \lambda(x_{.2}), \dots, \lambda(x_{.d}))$. Since there is no inequality in X_λ, I should assign the value 0 to X_λ. We state this property formally as follows:

Normalization: For all $n \in \hat{N}, X_\lambda \in M^n, I(X_\lambda) = 0$.

Since an inequality index is unambiguously nonnegative, this is the situation of minimum inequality, showing the lower bound of the index. It is a cardinality principle because we can assign a different numerical value to the inequality index in this situation by taking an affine transformation of the index. Note that the original and the transformed indices will rank any two distribution matrices in the same way. Consequently, no information is lost if the inequality index is subjected to an affine transformation. However, because of the affine transformation taken, nonnegativity of the index value may not be ensured.

Finally, the following supposition is self-explanatory.

Continuity: For all $n \in \hat{N}, I$ varies continuously with respect to dimensional achievements.

2.3.1.2 Examples of Indices

The first example we analyze here is the one that corresponds to the multidimensional generalized entropy family characterized by Tsui (1998), using the multidimensional, aggregative principle, formally stated as follows:

Multidimensional Aggregative Principle For all $n_1, n_2 \in \hat{N}$, $X^1 \in M^{n_1}$, $X^2 \in M^{n_2}$, $I(X) = f(I(X^1), I(X^1); \underline{\lambda}(X^1), \underline{\lambda}(X^2); n_1, n_2)$, where the aggregative function f is continuous and increasing in first two arguments, $\underline{\lambda}(X^1) = (\lambda(x^1_{.1}), \lambda(x^1_{.2}), \dots, \lambda(x^1_{.d}))$ and $\underline{\lambda}(X^2) = (\lambda(x^2_{.1}), \lambda(x^2_{.2}), \dots, \lambda(x^2_{.d}))$ are respectively the vectors of means of dimensions corresponding to the achievement matrices X^1 and X^2, and $X = \begin{pmatrix} X^1 \\ X^2 \end{pmatrix}$, that is, the $(n_1 + n_2) \times d$ dimensional distribution matrix X is obtained by placing the matrices X^1 and X^2 from above to below.

Since $n_1 \geq 2$ and $n_2 \geq 2$, it follows that $n = n_1 + n_2 \geq 4$. If there are n_1 female workers and n_2 male workers in a society, then this postulate shows how we can calculate overall inequality in terms of multidimensional inequality levels of the two sexes and the corresponding vectors of dimensionwise means. As argued in the earlier section, such decomposition becomes useful for judging the impact of subgroup inequalities on overall inequality.

Tsui (1998) characterized the following aggregative multidimensional generalized entropy family on M_3:

$$I_{TME}(X) = \frac{c}{n}\sum_{i=1}^{n}\left(\prod_{j=1}^{d}\left(\frac{x_{ij}}{\lambda(x_{.j})}\right)^{c_j} - 1\right), \tag{2.9a}$$

where $n \geq 4$ and $X \in M_3^n$ are arbitrary; $c, c_1, c_2, \ldots, c_d$ and $\beta_j > 0$ for all $j \in Q$ are constants. The parameters c, $c_1, c_2, \ldots, c_d$ are required to satisfy some restrictions for inequality to decrease under a uniform majorization operation and to increase under a correlation-increasing switch. For instance, if $d = 2$, then $(c_1, c_2) \neq (0,0), (1,0), (0,1), cc_1(c_1 - 1) > 0, c_1c_2(1 - c_1 - c_2) > 0$, and $cc_1c_2 > 0$. Evidently, this symmetric, population replication invariant index is continuous and normalized.

If sensitivity to a correlation-increasing swap is not incorporated, then the resulting index will be (2.9a), or

$$I_{TME}(X) = \frac{1}{n}\sum_{i=1}^{n}\left(\frac{x_{im}}{\lambda(x_{.m})}\right)\left(\sum_{j=1}^{d} a_{mj}\log\left(\frac{x_{ij}}{\lambda(x_{.j})}\right)\right), \tag{2.9b}$$

or,

$$I_{TME}(X) = \frac{1}{n}\sum_{i=1}^{n}\sum_{j=1}^{d}\beta_j\log\left(\frac{\lambda(x_{.j})}{x_{ij}}\right), \tag{2.9c}$$

where $n \geq 4$ and $X \in M_3^n$ are arbitrary; $m \in Q$ and all the parameters in (2.9b) are required to obey some restrictions. In (2.9c), $\beta_j > 0$ for all $j \in Q$. For $d = 2$, the necessary parametric constraints in (2.9b) are $a_{11} > 0, a_{12}(a_{11} + a_{12}) < 0$, $a_{21} < 0$, and $a_{21}(a_{21} + a_{22}) < 0$. In (2.9a), for $d = 2$, we require only $c_1c_2(1 - c_1 - c_2) > 0$ and $c(c_1 - 1) > 0$. The inequality $cc_1c_2 > 0$ is no longer necessary now.

The third functional form (2.9c) is a straightforward multidimensional extension of Theil's second index. In (2.9c), individual dimensional indices constituting a dashboard are aggregated to arrive at a composite index. This dashboard consisting of Theil's second indices for different dimensional indices may be named as the mean logarithmic deviation dashboard. This family consisting of (2.9a)–(2.9c) may be regarded as a multidimensional extension of the Shorrocks (1980) univariate generalized entropy family.

Lasso de la Vega et al. (2010) characterized the multidimensional aggregative, unit-consistent inequality index that decreases under a uniform majorization transformation and increases under a correlation-increasing switch. For arbitrary $n \in \hat{N}, X \in M_3^n$, it is defined as

$$I_{DLU}(X) = \frac{c}{n\prod_{j=1}^{d}(\lambda(x_{.j}))^{c_j-\tau}} \sum_{i=1}^{n}\left(\prod_{j=1}^{d}(x_{ij})^{c_j} - \prod_{j=1}^{d}(\lambda(x_{.j}))^{c_j}\right), \quad (2.10a)$$

where $\tau \in \Re^1$, $c > 0$, and $c_j < 0$ for all $j \in Q$. I_{DVU} becomes a relative index (I_{TME} in (2.9a)) if and only if $\tau = 0$. A nonzero value of τ makes I_{DVU} a unit-consistent index, which is not relative. For any value of τ, I_{DLU} is not an absolute index. An equiproportionate increase in the quantities of an attribute for different individuals will increase or decrease inequality unambiguously according as $\tau > 0$ or $\tau < 0$. Evidently, (2.10a) is the unit-consistent variant of (2.9a).

As Diez et al. (2008) demonstrated, if the issue of interdimensional correlation is given up, then the resulting inequality index will be (2.10a), where $\tau \in \Re^1$, c, and c_j have to be chosen such that $c\prod_{j=1}^{d}(x_{ij})^{c_j}$ is strictly convex, or

$$I_{DLU}(X) = \frac{1}{n\prod_{j=1}^{d}(\lambda(x_{.j}))^{-\tau}} \times \sum_{i=1}^{n}\left(\frac{x_{im}}{\lambda(x_{.m})}\right)\left(\sum_{j=1}^{d} a_{mj}\log\left(\frac{x_{ij}}{\lambda(x_{.j})}\right)\right), \quad (2.10b)$$

where $m \in Q$, $\tau \in \Re^1$, and a_{mj} have to be chosen such that $\sum_{j=1}^{d}\frac{x_{im}a_{mj}}{\lambda(x_{.m})}\log\left(\frac{x_{ij}}{\lambda(x_{.j})}\right)$ is strictly convex, or

$$I_{DLU}(X) = \frac{1}{n\prod_{j=1}^{d}(\lambda(x_{.j}))^{-\tau}} \sum_{i=1}^{n}\left(\sum_{j=1}^{d}\beta_j\log\left(\frac{x_{ij}}{\lambda(x_{.j})}\right)\right), \quad (2.10c)$$

where $\tau \in \Re^1$ and $\beta_j > 0$ for all j. The functional forms given by (2.10b) or (2.10c) may be treated as unit-consistent twins of (2.9b) and (2.9c), respectively. For $d = 1$, all these indices are multidimensional generalizations of Zheng's (2007a) one-dimensional unit-consistent indices.

In another highly interesting contribution, Lasso de la Vega et al. (2010) established that a multidimensional aggregative relative inequality index satisfies the multidimensional transfer principle if and only if it will be either

$$I_{LUS}(X) = \frac{1}{n}\sum_{i=1}^{n}\left(\prod_{j=1}^{d}\left(\frac{x_{ij}}{\lambda(x_{.j})}\right)^{c_j} - 1\right), \quad (2.11a)$$

where all $n \in N$, $n \geq 4$, $X \in M_3^n$ are arbitrary; either $c_j > 1$ for all $j \in Q$ or $c_j < 0$ for all $j \in Q$ or

$$I_{LUS}(X) = \frac{1}{n} \sum_{i=1}^{n} \sum_{j=1}^{d} \beta_j \log \left(\frac{\lambda(x_{.j})}{x_{ij}} \right), \tag{2.11b}$$

where all $n \in N$, $n \geq 4$, $X \in M_3^n$ are arbitrary and $\beta_j > 0$ for all $j \in Q$. In (2.9a), if we choose $c = 1$ and $c_1, c_2 < 0$, then I_{TME} satisfies the multidimensional transfer axiom for $d = 2$. Hence, in this special case, the functional form in (2.9a) is formally equivalent to that in (2.11a). In addition, when the number of dimensions is two or more, (2.11b) coincides with the composite index (2.9c).

The general procedure of first aggregating across all individuals for each dimension, and then across dimensions at the second step, is also followed in the multidimensional generalized Gini index characterized by Gajdos and Weymark (2005). However, in the alternative approaches we have analyzed so far in this part of the subsection, no concept of social welfare has been utilized. In contrast, Gajdos and Weymark's (2005) derivation has an explicit normative basis.

To define the index formally, we assume that $M \in \{M_2, M_3\}$. Recall that for all $n \in \hat{N}$ and $X \in M^n$, X_λ stands for the achievement matrix, each of whose jth column entries is $\lambda(x_{.j})$, where $j \in Q$. Now, define $\Xi(X)$ tacitly by the equation $W(X_\lambda \Xi(X)) = W(X)$. The strong Pareto principle and continuity ensure that $\Xi(X)$ defined via the ethical indifference condition $W(X_\lambda \Xi(X)) = W(X)$ is well defined. In words, $\Xi(X)$ is a positive scalar, which, when multiplied by the ideal social matrix X_λ, makes the matrix X, showing the current distribution of totals of dimensional achievements across persons, ethically indifferent. It is a multidimensional translation of the Atkinson–Kolm–Sen ede income. The positive scalar $\Xi(X)$ attains its upper bounded 1 when each attribute is equally distributed among the individuals, that is, when $X = X_\lambda$ (Weymark, 2006).

Kolm's (1977) multidimensional inequality index $I_{KM} : M^n \to \mathfrak{R}^1$ is defined as

$$I_{KM}(X) = 1 - \Xi(X), \tag{2.12}$$

where $n \in \hat{N}$ and $X \in M^n$ are arbitrary. Suppose that following some policy recommendation, the society has decided to move its current achievement distributions, as registered by X, to X_λ. Analytically, such an operation can be performed by premultiplying X by the $n \times n$ bistochastic matrix, each of whose entry is $\frac{1}{n}$. This process can as well be executed sequentially. Suppose that X is reformed into X^1 by some equitable transformation, say, some uniform majorization operation. In consequence, the welfare position of the society improves. A second equitable reformation at the next step improves it further. Continuing this way, finally, we arrive at X_λ. Consequently, the standard I_{KM} determines the proportion of welfare improvement enjoyed by the society if it decides to move the actual matrix X of achievement profiles to the ideal matrix $X = X_{\lambda}$. Equivalently, I_{KM} determines the fraction of welfare lost through unequal distribution of dimensional achievement totals across persons. We can also say that it ascertains the proportion of total achievements in each dimension that could be saved if the society distributed these totals for different dimensions equally among persons without any loss of welfare. In the polar case where there is only one dimension, I_{KM} reduces to the one-dimensional Atkinson–Kolm–Sen inequality index. If the welfare function obeys continuity, symmetry, the strong Pareto principle and decreases under a Pigou–Dalton bundle of progressive transfers, then the continuous, symmetric index I_{KM} satisfies multidimensional transfer axiom. It is bounded between 0 and 1, where the lower bound is achieved if the distribution of achievements for each dimension is equal among persons. It is a relative index if W is linear homogeneous. In view of equation (2.12), we can interpret Ξ as the Kolm multidimensional equality index and under linear homogeneity, $\Xi(X) = \frac{W(X)}{W(X_{\lambda})}$.

To illustrate the construction of Ξ, we note that for the 4×3 distribution matrix $\tilde{X}$ considered earlier, the associated $\tilde{X}_{\lambda}$ matrix is given by

$$\tilde{X}_{\lambda} = \begin{bmatrix} 2575 & 60 & 700 \\ 2575 & 60 & 700 \\ 2575 & 60 & 700 \\ 2575 & 60 & 700 \end{bmatrix}.$$

Then $\Xi(\tilde{X})$ is defined implicitly by the equation

$$W\left(\begin{bmatrix} 2500 & 50 & 900 \\ 2600 & 70 & 800 \\ 2500 & 60 & 500 \\ 2700 & 60 & 600 \end{bmatrix}\right) = W\left(\Xi(\tilde{X})\begin{bmatrix} 2575 & 60 & 700 \\ 2575 & 60 & 700 \\ 2575 & 60 & 700 \\ 2575 & 60 & 700 \end{bmatrix}\right).$$

We will analyze the multidimensional Kolm relative indices associated with the Gajdos–Weymark homothetic welfare functions given by Eqs (1.10) and (1.11). Let us first illustrate the calculation of $\Xi(X)$ for the generalized Gini welfare standard given by (1.10). We replace x_{ij}^{0} in the equation of $W_{GWL}(X)$ by $\lambda(x_{.j})\Xi(X)$ and equate the resulting expression for welfare function with the actual form of the function to get

$$\left[\sum_{j=1}^{d} \gamma_j \left(\sum_{i=1}^{n} c_{ij}\lambda(x_{.j})\Xi(X)\right)^{k}\right]^{\frac{1}{k}} = \left[\sum_{j=1}^{d} \gamma_j \left(\sum_{i=1}^{n} c_{ij}x_{ij}^{0}\right)^{k}\right]^{\frac{1}{k}},$$

from which it follows that

$$\Xi(X) = \frac{\left[\sum_{j=1}^{d} \gamma_j \left(\sum_{i=1}^{n} c_{ij} x_{ij}^0\right)^k\right]^{\frac{1}{k}}}{\left|\sum_{j=1}^{d} \gamma_j \lambda(x_{,j})^k\right|^{\frac{1}{k}}}, \tag{2.13a}$$

where $k \in \Re^1, k \neq 0$. By a similar calculation,

$$\Xi(X) = \frac{\prod_{j=1}^{d} \left(\sum_{i=1}^{n} c_{ij} x_{ij}^0\right)^{\gamma_j}}{\prod_{j=1}^{d} \lambda(x_{,j})^{\gamma_j}}, \tag{2.13b}$$

where $k = 0$.

Consequently, the corresponding family of multidimensional Kolm (1977) relative inequality indices turns out to be

$$I_{GWR}(X) = 1 - \frac{\left[\sum_{j=1}^{d} \gamma_j \left(\sum_{i=1}^{n} c_{ij} x_{ij}^0\right)^k\right]^{\frac{1}{k}}}{\left|\sum_{j=1}^{d} \gamma_j \lambda(x_{,j})^k\right|^{\frac{1}{k}}}, \tag{2.14a}$$

where $k \in \Re^1, k \neq 0$. By a similar calculation,

$$I_{GWR}(X) = 1 - \frac{\prod_{j=1}^{d} \left(\sum_{i=1}^{n} c_{ij} x_{ij}^0\right)^{\gamma_j}}{\prod_{j=1}^{d} \lambda(x_{,j})^{\gamma_j}}, \tag{2.14b}$$

where $k = 0$; $n \in \hat{N}$ and $X \in M^n$ are arbitrary, and $d \geq 3$. The coefficients γ_j and c_{ij} in (2.13a)–(2.14b) fulfill the following restrictions: $\gamma_j > 0$ for all $j \in Q$ with $\sum_{j=1}^{d} \gamma_j = 1$; $c_{ij} > 0$ for all pairs $(i, j) \in \{1, 2, \ldots, n\} \times \{1, 2, \ldots, d\}$

with $c_{.j}$ increasing and $\sum_{i=1}^{n} c_{ij} = 1$ for all $j \in Q$; and as before, for any $j \in Q$, $x_{1j}^0 \geq x_{2j}^0 \geq \ldots \geq x_{nj}^0$. The functional forms, specified in (2.14a) and (2.14b), are the Gajdos–Weymark multidimensional generalized relative Gini inequality indices.

If $\gamma_j = \frac{1}{d}$ for all $j \in Q$ and $k = 1$, then (2.14a) reduces to

$$I_{GWR}(X) = \frac{\sum_{j=1}^{d} \lambda(x_{.j}) I_G(x_{.j})}{\sum_{j=1}^{d} \lambda(x_{.j})}, \tag{2.14c}$$

where $I_G(x_{.j})$ is the relative Gini index of the distribution of achievements in dimension $j \in Q$. If we denote $\left(\frac{\lambda(x_{.j})}{\sum_{j=1}^{d} \lambda(x_{.j})} \right)$ by $k_j(X)$, then we can rewrite (2.14c) as $I_{GWR}(X) = \sum_{j=1}^{d} k_j(X) I_G(x_{.j})$. Consequently, we can say that in this particular case, the individual dimensional indices framing the relative Gini inequality dashboard are aggregated to arrive at the Gajdos–Weymark multidimensional generalized relative Gini index. Following the discussion in Section 1.5, we can say that this is a frequency-based weighting scheme.

Clearly, it satisfies the following factor decomposability postulate:

Factor Decomposability For all $n \in \hat{N}$ and $X \in M_2^n$, $I(X) = \sum_{j=1}^{d} w_j(X) I(x_{.j})$, where $0 \leq w_j(X) \leq 1$ for all $j \in Q$, with at least one $w_j(X)$ being positive, and $\sum_{j=1}^{d} w_j(X) = 1$.

This postulate is quite alluring from policy standpoint. It becomes helpful in judging the contributions of individual dimensions to overall inequality and hence to locate the dimensions that cause higher inequality (see Shorrocks, 1982; Chantreuil and Trannoy 2013; Chakravarty and Lugo, 2016). The decomposition (2.14c) of the Gajdos–Weymark multidimensional generalized relative Gini index is different from the arithmetic average of dimensionwise relative Gini indices (see Koshevoy and Mosler, 1997).

Similarly, when $k = 0$ for $\gamma_j = \frac{1}{d}$ for all $j \in Q$, (2.14b) becomes

$$I_{GWR}(X) = 1 - \prod_{j=1}^{d} (1 - I_G(x_{.j}))^{\frac{1}{d}}, \tag{2.14d}$$

for arbitrary $n \in \hat{N}$ and $X \in M_2^n$. In this case, we subtract the geometric mean of relative Gini equality indices across dimensions from 1. This variant of factor decomposability states that the geometric mean $\prod_{j=1}^{d}(1-I_G(x_{.j}))^{\frac{1}{d}}$ of individual dimensional relative Gini equality indices produces the multidimensional generalized relative Gini equality index $(1-I_{GWR}(X))$.

It will now be worthwhile to discuss the absolute sister of I_{KM} suggested by Tsui (1995), which may be treated as a multidimensional translation of Kolm's (1976), one-dimensional inequality index. For $n \in \hat{N}$ and $X \in M_1^n$, let $\Phi(X)$ be the scalar that solves the equation

$$W(X_\lambda - \Phi(X)\mathbf{1}_{\mathbf{n\times d}}) = W(X), \tag{2.15}$$

where $\mathbf{1}_{\mathbf{n\times d}}$ is the $n \times d$ dimensional achievement matrix, each of whose entries equals 1. Satisfaction of continuity and the strong Pareto Principle by W make sure that Φ is well defined.

Then Tsui's multidimensional inequality index $I_{TM}: M \to \Re^1$ is defined as

$$I_{TM}(X) = \Phi(X). \tag{2.16}$$

where $n \in \hat{N}$ and $X \in M_1^n$ are arbitrary. I_{TM} measures inequality by the amount that can be taken away from each individual from the achievement in each dimension of the ideal achievement matrix such that the resulting matrix becomes ethically indifferent to the original distribution matrix. For $d = 1$, I_{TM} corresponds exactly to I_{KP}. It is bounded from below by 0. This lower bound is achieved if $X = X_\lambda$. It becomes an absolute index if W is translatable. Translatability of W establishes that $\Phi(X) = W(X_\lambda) - W(X)$.

To illustrate the calculation of Φ, we consider again the 4×3 distribution matrix $\tilde{X}$ and the associated ideal matrix $\tilde{X}_\lambda$. Then Φ is implicitly defined by

$$W\left(\begin{bmatrix} 2575-\Phi(X) & 60-\Phi(X) & 700-\Phi(X) \\ 2575-\Phi(X) & 60-\Phi(X) & 700-\Phi(X) \\ 2575-\Phi(X) & 60-\Phi(X) & 700-\Phi(X) \\ 2575-\Phi(X) & 60-\Phi(X) & 700-\Phi(X) \end{bmatrix}\right)$$

$$= W\left(\begin{bmatrix} 2500 & 50 & 900 \\ 2600 & 70 & 800 \\ 2500 & 60 & 500 \\ 2700 & 60 & 600 \end{bmatrix}\right).$$

We will now calculate $\Phi(X)$ for the Gajdos–Weymark translatable welfare function $W_{GWA}(X)$ given by (1.13). For this purpose, we need to replace x_{ij}^0 in the equation of $W_{GWA}(X)$ by $\lambda(x_{.j}) - \Phi(X)$ and equate the resulting expression for the welfare function with the actual form of the function to get

$$\frac{1}{k}\log\left[\sum_{j=1}^{d}\gamma_j' \exp\left(k\sum_{i=1}^{n}c_{ij}(\lambda(x_j) - \Phi(X))\right)\right]$$

$$= \frac{1}{k}\log\left[\sum_{j=1}^{d}\gamma_j' \exp\left(k\sum_{i=1}^{n}c_{ij}x_{ij}^0\right)\right],$$

where $k \in \Re^1, k \neq 0$; $n \in \hat{N}$ and $X \in M_1^n$ are arbitrary, $d \geq 3$; so that

$$I_{GWA}(X) = \Phi(X) = \frac{1}{k}\log\left[\frac{\sum_{j=1}^{d} \gamma_j' \exp(k\lambda(x_{.j}))}{\sum_{j=1}^{d} \gamma_j' \exp\left(k\sum_{i=1}^{n} c_{ij}x_{ij}^0\right)}\right], \tag{2.17a}$$

where $k \in \Re^1, k \neq 0$; $n \in \hat{N}$ and $X \in M_1^n$ are arbitrary, $d \geq 3$. By a similar calculation, for the welfare function in (1.13),

$$I_{GWA}(X) = \Phi(X) = \left[\sum_{j=1}^{d} \gamma_j' \left(\lambda(x_{.j}) - \sum_{i=1}^{n} c_{ij}x_{ij}^0\right)\right], \tag{2.17b}$$

where $k = 0$; $n \in \hat{N}$ and $X \in M_1^n$ are arbitrary, $d \geq 3$. The coefficients γ_j' and c_{ij} in (2.17a) and (2.17b) fulfill the following restrictions: the sequence $\{\gamma_j'\}$ is positive, $c_{ij} > 0$ for all pairs $(i,j) \in \{1,2,\ldots,n\} \times \{1,2,\ldots,d\}$ with $c_{.j}$ increasing and $\sum_{i=1}^{n} c_{ij} = 1$ for all $j \in Q$; and as before, for any $j \in Q$, $x_{1j}^0 \geq x_{2j}^0 \geq \cdots \geq x_{nj}^0$. The functional forms (2.17a) and (2.17b) are the Gajdos–Weymark multidimensional generalized absolute Gini inequality indices.

If $\gamma_j' = \frac{1}{d}$ for all $j \in Q$, then (2.17b) becomes

$$I_{GWA}(X) = \sum_{j=1}^{d} \frac{1}{d} A_G(x_{.j}), \tag{2.17c}$$

where $n \in \hat{N}$ and $X \in M_1^n$ are arbitrary. In (2.17c), dimensionwise indices constituting the absolute Gini dashboard are averaged across dimensions to get the multidimensional generalized absolute index. The satisfaction of the factor decomposability property by the aggregated index in (2.17c) is evident. Implicit under the choice of this weighting sequence is the normative assessment that claims that all the metrics are equally important.

Several attempts to extend the relative Gini index to the multidimensional framework have generally been adopted by two broad procedures that rely on alternative formulations of the index.[7] Koshevoy and Mosler (1996) considered Lorenz zonoid as a multidimensional generalization of the one-dimensional Lorenz curve. A multidimensional Gini index can be calculated using the volume of the Lorenz zonoid. Arnold (1987), Koshevoy and Mosler (1997) and Anderson (2004) extended the Gini definition based on pairwise distances by proposing a multidimensional distance measure with the objective of

7 See Foster and Sen (1997), Yitzhaki (1998), and Chakravarty (2015) for discussions and interpretations of different formulations of the Gini index.

measuring distances across the vectors of outcomes. (See also Koshevoy (1997) and Banerjee (2010).) List (1999) defined the compensation matrix associated with $X \in M_2^n$ by replacing x_{ij}, the (i,j)th entry of X, by $\frac{x_{ij}}{\lambda(x_{.j})}$ for all pairs $(i,j) \in \{1,2,\ldots,n\} \times \{1,2,\ldots,d\}$. The multidimensional Gini index introduced by List is defined as a normalized value of the one-dimensional Gini index applied to the vector of nonnegative real numbers, with a positive mean, generated by taking some nonnegative-valued, continuous, increasing, and strictly concave transformation of the rows of the compensation matrix. However, it is not clear if all such indices can be interpreted in terms of loss of welfare since they have not been related to any notion of social welfare.

2.3.2 The Inclusive Measure of Well-being Approach

In this subsection, we study several multidimensional inequality indices that are explicitly dependent on the inclusive measure of well-being approach. According to this approach, which Kolm (1977) refers to as the individualistic approach, a real number summarizing the well-being of a person in all d dimensions of well-being is specified. These summary metrics of well-beings across persons are then combined using some aggregation rule to arrive at a level of well-being for the society as a whole. The society-level aggregated well-being is then employed to determine the extent of multidimensional inequality in the society.

As in Chapter 1, for any $x_{i.} = (x_{i1}, x_{i2}, \ldots, x_{id})$, $U(x_{i.})$ represents the extent of well-being derived by person i from possession of $x_{i.}$. For any $n \in \hat{N}$, $X \in M^n$, we refer to $(U(x_{1.}), U(x_{2.}), \ldots, U(x_{n.}))$ as the portfolio of well-being standards of the population.

The job of a social welfare function W here is to rank achievement matrices in terms of underlying well-being portfolios. More precisely, for all $n \in \hat{N}$, $X, Y \in M^n$, X is regarded as at least as good as Y if and only if W arrays the well-being portfolio associated X as at least as good as that corresponding to Y (see Chakravarty and Lugo, 2016). This approach is, in fact, the welfarist approach, which involves aggregation of individual well-being indices (see Chapter 1).

One way of implementing the inclusive measure approach in the current context, is to specify a social welfare function W, which is then employed to design the underlying inequality index. The first illustration we provide for this approach is the multidimensional Atkinson index, characterized by Tsui (1995).

Let us calculate the $\Xi(X)$ values for the homothetic welfare functions $W(X) = \sum_{i=1}^{n} U(x_{i.})$, characterized by Tsui (1995), where U are of the forms (1.7) and (1.8). For the utility function in (1.7) we have, $\sum_{i=1}^{n}\left(a + b\prod_{j=1}^{d}[\Xi(X)\lambda(x_{.j})]^{\theta_j}\right) = \sum_{i=1}^{n}\left(a + b\prod_{j=1}^{d} x_{ij}^{\theta_j}\right)$, from which it follows that

$\Xi(X) = \left[\frac{1}{n}\sum_{i=1}^{n}\prod_{j=1}^{d}\left(\frac{x_{ij}}{\lambda(x_{.j})}\right)^{\theta_j}\right]^{\frac{1}{\sum_{j=1}^{d}\theta_j}}$. Similarly, for (1.8), we derive $\Xi(X) = \left[\frac{1}{n}\prod_{i=1}^{n}\prod_{j=1}^{d}\left(\frac{x_{ij}}{\lambda(x_{.j})}\right)^{\frac{c_j}{\sum_{j=1}^{d}c_j}}\right]^{\frac{1}{n}}$. In these specifications of $\Xi(X)$, it is assumed that $n \in \hat{N}$ and $X \in M_3^n$ are arbitrary.

By plugging these forms of $\Xi(X)$ into (2.12), we get the following functional forms of the Kolm inequality quantifier associated respectively with the welfare functions (1.7) and (1.8):

$$I_{AM}(X) = 1 - \left[\frac{1}{n}\sum_{i=1}^{n}\prod_{j=1}^{d}\left(\frac{x_{ij}}{\lambda(x_{.j})}\right)^{\theta_j}\right]^{\frac{1}{\sum_{j=1}^{d}\theta_j}}, \tag{2.18a}$$

and

$$I_{AM}(X) = 1 - \left[\frac{1}{n}\prod_{i=1}^{n}\prod_{j=1}^{d}\left(\frac{x_{ij}}{\lambda(x_{.j})}\right)^{\frac{c_j}{\sum_{j=1}^{d}c_j}}\right]^{\frac{1}{n}}, \tag{2.18b}$$

where $n \geq 3$ and $X \in M_3^n$ are arbitrary, $c_j > 0$ for all $j \in Q$, and θ_j is appropriately restricted so that it increases with respect to a correlation-increasing swap and decreases under a uniform majorization change. For instance, if $d = 2$, $0 < \theta_1 < 1$ and $\theta_2 < (1 - \theta_1)$ should hold. This symmetric, normalized, population replication invariant relative index is the multidimensional Atkinson index of inequality. For $d = 1$, the formula coincides with the one-dimensional Atkinson (1970) index.

Lasso de la Vega et al. (2010) established that if we invoke the multidimensional transfer principle instead of the uniform majorization principle as the redistributive criterion, then the parametric restrictions in (2.18a) and (2.18b) become $\theta_j < 0$ and $c_j > 0$ for all $j \in Q$. The restriction $\theta_j < 0$ here is much simpler than that required in (2.18a).

Our subsequent illustration of the Kolm index is based on the double-class constant elasticity of substitution (CES) social welfare function proposed by Bosmans et al. (2015). Since some of the notation used in the current subsection are slightly different from that employed in Section 1.6, we explicitly mention the individual well-being metrics chosen by these authors. This also makes our discussion here self-contained.

The identical individual well-being standard considered is

$$U(x_{i.}) = \left(\sum_{j=1}^{d} w_j x_{ij}^{\beta}\right)^{\frac{1}{\beta}}, \quad \beta < 1, \ \beta \neq 0, \tag{2.19a}$$

or,

$$U(x_{i.}) = \prod_{j=1}^{d} x_{ij}^{w_j}, \quad \beta = 0, \tag{2.19b}$$

where $n \in \hat{N}$, $i \in \{1, 2, \ldots, n\}$, and $X \in M_3^n$ are arbitrary, $w_j > 0$ for all $j \in Q$, and $\sum_{j=1}^{d} w_j = 1$. The parameter β is related to the elasticity of substation between dimensions. The CES between any two dimensions is given by $\frac{1}{1-\beta}$. The private welfare standards given by (2.19a) and (2.19b) are continuous, increasing, linear homogeneous, and strictly concave.

In each of (2.19a) and (2.19b), a CES aggregation is employed to arrive at the social well-being standard. The corresponding social welfare function is defined as

$$W(X) = \left(\frac{1}{n}\sum_{i=1}^{n} U(x_{i.})^{\alpha}\right)^{\frac{1}{\alpha}}, \quad \alpha < 1, \ \alpha \neq 0, \tag{2.20a}$$

or,

$$W(X) = \prod_{i=1}^{n} (U(x_{i.}))^{\frac{1}{n}}, \quad \alpha = 0. \tag{2.20b}$$

At the second stage, another CES aggregator is invoked on the individual well-being levels for determining the social welfare function. These welfare standards are continuous, linear homogeneous, and strictly S-concave. They obey the strong Pareto principle as well.

For the welfare function defined by (2.20a), the appropriate form of $\Xi(X)$ satisfies the equation

$$\left(\frac{1}{n}\sum_{i=1}^{n}\left(\left(\sum_{j=1}^{d} w_j(\Xi(X)\lambda(x_{.j}))^{\beta}\right)^{\frac{1}{\beta}}\right)^{\alpha}\right)^{\frac{1}{\alpha}} = \left(\frac{1}{n}\sum_{i=1}^{n}\left(\left(\sum_{j=1}^{d} w_j x_{ij}^{\beta}\right)^{\frac{1}{\beta}}\right)^{\alpha}\right)^{\frac{1}{\alpha}},$$

which leads to

$$\Xi(X) = \left(\frac{1}{n}\sum_{i=1}^{n}\left(\frac{\sum_{j=1}^{d} w_j x_{ij}^{\beta}}{\sum_{j=1}^{d} w_j \lambda(x_{.j})^{\beta}}\right)^{\frac{\alpha}{\beta}}\right)^{\frac{1}{\alpha}}. \tag{2.21}$$

The resulting inequality quantifier turns out to be

$$I_{BDO}(X) = 1 - \left(\frac{1}{n} \sum_{i=1}^{n} \left(\frac{\sum_{j=1}^{d} w_j x_{ij}^{\beta}}{\sum_{j=1}^{d} w_j \lambda(x_{.j})^{\beta}} \right)^{\frac{\alpha}{\beta}} \right)^{\frac{1}{\alpha}}. \tag{2.22}$$

for $\alpha < 1$, $\alpha \neq 0$ and $\beta < 1$, and $\beta \neq 0$. (For reasons stated in the discussion after Eq. (1.17), we do not pursue the cases $\alpha = 0$ and $\beta = 0$ further.)

The relative, symmetric, replication invariant Bosmans–Decancq–Ooghe multidimensional inequality index, given by (2.22), changes under a uniform majorization transformation to the correct direction and increases under a correlation-increasing switch if and only if $\alpha < \beta < 1$.

Following Bosmans et al. (2015), we will now provide Graaff 's (1977) decomposition of equality into efficiency and equity components for the general equality index Ξ and then apply it to (2.21). We follow the inclusive measure of well-being approach. For this, assume that both U and W are continuous, increasing in individual achievements, and linear homogeneous. Further, strict concavity and strict S-concavity are assumed respectively for the individual and social well-being standards. For any $n \in \hat{N}$ and $X \in M_3^n$, denote the $1 \times d$ dimensional vector of means of achievements in different dimensions by $\lambda(X)$.

Definition 2.1 For any $n \in \hat{N}$ and $X \in M_3^n$, let $s(X)$ be the smallest positive real number for which there exists a social distribution $X' \in M_3^n$ such that $U(x_{i.}) = U(x'_{i.})$ for all $i \in \{1, 2, \ldots, n\}$ and $\lambda(X) \times s(X) = \lambda(X')$. Then $s(X)$ is the level of efficiency associated with X.

The distribution matrix X' in the aforementioned definition is perfectly efficient in the sense that $s(X')$ takes on the value 1, the maximum possible value that s can assume. However, X and X' are equally unequal since the individual well-being levels are the same in the two matrices. Consequently, $s(X)$ determines the smallest fraction of the total quantities of achievements across dimensions in X required to preserve individual well-being levels associated with X. This notion of efficiency has close similarity with Debreu's (1951) coefficient of resource utilization. The nonnegative number $(1 - s(X))$ is a determinant of the extent of inefficiency represented by X.

The level of equity associated with X can be measured by the smallest fraction of the dimensional achievement totals in X' necessary to uphold the level of social welfare indicated by X'. Formally,

Definition 2.2 For any $n \in \hat{N}$ and $X \in M_3^n$, let $X' \in M_3^n$ be the social distribution given by Definition 2.1. Let $h(X)$ be the smallest positive real number for which there exists a distribution matrix X'' such that $W(X'') = W(X')$ and $\lambda(X') \times h(X) = \lambda(X'')$. Then $h(X)$ is the level of equity associated with X and $(1 - h(X))$ is the corresponding inequity quantifier.

Observe that if we denote the distribution $X_{\lambda}\Xi(X)$ associated with $X \in M_3^n$ by X^*, then it is immediate that $W(X^*) = W(X)$ and $\lambda(X) \times \Xi(X) = \lambda(X^*)$. It, thus, follows that equity in the social matrix X is obtained by applying the definition of $\Xi(X)$ to the matrix X'. Observe also that "X^* must coincide with X''" in Definition 2.2 (Bosmans et al., 2015, p. 97). Combining $\lambda(X') \times h(X) = \lambda(X'')$ and $\lambda(X) \times s(X) = \lambda(X')$, we get $\lambda(X'') = \lambda(X) \times h(X) \times s(X)$. Since, in view of definition of X^*, $\lambda(X'') = \lambda(X') = \Xi(X) \times \lambda(X)$, it follows that $\Xi(X) = h(X) \times s(X)$.

The efficiency and equity components associated with (2.21) are given respectively by $s(X) = \frac{1}{n}\sum_{i=1}^{n}\left(\frac{\sum_{j=1}^{d} w_j x_{ij}^{\beta}}{\sum_{j=1}^{d} w_j \lambda(x_{.j})^{\beta}}\right)^{\frac{1}{\beta}}$ and $h(X) = \frac{\left(\frac{1}{n}\sum_{i=1}^{n}\left(\sum_{j=1}^{d} w_j x_{ij}^{\beta}\right)^{\frac{\alpha}{\beta}}\right)^{\frac{1}{\alpha}}}{\frac{1}{n}\sum_{i=1}^{n}\left(\sum_{j=1}^{d} w_j x_{ij}^{\beta}\right)^{\frac{1}{\beta}}}$.

The next illustration of this approach, we provide, is based on the Decancq and Lugo (2012) multidimensional S-Gini welfare function W_{DL}^2, defined by Eq. (1.19). For this, let us first substitute $\lambda(x_{.j})\Xi(X)$ for x_{ij} in (1.19) and equate the resulting expression with the actual form of W_{DL}^2 to obtain

$$\sum_{i=1}^{n}\left[\left(\frac{r^i}{n}\right)^{\rho} - \left(\frac{r^i - 1}{n}\right)^{\rho}\right]\left(\sum_{j=1}^{d} w_j(\Xi(X)\lambda(x_{.j}))^{\beta}\right)^{\frac{1}{\beta}}$$
$$= \sum_{i=1}^{n}\left[\left(\frac{r^i}{n}\right)^{\rho} - \left(\frac{r^i - 1}{n}\right)^{\rho}\right]\left(\sum_{j=1}^{d} w_j x_{ij}{}^{\beta}\right)^{\frac{1}{\beta}},$$

from which we deduce the following form of the equality index:

$$\Xi(X) = \frac{\sum_{i=1}^{n}\left[\left(\frac{r^i}{n}\right)^{\rho} - \left(\frac{r^i - 1}{n}\right)^{\rho}\right]\left(\sum_{j=1}^{d} w_j x_{ij}{}^{\beta}\right)^{\frac{1}{\beta}}}{\left(\sum_{j=1}^{d} w_j \lambda(x_{.j})^{\beta}\right)^{\frac{1}{\beta}}}. \tag{2.23}$$

Consequently, the Decancq–Lugo multidimensional S-Gini inequality index becomes

$$I_{DL}(X) = 1 - \frac{\sum_{i=1}^{n}\left[\left(\frac{r^i}{n}\right)^{\rho} - \left(\frac{r^i - 1}{n}\right)^{\rho}\right]\left(\sum_{j=1}^{d} w_j x_{ij}{}^{\beta}\right)^{\frac{1}{\beta}}}{\left(\sum_{j=1}^{d} w_j \lambda(x_{.j})^{\beta}\right)^{\frac{1}{\beta}}}, \tag{2.24}$$

where $n \in \hat{N}$ and $X \in M_3^n$ are arbitrary; r^i is the rank of individual i in the distribution of well-being levels $\left(\sum_{j=1}^{d} w_j x_{ij}{}^{\beta}\right)^{\frac{1}{\beta}}$, which are assumed to be nonincreasingly ordered; w_j is the positive weight attached to his transformed achievement $x_{ij}{}^{\beta}$ in dimension j, $\sum_{j=1}^{d} w_j = 1$; $\rho > 1$ and $\beta < 1, \beta \neq 0$ are parameters.

Decancq and Lugo (2012) proposed an alternative multidimensional S-Gini welfare function W_{DL}^1, defined by Eq. (1.18). The related Kolm multidimensional inequality measure, defined next, is not a member of the family that uses the direct approach since the underlying welfare evaluation is done in two stages. It is not a representative of the inclusive measure of well-being class as well. Instead, it relies on dimension-by-dimension dashboard formulation. However, we provide a discussion on this for the sake of completeness.

For the welfare standard specified in (1.18), it follows that

$$\left[\sum_{j=1}^{d} w_j \left(\sum_{i=1}^{n}\left[\left(\frac{r_j^i}{n}\right)^{\rho} - \left(\frac{r_j^i - 1}{n}\right)^{\rho}\right] \lambda(x_{.j})\Xi(X)\right)^{\beta}\right]^{\frac{1}{\beta}}$$

$$= \left[\sum_{j=1}^{d} w_j \left(\sum_{i=1}^{n}\left[\left(\frac{r_j^i}{n}\right)^{\rho} - \left(\frac{r_j^i - 1}{n}\right)^{\rho}\right] x_{ij}^0\right)^{\beta}\right]^{\frac{1}{\beta}},$$

which produces

$$I_{DL}^1(X) = 1 - \Xi(X) = 1 - \frac{\left[\sum_{j=1}^{d} w_j \left(\sum_{i=1}^{n}\left[\left(\frac{r_j^i}{n}\right)^{\rho} - \left(\frac{r_j^i - 1}{n}\right)^{\rho}\right] x_{ij}^0\right)^{\beta}\right]^{\frac{1}{\beta}}}{\left[\sum_{j=1}^{d} w_j \lambda(x_{.j})^{\beta}\right]^{\frac{1}{\beta}}}, \tag{2.25}$$

where $n \in \hat{N}$ and $X \in M_3^n$ are arbitrary; r_j^i is the rank of individual i in nonincreasingly ordered permutation of the distribution $x_{.j}$; w_j, $\rho > 1$, and β are the same as in (2.24). For $d = 1$, the two indices reduce the Donaldson and Weymark (1980) S-Gini inequality index. In general, one cannot claim that the two indices will make a distribution matrix equally unequal (see Decancq and Lugo, 2012, p. 733).

The next element of the inclusive measure of well-being category we scrutinize is the multidimensional Kolm–Pollak absolute index characterized by Tsui (1995). It corresponds to the utilitarian social welfare function $W(X) = \sum_{i=1}^{n} U(x_{i.})$, defined by Eq. (1.9). Recall that the underlying utility function is given by

$$U(x_{i.}) = a + b\prod_{j=1}^{d} \exp(v_j x_{ij}),$$

where $n \geq 3$ and $X \in M_1^n$ are arbitrary, and a is an arbitrary constant. The parameters b and v_j, $j \in Q$, are chosen such that U is increasing and strictly concave (see Chapter 1).

In consequence, $\Phi(X)$ must satisfy the equation

$$b\prod_{j=1}^{d} \exp(v_j(\lambda(x_{.j}) - \Phi(X))) = b\prod_{j=1}^{d} \exp(v_j x_{ij}), \tag{2.26}$$

from which it follows that

$$I_{KPM}(X) = \Phi(X) = \frac{1}{\sum_{j=1}^{d} v_j} \log\left[\frac{1}{n}\sum_{i=1}^{n} \exp\left(\sum_{j=1}^{d} v_j(\lambda(x_{.j}) - x_{ij})\right)\right]. \tag{2.27}$$

Since the index in (2.27) coincides with univariate Kolm index if $d = 1$, it may be treated as the multidimensional analog of the Kolm (1976) index.

A variant of inclusive measure of well-being approach was suggested by Maasoumi (1986). He directly employed a two-stage aggregation procedure to suggest a multidimensional inequality index on the domain M_3. His approach relies on the theory of information. The index is constructed first by aggregating dimension-by-dimension achievements for each person and then applying an aggregation across persons. The dimensional achievements of individual i are aggregated first using a utility function $\sigma_i = \left(\sum_{j=1}^{d} w_j x_{ij}^{\beta}\right)^{\frac{1}{\beta}}$, where the positive weights w_js add up to 1 across dimensions, the parameter $\beta < 1$ is related to substitutability between dimensions. For $\beta = 0$, we get the Cobb–Douglas utility function $\sigma_i = \prod_{j=1}^{d} x_{ij}^{w_j}$.

At the second stage Maasoumi (1986) employed Shorrocks (1980) generalized entropy-type aggregation on σ_is. That is, the multidimensional inequality index proposed by Maasoumi (1986) is given by

$$I_{MM}(X) = \begin{cases} \frac{1}{nc(c-1)}\sum_{i=1}^{n}\left[\left(\frac{\sigma_i}{\lambda(\sigma)}\right)^c - 1\right], & c \neq 0,1, \\ \frac{1}{n}\sum_{i=1}^{n}\left[\log\left(\frac{\lambda(\sigma)}{\sigma_i}\right)\right], & c = 0, \\ \frac{1}{n}\sum_{i=1}^{n}\left[\left(\frac{\sigma_i}{\lambda(\sigma)}\right)\log\left(\frac{\sigma_i}{\lambda(\sigma)}\right)\right], & c = 1. \end{cases} \tag{2.28}$$

Here $\lambda(\sigma)$ denotes the mean of the utility vector $\sigma = (\sigma_1, \sigma_2, \dots, \sigma_n)$, and the parameter c reflects different perceptions of inequality. Dardanoni (1996) demonstrated that the Maasoumi multidimensional index given by (2.28) may not respond properly to a change desired under a uniform majorization operation. However, I_{MM} is symmetric, population replication invariant, and ratio-scale invariant.

Bourguignon (1999) suggested an inequality index that can be interpreted in terms of fraction of welfare lost through unequal distribution of achievements. In order to explain the role of interdimensional association, for simplicity of exposition, we assume at the outset that $d = 2$. The utility function associated with the symmetric utilitarian social welfare function $W(X) = \sum_{i=1}^{n} U(x_{i.})$ is given by

$$U(x_{i.}) = \left(w_1 x_{i1}^{\beta} + w_2 x_{i2}^{\beta}\right)^{\frac{(1+c)}{\beta}}, \tag{2.29}$$

where $n \in \hat{N}$ and $X \in M^n$ are arbitrary, $-1 < c < 0$ is an inequality sensitivity parameter, $\beta < 1, \beta \neq 0$ reflect the degree of substitutability between the two dimensions, and w_j is the positive weight assigned to the achievement in the dimension j, where $j = 1{,}2$.

The Bourguignon (1999) inequality index is defined as

$$I_{BM}(X) = 1 - \frac{\sum_{i=1}^{n} \left(w_1 x_{i1}^{\beta} + w_2 x_{i2}^{\beta}\right)^{\frac{(1+c)}{\beta}}}{n\left(w_1(\lambda(x_{.1}))^{\beta} + w_2(\lambda(x_{.2}))^{\beta}\right)^{\frac{(1+c)}{\beta}}}. \tag{2.30}$$

When achievements are equally distributed across persons, welfare is maximized, and this value is given by $n(w_1(\lambda(x_{.1}))^{\beta} + w_2(\lambda(x_{.2}))^{\beta})^{\frac{(1+c)}{\beta}}$. Consequently, in this case, inequality is 0. Inequality is positive for any distribution matrix, which is different from X_{λ}. Hence, I_{BM} determines the proportion of welfare loss arising from unequal distribution of achievements. This symmetric, population replication invariant, and uniformly majorized statistic satisfies the ratio-scale invariance axiom. For a correlation-increasing switch, condition to reduce inequality is $(1 - \beta + c) > 0$. By strict quasiconcavity of U, we have $\beta < 1$ and $c < 0$. Values of these parameters can be chosen appropriately to ensure increasing or decreasing inequality under a correlation-increasing switch. This is an advantage of this index. The flexibility of choice of parameters enables us to look at interdimensional association from different perspectives. One common feature of the functions (2.28) and (2.30) is that although they specify individual well-being levels at the first stage, their final aggregations do not permit us to interpret them in the inclusive measure of well-being framework directly.

2.4 Concluding Remarks

Several functional forms representing multivariate inequality have been suggested in the literature. This chapter may be regarded as an endeavor toward the presentation of an analytical scrutiny on them.

A great deal remains to be explored. There have been some efforts to study ordinal inequality in the univariate case.[8] This area remains to be investigated in the multivariate context.

A second aspect of worth investigation is ordering of achievement matrices for a fixed number of dimensions with respect to multidimensional inequality. Since several multivariate indices have been suggested in the literature, ranking of two different matrices by two different indices may be of opposite directional (see Decancq and Lugo, 2012). Muller and Trannoy (2012) addressed the problem of multidimensional inequality comparisons from a compensation perspective. Under some well-defined notion of compensation, they developed ordering conditions in terms of second order stochastic dominance. A similar line of investigation here is to order achievement matrices in terms of inequality by taking into account some notion of redistributive criterion, interdimensional association and variability of the population size, and totals of achievements across dimensions.

Analysis of univariate inequality in an uncertain environment has been performed in the literature (see, e.g., Ben-Porath et al., 1997). Weymark (2006) argued that it is possible to develop similar analysis in the multivariate structure. In Chapter 6, we consider an uncertain framework and study expected poverty that results from the risk of an individual's dimensional achievements falling below corresponding threshold limits that are exogenously given.

One very important issue that we have not discussed in this chapter is inequality in the distribution of opportunities. An opportunity is assumed to be desirable in the sense that with greater opportunity, quality of a person's living condition does not go down. Reduction of disparities in the distribution of opportunities is an unquestioned doctrine of distributive justice.

Opportunities can be specified in various forms. For instance, an expansion in a person's income/wealth may increase his opportunities in many ways, say, greater access to higher education, better health care, higher chances for holiday trips, and so on. Evidently, an individual's opportunities are described by a set rather than by numbers, as specified in the person's multidimensional achievement profile.

Opportunities or advantages, which are also referred to as outcomes, can be circumstantial and noncircumstantial or effort-based (see Roemer, 1998;

---

8 See, for example, Ebert (1987), Chakravarty (1990, 2009), Dutta and Esteban (1992), Blackorby et al. (1999) and Dutta (2002).

Weymark, 2003; Yalonetzky, 2012). Opportunities identified by the former category are given exogenously. These are the outcomes over which individuals cannot exert control. Examples include ethnicity, gender, religion, parental education. They all are circumstantial opportunities. Combinations of such outcomes determine types of individuals. Opportunities spotted by the latter category do not mean that their attainability by some individuals of a specific type makes them enjoyable by all persons of the type. Their collection constitutes the class of noncircumstantial opportunities. Examples are health status, education, and earning. Consequently, as a source of opportunity inequality, circumstantial opportunities should not be held responsible; they are ethically irrelevant to the measurement of opportunity inequality (see Hild and Voorhoeve, 2004 and Yalonetzky, 2012).[9]

References

Aaberge, R., M. Mogstad and V. Peragine. 2011. Measuring Long-term Inequality of Opportunity. *Journal of Public Economics* 95: 193–204.

Adler, M.D. and M. Fleurbaey (eds.). 2016. *Oxford Handbook of Well-Being and Public Policy*. New York: Oxford University Press.

Almas, I., A.W. Cappelen, J.T. Lind, E. Sorensen and B. Tungodden 2011. Measuring Unfair (in) Equality. *Journal of Public Economics* 95: 488–499.

Anderson, G. 2004. Indices and Tests for Multidimensional Inequality: Multivariate Generalizations of the Gini Coefficient and Kolomorgov-Smirnov Two-Sample Test. *28th General Conference of the International Association for Research in Income and Wealth*: Cork. Ireland.

Arlegi, R. and J. Nieto. 1990. Equality of Opportunity: Cardinality-based Criteria. In H. de Swart (ed.) *Logic, Game Theory and Social Choice*. Tilburg: Tilburg University Press, 458–481.

Arnold, B. 1987. *Majorization and the Lorenz Order: A Brief Introduction*. New York: Springer.

Atkinson, A.B. 1970. On the Measurement of Inequality. *Journal of Economic Theory* 2: 244–263.

Atkinson, A.B. and F. Bourguignon. 1982. The Comparison of Multidimensioned Distributions of Economic Status. *Review of Economic Studies* 49: 183–201.

9 For influential contributions along this line, see Kranich (1996) and Roemer (1998) Highly valuable contributions also came from Herrero (1997), Ok (1997), Gravel (1994, 1998), Herrero et al. (1998), Ok and Kranich (1998), Peragine (1999, 2002, 2004), Arlegi and Nieto (1990), Weymark (2003), Hild and Voorhoeve (2004), Ooghe et al. (2007), Savaglio and Vannucci (2007), Lefranc et al. (2008, 2009), Foster (2010), Aaberge et al. (2011), Almas et al. (2011), Ferreira and Gignoux (2011), Fleurbaey and Maniquet (2012), Pignataro (2012), Singh (2012), Yalonetzky (2012), Roemer and Trannoy (2015), Fajardo-Gonzalez (2016), Ferreira and Peragine (2016), Fleurbaey (2016), Kanbur and Stiglitz (2016), and others.

Atkinson, A.B. and F. Bourguignon (eds.). 2015a. *Handbook of Income Distribution,* Vol. 2A. Amsterdam: North Holland.

Atkinson, A.B. and F. Bourguignon (eds.). 2015b. *Handbook of Income Distribution,* Vol. 2B. Amsterdam: North Holland.

Atkinson, A.B., B. Cantillon, E. Marlier and B. Nolan. 2002. *Social Indicators: The EU and Social Exclusion*. Oxford: Oxford University Press.

Banerjee, A.K. 2010. A Multidimensional Gini Index. *Mathematical Social Sciences* 60: 87–93.

Ben-Porath, E., I Gilboa and D. Schmeidler. 1997. On the Measurement of Inequality under Uncertainty. *Journal of Economic Theory* 75: 194–204.

Bhattacharya, N. and B. Mahalanobis. 1967. Regional Disparities in Household Consumption in India. *Journal of the American Statistical Association* 62: 143–161.

Blackorby C., W. Bossert and D. Donaldson. 1999. Income Inequality Measurement: The Normative Approach. In J. Silber (ed.) *Handbook of Income Inequality Measurement*. Boston: Kluwer, 133–157.

Blackorby, C. and D. Donaldson. 1978. Measures of Relative Equality and Their Meaning in Terms of Social Welfare. *Journal of Economic Theory* 18: 59–80.

Blackorby, C. and D. Donaldson. 1980. A Theoretical Treatment of Indices of Absolute Inequality. *International Economic Review* 21: 107–136.

Blackorby, C., D. Donaldson and M. Auersperg. 1981. A New Procedure for the Measurement of Inequality within and among Population Subgroups. *Canadian Journal of Economics* 14: 665–685.

Blam, I. and S. Kovalev. 2006. Spontaneous Commercialisation, Inequality and the Contradictions of Compulsory Medical Insurance in Transitional Russia. *Journal International Development* 18: 407–423.

Bosmans, K. and F.A. Cowell. 2010. The Class of Absolute Decomposable Inequality Measures. *Economics Letters* 109: 154–156.

Bosmans, K., K. Decancq and E. Ooghe. 2015. What do Normative Indices of Multidimensional Inequality Really Measure? *Journal of Public Economics* 130: 94–104.

Bourguignon, F. 1979. Decomposable Income Inequality Measures. *Econometrica* 47: 901–920.

Bourguignon, F. 1999. Comment on Multidimensional Approaches to Welfare Analysis by E. Maasoumi. In J. Silber (ed.) *Handbook of Income Inequality Measurement*. London: Kluwer Academic, 477–484.

Bourguignon, F. and S.R. Chakravarty. 2003. The Measurement of Multidimensional Poverty. *Journal of Economic Inequality* 1: 25–49.

Chakravarty, S.R. 1990. *Ethical Social Index Numbers*. New York: Springer.

Chakravarty, S.R. 2009. *Inequality, Polarization and Poverty: Advances in Distributional Analysis*. New York: Springer.

Chakravarty, S.R. 2015. *Inequality, Polarization and Conflict: An Analytical Study*. New York: Springer.

Chakravarty, S.R. and C. D'Ambrosio. 2013. A Family of Unit Consistent Multidimensional Poverty Indices. In V. Bérenger and F. Bresson (eds.) *Monetary Poverty and Social Exclusion around the Mediterranean Sea*. New York: Springer, 75–88.

Chakravarty, S.R. and M.A. Lugo. 2016. Multidimensional Indicators of Inequality and Poverty. In M.D. Adler and M. Fleurbaey, 246–285.

Chakravarty, S.R. and S. Tyagarupananda. 2009. The Subgroup Decomposable Intermediate Indices of Inequality. *Spanish Economic Review* 11: 83–97.

Chantreuil, F. and A. Trannoy. 2013. Inequality Decomposition Values: The Trade-off Between Marginality and Efficiency. *Journal of Economic Inequality* 11: 83–98.

Cowell, F.A. 1980. On the Structure of Additive Inequality Measures. *Review of Economic Studies* 47: 521–531.

Cowell, F.A. 2016. Inequality and Poverty Measures. In M.D. Adler and M. Fleurbaey (eds.), 82–125.

Dardanoni, V. 1996. On Multidimensional Inequality Measurement. *Research on Economic Inequality* 6: 201–205.

Debreu, G. 1951. The Coefficient of Resource Utilization. *Econometrica* 19: 273–292.

Decancq, K. and M.A. Lugo. 2012. Inequality of Well-Being: A Multidimensional Approach. *Economica* 79: 721–746.

Diez, H, M.C. Lasso de la Vega and A. Urrutia. 2008. Multidimensional Unit- and Subgroup Consistent Inequality and Poverty Measures: Some Characterization Results. *Research on Economic Inequality* 16: 189–211.

Donaldson D. and J.A. Weymark 1980. A Single Parameter Generalization of the Gini indices of inequality. *Journal of Economic Theory* 22: 67–86.

Dutta, B. 2002. Inequality, Poverty and Welfare. In K.J. Arrow, A.K. Sen and K. Suzumura (eds.) *Handbook of Social Choice and Welfare*, Vol 1. Amsterdam: North Holland, 597–633.

Dutta B. and J.M. Esteban. 1992. Social Welfare and Equality. *Social Choice and Welfare* 9: 267–276.

Dutta, I., P.K. Pattanaik and Y. Xu. 2003. On Measuring Deprivation and the Standard of Living in a Multidimensional Framework on the Basis of Aggregate Data. *Economica* 70: 197–221.

Ebert, U. 1987. Size and Distributions of Income as Determinants of Social Welfare. *Journal of Economic Theory* 41: 23–33.

Ebert, U. 1988. Measurement of Inequality: An Attempt at Unification and Generalization. *Social Choice and Welfare* 5: 147–169.

Ebert, U. 2010. The Decomposition of Inequality Reconsidered: Weakly Decomposable Measures. *Mathematical Social Sciences* 60: 94–103.

Fahey, T., C.T. Whelan and B. Maître. 2005. *First European Quality of Life Survey: Inequalities and Deprivation*. Luxembourg: Office for Official Publications of the European Communities.

Fajardo-Gonzalez, J. 2016. Inequality of Opportunity in Adult Health in Colombia. *Journal of Economic Inequality* 14: 395–416.
Ferreira, F.H.G. and J. Gignoux. 2011. The Measurement of Inequality of Opportunity: Theory and Application to Latin America. *Review of Income and Wealth* 57: 622–657.
Ferreira, F.H.G. and V. Peragine. 2016. Individual Responsibility and Equality of Opportunity. In M.D. Adler and M. Fleurbaey (eds.), 746–784.
Fleurbaey, M. 2016. Equivalent Income. In M.D. Adler and M. Fleurbaey (eds.), 746–784.
Fleurbaey, M and F. Maniquet. 2012. *Equality of Opportunity: The Economics of Responsibility*. New Jersey: World Scientific.
Foster, J.E. 1983. An Axiomatic Characterization of the Theil Measure of Inequality. *Journal of Economic Theory* 31: 105–121.
Foster, J.E. 2010. Freedom, Opportunity and Wellbeing. In K.J. Arrow, A.K. Sen and K. Suzumura (eds.) *Handbook of Social Choice and Welfare*, Vol. 2. Amsterdam: North Holland, 687–728.
Foster, J.E. and A.K. Sen. 1997. *On Economic Inequality: After a Quarter Century, Annex to Enlarged Edition of On Economic Inequality by A.K. Sen.* Oxford: Clarendon Press.
Foster, J.E. and A. Shneyerov. 1999. A General Class of Additively Decomposable Inequality Measures. *Economic Theory* 14: 89–111.
Gajdos, T. and J.A. Weymark. 2005. Multidimensional Generalized Gini Indices. *Economic Theory* 26: 471–496.
Gorodnichenko, Y., K. Sabirianova Peter and D. Stolyarov. 2008. A Bumpy Ride along the Kuznets Curve: Consumption and Income Inequality Dynamics in Russia. *Mimeographed.*
Graaff, J.de V. 1977. Equity and Efficiency as Components of the General Welfare. *South African Journal of Economics* 45: 362–375.
Gravel, N. 1994. Can a Ranking of Opportunity Sets Attach an Intrinsic Importance to Freedom of Choice? *American Economic Review* 84: 454–458.
Gravel, N. 1998. Ranking Opportunity Sets on the Basis of Their Freedom of Choice and Their Ability to Satisfy Preferences: A Difficulty. *Social Choice and Welfare* 15: 371–382.
Herrero, C. 1997. Equitable Opportunities: An Extension. *Economics Letters* 55: 91–95.
Herrero, C., I. Iturbe-Ormaetxe and J. Nieto. 1998. Ranking Opportunity Profiles on the Basis of 'Common Opportunities. *Mathematical Social Sciences* 35: 273–289.
Hild, M. and A. Voorhoeve. 2004. Equality of Opportunity and Opportunity Dominance. *Economics and Philosophy* 20: 117–145.
Kanbur, R. 2006. The Policy Significance of Inequality Decompositions. *Journal of Economic Inequality* 4: 367–374.

Kanbur, R. and J.E. Stiglitz. 2016. Dynamic Inequality, Mobility and Equality of Opportunity. *Journal of Economic Inequality* 14: 419–434.

Kolm, S.C. 1969. The Optimal Production of Social Justice. In J. Margolis and H. Guitton (eds.) *Public Economics*. London: Macmillan, 145–200.

Kolm, S.C. 1976. Unequal Inequalities I. *Journal of Economic Theory* 12: 416–442.

Kolm, S.C. 1977. Multidimensional Egalitarianism. *Quarterly Journal of Economics* 91: 1–13.

Koshevoy, G. 1997. Multivariate Gini Indices. *Journal of Multivariate Analysis* 60: 252–276.

Koshevoy, G. and K. Mosler. 1997. The Lorenz Zonoid of a Multivariate Distribution. *Journal of the American Statistical Association* 91: 873–882.

Kranich, L. 1996. Equitable Opportunities: An Axiomatic Approach. *Journal of Economic Theory* 71: 131–147.

Lasso de la Vega, M.C., A. Urrutia and A. Sarachu. 2010. Characterizations of Multidimensional Inequality Measures Which Fulfill the Pigou-Daltom Bundle Principle. *Social Choice and Welfare* 35: 319–329.

Lefranc, A., N. Pistolesi and A. Trannoy. 2008. Inequality of Opportunities vs. Inequality of Outcomes: Are Western Societies All Alike? *Review of Income and Wealth* 54: 513–546.

Lefranc, A., N. Pistolesi and A. Trannoy. 2009. Equality of Opportunity and Luck: Definitions and Testable Conditions, with an Application to Income in France. *Journal of Public Economics* 93: 1189–1207.

List, C. 1999. *Multidimensional Inequality Measurement*. Oxford: Nuffield College.

Lokshin, M. and M. Ravallion. 2008. Testing for an Economic Gradient in Health Status using Subjective Data. *Health Economics* 17: 1237–1259.

Lugo, M.A. 2007. Comparing Multidimensional Indices of Inequality: Methods and Application. *Research on Economic Inequality* 14: 213–236.

Maasoumi, E. 1986. The Measurement and Decomposition of Multidimensional Inequality. *Econometrica* 54: 991–997.

Muller, C. and A. Trannoy. 2012. Multidimensional Inequality Comparisons: A Compensation Perspective. *Journal of Economic Theory* 147: 1427–1449.

O'Donnell, O., E. Van Doorslaer and T. Van Ourti. 2015. Health and Inequality. In A.B. Atkinson and F. Bourguignon (eds.) *Handbook of Income Distribution*, Vol. 2B, Amsterdam: North-Holland, 1419–1534.

Ok, E. 1997. On Opportunity Inequality Measurement. *Journal of Economic Theory* 77: 300–329.

Ok, E. and L. Kranich. 1998. The Measurement of Opportunity Inequality: A Cardinality-based Approach. *Social Choice and Welfare* 15: 263–287.

Ooghe, E., E. Schokkaert and D. Van de Gear. 2007. Equality of Opportunity versus Equality of Opportunity Sets. *Social Choice and Welfare* 28: 209–230.

Pattanaik, P.K., S. Reddy and Y. Xu. 2012. On Measuring Deprivation and Living Standards of Societies of in a Multi-attribute Framework. *Oxford Economic Papers* 64: 43–56.
Peragine, V. 1999. The Distribution and Redistribution of Opportunity. *Journal of Economic Surveys* 13: 37–69.
Peragine, V. 2002. Opportunity Egalitarianism and Income Inequality. *Mathematical Social Sciences* 44: 45–64.
Peragine, V. 2004. Measuring and Implementing Equality of Opportunity for Income. *Social Choice and Welfare* 22: 187–210.
Pignataro, G. 2012. Equality of Opportunity: Policy and Measurement Paradigms. *Journal of Economic Surveys* 26: 800–834.
Roemer, J.E. 1998. *Equality of Opportunity*. Cambridge, MA: Harvard University Press.
Roemer, J.E. and A. Trannoy. 2015. Equality of Opportunity. In A.B. Atkinson and F. Bourguignon (eds.) *Handbook of Income Distribution*, Vol. 2A, Amsterdam: North-Holland, 217–300.
Savaglio, E., S. Vannucci. 2007. Filtral Preorders and Opportunity Inequality, *Journal of Economic Theory* 132: 474–492.
Sen, A.K. 1973. *On Economic Inequality*. New York: Norton.
Shorrocks, A.F. 1980. The Class of Additively Decomposable Inequality Measures. *Econometrica* 48: 613–625.
Shorrocks, A.F. 1982. Inequality Decomposition by Factor Components. *Econometrica* 50: 193–211.
Shorrocks, A.F. 1984. Inequality Decomposition by Population Subgroups. *Econometrica* 52: 1369–1859.
Singh, A. 2012. Inequality of Opportunity in Earnings and Consumption Expenditure: The Case of Indian Men. *Review of Income and Wealth* 58: 79–106.
Smolentseva, A. 2007. Educational Inequality in Russia. In R. Teese, S. Lamb and M. Duru-Bellat (eds.) *International Studies in Educational Inequality, Theory and Policy* Vol. 2: *Inequality in Education Systems*. Heidelberg: Springer, 476–489.
Theil, H. 1967. *Economics and Information Theory*, Amsterdam: North Holland.
Theil, H. 1972. *Statistical Decomposition Analysis*. Amsterdam: North Holland.
Tsui, K.-Y. 1995. Multidimensional Generalizations of the Relative and Absolute Indices: The Atkinson-Kolm-Sen Approach. *Journal of Economic Theory* 67: 251–265.
Tsui, K.-Y. 1998. Multidimensional Inequality and Multidimensional Generalized Entropy Measures: An Axiomatic Derivation. *Social Choice and Welfare* 16: 145–157.
Wagstaff, A. 2002. Inequality Aversion, Health Inequalities, and Health Achievement. *Journal of Health Economics* 21: 627–641.

Wagstaff, A., P. Paci, and E. van Doorslaer. 1991. On the Measurement of Inequalities in Health. *Social Science and Medicine* 33: 545–557.

Weymark, J.A. 2003. Generalized Gini Indices of Equality of Opportunity. *Journal of Economic Inequality* 1: 5–24.

Weymark, J.A. 2006. The Normative Approach to the Measurement of Multidimensional Inequality. In F. Farina and E. Savaglio (eds.) *Inequality and Economic Integration*. London: Routledge, 303–328.

Wilkinson, R.G. 1996. *Unhealthy Societies: the Afflictions of Inequality*. London: Routledge.

World Bank. 2005. *World Development Report 2006: Equity and Development*. Washington, DC: World Bank Publications.

Yalonetzky, G. 2012. A Dissimilarity Index of Multidimensional Index of Opportunity. *Journal of Economic Inequality* 10: 343–373.

Yitzhaki, S. 1998. More than a Dozen Alternative Ways of Spelling Gini. *Research on Economic Inequality* 8: 13–30.

Zheng, B. 2007a. Unit-consistent Decomposable Inequality Measures. *Economica* 74: 97–111.

Zheng, B. 2007b. Unit-consistent Poverty Indices. *Economic Theory* 31: 113–142.

3

A Synthesis of Multidimensional Poverty

3.1 Introduction

Poverty remains a burning problem in many countries of the world even in the early twenty-first century. Many people in such countries and in many relatively rich countries as well need to struggle in making ends meet. Consequently, removal of poverty continues to be one of the major economic policies for many people in the world.

We have argued explicitly in earlier chapters that well-being of a population is a multidimensional phenomenon (see Stiglitz et al., 2009). Hence, poverty can be regarded as a manifestation of insufficiency of achievements in different dimensions of well-being. The emphasis on multidimensionality of poverty arises from the cognizance that income by itself cannot capture many important factors that may downgrade a person to poverty. Reckless spending by a very wealthy person on consumption of unhealthy food items is likely to deteriorate health status. In other words, this income-rich person becomes deprived in health dimension of well-being. A wealthy person cannot increase the quantity of an inadequately supplied public good by spending money on his own.

In a study for Montevideo, the capital of Uruguay, Katzman (1989) noted that 13% of households were poor in the income dimension but did not encounter deprivation with respect to basic needs and the opposite happened for 7.5% of the households. Ruggeri Laderchi (1997) employed Chilean data to conclude that income alone is unable to furnish an all-inclusive picture of poverty. In their study, Stewart et al. (2007) noted that 53% of undernourished Indian children did not belong to income-poor households. It was noted as well that 53% of the children coming from the households that were poverty stricken in the income dimension were not undernourished. These studies clearly indicate income in itself does not convey deprivations in nonmonetary dimensions (see also Bradshaw and Finch, 2003 and Alkire et al., 2015).

Attempts to cluster dimensional achievements, using prices as respective weights, into a composite figure indicating overall achievement performance

Analyzing Multidimensional Well-Being: A Quantitative Approach, First Edition. Satya R. Chakravarty.

may not be unambiguously acceptable. The reason behind this is that there may not exist a suitable price system that enables us to aggregate individual achievements into a single number, which can be compared with an income poverty line to judge whether the person is poor or not. This is the well-known income method adopted in many earlier studies. This may be due to nonexistence of markets for some dimensions. Examples include public goods, consumption and production externalities, and informational asymmetry. This is true as well for rationed goods (see Tsui, 2002 and Bourguignon and Chakravarty, 2003).

A very important reason for assessing poverty from multidimensional perspective is based on a concrete recommendation made by the European Union. In March 2000, in the Lisbon European Union Council, it was decided to shift poverty measurement policy from income dimension to a multidimensional framework. Five objectives on employment, innovation, education, social exclusion, and climate/energy, to be achieved by 2020, were laid by the European Union.

Among different methods, suggested for the measurement of multidimensional poverty, are the basic needs, social exclusion, and capability approaches. The basic needs formulation to multidimensional poverty is concerned with the definitions of minimum resources required to maintain barely "physical efficiency" (Townsend, 1954, p. 131; see also Streeten et al., 1981). At the individual level, social exclusion can be regarded as a person's exclusion from participation in primary economic and social activities of human well-being (see, among others, Akerlof, 1997; Atkinson, 1998; Atkinson et al., 2002, 2017). According to Sen (1993), the capability approach relies on an outlook of living as a mixture of different "doings" and "things". Quality of life needs to be evaluated with respect to attainment of valuable functiongs. (See also Sen, 1987). In this method, functionings and capability are two integral aspects of poverty measurement. Capability deprivation incorporates the true concept of poverty experienced by people in everyday life (Sen, 1999, p. 87). The deprived individuals are declined access to many primary social and political rights. Poverty can be conceived as an overall construct involving different aspects of living conditions.

In the direct method, each person possesses a vector of quantities of needs that serve as different dimensions of human well-being and a direct procedure of pinpointing the poor substantiates whether the person has "minimally acceptable levels" (Sen, 1992, p. 139) of achievements in these dimensions. These "minimally acceptable" quantities appear as the threshold limits or cutoff points for different dimensions. These demarcation lines are assumed to be exogenously given; they do not depend on the distributions of achievements in different dimensions. They are determined independently of the achievement distributions. A person whose achievements in different dimensions do not fall below the corresponding threshold limits is treated as nonpoor. On the other hand, if a person's achievement in a dimension is lower than the associated threshold limit, then he is counted as deprived in the dimension. Given a well-defined rule of diagnosing the set of poor persons, the construction of a poverty index involves aggregation of shortfalls of dimensional achievements from respective thresholds, in other words, of the dimensionwise deprivations. More generally, in the direct method, joint distributions of disadvantages and interconnections between disadvantages are taken into account.

It will now be worthwhile to make a systematic comparison between the income method and the direct method. In the income method, under aggregation, low achievements in some dimensions may be counterbalanced by high achievements in some other dimensions. However, dimensions demonstrating low achievements may be of policy relevance. For instance, in India, aggregate consumption is on the rise and the head-count ratio, the proportion of population living in poverty, is reducing, but still many children remain undernourished (see Foster et al., 2013b). In contrast, in the direct method, dimensionwise achievements are integrated, and hence, the possibility of offsetting higher deprivations by lower ones is ruled out.[1]

Poverty in a society can be regarded as withdrawal of human rights from the affected persons. It is not an implication of the option "not to do." To understand this in greater detail, recall the example on distinction between starvation and fasting, considered in Chapter 1. An individual who is not deprived in any dimension of well-being may be fasting to pay respect to some religious custom. Consider also a second individual who is starving because he is poor. Thus, for the first individual, fasting is not a consequence of the inability to possess food. In contrast, for the second individual, it arises out of enforced inability to achieve minimal level of food items resulting from deprivation. Such a person is unable to maintain a decent standard of living.

Since poverty alleviation is one of the economic policies of high concern in many countries of the world, it becomes worthwhile to identify the causal factors of poverty. People may get into poverty for many reasons including unemployment, family breakdown, death of a major earning member of the family, low earning as a consequence of low education, bad health status, and so on. People may earn low incomes because of existing minimum wage laws of the country. These may force some people to fall into poverty. Breakdown of the poverty index by dimensions, say, by health condition, educational qualification, income, and so on, will empower us to locate which of the dimensions considered contribute more to overall poverty. All poverty indices obeying this breakdown characteristic are known as factor decomposable.

Often, a subgroup of a population with a low fraction of population turns out to be highly poverty stricken, and its dissemination to overall poverty is also

---

1 For excellent discussions on inconsistencies between income deprivation and deprivations in several other dimensions, see Ruggeri Laderchi (1997), Klasen (2000, 2008), Whelan et al. (2014), Bradshaw and Finch (2003), Wolff and De-Shalit (2007), Nolan and Whelan (2011), and Alkire et al. (2015).

quite high. Elimination or reduction of poverty in such subgroups will certainly reduce national poverty to a large extent. This alternative notion of policy can be implemented if the underlying poverty index is subgroup decomposable; for any separation of the population into subgroups with respect to an attribute, say, age, sex, race, region, and so on, overall poverty is the population share weighted average of subgroup poverty values.[2] For instance, when we split up population with respect to sex, poverty reduction may be possible by pursuing policies that equalize opportunities between men and women.

The objective of this chapter is to present an analytical discussion on the axiomatic approach to the measurement of multidimensional poverty.[3] The next section is concerned with a brief review of income poverty analysis. The background materials of the multidimensional analysis are introduced in Section 3.3. The problem of identification of the poor is discussed meticulously in Section 3.4. An investigation of the postulates for a multidimensional poverty index is carried out methodically in Section 3.5. Some implications of these postulates are also studied. In Section 3.6, a rigorous evaluation of multidimensional poverty indices is offered. The explored functional forms can be subdivided into three categories: dashboard-reliant composite indices, directly formulated indices, and the ones adopting inclusive measure of well-being approach. It often becomes worthwhile to investigate if a particular poverty index can rank two different distribution matrices in the same way for a range of poverty thresholds. This problem of multidimensional poverty ordering is studied in Section 3.7. We have noted that several dimensions of well-being possess ordinal characteristics. Poverty measurement in such a case requires a different treatment. We explore this matter in Section 3.8. Section 3.9 deals

---

2 In its June and September 2011 issues, Journal of Economic Inequality has published a sequence of forum articles on multidimensional achievement and poverty indices. These highly innovative contributions nicely illuminate conceptual problems on related matters. See Alkire et al. (2011), Birdsall (2011), Ferreira (2011), Lustig (2011a,b), Ravallion (2011), and Thorbecke (2011). See also Roodman (2011).

3 Different approaches to multidimensional poverty measurement have been suggested, among others, by Streeten et al. (1981), Mack and Lansley (1985), Stewart (1985), Ringen (1987, 1988), Boltvinik (1992, 2012), Muffels et al. (1992), Callan et al. (1993), Ravallion (1996), Bauman (1999), Gordon et al. (2000), Pradhan et al. (2000), Svedberg (2000), Gordon et al. (2001), Schreiner (2002, 2004, 2006), Gordon et al. (2003), Ruggeri Laderchi et al. (2003), Gunewardena (2004), Deutsch and Silber (2005, 2008), Gönner et al. (2007), van Praag and Ferrer-i-Carbonell (2008), Bresson (2009), Cohen (2010), Khan and Qutub (2010), D'Ambrosio et al. (2011), Ferreira (2011), Labar and Bresson (2011), Anaka and Kobus (2012), Permanyer (2011, 2012), Rahman et al. (2011), Saisana and Saltelli (2010), Silber (2011), Boyden and Bourdillon (2012), Callander et al. (2012a,b), Deutsch et al. (2012), Rippin (2012), Siegel and Waidler (2012), Smith (2012), Azevedo and Robles (2013), Batana (2013), Battison et al. (2013), Bérenger and Bresson (2013a,b), Bérenger et al. (2013a,b), Gasparini et al. (2013), Trani et al. (2013), Ferreira and Lugo (2013), Mitra et al. (2013a,b), Santos (2013), Shaffer (2013), Siani Tchouametieu (2013), Trani and Cannings (2013), Yu (2013), Cohen and Saisana (2014), Wagle (2014), Whelan et al. (2014), World Bank (2014), Bérenger (2016) and Santos and Villatoro (2016).

with ordering of distribution matrices using individual deprivation counts, the numbers of dimensions in which different individuals are deprived. The subject of Section 3.10 is aggregation of individual deprivation counts when the dimensions are of materialistic nature. Finally, Section 3.11 concludes the discussion.

3.2 A Brief Review of One-Dimensional Analysis

Since the one-dimensional analysis of poverty measurement has close relations with its multidimensional counterpart, in this section, we present a brief discussion on the former. It is assumed throughout the section that income is the only dimension of human well-being.

Let $\mathfrak{R}^n_+$, the nonnegative orthant of the n-dimensional Euclidean space $\mathfrak{R}^n$, stand for the set of income distributions in the n person society, we consider for our purpose, where $n \in N$ is arbitrary and N is the set of positive integers. Sometimes, it will be necessary to choose $\mathfrak{R}^n_{++}$, $\mathfrak{R}^n_+$ with the origin deleted, or D^n, the positive part of $\mathfrak{R}^n_{++}$, as the income domain in an n-person society. The associated sets for all possible population sizes are indicated by $\mathfrak{R}_+$, $\mathfrak{R}_{++}$, and D, respectively. We will write $u = (u_1, u_2, \dots , u_n)$, where u_i represents person i's income, for an arbitrary income distribution in an n person society.

Often, an absolute threshold income, called the poverty line, is used for poverty assessments of income distributions. An absolute poverty line is an exogenously given cutoff limit and is not affected by any change in the income distribution whose poverty is to be assessed. Given the income distribution, a person is identified as poor if his income falls below the threshold limit. In many developing countries of the world, individual absolute poverty lines are employed for poverty evaluations in the respective countries. Following a suggestion, put forward by Ravallion et al. (1991), a \$1 per day poverty line was used by the World Bank for the developing world, and in a later contribution by Ravallion et al. (2009), this threshold was revised to \$1.25 a day at the 2005 purchasing power parity (PPP). Deaton (2010) mentioned several problems associated with the construction of a global poverty line and the use of PPP exchange rates to correct international price differences. More recently, a new international poverty line of \$1.90 was adopted by the World Bank (see Ferreira et al., 2015).

In contrast to the absolute poverty line, the relative poverty line depends on the income distribution and hence is responsive to alterations in the distributions. Examples of such poverty lines are 50% of the median (Fuchs, 1969) and 50% of the mean (O'Higgins and Jenkins, 1990). In Atkinson and Bourguignon (2001), a relative poverty line equal to the 0.37 times the mean income (or expenditure) was considered. Chen and Ravallion (2001), on the other hand, used 0.33 instead of 0.37 as the multiplicative coefficient. The EU standard posited the poverty line as 60% of the median. To the contrary, in the United States, since the 1960s, official poverty rates were determined using an individual's or family's pretax income and an absolute cutoff limit (Orshansky, 1965). In recent periods, a new supplemental poverty measure, which uses more general definitions and incorporates additional items such as tax payments and work experiences in the estimation of family's resources, has been proposed since 2011. In India, separate absolute thresholds are used for the rural and urban sectors (Subramanian, 2011).[4]

Throughout the section, we assume the existence of an absolute threshold limit and denote it by $z > 0$. Assume further that $z \in [z_-, z_+] \subset \mathfrak{R}^1_+$, where $\mathfrak{R}^1_+$ is the nonnegative part of the real line $\mathfrak{R}^1$. In words, z presupposes values in a finite nondegenerate positive interval $[z_-, z_+]$ of $\mathfrak{R}^1_+$. Now, person i is regarded as poor in $u \in \mathfrak{R}^n_+$, if $u_i < z$. Equivalently, we can say that person i has a feeling of deprivation since his income falls below the threshold point z. The person is nondeprived in income when u_i is at least z, which means that $u_i \geq z$. Thus, z is the level of income that a person requires minimally to be nondeprived in income.

Evidently, the concept of deprivation here arises from the comparison of an individual's income with that of another whose income meets the subsistence limit z. Equivalently, all those persons whose incomes fall below z regard z as their reference limit, and all those whose incomes are at least z may be assumed to constitute the reference group.[5,6]

For any $u \in \mathfrak{R}^n_+$, we write $\pi(u; z)$ for the set of poor persons in u. Analytically, $\pi(u; z) = \{i \in \{1, 2, \dots, n\} | u_i < z\}$. Then the number of persons in $\pi(u; z)$, $|\pi(u; z)| = |\{i \in \{1, 2, \dots, n\} | u_i < z\}|$, is the total number of poor in u. If nobody is poor in $u \in \mathfrak{R}^n_+$, then $\pi(u; z)$ is an empty set. In contrast, if all the n persons in $u \in \mathfrak{R}^n_+$ are poor, $|\pi(u; z)| = n$.

In his pioneering contribution, Sen (1976) argued that measurement of poverty involves two main steps: identification and aggregation. The concern of

4 In a recent contribution, Klasen (2016) reviewed alternative ways of determining an Asia-specific poverty line that can take care of some of the shortcomings of $1.25 a day poverty line. He argued in favor of establishing a process where national poverty lines are expressed in national currencies and aggregating poor across countries in a consistent way, given that the poverty lines are derived consistently.

5 Runciman (1967) referred to a reference group as a "social class." For an income distribution, Yitzhaki (1979) considered reference group of a person as the set of those who have higher incomes than him. For related contributions, see, among others, Kakwani (1984), Berrebi and Silber (1985), Chakravarty and Mukherjee (1999), Chakravarty and Moyes (2003), Bossert and D'Ambrosio (2007), Zheng (2007a), Whelan and Maître (2009), and Anderson and Esposito (2014).

6 The notion of deprivation was introduced into the poverty measurement literature by Sen (1976). Chen and Ravallion (2013) argued in favor of using different reference limits. Foster (1998) suggested an amalgam threshold limit that involves a reference line as a component. For a recent axiomatic characterization along this line, see Chakravarty et al. (2016). A multidimensional treatment of the issue is available in Bellani (2013).

the issue of identification is the isolation of the set of poor. Consequently, given $u \in \Re^n_+$, identification requires determination of the set $\pi(u; z)$. The problem of aggregation is to summarize poverty information on the individuals in the society. More precisely, for any $u \in \Re^n_+$, the issue is to prepare a summary statistic of the extent of poverty suffered by the individuals in $\pi(u; z)$.

The most widely used summary statistic of poverty is the so-called head count, the proportion of poor people in the population. A second commonly used measure of income poverty is the poverty gap measure, the average of the proportionate income gaps of the poor from the poverty line multiplied by the head-count ratio. As Sen (1976) pointed out, these measures are violators of a basic postulate, which a useful poverty index should verify. This property, the transfer axiom, suggested by Sen himself, requires poverty to increase unambiguously under a transfer of income from a poorer poor to a richer poor such that the recipient does not become rich because of the transfer. Another basic poverty postulate suggested by Sen is the monotonicity axiom, of which the head-count ratio is a violator but not the poverty gap measure. This property demands poverty to increase whenever the income of a poor goes down. Sen also suggested a more sophisticated index that fulfills these desirable properties.[7]

Although each of the head-count ratio and poverty gap measure is a violator of at least one of the two basic postulates suggested by Sen, they have one attractive property, subgroup decomposability. According to subgroup decomposability, for any partitioning of the population into two or more population subgroups, the overall poverty is the population share weighted average of subgroup poverty levels.[8] (See Chapter 2, for a formal discussion on subgroup partitioning of a population.) The contribution of a subgroup to overall poverty can be defined as the subgroup's poverty multiplied by the population share of the subgroup divided by the overall poverty value. Since the multidimensional analog of this property, including its policy implications, will be investigated extensively in a later section, we do not elaborate it further here.

We will wind up this section with a brief discussion on three well-known subgroup-decomposable indices whose multidimensional extensions will be analyzed in one of the following sections. Consequently, this brief introduction serves as a background material.

For this purpose, we need some more preliminaries. Let $\hat{u}_i = \min(u_i, z)$ be the censored income related to u_i. Denote the censored income distribution associated with $u \in \Re^n_+$ by $\hat{u}$. In a censored income distribution, each income is replaced by poverty line if the income value does not fall below the poverty line. Otherwise, the income quantity remains unchanged (see Takayama, 1979). In

7 Alternatives and variations of the Sen index were suggested, among others, by Takayama (1979), Thon (1979), Blackorby and Donaldson (1980), Kakwani (1980), and Clark et al. (1981). See Sen (1979), Chakravarty (1990), Zheng (1997), Foster (2006) and Cowell (2016), for discussion.

8 See Anand (1983, 1997), Chakravarty (1983), and Foster et al. (1984).

our presentation of subgroup-decomposable indices, we will restrict attention on censored income distributions. Since a poverty index should focus on the incomes of the poor, this is a sensible assumption (Sen, 1981). This, however, does not rule out the possibility of dependence of the index on the nonpoor population size.

The poverty shortfall of person i may be measured using the absolute difference $(z - \hat{u}_i)$. This shortfall is 0 if person i is nonpoor and positive otherwise. When expressed in relative or proportionate term, it is given by $g_i = \frac{z-\hat{u}_i}{z}$; $1 \leq i \leq n$. By definition, each g_i is homogeneous of degree 0, that is, invariant under equiproportionate changes in $\hat{u}_i$ and the threshold limit z. It is continuous and decreasing in the censored income level $\hat{u}_i$. We refer to g_i as the deprivation index of person i. It is a measure of the extent of deprivation suffered by person i in the profile $u \in \Re^n_+$.

The entire family of subgroup-decomposable income poverty indices can be written as $\frac{1}{n}\sum_{i=1}^{n}\psi(g_i)$, where $u \in \Re^n_+$ is arbitrary and $\psi : [0, 1] \rightarrow \Re^1_+$ satisfying $\psi(0) = 0$ is a transformed deprivation indicator. It is also assumed to be decreasing, continuous, and strictly convex in incomes of the poor. As we derive $\psi(g_i)$ from person i's deprivation by applying the transformation ψ, we can ascribe $\psi(g_i)$ as his transformed income deprivation. Since $\psi(0) = 0$, in the amalgamated formula $\frac{1}{n}\sum_{i=1}^{n}\psi(g_i)$, only deprivations of the poor are taken into account. Decreasingness and strict convexity of ψ are necessary to ensure that the poverty index fulfills respectively the monotonicity and transfer axioms. For $\psi(g_i) = 1 - (1 - g_i)^e$ and $\psi(g_i) = g_i^{\alpha}$, where $0 < e < 1$ and $\alpha > 1$ are parameters, the resulting indices turn out respectively to be

$$P_C(u;\, z) = \frac{1}{n}\sum_{i=1}^{n}\left(1 - \left(\frac{\hat{u}_i}{z}\right)^e\right) \tag{3.1}$$

and

$$P_{FGT}(u;z) = \frac{1}{n}\sum_{i=1}^{n}\left(1 - \frac{\hat{u}_i}{z}\right)^{\alpha}. \tag{3.2}$$

The measuring devices P_C and P_{FGT} are respectively the Chakravarty (1983) and Foster et al. (1984) income poverty indices. For $e = 1$ and $\alpha = 1$, they coincide with the poverty gap measure. For $\alpha = 0$, P_{FGT} reduces to the head-count ratio. While P_{FGT} is defined directly on the deprivations of the poor, P_C is a normalized version of the utilitarian gap $\sum_{i=1}^{n}(U(z) - U(\hat{u}_i))$, where U is a continuous, increasing, and strictly concave identical utility function. The constant elasticity of the underlying marginal utility function is given by $(e - 1)$. Both e and α capture different aspects of income poverty. For all $0 < e < 1$ and $\alpha > 2$, under a transfer of income from a poorer poor to a richer poor, increase in poverty becomes higher, the poorer the donor is.[9]

Finally, consider the transformation $\psi(g_i) = -\log(g_i)$, where $u \in D^n$, which means that in this case, the domain of ψ is (0, 1]. Then the underlying measuring instrument becomes the Watts (1968) index of income poverty:

$$P_W(u;z) = \frac{1}{n}\sum_{i=1}^{n} \log\left(\frac{z}{\hat{u}_i}\right). \tag{3.3}$$

One common feature of all the three indices is that they assume the minimum value 0 when nobody is deprived in the society ($u_i \geq z$ for all i). Both P_C and P_{FGT} reach the upper bound 1 when everybody in the society is maximally deprived ($u_i = 0$ for all i). However, P_W is undefined in this situation. This index is unambiguously more sensitive to income transfers lower down the income scale.[10]

3.3 Preliminaries for Multidimensional Poverty Analysis

To formulate and discuss the preliminaries rigorously, we follow the notation adopted in Chapters 1 and 2. As before, the number of dimensions of well-being in an $n \in N$ -person society is given by $d \geq 2$, where N is the set of positive integers. Each dimension may be regarded as representing some basic need of human well-being. In this n-person society with d dimensions of well-being, a typical distribution matrix or an achievement matrix, which we also refer to as a social matrix or social distribution, is denoted by $X = (x_{ij})_{n\times d}$. The quantity $x_{ij} \geq 0$, the (i, j)th entry of X, indicates the achievement of person i in dimension j, where $1 \leq i \leq n, 1 \leq j \leq d$. The matrix X is assumed be an element of M^n, that is, $X \in M^n$. The set M^n is the restriction of the general set M when the

9 In several recent studies, measurement of richness at the top of an income distribution as a complement to poverty at the bottom of the profile has become a cornerstone of investigation (see, e.g., Piketty and Saez, 2006; Atkinson, 2007; Peichl and Pestel, 2013a,b). Among the various reasons for which evaluation of richness has got to be a focus of attention are collection of higher taxes from the people at the top with the objection of facilitating improvement in the quality/service of public goods and providing new public goods. Higher revenue collection also leads to reduction of inequality and polarization, hence likelihood of social conflict. This can as well be achieved by directly subsidizing the poor with higher revenue (Atkinson, 2007; Medeiros, 2006; Leigh, 2009; Brzezinski, 2010, provides further discussion along this line). Peichl et al. (2010) analyzed the affluence twins of the Foster et al. (1984) and Chakravarty (1983) indices of poverty.

10 Attempts to construct income poverty maps that harmonize census with household survey information to forecast income poverty are available in the literature (Elbers et al., 2002). For critical evaluation, see Tarozzi and Deaton (2009). See also Bedi et al. (2007) and Elbers et al. (2007).

population size is fixed n, where $M = \bigcup_{n \in N} M^n$. The necessity of the general set M arises whenever poverty comparisons involve differing population sizes. The general set M can be anyone of the three matrices in the set $\{M_1, M_2, M_3\}$, where M_1, M_2, and M_3 are the same as in Section 1.2. The column vector $x_{.j}$ of X represents the distribution of achievements in dimension j among n-persons. On the other hand, person i's achievement profile, the achievements of person i in d dimensions, is denoted by the row vector $x_{i.}$, the ith row of X.

In the multidimensional framework under consideration for each dimension j, there is a unique (exogenously given) poverty threshold $z_j > 0$, which represents means of supporting a person's level of living at a minimal level with respect to dimension j. Often, we will refer to z_j as dimension j's reference limit or cutoff limit. Since z_j represents the least possible quantity of achievement in dimension j for a subsistence level of living with respect to the dimension, we can say that a person whose achievement falls below this barely adequate quantity will regard z_j as his targeted achievement in the dimension. Consequently, person i feels deprived in dimension j, or the dimension is meager for the person if his achievement x_{ij} falls below the corresponding threshold z_j, that is, if $x_{ij} < z_j$. The person is nondeprived in the dimension in the case when his achievement x_{ij} is at least z_j, which means that $x_{ij} \geq z_j$. Thus, z_j is the level of achievement that a person requires minimally to be nondeprived in dimension j. Person i's deprivation in dimension j is maximal if $x_{ij} = 0$.

Evidently, relativity in the concept of deprivation in a dimension arises from the comparison of an individual's achievement in the dimension with that of another whose achievement meets at least the subsistence limit. Equivalently, all those persons whose achievements in dimension j fall below z_j regard z_j as their dimensional reference limit, and all those whose achievements are at least z_j may be assumed to constitute the dimensional reference group.

The threshold limits taken together for all the dimensions constitute the vector $\underline{z} = (z_1, z_2, \dots, z_d)$, which is assumed to be an element of Z, a finite subset of D^d, the strictly positive part the d-dimensional Euclidean space. More precisely, $\underline{z} = (z_1, z_2, \dots, z_d) \in Z \subset D^d$.

The aforementioned method of determination of multidimensional poverty in terms of dimensional deprivations using the vector $\underline{z}$ of dimensional reference limits is known as the direct method (Sen, 1981). In contrast, in the income method (Sen, 1981), the poverty line incorporates the monetary values of some necessaries required to maintain a minimal standard of living (see Townsend, 1954). (See also Booth, 1894, 1903; Rowntree, 1901; Bowley and Burnett-Hurst, 1915 and Gillie, 1996.) Evidently, "a commodity focussed concept of basic needs underlay the income method..., as the poverty line indicated the minimum amount of resources to cover such needs" (Alkire et al., 2015, p. 125).

For any person $i \in \{1, 2, \dots, n\}$ and any dimension $j \in \{1, 2, \dots, d\}$, let $\hat{x}_{ij} = \min(x_{ij}, z_j)$ stand for the censored quantity of achievement in dimension j

enjoyed by person i. Then the deprivation indicator of person i in dimension j is specified by $g_{ij} = \left(1 - \frac{\hat{x}_{ij}}{z_j}\right)$. We will also refer to g_{ij} as the proportionate deprivation, the proportionate shortfall of the achievement in the dimension from the dimensional cutoff limit. Hence, if individual i is deprived in dimension j, then he encounters a positive deprivation; otherwise, his deprivation is zero.

3.4 Identification of the Poor and Deprivation Counting

Identification of the poor in a multidimensional framework is not as simple as in the one-dimensional case. In the one-dimensional situation, given the unique income poverty line and a person's income, it can be unambiguously claimed that the person is poor (respectively, nonpoor) if his income falls below (respectively, not below) the poverty line. Since in a multivariate setup, the number of dimensions is at least 2, the selection of the number of deprived dimensions for judging whether a person is in poverty or not becomes an issue of natural discussion.

There can be two extreme positions in this context, each one possessing arguments for and against it. The first is the union approach that counts a person as poor if he is deprived in at least one dimension. On the other hand, we have the intersection criterion that regards a person as poor if all his achievements are simultaneously below the corresponding reference limits (see Tsui, 2002, Atkinson, 2003 and Bourguignon and Chakravarty, 2003). Finally, there is an intermediate way that can be reckoned as a compromise between the two extremes. In this case, the number of dimensions for which individual achievements have to be compared with the corresponding dimensional reference limits can vary from the minimum to the maximum (see Mack and Lansley, 1985; Nolan and Whelan, 1996; Gordon et al., 2003 and Alkire and Foster, 2011a,b).

To analyze the recommendations formally, following Bourguignon and Chakravarty (2003), let us define a deprivation identification function for each of them. The formulation will be presented in terms of an arbitrary element M of the set $\{M_1, M_2, M_3\}$. For the union mode, the identification function ρ_{UN} can be rigorously defined as follows. For all $n \in N$, $X \in M^n, \underline{z} \in Z, i \in \{1, 2, \ldots, n\}$,

$$\rho_{UN}(x_{i.}; \underline{z}) = \begin{cases} 1 \text{ if } \exists j \in Q \rightarrow x_{ij} < z_j, \\ 0, \text{ otherwise.} \end{cases} \tag{3.4}$$

In other words, $\rho_{UN}(x_{i.}; \underline{z})$ takes on the value 1 if person i is deprived in at least one dimension; otherwise, its value is 0. We designate ρ_{UN} as a deprivation identification function since it clearly indicates whether the person is deprived in some dimension. It is definitely not necessary to check whether deprivation occurs in all the dimensions. One goes on searching for a dimension in which deprivation prevails, and once this is established, the search stops. The person is then regarded as poor by the union criterion. Accordingly, the number of persons who are counted as poor in X by the union criterion is given by the sum $\sum_{i=1}^{n} \rho_{UN}(x_{i.}; \underline{z})$.

The set of persons who are regarded as poor by the union criterion, the set of union poor, in $X \in M^n$ is given by $\Pi_{UN}(X; \underline{z}) = \{i \in \{1, 2, \ldots, n\} | \rho_{UN}(x_{i.}; \underline{z}) = 1\}$. Consequently, the number of union poor persons in X can alternatively be expressed as $|\Pi_{UN}(X; \underline{z})|$, the number of persons in $\Pi_{UN}(X; \underline{z})$.

Consider a person who is nondeprived in all the dimensions except one with a low shortfall from the reference limit will be counted as poor by the union rule. In the aggregation, his contribution to total poverty will be quite low. This can be checked easily if the poverty index satisfies subgroup decomposability, an axiom that has attractive policy appeals. Isolation of such minor contributions is not a problem under subgroup decomposability. If the population size is large, the set of union poor may also be large. But identification of the set of poor with low deprivations, under subgroup decomposability, is an extremely easy task.

In the intersection mode, the poor are identified as those persons who experience deprivation in each dimension. As a result, the corresponding deprivation identification function ρ_{IN} can be formally defined as follows. For all $n \in N, X \in M^n, \underline{z} \in Z, i \in \{1, 2, \ldots, n\}$,

$$\rho_{IN}(x_{i.}; \underline{z}) = \begin{cases} 1 \text{ if } \forall j \in Q,\ x_{ij} < z_j, \\ 0, \text{ otherwise.} \end{cases} \tag{3.5}$$

In consequence, the set of intersection poor in X becomes $\Pi_{IN}(X; \underline{z}) = \{i \in \{1, 2, \ldots, n\} | \rho_{IN}(x_{i.}; \underline{z}) = 1\}$, and the number of persons suffering from deprivation in all the dimensions in the matrix X is $\sum_{i=1}^{n} \rho_{IN}(x_{i.}; \underline{z})$.

In this alternative identification arrangement, a person is poor if he is deprived in all the dimensions, and this leads us to identify the number of poor as the total number of persons who are deprived in all the dimensions. A person deprived in one dimension but nondeprived in another is not designated as poor by the intersection method. But trade-off between achievements in the two dimensions may not be possible. Shortage of essential durables cannot be neutralized by housing. Consider a person with high deprivations in all dimensions except one, and in the nondeprived dimension, his achievement is at the corresponding reference point. Although this person is assigned a nonpoverty status by the intersection criterion, from antipoverty policy perspective, this may be difficult to accept. An old street beggar who does not even earn hand-to-mouth daily by begging is judged as nonpoor by the intersection system because of high life expectancy. But overall, he maintains a very low level of living and is definitely a union poor. Consequently, treating a person as poor if he is deprived in at least one dimension appears to be more sensible.

In between the union and intersection procedures, there lies the intermediate identification system, which treats a person as poor if he has a minimum deprivation score of $\bar{l}$. For any $n \in N, X \in M^n$, the deprivation score l_i of person $i \in \{1, 2, \ldots, n\}$ is defined as $l_i = \sum_{j=1}^{d} w_j (g_{ij})^0$, where $g_{ij} = \left(1 - \frac{\hat{x}_{ij}}{z_j}\right)$ is the deprivation indicator of person i in dimension j, $w_j > 0$ is the weight assigned to dimension j, and $\sum_{j=1}^{d} w_j = 1$. Note that $(g_{ij})^0 = 1$ if person i is deprived in dimension j; otherwise, it takes on the value 0. Hence, $0 \leq l_i \leq 1$, where the lower and upper bounds are attained respectively in the extreme cases when the person is nondeprived and deprived in all the dimensions. Following Duclos and Tiberti (2016), we refer to l_i as the weighted proportion of deprived dimensions for person i. If all the dimensions are equally weighted, that is, $w_j = \frac{1}{d}$ for all $j \in Q$, then l_i becomes the person's deprivation count, the number of dimensions in which the person is deprived, divided by the maximum attainable value of the deprivation count.

Alkire and Foster (2011a,b) defined person i as multidimensionally poor if the inequality $l_i \geq \bar{l}$ holds, where the poverty cutoff $\bar{l}$ is a threshold parameter. Formally, the intermediate deprivation identification function ρ_{INT} can be formally defined as follows. For all $n \in N, X \in M^n, \underline{z} \in Z, i \in \{1, 2, \ldots, n\}$,

$$\rho_{INT}(x_{i.}; \underline{z}) = \begin{cases} 1 \text{ if } l_i \geq \bar{l}, \\ 0, \text{ otherwise.} \end{cases} \tag{3.6}$$

Hence, the set of persons in X who are regarded as poor by the intermediate system of identification is given by $\Pi_{INT}(X; \underline{z}) = \{i \in \{1, 2, \ldots, n\} \mid \rho_{INT}(x_{i.}; \underline{z}) = 1\}$, and the number of such persons in the matrix is $\sum_{i=1}^{n} \rho_{INT}(x_{i.}; \underline{z})$. This intermediate identification criterion coincides with the union mode if the poverty cutoff does not exceed the minimum of the weights: $0 < \bar{l} \leq \min_{j \in Q}\{w_j\}$. On the other hand, the intersection mode drops out as a particular case of the intermediate norm if $\bar{l} = 1$. For $w_j = \frac{1}{d}$, this intermediate identification criterion coincides with the union or the intersection rule depending on whether $\bar{l} = \frac{1}{d}$ or $\bar{l} = 1$. For the intermediate mode to be different from the union and intersection methods, the number of dimensions should be at least 3. The choice of $\bar{l}$ and the weights are matters of value judgment. (See Duclos and Tiberti, 2016, for further discussions on this criterion of identification and its implications.)

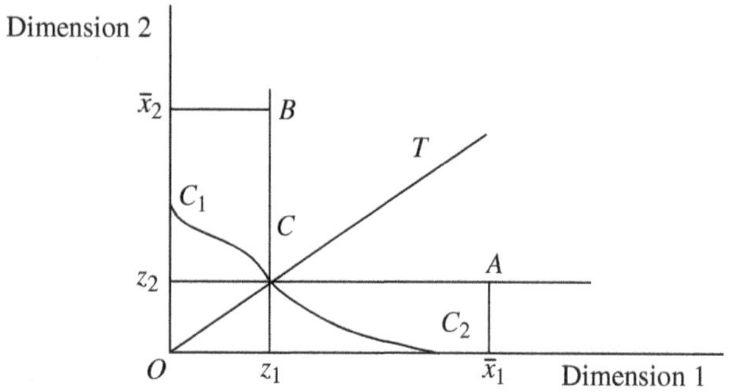

Figure 3.1 Identification of the poor.

Under the equal weighting scheme in the intermediate technique, we assign equal importance to each dimension by treating them symmetrically. Under symmetry, it becomes necessary to look at a person's deprivation count. As soon the count leads us to $\bar{l}$, the person is labeled as poor by the intermediate process. (More extensive applications of deprivation counts are available in Sections 3.8–3.10.)[11]

We may now illustrate the union, intersection, and intermediate practices of identification graphically. In Figure 3.1, the horizontal and vertical axes represent the achievements in dimensions 1 and 2, respectively. Their upper bounds are denoted respectively by $\bar{x}_1$ and $\bar{x}_2$. The positions of the respective cutoff limits are indicated by the horizontal and vertical lines z_1 and z_2. All those individuals whose achievements are in the two-dimensional poverty space-$TDPS(z_1, z_2)$, exhibited by the region Oz_2Cz_1, are enumerated as poor by the intersection criterion. Since the union rule recognizes someone as poor if he is deprived in either of the two dimensions, all individuals with achievements below the line z_2A or to the left of the line z_1B become poor by this criterion. Finally, the curve C_2CC_1 illustrates an intermediate approach.

11 The counting approach to identify the deprived has been implemented extensively. See, for example, Kast and Molina (1975), Altimir (1979), Townsend (1979), Mack and Lansley(1985), Ringen (1987, 1988), Katzman (1989), Mayer and Jencks (1989), Muffels and Vriens (1991), Callan et al. (1993), Erikson (1993), Halleröd (1994, 1995), Nolan and Whelan (1996), Davies (1997), Bauman (1998, 1999), Davies and Smith (1998), Gordon et al. (2000), Layte et al. (2000), Gordon et al. (2001), Nteziyaremye and MkNelly (2001), Eurostat (2002), Vranken (2002), Gordon et al. (2003), Hirway (2003), Sundaram (2003), Coady et al. (2004), Guio (2005, 2009), Jain (2004), Mukherjee (2005), Abbe (2006), Chakravarty and D'Ambrosio (2006), Guio and Maquet (2006), Eurobarameter (2007), Jalan and Murgai (2007), Alkire and Seth (2008, 2013a,b, 2015), Wright (2008), Thomas et al. (2009), Drèze and Khera (2010), Apablaza and Yalonetzky (2011), Gardiner and Evans (2011), Roy (2011), Sharan (2011), Alkire and Roche (2012), Boyden and Bourdillon (2012), Minujin and Nandy (2012), Angulo Salazar et al. (2013), Decancq et al. (2013), Roche (2013), Trani et al. (2013), Alkire et al. (2014), Robano and Smith (2014) and Dickerson and Popli (2015).

The two one-dimensional poverty spaces $SDPS(z_1)$ and $SDPS(z_2)$ are displayed by the regions $Oz_2A\bar{x}_1$ and $O\bar{x}_2Bz_1$, respectively. While in the former region, a person is deprived in dimension 2, in the latter, deprivation arises from low achievement in dimension 1. The intersection of the two one-dimensional spaces generates the two dimensional space Oz_2Cz_1. However, by summing up the numbers of individuals whose achievements lie inside the space, $(SDPS(z_1) + SDPS(z_2))$ will overestimate the number of poor. The reason behind is that the number of persons whose achievements lie inside Oz_2Cz_1 is counted twice. Suppose that a person's achievements in the first $(d-1)$ dimensions are zero and the achievement in the remaining dimension coincides with its threshold limit. This person is not counted as poor by the intersection method, however large or small the value of d may be. Thus, although the person is maximally deprived in all the dimensions except one and he is nondeprived in only one dimension, he is intersection nonpoor. This clearly indicates a shortcoming of the intersection rule as an identification criterion. Nevertheless, the union method identifies this person as poor.

In the following discussion, we follow the union criterion of identification. This mechanism has installed itself as a notable identification criterion because of its easy implementation and long usage. For any $n \in N$, $X \in M^n$, $\underline{z} \in Z$, we denote the set of all poor persons in X by $\Pi(X;\underline{z})$. For any given $\underline{z} \in Z$, we write the number of poor persons in $X \in M^n$ by $|\Pi(X;\underline{z})|$. The head-count ratio, the proportion of persons in poverty, is $\frac{|\Pi(X;\underline{z})|}{n}$.

3.5 Axioms for a Multidimensional Poverty Metric

A multidimensional poverty index P is required to aggregate the deprivations of the individuals in a society along different dimensions of well-being in terms of a nonnegative scalar. For any vector of exogenously given threshold limits and an achievement matrix, this scalar signifies the extent of poverty related to the matrix. More precisely, it is a summary statistic of the distributions of individual deprivations in different dimensions of well-being. Unless specified explicitly, we assume that the set of all distribution matrices is given by $M = M_1$. Then $P : M \times Z \to \mathfrak{R}^1_+$. For any $n \in N, X \in M^n$, the scalar $P(X;\underline{z})$ is the level of poverty associated with social matrix $X \in M^n$, where $\underline{z} \in Z$ is arbitrary.

The structure of the current section, whose subject is the analysis of the properties for a multidimensional poverty index, parallels that of Part 2.3.1.1 of Section 2.3.1. Most of the postulates discussed next for an arbitrary P are generalizations of different postulates suggested for an income poverty index. However, any axiom that necessitates existence of at least two dimensions does not have any unidimensional sister.

3.5.1 Invariance Axioms

The axioms scrutinized in this subsection do not indicate any change in the extent of poverty when some allowable changes are made in achievement matrices.

The first of them indicates invariance of poverty if there are proportionate changes in the achievement quantities and threshold limits, where the proportionality factors may not be the same across dimensions.

Strong Ratio-Scale Invariance: For all $n \in N, X \in M^n$, $\underline{z} \in Z, P(X;\underline{z}) = P(X\Omega; (\eta_1 z_1, \eta_2 z_2, \ldots, \eta_d z_d))$, where $\Omega = \text{diag}(\eta_1, \eta_2, \ldots, \eta_d)$, $\eta_i > 0$ for all i.

To illustrate the axiom, consider the 4×3 social matrix $X_1 = \begin{bmatrix} 9 & 5 & 90 \\ 6 & 4 & 80 \\ 7 & 6 & 50 \\ 2 & 3 & 40 \end{bmatrix}$. Assume that the vector of threshold limits is given by $\underline{z} = (9, 5, 50)$. By the union rule of identification, the second, third, and fourth persons are poor. This is because each of these three persons is deprived in at least one dimension. While person 2 is deprived in dimensions 1 and 2, the only source of deprivation of person 3 is dimension 1. On the other hand, person 4 is deprived in all the three dimensions. The intersection mode, in contrast, will detect only the fourth person as poor.

Now, suppose that $\Omega = \begin{bmatrix} 2 & 0 & 0 \\ 0 & 3 & 0 \\ 0 & 0 & 1 \end{bmatrix}$ so that $X_1\Omega = \begin{bmatrix} 18 & 15 & 90 \\ 12 & 12 & 80 \\ 14 & 18 & 50 \\ 4 & 9 & 40 \end{bmatrix}$ and $(\eta_1 z_1, \eta_2 z_2, \eta_3 z_3) = (18, 15, 50)$. Then strong ratio-scale invariance demands that $P\left(\begin{bmatrix} 9 & 5 & 90 \\ 6 & 4 & 80 \\ 7 & 6 & 50 \\ 2 & 4 & 40 \end{bmatrix}; (9, 5, 50)\right) = P\left(\begin{bmatrix} 18 & 15 & 90 \\ 12 & 12 & 80 \\ 14 & 18 & 50 \\ 4 & 9 & 40 \end{bmatrix}; (18, 15, 50)\right)$.

If the proportionality factors are assumed to be the same across dimensions, that is, if $\eta_i = \eta > 0$ for all $i \in \{1, 2, \ldots, d\}$, then we get the weaker form of the aforementioned axiom. We refer to this weaker variant of strong ratio-scale invariance as ratio-scale invariance, and a multidimensional poverty index satisfying this postulate will be known as a relative index. Evidently, all one-dimensional measures analyzed in Section 2.2 are of relative type.

Instead of assuming proportionate changes in achievement quantities, we can alternatively allow the possibility that these quantities can change by absolute amounts. More precisely, poverty will not change when dimensional achievement figures and threshold levels are changed by absolute quantities, where these absolute amounts may vary across dimensions. Formally,

Strong Translation-Scale Invariance: For all $n \in N, X \in M^n, \underline{z} \in Z, P(X;\underline{z}) = P(X + A; (z_1 + \kappa_1, z_2 + \kappa_2, \ldots, z_d + \kappa_d))$, where A is an $n \times d$ matrix with identical rows given by $(\kappa_1, \kappa_2, \ldots, \kappa_d)$ such that $X + A \in M^n$ and $z_j + \kappa_j \geq 0$ for all $j \in Q$.

For the 4×3 translation matrix $A = \begin{bmatrix} 1 & 0 & -2 \\ 1 & 0 & -2 \\ 1 & 0 & -2 \\ 1 & 0 & -2 \end{bmatrix}$, we have $X_1 + A = \begin{bmatrix} 10 & 5 & 88 \\ 7 & 4 & 78 \\ 8 & 6 & 48 \\ 3 & 3 & 38 \end{bmatrix}$ and $(\kappa_1 + z_1, \kappa_2 + z_2, \kappa_3 + z_3) = (10, 5, 48)$. Consequently, strong translation-scale invariance claims that $P\left(\begin{bmatrix} 9 & 5 & 90 \\ 6 & 4 & 80 \\ 7 & 6 & 50 \\ 2 & 3 & 40 \end{bmatrix}; (9, 5, 50)\right) = P\left(\begin{bmatrix} 10 & 5 & 88 \\ 7 & 4 & 78 \\ 8 & 6 & 48 \\ 3 & 3 & 38 \end{bmatrix}; (10, 5, 48)\right)$. A weaker form of the postulate, translation-scale invariance axiom, requires that $\kappa_j s$ are not variable across dimensions. A poverty index satisfying this weaker axiom is called an absolute index.

Sometimes, comparison between two societies with respect to their poverty levels becomes necessary. It is desirable that the poverty ranking remains unaltered even if the dimensional achievements and poverty cutoff limits in the two social matrices are expressed in differing measuring units. This requirement is ensured by the strong unit consistency axiom (Zheng, 2007a,b). To grasp the problem in greater detail, suppose that a policy-maker needs to rank social distributions of two countries in terms of their multidimensional poverty levels, where the dimensions included in the distributions are life expectancy and income. For illustrative purpose, assume that income is measured in dollar, and life expectancy is measured in years. It is noted that the former country has higher poverty compared to the latter. Now, if the policy-maker decides to change the measurement unit of income from dollar to euro and that of life expectancy from years to months, then strong unit consistency will require that the already observed poverty ranking should not alter as a consequence of these shifts in the measurement units of the dimensional achievements. Formally, the strong unit consistency axiom can be stated as:

Strong Unit Consistency: For all $n \in N, X^1, X^2 \in M$ and $\underline{z}^1, \underline{z}^2 \in Z$, if $P(X; \underline{z}^1) < P(Y; \underline{z}^2)$, then $P(X^1\Omega; \underline{z}^1\Omega) < P(X^2\Omega; \underline{z}^2\Omega)$ for all $\Omega = \text{diag}(\omega_1, \omega_2, \ldots, \omega_d), \omega_i > 0$ for all $i. \in Q$.

Evidently, all strongly ratio-scale invariant multidimensional poverty indices are strongly unit consistent. However, the converse is not true. More precisely, there may exist strongly unit-consistent multidimensional poverty indices that are not strongly ratio-scale invariant. If in the aforementioned axiom the positive scalars ω_is are the same across dimensions, then we refer to it as unit consistency.

In the invariance axioms analyzed above we allow changes in all dimensional quantities, irrespective of whether they correspond to deprived or nondeprived dimensions. In the next two postulates, the focus axioms, changes only in nondeprived dimensional quantities are permitted. These two axioms were suggested by Bourguignon and Chakravarty (2003).[12]

Weak Focus: For all $n \in N, X, Y \in M^n, \underline{z} \in Z$, if for some $i \in \{1, 2, \ldots, n\}$, $x_{ij} \geq z_j$ for all $j \in Q$, for some pair $(i, j) \in \{1, 2, \ldots, n\} \times \{1, 2, \ldots, d\}$, $y_{ij} = x_{ij} + c_{ij}$, where c_{ij} is a scalar such that $y_{ij} \geq z_j$ and $y_{hk} = x_{hk}$ for all $(h, k) \in \{1, 2, \ldots, n\} \times \{1, 2, \ldots, d\} / \{(i, j)\}$, then $P(X; \underline{z}) = P(Y; \underline{z})$.

According to this postulate, for a rich person, who is not deprived in any dimension, a change in a dimensional quantity that does not make the person deprived in the dimension should not affect poverty. This is natural since poverty is concerned with the deprivations of the poor.

To illustrate this axiom, note that person 1 is nondeprived in all the three dimensions in X_1. If we reduce his achievement quantity in dimension 3 from 90 to 80, then poverty should not change since the reduced quantity is much above the dimensional threshold limit, 50. If we denote the resulting distribution matrix by Y_1, then $Y_1 = \begin{bmatrix} 9 & 5 & 80 \\ 6 & 4 & 80 \\ 7 & 6 & 50 \\ 2 & 3 & 40 \end{bmatrix}$. The weak focus axioms stipulates that $P(X_1; (9, 5, 50)) = P(Y_1; (9, 5, 50))$.

In the next axiom, we consider a change in a nondeprived dimensional achievement of a person such that the change does make the person deprived in the dimension. Formally,

Strong Focus: For all $n \in N, X, Y \in M^n, \underline{z} \in Z$, if for some pair $(i, j) \in \{1, 2, \ldots, n\} \times \{1, 2, \ldots, d\}, y_{ij} = x_{ij} + c_{ij}$, where $x_{ij} \geq z_j$ and c_{ij} is a scalar such that $y_{ij} \geq z_j$ and $y_{hk} = x_{hk}$ for all $(h, k) \in \{1, 2, \ldots, n\} \times \{1, 2, \ldots, d\} / \{(i, j)\}$, then $P(X; \underline{z}) = P(Y; \underline{z})$.

Note that here in X_1 the possibility that person i is poor is not excluded. This axiom has an interesting implication with respect to trade-off between nondeprived and deprived dimensional quantities of a poor person. When the level of achievement in a nondeprived dimension of a poor is reduced such that the resulting achievement quantity does not fall below the corresponding

12 The strong version of the axiom was considered also by Tsui (2002).

threshold limit, in exchange the person is not made better off in a deprived dimension. Consequently, trade-off between two dimensional achievements of a poor person who is deprived in one but nondeprived in the other is not possible. This definitely does not rule out potentiality of trade-off between two deprived dimensional quantities. The two focus axioms do not as well claim that the poverty index is independent of the nonpoor population size. (See Bourguignon and Chakravarty, 2003, for extensive discussions along this line.)

In X_1 person 2 is nondeprived only in dimension 3 and hence he is poor by the union mode of identification. Now, the matrix $Y_2 = \begin{bmatrix} 9 & 5 & 90 \\ 6 & 4 & 75 \\ 7 & 6 & 50 \\ 2 & 3 & 40 \end{bmatrix}$ is obtained from X_1 by reducing only person 2's achievement level in dimension 3 from 80 to 75 so that he is still nondeprived in the dimension. Then according to the strong focus axiom, this alteration does not change the quantity of overall poverty. More precisely, $P(X_1; (9, 5, 50)) = P(Y_2; (9, 5, 50))$.

The reduction in achievement of the person in dimension 3 by 5 units is unable to reduce his deprivation in a deprived dimension.

The next two invariance axioms are poverty sisters of inequality symmetry and population replication invariance postulates, respectively.

Symmetry: For all $n \in N, X, Y \in M^n, \underline{z} \in Z$, if $Y = \Gamma X$, where Γ is any permutation matrix of order n, then $P(X; \underline{z}) = P(Y; \underline{z})$.

Population Replication Invariance: For all $n \in N, X \in M^n$, $\underline{z} \in Z, P(X; \underline{z}) = P(Y; \underline{z})$, where Y is any k-fold replication of X, $k \geq 2$ being any finite integer.

Our discussions so far have been on axioms that do not allow any change in the poverty intensity under some specific type of alternations in an achievement matrix. Next, we analyze distributional axioms that indicate directional movements of a poverty index resulting from some transformations in a distribution matrix.

3.5.2 Distributional Axioms

Suppose that there is a curtailment in the achievement of a deprived dimension of a poor. Since such degradation in the achievement is undesirable from poverty reduction perspective, we can claim enhancement of poverty in this situation. In other words, a poverty index should increase under this state of affairs.

The following axiom addresses the impact of debasement in the attainment of a deprived dimension of a poor.

Monotonicity: For all $n \in N, X, Y \in M^n, \underline{z} \in Z$, if for some pair $(i,j) \in \{1, 2, \ldots, n\} \times \{1, 2, \ldots, d\}$, $y_{ij} = x_{ij} - c$, where $0 < x_{ij} < z_j$, $y_{hk} = x_{hk}$ for all $(h, k) \in \{1, 2, \ldots, n\} \times \{1, 2, \ldots, d\}/\{(i, j)\}$ and $c > 0$, then $P(X; \underline{z}) < P(Y; \underline{z})$.

The social distribution $Y_3 = \begin{bmatrix} 9 & 5 & 90 \\ 6 & 4 & 80 \\ 6 & 6 & 50 \\ 1 & 3 & 40 \end{bmatrix}$ is deduced from X_1 by a cutback of person 3's achievement in dimension 1, a deprived dimension for the person, by 1 unit. According to the monotonicity axiom, $P(Y_3; \underline{z}) > P(X_1; \underline{z})$.

Often, it becomes desirable to ensure that a contraction in the achievement of a poor should increase poverty by a larger amount, the more deprived the person is. Similarly, an improvement in an achievement should lead to a greater diminution of poverty, the more deprived the poor is. This supports the view that the poorest subgroups in a society should receive maximum attention from antipoverty policy perspective. This plausible view is presented analytically in the next axiom (see Lasso de La Vega and Urrutia, 2012).

Let $S_{ih}(X; \underline{z})$ be the identical set of dimensions in which the poor persons i and h are deprived, that is, $S_{ih}(X; \underline{z}) = \{j \in Q \,|x_{hj} < z_j\} = \{j \in Q|x_{ij} < z_j\}$, where $i, h \in \{1, 2, \ldots, n\}$ are arbitrary. Assume further that all deprivations of h are higher than the corresponding deprivations of i in $S_{ih}(X; \underline{z})$. Formally, for all $j \in S_{ih}(X; \underline{z})$, $x_{hj} < x_{ij} < z_j$.

Definition 3.1 A multidimensional poverty index $P : M \times Z \to \mathfrak{R}^1_+$ is said to satisfy monotonicity sensitivity property if

i) all $n \in N, n > 1$, $X \in M^n, \underline{z} \in Z$, there exist multidimensionally poor persons $h, i \in \{1, 2, \ldots, n\}$ such that $S_{ih}(X; \underline{z})$ is nonempty,
ii) there corresponds $Y, \tilde{Y} \in M^n$ to $X \in M^n$ such that (a) $y_{p.}, \tilde{y}_{p.} = x_{p.}$ for all $p \neq h, i$; (b) $y_{h.} = x_{h.} - \delta, \tilde{y}_{i.} = x_{i.} - \delta$, where $\delta = (\delta_1, \delta_2, \ldots, \delta_d)$; (c) $\delta_j = 0$ for all $j \in Q \backslash S_{ih}(X\,;\,\underline{z})$; (d) $\delta_j \geq 0$ for all $j \in S_{ih}(X\,;\,\underline{z})$, with $>$ for at least one $j \in S_{ih}(X; \underline{z})$ and $x_{hj} > 0$ is accompanied by $\delta_j > 0$; and (e) $y_{i.} = x_{i.}, \tilde{y}_{h.} = x_{h.}$, then $P(Y; \underline{z}) - P(X; \underline{z}) > P(\tilde{Y}; \underline{z}) - P(X; \underline{z})$.

We assume that of two multidimensionally poor persons i and h, person h has higher deprivations than person i in some dimensions in X (condition (i)). Part (a) of condition (ii) states that in the three matrices X, Y, and $\tilde{Y}$, any person other than persons h and i has identical profile. Part (b) of the condition indicates that achievements in dimension j in Y and $\tilde{Y}$ of persons h and i, respectively, are obtained by reducing the corresponding dimensional achievements in X by the same quantity, and this holds for all $j \in S_{ih}(X; \underline{z})$. In part (c) of the condition, it is stated that achievements of each of the persons i and h in dimensions that are not in $S_{ih}(X; \underline{z})$ remain unaltered. In part (d) of the condition, it is claimed explicitly that amounts by which achievements of persons i and h in different dimensions in $S_{ih}(X; \underline{z})$ are reduced are nonnegative and positive for some dimensions, and these amounts need not be the same across the dimensions. Finally, in part (e) of the condition, it is demanded that profiles of person i in X and Y are the same and those of person h are identical in X and $\tilde{Y}$. Since $\tilde{Y} \in M^n$, nonnegativity of achievement of person h in $\tilde{Y}$ in any dimension in $S_{ih}(X; \underline{z})$ is ensured.

We are now in a position to state the following axiom:

Monotonicity Sensitivity: The poverty index $P : M \times Z \rightarrow \Re^1_+$ satisfies the monotonicity sensitivity property.

This axiom says that we consider shrinkage in the achievements in dimensions in $S_{ih}(X; z)$ that applies identically to both i and h. The shrinkage operation is performed separately for the affected persons, and poverty increment is higher when it applies to the more deprived person h.

In X_1, persons 2 and 4 are poor and both are deprived in dimensions 1 and 2. Person 2 has lower deprivation than person 4 in each of these dimensions. We get $Y_4 = \begin{bmatrix} 9 & 5 & 90 \\ 5 & 3 & 80 \\ 6 & 6 & 50 \\ 2 & 3 & 40 \end{bmatrix}$ and $Y_5 = \begin{bmatrix} 9 & 5 & 90 \\ 6 & 4 & 80 \\ 7 & 6 & 50 \\ 1 & 2 & 40 \end{bmatrix}$ from X_1 by curtailing, respectively, the achievements of persons 2 and 4 in each of these dimensions by 1 unit. The monotonicity sensitivity axiom demands that $P(Y_5; \underline{z}) - P(X_1; \underline{z}) > P(Y_4; \underline{z}) - P(X_1; \underline{z})$.

The next axiom, suggested by Alkire and Foster (2011a), is concerned with the effect of increasing the number of deprived dimensions of a poor. It requires that when a nondeprived dimension of a poor person, who is not deprived in all dimensions, becomes deprived, then poverty should increase. Formally,

Dimensional Monotonicity: For all $n \in N, X \in M^n, \underline{z} \in Z$, if $Y \in M^n$ is obtained from X such that for some pair $(i, j) \in \{1, 2, \ldots, n\} \times \{1, 2, \ldots, d\}$, $y_{ij} < z_j \leq x_{ij}$, where person i is deprived in X in at least dimension different from j and $y_{pk} = x_{pk}$ for all pairs $(p, k) \in \{1, 2, \ldots, n\} \times \{1, 2, \ldots, d\}/\{(i, j)\}$, then $P(Y; \underline{z}) > P(X; \underline{z})$.

Person i, who is poor and nondeprived in dimension j in X, becomes deprived in the dimension in Y. However, all other achievement levels for all persons in $\{1, 2, \ldots, n\}$ are the same in both X and Y. Now, under the change considered in the axiom, in Y, person i will be deprived in dimension j, a nondeprived dimension for the person in X. Hence, poverty should go up.

In our achievement matrix X_1, dimension 2 is a nondeprived dimension for person 3, a poor person in X_1. If his achievement in the dimension reduces from 6 to 4, he becomes deprived in this dimension in the transformed matrix $Y_6 = \begin{bmatrix} 9 & 5 & 90 \\ 6 & 4 & 80 \\ 7 & 4 & 50 \\ 2 & 3 & 40 \end{bmatrix}$. Dimensional monotonicity axiom demands that $P(Y_6; \underline{z}) > P(X_1; \underline{z})$.

Definition 3.2 For all $n \in N, n > 1$, $X \in M^n, \underline{z} \in Z$, $Y \in M^n$ is said to be obtained from X by a Pigou–Dalton bundle of regressive transfers between two multidimensionally poor persons if

i) There exist multidimensionally poor persons $h, i \in \{1, 2, \dots, n\}$ such that $S_{ih}(X; \underline{z})$ is nonempty,
ii) $y_{p.} = x_{p.}$ for all $p \neq h, i$;
iii) $y_{h.} = x_{h.} - \delta$, $y_{i.} = x_{i.} + \delta$, where $\delta = (\delta_1, \delta_2, \dots, \delta_d)$; (a) $\delta_j = 0$ for all $j \in Q \backslash S_{ih}(X; \underline{z})$; (b) $\delta_j \geq 0$ for any $j \in S_{ih}(X; \underline{z})$, with $>$ for at least one j, and $y_{ij} < z_j$ for all $j \in S_{ih}(X; \underline{z})$.

Condition (i) ensures that there is at least one element in the alike set of deprived dimensions of the poor persons h and i. By assumption, of the two persons, the former has higher deprivations than the latter in this set. According to condition (ii), all individuals except persons h and i have identical achievements in all the dimensions in both X and Y. Part (a) of condition (iii) asserts that each of persons h and i has identical achievements in all dimensions that are not included in the set $S_{ih}(X; \underline{z})$. Part (b) of condition (iii) means that transfers of achievements from person h to person i along dimensions in $S_{ih}(X; \underline{z})$ generate appropriate entries of $y_{h.}$ and $y_{i.}$ from the corresponding entries of $x_{h.}$ and $x_{i.}$, respectively, where the size of the transfer is nonnegative for any dimension in the set, and for at least one dimension of this type, the transfer has a positive size. Finally, in part (b) of condition (iii), it is ensured that the size of the transfer in any dimension does not allow the recipient to be nondeprived in the corresponding dimension. Since for any $j \in S_{ih}(X; \underline{z})$, $\delta_j \geq 0$ can at most be x_{hj}, it is guaranteed that $0 \leq y_{hj} \leq y_{ij}$. The transfer operation takes place between the multidimensionally poor individuals i and h only in their common set of deprived dimensions. Equivalently, X is obtained from Y by a Pigou–Dalton bundle of progressive transfers.

In the distribution matrix X_1, $S_{24}(X; \underline{z})$, the identical set of deprived dimensions of persons 2 and 4, contains dimensions 2 and 1. Further, in each of these two dimensions, person 2 has higher achievement than person 4. Now, regressive transfers of 1 and 0.5 units of achievements in dimension 1 and 2, respectively, from person 4 to person 2, transform the matrix X_1 into $Y_7 = \begin{bmatrix} 9 & 5 & 90 \\ 7 & 4.5 & 80 \\ 7 & 6 & 50 \\ 1 & 2.5 & 40 \end{bmatrix}$. We then say that Y_7 is deduced from X_1 by a Pigou–Dalton bundle of regressive transfers between two persons.

The following transfer postulate for a multidimensional poverty index can now be stated.

Multidimensional Transfer: For all $n \in N, n > 1, X \in M^n, \underline{z} \in Z$, if $Y \in M^n$ is obtained from X by a Pigou–Dalton bundle of regressive transfers between two multidimensionally poor persons, then $P(Y; \underline{z}) > P(X; \underline{z})$.

This postulate may be regarded as a multidimensional translation of the Donaldson and Weymark (1986) weak transfer axiom. For the illustrative example, where we derive Y_7 from X_1 by a Pigou–Dalton bundle of regressive transfers between the multidimensionally poor persons 2 and 4, the transfer axiom demands that $P(X_1; \underline{z}) < P(Y_7; \underline{z})$.

The final axiom in this subsection, we consider, has relevance only to multidimensional poverty and depends on the association between deprivations.

Definition 3.3 For all $n \in N, n > 1, X \in M^n, \underline{z} \in Z$, suppose that persons i and p are deprived in dimensions j and q in X, that is, $x_{ij}, x_{pj} < z_j$ and $x_{iq}, x_{pq} < z_q$. Assume also that $x_{ij} > x_{pj}$, $x_{iq} < x_{pq}$, and $x_{it} \le x_{pt}$ for all $t \in Q/\{j, q\}$. We then say that $Y \in M^n$ is obtained from X by a correlation-increasing switch in a domain of deprivations if (i) $y_{ij} = x_{pj}$, (ii) $y_{pj} = x_{ij}$, (iii) $y_{rj} = x_{rj}$ for all $r \ne i, p$, and (iv) $y_{rs} = x_{rs}$ for all $r \in \{1, 2, \dots, n\}$ and for all $s \in Q/\{j\}$.

In Definition 3.3, conditions (i) and (ii) along with condition (iv) for $r = i, p$ and $s = q$ indicate that the multidimensionally poor person p who had less achievement in dimension j and more achievement in dimension q than the multidimensionally poor person i in X has higher achievements in both the dimensions in Y. It is also known that in all the remaining dimensions, achievements of person p are at least as high as the corresponding achievements of person i. Condition (iii) says that achievements for the remaining individuals in dimension j are the same in both the distribution matrices X and Y. Finally, condition (iv) demands that achievements of all persons in all the dimensions except j are the same in both the achievement matrices. We obtain Y from X by a switch of achievements in dimension j between persons i and p. In the postswitch setting, person p has at least as much achievement as person i in every dimension and strictly more in at least one dimension. Since both j and q are deprived dimensions for the poor persons i and p who are affected by the switch, we say that the switch is performed in a domain of deprivations. The switch of achievements in dimension j, defined by (i) and (ii), increases the correlation between dimensions. That is why, we refer to the switch as a correlation-increasing switch in a domain of deprivations. The switch does not modify the total of the achievements in the dimension on which it operates. In the two-dimensional situation, a correlation-increasing switch, as presented in Definition 3.3, holds only in the two-dimensional poverty space $TDPS(z_1, z_2)$.

If the two dimensions are substitutes, then one counterbalances the deficiency of the other. Since one person (person p), who was originally richer than the other person (person i) in dimension q, is becoming richer in the other dimension (dimension j) also after the switch and the two dimensions represent similar aspect of well-being, the switch should increase poverty. For the other person (person i), the inability to offset the shortage in one dimension by the other now increases because he is now poorer in both the dimensions.

The aforementioned discussion enables us to state the following axiom:

Increasing Poverty under Correlation-Increasing Switch: For all $n \in N$, $n > 1, X, Y \in M^n, \underline{z} \in Z$, if Y is obtained from X by a correlation-increasing switch in a domain of deprivations, then $P(X; \underline{z}) < P(Y; \underline{z})$ if the dimensions involved in the switch are substitutes.

The corresponding postulate when the dimensions are complements requires poverty to decrease under such a switch. The switch will not affect poverty at all if the involved dimensions are independents.

3.5.3 Decomposability Axioms

A decomposability postulate deals with disaggregation of a poverty index by employing some well-defined procedure. They are helpful in monitoring poverty, targeting poor people, and implementing antipoverty policies. According to the first of these, subgroup decomposability, for any attribute-dependent split-up of the population into two or more subgroups, overall poverty can be expressed as the weighted average of subgroup poverty levels, where the weights are population shares of respective subgroups. (See Chapter 2 for a related discussion in the context of inequality.)

Formally,

Subgroup Decomposability: For any $X^1, X^2, \ldots, X^l \in M$ and $\underline{z} \in Z$, $P(X; \underline{z}) = \sum_{i=1}^{l} \frac{n_i}{n} P(X^i; \underline{z})$, where $X = \begin{pmatrix} X^1 \\ X^2 \\ \vdots \\ X^l \end{pmatrix} \in M$, n_i is the population size associated with X^i and $\sum_{i=1}^{l} n_i = n$.

To understand this, suppose that the population has been broken down into l subgroups using region as a social characteristic. Then X^i is the distribution matrix of region i, $P(X^i; \underline{z})$ is the corresponding poverty level, $\frac{n_i}{n}$ is the proportion of the total population belonging to this region, and $P(X; \underline{z})$ is the level of overall poverty, that is, the extent of poverty that arises when all the regions are taken together. Under repeated application of subgroup decomposability, we have $P(X; \underline{z}) = \frac{1}{n} \sum_{i=1}^{n} P(x_{i.}; \underline{z})$. Population poverty becomes disaggregated as the average of individual poverty levels. Since $P(x_{i.}; \underline{z})$ depends only on individual i's achievement profile, it is often referred to as individual poverty function.

The breakdown $P(X; \underline{z}) = \frac{1}{n} \sum_{i=1}^{n} P(x_{i.}; \underline{z})$ clearly establishes that a subgroup-decomposable poverty index is population replication invariant and symmetric. But the converse is not true.

For illustrative purpose, consider again the four-person distribution matrix X_1. Assume that the population has been divided into two subgroups using sex as the characteristic of division. Let the submatrices $X_1^F = \begin{bmatrix} 9 & 5 & 90 \\ 6 & 4 & 80 \end{bmatrix}$ and $X_1^M = \begin{bmatrix} 7 & 6 & 50 \\ 2 & 3 & 40 \end{bmatrix}$ denote respectively the distribution matrices of the female and male populations. Then under the assumption that the threshold limit vector is given by $(9, 5, 50)$, subgroup decomposability requires that $P(X_1; (9, 5, 50)) = \frac{1}{2}P(X_1^F; (9, 5, 50)) + \frac{1}{2}P(X_1^M; (9, 5, 50))$.

This type of breakdown of population poverty enables us to evaluate the impact of subgroup poverty levels on overall poverty. In other words, one can determine the contribution of a subgroup's poverty to total poverty. Analytically, the contribution of subgroup i to global poverty is $\left(\frac{n_i P(X^i; \underline{z})}{nP(X; \underline{z})}\right)$. Such contributions made by different subgroups become helpful in isolating subgroups that are more stressed by multidimensional poverty and hence to implement antipoverty at local levels. Some of the subgroups get identified as highly contributing subgroups because of large population proportions although their poverty levels are low. In contrast, there may be subgroups with low population shares but high poverty levels so that they are treated as high-poverty-contributing subgroups. This should be kept in mind while implementing the underlying targeted poverty alleviation policy. More precisely, subgroups with low population fractions and high poverty levels should be primary targets from antipoverty policy perspective. Given that population poverty turns out to be the average of individual poverty levels, determination of individual contributions is possible, which sometimes may be useful. This is certainly true when the community population size is not very high, and we are concentrating on household poverty levels.

The objective of the second decomposability postulate, factor decomposability, is to assess the contributions of individual dimensions to overall poverty. In other words, it enables us to identify the causal factors of poverty using dimension-by-dimension breakdown. Formally,

Factor Decomposability: For all $n \in N$, $X \in M^n, \underline{z} \in Z$, $P(X; \underline{z}) = \sum_{j=1}^{d} w_j P(x_{.j}; z_j)$, where $0 < w_j < 1$ for all $j \in Q$ and $\sum_{j=1}^{d} w_j = 1$.

In other words, overall poverty is the weighted average of dimensional poverty values, where the weight attached to each of the dimensional poverty levels is positive (Chakravarty et al. 1998). This postulate may be regarded as the poverty counterpart to the inequality factor decomposability axiom proposed in Chapter 2. The weight w_j allotted to dimension j's poverty may be interpreted as the importance a policy-maker assigns to the role of the dimension in poverty assessment. The weights may depend on achievement distributions. We may as well follow the normative criterion of assigning equal weight to the dimensional indices so that $w_j = \frac{1}{d}$ for all $j \in Q$ (see Chapter 1).

The contribution of weighted poverty in dimension j to overall poverty turns out to be $\frac{w_j P(x_{.j}; z_j)}{P(X; \underline{z})}$. This contribution reduces to 0 if nobody is deprived in the dimension. We are following here the union poverty criterion. Alternatively, if we choose the intersection poverty rule, then for positivity of contribution of a dimensional poverty, it is necessary that everybody is deprived in the dimension. Each of these dimensionwise statistics is important from policy perspective since using them we can judge which dimensions are contributing more. This is especially attractive for designing antipoverty policy at dimension levels.

A factor-decomposable poverty index is a composite index; it assembles the components of the dimensional dashboard $(P(x_{.1}; z_1), P(x_{.2}; z_2), \ldots, P(x_{.d}; z_d))$ using the positive weights w_j assigned across dimensions in $P(X; \underline{z}) = \sum_{j=1}^{d} w_j P(x_{.j}; z_j)$. Consequently, a multidimensional poverty index satisfying the factor decomposability postulate is insensitive to a correlation-increasing switch.

Often, a country's budget for elimination of poverty from one highly contributing subgroup or from one highly contributing dimension for the population as a whole may not be sufficient. In such a case, identification of the highly contributing dimension within a highly contributing subgroup may be appropriate, given that the allocated budget is sufficient to eliminate poverty associated with this (subgroup, dimension) combination.

Analytically, suppose that in a population partitioned into l subgroups, $\frac{n_k}{n} P(X^k; \underline{z})$, the contribution of subgroup k is the highest among the subgroups. The source of this high contribution is a very high value of the subgroup poverty $P(X^k; z)$ although $\frac{n_k}{n}$, the population fraction of the subgroup, is rather low. Consequently, from antipoverty policy perspective, elimination of poverty from this subgroup should get top priority. However, the limited allocated budget does not enable the administration to perform the job. Evidently, in such a case, identification of the highest contributing dimension within this subgroup is necessary.

Note that under factor decomposability, we can split $P(X^k; \underline{z})$ into dimensionwise components as $P(X^k; \underline{z}) = (w_1 P(x^k_{.1}; z_1) + w_2 P(x^k_{.2}; z_2) + \cdots + w_d P(x^k_{.d}; z_d))$, where $x^k_{.j}$ is the jth column of the distribution matrix X^k, indicating the distribution of achievements in dimension $j \in Q$ in X^k. Now, suppose that among all the components of $P(X^k; \underline{z})$, $P(x^k_{.p}; z_p)$ assumes the highest value. Formally, $\max_{j \in Q}\{P(x^k_{.j}; z_j)\} = P(x^k_{.p}; z_p)$. In other words, among all dimensionwise components of $P(X^k; \underline{z})$, the maximum contributor turns out to be $P(x^k_{.p}; z_p)$, poverty arising from distribution of achievements in dimension p in X^k.

Consequently, the subgroup–dimension combination that deserves maximum attention from poverty alleviation perspective is (k, p). If poverty is eliminated from this subgroup–dimension combination, then overall poverty reduces by the quantity $\frac{n_k}{n}(w_p P(x^k_{.p}; z_p))$.

An illustration will make the idea clearer. Assume that in the decomposition of $P(X_1; (9, 5, 50))$ by sex, $P(X_1^F; (9, 5, 50)) < P(X_1^M; (9, 5, 50))$. Assume further that among the three dimensionwise components $P\left(\begin{pmatrix}7\\2\end{pmatrix}; (9)\right)$, $P\left(\begin{pmatrix}6\\3\end{pmatrix}; (5)\right)$ and $P\left(\begin{pmatrix}50\\40\end{pmatrix}; (50)\right)$ of $P(X_1^M; (9, 5, 50))$, the highest contribution comes from $P\left(\begin{pmatrix}7\\2\end{pmatrix}; (9)\right)$. More precisely, $\max\left\{P\left(\begin{pmatrix}7\\2\end{pmatrix}; (9)\right), P\left(\begin{pmatrix}6\\3\end{pmatrix}; (5)\right), P\left(\begin{pmatrix}50\\40\end{pmatrix}; (50)\right)\right\} = P\left(\begin{pmatrix}7\\2\end{pmatrix}; (9)\right)$. This in turn enables us to conclude that the (subgroup–dimension) pair that requires maximum attention from poverty remedial point of view is (male, 1).

3.5.4 Threshold Limit Sensitivity Axiom

The axioms stated so far assume constancy of threshold limits. However, sometimes, a policy-maker may recommend revision of one or more threshold limits, say, following some steady changes in the prices of the achievements in the corresponding dimensions. In such a case, it becomes necessary to investigate how the level of existing poverty alters under such changes.

Nondecreasingness in Poverty Thresholds: For all $n \in N, X \in M^n, \underline{z} \in Z$, let $\underline{\tilde{z}} = (\tilde{z}_1, \tilde{z}_2, \dots, \tilde{z}_d) \in Z$ be such that $\tilde{z}_j = z_j + c, c > 0$ for some $j \in Q$, $\tilde{z}_k = z_k, k \in Q, k \neq j$. Then $P(X; \underline{z}) \leq P(X; \underline{\tilde{z}})$.

If a dimension is already deprived for some individuals, then an increase in its threshold limit can lead to increase in dimensional deprivations of these persons. Further, newer persons may become deprived. Consequently, multidimensional poverty may increase. In the society with the social distribution X_1 and vector of poverty cutoff points $(9, 5, 50)$, suppose that the cutoff limit in dimension 3 increases from 50 to 60, then person 3 who was nondeprived originally in the dimension becomes deprived. Further, person 4's deprivation in the dimension deepens. Consequently, it is legitimate to claim that $P(X_1; (9, 5, 50)) \leq P(X_1; (9, 5, 60))$.

The final subsection of this section deals with two technical postulates. The first of these, boundedness, is a cardinality principle. This axiom says that if nobody is deprived in any dimension, then the index takes on the minimum value 0. In other words, the poverty index achieves its lower bound 0 if nobody is deprived in any dimension. In particular, in a subgroup-decomposable index, if for a nonpoor person, who is nondeprived in all dimensions, the associated individual poverty function assumes the value 0, then the index achieves this lower bound.

On the other hand, the upper bound 1 is achieved if everybody's deprivation is maximal in each dimension. Maximal deprivation for each person in each dimension is a sensible requirement for a poverty index to reach its upper bound. It is a cardinality principle because we can also make the poverty index bounded in some other interval of the set of real numbers by taking an affine transformation of the index. The second property, continuity, requires that there should not be any sudden upward or downward movements of the poverty index for small changes in the deprived achievement levels, under ceteris paribus conditions. Rather, the poverty quantity should change by a negligible amount in this scenario.

3.5.5 Technical Axioms

Boundedness: For all $n \in N$, $X \in M^n$, $\underline{z} \in Z$, $P(X;\underline{z})$ is bounded between 0 and 1, where the lower bound is attained if $X \in M$ is such that $\Pi(X;\underline{z})$, the set of poor persons in X, is empty. The upper bound is attained if everybody is maximally deprived in each dimension.

Continuity: For all $n \in N, \underline{z} \in Z, P$ varies continuously with respect to changes in achievements of the poor, provided that the poverty statuses of the individuals are not affected as a result of achievement variations.

We now study an interesting implication of some of the postulates analyzed earlier. This property indicates a particular directional change in poverty resulting from an increase in nonpoor population size. For any $n \in N, Y \in M^n, \underline{z} \in Z$, consider $X = \begin{pmatrix} Y \\ x_{(n+1).} \end{pmatrix}$, where $x_{(n+1).} = (x_{(n+1)1}, x_{(n+1)2}, \ldots, x_{(n+1)d})$ is the achievement profile of the $(n+1)$th person in $X \in M^{n+1}$ and $x_{(n+1)j} \geq z_j$ for all $j \in Q$. In other words, X is obtained from Y by adding a rich person to the society. Suppose that P is subgroup decomposable and achieves the lower bound 0 in the situation described in the axiom. Now, $P(X;\underline{z}) = \frac{1}{(n+1)} \sum_{i=1}^{n} P(y_{i.};\underline{z}) + \frac{1}{(n+1)} P(x_{(n+1).};\underline{z})$. Since the $(n+1)$th person is not deprived in any dimension, $P(x_{(n+1).};z) = 0$. In consequence, it follows that $P(X;\underline{z}) = \frac{1}{(n+1)} \sum_{i=1}^{n} P(y_{i.};\underline{z}) < \frac{1}{n} \sum_{i=1}^{n} P(y_{i.};\underline{z}) = P(Y;\underline{z})$. This demonstration claims that if a rich person migrates to the society, then a subgroup-decomposable poverty index achieving the lower bound 0 for a society with nonpoor persons will indicate lower poverty for the enlarged society than for the original one.

To understand the property explicitly, suppose that a person with achievement profile (10, 8, 60) migrates to the four-person society whose social matrix is X_1. This person is nonpoor. Hence, $P((10,8,60);(9,5,50)) = 0$. We denote the resulting social matrix by Y_8 so that $Y_8 = \begin{pmatrix} X_1 \\ (10, 8, 60) \end{pmatrix} = \begin{bmatrix} 9 & 5 & 90 \\ 6 & 4 & 80 \\ 7 & 6 & 50 \\ 2 & 3 & 40 \\ 10 & 8 & 60 \end{bmatrix}$.

The property then demands that under subgroup decomposability, $P(Y_8; (9, 5, 50)) < P(X_1; (9, 5, 50))$. We can refer to this property of a multidimensional poverty index as nonpoverty population growth axiom.

3.6 Multidimensional Poverty Measurement

In this section, we analyze some functional forms for multidimensional poverty indices. Each of these functional specifications is a summary statistic of deprivations of the poor along different dimensions of well-being in terms of a real number. We begin by presenting dashboard-based composite indices. Next, we discuss the direct approach, the main method adopted in the literature, in which axioms and poverty measures are defined directly on multidimensional matrices (see also Duclos and Tiberti, 2016). We then turn to the indices that can be interpreted from the inclusive measure of well-being perspective.

3.6.1 The Dashboard Approach

The example we consider in this subsection is based on a dashboard of dimensional indices. For any $n \in N, X \in M^n, \underline{z} \in Z, P(x_{.j})$ signifies the level of poverty associated with $x_{.j}$, the distribution of achievements in dimension j. (Unless stated, the assumption $X \in M^n$ will be maintained throughout the section.) The $1 \times d$ dimensional poverty dashboard is given by $(P(x_{.1}), P(x_{.2}), \dots, P(x_{.d}))$. For illustrative purpose, assume that the dimensional metrics are given by $\frac{1}{n}\sum_{i=1}^{n} \psi(g_{ij})$, where $j \in Q$ is arbitrary and the transformation $\psi : [0, 1] \to \Re^1_+$ satisfies $\psi(0) = 0$. Since g_{ij} indicates person i's deprivation in dimension j, $\psi(g_{ij})$ is the corresponding transformed deprivation indicator. It is also assumed to be decreasing, continuous, and strictly convex in the concerned dimensional achievements of the poor. Each of the d dimensional metrics is the arithmetic average of transformed deprivations in the dimension. The resulting dashboard then becomes $\left(\frac{1}{n}\sum_{i=1}^{n}\psi(g_{i1}), \frac{1}{n}\sum_{i=1}^{n}\psi(g_{i2}), \dots, \frac{1}{n}\sum_{i=1}^{n}\psi(g_{id})\right)$. Evidently, $P(x_{.j}) = 0$ if nobody is deprived in dimension j.

Decreasingness of ψ ensures that a reduction in the achievement of a poor person in any deprived dimension $j \in Q$ increases $P(x_{.j})$. Strict convexity of ψ guarantees that a transfer of achievement from a poor person to a richer poor person such that the poverty status of the recipient does not change increases

$P(x_{.j})$, where the deprived dimension $j \in Q$ is arbitrary. This implies that if each component $j \in Q$ of the dashboard $\left(\frac{1}{n}\sum_{i=1}^{n}\psi(g_{i1}), \frac{1}{n}\sum_{i=1}^{n}\psi(g_{i2}), \ldots, \frac{1}{n}\sum_{i=1}^{n}\psi(g_{id})\right)$ is increasingly related to the composite poverty index to be designed from the dashboard, then the underlying composite index satisfies the Bourguignon and Chakravarty (2003) one-dimensional transfer principle. The one-dimensional transfer principle necessitates a raise of multidimensional poverty under a regressive transfer of achievement in a deprived dimension from a poorer poor to a richer poor, given that the poverty status of the richer person, achievements of the two affected persons in all other dimensions, and achievements of all the remaining persons are kept unchanged.

Sequential applications of one-dimensional transfers miss the essence of multidimensionality and hence are not suitable in the current context. The appropriate notion of redistribution is the multidimensional transfer axiom.

An extremely simple way to arrive at a composite index is to take a weighted average of dimensional indices incorporated into the dashboard. Formally, the formula for the composite index turns out to be

$$P_{CMR}(X; \underline{z}) = \sum_{j=1}^{d} w_j \frac{1}{n}\sum_{i=1}^{n}\psi(g_{ij}), \tag{3.7}$$

which can alternatively be expressed as

$$P_{CMR}(X; \underline{z}) = \frac{1}{n}\sum_{i=1}^{n}\sum_{j=1}^{d} w_j\psi(g_{ij}), \tag{3.7a}$$

where $w_j > 0$ is the weight assigned to poverty assessed in dimension j, $\sum_{j=1}^{d} w_j = 1$. Chakravarty et al. (1998) suggested (3.7a) assuming subgroup decomposability and factor decomposability at the outset. But it emerges that P_{CMR} in (3.7a) can also be accommodated within the dashboard framework.

By assigning positive weights to individual dimensional poverty amounts in the dashboard, we implicitly assume that all the dimensions are important in global poverty evaluation. However, any choice of the weights will reflect a particular value judgment. (See Section 1.5 for a discussion. See also Aaberge and Brandolini, 2015.) For instance, if we choose $w_j = \frac{1}{d}$, then all the dimensions are marked as equally important.

By construction, the symmetric, population replication invariant, dashboard-based family P_{CMR} satisfies monotonicity. It as well satisfies monotonicity sensitivity and dimensional monotonicity axioms. It expands if the threshold limit of a dimension in which there is at least one deprived person goes up.

Although it verifies the multidimensional transfer principle, it does not change under a correlation-increasing switch and hence treats the dimensions as "independents."

Several members of the family (3.7) are worthy of investigation. For the transformation $\psi(g_{ij}) = -\log(g_{ij})$, where $X \in M_3^n$, the underlying measuring instrument becomes the Watts (1968) index of multidimensional poverty:

$$P_W(X;\underline{z}) = \frac{1}{n}\sum_{i=1}^{n}\sum_{j=1}^{d} w_j \log\left(\frac{z_j}{\hat{x}_{ij}}\right). \tag{3.8}$$

In order to develop a characterization of this index, Tsui (2002) assumed in the first place that a poverty index is symmetric, population replication invariant, strongly focussed, monotonic, and continuous in achievements. He then demonstrated that axioms of strong ratio-scale invariance, decreasingness under a uniform majorization operation among the poor, nondecreasingness with respect to a correlation-increasing switch among the poor, subgroup consistency, and poverty criterion invariance hold together if and only if P_W is one of the members of a two-member family. Subgroup consistency requires that for any partitioning of the population into two or more subgroups, if poverty in one subgroup goes down and stays fixed in the other subgroups, then global poverty should reduce as well (see Foster and Shorrocks, 1991). Poverty criterion invariance demands that there should be no change in poverty ranking if one or more threshold limits change, keeping the number of poor unaltered.

Chakravarty and Silber (2008) characterized this index from a welfare theoretic perspective. Poverty index is defined as welfare loss generated as a consequence of shortfall of dimensional achievements of the poor from the respective cutoff limits. It was then demonstrated that the only strongly focused poverty index satisfying subgroup decomposability, strong ratio-scale invariance, monotonicity, and continuity in achievements is P_W.

An attractive feature of the Watts index is that we can split up the change in poverty between two periods into its multidimensional growth and multidimensional redistribution components (see Chakravarty et al., 2008). Inquiry concerning relationships among poverty, economic growth, and inequality is highly motivated by policy-related issues including "trickle-down" eventualities of economic growth and impact of structural adjustment plans for stabilizing the economy (See, e.g., Ravallion and Huppi, 1991; Datt and Ravallion, 1992; Kakwani 1993 and Lipton and Ravallion, 1995.) To diagnose the growth and redistribution ingredients explicitly, suppose that X^1 and X^2 stand for the achievement matrices of a society in periods 1 and 2, and let the corresponding population sizes be n_1 and n_2, respectively. Then assuming that the threshold limits stay put, the poverty change between the two periods happens to be

$$
\begin{aligned}
\Delta P &= P_W(X^2;\underline{z}) - P_W(X^1;\underline{z}) \\
&= \left[\frac{|\Pi(X^2;\underline{z})|}{n_2}\left(\frac{1}{|\Pi(X^2;\underline{z})|}\sum_{j=1}^{d}\sum_{i\in\Pi(X^2;\underline{z})} w_j \log\frac{\lambda_j^2(p)}{x_{ij}^2}\right)\right. \\
&\quad \left. - \frac{|\Pi(X^1;\underline{z})|}{n_1}\left(\frac{1}{|\Pi(X^1;\underline{z})|}\sum_{j=1}^{d}\sum_{i\in\Pi(X^1;\underline{z})} w_j \log\frac{\lambda_j^1(p)}{x_{ij}^1}\right)\right] \\
&\quad + \left[\frac{|\Pi(X^2;\underline{z})|}{n_2}\sum_{j=1}^{d} w_j \log\frac{z_j}{\lambda_j^2(p)} - \frac{|\Pi(X^1;\underline{z})|}{n_1}\sum_{j=1}^{d} w_j \log\frac{z_j}{\lambda_j^1(p)}\right],
\end{aligned}
\tag{3.9}
$$

where $\lambda_j^t(p)$ stands for the mean of the jth dimensional achievements of the poor in period t ($t = 1, 2$). The first third bracketed term on the right-hand side of (3.9) represents the redistribution factor showing the change in poverty resulting from a change in inequality among the poor, given that the means of their dimensional achievements stay put. The inequality index that appears here is a member of the multidimensional generalized entropy family (see Equation (2.9c)). It is a multidimensional extension of Theil's mean logarithmic deviation (see Equation (2.8)). The second third bracketed term of the right-hand expression is the growth ingredient of the decomposition. It signifies the change in the poverty that follows from changes in means of achievements of the poor under the a priori assumption that inequality stays fixed (see also Chakravarty, 2009). It shows the effectiveness of economic growth on poverty change.[13]

A multidimensional generalization of the one-dimensional Chakravarty (1983) index was suggested by Chakravarty et al. (1998) entailing additivity over transformed individual dimensional deprivations. It corresponds to the transformation $\psi(g_{ij}) = 1 - (1 - g_{ij})^e$, where $0 < e < 1$ is a constant. The resulting summary measure becomes

$$
P_{CMRe}(X;\underline{z}) = \frac{1}{n}\sum_{i=1}^{n}\sum_{j=1}^{d} w_j\left(1 - \left(\frac{\hat{x}_{ij}}{z_j}\right)^e\right) \tag{3.10}
$$

For any value of $e \in (0,1)$, the index satisfies the monotonicity sensitivity property. For $e = 1$, overall poverty assumes the form of weighted average of dimensional deprivations of an average person. Although the transfer principle is violated in this case, it may be worthwhile to note that for computational purpose, we only need information on dimensionwise deprivations of different individuals and the dimensional weights.

13 Excellent discussions on how economic growth influences basic needs can be found in Commission on Growth and Development (2008), Stiglitz et al. (2009), and Drèze and Sen (2013).

Finally, consider the specification $\psi(g_{ij}) = (g_{ij})^{\alpha}$, where $\alpha > 1$ is a parameter. The consequential multidimensional index comes out to be

$$P_{CMR\alpha}(X;\underline{z}) = \sum_{i=1}^{n}\sum_{j=1}^{d} w_j\left(1-\frac{\hat{x}_{ij}}{z_j}\right)^{\alpha}. \tag{3.11}$$

This is a simple multidimensional extension of the Foster–Greer–Thorbecke unidimensional index (see Foster et al., 1984). It satisfies the monotonicity sensitivity axiom for all $\alpha > 1$. The values P_{CMRe} and $P_{CMR\alpha}$ coincide when $e = \alpha = 1$.

3.6.2 The Direct Approach

The first example we provide in this subsection is the second member of the Tsui (2002) family, defined as

$$P_{TR(r)}(X;\underline{z}) = \frac{1}{n}\sum_{i=1}^{n}\left[\prod_{j=1}^{d}\left(\frac{z_j}{\hat{x}_{ij}}\right)^{r_j} - 1\right], \tag{3.12}$$

where $X \in M_3^n$ is arbitrary and the parameters r_j are positive for all $j \in Q$. The subscript TR indicates that this strongly relative (more generally, strongly ratio-scale invariant) index was proposed by Tsui, and (r) stands for the d dimensional vector of parameters $(r_1, r_2, \ldots, r_d)$. This quantifier of poverty is an alternative multivariate extension of the one-dimensional Chakravarty (1983) index. (See Eq. (3.1)). While the first member of the Tsui family involves additive aggregation both across dimensions and across individuals, in (3.12), a multiplicative aggregation across dimensions is employed. The parameters r_j have to obey some inequality restrictions for the fulfillment of different axioms. For $d = 2$, verification of the transfer axiom is ensured by the restrictions $r_1(r_1+1) > 0$ and $r_1r_2(r_1r_2+1) > 0$. It is unambiguously increasing with reference to a correlation-increasing switch.

The next proposal we wish to analyze is the Bourguignon and Chakravarty (2003) index $P_{BC(\alpha,\theta)}(X;\underline{z})$, one of the most widespread indices of multidimensional poverty:

$$P_{BC(\alpha,\theta)}(X;\underline{z}) = \frac{1}{n}\sum_{i-1}^{n}\left[\sum_{j=1}^{d} w_j\left(1-\frac{\hat{x}_{ij}}{z_j}\right)^{\theta}\right]^{\frac{\alpha}{\theta}}, \tag{3.13}$$

where the parameters α and θ are positive, and $0 < w_j < 1$ is the weight assigned to the transformed deprivation indicator $\left(1-\frac{\hat{x}_{ij}}{z_j}\right)^{\theta}$ of dimension j, $\sum_{j=1}^{d} w_j = 1$. Accordingly, the individual poverty function $\left[\sum_{j=1}^{d} w_j\left(1-\frac{\hat{x}_{ij}}{z_j}\right)^{\theta}\right]^{\frac{\alpha}{\theta}}$ in (3.13) is obtained by raising the weighted average of such indicators across dimensions to the power $\frac{\alpha}{\theta}$. Multidimensional poverty is then defined as the simple arithmetic average of individual poverty functions. As a consequence, by construction, the index comes to be subgroup decomposable (hence symmetric and population replication invariant). Further, it is continuous, bounded, strongly ratio-scale invariant, and dimensionally monotonic. It also gladdens the monotonicity sensitivity (hence monotonicity) and threshold limit sensitivity axioms. The transfer axiom is satisfied when θ is greater than 1. For a given θ, as the value of α increases, sensitivity of dimensionwise regressive transfers at lower down the distributions of achievements increases. It may be viewed as a simple parametric generalization of the Foster et al. (1984) one-dimensional index to the multidimensional framework.

Its value increases or decreases under a correlation-increasing switch depending on whether α is greater or less than θ. As a result, while under the restriction $\alpha > \theta$, the dimensions affected by the switch are treated as substitutes, they are counted as complements whenever the reverse restriction $\alpha < \theta$ holds. That is why, $P_{BC(\alpha,\theta)}$ is referred to as the "Bourguignon–Chakravarty substitutes" index for $\alpha > \theta$, and it is known as the "Bourguignon–Chakravarty complements" index for $\alpha < \theta$ (Vélez and Robles, 2008, p. 217).

For $\alpha = \theta$, $P_{BC(\alpha,\theta)}$ coincides with $P_{CMR\alpha}$ in (3.11) and hence gets converted into a composite index, which shows insensitivity to a correlation-increasing switch. Bourguignon and Chakravarty (2003) proposed and analyzed this index extensively by assuming that the deprivation indicator of person i in dimension j is given by $\left(1 - \frac{\hat{x}_{ij}}{z_j}\right)^{\alpha_j}$, where $\alpha_j > 1$ for all $j \in Q$, and they need not be the same across dimensions. The resulting index, which Alkire et al. (2015) denoted as P_{BC1}, comes to be $P_{BC1}(X;\underline{z}) = \frac{1}{n}\sum_{i=1}^{n}\left[\sum_{j=1}^{d} w_j\left(1 - \frac{\hat{x}_{ij}}{z_j}\right)^{\alpha_j}\right]$. We can as well obtain it by assuming first parametric variability in $P_{BC(\alpha,\theta)}$. More precisely, first α is replaced by α_j and θ is replaced by θ_j where $j \in Q$ is arbitrary, and variability of these 2d such parameters across dimensions is allowed. At the second step, we assume that $\alpha_j = \theta_j$ for all $j \in Q$ and deduce $P_{BC1}(X;\underline{z})$. Alkire et al. (2015) refer to $P_{BC(\alpha,\theta)}$, which is known in the literature as the Bourguignon–Chakravarty index, as P_{BC2}. For $\alpha = 1$, $\theta = 1$, the value of $P_{BC(\alpha,\theta)}$ matches with those of P_{CMRe} and $P_{CMR\alpha}$ when $e = \alpha = 1$, indicating its insensitivity to a correlation-increasing swap as well as transfers.

The parameter θ is directly related to the curvature of an isopoverty contour, a locus of achievements in $TDPS(z_1, z_2)$ that generate the same value of the individual poverty function. For any $\theta \in (1, \infty)$, an isopoverty contour becomes strictly convex to the origin. As the value of θ over the interval $(1, \infty)$ rises, convexity of the contour increases under ceteris paribus assumptions. Because of this, the marginal rate of substitution, the trade-off between the proportionate deprivations in the given dimensions, becomes increasingly difficult with an increase in the value of θ.

The constant elasticity of substitution between proportionate shortfalls associated with the two dimensions is $\frac{1}{\theta-1}$. For $\theta = 1$, there is perfectly elastic trade-off between the proportionate deprivations; the isopoverty contour becomes a straight line in this polar situation. At the other extreme, as $\theta \to \infty$, we get the rectangular isopoverty contour.

Given α, in the limit as $\theta \to \infty$, $P_{BC(\alpha,\theta)}(X; \underline{z})$ approaches

$$P_{BC(\alpha,\theta)}(X; \underline{z}) = \begin{cases} \frac{1}{n}\sum_{i=1}^{n}\left[1 - \min_{j\in Q}\left\{\frac{\hat{x}_{ij}}{z_j}\right\}\right]^{\alpha} \\ \frac{1}{n}\sum_{i=1}^{n}\left[\max_{j\in Q}\left\{1 - \frac{\hat{x}_{ij}}{z_j}\right\}\right]^{\alpha} \end{cases}. \tag{3.14}$$

As the two-dimensional individual isopoverty curves corresponding to the formula (3.14) are of rectangular shape, substitution between the two relative shortfalls is ruled out. The information required for this representation of multidimensional poverty is rather basic; knowledge of the proportionate shortfalls is sufficient to perform the underlying aggregation. (See Bourguignon and Chakravarty, 1999, for further discussion.) In consideration of the fact that $P_{BC(\alpha,\theta)}$ in (3.14) employs a Leontief-type aggregation, Vélez and Robles (2008, p. 217) refer to it as the "Bourguignon–Chakravarty–Leontief" index. The second expression of (3.14) clearly demonstrates that in this limiting case, $P_{BC(\alpha,\theta)}$ is the average of the relative maximin individual poverty functions.

Bourguignon and Chakravarty (2003) considered extensions of $P_{BC(\alpha,\theta)}$ in (3.13) by allowing variation of the elasticity of substitution between dimensional proportionate shortfalls with the level of poverty. For instance, if a person is highly deprived in one dimension but is characterized with a very low level of deprivation in a second dimension, then elasticity of substitution may be of minor significance. This is because deprivation in the first dimension becomes a major determinant of overall poverty. But if the extents of deprivations are low in both the dimensions, then the roles of deprivations in both the dimensions are important. One may assume the opposite as well; scope of substitution decreases with the level of poverty. These two positions can be incorporated into the general Bourguignon–Chakravarty index (3.13) by assuming that the parameter θ depends on the level of poverty. More precisely, we replace θ in (3.13) by $a(P)$, a positive-valued function of the extent of poverty P. The consequential variant of $P_{BC(\alpha,\theta)}$ in (3.13) that emerges under this assumption about the value of θ is

$$P_{BC(\alpha,a(P))}(X; \underline{z}) = \frac{1}{n}\sum_{i=1}^{n}\left[\sum_{j=1}^{d} w_j\left(1 - \frac{\hat{x}_{ij}}{z_j}\right)^{a(P)}\right]^{\frac{\alpha}{a(P)}}. \tag{3.15}$$

Two simple forms of $a(P)$ that will ensure decreasingness and increasingness of the elasticity of substitution as poverty level increases are, respectively,

$a(P) = \frac{1}{1-P}$ and $a(P) = \frac{1}{1+P}$. (P here stands for $P_{BC(\alpha,a(P))}$ and hence is bounded so that the examples of $a(P)$ we have considered are well defined.) Under these specifications of $a(P)$, we can solve equation (3.15) numerically. The variant (3.15) of (3.13) inherits all postulates of the original poverty representation (3.13), except unambiguous change under a correlation-increasing swap between two poor persons. The swap may increase or decrease overall poverty depending on whether the affected persons are very poor or moderately poor.

In their excellent contributions, Lasso de la Vega and Urrutia (2011, 2009) characterized $P_{BC(\alpha,\theta)}$ axiomatically as a multidimensional deprivation index by employing several intuitively understandable axioms defined on the set of deprivations of the individuals in different dimensions of well-being. The set of axioms invoked in the characterization includes continuity, monotonicity, weak dimension separability, homotheticity, subgroup decomposability, and normalization. The first axiom, continuity, stresses continuous variation in the index with respect to its arguments. The next axiom, monotonicity, says that overall deprivation is increasing with respect to dimensionwise deprivations. The third axiom, weak dimension separability, requires that for any separation of the set of dimensions Q into two or more subgroups, if deprivation for one subgroup goes up, while deprivations in the other subgroups stay put, then global deprivation should go up as well. According to homotheticity, multiplication of all dimensionwise deprivations in two different societies, by the same positive scalar, will not reverse the original deprivation ranking of the societies. The normalization axiom parallels the boundedness axiom of multidimensional poverty. Since $P_{CMR\alpha}$ when $\alpha = 1$ coincides with $P_{BC(\alpha,\theta)}$ for $\alpha = \theta = 1$, the framework also includes a member of the Chakravarty et al. (1998) family. A highly novel characteristic of their axiomatization is its generality; many perceptions of deprivation, including multidimensional poverty, can be accommodated within their general framework.

For any $n \in N$, $X \in M^n, \underline{z} \in Z$, and the poverty threshold $\bar{l}$ denote the set of persons who are treated as poor by the intermediate identification rule by $\prod_{INT}(X; \underline{z}; \bar{l})$. Then the Alkire and Foster (2011a,b) multidimensional poverty index P_{AFM} is the simple average of the deprivation scores of the individuals in a population. Formally,

$$P_{AF\alpha}(X; \underline{z}; \bar{l}) = \frac{1}{n} \sum_{i=1}^{n} \sum_{j=1}^{d} w_j g_{ij}^{\alpha}(\bar{l}), \tag{3.16}$$

where $\alpha > 0$ and

$$g_{ij}^{\alpha}(\bar{l}) = \begin{cases} \left(\dfrac{z_j - \hat{x}_{ij}}{z_j} \right)^{\alpha} \text{if } l_i \geq \bar{l}, \\ 0, \text{ otherwise.} \end{cases} \tag{3.17}$$

In other words, the deprivation scores that are not lower than the poverty threshold $\bar{l}$ are included in the aggregation involved in (3.16). This strongly focused subgroup-decomposable index is strong ratio-scale invariant, normalized, continuous, symmetric, population replication invariant, insensitive to a correlation-increasing switch, and monotonic in dimensions and achievements of the poor. It meets transfer postulate for $\alpha > 1$ and increases if the cutoff limit of a deprived dimension of a poor goes up. For $\alpha = 0$, $P_{AF\alpha}$ simplifies to the adjusted head-count ratio, the product of the head-count ratio $\frac{|\Pi_{INT}(X;\underline{z};\bar{l})|}{n}$, and the average deprivation score of the poor $\frac{1}{|\Pi_{INT}(X;\underline{z};\bar{l})|}\sum_{i=1}^{n}\sum_{j=1}^{d} w_j g_{ij}^0(\bar{l})$ (see Alkire et al., 2015). Since an increase in the number of deprived dimensions of a poor increases the average deprivation score, this product functional representation endorses the dimensional monotonicity property, although it is a violator of the monotonicity and the transfer postulates. For $\alpha = 1$, P_{AFM} coincides with the adjusted poverty gap, the product of the head-count ratio, and the average deprivation of the poor.

Evidently, under the union rule of spotting the set of poor persons, $P_{AF\alpha}$ coincides with $P_{BC(\alpha,\theta)}$ when $\theta = 1$. A similar observation reveals that $P_{AF\alpha}$ equates with $P_{CMR\alpha}$ if the union criterion of isolating the set of poor persons is adopted.

The strong ratio-scale invariance axiom is a representative of some particular concept related to poverty evaluation. An alternative reflection of poverty assessment arises through gratification of strong translation-scale invariance, a postulate that requires invariance of poverty under equal absolute changes in achievements and threshold limits, where the absolute amounts need not be the same across dimensions. Thus, while the strong ratio-scale invariance postulate summarizes poverty with respect to proportionate shortfalls, the strong translation invariance axiom treats poverty in terms of absolute shortfalls $(z_j - x_{ij})$.

Tsui (2002) characterized the following class of strongly translation-scale invariant multidimensional absolute indices:

$$P_{TA}(X;\underline{z}) = \begin{cases} \frac{1}{n}\sum_{i=1}^{n}\left[\prod_{j=1}^{d}\exp c_j(z_j - \hat{x}_{ij}) - 1\right] \\ \frac{1}{n}\sum_{i=1}^{n}\left[\sum_{j=1}^{d} h_j(z_j - \hat{x}_{ij})\right] \end{cases} \tag{3.18}$$

where $n \in N, X \in M^n, \underline{z} \in Z$ are arbitrary, and $c_j, h_j > 0$ for all $j \in Q$. The positive parameters c_j are also assumed to obey the condition that $\prod_{j=1}^{d}\exp c_j(z_j - \hat{x}_{ij})$ is strictly convex. While the first functional form in (3.18) is a multidimensional extension of the Zheng (2000a,b) income poverty index, the second expression is a multidimensional generalization of the absolute poverty gap.

Often, for many policy purposes, we need to assess poverty using unit-consistent indices. The following family of strongly unit-consistent multidimensional poverty indices, fulfilling subgroup decomposability and continuity, has been characterized axiomatically independently by Diez et al. (2008) and Chakravarty and D'Ambrosio (2013):

$$P_{UC}(X;\underline{z}) = \frac{c}{n\prod_{j=1}^{d} z_j^{b_j-t}} \sum_{i=1}^{n}\left[\prod_{j=1}^{d} z_j^{b_j} - \prod_{j=1}^{d} \hat{x}_{ij}^{b_j}\right], \tag{3.19}$$

where $n \in N$, $X \in M^n$, $\underline{z} \in Z$ are arbitrary; t is a real number; and choices of the parameters c and b_j are dictated by the constraints $cb_j > 0$ for all $j \in Q$. It increases (respectively, decreases) under a correlation-increasing exchange between two poor persons if and only if $cb_i b_j > 0$ (respectively, $cb_i b_j < 0$), where $i \neq j \in Q$.

Given b_j, the necessary and sufficient condition for P_{UC} to fulfill the strong ratio-scale invariance axiom is $t = 0$. Since strong ratio-scale invariance implies strong unit consistency, for any real t, strong unit consistency is fulfilled. Consequently, the family of strongly unit-consistent multidimensional poverty indices given by (3.19) is rather large. Nevertheless, no suitable choices of c and b_j will empower P_{UC} to fulfill strong translation-scale invariance, where $j \in Q$ is arbitrary.

If there are only two dimensions, the transfer axiom holds if and only if $cb_1(b_1 - 1) < 0$ and $b_1 b_2(1 - b_1 - b_2) < 0$. If P_{UC} decreases under a correlation-increasing swap (the two dimensions are regarded as complements), for expositional ease, the value of c may be chosen as 1. Then satisfaction of all the conditions stipulated earlier are ensured for all choices of $b_1, b_2 \in (0.5, 1)$. The index increases by a larger quantity under a bundle of regressive transfers, the higher is the value of b_j over the interval (0.5, 1) However, if P_{UC} increases under the swap (the two dimensions are treated as substitutes), a suitable choice of c may be -1. In such a situation, if $b_1, b_2 \in (-1, -0.5)$, then all the conditions are satisfied. To establish this formally, observe that for $c = -1$, the necessary and sufficient condition for P_{UC} to increase with respect to the swap is $b_1 b_2 > 0$. The necessary and sufficient conditions for the transfer postulate to hold get modified as $b_1(b_1 - 1) > 0$ and $b_1 b_2(1 - b_1 - b_2) < 0$. These three inequalities hold at the same time for any $b_1, b_2 \in (-1, -0.5)$.

If there is only one dimension, P_{UC} may be treated as a multidimensional extension of the Zheng (2007b) unit-consistent income poverty index. A worthwhile observation here is that the Zheng index itself is a two-parameter generalization of the Chakravarty and the Clark et al. (1981) ratio-scale invariant income poverty indices.

3.6.3 The Inclusive Measure of Well-being Approach

A natural question that arises is whether it is possible to interpret multidimensional poverty indices from the inclusive measure of well-being perspective. The objective of this subsection is to explore this possibility. It is necessary to check whether a standard multidimensional poverty quantifier relying on the direct method corresponds to a one-dimensional poverty measure computed using a vector of individual well-being numbers. (See also Ravallion, 1994, for a discussion.)

We can illustrate the issue using some examples. The first example we consider is based on the welfare theoretic characterization of the Watts multidimensional poverty index. Chakravarty and Silber (2008) argued that the index can be deduced as a normalized value of the welfare difference $\sum_{i=1}^{n}[U(\underline{z}) - U(\hat{x}_{i.})]$, where U is a metric of individual well-being and $\hat{x}_{i.}$ is the $1 \times d$ dimensional profile of censored achievements of person i. But use of the symmetric utilitarian well-being function for poverty assessment here is not logically acceptable when one adopts the inclusive measure disposition. The reason behind this is that it does not demonstrate uniform sensitivity to a person's dimensional achievements below and above the corresponding cutoff limits. All dimensional achievements above appropriate cutoff limits are replaced by the cutoff points themselves, and this is done irrespective of how large or small they are. Consequently, any change in such achievements provided that they never fall below the respective cutoff points is completely ignored. Consequently, the Watts index cannot be treated as an inclusive measure of well-being approach-based index.

As a second example, we may consider Tsui's (2002) generalization of the Chakravarty index (Chakravarty, 1983). From the functional form, it appears that at the initial stage for each person, a product-type well-being function is employed to cluster allocation of the d dimensions into a metric of personal well-being, and then at the second stage, transformed values of individual well-being levels are clumped by using simple arithmetic averaging rule. But the same problem, as we have encountered in the context of the Watts index, arises here as well. The same remark can be made for the Chakravarty et al. (1998), the Bourguignon and Chakravarty (2003), and the Alkire and Foster (2011a, 2011b) indices as well.

Maasoumi and Lugo (2008) suggested a family of multidimensional poverty measures by employing the Bourguignon and Chakravarty (2003) index within an information theory framework. Subgroup decomposability of the family is assumed in the first place. The individual well-being function, which requires aggregation across achievements of a person, was derived by using the same aggregation technique considered by Maasoumi (1986) (see Equation (2.29)). The same transformations that were employed for accumulating dimensional achievements were used to pile the threshold limits as well. The individual poverty function was then defined as the relative gap between one and the individual well-being function and the compounded poverty limit. The overall index, which was assumed to be increasingly related to the individual indices, was deduced by combining these individual components using a Foster et al. (1984) type transformation.

Formally, the family is given by

$$P_{LM}(X;\underline{z}) = \begin{cases} \frac{1}{n}\sum_{i=1}^{n}\left(\frac{\left(\sum_{j=1}^{d} w_j(z_j)^{-c}\right)^{\frac{-1}{c}} - \left(\sum_{j=1}^{d} w_j(\hat{x}_{ij})^{-c}\right)^{\frac{-1}{c}}}{\left(\sum_{j=1}^{d} w_j(z_j)^{-c}\right)^{\frac{-1}{c}}}\right)^{\alpha}, c \neq 0, \\ \frac{1}{n}\sum_{i=1}^{n}\left(\frac{\prod_{j=1}^{d}(z_j)^{w_j} - \prod_{j=1}^{d}(\hat{x}_{ij})^{w_j}}{\prod_{j=1}^{d}(z_j)^{w_j}}\right)^{\alpha}, \quad c = 0, \end{cases} \tag{3.20}$$

where $X \in M_3^n$, $w_j s$ are positive weights that add up to 1, $\underline{z} \in Z$, $c > -1$, and $\alpha > 0$ are parameters. The denominator of each of the two members of the family can be regarded as the comprehensive poverty line. This is essentially a one-dimensional threshold limit.

The first bracketed term in the second member of the family is the shortfall of the ratio between a Cobb–Douglas function of censored achievements and the composite poverty line from unity. Hence, this notion of averaging is different from the usual ones where dimensionwise deprivations are calculated for each person, which are then amalgamated across dimensions and persons. An analogous sequential compounding process is performed for the first functional form as well. As a result, under this notion of composition, some degree of substitution between dimensional achievements is permitted before related deprivations are deduced from them. From poverty assessment perspective, this requires careful analysis. For $\alpha = 0$, the index value becomes 1 for all distribution matrices. For all values of $\alpha > 0$, it is sensitive to dimensional achievements.

By construction, an IMWB-based index is a violator of the strong focus axiom. One way to resolve this issue is to adopt the suggestion put forward by Decancq et al. (2015). In a different approach, these authors proposed to use heterogamous preferences in poverty evaluation analysis. Since their framework does not start with existence of dimensionwise threshold limits, it deviates substantially from the direct methodology. Instead, it is assumed that there exists a common cutoff bundle with regard to minimum degree of satisfaction of individual preferences.

They have demonstrated that the only way of measuring poverty is by imposing a minimum consumption bundle, which is the same for all. Consequently, if a person's consumption bundle turns out to be worse than the common minimum bundle $\underline{z}$, then he is regarded as poor; otherwise, he is counted as nonpoor. Their preference-based axiomatic study imposes a strong decomposition restriction on the poverty standard. The central idea is to look at individual preferences in order to identify the poor and aggregate dimensional achievements. Consequently, this contribution offers a two-fold suggestion: endogenizing the poverty thresholds and using individual preferences in the context of identification of the poor.

Under these authors' proposition, the strong Pareto principle is satisfied among the poor. Furthermore, the assessment of complementarity or substitutability between dimensions is left to the individuals themselves. This contrasts with the direct approach where the complementarity–substitutability issue is resolved by imposing parametric restrictions in the aggregated standard, which may or may not respect individual preferences (see Bourguignon and Chakravarty, 2003).

We denote the preference relation of person i, defined on the bundles of d-dimensional private consumption goods, by R_i. For any two bundles x_i and x_i', $x_i R_i x_i'$ indicates that person prefers x_i to x_i'. The matrix $(x_1, x_2, \dots, x_n)$ of allocation of private consumption goods among n individuals in the society is denoted by x. We write $R_{(n)}$ for the vector of preferences of the persons. In this model, an economic situation is represented by $(x, R_{(n)})$. Let I_i stand for the indifference component of R_i. The only preference relation identified by their axiomatic characterization is the Leontief preference relation, and the resulting index emerges as

$$P(x; R_{(n)}) = f\left[\frac{1}{n}\sum_{i=1}^{n}\varphi(1 - \min\{1, \mu(x_i, R_i)\})\right], \tag{3.21}$$

where $f \rightarrow [0,1] \rightarrow \Re^1_+$ is continuous and increasing, $\varphi \rightarrow [0,1] \rightarrow [0,1]$ is continuous, decreasing, and convex and $\mu(x_i, R_i) = \mu$ if and only if $x_i I_i \mu z$. Here the individual poverty function φ can be any decreasing, convex function worked out from the proportion μ of z to which a person shows indifference.[14] By accommodating preference relations in the formulation, the model subsumes high degree of flexibility in the context of the choice of the minimal consumption vector. (Maniquet, 2016, provides an excellent discussion on this scheme.)

3.7 Multidimensional Poverty Orderings

As we have noted, given the threshold limits, there may exist several poverty indices that fulfill a set of desirable axioms. However, often subjective opinions may dictate the selection of such reference limits. (See the discussion presented

14 This procedure for measuring individual poverty bears similarity with the ray index suggested by Samuelson (1947) and the concept of egalitarian equivalence advocated by Panzer and Schmeidler (1979).

in Section 3.2.) As a result, involvement of arbitrariness in the choice of the lines of demarcation may lead to unreliable conclusions based on that index. For instance, it may happen that a poverty index ranks two achievement matrices in different directions for two different threshold limit vectors. In consequence, it becomes worthwhile to verify if two achievement matrices may be ordered commonly by the same poverty index when the threshold limit vectors are allowed to vary within some reasonable limits. We refer to this notion of ordering as poverty-line limits ordering.

An alternative concept of ordering is to rank two achievement matrices unanimously by a family of poverty indices satisfying a set of plausible postulates, when the threshold limits are assumed to be fixed. This natural line of investigation is a consequence of existence of too many poverty indices satisfying such postulates, and emergence of opposite directional ordering of two different matrices by two alternative members of the family is quite likely. We term this concept of ordering as poverty-measure ordering[15] (see Zheng, 2000a,b).

In this section of the chapter, we address the former notion of ordering. We begin by presenting a brief review of one-dimensional orderings along this line. This serves as the background material of the analysis carried out for multidimensional orderings.

3.7.1 A Brief Outline of One-Dimensional Orderings

In the one-dimensional framework, the problem is to judge whether one distribution of income does not have lower poverty than the other for all poverty lines. (For simplicity of exposition, we use income as the dimension of well-being. The analysis applies equally to any other dimension.) In such a case, we say that the former distribution poverty dominates the latter or the latter is poverty dominated by the former.

Let u^{I} and u^{II} be two nondecreasingly ordered distributions of income over a given population size. These distributions can as well be represented by the respective cumulative distribution functions G^{I} and G^{II} (distribution functions, for short). Then the value $G^i(v)$ of G^i at the income level v stands for the cumulative proportion of persons with income not exceeding v, G^i is nondecreasing, $G^i(0) = 0$ and $G^i(v^*) = 1$, where v^* is the maximum value that incomes can assume, where $i = \mathrm{I}, \mathrm{II}$.

Assume that the poverty lines can vary over the interval $[0, v^*]$. For any $z \in [0, v^*]$ and a poverty index P, we write $P(G^i, z)$ for the poverty level associated with the distribution function G^i. Then we say that G^{II} poverty dominates G^{I} with respect to the poverty index P if and only if $P(G^{\mathrm{I}}, z) \leq P(G^{\mathrm{II}}, z)$ for all $z \in [0, v^*]$.

15 See Atkinson (1987), Spencer and Fisher (1992), Jenkins and Lambert (1997, 1998a,b), Shorrocks (1998), Zheng (2000a), and Fields (2001), among others.

Suppose that poverty evaluation is done using the head-count ratio. In terms of the distribution functions, this means that $P(G^i, z) = G^i(z)$. In other words, the value of the head-count ratio for u^i when the poverty line is z is simply the value of G^i at z. Accordingly, poverty dominance of G^{II} over G^I with respect to the head-count ratio holds if and only if $G^{I(z)} \leq G^{II(z)}$ for all $z \in [0, v^*]$. As Foster and Shorrocks (1988) noted, this is the same as the condition that G^I with first order stochastic dominates G^{II}. Atkinson (1987) demonstrated that of two income distributions, if one first order stochastic dominates the other, then the former cannot have higher poverty than the latter for all subgroup-decomposable poverty indices that are nonincreasing in incomes of the poor. Graphically, first order stochastic dominance means that the graph of G^{II} never lies below that of G^I. In other words, we need pointwise dominance of the curve of G^{II} over that of G^I (see Figure 3.2).

Next, assume that poverty assessment is performed with the poverty gap ratio. Foster and Shorrocks (1988) demonstrated that dominance of G^{II} over G^I with respect to the poverty gap ratio is equivalent to the requirement that G^I second order stochastic dominates G^{II}. Graphically, at any income, the area under the curve of G^I never exceeds the corresponding area under the curve of G^{II} (see Figure 3.3). Equivalently, we say that areawise dominance of the graph of G^{II} over that of G^I has to hold.[16] Second order stochastic dominance of G^I over G^{II} is also equivalent to the condition that G^I is not generalized Lorenz inferior to G^{II}; the generalized Lorenz curve of G^I does not lie below that of G^{II}.

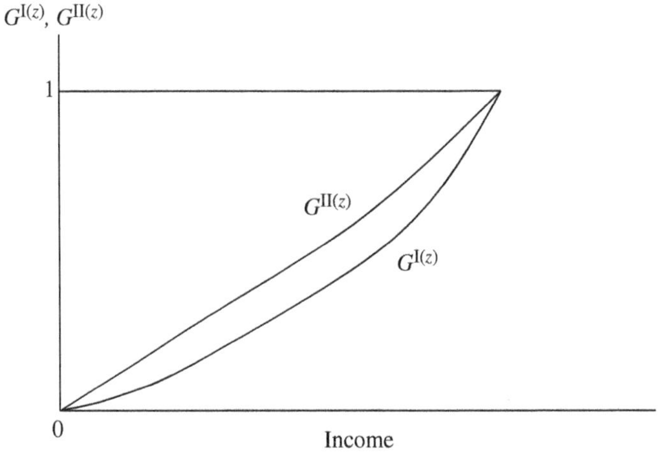

Figure 3.2 First order stochastic dominance.

16 In fact, these two poverty orderings correspond to the members of P_{FGT} in (3.2) for $\alpha = 0$ and 1, respectively. See also Tungodden (2005). Foster and Jin (1998) developed poverty ordering of income distributions using indices that are based on utility gaps. The set of poverty indices considered for this purpose includes the Watts and Chakravarty indices.

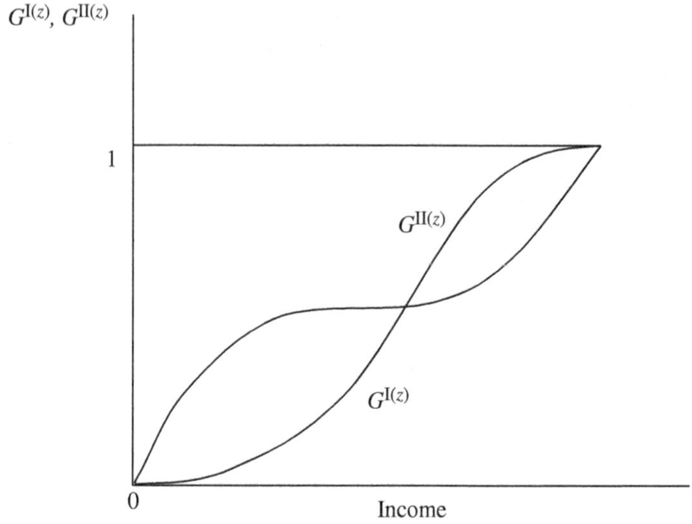

Figure 3.3 Second order stochastic dominance.

From Figure 3.3, it follows clearly that up to any level of income z, the area under the curve of G^{II} is not lower than the corresponding area under the curve of G^{I}. Hence, second order stochastic dominance of G^{I} over G^{II} holds. From the figures, it also follows that first order dominance implies the second order dominance, but the converse is not true. In other words, first order dominance is a sufficient but not a necessary condition for second order dominance. This shows that as we move from the first order condition to the next higher order condition, the ranking power becomes thinner. The reason behind this is that in the case of the latter, we need areawise dominance starting from the initial income level. As a result, one or more intersections between the curves of the distribution functions are permissible; the only restriction we need to follow is that area under G^{I} does not exceed the area under G^{II} at any income level. But for the first order dominance to hold, we need pointwise dominance, and as a result, no intersection between the curves is allowed.[17] (Formal treatments of stochastic dominance relations are available in Hadar and Russell, 1969; Whitmore, 1970; Levy, 2006; Shaked and Shanthikumar, 2006 and Chakravarty, 2013.)

17 If in the first order dominance we require $F(z) < G(z)$ for at least one $z \in [0, v^*]$, we get the strong form of the dominance. Similarly, we can have strong form for the second order rule. However, in empirical investigations, some statistical tests are unable to make a clear distinction between weak and strong inequalities (Davidson, 2008; Davidson and Duclos, 2000).

3.7.2 Multidimensional Orderings

Duclos et al. (2006a) and Bourguignon and Chakravarty (2009) developed conditions for poverty ranking of alternative multivariate distributions of achievements. Recall that each column of an achievement matrix represents the marginal distribution of a particular dimension (see Section 3.3). Ranking of dimension-wise marginal distributions in two distribution matrices ignores association among dimensions, an important characteristic in multidimensional well-being analysis. Duclos et al. (2006a) compared child poverty in two dimensions between Madagascar and Cameroon and noted statistically significant dominations for each of the two marginal distributions. Nevertheless, no unambiguous domination was observed for the joint distributions. This clearly confirms that simple comparisons of marginal distributions across social matrices do not give us a comprehensive picture of the issue. In consequence, the ranking analysis should explicitly involve the matrices as a whole.

Gravel and Mukhopadhyay (2010) employed generalizations, to three dimensions or more, of the Atkinson and Bourguignon (1982) first and second order dominance criteria to provide a normative assessment of growth in India over the 1987–2002 period. The four dimensions, considered in their analysis, are real consumption (measured at the individual level), literacy rate, under-5 mortality, and violent crime rates (all measured at the district levels). Their findings indicate that India was better off in 2002 than in 1995 or 1987 by the second order dominance rule. However, if violent crime rates are excluded from the list of dimensions, the dominance was found to be steady over the entire period.[18]

As we have observed, in a multidimensional setup, identification of the poor is an important ingredient of poverty evaluation. A "poverty frontier," defined as alternative combinations of all dimensional achievements that produce an overall achievement, which equals an aggregate or comprehensive poverty line, is taken as the identification indicator. The comprehensive poverty line is assumed to render a subsistence standard of living. It is gathered by aggregating the poverty cutoff limits across all dimensions, where the underlying aggregation function is the same as that employed to deduce an overall achievement. Subsequently, a person is identified as poor if his achievements in all the dimensions generate a lower level of aggregated achievement than the comprehensive poverty line. The frontier, thus, separates the poor from the nonpoor.

Given a particular poverty frontier, of two social distributions $X, Y \in M$, X is said to be poverty dominated by Y in the Duclos–Sahn–Younger sense if and only if $P(X; z) \leq P(Y; z)$ for all $z \in Z$. We denote this relation by $XP^{D}Y$.

---

18 Applications of multidimensional dominance criteria can also be found in Duclos et al. (2006b, 2007, 2008, 2011), Batana and Duclos (2010, 2011), Duclos and Échevin (2011), Gräb and Grimm (2011), Labar and Bresson (2011), Anaka and Kobus (2012), Garcia-Diaz (2013), and others. See Alkire et al. (2015) for further discussion.

Duclos et al. (2006a) developed stochastic dominance-based poverty ordering results for achievement matrices with two dimensions of well-being. To analyze these results, let us denote the achievements in the two dimensions by x_1 and x_2, respectively, assuming that the dimensions are substitutes. Let $G(x_1;x_2)$ stand for the joint distribution of x_1 and x_2. Formally, $G(q_1;q_2) = \text{Prob}(x_1 \leq q_1; x_2 \leq q_2)$. The joint distribution shows simultaneously the proportion of population enjoying achievement levels x_1 and x_2 not exceeding q_1 and q_2, respectively. The marginal distribution of x_i is expressed by $G(q_i) = \text{Prob}(x_i \leq q_i)$, where $i = 1,2$.

Duclos et al. (2006a) showed that under substitutability assumption between the dimensions, if $G_Y(q_1;q_2) \geq G_X(q_1;q_2)$ for all $q_1, q_2 > 0$, then XP^DY holds for all two dimensional subgroup-decomposable poverty indices that are nonincreasing in dimensional achievements, where G_Y (respectively, G_X) is the joint cumulative distribution function for Y (respectively, X). The inequality $G_Y(q_1;\, q_2) \geq G_X(q_1;\, q_2)$ means that the joint cumulative distribution function of Y does not lie below that of X cumulated up to $(q_1;\, q_2)$. The underlying class of indices includes the family of indices suggested by Chakravarty et al. (1998), Tsui (2002), Chakravarty et al. (2008), Alkire and Foster (2011a,b) and some members of the family proposed by Bourguignon and Chakravarty (2003) (see also Bresson and Duclos, 2015).

The poverty frontier is implicitly defined by a locus $\Lambda(x_1;\, x_2) = 0$, where the aggregator is continuous and nondecreasing in its arguments. Bidimensional poverty is now defined by the $(x_1;\, x_2)$ combinations for which $\Lambda(x_1;\, x_2) \leq 0$, and the poverty domain is given by $S(\Lambda) = \{(x_1;\, x_2) \in \Re^2_+ \,|\, \Lambda(x_1;\, x_2) \leq 0\}$.

In Figure 3.4, the poverty frontier is represented by the curve A. Since $G_Y(q_1;\, q_2)$(respectively, $G_X(q_1;\, q_2)$) signifies the proportion of population with achievements simultaneously less than or equal to q_1 in dimension 1 and q_2 in dimension 2, under G_Y (respectively, G_X), the inequality $G_Y(q_1;\, q_2) \geq G_X(q_1;\, q_2)$ is an intersection type condition. If $G_Y(q_1;\, q_2)$ is not lower than $G_X(q_1;\, q_2)$ for all rectangles B, C, and so on that fit within $S(\Lambda)$, then the dominance XP^DY follows. Hence, an attractive feature of this dominance condition is that we only need to check intersection-type conditions.

Bourguignon and Chakravarty (2009) developed related first order bidimensional dominance conditions involving the joint distributions and the marginal distributions. In their highly innovative contribution, Aaberge and Brandolini (2015) provided an excellent overview of the Bourguignon–Chakravarty orderings. Here we furnish a sketch of their main findings. They demonstrated that poverty dominance for two bidimensional achievement matrices for all poverty indices that are strongly focussed, symmetric, subgroup decomposable, population replication invariant, nonincreasing in achievements of the poor, and nondecreasing under a correlation-increasing switch (substitutability) holds if and only if there is unambiguous dominance for each marginal distribution and the intersection area. Graphically, the areas of all intersection rectangles

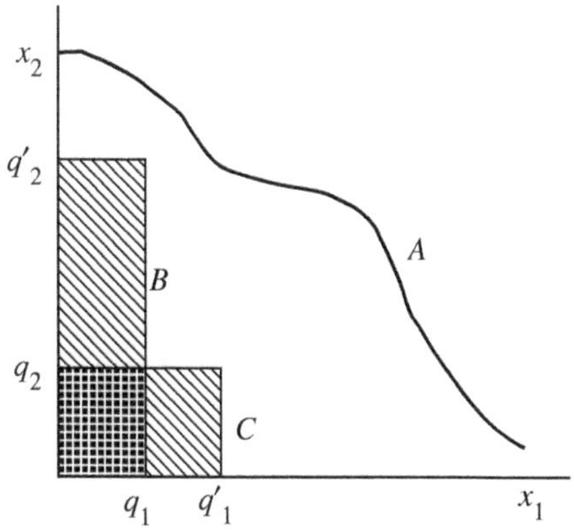

Figure 3.4 Bidimensional poverty ordering.

for the dominant matrix should not be less than the corresponding areas of the dominated ones, and the marginal distribution function for each dimension in the dominated matrix cannot lie above that of the dominant one. (See Figure 3.4.)

In a subsequent result, Bourguignon and Chakravarty (2009) retained all the poverty postulates stated earlier except nondecreasingness under a correlation-increasing switch, which has been replaced by nonincreasingness under the switch (complementarity). They then established that necessary and sufficient conditions in such a situation are dominance for each marginal distribution and dominance with respect to joint distribution in union area (see Figure 3.1).

3.8 Dimensions of Well-Being with Ordinal Significance and Multidimensional Poverty

It has already been observed in Chapter 1 that values of ordinally measurable dimensions are only indicators of order. Specific numerical values assigned to represent the ordering are insignificant. Recall that each notion of measurability allows some admissible transformation that can be applied to dimensional achievements so that no loss of information occurs. In other words, the value of a quantifier that relies on dimensional achievements remains unaltered when we transform the achievements by applying some admissible transformations.

We write Q_O for the set of all dimensions of well-being that are measurable on ordinal scale. The corresponding set of dimensional thresholds is denoted by Z_O. Let $|Q_O| = k$ (say) be the number of elements in Q_O. This is the exogenously given number of dimensions of well-being with ordinal significance. For any $n \in N$, let M_O^n stand for the set of all $n \times k$ dimensional matrices of achievements in different dimensions. The set of all such matrices is given by M_O, where

$M_O = \bigcup_{n \in N} M_O^n$. A multidimensional poverty index P_O in an ordinal framework is a real-valued function defined on M_O. More precisely, $P_O : M_O \times Z_O \to \Re_+^1$. In other words, for any $n \in N$, $(X_O; \underline{z_O}) \in M_O^n \times Z_O$, $P_O(X_O; \underline{z_O})$ is the level of poverty that exists in the society given that the dimensions of well-being are ordinally significant.

The information invariance assumption can now be analytically stated as follows. For any $n \in N$, $(X_O; \underline{z_O}) \in M_O^n \times Z_O$, we say that $(X_O'; \underline{z_O'}) \in M_O^n \times Z_O$ is derived from $(X_O; \underline{z_O})$ using a permissible transformation if for each $j \in Q_O$, there exists an increasing transformation f_j such that $x_{ij}' = f_j(x_{ij})$ and $z_{0j}' = f_j(z_{0j})$, where z_{0j} is the threshold point of $j \in Q_O$. In other words, z_{0j} is the jth coordinate of the vector $\underline{z_0} \in Z_0$. We do not assume that the transformations f_js are the same across dimensions. The ordinality property, which we also refer to as ordinal information invariance assumption, then requires that $P_O(X_O; \underline{z_O}) = P_O(X_O'; \underline{z_O'})$.

Essentials to the construction of a multidimensional poverty index when dimensions have ordinal significance are deprivation counts of the individuals. The deprivation count of a person relies on a dichotomous or binary variable. A variable may be binary by definition: for instance, whether a person is a citizen of a given country or not. But often it may be useful to derive binary variables from nonbinary variables. For instance, weights of individuals in a region can assume more than two values. However, we can segregate these persons into two subgroups: those who weigh less than 60 kilograms and those weighing at least 60 kilograms. This is a simple creation of a binary variable from a nonbinary variable.

In the current context, we dichotomize each ordinal dimension by comparing a person's achievement in the dimension with its norm, the threshold limit. If somebody's achievement in the dimension is associated with a category that has a lower rank than the category to which the threshold limit corresponds, then he is deprived in the dimension, given that the categories are ranked in increasing order of preferences, that is, from the worst to the best. Otherwise, the person is nondeprived in the dimension. We assign the values 1 and 0, respectively, to indicate deprivation and nondeprivation of a person in a dimension possessing ordinal characteristic.

For any $n \in N$, $(X_O; \underline{z_O}) \in M_O^n \times Z_O$, $i \in \{1, 2, \ldots, n\}$, let $\xi_{ij}^O(X_O)$, (ξ_{ij}^O, for short) denote person i's deprivation metric for $j \in Q_O$. More precisely, $\xi_{ij}^O = 1$ if person i is deprived in the ordinal dimension j and $\xi_{ij}^O = 0$, otherwise. Then the deprivation profile of the person associated with the ordinal dimensions in the set Q_O is $(\xi_{i1}^O, \xi_{i2}^O, \ldots, \xi_{ik}^O)$, where $k = |Q_O|$. Then the deprivation count of person i in ordinal dimensions is $\xi_i^O = \sum_{j \in Q_O} \xi_{ij}^O$. Clearly, ξ_i^O is a nonnegative integer bounded between 0 and k. The lower bound is achieved if the person is not deprived in ordinal dimensions, and the upper bound is attained when he has deprivations in all the dimensions. The distribution of deprivation counts in ordinally significant dimensions across individuals in the society is given by $(\xi_1^O, \xi_2^O, \ldots, \xi_n^O)$. Person i is regarded as union poor in this ordinal framework if $\xi_i^O \geq 1$. However, the intersection rule treats the person as poor if $\xi_i^O = k$. (See Cappellari and Jenkins, 2007, for a discussion.)

As an illustrative example, assume that in a four-person society, there are only two dimensions of well-being: self-reported health status and literacy grade. In the dimension self-reported health condition, we assign the numbers 1, 4, 9, 16, 25, and 36 to the six health categories "very poor," "poor," "fair," "good," "very good," and "excellent" to indicate that a higher number is assigned to a better category.[19] Suppose that the category "good" represents the threshold category, and it is identified with the number 16. Assume that out of four individuals in the society, the first and third individuals have health conditions characterized by the categories "very poor," "poor" so that they suffer from health deprivation. The heath conditions of the second and fourth persons belong to the categories "excellent" and "good," respectively. Consequently, they are not health-deprived. For the second dimension, literacy level, the numbers assigned to the categories "illiteracy," "knowledge just to read and write," "elementary school graduation," "high school graduation," and "college graduation" are respectively 0, 0.1, 0.2, 0.3, and 0.4. The threshold limit of this dimension is 0.1, that is, the ability just to read and write only is taken as the threshold education category. Assume that the levels of education of the four persons are respectively "illiteracy," "high school graduation," "knowledge just to read and write," and "college graduation." Then the threshold education level is identified by the number 0.1. If we denote the two dimensions by 1 and 2, respectively, and the distribution matrix by Y_O, then $Y_O = \begin{bmatrix} 1 & 0 \\ 36 & 0.3 \\ 4 & 0.1 \\ 16 & 0.4 \end{bmatrix}$ and $\underline{z_O} = (16, 0.1)$.

In Y_O, while person 1 is deprived in both the dimensions, person 3 is deprived only in dimension 1. On the other hand, none of persons 2 and 4 is deprived in any dimension. Consequently, the deprivation profiles of these four persons are given, respectively, by $(1,1)$, $(0,0)$, $(1,0)$, and $(0,0)$. This in turn shows that the deprivation counts of the four persons, the numbers of dimensions in which they are deprived are given respectively by 2, 0, 1, and 0.

Now, let us assign the numbers 1, 2, 3, 4, 5, and 6 to the self-reported health categories by taking square roots of the previously assigned numbers. Similarly, we assign the numbers 0.01, 0.04, 0.09, and 0.16 by simply squaring the numbers allotted earlier to the grades of literacy. Formally, we transform

19 For the purpose at hand, categorical variables data need to be ordered (see Asselin, 2009, p. 32).

the dimensional achievements in these two dimensions by applying the increasing transformations $f_1(t) = \sqrt{t}$ and $f_2(t) = t^2$, where f_j is the increasing transformation applied to the achievements in dimension $j = 1,2$ and t denotes a dimensional achievement. The threshold limit vector $\underline{z_O} = (16, 0.1)$ gets converted into $\underline{z'_O} = (4, 0.01)$ and the transformed achievement matrix becomes $Y'_O = \begin{bmatrix} 1 & 0 \\ 6 & 0.09 \\ 2 & 0.01 \\ 4 & 0.16 \end{bmatrix}$. It is easy to check that the individual deprivation counts remain unchanged under these ordinal transformations of dimensional achievements.

Hence, union poverty head-count ratio turns out to be $\frac{|\Pi_O(Y_O;\underline{z_O})|}{4} = \frac{2}{4}$, whereas according to the intersection rule, this ratio becomes $\frac{1}{4}$. The ordinal information invariance assumption demands that $P_O(Y_O; (16, 0.1)) = P_O(Y'_O; (4, 0.01))$.

It is then easy to check that the values of the union and the intersection head-count ratios are the same for Y_O and Y'_O, given that the corresponding threshold limit vectors are $(16, 0.1)$ and $(4, 0.01)$, respectively. In other words, the head-count ratio remains unaltered under allowable transformations in the ordinal framework. In consequence, the head-count ratio measure of multidimensional poverty has an advantage over many other indices of multidimensional poverty indices in the sense of its fulfillment of the ordinality property. This holds irrespective of whether the union, intersection, or the intermediate identification rule is employed to determine the set of poor persons. A second index that fulfils this property is the Alkire and Foster (2011a,b) adjusted head-count ratio. This index satisfies dimensional monotonicity property as well, whereas the head-count ratio is a violator of the postulate.

3.9 Orderings Based on Deprivations Counts

Chakravarty and Zoli (2012) used an axiomatic framework to derive some integer majorization results that can be easily transformed into deprivation profile ranking structure. These results apply to both ordinal and nonordinal dimensions of well-being. Consequently, the set of dimensions can include pension income, interest income, public goods, environmental conditions, and so on. Given that there are $(d + k)$ such dimensions of well-being, denote the functioning score of person $i \in \{1, 2, \dots, n\}$ by τ_i, where $n \in N$ is arbitrary. In other words, τ_i is the number of dimensions in which person i is not deprived. Evidently, $\tau_i \in \overline{Q} = Q \cup Q_O \cup \{0\} = \{0, 1,2, \dots, d, d + 1, \dots, d + k\}$. The lower bound 0 of τ_i arises when the person is deprived in all the dimensions. On the other hand, the upper bound $(d + k)$ is achieved whenever the individual becomes nondeprived in all the dimensions. Let $\tau = (\tau_1, \tau_2, \dots, \tau_n)$ be a profile of functioning scores of the persons in the society. The functioning score distribution τ is an element of $\overline{Q}^n$, the n-fold Cartesian product of $\overline{Q}$. Clearly, the deprivation count ξ_i of person $i \in \{1, 2, \dots, n\}$ is given by $(d + k - \tau_i)$. That is, given any profile $\tau \in \overline{Q}^n$ of functioning scores, we can write its deprivation counterpart as $\xi = (d + k).1^n - \tau$, where 1^n is the n-coordinated vector of 1s. It then follows that the profile $\xi = (\xi_1, \xi_2, \dots, \xi_n)$ of deprivation counts is also an element of $\overline{Q}^n$.

The nonincreasingly ordered permutation of τ is denoted by τ^0, that is, $\tau^0 = (\tau_1^0, \tau_2^0, \dots, \tau_n^0)$ and $\tau_1^0 \geq \tau_2^0 \geq \dots \geq \tau_n^0$. Similarly, we write $\tilde{\tau}$ for the nondecreasingly ordered permutation of τ, that is, $\tilde{\tau}_1 \leq \tilde{\tau}_2 \leq \dots \leq \tilde{\tau}_n$. Similarly ordered permutations of ξ are denoted by ξ^0 and $\tilde{\xi}$, respectively.

Chakravarty and Zoli (2012) considered distributions of functioning scores across persons and established the equivalence between five dominance conditions. Of particular interest is their demonstration that if one vector of functioning scores generalized Lorenz dominates that of another, then the former is preferred to the latter by the generalized Gini welfare function. The converse is true as well.

As a background material of deprivation count ordering, we now analyze the Chakravarty–Zoli dominance results. Of two profiles of functioning scores $\tau, \tau' \in \overline{Q}^n$, we say that τ is obtained from τ' by a favorable composite change if there exists individuals $i, j \in \{1, 2, \dots, n\}$ such that $\tau_i' - \tau_j' \geq 2$ and $\tau_i = \tau_i' - 1, \tau_j = \tau_j' + 1$ and $\tau_k = \tau_k'$ for all $k \neq i, j$. In τ', person i's functioning score exceeds that of person j by at least 2, and τ' is transformed into τ by reducing i's functioning score by 1 and increasing that of j by 1. The transformation decreases the variance of the distribution of functioning scores without changing the mean. Consequently, it leads to an improvement in well-being of the society. The restriction $\tau_i' - \tau_j' \geq 2$ ensures that $\tau_i \geq \tau_j$, that is, the relative position of the affected individuals remains the same. (See Chakravarty and D'Ambrosio, 2006 and Chakravarty and Zoli, 2012.)

We say that τ is obtained from $\tau' \in \overline{Q}^n$ by a simple increment if for some $j \in \{1, 2, \dots, n\}$ such that $\tau_j' < d + k$, $\tau_j = \tau_j' + 1$ and $\tau_k = \tau_k'$ for all $k \neq j$. In other words, we deduce τ is from τ' by increasing person j's functioning score by 1 and keeping all other persons' scores unchanged.

Now, consider a functioning evaluation standard F_E, a nonnegative real-valued function defined on $\overline{Q}^n$. Formally, $F_E : \overline{Q}^n \to \Re^1_+$. For any $\tau \in \overline{Q}^n$, $F_E(\tau)$ indicates the extent of well-being enjoyed by the individuals in the society corresponding to the distribution τ of functioning scores across the individuals. A standard F_E is said to be increasing if $F_E(\tau) > F_E(\tau')$ whenever τ is obtained from τ' by a simple increment. It satisfies the principle of favorable composite change if its value increases under a favorable composite change.

The following dominance theorem of Chakravarty and Zoli (2012) can now be stated.

Theorem 3.1 Let $\tau, \tau' \in \overline{Q}^n$, where $\tau \neq \tau'$, be arbitrary. Then the following statements are equivalent:

i) $\sum_{i=1}^{n} v_i^n \tilde{\tau}_i > \sum_{i=1}^{n} v_i^n \tilde{\tau}'_i$ for all $v_i^n > v_{i+1}^n > 0$.
ii) $\sum_{i=1}^{j} \tilde{\tau}_i \geq \sum_{i=1}^{j} \tilde{\tau}'_i$ for all $j = 1,2, \ldots, n$, with $>$ for at least one j.
iii) $F_E(\tau) > F_E(\tau')$ for all functioning evaluation standards $F_E : \overline{Q}^n \rightarrow \Re^1_+$ that are increasing, symmetric and that satisfy the principle of favorable composite change.
iv) $\sum_{i=1}^{n} f_E(\tau_i) > \sum_{i=1}^{n} f_E(\tau'_i)$ for all individual functioning evaluation standards f_E : $\overline{Q} \rightarrow \Re^1_+$ that are increasing in individual arguments and obey the principle of favorable composite change.
v) $\tilde{\tau}$ can be obtained from $\tilde{\tau}'$ by a finite sequence of rank-preserving simple increments and a finite sequence of rank-preserving favorable composite changes or simply by a sequence of rank-preserving simple increments.

In condition (i), decreasingness of the population-size-dependent positive sequence $\{v_i^n\}$ ensures that the value of generalized Gini functioning evaluation is higher for the profile τ compared to that for the profile τ' (see Weymark, 1981 and Yaari, 1987). According to condition (ii), of two distributions τ and τ' of functioning scores, the former integer generalized Lorenz dominates that of the latter, that is, the generalized Lorenz curve of the former lies nowhere below that of the latter and lies above in at least some places. Condition (iii) says that the profile τ is regarded as socially better than the profile τ' by all evaluation standards that are increasing, symmetric, and increasing under favorable composite changes. Conditions (iv) and (v) are self-explanatory. Conditions (ii)–(v) can be regarded as integer counterparts of some well-known majorization results existing in the literature on univariate inequality measurement (see Marshall et al., 2011, p. 14 and p. 87).[20]

To illustrate condition (v), consider the functioning score profile $\tau' = (6, 4, 4, 1)$. The profile $\tau = (7, 4, 3, 2)$ is deduced from τ' by increasing person 1's score by 1 accompanied by a rank-preserving favorable composite change involving persons 3 and 4.

Recall that for all $i \in \{1, 2, \ldots, n\}$, $\tau_i = d + k - \xi_i$. In consequence, we can easily convert the dominance conditions of vectors of functioning scores into ordering of deprivation count distributions. Note that for any $i \in \{1, 2, \ldots, n\}$, $\tilde{\tau}_i = d + k - \xi_i^0$. Let $\xi \in \overline{Q}^n$ and $\xi' \in \overline{Q}^n$, respectively, be the deprivation

20 While Muirhead's (1903) integer majorization result deals with a constant total, Theorem 3.1 assumes variability of the total. Related contributions were made among others, by Milne and Neave (1994), Fishburn and Lavalle (1995), Bossert and Fleurbaey (2002), Aboudi and Thon (2006), Savaglio and Vannucci (2007), and Deineko et al. (2009).

counterparts of the profiles τ and τ' of functioning scores. If $\tau \in Q^n$ is obtained from $\tau' \in \overline{Q}^n$ by a simple increment, an increment in functioning score of a person, we can equivalently say that ξ' is deduced from $\xi \in Q^n$ by an increment in his deprivation count. Similarly, if $\tau \in Q^n$ is deduced from τ' by a favorable composite change affecting functioning scores of two individuals, we can as well say that ξ' is derived from ξ by an unfavorable composite change that affects deprivation counts of the concerned persons. In the example, $\tau' = (6, 4, 4, 1)$ and $\tau = (7, 4, 3, 2)$ assume that $d + k = 8$. We can then say that $\xi = (1, 4, 5, 6)$ is transformed into $\xi' = (2, 4, 4, 7)$ by increasing person 1's deprivation count by 1 and an unfavorable composite change entailing persons 4 and 3. (We increase the deprivation count of person 4, the most deprived person in terms of counting, by 1 and reduce that of person 3, who is less deprived than person 4, by 1.)

Then condition (ii) of Theorem 3.1 can be restated in terms of dominance between the integer inverse generalized Lorenz curves of the distribution of deprivation counts.[21] Formally, this condition becomes (ii) $\sum_{i=1}^{j} \xi'^0_i \geq \sum_{i=1}^{j} \xi^0_i$ for all $j = 1,2, \dots, n$, with $>$ for at least one j. This is the same as the condition that the integer inverse generalized Lorenz curve of ξ' dominates that of ξ. Condition (i) of the theorem can be rewritten as $\sum_{i=1}^{n} v^n_i \xi'^0_i > \sum_{i=1}^{n} v^n_i \xi^0_i$. In the aggregation, higher weight is assigned higher deprivation counts. This inequality means that the value of the generalized Gini index of deprivation count distribution ξ' is higher than that of the distribution ξ.

In general, a deprivation count assessment metric F_D is a nonnegative real-valued function defined on the set of profiles of deprivation count. Formally, $F_D : \overline{Q}^n \rightarrow \Re^1_+$. Such an index provides a social assessment of deprivation counts existing at the individual levels.

Conditions (iii)–(v) of the Theorem 3.1 can be modified analogously. Hence, the following theorem, which may be regarded as the deprivation count twin of Theorem 3.1, can now be stated.

Theorem 3.2 Let $\xi, \xi' \in \overline{Q}^n$, where $\xi \neq \xi'$, be arbitrary. Then the following statements are equivalent:

i) $\sum_{i=1}^{n} v^n_i \xi'^0_i > \sum_{i=1}^{n} v^n_i \xi^0_i$ for all $v^n_i > v^n_{i+1} > 0$.

ii) $\sum_{i=1}^{j} \xi'^0_i \geq \sum_{i=1}^{j} \xi^0_i$ for all $j = 1,2, \dots, n$, with $>$ for at least one j.

---

21 The inverse generalized Lorenz curve $IGL\left(u, \frac{j}{n}\right)$ of an income distribution $u \in \Re^n_+$ is a plot of $\sum_{i=1}^{j} u^0_i/n$ against $\frac{j}{n}$, where $j = 0,1, \dots, n$ and $IGL(u, 0) = 0$. In other words, it indicates the cumulative income, normalized by the population size, enjoyed by the top $\frac{j}{n}$ proportion of the population, where 0 proportion of the population enjoys 0 income. See Jenkins and Lambert (1997).

iii) $F_D(\xi') > F_D(\xi)$ for all deprivation count assessment metrics $F_D : \overline{Q}^n \to \Re^1_+$ that are increasing, symmetric in deprivation counts and whose values increase under unfavorable composite changes in deprivation counts.
iv) $\sum_{i=1}^{n} f_D(\xi'_i) > \sum_{i=1}^{n} f_D(\xi_i)$ for all individual deprivation count assessment metrics $f_D : \overline{Q} \to \Re^1_+$ that increase with respect to increments in deprivation counts and unfavorable composite changes.
v) ξ'^0 can be obtained from ξ^0 by a finite sequence of rank-preserving deprivation count increments and a finite sequence of rank-preserving unfavorable composite changes or by a sequence of rank-preserving deprivation increments.

The most attractive feature of Theorem 3.2 is equivalence of integer inverse generalized Lorenz ordering with the remaining four conditions each of which has its own merit. Once the dominance condition between integer inverse generalized Lorenz curves of two social matrices hold, we can be sure about their ranking by the generalized Gini deprivation index, where the positive increasing weights assigned to nondecreasingly ordered deprivation counts are arbitrary. Similar remarks hold for other equivalent conditions (see Chakravarty and Zoli, 2012).

Lasso de La Vega (2010) examined dominance conditions to ensure unanimous poverty ranking in a counting framework. These orderings coincide with the integer first and second order stochastic dominance orderings. Theorem 3.2 of the current section is formally equivalent to the integer second order stochastic dominance condition. However, its equivalence with ranking in terms of the generalized Gini index of the count distribution has not been demonstrated rigorously earlier (see also Silber and Yalonetzky, 2014 and Yalonetzky, 2014). Aaberge and Peluso (2011) compared distributions of deprivation counts by employing summary measures of deprivation within the rank-dependent social evaluation framework (Sen, 1974; Yaari, 1987).

3.10 Multidimensional Material Deprivation

Material deprivation can be regarded as a situation of economic condition, which follows as a consequence imposed incapability of an individual to acquire achievements not below cutoff limits in different dimensions related to material living conditions. More precisely, multidimensional material deprivation deals with deprivations in dimensions of well-being regarding material conditions.[22]

22 See, among others, Layte et al. (2001), Whelan et al. (2001, 2001a), Guio (2005, 2009), Boarini and d'Ercole (2006), Guio and Maquet (2006), Guio et al. (2009), Guio et al. (2012), Fusco et al. (2013), and Deutsch et al. (2015).

We refer to such a dimension as a material dimension. Consequently, qualitative dimensions such as communing with friends and political participation are excluded from the domain of the material deprivation measurement. As maintained by EU policy, indices of material deprivation are to be consolidated with income-dependent poverty measures and quantifiers of low employment.

Examples of material deprivations in nonmonetary dimensions of well-being considered in the "The European Union Statistics on Income and Living Conditions (EU-SILC)" project are incapability to face unexpected required expenses, inability to bear expenses to have a meal with meat, chicken, fish (or vegetarian protein equivalent) every second day, lacking capacity to afford to pay for a one-week annual holiday from residence, not having a durable good such as color television, washing machine, telephone, or car, and so on.

Bossert, Chakravarty and D'Ambrosio (2013) developed an axiomatic characterization of a multidimensional index of material deprivation that relies on the union mode to the identification of the poor. The suggested index turns out to be a weighted sum of material deprivation counts of the individuals, where the material deprivation count of a person is defined as the number of relevant dimensions from which the person is deprived.[23]

The framework considered deprivation counts because the dimensions were assumed to be discrete in nature. Consequently, it was not possible to determine deprivation in a dimension in terms of shortfall from its threshold limit, which is also nonquantifiable. For instance, possession of a durable good was taken as the threshold limit of the corresponding dimension, and its nonpossession was regarded as deprivation in the dimension. As a result, it was simply necessary to check whether the person has achievement in the dimension or not. The material deprivation count of a person is deduced by calculating the number of material dimensions in which he is deprived. The model rules out the possibility of using continuous dimensions so that an axiom such as ratio-scale invariance becomes inappropriate.

Since the union poverty rule has been employed, a person becomes materially deprived if his deprivation count in appropriate dimensions is at least 1. As a result, for a person to be materially nondeprived, it is necessary that he is not deprived in any accordant dimension, and in such a case, the person's deprivation count is 0. This does not rule the possibility that he is not multidimensionally poor; he may be deprived in one or more nonmaterial living conditions.

---

23 Bossert et al. (2013) applied this index to the European Union member counties where the idea of material deprivation was pioneered. Layte et al. (2001) developed a material deprivation index using European Community Household Panel data for looking at association between income deprivation and material deprivation. Using panel data for nine European countries, Whelan et al. (2011, 2014) observed mismatch between persistently income deprived and persistently materially deprived.

Of the three axioms that were employed in the characterization result, the first, zero normalization is a cardinality property. According to this postulate, the index takes on the value zero whenever in a one-person society, the person is not deprived in any dimension. The second axiom is the factor decomposability postulate introduced by Chakravarty et al. (1998). The third axiom is population subgroup decomposability.

To present the index analytically, we assume that there are $\overline{k}$ material dimensions of well-being and denote the material deprivation count of person $i \in \{1, 2, \dots, n\}$ by ξ_i^m. The superscript m signifies that our concern here is with material deprivation. Clearly, ξ_i^m is a nonnegative integer bounded between 0 and $\overline{k}$, the total number of materialistic dimensions. The lower bound is achieved if the person is not materially deprived and the upper bound is attained when he has deprivations in all the dimensions. The material deprivation profile in an n-person society is denoted by $\xi^m = (\xi_1^m, \xi_2^m, \dots, \xi_n^m)$. The vector ξ^m is an element of the set Q_m^n, the n-fold Cartesian product of the set $Q_m = \{0, 1, 2, \dots, \overline{k}\}$.

The Bossert et al. (2013) material deprivation index is defined as

$$B_m(\xi^m) = \frac{1}{n} \sum_{i \in S(\xi^m)} \sum_{j=1}^{\overline{k}} w_j, \tag{3.22}$$

where $n \in N$, $\xi^m \in Q_m^n$ are arbitrary, $S(\xi^m)$ is the set of all persons who are materially deprived in $\{1, 2, \dots, n\}$, and $w_j > 0$ is the weight assigned to the jth material dimension. It represents the importance assigned to dimension j in the aggregation. The index in (3.22) satisfies a monotonicity property; if a person who was deprived in a material dimension now becomes nondeprived in it because of, improvement in living conditions, say, then value of B_m reduces. The individuals are treated symmetrically in (3.22) in the sense that if two individuals are deprived in the same set of material dimensions, then their material deprivation counts are the same. If $w_j = \frac{1}{(\overline{k})}$ for all material dimensions j, then B_m is simply the head-count ratio of material deprivation, the proportion of persons who are materially deprived.

Earlier Chakravarty and D'Ambrosio (2006) characterized the following measure of social exclusion, which can be regarded as a material deprivation metric:

$$C_m(\xi^m) = \frac{1}{n} \sum_{i \in S(\xi^m)} f(\xi_i^m), \tag{3.23}$$

where $f : Q_m \to \Re_+^1$, $f(0) = 0$ and f is increasing. Increasingness of f guarantees that the value of C_m increases if the material deprivation count of a person goes up.

A functional form of f under which increasingness of material deprivation index holds is $f(\xi_i^m) = (\xi_i^m)^\alpha$, where $\alpha > 0$ is a parameter. The resulting functional form of C_m becomes $C_m(\xi^m) = \frac{1}{n} \sum_{i \in S(\xi^m)} (\xi_i^m)^\alpha$. The parametric restriction $\alpha > 0$ ensures that $\frac{1}{n} \sum_{i \in S(\xi^m)} (\xi_i^m)^\alpha$ is monotonic. (Jayaraj and Subramanian (2010) applied the index C_m to study multidimensional deprivation in India using data from National Family Health Surveys.)

An example of a nonadditive material deprivation index is the generalized Gini index defined by $\sum_{i \in S(\xi^m)} v_i^{|S(\xi^m)|} (\xi_i^m)^0$, where the decreasing, positive sequence $\{v_i^{|S(\xi^m)|}\}$ depends on the population size $|S(\xi^m)|$ affected by material deprivation, and $(\xi^m)^0$ is the nonincreasingly ordered permutation of ξ^m, that is, $(\xi_i^m)^0 \geq (\xi_{i+1}^m)^0$ for all $i, i+1 \in S(\xi^m)$. Assignment of higher weights to higher material deprivation counts in the generalized Gini index reflects the idea that the deprivation index has an increasing marginal.

To state the increasing marginal material deprivation property formally, consider the change in material deprivation when person i's materialistic deprivation count increases by 1, where $i \in S(\xi^m)$ is arbitrary. Analytically, given $\xi^m = (\xi_1^m, \xi_2^m, \dots, \xi_{\overline{k}}^m)$, this change is given by $F_m(\xi_1^m, \xi_2^m, \dots, \xi_{i-1}^m, \xi_i^m + 1, \xi_{i+1}^m, \dots, \xi_{\overline{k}}^m) - F_m(\xi^m)$. Since this difference in the deprivation index arises from a marginal increase in person i's deprivation count in materialistic dimensions, we refer to it as marginal material deprivation. Of two arbitrary persons $i, j \in S(\xi^m)$, if the material deprivation of each of them increases by 1, where i has higher number of deprivation count than j in the relevant dimensions, then increasingness of marginal material deprivation means that $F_m(\xi_1^m, \xi_2^m, \dots, \xi_{i-1}^m, \xi_i^m + 1, \xi_{i+1}^m, \dots, \xi_{\overline{k}}^m) - F_m(\xi^m) > F_m(\xi_1^m, \xi_2^m, \dots, \xi_{j-1}^m, \xi_j^m + 1, \xi_{j+1}^m, \dots, \xi_{\overline{k}}^m) - F_m(\xi^m)$, which we can rewrite as $F_m(\xi_1^m, \xi_2^m, \dots, \xi_{i-1}^m, \xi_i^m + 1, \xi_{i+1}^m, \dots, \xi_{\overline{k}}^m) > F_m(\xi_1^m, \xi_2^m, \dots, \xi_{j-1}^m, \xi_j^m + 1, \xi_{j+1}^m, \dots, \xi_{\overline{k}}^m)$. Under additivity of F_m, that is, if it is of the type $\frac{1}{n} \sum_{i \in S(\xi^m)} f(\xi_i^m)$, where $f : Q_m \to \mathfrak{R}_+^1$, then increasingness of marginal evaluation requires the satisfaction of the inequality $f(\xi_i^m + 1) - f(\xi_i^m) > f(\xi_j^m + 1) - f(\xi_j^m)$, where $\xi_i^m > \xi_j^m$ and $i, j \in \{1, 2, \dots, n\}$ are arbitrary.

We can now formally say that the index F_m satisfies the increasing marginal material deprivation property if for all $i, j \in S(\xi^m)$, $F_m(\xi_1^m, \xi_2^m, \dots, \xi_{i-1}^m, \xi_i^m + 1, \xi_{i+1}^m, \dots, \xi_{\overline{k}}^m) > F_m(\xi_1^m, \xi_2^m, \dots, \xi_{j-1}^m, \xi_j^m + 1, \xi_{j+1}^m, \dots, \xi_{\overline{k}}^m)$, where $\overline{k} > \xi_j^m$.

We note that the material deprivation count of each of the two persons i and j increases by 1 and j has lower count than i. Then increasingness of material deprivation demands that the increase in society material deprivation resulting from worsening in person i's deprivation count in material dimensions is higher than the corresponding increase that arises as a result of similar aggravation in person *j*'s position. In other words, higher weight is assigned to increase in social assessment of material deprivations as the number of materially deprived dimensions of a person increases.[24] Recall that this has been done in the generalized Gini material deprivation index $\sum_{i \in S(\xi^m)} v_i^{|S(\xi^m)|}(\xi_i^m)^0$. For the additive index $\frac{1}{n} \sum_{i \in S(\xi^m)} (\xi_i^m)^\alpha$, the parametric restriction $\alpha > 1$ is necessary and sufficient for fulfillment of this postulate.[25]

3.11 Concluding Remarks

Several methodologies have been proposed in the literature for the evaluation of poverty from multidimensional standpoints. Each of them has its own objectives and represents a particular mode of assessing poverty using specific means. None of them is designed to overthrow one or more of the others.

In the dashboard mechanism, valuation of poverty is carried out in a primitive framework; the dashboard comprises dimension-by-dimension poverty figures. In the axiomatic approach to the evaluation of multidimensional poverty, a set of desirable postulates for alternative poverty indices is proposed at the outset. Each of these indices or quantifiers is a summary measure of the levels of deprivations arising from insufficiency of achievements in different dimensions of well-being. Broadly speaking, the job then becomes scrutiny of a measure with respect to gratification of one or more of these desiderata. A related issue is to order two or more social matrices, which describe different individuals' positions in terms of their achievements in given dimensions of well-being, indicating society's preference for lower poverty. Several notions of ordering depend on a cumulative joint distribution function, a statistical concept, of a social matrix. Further, it also often becomes necessary to enquire whether poverty ranking by cumulative distribution functions agrees with that produced by axiomatic indices. Consequently, sometimes the ordering process may be interpreted as a mixture of axiomatic and statistical designs, where the latter incorporates many tools that can be invoked for the purpose of poverty evaluation. A second example of a statistical technique employed within the

---

24 Formal equivalence between this postulate, when reformulated for functioning scores, and condition (ν) of Theorem 3.1 has been demonstrated rigorously in Chakravarty and Zoli (2012).

25 In a recent contribution, Dhongde et al. (2016) characterized the average of a real-valued increasing function of a weighted average of 0–1 dimensional deprivation counts of different individuals. They have also determined the implications of imposing the requirement that a deprivation-decreasing switch, defined in an unambiguous way, should reduce overall deprivation, on the measure.

axiomatic framework is the correlation between dimensional achievements that judges interdimensional association.

Additional examples of statistical techniques include principle component analysis; factor analysis (see Chapter1); multiple correspondence analysis used to reveal veiled structures in a given data set; cluster analysis, concerned with grouping of individuals bearing similarity with respect to multidimensional deprivations and structural equations models that are capable of intimating relationships between latent and observed variables.[26]

Another well-accepted process that exists in the literature is the fuzzy set approach that arises when information concerning the identification of the poor is incomplete (see Chapter 4). Multidimensional poverty analysis sometimes also makes use of information-theory-based technique that relies on information function and related entropies. (See Maasoumi and Lugo, 2008; Roelen et al., 2009; Alkire et al., 2015; Chakravarty and Lugo, 2016 and Section 3.5 of this chapter.) An alternative mention worthy technique employed in this context is the distance function that looks at the distance between achievements of an individual and a yardstick vector (see, e.g., Anderson et al., 2008 and Ramos, 2008). In the Venn diagram method, joint distributions of deprivations of the individuals are presented diagrammatically when the number of dimensions does not exceed 3 (see Alkire et al., 2015).[27]

References

Aaberge, R. and A. Brandolini. 2015. Multidimensional Poverty and Inequality. In A.B. Atkinson and F. Bourguignon (eds.) *Handbook of Income Distribution*, Vol. 2A. Amsterdam: North-Holland, 141–216.

Aaberge, R. and E. Peluso. 2011. A Counting Approach for Measuring Multidimensional Deprivation. University of Verona, Department of Economia, *WP No.* 7.

Abbe, A. 2006. *Empirical Analysis of Relative Deprivation and Poverty in Japan.* Tokyo, National Institute of Population and Social Security Research.

26 For applications of statistical techniques in poverty measurement analysis, see, among others, Sahn and Stifel (2000), Lelli (2001), Kuklys (2005), McKenzie (2005), Di Tommaso (2007), Stifel and Christiaensen (2007), Anderson (2008), Asselin and Anh (2008), Booysen et al. (2008), Fusco and Dickes (2008), Klasen (2008), Luzzi et al. (2008), Krishnakumar (2008), Krishnakumar and Ballon (2008), Nardo et al. (2008), Roche (2008), Wagle (2008), Batana and Duclos (2010), Ballon and Krishnakumar (2011), Rahman et al. (2011), Deutsch et al. (2012), Anderson and Hachem (2013), Bennett and Mitra (2013), Davidson and Duclos (2013), Ezzrari and Verme (2013), Foster et al. (2013a), Maasoumi and Yalonetzky (2013), Yalonetzky (2013), Ballon and Duclos (2015) and Deutsch et al. (2015).

27 The remarks made in this section on alternative methodologies apply as well to the analyses presented in the earlier and subsequent chapters.

Aboudi, R. and D. Thon. 2006. Refinements of Muirhead's Lemma and Income Inequality. *Mathematical Social Sciences* 51: 201–216.

Adler, M.D. and M. Fleurbaey (eds.) 2016. *Oxford Handbook of Well-Being and Public Policy*. New York: Oxford University Press.

Akerlof, G. 1997. A Model of Social Distance and Social Decisions. *Econometrica* 65: 1005–1028.

Alkire, S., M. Apablaza, and E. Jung. 2014. Multidimensional Poverty Measurement for EU-SILC Countries. *Research in Progress Series 36c*: OPHI.

Alkire, S. and J.E. Foster. 2011a. Counting and Multidimensional Poverty Measurement. *Journal of Public Economics* 95: 476–487.

Alkire S. and J.E. Foster. 2011b. Understandings and Misunderstandings of Multidimensional Poverty Measurement. *Journal of Economic Inequality* 9: 289–314.

Alkire S, J.E. Foster, and M. Santos. 2011. Where Did Identification Go? *Journal of Economic Inequality* 9: 501–505.

Alkire, S., J.E. Foster, S. Seth, M.E. Santos, J.M. Roche, and P. Ballon. 2015. *Multidimensional Poverty Measurement and Analysis*. Oxford: Oxford University Press.

Alkire, S. and J.M. Roche. 2012. Beyond Headcount: Measures that Reflect the Breadth and Components of Child Poverty. In A. Minujin and S. Nandy (eds.), 103–134.

Alkire, S. and S. Seth. 2008. Determining BPL Status: Some Methodological Improvements. *Indian Journal of Human Development* 2: 407–424.

Alkire, S. and S. Seth. 2013a. Identifying the BPL Households. *Economic and Political Weekly* 48: 49–67.

Alkire, S. and S. Seth. 2013b. Selecting a Targeting Method to Identify BPL Households in India. *Social Indicators Research* 112: 417–446.

Alkire, S. and S. Seth. 2015. Multidimensional Poverty Reduction in India Between 1999-2006: Where and How? *World Development* 72: 93–108.

Altimir, O. 1979. *La Dimensión de la Pobreza en América Latina*. Cuadernos de la Cepal No. 27, Naciones Unidas, Santiago de Chile.

Anaka, M. and M. Kobus. 2012. Multidimensional Poverty Analysis in Polish Gminas. *Ekonomista* 112: 101–117.

Anand, S. 1983. *Inequality and Poverty in Malaysia: Measurement and Decomposition*. New York: Oxford University Press.

Anand, S. 1997. Aspects of Poverty in Malaysia. *Review of Income and Wealth* 23: 1–16.

Anderson, G., 2008. The Empirical Assessment of Multidimensional Welfare, Inequality and Poverty: Sample Weighted Multivariate Generalizations of the Kolomogorov-Smirnov Two Sample Test for Stochastic Dominance. *Journal of Economic Inequality* 6: 73–87.

Anderson, G., I. Crawford, and A. Leicester. 2008. Efficiency Analysis and the Lower Convex Hull Approach. In N. Kakwani and J. Silber (eds.), 191–196.

Anderson, E. and L. Esposito. 2014. On the Joint Evaluation of Absolute and Relative Deprivation. *Journal of Economic Inequality* 12: 411–428.
Anderson, G. and K. Hachem. 2013. Institutions and Economic Outcomes: A Dominance-Based Analysis. *Econometric Reviews* 32: 164–182.
Angulo Salazar, R.C., B.Y. Diaz, and R. Pardo Pinzón. 2013. A Counting Multidimensional Poverty Index in Public Policy Context: The Case of Colombia. *Working Paper* 62: OPHI.
Apablaza, M. and G. Yalonetzky. 2011. Measuring the Dynamics of Multiple Deprivations among Children: The Cases of Andhra Pradesh, Ethiopia, Peru and Vietnam: OPHI.
Asselin, L.M. 2009. *Analysis of Multidimensional Poverty: Theory and Case Studies*. Dordrecht: Springer.
Asselin, L.M. and V.T. Anh. 2008. Multidimensional Poverty and Multiple Correspondence Analysis. In N. Kakwani and J. Silber (eds.), 80–103.
Atkinson, A.B.. 1987. On the Measurement of Poverty. *Econometrica* 55: 749–764.
Atkinson, A.B. 1998. Social Exclusion, Poverty and Unemployment. CASE/4. Centre for Analysis of Social Exclusion. London School of Economics: 1–20.
Atkinson, A.B. 2003. Multidimensional Deprivation: Contrasting Social Welfare and Counting Approaches. *Journal of Economic Inequality* 1: 51–65.
Atkinson, A.B. 2007. Measuring Top Incomes: Methodological Issues. In A.B. Atkinson and T. Piketty (eds.) *Top Incomes over the Twentieth Century*. Oxford: Oxford University Press, 18–42.
Atkinson, A.B. and F. Bourguignon. 1982. The Comparison of Multidimensioned Distributions of Economic Status. *Review of Economic Studies* 49: 183–201.
Atkinson, A.B. and F. Bourguignon. 2001. Poverty and Inclusion from a World Perspective. In J.E. Stiglitz and P.A. Muet (eds.) *Governance, Equity and Global Markets*. New York: Oxford University Press.
Atkinson, A.B. and F. Bourguignon (eds.). 2015. *Handbook of Income Distribution*, Vol. 2A. Amsterdam: North-Holland.
Atkinson, A.B., B. Cantillon, E. Marlier, and B. Nolan. 2002. *Social Indicators: The EU and Social Inclusion*. Oxford: Oxford University Press.
Atkinson, A.B., A.-C. Guio, and E. Marlier (eds) (2017) *Monitoring Social Inclusion in Europe*. Luxembourg: Publications office of the European Union.
Azevedo, V. and M. Robles. 2013. Multidimensional Targeting: Identifying Beneficiaries of Conditional Cash Transfer Program. *Social Indicators Research* 112: 447–475.
Ballon, P. and J.-Y. Duclos. 2015. Multidimensional Poverty in Sudan and South Sudan. Working Paper 93: OPHI.
Ballon, P. and J. Krishnakumar. 2011. Measuring Capability Poverty: A Multidimensional Model-Based Index. In P. Ballon *Model-Based Multidimensional Poverty Indices: Theoretical Construction and Statistical Properties*. Doctoral Dissertation: University of Geneva.

Batana, Y.M. 2013. Multidimensional Measurement of Poverty among Women in Sub-Saharan Africa. *Social Indicators Research* 112: 337–362.

Batana, Y.M. and J.-Y. Duclos. 2010. Multidimensional Poverty among West African Children: Testing for Robust Poverty Comparisons. In J. Cockburn and J. Kabubo-Mariara (eds.) *Child Welfare in Developing Countries.* New York: Springer, 95–122.

Batana, Y.M. and J.-Y. Duclos. 2011. Comparing Multidimensional Poverty with Qualitative Indicators of Well-Being. In J. Deutsch and J. Silber (eds.) *The Measurement of Individual Well-Being and Group Inequalities: Essays in Memory of Z.M. Berrebi.* London: Routledge, 280–297.

Battison, D., G. Cruces, L.F. Lopez-Calva, M.A. Lugo, and M.E. Santos. 2013. Income and Beyond: Multidimensional Poverty in Six Latin American Countries. *Social Indicators Research* 112: 291–314.

Bauman, K. 1998. Direct Measures of Poverty as Indicators for Economic Need: Evidence from the Survey of Income and Program Participation. *Population Division Working Paper 30.* US Census Bureau.

Bauman, K. 1999. Extend Measures of Well-being: Meeting Basic Needs. *Households Economic Studies.* US Department of Commerce.

Bedi, T., A. Coudouel, and A. Smile (eds.) 2007. *More Than a Pretty Picture: Using Poverty Maps to Design Better Policies and Interventions.* Washington, DC: World Bank.

Bellani, L. 2013. Multidimensional Indices of Deprivation: The Introduction of Reference Groups Weights. *Journal of Economic Inequality* 11: 495–516.

Bennett, C.J. and S. Mitra. 2013. Multidimensional Poverty: Measurement, Estimation and Inference. *Econometric Reviews* 32: 57–83.

Bérenger, V. 2016. Measuring Multidimensional Poverty in Three South Asian Countries Using Ordinal Variables. In J. Silber and G. Wan (eds.), 149–214.

Bérenger, V. and F. Bresson (eds.) 2013a. *Monetary Poverty and Social Exclusion Around the Mediterranean Sea.* New York: Springer.

Bérenger, V. and F. Bresson. 2013b. Axiomatic and Robust Multidimensional Poverty Measurements in Five Southern Mediterranean Countries. In V. Bérenger and F. Bresson (eds.), 3–42.

Bérenger, V., F. Bresson, P. Makdissi, and M. Yazbeck. 2013a. Regional and Sectoral Distribution of Poverty in Lebanon, 2004. In V. Bérenger and F. Bresson (eds.), 109–141.

Bérenger, V., J. Deutsch, and J. Silber. 2013b. Durable Goods, Access to Services and the Derivation of an Asset Index. *Economic Modeling* 35: 881–891.

Berrebi, Z.M. and J. Silber. 1985. Income Inequality Indices and Deprivation: A Generalisation. *Quarterly Journal of Economics* 100: 807–810.

Birdsall, N. 2011. Comment on Multidimensional Indices. *Journal of Economic Inequality* 9: 489–491.

Blackorby C. and D. Donaldson. 1980. Ethical Indices for the Measurement of Poverty. *Econometrica* 58: 1053–1060.

Boarini, R. and M.M. d'Ercole. 2006. Measures of Material Deprivation in OECD Countries. *OECD Social, Employment and Migration Working Paper* 37.

Boltvinik, J. 1992. El Metodo de Medición Integrada dela Pobreza: Una propuesta para su desarrollo. *Comercio Exterior* 42: 354–365.

Boltvinik, J. 2012. Medición Multidimensional de la Pobreza. América Latina, de precursora a rezagada. La experiencia contrastante de México: una guía para la región?. Paper presented at the Seminario International Multidimencionalidad di la pobreza, 'Alcances para su definición y evaluación en América Latina y el Caribe'. Universidad de Chile 22–23 November.

Booth, C. 1894. *The Aged Poor: Condition.* London: Macmillan.

Booth, C. 1903. *Life and Labor of the People in London.* London: Macmillan.

Booysen, F., R. Servass Van Derberg, M. Von Maltitz, and G. Du Rand. 2008. Using an Asset Index to Assess Trends in Poverty in Seven Sub-Saharan African Countries. *World Development* 36: 1113–1130.

Bossert, W., S.R. Chakravarty, and C. D'Ambrosio. 2013. Multidimensional Poverty and Material Deprivation. *Review of Income and Wealth* 59: 29–43.

Bossert, W. and C. D'Ambrosio. 2007. Dynamic Measures of Individual Deprivation. *Social Choice and Welfare* 28: 77–88.

Bossert, W. and M. Fleurbaey. 2002. Equitable Insurance Premium Schemes. *Social Choice and Welfare* 19: 113–125.

Bourguignon, F. and S.R. Chakravarty. 1999. A Family of Multidimensional Poverty Measures. In D.J. Slottje (ed.) *Advances in Econometrics, Income Distribution and Scientific Methodology: Essays in Honor of C. Dagum.* Heidelberg: Physica-Verlag, 331–342.

Bourguignon, F. and S.R. Chakravarty. 2003. The Measurement of Multidimensional Poverty. *Journal of Economic Inequality*, 1, 25–49.

Bourguignon, F. and S.R. Chakravarty. 2009. Multidimensional Poverty Orderings: Theory and Applications. In K. Basu and R. Kanbur (eds.) *Arguments for a Better World: Essays in Honor of Amartya Sen, Volume 1: Ethics, Welfare and Measurement.* Oxford: Oxford University Press, 337–361.

Bowley, A.L. and A.R. Burnett-Hurst. 1915. *Livelihood and Poverty: A Study in the Economic and Social Conditions of Working Class Households in Northampton, Warrington, Stanley, Reading (and Bolton).* London: King.

Boyden, J. and M. Bourdillon. 2012. *Childhood Poverty: Multidisciplinary Approaches.* Basingstoke: Palgrave Macmillan.

Bradshaw, J. and N. Finch. 2003. Overlaps in Dimensions of Poverty. *Journal of Social Policy* 32: 513–525.

Bresson, F. 2009. *Multidimensional Poverty Measurement without the Strong Focus Axiom.* Université de Nice Sophia Antipolis.

Bresson, F. and J.-Y. Duclos. 2015. Intertemporal Poverty Comparisons. *Social Choice and Welfare* 44: 567–616.

Brzezinski, M. 2010. Income Affluence in Poland. *Social Indicators Research* 99: 285–299.

Callan, T., B. Nolan, and C.T. Whelan. 1993. Resources Deprivation and the Measurement of Poverty. *Journal of Social Policy* 22: 141–172.

Callander, E.J., D.J. Schofield, and R.N. Shrestha. 2012a. Multiple Disadvantages among Older Citizens: What a Multidimensional Measure of Poverty Can Show? *Journal of Aging and Social Policy* 24: 368–383.

Callander, E.J., D.J. Schofield, and R.N. Shrestha. 2012b. Towards a Holistic Understanding of Poverty: A New Multidimensional Measure of Poverty for Australia. *Health and Sociology Review* 21: 141–155.

Cappellari, L. and S.P. Jenkins. 2007. Summarizing Multiple Deprivation Indicators. In: S.P. Jenkins and J. Micklewright (ed.) *Inequality and Poverty Re-Examined*. Oxford: Oxford University Press, 166–184.

Chakravarty, S.R. 1983. A New Index of Poverty. *Mathematical Social Sciences* 6: 307–313.

Chakravarty, S.R. 1990. *Ethical Social Index Numbers*. New York: Springer.

Chakravarty, S.R. 2009. *Inequality, Polarization and Poverty: Advances in Distributional Analysis*, New York: Springer.

Chakravarty, S.R. 2013. *An Outline of Financial Economics.* New York: Anthem Press.

Chakravarty, S.R., N. Chattopadhyay, J. Deutsh, Z. Nissanov, and J. Silber. 2016. Reference Groups and the Poverty Line: An Axiomatic Approach with an Empirical Illustration. *Research on Economic Inequality* 24: 1–27.

Chakravarty, S.R. and C. D'Ambrosio. 2006. The Measurement of Social Exclusion. *Review of Income and Wealth* 52: 377–398.

Chakravarty, S.R. and C. D'Ambrosio. 2013. A Family of Unit Consistent Multidimensional Poverty Indices. In V. Berenger and F. Bresson (eds.), 75–88.

Chakravarty S.R., J. Deutsch, and J. Silber. 2008. On the Watts Multidimensional Poverty Index and Its Decomposition. *World Development* 36: 1067–1077.

Chakravarty, S.R. and M.A. Lugo. 2016. Multidimensional Indicators of Inequality and Poverty. In M.D. Adler and M. Fleurbaey (eds.), 246–285.

Chakravarty, S.R. and P. Moyes. 2003. Individual Welfare, Social Deprivation and Income Taxation. *Economic Theory* 21: 843–869.

Chakravarty, S.R. and D. Mukherjee. 1999. Measures of Deprivation and Their Meaning in Terms of Social Satisfaction. *Theory and Decision* 47: 89–100.

Chakravarty, S.R., D. Mukherjee, and R. Ranade. 1998. On the Family of Subgroup and Factor Decomposable Measures of Multidimensional Poverty. *Research on Economic Inequality* 8: 175–194.

Chakravarty, S.R. and J. Silber. 2008. Measuring Multidimensional Poverty: The Axiomatic Approach. In N. Kakwani and J. Silber (eds.), 192–209.

Chakravarty, S.R. and C. Zoli. 2012. Stochastic Dominance Relations for Integer Variables. *Journal of Economic Theory* 147: 1331–1341.

Chen, S. and M. Ravallion. 2001. How did the World's Poorest Fare in the 1990s? *Review of Income and Wealth* 47: 283–300.

Chen, S. and M. Ravallion. 2013. More Relatively-Poor People in a Less Absolutely-Poor World. *Review of Income and Wealth* 59: 1–28.
Clark, S., R. Hemming, and D. Ulph. 1981. On Indices for the Measurement of Poverty. *Economic Journal* 91: 515–526.
Coady, D., M. Grosh, and J. Hoddinot. 2004. *Targeting of Transfers in Developing Countries: Review of Lessons and Experience.* Washington, DC: World Bank.
Cohen, A. 2010. The Multidimensional Poverty Assessment Tool: A New Framework for Measuring Rural Poverty. *Development in Practice* 20: 887–897.
Cohen, A. and M. Saisana. 2014. Quantifying the Qualitative: Eliciting Expert Input to Develop the Multidimensional Poverty Assessment Tool. *Journal of Development Studies* 50: 35–50.
Commission on Growth and Development. 2008. *The Growth Report: Strategies for Sustained Growth and Inclusive Development.* Washington, DC: World Bank.
Cowell, F.A. 2016. Inequality and Poverty Measures. In M.D. Adler and M. Fleurbaey (eds.), 82–125.
D'Ambrosio, C., J. Deutsch, and J. Silber. 2011. Multidimensional Approaches to Poverty Measurement: An Empirical Analysis of Poverty in Belgium, France, Germany Italy and Spain, Based on European Panel. *Applied Economics* 43: 951–961.
Datt, G. and M. Ravallion. 1992. Growth and Redistribution Components of Change in Poverty Measures: A Decomposition with Applications to Brazil and India in the 1980s. *Journal of Development Economics* 38: 275–295.
Davidson, R. 2008. Stochastic Dominance. In S.N. Durlauf and L.E. Blume (eds.) *The New Palgrave Dictionary of Economics,* Second Edition. London: Palgrave Macmillan.
Davidson, R. and J.E. Duclos. 2000. Statistical Inference for Stochastic Dominance and for the Measurement of Poverty and Inequality. *Econometrica* 68: 1435–1464.
Davidson, R. and J.E. Duclos. 2013. Testing for Restricted Stochastic Dominance. *Econometric Reviews* 32: 84–125.
Davies, R. 1997. Beyond Wealth Ranking: The Democratic Definition and the Measurement of Poverty. Briefing Note Prepared for the ODI Workshop 'Indicators of Poverty: Operational Significance' in London, October.
Davies, R. and W. Smith. 1998. *The Basic Necessities Survey (BNS): The Experience of Action Aid Vietnam.* Hanoi: Action Aid.
Deaton A. 2010. Price Indexes, Inequality, and the Measurement of World Poverty. *American Economic Review* 100: 5–34.
Decancq, K., M. Fleurbaey, and F. Maniquet. 2015. *Multidimensional Poverty Measurement: Shouldn't We Take Preferences into Account? mimeographed,* Brussels: CORE.
Decancq, K., T. Goedemé, K. Van den Bosch, and J. Vanhille. 2013. The Evolution of Poverty in the European Union: Concepts, Measurement and Data. Methodological Paper No. 13/01, ImPRoveE.

Deineko, V.G., B. Klinz, and G.J. Woeginger. 2009. The Complexity of Computing the Muirhead-Dalton Distance. *Mathematical Social Sciences* 57: 282–284.

Deutsch, J., A.-C. Guio, M. Pomati, and J. Silber. 2015. Material Deprivation in Europe: Which Expenditures Are Curtailed First? *Social Indicators Research* 120: 723–740.

Deutsch, J. and J. Silber. 2005. Measuring Multidimensional Poverty: An Empirical Comparison of Various Approaches. *Review of Income and Wealth* 51: 145–174.

Deutsch, J. and J. Silber. 2008. The Order of Acquisition of Durable Goods and the Measurement of Multidimensional Poverty. In N. Kakwani and J. Silber (eds.), 226–243.

Deutsch, J., J. Silber, and P. Verme. 2012. On Social Exclusion in Macedonia: Measurement and Determinants. In C. Ruggeri Laderchi and S. Savastano (eds.) *Poverty and Exclusion in the Western Balkans: New Directions in Measurement and Policy.* New York: Springer.

Dhongde, S., Y. Li, P.K. Pattanaik, and Y. Xu. 2016. Binary Data, Hierarchy of Attributes, and Multidimensional Deprivation. *Journal of Economic Inequality* 14: 363–378.

Di Tommaso, M. 2007. Children Capabilities: A Structural Equation Model for India. *Journal of Socio-Economics* 36: 436–450.

Dickerson, A. and G. Popli. 2015. The Many Dimensions of Child Poverty: Evidence from the UK Millennium Cohort Study. *Sheffield Economic Research Paper Series* no. 2015-09: Institute for Economic Analysis and Decision Making, University of Sheffield.

Diez, H., M.C. Lasso de la Vega, and A. Urrutia. 2008. Multidimensional Unit- and Subgroup Consistent Inequality and Poverty Measures: Some Characterization Results. *Research on Economic Inequality* 16: 189–211.

Donaldson, D. and J.A. Weymark. 1986. Properties of Fixed-Population Poverty Indices. *International Economic Review* 27: 667–688.

Drèze, J. and R. Khera. 2010. The BPL Census and a Possible Alternative. *Economic and Political Weekly* 45: 54–63.

Drèze, J. and A.K. Sen. 2013. *Uncertain Glory:India and Its Contradictions.* London: Allen Lane.

Duclos, J.-Y. and D. Échevin. 2011. Health and Income: A Robust Comparison of Canada and the US. *Journal of Health Economics* 30: 293–302.

Duclos, J.-Y., D.E. Sahn, and S.D. Younger. 2006a. Robust Multidimensional Poverty Comparisons. *Economic Journal* 116: 943–968.

Duclos, J.-Y., D.E. Sahn, and S.D. Younger. 2006b. Robust Multidimensional Spatial Poverty Comparisons in Ghana, Madagascar, and Uganda. *World Bank Economic Review* 20: 91–113.

Duclos, J.-Y., D.E. Sahn, and S.D. Younger. 2007. Robust Multidimensional Poverty Comparisons with Discrete Indicators of Well-Being. In S.P. Jenkins and J. Micklewright (eds.) *Inequality and Poverty Re-examined.* Oxford: Oxford University Press.

Duclos, J.-Y., D.E. Sahn, and S.D. Younger. 2008 Using an Ordinal Approach to Multidimensional Poverty Analysis. In N. Kakwani and J. Silber (eds.), 244–261.

Duclos, J.-Y., D.E. Sahn, and S.D. Younger. 2011. Partial Multidimensional Inequality Orderings. *Journal of Public Economics* 95: 225–238.

Duclos, J.-Y. and L. Tiberti. 2016. Multidimensional Poverty Indices: A Critical Assessment. In M.D. Adler and M. Fleurbaey (eds.) *The Oxford Handbook of Well-Being and Public Policy*. Oxford University Press, 677–708.

Elbers, C., T. Fuji, P. Lanjouw, B. Özler, and W. Yin 2007. Poverty Alleviation Through Geographic Targeting: How Much Does Disaggregation Help? *Journal of Development Economics* 71: 355–364.

Elbers, C., J.O. Lanjouw, and P. Lanjouw. 2002. Micro-Level Estimation of Poverty and Inequality. *Econometrica* 71: 355–364.

Erikson, R. 1993. Descriptions of Inequality: The Swedish Approach to Welfare Research. In M. Nussabaum and A.K. Sen (eds.) *The Quality of Life.* New York: Oxford University Press, 67–83.

Eurobarameter. 2007. *Special Eurobarameter 279/Wave 67/1: Poverty and Exclusion;* Report. European Commission.

Eurostat. 2002. *Statistiques Sociales Européennes: Deuxième rapport sur le revenu, la pauvreté et l'exclusion sociale.* Luxembourg: Office des publications officielles des communnautés européennes.

Ezzrari, A. and P. Verme. 2013. A Multiple Correspondence Analysis Approach to the Measurement of Multidimensional Poverty in Morocco 2001–2007. In V. Berenger and F. Bresson (eds.), 181–209.

Ferreira, F.H.G. 2011. Poverty is Multidimensional. But What Are We Going to Do about It? *Journal of Economic Inequality* 9: 493–495.

Ferreira, F.H.G., S. Chen, A. Dabalen, Y. Dikhanov, N. Hamadeh, D. Jolliffe, A. Narayan, E. Beer Prydz, A. Revenga, P. Sangraula, U. Serajuddin and N. Yoshida. 2015. A Global Count of the Extreme Poor in 2012: Data Issues, Methodology and Initial Results. IZA DP No. 9442.

Ferreira, F.H.G. and M.A. Lugo. 2013. Multidimensional Poverty Analysis: Looking for a Middle Ground. *World Bank Research Observer* 28: 220–235.

Fields, G.S. 2001. *Distribution and Development: A New Look at the Developing World.* Cambridge, MA: MIT Press.

Fishburn, P. and I.H. Lavalle. 1995. Stochastic Dominance on Unidimensional Grids. *Mathematics of Operations Research* 20: 513–525.

Foster, J.E. 1998. Absolute versus Relative Poverty. *American Economic Review* 88: 335–341.

Foster, J.E. 2006. Poverty Indices. In A. de Janvry, R. Kanbur (eds.) *Poverty, Inequality and Development: Essays in Honor of Erik Thorbecke.* New York: Springer, 41–65.

Foster, J.E., J. Greer, and E. Thorbecke. 1984. A Class of Decomposable Poverty Measures. *Econometrica* 42: 761–766.

Foster J.E., Jin Y. 1998. Poverty Orderings for the Dalton Utility-gap Measures. In: S.P. Jenkins, A. Kapteyn, and B. Van Praag (eds.), 268–285.

Foster, J.E., M. McGillivray, and S. Seth. 2013a. Composite Indices: Rank Robustness, Statistical Association and Redundancy. *Econometric Reviews* 22: 35–56.

Foster, J.A., S. Seth, M. Lokshin, and Z. Sajaia. 2013b. *A Unified Approach to Measuring Poverty and Inequality: Theory and Practice.* Washington, DC: World Bank.

Foster J.E. and A.F. Shorrocks. 1988. Poverty Orderings. *Econometrica* 56: 173–177.

Foster, J.E. and A.F. Shorrocks. 1991. Subgroup Consistent Poverty Indices. *Econometrica* 59: 687–709.

Fuchs, V. 1969. Comment on Measuring the Size of the Low-Income Population. In L. Soltow (ed.) *Six Papers on the Size Distribution of Wealth and Income.* New York: National Bureau of Economic Research, 198–202.

Fusco, A. and P. Dickes. 2008. The Rasch Model and Multidimensional Poverty Measurement. In N. Kakwani and J. Silber (eds.), 49–62.

Fusco, A., A.-C. Guio, and E. Marlier. 2013. Building a Material Deprivation Index in a Multidimensional Context: Lessons from the EU Experience. In V. Berenger and F. Bresson (eds.), 43–71.

Garcia-Diaz, R. 2013. Poverty Orderings with Asymmetric Attributes. *B. E. Journal of Theoretical Economics* 13: 347–361.

Gardiner, K. and M. Evans. 2011. Exploring Poverty Gaps among Children in the UK. *Department for Work and Pensions Working Paper* No 103.

Gasparini, L., W. Sosa-Escudero, M. Marchionni, and S. Olivieri. 2013. Multidimensional Poverty in Latin America and the Caribbean: New Evidence from the Gallup World Poll. *Journal of Economic Inequality* 11: 195–214.

Gillie, A. 1996. The Origin of the Poverty Line. *Economic History Review* 49: 715–730.

Gönner, C., A. Cahyat, M. Haug, and G. Limberg. 2007. *Towards Wellbeing: Monitoring Poverty in Kutai Barat, Indonesia.* Bogor, Indonesia: Center for International Forestry Research.

Gordon, D., R. Levitas, C. Pantazis, D. Patsios, S. Payne, and P. Townsend. 2000. *Poverty and Social Exclusion in Britain.* York: Joseph Rowntree Foundation.

Gordon, D., S. Nandy, C. Pantazis,S. Pemberton, and P. Townsend. 2003. *Child Poverty in the Developing World.* Bristol: Policy Press.

Gordon, D., C. Pantazis, and P. Townsend. 2001. *Child Rights and Child Poverty in Developing Countries.* University of Bristol, Centre for International Poverty Research.

Gräb, J. and M. Grimm. 2011. Robust Multiperiod Poverty Comparisons. *Journal of Statistics: Advances in Theory and Applications* 6: 19–54.

Gravel, N. and A. Mukhopadhyay. 2010. Is India Better Off Today Than 15 Years Ago? A Robust Multidimensional Answer. *Journal of Economic Inequality* 8: 173–195.
Guio, A.-C. 2005. Material Deprivation in the EU. *Statistics in Focus, Population and Social Conditions, Living Conditions and Welfare,* 21/2005. Luxembourg.
Guio, A.-C. 2009. What Can Be Learned from Deprivation Indicators in Europe. Paper presented at the Indicator Subgroup of the Social Protection Committee, 10 February.
Guio, A.-C., A. Fusco, and E. Marlier. 2009. An EU Approach to Material Deprivation using EU-SILC and Eurobarometer Data. *IRISS Working Paper* 2009–19.
Guio, A.-C., D. Gordon, and E. Marlier. 2012. Measuring Material Deprivationin the EU: Indicators for the Whole Population and Child Specific Indicators. *Mimeographed.*
Guio, A.-C. and I.E. Maquet. 2006. Material Deprivation and Poor Housing: What Can be Learned from the EU-SLIC 2004 Data? How Can EU-SLIC be Improved in This Matter? Draft Paper for the Conference 'Comparative EU Statistics on Income and Living Conditions: Issues and Challenges'. Helsinki.
Gunewardena, D. 2004. *Poverty Measurement: Meanings, Methods and Requirements.* Colombo: Centre for Poverty Analysis.
Hadar, J. and W.R. Russell. 1969. Rules for Ordering Uncertain Prospects. *American Economic Review* 59: 25–34.
Halleröd, B. 1994. A New Approach to Direct Measurement of Consensual Poverty. *SSRC Discussion Paper* 50.
Halleröd, B. 1995. The Truly Poor: Direct and Indirect Consensual Measurement of Poverty in Sweden. *Journal of European Social Policy* 5: 111–129.
Hirway, I. 2003. Identification of BPL Households for Poverty Alleviation Programs. *Economic and Political Weekly* 38: 4803–4838.
Jain, S.K. 2004. Identification of the Poor: Flaws in Government Surveys. *Economic and Political Weekly* 39: 4981–4984.
Jalan, J. and R. Murgai. 2007. *An Effective "Targeting Shortcut"? An Assessment of the 2002 Below-Poverty Line Census Method.* World Bank.
Jayaraj, D. and S. Subramanian. 2010. A Chakravarty-DAmbrosio View of Multidimensional Deprivation: Some Estimates for India. *Economic and Political Weekly* 45: 53–65.
Jenkins, S.P., A. Kapteyn, and B. Van Praag (eds.). 1998. *The Distributions of Welfare and Household Production: International Perspective.* Cambridge: Cambridge University Press.
Jenkins S.P. and P.J. Lambert. 1997. Three 'I's of Poverty Curves, with an Analysis of UK Poverty Trends. *Oxford Economic Papers* 49: 317–327.
Jenkins S.P. and P.J. Lambert. 1998a. Ranking Poverty Gap Distributions: Further TIPs for Poverty Analysis. *Research on Economic Inequality* 8: 31–38.

Jenkins S.P. and P.J. Lambert. 1998b. Three 'I's of Poverty Curves and Poverty Dominance: TIP for Poverty Analysis. *Research on Economic Inequality* 8: 39–56.

Kakwani, N.C. 1980. On a Class of Poverty Measures. *Econometrica,* 48: 437–446.

Kakwani, N.C. 1984. The Relative Deprivation Curve and Its Applications. *Journal of Business and Economic Statistics* 2: 384–405.

Kakwani, N.C. 1993. Poverty and Economic Growth with Application to Côte d'Ivoire. *Review of Income and Wealth* 39: 121–139.

Kakwani, N. and J. Silber (eds.). 2008. *Quantitative Approaches to Multidimensional Poverty Measurement*. New York: Palgrave Macmillan.

Kast, M. and S. Molina. 1975. *Mapa de la Extrema Pobreza.* Santiago: Odeplan, Escuela de Economia Pontificia Universidad Católica de Chile.

Katzman, R. 1989. La Heterogeneidad de la Pobreza. El Casode Montevideo. *Rivistade la Cepal* 37: 141–152.

Khan, S.N. and S. Qutub. 2010. *The Benazir Income Support Programme and the Zakat Programme: A Political Economy of Gender*. London: Overseas Development Institute.

Klasen, S. 2000. Measuring Poverty and Deprivation in South Africa. *Review of Income and Wealth* 46: 33–58.

Klasen, S. 2008. Economic Growth and Poverty Reduction: Measurement Using Income and Non-Income Indicators. *World Development* 36: 420–445.

Klasen, S. 2016. An Asian Poverty Line? Issues and Options. In J. Silber and G. Wan (eds.), 13–29.

Krishnakumar, J. 2008. Multidimensional Measures of Poverty and Well-Being Based on Latent Variable Models. In N. Kakwani and J. Silber (eds.), 118–134.

Krishnakumar, J. and P. Ballon. 2008. Estimating Basic Capabilities: A Structural Equation Model Approach Applied to Bolivian Data. *World Development* 36: 992–1010.

Kuklys, W. 2005. *Amartya Sen's Capability Approach: Theoretical Insights and Empirical Applications.* Berlin: Springer Science & Business Media.

Labar, K. and F. Bresson. 2011. A Multidimensional Analysis of Poverty in China from 1991 to 2006. *China Economic Review* 22: 646–668.

Lasso de la Vega, M.C. 2010. Counting Poverty Orderings and Deprivation Curves. *Research on Economic Inequality* 18: 153–172.

Lasso de la Vega, M.C. and A.M. Urrutia. 2011. Characterizing How to Aggregate the Individuals' Deprivations in a Multidimensional Framework. *Journal of Economic Inequality* 9: 183–194.

Lasso de La Vega, M.C. and A. Urrutia. 2012. A Note on Multidimensional Distribution Sensitive Poverty Axioms. *Research on Economic Inequality* 20: 161–173.

Lasso de la Vega, M.C., A.M. Urrutia, and A. Sarachu. 2009. The Bourguignon and Chakravarty Multidimensional Poverty Family: A Characterization, ECINEQ WP 2009-109.

Layte, R., B. Maître, B. Nolan, D. Watson, J. Williams, and B. Casey. 2000. Monitoring Poverty Trends: Results from the 1998 Living in Ireland Survey. *ESRI Working Paper* 132.

Layte, R., B. Maître, D. Nolan, and C. Whelan. 2001. Persistent and Consistent Poverty in the 1994 and 1995 Waves of the European Community Household Panel Survey. *Review of Income and Wealth* 47: 427–449.

Leigh, A. 2009. Top Incomes. In B. Nolan, W. Salvedra, and T. Smeeding (eds.) *The Oxford Handbook of Economic Inequality*. Oxford: Oxford University Press, 150–174.

Lelli, S. 2001. Factor Analysis versus Fuzzy Sets Theory: Assessing the Influence of Different Techniques on Sen's Functioning Approach. Centre for Economic Studies Discussion Paper 01.21.

Levy, H. 2006. *Stochastic Dominance, Investment Decisions Making under Uncertainty*. Second Edition. New York: Springer.

Lipton, M. and M. Ravallion. 1995. Poverty and Policy. In J. Behrman and T.N. Srinivasan (eds.) *Handbook of Development Economics*, Vol. 3, Amsterdsam: North-Holland, 2551–2567.

Lustig, N. 2011a. Multidimensional Indices of Achievements and Poverty: What Do We Gain and What Do We lose? An Introduction in JOEI Forum on Multidimensional Poverty. *Journal of Economic Inequality* 9: 227–234.

Lustig, N. 2011b. Multidimensional Indices of Achievements and Poverty: Comments. *Journal of Economic Inequality* 9: 469.

Luzzi, G.F., Y. Flükgier, and S. Weber. 2008. A Cluster Analysis of Multidimensional Poverty in Switzerland. In N. Kakwani and J. Silber (eds.), 63–79.

Maasoumi, E. 1986. The Measurement and Decomposition of Multidimensional Inequality. *Econometrica* 54: 991–997.

Maasoumi, E. and M.A. Lugo. 2008. The Information Basis of Multivariate Poverty Assessments. In N. Kakwani and J. Silber (eds.), 1–29.

Maasoumi, E. and G. Yalonetzky. 2013. Introduction to Robustness in Multidimensional Analysis. *Econometric Reviews* 32: 1–6.

Mack, J. and S. Lansley. 1985. *Poor Britain*. London: Allen and Unwin.

Maniquet, F. 2016. Social Ordering Functions. In Adler, M.D. and M. Fleurbaey (eds.), 227–245.

Marshall, A.W., I. Olkin, and B.C. Arnold. 2011. *Inequalities: Theory of Majorization and Its Applications*. New York: Springer.

Mayer, S.E. and C. Jencks. 1989. Poverty and the Distribution of Material Hardship. *The Journal of Human Resources* 24: 88–114

McKenzie, D. 2005. Measuring Inequality with Asset Indicators. *Journal of Population Economics* 18: 229–260.

Medeiros, M. 2006. The Rich and the Poor: The Construction of an Affluence Line from the Poverty Line. *Social Indicators Research* 78: 1–18.

Milne, F. and E. Neave. 1994. Dominance Relations among Standardized Variables. *Management Science* 40: 1343–1352.

Minujin, A. and S. Nandy (eds.). 2012. *Global Child Poverty and Well-Being: Measurement, Concepts, Policy and Action.* Bristol: Policy Press.

Mitra, S., K. Jones, B. Vick,D. Brown,E. McGinn, and M.J. Alexander. 2013a. Implementing a Multidimensional Poverty Using Mixed Method and Participatory Framework. *Social Indicators Research* 110: 1061–1081.

Mitra, S., A. Posarac, and B. Vick. 2013b. Disability and Poverty in Developing Countries: A Multidimensional Study. *World Development* 41: 1–18.

Muffels, R. and M. Vriens. 1991. The Elaboration of a Deprivation Scale and the Definition of a Subjective Poverty Line. Annual Meeting of the European Society for Population Economics, June, Tilburg University.

Muffles, R., J. Berghman, and H.-J. Driven, 1992. A Multi-Method Approach to Monitor the Evolution of Poverty. *Journal of the European Social Policy* 2: 193–213.

Muirhead, R.F. 1903. Some Methods Applicable to Identities and Inequalities of Symmetric Algebraic Functions of n Letters, *Proceedings of the Edinburgh Mathematical Society* 21: 144–167.

Mukherjee, N. 2005. *Political Corruption in India's Below the Poverty Line (BPL Exercise): Grassroots Perspectives on BPL in Perpetuating Poverty and Social Exclusion.* New Delhi: Development Tracks in Research, Training and Consultancy.

Nardo, M., M. Saisana, A. Saltelli, and S. Tarantola, A. Hoffman and E. Giovannini. 2008. *Handbook on Constructing Composite Indicators: Methodology and User Guide.* OECD Publishing.

Nolan, B. and C. Whelan. 1996. *Resources, Deprivation and Poverty.* Oxford: Oxford University Press.

Nolan, B. and C. Whelan. 2011. *Poverty and Deprivation in Europe.* Oxford: Oxford University Press.

Nteziyaremye, A. and B. MkNelly. 2001. *Mali Poverty Outreach Study of the Kafo Jiginew and Nyèsigiso Credit and Savings with Education Programs. Freedom from Hunger Research Paper 7.* Davis, CA: Freedom from Hunger.

O'Higgins, M. and S. Jenkins. 1990. Poverty in the EC: Estimates for 1975, 1980 and 1985. In R. Teekens and B.M.S. Van Praag (eds.) *Analysing Poverty in the European Community: Policy Issues, Research Options, and Data Sources.* Luxembourg: Office of Official Publications of the European Communities, 187–212.

Orshansky, M. 1965. Counting the Poor: Another Look at the Poverty Profile. *Social Security Bulletin* 28: 3–29.

Pazner, E. and D. Schmeidler. 1978. Egalitarian Equivalent Allocation: A New Concept of Economic Equity. *Quarterly Journal of Economics* 92: 671–687.

Peichl, A. and N. Pestel. 2013a. Multidimensional Well-being at the Top: Evidence for Germany. *Fiscal Studies* 34: 355–371.

Peichl, A. and N. Pestel. 2013b. Multidimensional Affluence: Theory and Applications to Germany and the US. *Applied Economics* 45: 591–601.
Peichl, A., T. Schaefer, and C. Scheicher. 2010. Measuring Richness and Poverty: A Micro Data Application to Europe and Germany. *Review of Income and Wealth* 56: 597–619.
Permanyer, I. 2011. Assessing the Robustness of Composite Indices Rankings. *Review of Income and Wealth* 57: 306–326.
Permanyer, I. 2012. Uncertainty and Robustness in Composite Indices Rankings. *Oxford Economic Papers* 64: 57–79.
Piketty, T. and E. Saez. 2006. The Evolution of Top Incomes: A Historical and Inter-national Perspective. *American Economic Review* 96: 200–205.
Pradhan, M., A. Suryahadi, S. Sumerto, L. Pritchett. 2000. *Measurement of Poverty in Indonesia-1996, 1999, and Beyond. Policy Research Working Paper.* Washington, DC: World Bank.
Rahman, T., R.C. Mittelhammer, and P. Wandscheider. 2011. Measuring the Quality of Life Across Countries: A Multiple Indicators and Multiple Causes Approach. *Journal of Socio-Economics* 40: 43–52.
Ramos, X. 2008. Using Efficiency Analysis to Measure Individual Well-Being with an Illustration for Catalonia. In N. Kakwani and J. Silber (eds.), 155–175.
Ravallion, M. 1994. Measuring Social Welfare with and without Poverty Lines. *American Economic Review* 84: 359–364.
Ravallion, M. 1996. Issues in Measuring and Modeling Poverty. *Economic Journal* 106: 1328–1343.
Ravallion, M. 2011. On Multidimensional Indices of Poverty. *Journal of Economic Inequality* 9: 235–248.
Ravallion, M., S. Chen and P. Sangraula, 2009.Dollar a Day Revisited. *The World Bank Economic Review* 23: 163–184.
Ravallion, M., G. Datt and D. van de Walle. 1991. Quantifying Absolute Poverty in the Developing World. *Review of Income and Wealth,* 37: 345–361.
Ravallion, M. and M. Huppi 1991. Measuring Changes in Poverty: A Methodological Case Study of Indonesia During an adjustment Period. *World Bank Economic Review* 5: 57–82.
Ringen, S. 1987. *The Possibility of Politics.* New York: Oxford University Press.
Ringen, S. 1988. Direct and Indirect Measures of Poverty. *Journal of Social Policy* 17: 351–366.
Rippin, N. 2012. *Considerations of Efficiency and Distributive Justice in Multidimensional Poverty Measurement.* Ph.D. Dissertation. Göttingen: Georg-August Universität.
Robano, V. and S.C. Smith. 2014. Multidimensional Targeting and Evaluation: A General Framework with an Application to a Poverty Program in Bangladesh. *Working Paper* 65: OPHI.

Roche, J.M. 2008. Monitoring Inequality among Social Groups: A Methodology Combining Fuzzy Set Theory and Principal Component Analysis. *Journal of Human Development and Capabilities* 9: 427–452.
Roche, J.M. 2013. Monitoring Progress in Child Poverty Reduction: Methodological Insights and Illustration to the Case Study of Bangladesh. *Social Indicators Research* 112: 363–390.
Roelen, K., F. Gassmann, and C. de Neubourg. 2009. The Importance of Choice and Definition for the Measurement of Child Poverty: The Case of Vietnam. *Child Indicators Research* 2: 245–263.
Roodman, D. 2011. Composite Indices. *Journal of Economic Inequality* 9: 483–484.
Rowntree, B.S. 1901. *Poverty: A Study of Town Life*. London: Macmillan.
Roy, I. 2011. 'New' Lists for 'Old': Re-Constructing the Poor in the BPL Census. *Economic and Political Weekly* 46: 82–91.
Ruggeri Laderchi, C. 1997. Poverty and Its Many Dimensions: The Role of Income as an Indicator. *Oxford Development Studies* 25: 345–360.
Ruggeri Laderchi, C., R. Saith, and F. Stewart. 2003. Does It Matter that We Don't Agree on the Definition of Poverty? A Comparison of Four Approaches. *Oxford Development Studies* 31: 243–274.
Runciman, W.G. 1967. *Relative Deprivation and Social Justice*. London: Routledge.
Sahn, D.E. and D. Stifel. 2000. Poverty Comparisons over Time and Across Countries in Africa. *World Development* 28: 2123–2155.
Saisana, M. and A. Saltelli. 2010. The Multidimensional Poverty Assessment Tool (MPAT): Robustness Issues and Critical Assessment. *Scientific and Technical Report JRC* 56806 (EUR 24310 EN). Publications Office of the European Union.
Samuelson, P.A. 1947. *Foundations of Economic Analysis*. Cambridge, MA: Harvard University Press.
Santos, M.E. 2013. Tracking Poverty Reduction in Bhutan: Income Deprivation Alongside Deprivation in Other Sources of Happiness. *Social Indicators Research* 112: 259–290.
Santos, M.E. and P. Villatoro. 2016 A Multidimensional Poverty Index for Latin America. *Review of Income and Wealth* DOI: 10.1111/roiw.12275.
Savaglio, E., S. Vannucci. 2007. Filtral Preorders and Opportunity Inequality. *Journal of Economic Theory* 132: 474–492.
Schreiner, M. 2002. Scoring: The Next Breakthrough in Microfinance? *Consultative Group to Assist the Poorest Occasional Paper*.
Schreiner, M. 2004. Benefits and Pitfalls of Statistical Credit Scoring for Microfinance. *Savings and Development* 28: 63–86.
Schreiner, M. 2006. A Simple Poverty Scorecard for Bangladesh. Report to Grameen Foundation.
Sen, A.K. 1974. Informational bases of Alternative Welfare Approaches : Aggregation and Income Distribution. *Journal of Public Economics* 3: 387–403.
Sen, A.K. 1976. Poverty: An Ordinal Approach to Measurement. *Econometrica* 44: 219–231.

Sen, A.K. 1979. Issues in the Measurement of Poverty. *Scandinavian Journal of Economics* 81: 285–307.

Sen, A.K. 1981. *Poverty and Famines*. Oxford: Clarendon Press.

Sen, A.K. 1987. *Standard of Living*. Cambridge: Cambridge University Press.

Sen, A.K. 1992. *Inequality Re-Examined.* Cambridge, MA: Harvard University Press.

Sen, A.K. 1993. Capability and Well-Being. In M.C. Nussbaum and A.K. Sen (eds.) *The Quality of Life.* Oxford: Oxford University Press, 9–29.

Sen, A.K. 1999. *Development as Freedom.* Oxford: Oxford University Press.

Shaffer, P. 2013. Ten Years' of "Q-Squared": Implications for Understanding and Explaining Poverty. *World Development* 45: 269–285.

Shaked, M. and G. Shanthikumar. 2006. *Stochastic Orders*. New York: Springer.

Sharan, M.R. 2011. Identifying BPL Households: A Comparison of Competing Approaches. *Economic and Political Weekly* 46: 256–262.

Shorrocks A.F. 1998. Deprivation Profiles and Deprivation Indices. In: S.P. Jenkins, A. Kapteyn, and B.M.S. Van Praag (eds.), 250–267.

Siani Tchouametieu, J.R. 2013. Has Poverty Decreased in Cameroon Between 2001 and 2007? An Analysis Based on Multidimensional Poverty Measures. *Economics Bulletin* 33: 3059–3069.

Siegel, M. and J. Waidler. 2012. Migration and Multidimensional Poverty in Moldovan Communities. *Eastern Journal of European Studies* 3: 105–119.

Silber, J. 2011. A Comment on the MPI Index. *Journal of Economic Inequality* 9: 479–481.

Silber, J. and G. Wan (eds.) 2016. *The Asian 'Poverty Miracle': Impressive Accomplishments or Incomplete Achievements?* Cheltenham: Edward Elgar.

Silber, J and G. Yalonetzky. 2014. Measuring Multidimensional Deprivation with Dichotomized and Ordinal Variables. In G. Betti and A. Lemmi (eds.) *Poverty and Social Exclusion: New Methods of Analysis.* London: Routledge, 9–37.

Smith, S.C. 2012. The Scope of NGOs and Development Programme Design: Applications to Problems of Multidimensional Poverty. *Public Administration and Development* 32: 357–370.

Spencer, B. and S. Fisher. 1992. On Comparing Distributions of Poverty Gaps. *Sankhya B. The Indian Journal of Statistics* 54: 114–126.

Stewart, F. 1985. *Basic Needs in Developing Countries.* Baltimore, MD: Johns Hopkins University Press.

Stewart, F., R. Saith, and B. Harris-White. 2007.*Definig Poverty in Developing Countries.* Basingstoke: Palgrave Macmillan.

Stifel, D. and L. Christiaensen. 2007. Tracking Poverty over Time in the Absence of Comparable Consumption Data. *World Bank Economic Review* 21: 317–341.

Stiglitz, J.E., A. Sen, and J.-P. Fitoussi .2009. *Report by the Commission on the Measurement of Economic Performance and Social Progress.* www.stiglitz-sen-fitoussi.fr.

Streeten, P., J.S. Burki, M.U. Haq, N. Hicks, and F. Stewart. 1981. *First Things First: Meeting Basic Human Needs in Developing Countries.* Oxford: Oxford University Press.

Subramanian, S. 2011. The Poverty Line: Getting It Wrong Again. *Economic and Political Weekly,* 46: 37–42.

Sundaram, K. 2003. On Identification of Households Below Poverty Line in BPL Census 2002: Some Comments on Proposed Methodology. *Economic and Political Weekly* 38: 896–901.

Svedberg, P. 2000. *Poverty and Undernutrition: Theory, Measurement and Policy.* Oxford: Oxford University Press.

Takayama, N. 1979. Poverty, Income Inequality, and Their Measures: Professor Sen's Axiomatic Approach Reconsidered. *Econometrica* 47: 747–760.

Tarozzi, A. and A. Deaton. 2009. Using Census and Survey Data to Estimate Poverty and Inequality for Small Areas. *Review of Economics and Statistics* 91: 773–792.

Thomas, B.K., R. Muradian, G. de Groot, and A. de Ruijter. 2009. Multidimensional Poverty and Identification of Poor Households: A Case from Kerala, India. *Journal of Human Development and Capabilities* 10: 237–257.

Thon, D. 1979. On Measuring Poverty. *Review of Income and Wealth* 25: 429–440.

Thorbecke, E. 2011. A Comment on Multidimensional Poverty Indices. *Journal of Economic Inequality* 9: 485–487.

Townsend, P. 1954. Measuring Poverty. *British Journal of Sociology* 5: 130–137.

Townsend, P. 1979. *Poverty in the United Kingdom: A Survey of Household Resources and Standards of Living.* London: Penguin Books.

Trani, J.-F., M. Biggeri, and V. Mauro. 2013. The Multidimensionality of Child Poverty: Evidence from Afghanistan. *Social Indicators Research* 112: 391–416.

Trani, J.-F. and T.I. Cannings. 2013. Child Poverty in an Emergency and Conflict Context: A Multidimensional Profile and Identification of the Poorest Children in Western Darfur. *World Development* 48: 48–70.

Tsui, K.-Y. 2002. Multidimensional Poverty Indices. *Social Choice and Welfare* 19: 69–93.

Tungodden B. 2005. Poverty Measurement: The Critical Comparison Value. *Social Choice and Welfare* 25: 75–84.

van Praag, B.M.S. and A. Ferrer-i-Carbonell. 2008. *A Multidimensional Approach to Subjective Poverty.* In N. Kakwani and J. Silber (eds.), 135–154.

Vélez, C.E. and M. Robles. (2008). Determining the Parameters of Axiomatically Derived Multidimensional Poverty Indices: An Application Based on Reported Well-Being in Colombia. In N. Kakwani and J. Silber (eds.) 210–225.

Vranken, J. 2002. Belgian Reports on Poverty. Paper Presented at the Conference "Reporting on Income Distribution and Poverty – Perspectives from a German and a European Point of View" organized by the Hans Böckler Stiftung, Berlin.

Wagle, U.R. 2008. *Multidimensional Poverty Measurement: Concepts and Applications.* New York: Springer.

Wagle, U.R. 2014. The Counting-Based Measurement of Multidimensional Poverty: The Focus on Economic Resources, Inner Capabilities and Relation Resources in the United States. *Social Indicators Research* 115: 223–240.

Watts, H. 1968. An Economic Definition of Poverty. In D.P. Moynihan (ed.) *On Understanding Poverty*. New York: Basic Books, 316–329.

Weymark, J.A. 1981. Generalized Gini Inequality Indices. *Mathematical Social Sciences* 1: 409–430.

Whelan, C.T., R. Layte, B. Maître, and B. Nolan. 2001. Income, Deprivation and Economic Stain: An Analysis of the European Community Household Panel. *European Sociological Review* 19: 357–372.

Whelan, C.T. and B. Maître. 2009. Europeanization of Inequality and European Reference Groups. *Journal of European Social Policy* 19: 117–130.

Whelan, C.T., B. Nolan, and B. Maître. 2014. Multidimensional Poverty Measurement in Europe: An Application of the Adjusted Headcount Approach. *Journal of European Social Policy* 24: 183–197.

Whitmore, G.A. 1970. Third Degree Stochastic Dominance. *American Economic Review* 60: 457–459.

Wolff, J. and A. De-Shalit. 2007. *Disadvantage*. New York: Oxford University Press.

World Bank. 2014. *World Development Indicators*. Washington, DC: World Bank.

Wright G. 2008. *Findings from the Indicators of Poverty and Social Exclusion Project: A Profile of Poverty using the Socially Perceived Necessities Approach*. Key Report 7. Pretoria: Department of Social Development.

Yaari, M.E. 1987. The Dual Theory of Choice under Risk. *Econometrica* 55:95–115.

Yalonetzky, G. 2013. Stochastic Dominance with Ordinal Variables: Conditions and a Test. *Econometric Reviews* 32: 126–163.

Yalonetzky, G. 2014. Conditions for the Most Robust Multidimensional Poverty Comparisons using Counting Measures and Ordinal Variables. *Social Choice and Welfare*, 43: 773–807.

Yitzhaki, S. 1979. Relative Deprivation and the Gini Coefficient. *Quarterly Journal of Economics* 93: 321–324.

Yu, J. 2013. Multidimensional Poverty in China: Findings Based on CNHS. *Social Indicators Research* 112: 315–316.

Zheng, B. 1997. Aggregate Poverty Measures. *Journal of Economic Surveys* 11: 123–162.

Zheng, B. 2000a. Minimum Distribution-Sensitivity, Poverty Aversion and Poverty Orderings. *Journal of Economic Theory* 95: 116–137.

Zheng B. 2000b. Poverty Orderings: A Review. *Journal of Economic Surveys* 14: 427–466.

Zheng, B. 2007a. Utility-Gap Dominances and Inequality Orderings. *Social Choice and Welfare* 28: 255–280.

Zheng, B. 2007b. Unit-Consistent Poverty Indices. *Economic Theory* 31: 113–142.

4

Fuzzy Set Approaches to the Measurement of Multidimensional Poverty

4.1 Introduction

It often becomes impossible to gain sufficient information on achievement levels in different dimensions of well-being. This, therefore, may make the poverty status of a person quite ambiguous. To understand this, consider a person who has sufficiently high income so that he can certainly be regarded as income-rich. It is likely that he will remain rich if his income reduces by a tiny amount. But if this tiny reduction process continues, he will be poor after some time. In the process of these sequential reductions, we may classify him as "marginally poor" or "borderline poor" at some stage. However, there may not be a clear borderline or line of demarcation that will unambiguously partition the population into sets of poor and rich. Therefore, the predicate "poor" may often involve vagueness. Often, the respondents may be reluctant to supply correct data on achievement levels, particularly, on income and wealth holdings. There can be a wide range of threshold limits for achievement levels, which may be socially acceptable. The possibility that there is lack of relevant information on achievement quantities indicates that there is a degree of unclearness in the concept of poverty.

Now, if there is some vagueness in a concept, then vagueness is preserved by a clear-cut representation of that ambiguous concept. Fuzzy set theory has been introduced an equipment for tackling problems in which uncertainty resulting from a sort of unclearness plays a major role (see Zadeh, 1965). Consequently, given that the notion of poverty itself is dubious, the poverty position of a person is intrinsically fuzzy. This in turn demonstrates that the fuzzy set approach to the measurement of poverty can be advocated logically. Given the multidimensionality of poverty, we can regard the problem as one of fuzzy capability deprivation. This contention is addressed in this chapter of the book.

For each dimension, there is no unique threshold limit that can identify whether the person is deprived or nondeprived in the dimension. Thus, there may be ambiguity in identifying the status of a person uniformly in a dimension. There is an interval such that the positions of a person are unambiguous

Analyzing Multidimensional Well-Being: A Quantitative Approach, First Edition. Satya R. Chakravarty.

when his achievement in the dimension lies above the upper limit and below the lower limit. More precisely, the person is unambiguously deprived or nondeprived depending on whether his achievement in the dimension lies below or above the respective threshold limit. Equivalently, if we arrange the individual achievement levels in the dimension nondecreasingly, then there is a partitioning of the population into subgroups with respect to dimensional achievement with clear presumption about the statuses of individual deprivations in the dimension in the first and third subgroups. In the second subgroup, the extent of deprivation of a person in the specified dimension is determined by employing a fuzzy membership function. This clear partitioning of the population shows that one of the innovative features of the fuzzy set approach lies at the stage of identifying the poor. By providing a systematic treatment of vagueness arising in the context of identification problem, the fuzzy set approach establishes its clear merit. Standard poverty measurement methodologies that rigidly dichotomize the population into the poor and nonpoor using threshold limits disregard any ambiguity that may emerge in connection with identification of the poor and hence cause loss of information.

Application of fuzzy sets to the measurement of poverty, which has already gained considerable popularity, was pioneered by Cerioli and Zani (1990). Further contributions along this line came from Chiappero-Martinetti (1994, 1996, 2000, 2008), Cheli and Lemmi (1995), Makdissi and Wodon (2004), Lelli (2001), Deutsch and Silber (2005, 2006), Baliamoune-Lutz and MacGillivray (2006), Bérenger and Celestini (2006), Betti et al. (2006a,b), Chakravarty (2006), Molnar et al. (2006), Miceli (2006), Panek (2006), Qizilbash (2006), Vero (2006), Bérenger and Verdier-Chouchane (2007), Betti and Verma (2008), Roche (2008), Amarante et al. (2010), Belhadj and Matoussi (2010), Clark and Hulme (2010), D'Ambrosio et al. (2011), Belhadj and Limam (2012), and Zheng (2015), and others. While some of these contributions deal with theoretical issues, the concern of others is empirical analysis across methodologies. The contribution by Makdissi and Wodon (2004) deals with a suggestion for fuzzy targeting applied to Chile. A recent survey by Alkire et al. (2015) provides a critical evaluation of some methodological aspects.

It may be worthwhile to mention here that apart from the measurement of poverty, the theory of fuzzy sets has been applied to many areas of research, including, learning (Wee and Fu, 1969), philosophy (Goguen, 1969), control systems (Zadeh, 1965), linguistics (Lee and Zadeh, 1969), management science (Bellman and Zadeh, 1970), income inequality (Basu, 1987 and Ok, 1996), and social choice theory (Mordeson et al., 2015).

The next section of the chapter presents an analytical discussion on the fuzzy membership function that quantifies the degree of belongingness of a person to the poverty population. As we will observe, there can be many choices of membership functions. It is, therefore, necessary to justify a particular choice using intuitively reasonable arguments. This matter is also a subject of discussion of the section. The concern of Section 4.3 is the set of axioms for a fuzzy multidimensional poverty index. These axioms are fuzzy twins to their nonfuzzy sisters. Section 4.4 analyzes some examples of fuzzy multidimensional poverty indices. It may be necessary to verify if these indices satisfy these properties. As we will observe, satisfaction of the basic properties by the proposed indices will narrow down the choice of membership functions. While the general functional form scrutinized in this section is insensitive to a correlation increasing switch, we also analyze an index using the Bourguignon–Chakravarty aggregation criterion that clearly indicates sensitivity to such a switch.

Often, it may be worthwhile to investigate whether one population is characterized by no more poverty compared to another for a given membership function. In other words, for a given membership function, the objective is to establish dominance conditions under which one distribution does not have higher poverty compared to another for all fuzzy poverty indices. In such a case, for this membership function, it is not necessary to calculate the values of the poverty indices to rank distributions in terms of poverty. Once the dominance conditions hold, we can clearly infer if one distribution has no more poverty compared to another. A similar line of investigation is to order distributions in terms of fuzzy poverty for a class of membership functions when the poverty index is given. A worthwhile exercise here is poverty ranking of distributions when both membership functions and poverty indices are allowed to vary. Following Zheng (2015), we investigate these issues in Section 4.5 when income is taken as the only dimension of well-being.

4.2 Fuzzy Membership Function

Before presenting an analytical discussion on the fuzzy membership function, the degree of membership of a person of the poor population, we give some simple examples to illustrate how vagueness arises often in different situations. Consider a heap of very small stone chips. If one chip is taken away from this pile, it still remains a heap. If we continue this "taking away" job with patience, then at the last but one step, only one chip will be left, which definitely does not constitute a heap. Evidently, at some stage of this "taking away" assignment, the pile became a "borderline" heap. But precise formulation of this "borderline" notion may not be unambiguous, which clearly indicates the presence of imprecision here. As pointed out in Keefe and Smith (1996) and Qizilbash (2006), such a vague predicate possesses three characteristics: it includes "borderline" positions, where one cannot decide emphatically between "heap" and "not heap"; a sharp boundary between "heap" and "not heap" cannot be drawn; and the presence of Sorties paradox – reducing the size of the heap by one chip keeps the pile "heap" but repeating the same step many times will make the pile "heap" or "not heap." For the linguistic variable "tall," we cannot assuredly distinguish between "tall" and "not tall" in borderline situations; a clear barrier between "tall" and "not tall" cannot be built; and the Sortie paradox holds. This clearly demonstrates that "tall" is a vague predicate. Similar remarks apply also to the linguistic variable "bald." Human qualities such as "being nice," "politeness," "generosity" can as well be regarded as vague predicates.

In the "income-rich" example we considered in Section 4.1, since the notion of "poverty" fulfils all the three criteria discussed earlier, it is a vague predicate (Qizilbash, 2006). Vagueness is also relevant to the predicate "poor" in the multidimensional framework. We assume that there is no ambiguity with respect to definition of the identification of the poor. To illustrate the situation, let us assume that there are only two dimensions of well-being, income and nourishment. As Sen (1981, p. 13) argued, nutritional requirement is a rather imprecise concept. Following Chiappero-Martinetti (2006), we assume that for the dimension "nourishment," possible specifications of "being nourished" ranked in increasing order are as follows: (i) starvation, (ii) very seriously undernourished, (iii) malnourishment, (iv) almost achievement of minimum calorie intake, (v) achievement of minimum calorie intake without fully balanced diet, (vi) achievement of minimum calorie intake with quite balanced diet, and (vii) achievement of nutritional level intake and balanced diet. It should be clear that a sharp difference between two consecutive specifications can barely be appropriated using some threshold. Thus, here also we recognize the presence of vagueness.

To formulate and discuss the membership function rigorously, we follow the notation adopted in Chapters 1 and 3. As in Chapters 1, 2, and 3, the number of persons in the society is denoted by $n \geq 1$ and the number of dimensions of well-being is $d \geq 2$. We denote the set of all dimensions $\{1, 2, \dots, d\}$ by Q. The achievement of any person i in dimension j, denoted by $x_{ij} \geq 0$, is the (i, j)th entry of an $n \times d$ achievement matrix $X \in M^n$, where $n \in N$ is arbitrary and $M \in \{M_1, M_2, M_3\}$ (see Chapter 1). Person i is a member of a crisp population set for dimension j if his achievement in the dimension falls below the corresponding threshold limit, that is, if he is deprived in the dimension. Recall from Chapter 3 that in such a case, we can partition $[0, \infty)$, the domain of definition of achievement in dimension j, as $[0, z_j) \cup [z_j, \infty)$, where, as before, $z_j > 0$ is the threshold limit for the dimension. The deprivation status of a person i in dimension j can be indicated using a two-valued characteristic function $\mathfrak{J}_j : [0, z_j) \cup [z_j, \infty) \to \{0, 1\}$ defined as follows:

$$\mathfrak{J}_j(x_{ij}) = \begin{cases} 1 & \text{if } x_{ij} < z_j, \\ 0 & \text{if } x_{ij} \geq z_j. \end{cases}$$

Thus, while for a person who is deprived in dimension j, the characteristic function $\mathfrak{J}_j$ assigns the value 1; for a nondeprived person, the assigned value is 0. Since person i is arbitrary in the population set, it follows that the characteristic function explicitly dichotomizes the entire population into two subgroups that are respectively deprived and nondeprived with respect to dimension j. In the case of income poverty, the characteristic function partitions the population into income-poor and -rich subgroups.

As we have argued, in the multidimensional framework, the job of making distinction between deprived and nondeprived in a dimension often becomes difficult. Unambiguity in poverty measurement can be captured using a poverty membership function, which assigns the value 0 or 1 when there is complete information that the person is nondeprived or deprived in the dimension. However, when there is lack of perfect information arising from uncertainty, on a person's deprivation status in the dimension, the membership function counts him as partially deprived by assigning a number lying between 0 and 1.

Note that the magnitudes of x_{ij} vary over the interval $[0, \infty)$, and doubtfulness regarding deprivation position of a person in the dimension emerges for denominations of x_{ij} for which he is neither deprived nor nondeprived unambiguously. Then, given that deprivation is a decreasing function of x_{ij}, it must be the situation that there exists an interval (z_j^l, z_j^u), a nonempty subset of $[0, \infty)$, such that the person is unequivocally deprived or nondeprived for x_{ij} quantities not above z_j^l or not below z_j^u. In other words, we need to specify two achievement quantities z_j^l and z_j^u such that any person with achievement not more than z_j^l will be counted as certainly deprived in dimension j and any person with achievement not less than z_j^u will be unambiguously treated as nondeprived in the dimension. For any x_{ij} quantity in the interval (z_j^l, z_j^u), a partial degree of certainty about the stature of a person in terms of deprivation is specified by assigning a number between 0 and 1, and in such a case, we say that person i is partially deprived in dimension j. This numbering assignment is done by the fuzzy membership function, which is at the core of the fuzzy poverty measurement. The specification of the membership function relies on the source of fuzziness. We can refer to z_j^l and z_j^u as respectively the lower and upper fuzzy boundaries for dimension j. The vector $((z_1^l, z_1^u), (z_2^l, z_2^u), \dots, (z_d^l, z_d^u))$ of ordered pairs of lower and upper fuzzy boundaries taken together for all the dimensions is denoted by z^{lu}, which is assumed to be an element of Z^{lu}, a finite set of vectors of d ordered pairs, where each number of a pair is positive and the second number is greater than the first number. That is, $z^{lu} \in Z^{lu}$.

Since the interval (z_j^l, z_j^u), which we refer to as fuzzy poverty region for dimension j, is open, we have $z_j^l < z_j^u$. Otherwise, $z_j^l = z_j^u$, in which case, we have the standard multidimensional framework characterized by a unique threshold limit for each dimension. The domain $[0, \infty)$ of x_{ij} quantities can now be represented in terms of the union of three nonoverlapping sets as $[0, \infty) = [0, z_j^l] \cup (z_j^l, z_j^u) \cup [z_j^u, \infty)$.

We can summarize the earlier discussion on the values of an arbitrary membership function in the following definition:

Definition 4.1 A continuous, decreasing function $\mu_j : [0, z_j^l] \cup (z_j^l, z_j^u) \cup [z_j^u, \infty) \to [0, 1]$ is called a fuzzy membership function for dimension j if it satisfies the following assumptions:

$$\mu_j(x_{ij}) = \begin{cases} 1 \quad \text{if } x_{ij} \leq z_j^l, \\ h(x_{ij}, z_j^l, z_j^u), 0 < h(x_{ij}, z_j^l, z_j^u) < 1, \quad \text{if } z_j^l < x_{ij} < z_j^u, \\ 0, \quad \text{if } x_{ij} \geq z_j^u. \end{cases} \tag{4.1}$$

Evidently, the function h is the restriction of μ_j on (z_j^l, z_j^u), that is, $\mu_j(x_{ij}) = h(x_{ij}, z_j^l, z_j^u)$ for $z_j^l < x_{ij} < z_j^u$. Thus, for person i who is partially deprived in dimension j, $0 < \mu_j(x_{ij}) < 1$. By expressing h as a function of (x_{ij}, z_j^l, z_j^u), we recognize that for any achievement $x_{ij} \in (z_j^l, z_j^u)$, the membership grade $\mu_j(x_{ij})$ will depend on the achievement quantity itself and the lower and upper bounds z_j^l and z_j^u of the set (z_j^l, z_j^u). Continuity of the membership function ensures that negligible observational errors on achievement denominations will not give rise to steep changes in the value of the membership function. Decreasingness of the membership function reflects the view that as the quantity of achievement increases, the extent of deprivation decreases. Clearly, h is continuous and decreasing on (z_j^l, z_j^u). By continuity, as $x_{ij} \to z_j^l$, $h(x_{ij}, z_j^l, z_j^u) \to \mu_j(z_j^l) = 1$ and as $x_{ij} \to z_j^u$, $h(x_{ij}, z_j^l, z_j^u) \to \mu_j(z_j^u) = 0$. The function μ_j is homogeneous of degree 0 over the domain $[0, z_j^l] \cup [z_j^u, \infty)$. Clearly, Definition 4.1 enables us to say that $\mu_j(x_{ij})$ specifies the degree of belongingness of person i in the deprivation range of dimension j, where the deprivation range for any dimension is given by $\{0\} \cup (0, 1) \cup \{1\}$, the range of the function μ_j.

For each value of h, there corresponds a different membership function. The choice of the value of h is a matter of value judgment. Observe that we maintain the extreme conditions $\mu_j(x_{ij}) = 1$ if $x_{ij} \leq z_j^l$ and $\mu_j(x_{ij}) = 0$, if $x_{ij} \geq z_j^u$ as two defining conditions. This is not unrealistic because we have a clear idea about the extent of deprivation in these extreme cases, whereas our idea about the same is quite unclear in the intermediate region (z_j^l, z_j^u). Corresponding to each membership function, there will be a different fuzzy poverty index. Each index will be directly related to its associated membership function.

Two major concerns for poverty indices based on membership functions are the lower and upper bounds z_j^l and z_j^u. Selection of these bounds of the fuzzy poverty region (z_j^l, z_j^u) is a challenging job in this situation. Following Zheng (2015), we discuss here an illustrative example put forward for income poverty. In the European Income and Living Conditions survey, a household is requested to report "the very lowest net monthly income" that it would require for making "ends meet." Suppose that this monthly income, denoted by z, is interpreted as the income poverty line that each household regards. Let $v(z)$ be the cumulative proportion of voters in the society who believe that the income poverty line is less than or equal to z. Hence, $(1 - v(z))$ is the proportion of voters who opine that the income poverty line should be at least z. Then the minimum value of z that has been elected by the voters can be taken as z^l_{IN}, the lower bound of fuzzy income poverty region. On the other hand, z^u_{IN}, the upper bound of the fuzzy income poverty territory, can be taken as the maximum value of z chosen by the voters.

In some rich countries, such as in Western European countries, the income poverty line is taken as some proportion of the median income. In a society, individuals with incomes less than the median income may regard the median as a reference income, an income level with which they compare their own incomes and suffer from depression from a feeling that their incomes are lower. (The median of a nondecreasingly ordered n-person income distribution u^0 with odd number of observations is the $\left(\frac{n+1}{2}\right)$ th observation, the middle-most income. If the number of incomes is even, then the median is defined as the arithmetic mean of the $\left(\frac{n}{2}\right)$ th and $\left(\frac{n}{2}+1\right)$ th incomes.[1])

All individuals whose incomes belong to some small income range $(\text{me}(x) - \varepsilon, \text{me}(x) + \varepsilon)$ around the median are said to constitute the middle class of the society, where $\text{me}(x)$ is the median income and $\varepsilon > 0$ is small. It is highly likely that a poor person's reference group in a society is the middle class of the society. Now, a rich and large middle class is highly beneficial to the society in view of the high extent of its contribution to society's economic growth, education, public goods through provision of higher taxes, and so on. Therefore, a person with income less than the median income may regard the middle class as his targeted group since living conditions will be better then. The lower and upper limits of this income range, $\text{me}(x) - \varepsilon$ and $\text{me}(x) + \varepsilon$, may be considered as the lower and upper bounds z^l_{IN} and z^u_{IN}, of fuzzy income poverty domain. (See Chakravarty (2015, Chapter 2), for further discussion.) These discussions can be extended to the other dimensions of well-being under appropriate modifications.

In the general functional form, specified in (4.1), if $z^l_j = \min_i\{x_{ij}\}$ and $z^u_j = \max_i\{x_{ij}\}$, then the inequalities $x_{ij} \le z^l_j$ and $x_{ij} \ge z^u_j$ have to be replaced with the perfect equalities $x_{ij} = \min_i\{x_{ij}\}$ and $x_{ij} = \max_i\{x_{ij}\}$. In such a case, the ambiguous destitution domain for dimension j becomes $(\min_i\{x_{ij}\}, \max_i\{x_{ij}\})$.

Since estimation of fuzzy poverty indices relies on the choice of the membership functions, it is certainly necessary to justify the use of specific

1 For instance, if the distribution is $u^0 = (3, 9, 12)$, then the median is 9, the middle-most income, and if $u^0 = (5, 9, 15, 20)$, then the median of u^0 is 12, the arithmetic mean of 9 and 15.

membership functions. We briefly discuss here some suggestions made by Chiappero-Martinetti (2006) along this line. As we have argued earlier, in the case of (4.1), the choice of an explicit membership function will depend on the value of $h(x_{ij}, z_j^l, z_j^u)$. Such a choice is a matter of value judgment. For instance, if we assume that reduction in its value resulting from an increase in achievement is independent of the initial magnitude of achievement, then it implicitly represents the value judgment that $h(x_{ij}, z_j^l, z_j^u)$ is linear. Membership functions may be obtained from empirical evidence. One such example is the totally fuzzy and relative function, which we discuss later in greater length. This function, introduced by Cheli and Lemmi (1995), has its membership values dependent on the relative positions of the individuals in the distribution of the achievements in the dimension. A third way of choosing a membership function is to take opinions of external experts. For instance, doctors and dieticians may be requested to classify nutritional levels. The subjective questionnaire method, similar to that adopted by the European Income and Living Conditions survey, can also be an alternative move for selecting grades of a membership function.

We may explain the role of a membership function further using literacy as a dimension of well-being. In a household, a person is either literate or illiterate, where a literate person is assumed to be one who can read and write with grasp in some language. Often, an illiterate in a family can get literacy benefit if there are one or more literates in the family. For instance, such a situation arises if the illiterate is required to fill in some form. Following Basu and Foster (1998), we can refer to such a person as a proximate illiterate. On the other hand, if there is no literate person in a family, then a member of the family is called isolated illiterate. If we assign the number 1 or 0 depending on whether a person in a household is isolated illiterate or literate, then we can indicate the illiteracy grade of a proximate illiterate by a number a lying between 0 and 1, that is, $a \in (0, 1)$. The value of the pure positive fraction a depends on several external factors, including attitude and availability of literates in the family to help illiterates literally. As these external factors become more favorable to him, the value of $a \in (0, 1)$ should be lower for him. This indicates that the concept of proximate illiterate involves some factors, which themselves are dubious. In view of this, we can regard it as a fuzzy concept. The corresponding membership function takes on the value 0 or 1 depending on whether a person is literate or isolated illiterate. If the person is a proximate illiterate, then the membership grade is a number lying between 0 and 1. The fuzzy deprivation range for the dimension literacy is, therefore, given by (0, 1).

De Luca and Termini (1972) raised the interesting question of measuring the extent of fuzziness of a fuzzy set. Smithson (1982) argued that some transformation of a measure of variability of membership grades can be employed for measuring the level of fuzziness. A unified approach to this issue has been developed by Chakravarty and Roy (1985). Since in this chapter we are dealing with fuzzy multidimensional poverty, we only need to be concerned with the relevance of a membership function to the poverty measurement problem.

We now present some illustrations of membership functions that drop out as particular cases of the general membership function μ_j given by (4.1). For $h(x_{ij}, z_j^l, z_j^u) = \left(\frac{z_j^u - x_{ij}}{z_j^u - z_j^l}\right)^{\alpha_j}$, $\mu_j^C(x_{ij})$ reduces to the form suggested by Chakravarty (2006), where $\alpha_j > 1$ is a constant. The explicit form of this membership function is given by

$$\mu_j^C(x_{ij}) = \begin{cases} 1 & \text{if } x_{ij} \le z_j^l, \\ \left(\dfrac{z_j^u - x_{ij}}{z_j^u - z_j^l}\right)^{\alpha_j}, \alpha_j > 1, & \text{if } z_j^l < x_{ij} < z_j^u \\ 0, & \text{if } x_{ij} \ge z_j^u. \end{cases} \tag{4.2}$$

As we will see next, the parametric restriction $\alpha_j > 1$ can be justified in terms of satisfaction of several fuzzy poverty axioms. For $\alpha_j = 1$, (4.2) coincides with the Cerioli and Zani (1990) trapezoidal function given by

$$\mu_j^{CZ}(x_{ij}) = \begin{cases} 1 & \text{if } x_{ij} \le z_j^l, \\ \left(\dfrac{z_j^u - x_{ij}}{z_j^u - z_j^l}\right), & \text{if } z_j^l < x_{ij} < z_j^u, \\ 0, & \text{if } x_{ij} \ge z_j^u. \end{cases} \tag{4.3}$$

While μ_j^{CZ} is linear in achievement quantities over the uncertain poverty space, μ_j^C is strictly convex there. Thus, although for (4.2), the reduction in the membership grade resulting from an increase in achievement denomination in the territory (z_j^l, z_j^u) takes place at an increasing rate, for (4.3), the corresponding change occurs at a constant rate.

An alternative of interest arises from the stipulation $h(x_{ij}, z_j^l, z_j^u) = 1 - \left(\frac{(x_{ij} - z_j^u)}{(z_j^u - z_j^l)}\right)^{e_j}$, where $0 < e_j < 1$. In such a case, the resulting membership function turns out to be

$$\mu_j^{Ch}(x_{ij}) = \begin{cases} 1 & \text{if } x_{ij} \le z_j^l, \\ 1 - \left(\dfrac{x_{ij} - z_j^l}{z_j^u - z_j^l}\right)^{e_j}, & \text{if } z_j^l < x_{ij} < z_j^u, \\ 0, & \text{if } x_{ij} \ge z_j^u. \end{cases} \tag{4.4}$$

One similarity of μ_j^{Ch} with μ_j^{C} is its strict convexity on the fuzzy poverty territory in the achievement extent. The last of the three membership functions (4.2)–(4.4) expresses membership grades over the fuzzy region in terms of the excess $(x_{ij} - z_j^l)$ of achievement x_{ij} over the lower fuzzy limit z_j^l as a fraction of the length $(z_j^u - z_j^l)$ of the fuzzy region (z_j^l, z_j^u). This ensures homogeneity of degree 0 of the membership function over the entire domain. This common property of the three functions guarantees that the membership grades remain invariant if we change the unit of measurement of achievement quantities and the lower and upper fuzzy boundaries. Thus, if we convert the unit of energy consumption from calorie into joule, the membership grades of the dimension "energy" does not alter. Another characteristic of these membership functions is that they are translatable of degree 0 or translation invariant, which says that for an equal absolute change in the achievements and the fuzzy boundaries, the membership grades do not change. Hence, if each person's income and fuzzy income limits reduce by \$0.4, then the membership grades remain unaltered.

For an appropriate choice of $h(x_{ij}, z_j^l, z_j^u)$ in the fuzzy region (z_j^l, z_j^u), (4.1) generates the following specification of the membership function, which is a member of the class constructed by Dombi (1990, Theorem 2):

$$\mu_j^D(x_{ij}) = \begin{cases} 1 \quad \text{if } x_{ij} \le z_j^l, \\ \dfrac{(z_j^u - x_{ij})^2}{(x_{ij} - z_j^l)^2 + (z_j^u - x_{ij})^2}, \quad \text{if } \; z_j^l < x_{ij} < z_j^u, \\ 0, \quad \text{if } x_{ij} \ge z_j^u. \end{cases} \tag{4.5}$$

The function μ_j^D is unambiguously decreasing over the hazy slot (z_j^l, z_j^u), but it initially decreases at a decreasing rate and then decreases at an increasing rate. In other words, there exists a number $\zeta \in (z_j^l, z_j^u)$, such that it is strictly concave over (z_j^l, ζ) and strictly convex over (ζ, z_j^l). Equivalently, we say that this function has an inverted S-shape.

In the totally fuzzy and relative approach, advocated by Cheli and Lemmi (1995), the membership function for dimension j, μ_j^{TFR}, is defined as the shortfall of the dimension's distribution function F_j from its maximum attainable value so that it equals 1 for the poorest and 0 for the richest. Formally,

$$\mu_j^{TFR}(x_{ij}) = \begin{cases} 1 \quad \text{if } x_{ij} = \min_i\{x_{ij}\}, \\ 1 - F_j(x_{ij}), \quad \text{if } \min_i\{x_{ij}\} < x_{ij} < \max_i\{x_{ij}\}, \\ 0, \quad \text{if } x_{ij} = \max_i\{x_{ij}\}. \end{cases} \tag{4.6}$$

Thus, in this case, $h(x_{ij}, z_j^l, z_j^u) = 1 - F_j(x_{ij})$. Since a distribution function may not be increasing, although nondecreasing, μ_j^{TFR} is nonincreasing, if not decreasing, over the sphere $(\min_i\{x_{ij}\}, \max_i\{x_{ij}\})$. In addition, μ_j^{TFR} need not be continuous, since a monotone function has at most a countable number of points of discontinuity. If $\min_i\{x_{ij}\} = 0$, then the fuzzy sphere here should be $(0, \max_i\{x_{ij}\})$.

As we have argued earlier, the selection of a particular membership function may contemplate some value judgments implicit in the theoretical notion that we wish to delineate. One way of judging the choice of a particular form of the membership function is to develop an axiomatic characterization of the function so that the axioms represent the underlying subjective evaluation. An attempt along this line was made in Chakravarty (2006), where the linear membership function (4.3) has been characterized axiomatically.

4.3 Axioms for a Fuzzy Multidimensional Poverty Index

The objective of this section is to propose and analyze some desirable properties for fuzzy set theory–based poverty indices. Most of these properties, which we refer to as fuzzy poverty axioms, are fuzzy dittos to the multidimensional poverty axioms considered in Chapter 3.

Given that there are d dimensions of well-being and μ_j represents the fuzzy membership function for dimension j, we write $\boldsymbol{\mu}$ for the vector $(\mu_1, \mu_2, \dots, \mu_d)$ of membership functions when all the dimensions are considered together. Let M^F stand for the set of d dimensional vectors of membership functions, that is, $M^F = \{\boldsymbol{\mu} = (\mu_1, \mu_2, \dots, \mu_d) | \mu_j$ is the membership function for dimension $j \in Q\}$. For any achievement matrix X, let $\pi^p(X; z^{lu}; \boldsymbol{\mu})$ denote the set of persons who are only partially deprived in X. Formally, $\pi^p(X; z^{lu}; \boldsymbol{\mu}) = \{i \in \{1, 2, \dots, n\} | 0 < \mu_j(x_{ij}) < 1$ for at least one $j \in Q\}$. Similarly, $\pi^c(X; z^{lu}; \boldsymbol{\mu}) = \{i \in \{1, 2, \dots, n\} | \mu_j(x_{ij}) = 1$ for at least one $j \in Q\}$ stands for the set of persons who are only certainly deprived in X. The sets of partially and certainly deprived persons in X corresponding to dimension j are respectively $\pi_j^p(X; (z_j^l, z_j^u); \mu_j) = \{i \in \{1, 2, \dots, n\} | 0 < \mu_j(x_{ij}) < 1\}$ and $\pi_j^c(X; (z_j^l, z_j^u); \mu_j) = \{i \in \{1, 2, \dots, n\} | \mu_j(x_{ij}) = 1\}$. The set of dimensions in which person i is certainly deprived is given by $\{j \in Q | \mu_j(x_{ij}) = 1\}$. Then $d_i^c(X) = |\{j \in Q | \mu_j(x_{ij}) = 1\}|$ indicates the number of dimensions in which person i is certainly deprived in X.

We follow the union method of identification of the poor. That is, a person i will be called fuzzy multidimensionally poor if he is deprived in at least one dimension, certainly or partially. Accordingly, the set $\pi^F(X; z^{lu}; \boldsymbol{\mu})$ of fuzzy poor persons in the society with the distribution matrix X is the union of the nonoverlapping sets $\pi^p(X; z^{lu}; \boldsymbol{\mu})$ and $\pi^c(X; z^{lu}; \boldsymbol{\mu})$. More precisely, $\pi^F(X; z^{lu}; \boldsymbol{\mu}) = \pi^p(X; z^{lu}; \boldsymbol{\mu}) \cup \pi^c(X; z^{lu}; \boldsymbol{\mu})$. Consequently, the number of fuzzy poor persons in X is $|\pi^F(X;z^{lu};\boldsymbol{\mu})| = |\pi^p(X;z^{lu};\boldsymbol{\mu})| + |\pi^c(X;z^{lu};\boldsymbol{\mu})|$. If for some pair $(i,j) \in \{1,2,\dots,n\} \times \{1,2,\dots,d\}$, there is at least one dimension j such that $z_j^l < x_{ij} < z_j^u$, which is the same as the requirement that $0 < \mu_j(x_{ij}) < 1$, and for no dimension, person i is certainly deprived, then we can call him strictly fuzzy poor, where $n \in N$ is arbitrary. We can also refer to this person as possibly multidimensionally poor, but not certainly poor. Clearly, $|\pi^F(X;z^{lu};\boldsymbol{\mu})| \le n$. The fuzzy head-count ratio in X, the proportion of fuzzy poor persons in X, is then given by $H^F(X;z^{lu};\boldsymbol{\mu}) = \frac{|\pi^F(X;z^{lu};\boldsymbol{\mu})|}{n}$. If all the deprived persons' achievements are in the corresponding fuzzy spaces, then $|\pi^c(X;z^{lu};\boldsymbol{\mu})| = 0$ so that $H^F(X;z^{lu};\boldsymbol{\mu})$ reduces to its strict fuzzy version $H^{SF}(X;z^{lu};\boldsymbol{\mu}) = \frac{|\pi^p(X;z^{lu};\boldsymbol{\mu})|}{n}$, the strict fuzzy head-count ratio. Then $H^{FA}(X;z^{lu};\boldsymbol{\mu}) = \frac{|\pi^F(X;z^{lu};\boldsymbol{\mu})|}{nd}$ and $H^{SFA}(X;z^{lu};\boldsymbol{\mu}) = \frac{|\pi^p(X;z^{lu};\boldsymbol{\mu})|}{nd}$ stand respectively for the dimension adjusted fuzzy head-count and its strict version.[2] We can also define here the fuzzy head-count ratio in dimension j as $H_j^F(X;(z_j^l,z_j^u);\mu_j) = \frac{|\pi_j^p(X;(z_j^l,z_j^u);\mu_j)|+|\pi_j^c(X;(z_j^l,z_j^u);\mu_j)|}{n}$ and its strict form as $H_j^{SF}(X;(z_j^l,z_j^u);\mu_j) = \frac{|\pi_j^p(X;(z_j^l,z_j^u);\mu_j)|}{n}$. Their dimension-adjusted varieties are respectively $H_j^{FA}(X;(z_j^l,z_j^u);\mu_j) = \frac{|\pi_j^p(X;(z_j^l,z_j^u);\mu_j)|+|\pi_j^c(X;(z_j^l,z_j^u);\mu_j)|}{nd}$ and $H_j^{SFA}(X;(z_j^l,z_j^u);\mu_j) = \frac{|\pi_j^p(X;(z_j^l,z_j^u);\mu_j)|}{nd}$. Obviously, for any $n \in N$, $X \in M^n$, $z^{lu} \in Z^{lu}$, $\boldsymbol{\mu} \in \boldsymbol{M}^F$, $H^{SFA}(X;z^{lu};\boldsymbol{\mu}) \le H^{SF}(X;z^{lu};\boldsymbol{\mu}) \le H^F(X;z^{lu};\boldsymbol{\mu})$, $H^{SFA}(X;z^{lu};\boldsymbol{\mu}) \le H^{FA}(X;z^{lu};\boldsymbol{\mu})$. Similarly, for any $n \in N$, $X \in M^n$, $z^{lu} \in Z^{lu}$, $\boldsymbol{\mu} \in \boldsymbol{M}^F$ and $j \in Q$, $H_j^{SFA}(X;(z_j^l,z_j^u);\mu_j) \le H_j^{SF}(X;(z_j^l,z_j^u);\mu_j) \le H_j^F(X;(z_j^l,z_j^u);\mu_j)$ and $H_j^{SFA}(X;(z_j^l,z_j^u);\mu_j) \le H_j^{FA}(X;(z_j^l,z_j^u);\mu_j)$.

In order to distinguish the fuzzy approach from the standard approach, unless specified, we assume, throughout the chapter, that at least a person in the society is strictly fuzzy multidimensionally poor, that is, at least one person i is partially deprived in at least one dimension j. In other words, there exists at least one pair $(i,j) \in \{1,2,\dots,n\} \times \{1,2,\dots,d\}$ such that $z_j^l < x_{ij} < z_j^u$ indicating that $0 < \mu_j(x_{ij}) < 1$. Person i may be unambiguously deprived in one or more dimensions, but if none of his achievements is in the fuzzy space of a deprived dimension, then he is definitely poor but not strictly fuzzy poor. Therefore, if achievements in deprived dimensions of all the poor are below the corresponding fuzzy lower boundaries, the problem becomes one of standard poverty measurement.

By a fuzzy multidimensional poverty index P^F, we mean a nonconstant nonnegative real-valued function defined on the Cartesian product $M \times Z^{lu} \times \boldsymbol{M}^F$. More precisely, $P^F : M \times Z^{lu} \times \boldsymbol{M}^F \to \mathfrak{R}_+^1$, where $\mathfrak{R}_+^1$ is the nonnegative part of the set of real numbers $\mathfrak{R}^1$. For any $n \in N$, $X \in M^n$, $z^{lu} \in Z^{lu}$, $\boldsymbol{\mu} \in \boldsymbol{M}^F$, $P^F(X;z^{lu};\boldsymbol{\mu})$ determines the extent of poverty associated with the distribution

2 Zheng (2015) considers income as the only dimension of well-being and refers to our strict head-count ratio as the fuzzy head-count ratio.

matrix X, the vector of ordered pairs of fuzzy boundaries z^{lu}, and the vector of membership functions $\boldsymbol{\mu}$. By nonconstancy, P^F is assumed to take at least two different values. Otherwise, it becomes insensitive to achievement levels of the poor. A constant index P^F will assign the same value to all distribution matrices with the same dimensions, irrespective of whether the achievements are equal or not equal across individuals and dimensions.

The selection of a particular index of poverty will depend on the purpose we have in mind. For instance, suppose that we are interested in investigating how a poverty index changes under an increase in an achievement of a person in the fuzzy region of the corresponding dimension. This increase in achievement may be a consequence of improvement in some positive external factors that influence the membership grades. Similarly, it may be worthwhile to check how a poverty index responds following an increase in the membership grades in the fuzzy region of a dimension. Such changes in the membership grades may represent a policy evaluator's opinion on susceptibility about fuzziness in the dimension. In all these cases, we need some particular poverty indices that we have not analyzed in earlier chapters. We may also be interested in intersociety poverty comparisons for given membership functions and fuzzy boundaries and identifying subgroups and or dimensions that affect fuzzy poverty more.

As in Chapters 1, 2, and 3, following Chakravarty and Lugo (2016), we will subdivide the presentation of the relevant axioms into several subsections. First, we analyze the invariance postulates.

4.3.1 Invariance Axioms

The first invariance axiom, we discuss, is fuzzy ratio-scale invariance, which demands that the extent of poverty remains unaltered if there are changes in the units of measurement of achievement quantities.

4.3.1.1 Fuzzy Strong Ratio-Scale Invariance

For all $n \in N$, $X \in M^n, z^{lu} \in Z^{lu}$, $\boldsymbol{\mu} \in \boldsymbol{M}^F$, $P^F(X; z^{lu}; \boldsymbol{\mu}) = P^F(X\Omega; ((\eta_1 z_1^l, \eta_1 z_1^u), (\eta_2 z_2^l, \eta_2 z_2^u), \ldots, (\eta_d z_d^l, \eta_d z_d^u)); \boldsymbol{\mu})$, where $\Omega = \text{diag}(\eta_1, \eta_2, \ldots, \eta_d)$, $\eta_i > 0$ for all i.

The fuzzy strong ratio-scale invariance axiom requires that the distribution matrix, upon postmultiplication by a diagonal matrix accompanied by the condition that the fuzzy demarcation lines are also multiplied by the corresponding proportionality factors, does not change the extent of fuzzy poverty. In other words, fuzzy poverty remains invariant under positive proportional changes in achievements and fuzzy boundaries. As a result, if we change the units of measurements of dimensional quantities and fuzzy limits, the degree of poverty does not change. The scales of proportionalities need not be the same across dimensions because different achievements and hence fuzzy boundaries may have different units of measurements. This axiom is the fuzzy twin of the corresponding inequality axiom. A weaker form of this axiom is fuzzy ratio-scale invariance, which requires equality of proportionality factors across dimensions (see Chapter 2). A fuzzy poverty index satisfying the fuzzy ratio-scale invariance axiom is called a relative index.

In order to illustrate this axiom, let us assume that there are three dimensions of well-being, namely daily energy consumption by an adult male, per capita income, and life expectancy, measured respectively in calories, dollars, and years. With these three dimensions of well-being, we consider the following matrix X_1 as an example of a social matrix in a four-person economy:

$$X_1 = \begin{bmatrix} 2700 & 59.4 & 400 \\ 2500 & 65 & 900 \\ 2700 & 59.5 & 440 \\ 2700 & 62 & 600 \end{bmatrix}.$$

The first entry in row i of the given matrix shows person i's daily calorie intake. On the other hand, the second and third entries of the row exemplify respectively the person's life expectancy and income.

For illustrative purpose, let us assume that any calorie consumption level below 2000 will be referred to as "too low," whereas a consumption quantity in the interval (2000, 2700) may be regarded as "not too low," which is a fuzzy concept. On the other hand, the consumption magnitude 2700 is the optimum figure, which, for simplicity, is assumed to be the maximum. The fuzzy space of malnutrition arising from low calorie intake is, therefore, given by $(z^l_{EC}, z^u_{EC}) = (2000, 2700)$, where the subscript "EC" stands for energy consumption. The upper fuzzy boundary value z^u_{EC} is $\max_i\{x_{iEC}\} = 2700$. The fuzzy space for life expectancy is taken as $(z^l_{LE}, z^u_{LE}) = (59, 60)$, where the subscript "LE" symbolizes life expectancy. Finally, for income, this region is assumed to be $(z^l_{IN}, z^u_{IN}) = (450, 500)$, where the subscript "IN" appears for income.

Thus, although person 2's energy consumption is not too low, he does not have any feeling of destitution with respect to life expectancy and income. In contrast, person 4 has no sensuality of deprivation in any dimension. Similar interpretations hold for the other entries of the matrix.

For the three dimensions we have considered earlier, recall that for energy absorption dimension the fuzzy domain is $(z^l_{EC}, z^u_{EC}) = (2000, 2700)$. Since 1 calorie = 4.18 joules, the entries in the first column of X_1, starting from the first row, get transformed into 11286, 10450, 11286, and 11286 joules, respectively (see Chapter 2). Under this transformation, the fuzzy space (2000, 2700) gets transformed into (8360, 11286) and any $x_{iEC} \in (2000, 2700)$ becomes $4.18x_{iEC} \in (8360, 11286)$, where $i = 1, 2, 3, 4$. Next, suppose that we measure life expectancy in months and incomes in cents so that the entries in the second and third columns get transformed appropriately. This means that we are postmultiplying X_1 by the diagonal matrix diag(4.18, 12, 100) to obtain a new social matrix Y_1, where

$$Y_1 = X_1 \operatorname{diag}(4.18, 12, 100) = \begin{bmatrix} 2700 & 59.4 & 400 \\ 2500 & 65 & 900 \\ 2700 & 59.5 & 440 \\ 2700 & 62 & 600 \end{bmatrix} \operatorname{diag}(4.18, 12, 100)$$

$$= \begin{bmatrix} 11\,286 & 712.8 & 40\,000 \\ 10\,450 & 780 & 90\,000 \\ 11\,286 & 714 & 44\,000 \\ 11\,286 & 744 & 60\,000 \end{bmatrix}.$$

The fuzzy ratio-scale invariance property demands that Y_1 is fuzzy poverty equivalent to X_1.

4.3.1.2 Fuzzy Strong Translation-Scale Invariance

For all $n \in N$, $X \in M^n$, $z^{lu} \in Z^{lu}$, $\boldsymbol{\mu} \in M^F$, $P^F(X; z^{lu}; \mu) = P^F(X + A; ((z_1^l + \kappa_1, z_1^u + \kappa_1), (z_2^l + \kappa_2, z_2^u + \kappa_2), \dots, (z_d^l + \kappa_d, z_d^u + \kappa_d)); \boldsymbol{\mu})$, where A is an $n \times d$ matrix with identical rows given by $(\kappa_1, \kappa_2, \dots, \kappa_d)$ such that $X + A \in M^n, z^{lu} \in Z^{lu}$ and $z_j^l + \kappa_j > 0$ for all $j \in Q$.

This axiom needs that the fuzzy poverty index does not change if there are equal absolute additions/subtractions to all achievements and their fuzzy boundaries in a dimension. It parallels the strong translation invariance axiom in Chapter 2. Since we do not rule out the possibility that $\kappa_j = 0$ for one or more j, achievements in some of the dimensions and their fuzzy limits may remain unaltered under this operation. A weaker version of the axiom, fuzzy translation invariance axiom, requires constancy of the amounts κ_js across dimensions. A fuzzy poverty index satisfying this weaker postulate is called an absolute index. If a fuzzy poverty index is both relative and absolute, we call it a compromise index.

The next postulate, the fuzzy weak focus axiom, involves a change in the achievement in a dimension of a person who does not suffer from deprivation in any dimension, and the change does not make him deprived in the dimension.

4.3.1.3 Fuzzy Weak Focus

For all $n \in N$, $X, Y \in M^n$, $z^{lu} \in Z^{lu}$, $\boldsymbol{\mu} \in M^F$, if for some $i \in \{1, 2, \dots, n\}$, $x_{ij} \geq z_j^u$ for all $j \in Q$, for some pair $(i,j) \in \{1, 2, \dots, n\} \times \{1, 2, \dots, d\}$, $y_{ij} = x_{ij} + c$, where c is a scalar such that $y_{ij} \geq z_j^u$ and $y_{hk} = x_{hk}$ for all $(h, k) \neq (i,j) \in \{1, 2, \dots, n\} \times \{1, 2, \dots, d\}$, then $P^F(X; z^{lu}; \boldsymbol{\mu}) = P^F(Y; z^{lu}; \boldsymbol{\mu})$.

Since the change affects only a person who is nondeprived in all dimensions, it is similar to the Bourguignon–Chakravarty weak focus axiom considered in Chapter 3. (The person is neither certainly nor partially deprived in any dimension.) However, here in the formulation, we note the existence of membership functions and fuzzy lines of demarcation, which are assumed to be given. These characteristics, which are absent in the standard structure, enable us to refer to the property as fuzzy weak focus axiom instead of weak focus axiom.

To illustrate this axiom, suppose that income of person 4 in X_1 increases by 50. The resulting social matrix is given by

$$Y_2 = \begin{bmatrix} 2700 & 59.4 & 400 \\ 2500 & 65 & 900 \\ 2700 & 59.5 & 440 \\ 2700 & 62 & 650 \end{bmatrix}.$$

Since person 4 is nondeprived in all the dimensions, giving him more income should not affect global poverty assessment in any way.

The third postulate deals with an augmentation/diminution of achievement in a nondeprived dimension of a poor or a nonpoor person that does not make him deprived in the dimension. Formally,

4.3.1.4 Fuzzy Strong Focus

For all $n \in N$, $X, Y \in M^n$, $z^{lu} \in Z^{lu}$, $\boldsymbol{\mu} \in M^F$, if for some pair $(i,j) \in \{1,2,\dots,n\} \times \{1,2,\dots,d\}$, $y_{ij} = x_{ij} + c$, where $x_{ij} \geq z_j^u$, c is a scalar such that $y_{ij} \geq z_j^u$ and $y_{hk} = x_{hk}$ for all $(h,k) \neq (i,j) \in \{1,2,\dots,n\} \times \{1,2,\dots,d\}$, then $P^F(X; z^{lu}; \boldsymbol{\mu}) = P^F(Y; z^{lu}; \boldsymbol{\mu})$.

Note that here we do not rule out the possibility that person i is fuzzy poor. This axiom parallels the Bourguignon–Chakravarty strong focus axiom analyzed in Chapter 3.

The matrix Y_3, given as follows, is obtained from X_1 by increasing only person 2's income, a nondeprived dimension for the person. The person is, however, deprived in energy consumption. The fuzzy strong focus axiom insists that this augmentation does not change the evaluation of overall poverty.

$$Y_3 = \begin{bmatrix} 2700 & 59.4 & 400 \\ 2500 & 65 & 950 \\ 2700 & 59.5 & 440 \\ 2700 & 62 & 600 \end{bmatrix}$$

The additional income is unable to lift person 2 out of deprivation in calorie intake.

The next invariance postulate, which we refer to as fuzzy symmetry because it provides an impartial treatment of persons, can be stated as follows:

4.3.1.5 Fuzzy Symmetry

For all $n \in N$, $X, Y \in M^n$, $z^{lu} \in Z^{lu}$, $\boldsymbol{\mu} \in M^F$, if $Y = \Gamma X$, where Γ is any permutation matrix of order n, then $P^F(X; z^{lu}; \boldsymbol{\mu}) = P^F(Y; z^{lu}; \boldsymbol{\mu})$.

Clearly, in this case, we consider reordering of all the individuals, not necessarily of those who have achievements in the fuzzy regions. However, as in the focus axioms, we recognize the presence of membership functions and fuzzy boundaries. Precisely, because of this, we refer to this axiom as fuzzy symmetry.

For cross-population comparison of fuzzy poverty, we assume that the fuzzy boundaries and membership functions are the same in the two populations under comparison. Otherwise, the comparison is not meaningful. We can formally state this axiom as follows:

4.3.1.6 Fuzzy Population Replication Invariance

For all $n \in N$, $X \in M^n$, $z^{lu} \in Z^{lu}$, $\boldsymbol{\mu} \in \boldsymbol{M}^F$, $P^F(X; z^{lu}; \boldsymbol{\mu}) = P^F(Y; z^{lu}; \boldsymbol{\mu})$, where Y is any k-fold replication of X, $k \geq 2$ being any finite integer.

Under ceteris paribus assumptions, we consider replications of the entire population. Because of the presence of fuzziness in the structure, we call this property the axiom of fuzzy population replication invariance.

The following subsection concentrates on the analysis of desirable directional movements of a fuzzy poverty index under some sensible transformation in a social matrix.

4.3.2 Distributional Axioms

Given that we are dealing with fuzzy poverty measurement here, it is rational to assume that a scaling down of the achievement in the fuzzy region of a deprived dimension of a person should enlarge fuzzy poverty. Note that if the contraction takes place in the space where the person is certainly deprived, then the membership function remains insensitive to such a reduction.

The following axiom addresses the impact of debasement in the attainment lying in the fuzzy domain of a deprived dimension of a poor.

4.3.2.1 Fuzzy Monotonicity

For all $n \in N$, $X, Y \in M^n$, $z^{lu} \in Z^{lu}$, $\boldsymbol{\mu} \in \boldsymbol{M}^F$, if for some pair $(i,j) \in \{1,2,\ldots,n\} \times \{1,2,\ldots,d\}$, $y_{ij} = x_{ij} - c$, where $z_j^l < x_{ij} < z_j^u$, $y_{hk} = x_{hk}$ for all $(h,k) \neq (i,j) \in \{1,2,\ldots,n\} \times \{1,2,\ldots,d\}$ and $c > 0$, then $P^F(Y; z^{lu}; \boldsymbol{\mu}) > P^F(X; z^{lu}; \boldsymbol{\mu})$.

Here the reduced achievement y_{ij} will be either in the fuzzy region ($z_j^l < y_{ij} < z_j^u$) or in the certainly deprived region ($y_{ij} \leq z_j^l$) of the dimension.

The achievement matrix Y_4 given as follows is obtained from X_1 by a cutback of person 1's life expectancy, a deprived dimension for the person with its achievement in the fuzzy territory, by 0.1.

$$Y_4 = \begin{bmatrix} 2700 & 59.3 & 400 \\ 2500 & 65 & 900 \\ 2700 & 59.5 & 440 \\ 2700 & 62 & 600 \end{bmatrix}.$$

Fuzzy monotonicity axiom then demands that $P^F(Y_4; z^{lu}; \boldsymbol{\mu}) > P^F(X_1; z^{lu}; \boldsymbol{\mu})$.

Since existence of poverty can be regarded as withdrawal of human rights from the affected people, from policy point of view, it is appealing that reductions (respectively, increments) in achievements should raise (respectively, cutback) poverty by higher quantities, the poorer the affected persons are.

This plausible view is presented analytically in the following axiom.

4.3.2.2 Fuzzy Monotonicity Sensitivity

For all $n \in N$, $X, Y, \tilde{Y} \in M^n$, $z^{lu} \in Z^{lu}$, $\boldsymbol{\mu} \in \boldsymbol{M}^F$, if for some pair $(i,j) \in \{1,2,\ldots,n\} \times \{1,2,\ldots,d\}$, $y_{ij} = x_{ij} - c$, $y_{pk} = x_{pk}$ for all $(p,k) \neq (i,j) \in \{1,2,\ldots,n\} \times \{1,2,\ldots,d\}$, and for some pair $(h,j) \in \{1,2,\ldots,n\} \times \{1,2,\ldots,d\}$, $\tilde{y}_{hj} = x_{hj} - c$, and $\tilde{y}_{pk} = x_{pk}$ for all $(p,k) \neq (h,j) \in \{1,2,\ldots,n\} \times \{1,2,\ldots,d\}$, where $z_j^l < x_{hj} < x_{ij} < z_j^u$, and $c > 0$, then $P^F(\tilde{Y}; z^{lu}; \boldsymbol{\mu}) - P^F(X; z^{lu}; \boldsymbol{\mu}) > P^F(Y; z^{lu}; \boldsymbol{\mu}) - P^F(X; z^{lu}; \boldsymbol{\mu})$.

We assume that attainments of multidimensionally poor persons i and h in dimension j are in the fuzzy space of the dimension, and person h has a higher deprivation here. Then increase in poverty resulting from shrinkage in the dimensional achievement that applies identically to both i and h will be higher whenever it corresponds to person h who is more deprived in the dimension. Note that a decrement in the achievements of the two poor persons who are certainly deprived in the corresponding dimensions does not influence the value of a membership function. That is why we have restricted attention to the fuzzy dominion of the dimension.

Consider the achievement matrices

$$Y_5 = \begin{bmatrix} 2700 & 59.3 & 400 \\ 2500 & 65 & 900 \\ 2700 & 59.5 & 440 \\ 2700 & 62 & 600 \end{bmatrix}, \quad Y_6 = \begin{bmatrix} 2700 & 59.4 & 400 \\ 2500 & 65 & 900 \\ 2700 & 59.4 & 440 \\ 2700 & 62 & 600 \end{bmatrix}.$$

In X_1, both persons 1 and 3 are poor, and they are deprived in life expectancy whose values are in the fuzzy space. Person 3 had originally lower deprivation compared to person 1 in the dimension. We obtain Y_5 and Y_6 from the initial matrix X_1 by curtailing the life expectancy of persons 1 and 3, respectively, by 0.1. The fuzzy monotonicity sensitivity axiom appeals that $P^F(Y_5; z^{lu}; \boldsymbol{\mu}) - P^F(X_1; z^{lu}; \boldsymbol{\mu}) > P^F(Y_6; z^{lu}; \boldsymbol{\mu}) - P^F(X_1; z^{lu}; \boldsymbol{\mu})$.

The next axiom is concerned with the effect of increasing the number of deprived dimensions of a fuzzy poor. It requires that when a nondeprived dimension of a fuzzy poor person, who is not deprived in all dimensions, becomes partially or certainly deprived, then fuzzy poverty should increase. Formally,

4.3.2.3 Fuzzy Dimensional Monotonicity

For all $n \in N$, $X \in M^n$, $z^{lu} \in Z^{lu}$, $\boldsymbol{\mu} \in \boldsymbol{M}^F$, if $Y \in M^n$ is obtained from X such that for some pair $(i,j) \in \{1,2,\dots,n\} \times \{1,2,\dots,d\}$, $y_{ij} < z_j^u \leq x_{ij}$, where person i is partially deprived in X in at least one dimension different from j and $y_{pk} = x_{pk}$ for all pairs $(p,k) \neq (i,j) \in \{1,2,\dots,n\} \times \{1,2,\dots,d\}$, then $P^F(Y; z^{lu}; \boldsymbol{\mu}) > P^F(X; z^{lu}; \boldsymbol{\mu})$.

Person i, who is fuzzy poor and nondeprived in dimension j in X, comes to be deprived in the dimension in Y. Nevertheless, all other dimensional achievements for all persons in $\{1,2,\dots,n\}$ are the same in both X and Y. Now, under the change considered in the axiom, in Y, person i will be either partially or certainly deprived in dimension j, a nondeprived dimension for the person in X. Hence, fuzzy poverty should increase. This axiom may be treated as the fuzzy analog to the Alkire and Foster (2011) dimensional monotonicity axiom.

In our achievement matrix X_1, calorie intake is a nondeprived dimension for person 1, a fuzzy poor person in X_1. If this calorie intake now reduces from 2700 to 2450, person 1 becomes deprived in this dimension in the transformed matrix Y_7 given as follows:

$$Y_7 = \begin{bmatrix} 2450 & 59.4 & 400 \\ 2500 & 65 & 900 \\ 2700 & 59.5 & 440 \\ 2700 & 62 & 600 \end{bmatrix}.$$

Fuzzy dimensional monotonicity axiom demands that $P^F(Y_7; z^{lu}; \boldsymbol{\mu}) > P^F(X_1; z^{lu}; \boldsymbol{\mu})$.

Let $S_{ih}^F(X; z^{lu}; \boldsymbol{\mu})$ be the identical set of dimensions in which persons i and h are partially deprived, that is, $S_{ih}^F(X; z^{lu}; \boldsymbol{\mu}) = \{j \in Q | z_j^l < x_{hj} < z_j^u\} = \{j \in Q | z_j^l < x_{ij} < z_j^u\}$, where $i, h \in \{1,2,\dots,n\}$ are arbitrary. Assume further that all partial deprivations of h are higher than the corresponding deprivations of i. Formally, for all $j \in S_{ih}^F(X; z^{lu}; \boldsymbol{\mu})$, $z_j^l < x_{hj} < x_{ij} < z_j^u$.

Definition 4.2 For all $n \in N$, $n > 1$, $X \in M^n$, $z^{lu} \in Z^{lu}$, $\boldsymbol{\mu} \in \boldsymbol{M}^F$, $Y \in M^n$ is said to be obtained from X by a fuzzy Pigou–Dalton bundle of regressive transfers from person h to person i if

i) $S_{ih}^F(X; z^{lu}; \boldsymbol{\mu})$ is nonempty,
ii) $y_{p.} = x_{p.}$ for all $p \neq h, i$;
iii) $y_{h.} = x_{h.} - \delta$, $y_{i.} = x_{i.} + \delta$, where $\delta = (\delta_1, \delta_2, \dots, \delta_d)$; (a) $\delta_j = 0$ for all $j \in Q / S_{ih}^F(X; z^{lu}; \boldsymbol{\mu})$; (b) $\delta_j \geq 0$ for any $j \in S_{ih}^F(X; z^{lu}; \boldsymbol{\mu})$, with $>$ for at least one j, and $y_{ij} < z_j^u$ for all $j \in S_{ih}^F(X; z^{lu}; \boldsymbol{\mu})$.

According to condition (i), there is at least one element in the identical set of partially deprived dimensions of the persons h and i, where h has higher deprivations than i in this set. Condition (ii) declares that all individuals except persons h and i have identical achievements in all the dimensions in both X and Y. Part (a) of condition (iii) claims that achievements of each of the persons h and i remain the same in all the dimensions that are outside the set $S_{ih}^F(X; z^{lu}; \boldsymbol{\mu})$. In part (b) of the condition, it is indicated that we derive $y_{h.}$ and $y_{i.}$ from $x_{h.}$ and $x_{i.}$, respectively, by transfers of achievements from person h to person i for dimensions in $S_{ih}^F(X; z^{lu}; \boldsymbol{\mu})$,where the size of the transfer is nonnegative for any dimension in the set and positive for at least one dimension. Finally, part (b) of condition (iii) confirms that the size of the transfer in any dimension does not allow the recipient to cross the upper fuzzy boundary or to be even at the boundary itself. Since for any $j \in S_{ih}^F(X; z^{lu}; \boldsymbol{\mu})$, $\delta_j \geq 0$ can be no more than x_{hj}, it is ensured that $0 \leq y_{hj} < y_{ij}$. In the posttransfer distributions, both persons h and i may remain partially deprived in a dimension $j \in Q$ affected by the transfer so that $z_j^l < y_{hj} < y_{ij} < z_j^u$. Partial deprivation of the persons in dimension j shows that fuzzy environment exists for both the persons in the posttransfer situation as well. However, situations such as (c) $y_{hj} = z_j^l < y_{ij} < z_j^u$ and (d) $y_{hj} < z_j^l < y_{ij} < z_j^u$ are also possible. While in situation (c) of the posttransfer circumstance, person h's achievement in the dimension is exactly at the lower boundary of the fuzzy space of the dimension, in (d), this achievement is even lower. Note that the transfer activity applies only to the set of partially deprived dimensions of individuals i and h.

In the distribution matrix X_1, $S_{31}^F(X_1; z^{lu}; \boldsymbol{\mu}) = \{LE, IN\}$ and in each of the two dimensions in this identical set of deprived dimensions of persons 1 and 3, person 3 has higher achievement than person 1. Now, a regressive transfer of 5 units of income from person 1 to person 3, who are both partially deprived in the dimension, transforms the matrix X_1 into Y_8, given by

$$Y_8 = \begin{bmatrix} 2700 & 59.4 & 395 \\ 2500 & 65 & 900 \\ 2700 & 59.5 & 445 \\ 2700 & 62 & 600 \end{bmatrix}.$$

We then say that Y_8 is deduced from X_1 by a fuzzy Pigou–Dalton bundle of regressive transfers. The following postulate for a multidimensional fuzzy poverty index can now be stated.

4.3.2.4 Fuzzy Transfer

For all $n \in N$, $n > 1$, $X \in M^n$, $z^{lu} \in Z^{lu}$, $\boldsymbol{\mu} \in M^F$, if $Y \in M^n$ is obtained from X by a fuzzy Pigou–Dalton bundle of regressive transfers, then $P^F(X; z^{lu}; \boldsymbol{\mu}) < P^F(Y; z^{lu}; \boldsymbol{\mu})$.

For the illustrative example, where we derive Y_8 from X_1 by a fuzzy Pigou–Dalton regressive transfer, the fuzzy transfer axiom demands that $P^F(X_1; z^{lu}; \boldsymbol{\mu}) < P^F(Y_8; z^{lu}; \boldsymbol{\mu})$.

In Definition 4.2, we can alternatively assume that person h has higher deprivations than person i in their identical set of deprived dimensions, and in at least one dimension, person h is partially deprived. Then a Pigou–Dalton bundle of regressive transfers from h to i takes place in a fuzzy environment if the size of transfer of achievement from at least one partially deprived dimension is positive. Evidently, our formulation of the Pigou–Dalton bundle of regressive transfers presented in Definition 4.2 is quite simple and easy to understand.

The final axiom of the subsection is applicable only to multidimensional poverty in a fuzzy environment and depends on the association between deprivations.

Definition 4.3 For all $n \in N$, $n > 1$, $X \in M^n$, $z^{lu} \in Z^{lu}$, $\boldsymbol{\mu} \in \boldsymbol{M}^F$, suppose that persons i and p are partially deprived in dimensions j and q in X, that is, $z_j^l < x_{ij}, x_{pj} < z_j^u$ and $z_q^l < x_{iq}, x_{pq} < z_q^u$. Assume also that $x_{ij} > x_{pj}$, $x_{iq} < x_{pq}$, and $x_{it} \leq x_{pt}$ for all $t \in Q/\{j, q\}$. We then say that $Y \in M^n$ is obtained from X by correlation-increasing switch in a fuzzy poverty environment if (i) $y_{ij} = x_{pj}$, (ii) $y_{pj} = x_{ij}$, (iii) $y_{rj} = x_{rj}$ for all $r \neq i, p$, and (iv) $y_{rs} = x_{rs}$ for all $r \in \{1, 2, \ldots, n\}$ and for all $s \in Q/\{j\}$.

In Definition 4.3, conditions (i) and (ii) accompanied by condition (iv) for $r = i, p$ and $s = q$ specify that person p who had lower achievement in dimension j and higher achievement in dimension q than person i in X have higher achievements in both the dimensions in Y. It is also given that all the remaining dimensional achievements of person i are not higher than the corresponding dimensional achievements of person p. In condition (iii), it is asserted that achievements for the remaining individuals in dimension j are the same in both the social matrices X and Y. Finally, condition (iv) stipulates that achievements of all persons in all the dimensions except j are the same in the two social matrices. We deduce Y from X by an interchange of achievements in dimension j between persons i and p. In the postswitch situation, person p does not possess lower achievement than person i in each dimension and possesses strictly more achievement in at least one dimension. The swap of achievements in the fuzzy region of dimension j, defined by (i) and (ii), increases the correlation between dimensions. That is why, we refer to the switch as a correlation-increasing switch in a fuzzy poverty setting. The switch does not alter the total of the achievements in the dimension on which it applies.

If the two dimensions are substitutes, then one neutralizes the shortness of the other. Observe that one person (person p), who was originally richer than the other person (person i) in the fuzzy space of dimension q, is becoming richer in the fuzzy space of the other dimension (dimension j) as well after the switch. Since the two dimensions represent akin features of well-being, the switch should increase fuzzy poverty. For the other person (person i), the incapability to outweigh the deficiency in one dimension by the other now goes up since he is now poorer in both the dimensions.

The aforementioned discussion enables us to state the following axiom:

4.3.2.5 Increasing Fuzzy Poverty under Correlation-Increasing Switch

For all $n \in N$, $n > 1$, $X, Y \in M^n$, $z^{lu} \in Z^{lu}$, $\boldsymbol{\mu} \in \boldsymbol{M}^F$, if Y is obtained from X by a correlation-increasing switch in a fuzzy poverty environment, then $P^F(X; z^{lu}; \boldsymbol{\mu}) < P^F(Y; z^{lu}; \boldsymbol{\mu})$ if the dimensions involved in the switch are substitutes.

The corresponding postulate when the dimensions are complements requires fuzzy poverty to decrease under a correlation-increasing switch. The switch will not affect fuzzy poverty at all if the two dimensions are independents. These axioms are fuzzy versions of the corresponding Bourguignon–Chakravarty axioms for standard multidimensional poverty indices stated in Chapter 3.

To exemplify the aforementioned property, note that in $\tilde{X}_1$, the first person has more achievement than the third person in the third dimension, and the opposite inequality holds in the second dimension. The matrix Y_9 is derived from $\tilde{X}_1$ by a switch of achievements in dimension 2 between the two persons. In the postswitch social matrix Y_9, achievements of person 1 in dimensions 2 and 3 are higher than the corresponding quantities for person 3, and their achievements in dimension 1 are the same. Observe also that the achievements of each of the persons 1and 3 in dimensions 2 and 3 are in the corresponding fuzzy regions. As a result, we can claim that Y_9 has been obtained from $\tilde{X}_1$ by a correlation-increasing switch.

$$\tilde{X}_1 = \begin{bmatrix} 2700 & 59.4 & 440 \\ 2500 & 65 & 900 \\ 2700 & 59.5 & 400 \\ 2700 & 62 & 600 \end{bmatrix}, Y_9 = \begin{bmatrix} 2700 & 59.5 & 440 \\ 2500 & 65 & 900 \\ 2700 & 59.4 & 400 \\ 2700 & 62 & 600 \end{bmatrix}.$$

In consequence, $P^F(Y_9; z^{lu}; \boldsymbol{\mu}) > P^F(\tilde{X}_1; z^{lu}; \boldsymbol{\mu})$, if the second and third dimensions are regarded as substitutes. The reverse inequality or exact equality holds if the two dimensions are complements or independents.

The concern of the first axiom of the next set of two axioms is the relationship between overall poverty and poverty levels of two or more population subgroups that are formed by breaking down the population using some homogeneous characteristic. The second axiom deals with the connection between overall poverty and dimensional poverty levels. These two axioms consider respectively partitions of the population and dimensions keeping other characteristics such as membership functions and fuzzy limits unchanged.

4.3.3 Decomposability Axioms

4.3.3.1 Fuzzy Subgroup Decomposability

For any $X^i \in M^{n_i}$, $z^{lu} \in Z^{lu}$, $\boldsymbol{\mu} \in \boldsymbol{M}^F$, $P^F(X; z^{lu}; \boldsymbol{\mu}) = \sum_{i=1}^{m} \frac{n_i}{n} P^F(X^i; z^{lu}; \boldsymbol{\mu})$, where $\sum_{i=1}^{m} n_i = n$, $X \in M^n$ is obtained by placing $X^i \in M^{n_i}$ matrices from above to below for $i = 1,2,\ldots,m$, and for all $1 \le i \le m$, $n_i \ge 1$, where $m \ge 2$.

This axiom, which is a fuzzy variant of subgroup decomposability postulate for standard poverty indices, demands that global fuzzy poverty is the population share weighted average of subgroup fuzzy poverty levels. Here $\frac{n_i}{n} P^F(X^i; z^{lu}; \boldsymbol{\mu})$, is fuzzy poverty of subgroup i weighted by the corresponding population fraction. Aggregation of all such weighted numbers across population subgroups gives us the comprehensive fuzzy poverty. Following our arguments in Chapter 3, we can say that each of these numbers becomes important from policy perspective for mitigating fuzzy poverty.

Suppose that the social distribution X_1 is broken down into two submatrices X_1^1 and X_1^2 with population sizes 3 and 1, respectively, where

$$X_1^1 = \begin{bmatrix} 2700 & 59.4 & 400 \\ 2500 & 65 & 900 \\ 2700 & 59.5 & 440 \end{bmatrix} \text{ and } X_1^2 = \begin{bmatrix} 2700 & 62 & 600 \end{bmatrix}.$$

Then subgroup decomposability requires that $P^F(X_1; z^{lu}; \boldsymbol{\mu}) = \frac{3}{4} P^F(X_1^1; z^{lu}; \boldsymbol{\mu}) + \frac{1}{4} P^F(X_1^2; z^{lu}; \boldsymbol{\mu})$.

4.3.3.2 Fuzzy Factor Decomposability

For any $n \in N, X \in M^n, z^{lu} \in Z^{lu}, \boldsymbol{\mu} \in \boldsymbol{M}^F, P^F(X; z^{lu}; \boldsymbol{\mu}) = \sum_{j=1}^{d} b_j P^F(x_{.j}; (z_j^l, z_j^u); \boldsymbol{\mu}_j)$, where $b_j \ge 0$ is the weight assigned to dimension j and $\sum_{i=1}^{d} b_j = 1$.

This axiom, which is a fuzzy sister of the factor decomposability axiom introduced by Chakravarty et al. (1998), claims that total fuzzy poverty is the weighted average of dimension-wise fuzzy poverty levels, where the nonnegative weights add up to 1. As in the standard case, this axiom has also interesting policy applications.

This axiom empowers us to express the fuzzy poverty quantity of X_1 as

$$P^F(X_1; z^{lu}; \boldsymbol{\mu}) = b_1 P^F\left(\begin{bmatrix}2700\\2500\\2700\\2700\end{bmatrix}; (z_1^l, z_1^u); \mu_1\right) + b_2 P^F\left(\begin{bmatrix}59.4\\65\\59.5\\62\end{bmatrix}; (z_2^l, z_2^u); \mu_2\right) + b_3 P^F\left(\begin{bmatrix}400\\900\\440\\600\end{bmatrix}; (z_3^l, z_3^u); \mu_3\right).$$

The axioms presented so far assume the existence of fuzzy zone in each dimension of well-being. However, we did not analyze how poverty changes when we replace the existing membership function by a newer one that assigns higher values to deprivations in one or more fuzzy belts. This is the subject of our next subsection.

4.3.4 Fuzzy Sensitivity Axiom

Of two identical communities, the one in which at least one of the dimensions has higher membership grade in the fuzzy space should have a higher fuzzy poverty than the other. The reason behind this is that the former assigns a higher value to deprivations in the fuzzy territory of the dimension. Note that we are implicitly assuming here that there is at least one person in the community who is partially deprived in the dimension under consideration. Otherwise, the two membership functions will assign the same value to deprivations in the dimension. Evidently, this axiom does not parallel any poverty axiom that we analyzed in Chapter 3. From this perspective, it represents a unique feature of fuzzy multidimensional poverty. It clearly distinguishes the fuzzy approach to multidimensional poverty measurement from the standard approach.

The axiom can be formally stated as:

4.3.4.1 Increasing Fuzzy Poverty for Increased Membership Function

For all $n \in N, X \in M^n, z^{lu} \in Z^{lu}, \boldsymbol{\mu}, \boldsymbol{\mu}' \in \boldsymbol{M}^F$, suppose that $\mu_j > \mu_j'$ for some j in the fuzzy region, and there is at least one person i such that $z_j^l < x_{ij} < z_j^u$, and $\mu_q = \mu_q'$ for all $q \in Q/\{j\}$. Then $P^F(X; z^{lu}; \boldsymbol{\mu}) > P^F(X; z^{lu}; \boldsymbol{\mu}')$.

From (4.2) and (4.3), we note that $\mu_j^C(x_{ij}) < \mu_j^{CZ}(x_{ij})$, where $z_j^l < x_{ij} < z_j^u$ and $\alpha_j > 1$. Since in X_1, persons 1 and 3 are partially deprived in the second dimension, the increasing fuzzy multidimensional poverty for increased membership function axiom claims that $P^F(X_1; z^{lu}; (\mu_1^C, \mu_2^C, \mu_3^C)) < P^F(X_1; z^{lu}; (\mu_1^C, \mu_2^{CZ}, \mu_3^C))$.

The next two axioms are fuzzy parallels of the corresponding axioms scrutinized in Chapter 3. A fuzzy poverty quantifier attains its lower bound 0, if nobody is certainly or partially deprived. The upper bound 1 is attained if everybody is certainly deprived in each dimension. However, the extents of deprivations need not be the maximum. In contrast, in the standard case, each person should be maximally deprived in each dimension for a poverty index to reach its upper bound. The second property, fuzzy continuity, specifies that under minor changes in the achievement levels, the poverty index should register only minimal changes.[3]

4.3.5 Technical Axioms

4.3.5.1 Fuzzy Boundedness

For all $n \in N$, $X \in M^n$, $z^{lu} \in Z^{lu}$, $\boldsymbol{\mu} \in M^F$, $P^F(X; z^{lu}; \boldsymbol{\mu})$ is bounded between 0 and 1, where the lower bound is attained if $X \in M$ is such that $\pi(X; z^{lu}; \mu)$, the set of poor persons in X is empty. The upper bound is attained if everybody is certainly deprived in each dimension.

4.3.5.2 Fuzzy Continuity

For all $n \in N$, $z^{lu} \in Z^{lu}$, $\boldsymbol{\mu} \in M^F$, P^F varies continuously with changes in achievements provided that the poverty statuses of the individuals remain unaltered.

4.4 Fuzzy Multidimensional Poverty Indices

The fuzzy-set-based axiomatic approach to multidimensional poverty measurement involves indices that should fulfill axioms suggested in the earlier section. We will assume subgroup decomposability at the outset because of its interesting policy applications and discuss some indices possessing this property.

Repeated applications of subgroup decomposability shows that we can write an index satisfying this axiom as

$$P^F(X; z^{lu}; \boldsymbol{\mu}) = \frac{1}{n}\sum_{i=1}^{n} P^F(x_{i.}; z^{lu}; \boldsymbol{\mu}), \tag{4.7}$$

where $n \in N$, $X \in M^n$, $z^{lu} \in Z^{lu}$, $\boldsymbol{\mu} \in M^F$ are arbitrary. Here $P^F(x_{i.}; z^{lu}; \boldsymbol{\mu})$ is the individual fuzzy poverty function. Following Chakravarty (2006), we define $P^F(x_{i.}; z^{lu}; \boldsymbol{\mu}) = \frac{1}{d}\sum_{j=1}^{d} \mu_j(x_{ij})$, the average of grades of memberships of person i in different dimensions. Since $\mu_j(x_{ij})$ gives us the extent of deprivation of person i in dimension j, this definition of individual fuzzy poverty function is quite sensible. The choice $\frac{1}{d}$ of dimensional weights in the individual poverty function makes $P^F(X; z^{lu}; \boldsymbol{\mu})$ in (4.7) symmetric in dimensions; any reordering of dimensions does not change poverty.

3 This axiom is different from the notion of fuzzy continuity used in fuzzy set theory; see, for example, Mukherjee and Sinha (1990).

Substituting this definition of individual poverty function into (4.7), we obtain

$$P^F(X;z^{lu};\boldsymbol{\mu}) = \frac{1}{nd}\sum_{i=1}^{n}\sum_{j=1}^{d}\mu_j(x_{ij}) = \frac{1}{nd}\left[\sum_{j=1}^{d}\sum_{i:z_j^l<x_{ij}<z_j^u}\mu_j(x_{ij}) + \sum_{i=1}^{n}d_i^c(X)\right], \quad (4.8)$$

where $n \in N$, $X \in M^n, z^{lu} \in Z^{lu}$, $\boldsymbol{\mu} \in \boldsymbol{M}^F$ are arbitrary. The expression $\sum_{i:z_j^l<x_{ij}<z_j^u}\mu_j(x_{ij})$ in (4.8) means that the sum is taken over membership grades of all individuals $i \in \{1, 2, \ldots, n\}$ who are partially deprived in dimension j, and as before, $d_i^c(X)$ is the total number of dimensions in which person i is certainly deprived. In (4.8) at the outset, membership grades are aggregated across individuals. At the second stage, the individual averages derived at the first stage are aggregated across dimensions.

Given any membership function μ_j for dimension j, there corresponds a particular fuzzy poverty index of the type (4.8). It is given by the sum of grades of memberships of all persons in the society divided by nd, the maximum number of dimensions in which all the persons are certainly deprived. These indices will differ in the way we stipulate the membership grades in the dimension. For any arbitrary μ_j given by (4.1), the general index $P^F(X;z^{lu};\boldsymbol{\mu})$ in (4.8) treats any two dimensions as independents. For satisfaction of the fuzzy transfer axiom, we need strict convexity of μ_j over the corresponding fuzzy region. Strict convexity also ensures verification of the fuzzy monotonicity sensitivity axiom. The general index meets all other axioms unambiguously for any arbitrary μ_j of the type (4.1).

We can now state the following proposition:

Proposition 4.1 The subgroup and factor-decomposable general multidimensional index, given by (4.8), satisfies the following fuzzy poverty axioms: weak focus, strong focus, symmetry, population replication invariance, monotinicity, dimensional monotonicity, increasing fuzzy poverty for increased membership function, boundedness, and continuity. It is insensitive to a correlation-increasing switch in a fuzzy poverty situation. It satisfies the fuzzy transfer axiom if μ_j is strictly convex for all dimensions j on which the transfer operations are performed in the fuzzy regions of the corresponding dimensions. Strict convexity μ_j is also a sufficient condition for satisfaction of the fuzzy monotinicity sensitivity axiom given that the changes in the achievements take place in the fuzzy regions of the associated dimensions. It satisfies fuzzy ratio and translation-scale invariance axioms if the function h in the definition of μ_j is respectively homogeneous and translatable of degree 0 for all $j \in \{1, 2, \ldots, d\}$.

An explicit specification of the general family (4.8) can be provided using the membership function μ_j^C (4.2). In this case, (4.8) reduces to the following fuzzy version of the multidimensional extension of the Foster et al. (1984) index suggested by Chakravarty et al. (1998) and Bourguignon and Chakravarty (2003):

$$P^F_{FGT}(X; z^{lu}; \underline{\alpha}) = \frac{1}{nd}\left[\sum_{j=1}^{d} \sum_{i:z^l_j<x_{ij}<z^u_j} \left(\frac{z^u_j - x_{ij}}{z^u_j - z^l_j}\right)^{\alpha_j} + \sum_{i=1}^{n} d^c_i(X)\right], \tag{4.9}$$

where $n \in N, X \in M^n, z^{lu} \in Z^{lu}, \boldsymbol{\mu} \in \boldsymbol{M}^F$ are arbitrary. Here $\underline{\alpha} = (\alpha_1, \alpha_2, \dots, \alpha_d)$ reflects different attitudes toward poverty. Satisfaction of the transfer axiom by this compromise index in dimension j requires $\alpha_j > 1$, the necessary and sufficient condition for strict convexity of μ^C_j. For $\alpha_j = 0$ for all j, P^F_{FGT} becomes $H^F(X; z^{lu}; \boldsymbol{\mu})$, the fuzzy head-count ratio. If $\alpha_j = 1$ for all j, then P_{FGT} becomes

$$P^F_{FGT}(X; z^{lu}; \underline{\alpha}) = \left[\sum_{j=1}^{d} H^{SFA}_j \frac{1}{|\pi^p_j(X; (z^l_j; z^u_j); \mu_j)|} \sum_{i:z^l_j<x_{ij}<z^u_j} \mu^{CZ}_j + \frac{1}{nd}\sum_{i=1}^{n} d^c_i(X)\right]. \tag{4.10}$$

The quantity $\frac{1}{|\pi^p_j(X;(z^l_j;z^u_j);\mu_j)|} \sum_{i:z^l_j<x_{ij}<z^u_j} \mu^{CZ}_j$ is the average of membership grades of persons who are partially deprived in dimension j, where the grading is done using the Cerioli–Zani membership function given by (4.3). A weighed average of these grade averages across dimensions gives us the first term in the third bracketed expression on the right-hand side of (4.10), where the weights are the respective strict dimension-adjusted fuzzy head-count ratios in the dimensions. The second term is simply the fraction of dimensions in which an average person is certainly deprived. The sum of these two terms gives us the poverty index. For a given H^{SFA}_j, an increase in μ^{CZ}_j, say, following a reduction in x_{ij}, increases the index. This index satisfies the monotonicity axiom but not its sensitivity version. It is a transgressor of the transfer axiom as well.

A second member of the general index in (4.8) is obtained by using (4.3) as the membership function. The affiliated compromise index turns out to be

$$P_C(X; z^{lu}; \underline{e}) = \frac{1}{nd}\left[\sum_{j=1}^{d} \sum_{i:z^l_i<x_{ij}<z^u_j} \left(1 - \left(\frac{x_{ij} - z^l_j}{z^u_j - z^l_j}\right)^{e_j}\right) + \sum_{i=1}^{n} d^c_i(X)\right], \tag{4.11}$$

where $n \in N$, $X \in M^n, z^{lu} \in Z^{lu}$, $\boldsymbol{\mu} \in \boldsymbol{M}^F$ are arbitrary and $\underline{e} = (e_1, e_2, \dots, e_d)$. This index is a fuzzy translation of the multidimensional extension of the Chakravarty (1983) index suggested by Chakravarty, Mukherjee, and Ranade (1998). For a given X, for all $j \in Q$, it is increasing in e_j, as $e_j \to 0$, its value approaches the proportion of dimension in which an average person is certainly deprived and for $e_j = 1$ index coincides with the particular case of P_{FGT}

for $\alpha_j = 1, j \in Q$. For $0 < e_j < 1, j \in Q$, the index satisfies the transfer axiom and sensitivity version of the monontonicity axiom.

The general family (4.8) we have considered earlier is insensitive to a correlation-increasing switch. Given subgroup decomposability, the axiom that leads to such insensitivity property is factor decomposability. This can be avoided by using some suitable transformation of the membership functions employed in the aggregation. One such example is a Bourguignon and Chakravarty (2003) aggregation criterion. To see this more explicitly, assume that in μ_j^C given by (4.2) $\alpha_j = \alpha$ for all $j \in Q$. Then the following compromise index may be regarded as a fuzzy sister of a member of the Bourguignon–Chakravarty family of indices in the standard situation:

$$P_{BC}^F(X; z^{ld}; \alpha; \beta) = \frac{1}{n}\sum_{i=1}^{n}\left[\left[\frac{1}{d}\sum_{j:z_j^l<x_{ij}<z_j^u}\left(\frac{z_j^u - x_{ij}}{z_j^u - z_j^l}\right) + \frac{d_i^c(X)}{d}\right]^{\alpha}\right]^{\frac{\beta}{\alpha}}, \tag{4.12}$$

where $n \in N$, $X \in M^n$, $z^{lu} \in Z^{lu}$, $\boldsymbol{\mu} \in \boldsymbol{M}^F$ are arbitrary. Here $\sum_{j:z_j^l<x_{ij}<z_j^u}\left(\frac{z_j^u-x_{ij}}{z_j^u-z_j^l}\right)$ means that the sum is taken over all dimensional shortfalls $(z_j^u - x_{ij})$ as fractions of the lengths $(z_j^u - z_j^l)$ of the corresponding fuzzy regions (z_j^l, z_j^u) for all those dimensions j in which person i is partially deprived and $\beta > 0$ is a parameter. The parameter $\alpha > 1$ is the same as in (4.9), assuming that $\alpha_j = \alpha$ for all $j \in Q$. This index takes into account the joint distribution of achievements in an explicit manner. It increases or decreases in the fuzzy region under a correlation-increasing switch if $\beta > \alpha$ or $\beta < \alpha$. For $\beta = \alpha$, the index bears similarity with the one given in (4.9) and becomes insensitive to a switch. However, satisfaction of the transfer and monotonicity sensitivity axioms is ensured in all cases.

We now systematically compare our approach with an alternative approach suggested in the literature. This latter proposal mostly aggregates first dimensional deprivation membership values advocated by Cerioli and Zani (1990) and Cheli and Lemmi (1995). In terms of our notation, this aggregated membership value for person i is given by $\sum_{j=1}^{d}\frac{w_j\mu_j(x_{ij})}{\sum_{j=1}^{d}w_j}$, where w_j is the weight assigned to dimension j. As a fuzzy poverty index, Cerioli and Zani (1990) suggested the use of the arithmetic average of the individual membership values. More precisely, their index is given by $\sum_{i=1}^{n}\sum_{j=1}^{d}\frac{w_j\mu_j(x_{ij})}{n\sum_{j=}^{d}w_j}$. If we employ μ_j^{CZ} and μ_j^{TFR} for defining individual membership values, then the resulting indices become violators of the fuzzy transfer axiom. There is a possibility that index based on μ_j^{TFR} will not satisfy the fuzzy monotonicity axiom. It is a violator of the fuzzy subgroup decomposability property as well since it relies on relative frequency distributions and categorical rank orders (see Alkire et al., 2015).

As Chiappero-Martinetti (1996, 2000) argued, a more general aggregation for membership will be the use of weighted generalized mean. In fact, P^F_{Bc} employs a closely related aggregation. Evidently, the process of arriving at (4.8) has a different logic than the Cerioli–Zani suggestion. We consider subgroup decomposability at the outset and then substitute a particular form of the individual poverty function to obtain (4.8) (see Chakravarty, 2006).

4.5 Fuzzy Poverty Orderings

In this section, following Zheng (2015), we assume that income is the only dimension of well-being. The objective of the section is to obtain the dominance conditions, which ensure that for a given poverty index, one income distribution is not characterized as more poverty stricken than another for all membership functions. We will also analyze the dominance conditions under variability of poverty indices for a fixed membership function. Finally, it will be worthwhile to investigate dominance when both membership functions and poverty indices are variable.

We begin by assuming that each income v is an element of $[0, \infty)$, that is, $v \in [0, \infty)$. The lower and upper fuzzy boundaries for income are given respectively by z^l_{IN} and z^u_{IN}. A person with income below z^l_{IN} will definitely be counted as income-poor while a person with income above z^u_{IN} will definitely be treated as nonpoor. Since in this section we will assume continuous-type income distributions, it will be necessary to calculate the value of a fuzzy poverty index, obtained after some integration operation, at the limiting points z^l_{IN} and z^u_{IN}. Hence, anybody with income lying in the fuzzy interval $[z^l_{IN}, z^u_{IN}]$ will be counted as fuzzy poor. Thus, the domain of income $[0, \infty)$ can now be written as $[0, z^l_{IN}) \cup [z^l_{IN}, z^u_{IN}] \cup (z^u_{IN}, \infty)$. The fuzzy membership function is denoted by μ_{IN}.

Given that income distributions are defined on the continuum, let $G{:}[0, \infty) \to [0, 1]$ be the cumulative distribution function of income. Then $G(v)$ gives the proportion of persons with income less than or equal to v. G is nondecreasing, $G(0) = 0$ and $G(v_G) = 1$ for some $v_G < \infty$.

An additively decomposable income crisp poverty index with the unique poverty line $z > 0$ is

$$P(G; z) = \int_0^z P_I(v; z)\, dG(v), \tag{4.13}$$

where $P_I(v; z)$ is the individual income poverty function with $P_I(v; z) > 0$ for $v < z$ and $P_I(v; z) = 0$ for all $v \geq z$. Further, $P_I(v; z) > 0$ is nonincreasing in

$v < z$, that is, an increase in a poor person's income does not increase poverty, and $P_I(v; z)$ is convex in $v < z$, which means that a transfer of income from a poor person to a poorer person does not increase poverty, where the transfer does not reverse the ranks of the donor and the recipient. In the remainder of this section, we will assume that poverty indices are of additively decomposable type.

As Shorrocks and Subramanian (1994) proved, under ceteris paribus conditions, every crisp poverty index can be extended uniquely to a fuzzy poverty index

$$\Pi(G; \mu_{IN}) = \int_0^{\infty} P(G; z) d(1 - \mu_{IN}(z)). \tag{4.14}$$

Zheng (2015) refers to $\rho_{IN}(v) = \frac{d(1-\mu_{IN}(v))}{dv}$ for all $z^l_{IN} < v < z^u_{IN}$ and $\rho_{IN}(v) = 0$ for any $v \leq z^l_{IN}$ and $v \geq z^u_{IN}$, as the density function of the membership function μ_{IN}. Hence, we can rewrite $\Pi(G; \mu_{IN})$ as

$$\Pi(G; \mu_{IN}) = \int_{z^l_{IN}}^{z^u_{NI}} P(G; z)\rho_{IN}(z) dz. \tag{4.15}$$

For some of the dominance conditions, it will be necessary to consider poverty indices of two varieties: relative and absolute. An additively decomposable income poverty index given by (4.13) is of relative type if

$$P(G; z) = \int_0^{z} \tilde{P}_I\left(\frac{v}{z}\right) dG(v), \tag{4.16}$$

and of absolute type if

$$P(G; z) = \int_0^{z} \tilde{P}_I(z - v) dG(v), \tag{4.17}$$

for some individual poverty function $\tilde{P}_I$.

The following four subclasses of poverty indices will be used for presenting some of the dominance conditions:

$$\begin{aligned}
\Psi^r_1 &= \{P(G; z) | P \text{ is of the type (4.16) and } \tilde{P}_I \text{ is nonincreasing}\},\\
\Psi^r_2 &= \{P(G; z) | P \text{ is of the type (4.16) and } \tilde{P}_I \text{ is nonincreasing and}\\
&\qquad \text{convex}\},\\
\Psi^a_1 &= \{P(G; z) | P \text{ is of the type (4.17) and } \tilde{P}_I \text{ is nonincreasing}\},\\
\Psi^a_2 &= \{P(G; z) | P \text{ is of the type (4.17) and } \tilde{P}_I \text{ is nonincreasing and}\\
&\qquad \text{convex}\}.
\end{aligned}$$

The following proposition of Zheng (2015) identifies the partial ordering desiderata for all membership functions belonging to a general family.

Proposition 4.2 Let $\boldsymbol{IM}^F$ be the set of differentiable income membership functions $\mu_{IN}: [0, \infty) \rightarrow [0, 1]$ such that $\mu_{IN}(v) = 1$ for all $v \leq z^l_{IN}$, $\mu_{IN}(v) = 0$ for all $v \geq z^u_{IN}$, $0 \leq \mu_{IN}(v) \leq 1$ for all $z^l_{IN} < v < z^u_{IN}$, and $\mu'_{IN}(v) < 0$ for $z^l_{IN} < v < z^u_{IN}$, where μ'_{IN} is the derivative of μ_{IN}. Consider also any two income distributions represented by the cumulative distribution functions G^I and G^{II} defined on $[0, \infty)$ and any crisp poverty index P. Then the following statements are equivalent:

i) $\Pi(G^I; \mu_{IN}) \leq \Pi(G^{II}; \mu_{IN})$ for all $\mu_{IN} \in \boldsymbol{IM}^F$.
ii) $P(G^I; z) \leq P(G^{II}; z)$ for all $z \in [z^l_{IN}, z^u_{IN}]$.

According to Proposition 4.2, of two income distributions G^I and G^{II}, G^{II} has at least as high fuzzy poverty as G^I for all membership functions in $\boldsymbol{IM}^F$ if and only if for any crisp poverty index P, similar poverty ranking between G^I and G^{II} holds over the fuzzy area $z \in [z^l_{IN}, z^u_{IN}]$. We refer to this as fuzzy-membership ordering because it is independent of the specific form of the membership function in the set $\boldsymbol{IM}^F$. This is a first order condition. Zheng (2015) also derived a second order dominance condition using inverted S-shape membership functions. But this ordering is not relevant to our context, since use of such a membership function will lead to a clear violation of the fuzzy transfer axiom.

We can also derive fuzzy poverty-measure ordering for a given membership function. For this given membership function, we wish to look for the dominance conditions that will ensure that one distribution does not have higher poverty compared to another for all fuzzy poverty indices. In this context, Zheng (2015) established the following proposition for members of Ψ^r_1 and Ψ^r_2.

Proposition 4.3 Consider any two income distributions represented by the cumulative distribution functions G^I and G^{II} defined on $[0, \infty)$, and let $\mu_{IN} \in \boldsymbol{IM}_F$ be given. Then we have the following:

i) $\Pi(G^I; \mu_{IN}) \leq \Pi(G^{II}; \mu_{IN})$ holds for all poverty indices in Ψ^r_1 if and only if $\int_{z^l_{IN}}^{z^u_{IN}} \rho_{IN}(z) G^I_z(cz)\,dz \leq \int_{z^l_{IN}}^{z^u_{IN}} \rho_{IN}(z) G^{II}_z(cz)\,dz$ for all $c \in [0, 1]$, where $G^I_z(v)$ is G^I censored at z, that is, $G^I_z(v) = G^I(v)$ for $v < z$ and $G^I_z(v) = 1$ for $v \geq z$ (G^{II}_z is defined similarly),
ii) $\Pi(F; \mu_{IN}) \leq \Pi(G; \mu_{IN})$ holds for all poverty indices in Ψ^r_2 if and only if $\int_0^t \int_{z^l_{IN}}^{z^u_{IN}} \rho_I(z) G^I_z(cz)\,dz\,dc \leq \int_0^t \int_{z^l_{IN}}^{z^u_{IN}} \rho_I(z) G^{II}_z(cz)\,dz\,dc$ for all $t \in [0, 1]$.

Conditions (i) and (ii) of the aforementioned proposition extend the partial poverty orderings for relative crisp poverty indices to fuzzy poverty measurement. For condition (i), weighted censored cumulative distributions $\int_{z_{IN}^l}^{z_{IN}^u} \rho_{IN}(z)G_z^I(cz)\,dz$ and $\int_{z_{IN}^l}^{z_{IN}^u} \rho_{IN}(z)G_z^{II}(cz)\,dz$ are compared. Here scaling of incomes, $z \to cz$, is necessitated by the scale invariance property of the poverty indices. We can refer to this as first order fuzzy poverty-measure ordering. If the fuzzy poverty region reduces to a degenerate point, then this ordering coincides with the first order one-dimensional poverty ordering in the standard framework. We have similar remarks for condition (ii).

The following proposition of Zheng (2015) can be regarded as the absolute mate of Proposition 4.3:

Proposition 4.4 Consider any two income distributions represented by the cumulative distribution functions G^I and G^{II} defined on $[0, \infty)$, and let $\mu_{IN} \in \boldsymbol{IM}^F$ be given. Then we have the following:

i) $\Pi(G^I; \mu_{IN}) \leq \Pi(G^{II}; \mu_{IN})$ holds for all poverty indices in Ψ_1^a if and only if $\int_{z_{IN}^l}^{z_{IN}^u} \rho_{IN}(z)G_z^I(z-v)\,dz \leq \int_{z_{IN}^l}^{z_{IN}^u} \rho_{IN}(z)G_z^{II}(z-v)\,dz$ for all $v \in [0, z_{IN}^u]$, where $G_z^I(v)$ is G^I censored at z, that is, $G_z^I(v) = G^I(v)$ for $v < z$ and $G_z^I(v) = 1$ for $v \geq z$ (G_z^{II} is defined similarly),
ii) $\Pi(G^I; \mu_{IN}) \leq \Pi(G^{II}; \mu_{IN})$ holds for all poverty indices in Ψ_2^a if and only if $\int_0^v \int_{z_{IN}^l}^{z_{IN}^u} \rho_{IN}(z)G_z^I(z-c)\,dz\,dc \leq \int_0^v \int_{z_{IN}^l}^{z_{IN}^u} \rho_{IN}(z)G_z^{II}(z-c)\,dz\,dc$ for all $v \in [0, z_{IN}^u]$.

Finally, Zheng's (2015) following propositions establish dominance conditions under variability of both poverty indices and membership functions.

Proposition 4.5 Consider any two income distributions represented by the cumulative distribution functions G^I and G^{II} defined on $[0, \infty)$. Then,

i) $\Pi(G^I; \mu_{IN}) \leq \Pi(G^{II}; \mu_{IN})$ holds for all poverty indices in Ψ_1^r and for all membership functions $\mu_{IN} \in \boldsymbol{IM}^F$ if and only if $G^I(v) \leq G^{II}(v)$ for all $v \in [0, z_{IN}^u]$;
ii) $\Pi(G^I; \mu_{IN}) \leq \Pi(G^{II}; \mu_{IN})$ holds for all poverty indices in Ψ_2^r and for all membership functions $\mu_{IN} \in \boldsymbol{IM}^F$ if and only if $\int_0^v G^I(t)\,dt \leq \int_0^v G^{II}(t)\,dt$ for all $v \in [0, z_{IN}^u]$.

Proposition 4.6 Consider any two income distributions represented by the cumulative distribution functions G^I and G^{II} defined on $[0, \infty)$. Then,

i) $\Pi(G^I; \mu_{IN}) \leq \Pi(G^{II}; \mu_{IN})$ holds for all poverty indices in Ψ_1^a and for all membership functions $\mu_{IN} \in \boldsymbol{IM}^F$ if and only if $G^I(v) \leq G^{II}(v)$ for all $v \in [0, z_{IN}^u]$;
ii) $\Pi(G^I; \mu_{IN}) \leq \Pi(G^{II}; \mu_{IN})$ holds for all poverty indices in Ψ_2^a and for all membership functions $\mu_{IN} \in \boldsymbol{IM}^F$ if and only if $\int_0^v G^I(t)dt \leq \int_0^v G^{II}(t)dt$ for all $v \in [0, z_{IN}^u]$.

These orderings are referred to as fuzzy poverty-membership-measure orderings because of variability of both the poverty indices and membership functions. Clearly, we can arrive at this orderings using first poverty-measure ordering for a given membership function and then allowing membership function to vary or first looking at membership ordering for a given poverty index and later on considering all poverty indices.

4.6 Concluding Remarks

One issue that remains to be explored is to extend Zheng (2015)-type analysis to the multidimensional framework. We may examine the possibility of broadening the Duclos et al. (2006a,b) and Bourguignon and Chakravarty (2009) multidimensional poverty orderings to the fuzzy situation. Another issue of relevance here is assignment of membership grades to achievements in a dimension when the dimension is of ordinal nature (see Chapter 3). In a situation of this type, we can assign real numbers to fuzzy boundaries and membership grades using some specific ranking criterion. This numbering procedure is arbitrary in the sense that we need to ensure that the ranks of the fuzzy boundaries and grades should always be preserved. In such a case, formulation of some appropriate axioms and aggregation of membership grades across dimensions and individuals are our concerns. Information invariance assumption requires that the aggregated value remains invariant under renumbering of original boundaries and membership grades.

References

Alkire, S. and J.E. Foster. 2011. Counting and Multidimensional Poverty Measurement. *Journal of Public Economics* 95: 476–487.

Alkire, S., J.E. Foster, S. Seth, M.E. Santos, J.M. Roche, and P. Ballon. 2015. *Multidimensional Poverty Measurement and Analysis*. New York: Oxford University Press.

Amarante, V., R. Arim, and A. Vigorito. 2010. Multidimensional Poverty among Children in Uruguay. *Research on Economic Inequality* 18: 31–53.

Baliamoune-Lutz, M. and M. MacGillivray. 2006. Fuzzy Well-being Achievement in Pacific Area. *Journal of the Asia Pacific Economy* 11: 168–177.

Basu, K. 1987. Axioms for a Fuzzy Measure of Inequality. *Mathematical Social Sciences* 14: 275–288.

Basu, K. and J.E. Foster. 1998. On measuring Literacy. *Economic Journal* 108: 1733–1749.

Belhadj, B. and M. Limam. 2012. Unidimensional and Multidimensional Fuzzy Poverty Measures. *Economic Modelling* 29: 995–1002.

Belhadj, B. and M.S. Matoussi. 2010. Poverty in Tunisia: A Fuzzy Measurement Approach. *Swiss Journal of Economics and Statistics* 146: 431–450.

Bellman, R.E. and L.A. Zadeh. 1970. Decision-Making in a Fuzzy Environment. *Management Science* 17: BI41–BI64.

Bérenger, V. and F. Celestini. 2006. French Poverty Measures using Fuzzy Set Approaches. In A. Lemmi and G. Betti (eds.), 139–154.

Bérenger, V. and Verdier-Chouchane, A. 2007. Multidimensional Well-being: Standard of Living and Quality of Life across Countries. *World Development* 35: 1259–1276.

Betti, G., B. Cheli, A. Lemmi, and V. Verma. 2006a. Multidimensional and Longitudinal Poverty. In A. Lemmi and G. Betti (eds.), 115–137.

Betti, G., A. D'agostino, and L. Neri. 2006b. Modelling Fuzzy and Multidimensional Poverty Measures in the United Kingdom with Variance Components Panel Regression. In A. Lemmi and G. Betti (eds.), 257–275.

Betti, G. and V. Verma. 2008. Fuzzy Measures of the Incidence of Relative Poverty and Deprivation: A Multi-Dimensional Perspective. *Statistical Methods and Applications* 17: 225–250.

Bourguignon, F. and S.R. Chakravarty. 2003. The Measurement of Multidimensional Poverty. *Journal of Economic Inequality* 1: 25–49.

Bourguignon, F. and S.R. Chakravarty. 2009. Multidimensional Poverty Orderings: Theory and Applications. In K. Basu and R. Kanbur (eds.) *Arguments for a Better World: Essays in Honor of Amartya Sen ,Volume 1: Ethics, Welfare and Measurement*. Oxford: Oxford University Press, 337–361.

Cerioli, A. and Zani, S. 1990. A Fuzzy Approach to the Measurement of Poverty. In C. Dagum and M. Zenga (eds.) *Income and Wealth Distribution, Inequality and Poverty*. New York: Springer, 272–284.

Chakravarty, S.R. 1983. A New Index of Poverty. *Mathematical Social Sciences* 6: 307–313.

Chakravarty, S.R. 2006. An Axiomatic Approach to Multidimensional Poverty Measurement via Fuzzy Sets. In A. Lemmi and G. Betti (eds.), 49–72.

Chakravarty, S.R. 2015 *Inequality, Polarization and Conflict: An Analytical Study*. New York: Springer.

Chakravarty, S.R. and M.A. Lugo. 2016. Multidimensional Indicators of Inequality and Poverty. In M.D. Adler and M. Fleurbaey (eds.) *Oxford Handbook of Well-Being and Public Policy*. New York: Oxford University Press, 246–285.

Chakravarty, S.R., D. Mukherjee, and R. Ranade. 1998. On the Family of Subgroup and Factor Decomposable Measures of Multidimensional Poverty. *Research on Economic Inequality* 8: 175–194.

Chakravarty, S.R. and T. Roy. 1985. Measurement of Fuzziness: A General Approach. *Theory and Decision* 19: 163–169.

Cheli, B. and A. Lemmi. 1995. A "Totally" Fuzzy and Relative Approach to the Multidimensional Analysis of Poverty. *Economic Notes* 24: 115–133.

Chiappero-Martinetti, E. 1994. A New Approach to Evaluation of Well-Being and Poverty by Fuzzy Set Theory. *Giornale degli Economisti e Annali di Economia* 53: 367–388.

Chiappero-Martinetti, E. 1996. Standard of Living Evaluation Based on Sen's Approach: Some Methodological Suggestions. *Notizie di Politeia* 12: 37–53.

Chiappero-Martinetti, E. 2000. A Multidimensional Assessment of Well-Being Based on Sen's Functioning Approach. *Revista Internazionale de Sciencze Sociali* 108: 207–239.

Chiappero-Martinetti, E. 2006. Capability Approach and Fuzzy Set Theory: Description, Aggregation and Inference Issues. In A. Lemmi and G. Betti (eds.), 93–113.

Chiappero-Martinetti, E. 2008. Complexity and Vagueness in the Capability Approach: Strengths or Weaknesses? In F. Comin, M. Qizilbash, and S. Alkire (eds.) *The Capability Approach: Concepts, Applications and Measurement*. Cambridge: Cambridge University Press.

Clark, D.A. and D. Hulme. 2010. Poverty, Time and Vagueness: Integrating the Core Poverty and Chronic Poverty Frameworks. *Cambridge Journal of Economics* 34: 347–366.

D'Ambrosio, C., J. Deutsch, and J. Silber. 2011. Multidimensional Approaches to Poverty Measurement: An Empirical Analysis of Poverty in Belgium, France, Germany, Italy and Spain. *Applied Economics* 43: 951–961.

De Luca, A. and S. Termini. 1972. A Definition of Non-probabilistic Entropy in the Setting of Fuzzy Sets Theory. *Information and Control* 20: 301–312.

Deutsch, J. and J. Silber. 2005. Measuring Multidimensional Poverty: An Empirical Comparison of Various Approaches. *Review of Income and Wealth* 51: 145–174.

Deutsch, J. and J. Silber. 2006. The "Fuzzy Set" Approach to Multidimensional Poverty Analysis using the Shapley Decomposition to Analyze the Determinants of Poverty in Israel. In A. Lemmi and G. Betti (eds.), 155–174.

Dombi, J. 1990. Membership Functions as an Evaluation. *Fuzzy Sets and Systems* 35: 1–21.

Duclos, J.V., D.E. Sahn, and S.D. Younger. 2006a. Robust Multidimensional Poverty Comparisons. *Economic Journal* 116: 943–968.

Duclos, J.V., D.E. Sahn, and S.D. Younger. 2006b. Robust Multidimensional Spatial Poverty Comparisons in Ghana, Madagascar and Uganda. *World Bank Economic Review* 20: 91–113.

Foster, J.E., J. Greer, and E. Thorbecke. 1984. A Class of Decomposable Poverty Measures. *Econometrica* 52: 761–766.

Goguen, J.A. 1969. The Logic of Inexact Concepts. *Synthese* 19: 325–373.

Keefe, R. and P. Smith (eds.) 1996. *Vagueness: A Reader*. Cambridge, MA: MIT Press.

Lee, E.T. and L.A. Zadeh. 1969. Note on Fuzzy Languages. *Information Sciences* I: 421–434.

Lelli, S. 2001. Factor Analysis versus Fuzzy Sets Theory: Assessing the Influence of Different Techniques On Sen's Functioning Approach. Center of Economic Studies Discussion Paper 01.21.

Lemmi, A. and G. Betti (eds.) 2006. *Fuzzy Set Approaches to Multidimensional Poverty Measurement*. New York: Springer.

Makdissi, P. and Q. Wodon. 2004. Fuzzy Targeting Indices and Ordering. *Bulletin of Economic Research* 56: 41–51.

Miceli, D. 2006. Multidimensional and Fuzzy Poverty in Switzerland. In A. Lemmi and G. Betti (eds.), 195–209.

Molnar, M., F. Panduru, A. Vasile, and V. Duma. 2006. Multidimensional Fuzzy Set Approach to Poverty Estimates in Romania. In A. Lemmi and G. Betti (eds.), 175–194.

Mordeson, J.N., D.S. Malik, and T.D. Clark. 2015. *Applications of Fuzzy Logic to Social Choice Theory*. New York: CRC Press.

Mukherjee, M.N. and S.P. Sinha. 1990. On Some Strong Forms of Fuzzy Continuous Mappings on Fuzzy Topological Spaces. *Fuzzy Sets and Systems* 38: 375–387.

Ok, E. 1996. Fuzzy Income Inequality Measurement. *Economic Theory* 7: 513–530.

Panek, T. 2006. Multidimensional Fuzzy Relative Poverty Measures in Poland. In A. Lemmi and G. Betti (eds.), 233–255.

Qizilbash, M. 2006. Philosophical Accounts of Vagueness, Fuzzy Poverty Measures and Multidimensionality. In A. Lemmi and G. Betti (eds.), 9–28.

Roche, J.M. 2008. Monitoring Inequality among Social Groups: A Methodology Combining Fuzzy Set Theory and Principal Component Analysis. *Journal of Human Development and Capabilities* 9: 427–452.

Sen, A.K. 1981. *Poverty and Famines: An Essay on Entitlement and Deprivation*. New York: Oxford University Press.

Shorrocks, A.F. and S. Subramanian. 1994. *Fuzzy Poverty Indices*, Mimeographed, University of Essex.

Smithson, M. 1982. Applications of Fuzzy Set Concepts to Behavioral Sciences. *Mathematical Social Sciences* 2: 257–274.

Vero, J. 2006. A Comparison of Poverty According to Primary Goods, Capabilities and Outcomes: Evidences from French School Leavers' Surveys. In A. Lemmi and G. Betti (eds.), 211–231.

Wee, W.G. and K.S. Fu. 1969. A Formulation of Fuzzy Automata and its Application as a Model of Learning Systems. *IEEE Transactions on Systems Science and Cybernetics* SSC-5: 215–223.

Zadeh, L.A. 1965. Fuzzy Sets. *Information and Control* 8: 338–353.

Zheng, B. 2015. Poverty: Fuzzy Measurement and Crisp Ordering. *Social Choice and Welfare* 45: 203–229.

5

Poverty and Time: A Multidimensional Appraisal

5.1 Introduction

Our investigations on multidimensional poverty in Chapters 3 and 4 employ individual multidimensional achievements as inputs in a single period only. As a result, these atemporal studies do not convey us any information on the time span of poverty at the individual or society level. However, there are reasons not to regard poverty as a timeless concept, but to interpret it as a notion that undergoes evolution over time. It has a particular trajectory – a path with a past and a future. There are no reasons to expect that evolvement of income and nonincome dimensions of life will be the same over time (see Bourguignon and Morrison, 2002, and Decancq et al., 2006). If we restrict attention on each period of the trajectory independently of the past and future poverty experiences, then the assessment of the actual time path is ignored. In consequence, it becomes necessary to have knowledge on the durations and extents of poverty across persons. It has been stressed in the literature that continued periods of poverty are worse than scattered poverty occurrences over time (see Rodgers and Rodgers, 2003 and Jenkins, 2000). Prolonged poverty can be endemic if it arises because of political institutions and structure of the economy (Green and Hulme, 2005). A person, stricken by a long duration of poverty, may suffer from depression on finding that he is deprived even from "minimally acceptable levels" of one or more dimensions of human well-being necessary for leading a decent standard of living (Sen, 1992, p. 139). This feeling of depression may be accompanied by ruination of health and ailment. It is highly unlikely that such a socially excluded person will remain loyal to the society norms (Walker, 1995). This in turn may give rise to social turmoil. Consequently, from long-term policy perspectives, it becomes essential to look at the dynamics of individual and overall poverty.

A dynamic analysis of poverty should make a clear distinction between chronically poor and transiently poor. For effective implementation of antipoverty policy in the current context, it is necessary to pinpoint the chronically poor among the poor (Lybbert et al., 2004; Carter and Barrett, 2006).

Analyzing Multidimensional Well-Being: A Quantitative Approach, First Edition. Satya R. Chakravarty.

According to Hulme and Shepherd (2003), chronically poor persons may be characterized as those "people who remain poor for much of their life course, and who may 'pass on' their poverty to subsequent generations" (p. 405). Two criteria that have been suggested in the literature for developing quantifiers of chronic poverty that aggregate an individual's poverty positions over time are the spells or duration approach and the permanent income approach (see Yaqub, 2000a,b; Mckay and Lawson, 2003; Hoy et al., 2012). The former relies on the fraction of time a person is perceived to be in poverty.[1]

Foster (2009) employed the duration approach to suggest a family of income-based chronic poverty indices using an axiomatic framework. This class of indices, which is the chronic variant of the Foster et al. (1984) family of poverty indices, invokes an aggregation first across time and then over individuals. Chakravarty (2009) considered the entire one-dimensional subgroup-decomposable chronic poverty indices within this framework and investigated their properties.

The permanent income approach, also known as the components approach (Yaqub, 2000b), to the identification of the chronically poor persons, relies on the comparison between the resources that he has over time with the poverty line. Jalan and Ravallion (1998) defined a person as chronically poor if his resources, averaged over time, fall below an appropriate poverty line.[2]

As Foster and Santos (2014) noted, these two different desiderata to the identification of chronically poor persons can be clearly separated depending on the nature of substitutability between periods. While by concentrating simply on periodwise resources, the duration approach does not allow the transfer of resources across periods, the permanent income approach makes use of the average value of resources and hence implicitly allows perfect substitutability across periods. An expansion of the permanent income approach by incorporating savings and borrowings of an individual was suggested by Rodgers and Rodgers (2003). Foster and Santos (2014) put forward a new methodology for assessing chronic poverty that adopts the permanent income approach but incorporates explicitly imperfect degree of substitutability between periods. Porter and Quinn (2008) also replaced the perfect substitution assumption by an alternative supposition of increasing elasticity of substitution using a linear combination of constant elasticity of substitution functions. The family of indices advocated by Porter and Quinn (2014) takes into account the view that the lower the income of a poor person, the higher will be the negative effect of variations in well-being.

A person who is irregularly or occasionally poor over time can be treated as transiently poor. Such a person is poor in some of the periods but not in

1 See also Bane and Ellwood (1986), Gaiha (1989), Gaiha and Deolikar (1993), Morduch (1994), Levy (1997), Baluch and Masset (2003), Mehta and Shah (2003), and Carter and Barrett (2006), for discussion on duration issues.

2 The central idea underlying this methodology was suggested by Ravallion (1988).

other periods, and he is not also poor for a minimum number of periods so that he may not be regarded as chronically poor. A person, stricken by this notion of poverty, transiently falls below the poverty line. Transient poverty can be defined as the difference between average of the static periodwise poverty levels and the chronic poverty value (see Ravallion, 1988; Rodgers and Rodgers, 2003; Kurosaki, 2006; Foster, 2009). Time here becomes a characteristic for differentiating among the poor: chronic poverty is different from temporary poverty. The major source of transient poverty is income fluctuation over the periods. A transient poverty index represents a composite picture of fluctuations of income over time that force individuals to be in poverty transiently. In case there are no variations in income over time due to uncertainty, total poverty is determined by value of a poverty index using incomes observed with certainty across periods. It has been argued that transient poverty is equally significant as chronic poverty, and its relative significance varies across social groups and regions (Ravallion, 1988; Ravallion et al., 1995; Jalan and Ravallion, 1998; Baluch and Hoddinott, 2000; Kurosaki, 2006). Foster (2009) and Foster and Santos (2014) suggested transient poverty indices using, respectively, the duration and permanent income approaches to poverty measurement with shorter durations. Duclos et al. (2010) suggested aggregate chronic and transient poverty indices, and there is no identification yardstick for the chronically poor.

There is also a related literature on poverty dynamics that does not deal with chronic poverty but instead concentrates on lifetime or intertemporal poverty. In a recent contribution, Bossert et al. (2012) argued that a metric of individual intertemporal poverty should explicitly incorporate persistence in a state of poverty. The notion of persistence takes into account the durations of poverty spells along with the requisite that the states of affairs where poverty exists in consecutive periods should be regarded as more severe than comparatively the situations in which poverty occurs in separated periods. Thus, while chronic poverty is characterized by frequent occurrence of poverty states, persistence in poverty stipulates that in addition to frequency, consecutiveness of poverty appearance is also vital. To understand the difference between the duration and the persistence approaches in greater detail, let us refer to a cluster of k consecutive poverty (respectively, nonpoverty) spells as a poverty (respectively, nonpoverty) block of size k, where $k \geq 1$ is an integer. Now, suppose that, given income data for six consecutive periods, a person will be identified as chronically poor if he spends at least three periods in poverty. However, a person is found to be poor only in the first and second periods and out of poverty in all the other periods. While the duration approach does not regard him as chronically poor, the Bossert–Chakravarty–D'Ambrosio approach, which we refer to as the block approach (Zheng, 2012), treats him as intertemporally poor because in this approach, poverty blocks of any length are taken into account. Further, his total poverty is more here than in the situation if he would have experienced the same poverty extents in the first and third periods, that is, when an interchange of poverty values between the second and third periods takes place. In other words, a two-period poverty block is regarded as more damaging than two one-period poverty blocks that are separated by one or more nonzero poverty blocks. More precisely, severity of individual intertemporal poverty is an increasing function of the size of poverty blocks. This indicates that the negative effects of poverty are cumulative.

There are empirical evidences that support negative consequences of cumulative poverty. For instance, individuals characterized by persistent poverty are affected by capability deprivations with respect to education, health, and social capital (Chronic Poverty Research Center, 2004). Arranz and Cantó (2012) used Spanish longitudinal data to demonstrate that poverty exit rates are negatively affected by accumulation of poverty spells and length of past spells. It has been argued in the literature that when individuals are affected by poverty spells of long size, getting away from poverty becomes quite difficult (see Bane and Ellwood, 1986; Walker, 1995; Cappellari and Jenkins, 2004). Bossert et al. (2012) axiomatically characterized an individual's intertemporal poverty index given by the weighted sum of periodwise poverty levels, where the weights are the sizes of poverty blocks. In consequence, it reflects the views adopted in the block approach. In Lillard and Willis (1978) and Duncan and Rodgers (1991), proportion of persons with incomes below the permanent income has been taken as an index of persistent poverty, where permanent income has been estimated as a person's intercept in fixed-effects earnings model, and the transitory component was represented by the error term. Bossert et al. (2012) also axiomatically characterized an intertemporal poverty index for the society as a whole using the individual intertemporal indices. In Dutta et al. (2013), a variant of the Bossert–Chakravarty–D'Ambrosio approach was developed by discounting the effect of a period in poverty using the number of periods out of poverty that precede it.

The persistence issue has also been considered by Calvo and Dercon (2009), but their suggested index considers the poverty of the immediately preceding period only without taking into account the entire history of the individuals. Calvo and Dercon (2009) made a thorough presentation of several issues on lifetime poverty for an individual. The three critical features that were addressed in their study are as follows: aiding poverty spells by nonpoverty spells, treating consecutive poverty spells as more harmful than separated spells, and discounting instead of valuing all spells equally. They suggested several indices that provide different answers to these issues.

Hoy and Zheng (2011) attempted to provide an axiomatic framework to investigate the notion of lifetime poverty for an individual as well as for a society. A major difference between the duration approach and the Hoy–Zheng approach is that the latter does not directly identify the chronically poor; instead, it concentrates on closeness of poverty spells. The impact of closeness is maximized when all the spells constitute a block, and it is minimized if the spells are separated evenly over the entire period. For any situation in between these two extremes, the impact changes continuously. They also invoked an axiom that stresses that poverty in earlier phases of life not only produces an effect on incomes in later periods but also intensifies lifetime poverty. Their approach, which attaches importance on closeness of poverty spells, may be referred to as a closeness approach (Zheng, 2012). Similarly to the Bossert–Chakravarty–D'Ambrosio index, the Hoy and Zheng (2011) individual index of lifetime poverty is a weighted average of snapshot poverty levels with the weights being a decreasing and strictly concave function of the time period. For the society lifetime index, Hoy and Zheng (2011) demanded that aggregation first across individuals and then across time is equivalent to aggregation in the reverse order, that is, for each individual, intertemporal aggregation is done first, which is then followed by aggregation across individuals. This gives rise to the concept of "path independence."

Mendola and Busetta (2012) proposed a persistent individual poverty index that is based on a path dependence axiom. According to this axiom, different weight is assigned to each pair of years of poverty, irrespective of whether they are consecutive or not. It assigns a higher degree of (longitudinal) poverty to people who suffer from poverty in blocks, rather than in separated periods, for whom the gaps from the poverty line are larger through time and when the worst years are in blocks and/or recent. They also introduced an aggregate index of persistence in poverty with the objective of measuring the distribution of the persistence of poverty in the society. Gradin et al. (2012) made a methodological proposal to measure intertemporal poverty by suggesting a new family of poverty indices that attempts to harmonize the ways poverty is quantified in a static and a dynamic framework. Their index explicitly indicates social preference for equality in the distribution of poverty across periods through income transfer from one period to another.

Hojman and Kast (2009) developed an intertemporal index that relies on trade-off between levels of poverty and changes in poverty (gains and losses). The individual index characterized by Hojman and Kast (2009) turns out to be an increasing function of periodwise absolute poverty levels and changes in poverty. Bossert et al. (2014) suggested an index of individual intertemporal material deprivation as the sum of average material deprivation suffered by the individual over time and the average of weighted changes in material deprivation met by the person overt time, where weights can behave in a similar way as loss aversion. However, while the Hojman–Kast analysis is concerned with a single dimension of well-being, the Bossert et al. approach looks at material deprivations in different possible dimensions. In Bossert et al. (2014), it has also been explored how the Foster (2009) and block approaches can be utilized to ascertain material deprivation.

A generalization of the Chakravarty and D'Ambrosio (2006) counting approach to the measurement of social exclusion was considered by Nicholas and Ray (2011) for measuring multidimensional deprivation, building on the proposals of Bossert et al. (2012) and Gradin et al. (2012) for evaluating intertemporal poverty.

The objective of this chapter is to analyze alternative approaches that propose or develop specific indices of lifetime poverty in a multidimensional framework. All such indices may be regarded as indices of intertemporal capability deprivation. Now, when time and multidimensionality are simultaneously subsumed into the analysis of poverty measurement, the picture becomes quite complex. The principal reason behind this is that the identification of a poor in a multidimensional intertemporal setup itself is complicated. For instance, it becomes necessary to investigate whether we aggregate multidimensional poverty levels of an individual at different time periods to arrive at an overall measure, or periodwise dimensional deprivations of the persons are aggregated to get a comprehensive picture of his intertemporal poverty. Consequently, it becomes imperative to examine what matter in defining and conceptualizing the notion of multidimensional intertemporal poverty and how to record these features accurately.

Section 5.2 of the chapter reports the preliminaries and background materials. The concern of Section 5.3 is to extend the one-dimensional block approach advocated by Bossert et al. (2012) to a multidimensional framework. A comparative analysis with some one-dimensional variants of this approach, when it is adapted to the unidimensional case, is also presented in a subsection of the section. Two multidimensional counting approaches to the determination of intertemporal deprivation are examined in Section 5.4. Section 5.5 presents a deliberation on a generalization of Foster's (2009) chronic income poverty measurement proposal to a multidimensional situation, suggested by Alkire et al. (2017). A short subsection of Section 5.5 deals with one-dimensional chronic poverty measurement. The functional form of the multidimensional chronic poverty index we propose relies on the Bourguignon and Chakravarty (2003) approach to multidimensional poverty measurement. Its transient counterpart is also explored rigorously. One characteristic of this specific choice is that it can accommodate a scrutiny of relationship between any two dimensions of well-being in terms of substitutability and complementarity. A detailed investigation of the axioms considered for each case is made in the respective section. The objective of Section 5.6 is to study intertemporal poverty orderings explored by Bresson and Duclos (2015). Finally, Section 5.7 concludes the discussion.

5.2 Preliminaries

Assume availability of observations on d dimensions of well-being for n individuals at T consecutive time periods, where $n, T \in N$, with N being the set of natural numbers. We denote the set of all dimensions $\{1, 2, \ldots, d\}$ by Q. For any $T \in N$, we say that $(1, 2, \ldots, T)$ is a period profile of length T. The set $\{1, 2, \ldots, T\}$ denotes the set of periods in the profile $(1, 2, \ldots, T)$ of length T. Person i's achievement in dimension j in the tth period is denoted by x_{ij}^t, where $i \in \{1, 2, \ldots, n\}$, $j \in Q$ and $t \in \{1, 2, \ldots, T\}$ are arbitrary. These numbers constitute the basic ingredients of our analysis. Unless specified, it will be assumed that $x_{ij}^t \geq 0$. Given that we are concerned here with intertemporal analysis, it is likely that $T \geq 1$. For $T = 1$, we go back to the atemporal situation considered in Chapter 3. Assume also that no ambiguity arises with respect to the definition of a period, for instance, it can be a year or three-quarters of a year and so on. Each period is assumed to be sufficiently long for achievements to be observed and measured.

Let X^t stand for the $n \times d$ dimensional matrix whose ith row is $x_{i.}^t = (x_{i1}^t, x_{i2}^t, \ldots, x_{id}^t)$, which is a listing of the quantities in d dimensions that person i possesses in period t. More formally, for $t \in \{1, 2, \ldots, T\}$, $i \in \{1, 2, \ldots, n\}$, this $1 \times d$ matrix represents person i's achievements in different dimensions in the tth period. The number of dimensions d is assumed to be fixed. We refer to the $n \times d$ matrix X^t as the achievement or distributional matrix in period t. Often, we will refer to X^t as the social distribution or social matrix in the tth period. The distribution of achievements in dimension j in period t is depicted by the column vector $x_{.j}^t$. We write A^t for the set of all $n \times d$ achievement matrices in period t.

We assume at the outset that the dimensional achievements have been suitably tailored to take into consideration variations across time periods, for instance, by discounting. Consequently, for each dimension, a common threshold limit can be used. Let $\underline{z} = (z_1, z_2, \ldots, z_d)$ be the d dimensional vector (i.e., $1 \times d$ matrix) of time invariant threshold limits, where $z_j > 0$ for all $j \in Q$. The vector $\underline{z}$ is assumed to be an element of the set $Z \subset D^d$, strictly positive part of the d dimensional Euclidean space. Person i is regarded as deprived (respectively, nondeprived) with respect to dimension j in period t if $x_{ij}^t < z_j$ (respectively, $x_{ij}^t \geq z_j^t$). Equivalently, we say that dimension j is meager (respectively, nonmeager) for person i in period t. For any period t and each pair $(i, j) \in \{1, 2, \ldots, n\} \times \{1, 2, \ldots, d\}$, let $\hat{x}_{ij}^t = \min(x_{ij}^t, z_j)$ be the censored amount of achievement in dimension j possessed by person i in period t. Then the deprivation indicator of person i in the dimension–period pair $(j,t) \in \{1,2,\ldots,d\} \times \{1,2,\ldots,T\}$ is given by $g_{ij}^t = \left(1 - \frac{\hat{x}_{ij}^t}{z_j}\right)$. Thus, if individual i is deprived in dimension j at period t, then he experiences a positive deprivation; otherwise, his deprivation is zero.

Let X be the $nT \times d$ intertemporal achievement matrix of the n individuals for all the periods, whose typical entry is x_{ij}^t, person i's achievement in dimension j in period t. The first n rows of X indicate the achievements of n individuals in different dimensions in period 1, the second n rows, starting from the $(n+1)$th row to the $(2n)$th row, specify similar figures in period 2, and so on. Unless mentioned explicitly, it will be assumed that T, the number of periods over which observations are made, is given. It is also assumed that the choice of the vector of threshold limits $\underline{z} \in Z$ is arbitrary. The population size n is allowed to vary over the set of natural numbers N. Let M^{nT} stand for the set of all $nT \times d$ intertemporal achievement matrices. The set of intertemporal achievement matrices for all population sizes are given by M, that is, $\underset{n\in N}{\cup} M^{nT} = M$. We denote the n coordinated vector of ones by 1^n. For any $T, n \in N$, $X \in M$, $x_{i.}^{INT} = (x_{i.}^1, \ldots, x_{i.}^T)$ represents an intertemporal achievement profile for person i, where $x_{i.}^t$ is ith row of $X^t \in A^t$, with $t \in \{1,2,\ldots,T\}$, $i \in \{1,2,\ldots,n\}$, $n \in N$ being arbitrary.

We assume the union method of identifying the poor in each period in this multidimensional framework. In consequence, if a person is deprived in at least one dimension in a period, then he is regarded as poor in that period. Evidently, a person deprived in a dimension in a period may or may not be deprived in the same dimension next period.

5.3 The Block Approach

For expositional ease, we will subdivide our discussion in this section into several subsections.

5.3.1 Individual Multidimensional Intertemporal Poverty Index

The objective of this subsection is to develop an analytical formulation of the block approach to the quantification of intertemporal poverty for any arbitrary individual $i \in \{1,2,\ldots,n\}$. Essentials to the approach are the individual poverty profiles across periods. It is assumed that individual poverty indicators are observed in each of the periods under consideration. For each person i, the per-period poverty profile is a vector $p_i = (p_i^1, p_i^2, \ldots, p_i^T) \in \Re_+^T$, the non-negative part of the T-dimensional Euclidean space. We can as well say that p_i is person i's intertemporal poverty profile of length T. For any given period $t \in \{1,2,\ldots,T\}$, p_i^t represents person i's overall deprivation in the period, as determined by a nonconstant subgroup-decomposable multidimensional poverty index $F: A^t \times Z \to \Re_+^1$. More precisely, for any $(X^t; \underline{z}) \in A^t \times Z$,

$p_i^t = F(x_{i.}^t; \underline{z})$. That is, for any $X^t \in A^t$ and $\underline{z} \in Z$, $p_i^t = F(x_{i.}^t; \underline{z}) \geq 0$ gives the extent of poverty corresponding to $x_{i.}^t$ and the threshold vector $\underline{z}$. It takes on the minimal value 0 if person i is nondeprived in all the dimensions. We assume subgroup decomposability at the outset because of its appealing policy applications.

By assumption,

$$F(X^t; \underline{z}) = \frac{1}{n} \sum_{i=1}^{n} F(x_{i.}^t; \underline{z}) \tag{5.1}$$

The index F is ratio-scale invariant, strongly (hence weakly) focused, symmetric, population replication invariant, monotonic, monotonically sensitive, dimensionally monotonic, increasing under a Pigou–Dalton bundle of regressive transfers between two poor persons, increasing (respectively, decreasing) under a correlation-increasing switch if the underlying dimensions are substitutes (respectively, complements) and bounded. It varies continuously with respect to changes in achievement levels of the individual in the period provided that the person's poverty status remains unchanged in the period (period-restricted continuity). (See Chapter 3, for details.)

The individual poverty function considered next turns out to be satisfactory from these perspectives. It corresponds to a member of the Bourguignon–Chakravarty family and is formally defined as

$$F_{BC}\,(x_{i.}^t; \underline{z}) = \left[\sum_{j=1}^{d} \frac{1}{d} \left(1 - \frac{\hat{x}_{ij}^t}{z_j^t} \right)^{\alpha} \right]^{\frac{\beta}{\alpha}}, \tag{5.2}$$

where $\alpha > 1$ and $\beta > 0$ are parameters. Some restrictions on inequality between α and β have to be imposed for sensitivity under a correlation-increasing switch (see Chapter 3). For all t, $p_i^t = 0$ means that individual i is nonpoor in period t, whereas a positive value of p_i^t indicates that he is in poverty in this period.

It may often be necessary to compare intertemporal poverty profiles of different lengths. This type of comparison can be made if we assume that the individual intertemporal poverty index entertains time replication invariance, that is, it remains invariant under replication of the poverty profile with respect to time (see Shorrocks, 2009a). Fulfillment of this property also makes comparisons of individual intertemporal poverty meaningful when possibilities of profiles with different lengths, coming from populations with different sizes, are allowed. To state this principle, formally, we need to define an individual intertemporal index rigorously.

Let $\mathfrak{R}_+ = \bigcup_{T \in N} \mathfrak{R}_+^T$, where N is the set of natural numbers. Here $\mathfrak{R}_+$ represents the set of person i's intertemporal poverty profiles of all possible lengths.

Definition 5.1 An intertemporal poverty index P_i^{INT} for any individual $i \in \{1, 2, \ldots, n\}$ is a nonconstant nonnegative real-valued function defined on

$\mathfrak{R}_+$, where $n \in N$ is arbitrary. More formally, for any $i \in \{1, 2, \cdots, n\}$ and $n \in N$, intertemporal poverty is measured by the nonconstant function $P_i^{INT} : \mathfrak{R}_+ \rightarrow \mathfrak{R}_+^1$.

For any $T \in N$, $p_i = (p_i^1, p_i^2, \cdots, p_i^T) \in \mathfrak{R}_+^T$, $P_i^{INT}(p_i)$ determines the extent of intertemporal poverty suffered by person i over the time profile $(1, 2, \ldots, T)$. By defining P_i^{INT} over the set all poverty profiles of different lengths, we consider the possibility of allowing comparisons of intertemporal poverty profiles with different lengths using the metric P_i^{INT}.

The time replication principle may now be formally stated as follows:

Time Replication Principle: The intertemporal poverty index $P_i^{INT} : \mathfrak{R}_+ \rightarrow \mathfrak{R}_+^1$ is said to be time replication invariant if for all $T \in N$, $p_i = (p_i^1, p_i^2, \cdots, p_i^T) \in \mathfrak{R}_+^T$, $P_i^{INT}(p_i) = P_i^{INT}(p_i^{(k)})$,where $p_i^{(k)}$ is the $k-$ fold replication of p_i, and $k \geq 2$ is any integer.

In the replicated poverty profile $p_i^{(k)}$, each entry p_i^t of p_i is repeated k times so that $p_i^{(k)}$ has a length of Tk. In consequence, $p_i^{(k)} \in \mathfrak{R}_+^{Tk}$. Satisfaction of the time replication principle by an individual intertemporal poverty index means that intertemporal poverty is an average concept.

We now suggest two basic postulates for an individual intertemporal poverty index. The first property, monotonicity, involves a curtailment in a deprived dimension's achievement of the person in a period in which he is poor.

Definition 5.2 For all $T, n \in N$, and $i \in \{1, 2, \cdots, n\}$, consider an intertemporal achievement profile $x_{i.}^{INT} = (x_{i.}^1, x_{i.}^2, \ldots, x_{i.}^T)$, where for each $t \in \{1, 2, \cdots, T\}$, $x_{i.}^t$ is the ith row of $X^t \in A^t$. Then we say that the profile $y_{i.}^{INT} = (y_{i.}^1, y_{i.}^2, \ldots, y_{i.}^T)$ is obtained from the profile $x_{i.}^{INT}$, by a simple reduction in a deprived dimension's achievement of person i if (i) for some $t_1 \in \{1, 2, \ldots, \mathrm{T}\}$, $k \in \{1, 2, \cdots, d\}$, $y_{ik}^{t_1} = x_{ik}^{t_1} - c \geq 0$, where $0 < x_{ik}^{t_1} < z_k$ and $c > 0$, (ii) $y_{ij}^{t_1} = x_{ij}^{t_1}$ for all $j \in \{1, 2, \ldots, d\}/\{k\}$, and (iii) $y_{i.}^t = x_{i.}^t$ for all $t \in \{1, 2, \cdots, T\}/\{t_1\}$.

In Definition 5.2, person i is poor in period t_1 because of his positive deprivation in dimension k in the profile $x_{i.}^{INT}$ in period t_1, and his deprivation in the dimension in the same period is higher in the profile $y_{i.}^{INT}$. (Recall that we follow the union method of identification of the poor.) His achievements in all other dimensions in t_1 and also in all the dimensions in all other periods across the profiles remain unchanged. In consequence, $y_{i.}^{INT}$ should indicate a higher level of intertemporal poverty than $x_{i.}^{INT}$. This postulate, which may be treated as a multidimensional translation of the axiom "monotonicity in outcomes," suggested by Calvo and Dercon (2009), can now be formally stated as follows.

Period-Restricted Monotonicity: For all $T, n \in N$, and $i \in \{1, 2, \cdots, n\}$, $P_i^{INT}(p_i^1, p_i^2, \cdots, p_i^T) < P_i^{INT}(\tilde{p}_i^1, \tilde{p}_i^2, \cdots, \tilde{p}_i^T)$, given that for all $t \in \{1, 2, \cdots, T\}$,

$p_i^t = F(x_{i.}^t; \underline{z})$ and $\tilde{p}_i^t = F(y_{i.}^t; \underline{z})$, where F is an individual poverty function, and $y_{i.}^{INT} = (y_{i.}^1, y_{i.}^2, \ldots, y_{i.}^T)$ is obtained from $x_{i.}^{INT} = (x_{i.}^1, x_{i.}^2, \ldots, x_{i.}^T)$ by a simple reduction in the achievement in a deprived dimension of person i.

This axiom demands that a cutback in a deprived dimension's achievement of a person in any period leads to an augmentation in intertemporal poverty level of the person. To understand the axiom in greater detail, let $T = 3$ and $d = 3$. The three dimensions of well-being are daily energy consumption in calories by an adult male, per capita income, and life expectancy. The vector of respective thresholds limits is $\underline{z} = (2700, 60, 500)$. The achievement profiles of person i in the 3 periods are, respectively, $x_{i.}^1 = (2700, 59.4, 440)$, $x_{i.}^2 = (2700, 59.5, 490)$, and $x_{i.}^3 = (2500, 62, 600)$. In periods 1 and 2, the person is deprived in life expectancy and income. In period 3, he is deprived only in calorie consumption. In period 1, if life expectancy of the person goes down to 59, then the profile $y_{i.}^{INT} = ((2700, 59, 440), (2700, 59.5, 490), (2500, 62, 600))$ is obtained from the profile $x_{i.}^{INT} = ((2700, 59.4, 440), (2700, 59.5, 490), (2500, 62, 600))$ by a simple reduction in person i's life expectancy, a deprived dimension of the person, in period 1. The state-restricted monotonicity axiom demands that the former profile should be more intertemporally poverty stricken than the latter.

For $x_{i.}^{INT} = (x_{i.}^1, x_{i.}^2, \ldots, x_{i.}^T)$ and $y_{i.}^{INT} = (y_{i.}^1, y_{i.}^2, \ldots, y_{i.}^T)$ considered in Definition 5.2, assume that $c > 0$ is such $0 < y_{ik}^{t_1} < z_k$ and $\overline{y}_{ik}^{t_1} = y_{ik}^{t_1} - c = x_{ik}^{t_1} - 2c \geq 0$. Define $\overline{y}_{i.}^{INT} = (\overline{y}_{i.}^1, \overline{y}_{i.}^2, \ldots, \overline{y}_{i.}^T)$ as follows: (i) $\overline{y}_{ik}^{t_1} = y_{ik}^{t_1} - c = x_{ik}^{t_1} - 2c$, (ii) $\overline{y}_{ij}^{t_1} = y_{ij}^{t_1} = x_{ij}^{t_1}$ for all $j \in Q/\{k\}$, and (iii) $\overline{y}_{i.}^t = y_{i.}^t = x_{i.}^t$ for all $t \in \{1, 2, \cdots, T\}/\{t_1\}$. Then the shortfall of achievement in dimension k between the profiles $x_{i.}^{INT}$ and $y_{i.}^{INT}$ in period t_1 is identical to that between $y_{i.}^{INT}$ and $\overline{y}_{i.}^{INT}$. But in $y_{i.}^{INT}$, person i's achievement in the dimension is lower than that in the original profile $x_{i.}^{INT}$. One may argue that intertemporal poverty should hit a person harder if achievement loss takes at a lower level. To state this formally in terms of an axiom, for all $t \in \{1, 2, \cdots, T\}$, let $p_i^t = F(x_{i.}^t; \underline{z})$, $\tilde{p}_i^t = F(y_{i.}^t; \underline{z})$, and $\overline{p}_i^t = F(\overline{y}_{i.}^t; \underline{z})$, where F is an individual poverty function. Then the following postulate, which may be treated as a multidimensional twin of Calvo and Dercon's (2009) "increasing cost of hardship" axiom in the one-dimensional case, may be stated as follows:

Period-Restricted Monotonicity Sensitivity: For all $T, n \in N$, and $i \in \{1, 2, \ldots, n\}$, $P_i^{INT}(\tilde{p}_i^1, \tilde{p}_i^2, \ldots, \tilde{p}_i^T) - P_i^{INT}(p_i^1, p_i^2, \ldots, p_i^T) < P_i^{INT}(\overline{p}_i^1, \overline{p}_i^2, \ldots, \overline{p}_i^T) - P_i^{INT}(p_i^1, p_i^2, \ldots, p_i^T)$.

In the aforementioned example, suppose that person i's life expectancy in period 1 reduces further from 59 to 58.5. Then the period-restricted monotonicity sensitivity axiom appeals that the escalation in the person's intertemporal poverty when the intertemporal achievement profile modifies from $((2700, 59.4, 440), (2700, 59.5, 490), (2500, 62, 600))$ to $((2700, 59, 440),$

(2700, 59.5, 490), (2500, 62, 600)) is lower than that when it shifts from ((2700, 59, 440), (2700, 59.5, 490), (2500, 62, 600)) to ((2700, 58.6, 440), (2700, 59.5, 490), (2500, 62, 600)).

In the block approach, aggregation of the components of the individual per-period poverty profile into an individual intertemporal poverty index assumes, under ceteris paribus conditions, that longer breaks between poverty blocks will decrease intertemporal poverty. To understand this requirement, consider the per-period poverty profiles $\left(\frac{1}{2}, \frac{1}{4}, 0, \frac{1}{8}, 0, \frac{1}{2}\right)$ and $\left(\frac{1}{2}, \frac{1}{4}, 0, 0, \frac{1}{8}, 0, \frac{1}{2}\right)$. There are two breaks in each profile, but the first break in the second profile has higher length. This suggests that the second profile should have lower intertemporal poverty. More precisely, both the profiles are portrayed by a two-period block with poverty levels $\frac{1}{2}$ and $\frac{1}{4}$, respectively, one one-period block with a poverty value of $\frac{1}{8}$, and also one one-period block having a poverty value of $\frac{1}{2}$. But while in the former profile, there is one zero-poverty block between the sequences $\left(\frac{1}{2}, \frac{1}{4}\right)$ and $\frac{1}{8}$, in the latter profile, the same sequences are separated by a zero-poverty block of size 2. In order to make the presence of zero-poverty block significant in a situation of this type, from antipoverty perspective, it is desirable that the former profile should indicate higher individual intertemporal poverty than the latter, under ceteris paribus conditions. We refer to this property as sensitivity to the *length in poverty break*.

The second feature of the aggregation is that intertemporal poverty increases as the longer length of a poverty block increases at the expense of shorter length of a poverty block. To illustrate this, consider the profiles $\left(\frac{1}{2}, \frac{1}{4}, \frac{1}{8}, 0, \frac{1}{2}\right)$ and $\left(\frac{1}{2}, \frac{1}{4}, \frac{1}{8}, \frac{1}{2}, 0\right)$. In both the profiles, the positive poverty values $\frac{1}{2}$, $\frac{1}{4}$, and $\frac{1}{8}$ appear respectively twice, once, and once. In the first profile, the length of the first poverty block is 3 and that of the second poverty block is 1. Now, in the second profile, the length of the first poverty block increases to 4 and that of the second poverty block reduces to 0. Then the former profile should have less intertemporal poverty than the latter under ceteris paribus conditions. This property reflects sensitivity to the *length of poverty blocks*.

In sum, we have argued that evaluation of poverty over time from a multidimensional perspective is highly positively correlated with the lengths of individual poverty spells and negatively correlated with the lengths of breaks between two poverty spells.

Now, for any $t \in \{1, 2, \cdots, T\}$ such that $p_i^t > 0$ (respectively, $p_i^t = 0$), let $l_i^t(p_i)$ be the maximal number of consecutive periods including t with positive (respectively, zero) per-period poverty values. For instance, let $p_i = \left(\frac{1}{2}, \frac{1}{4}, 0\frac{1}{8}, 0, \frac{1}{2}\right)$. Since the individual is in poverty in the first two periods, $l_i^1(p_i) = l_i^2(p_i) = 2$. This is followed by a zero-poverty block of length 1 and hence, $l_i^3(p_i) = 1$. The individual is again in poverty in the next period and out of poverty then, which in turn implies that $l_i^4(p_i) = l_i^5(p_i) = 1$. The final period in which the person is in poverty is a single period after the fifth block with a zero poverty. This implies that $l_i^6(p_i) = 1$.

The Bossert et al. (2012) multidimensional intertemporal poverty index for person i can now be defined as

$$P_i^{BCD}(p_i) = \frac{1}{T}\sum_{t=1}^{T} l_i^t p_i^t. \tag{5.3}$$

Note that nonnegativity of p_i ensures that $P_i^{BCD} \in \Re_+^1$, where the lower bound 0 is achieved if nobody is deprived in any period ($x_{ij}^t \geq z_j^t$ for all triplets (i, j, t)). This time replication individual intertemporal index unambiguously reduces when profiles have longer breaks between poverty blocks and increases when the length of a poverty block increases. Now, each component p_i^t of p_i is the individual function, evaluated using person i's achievements, associated with a subgroup-decomposable multidimensional poverty index F. Given that l_i^t's are positive, all postulates of p_i^t are periodwise satisfied by P_i^{BCD}. In the discussion on sensitivity to length in poverty break, the two profiles, we have considered, are of lengths 5 and 7, respectively. The time replication invariance postulate empowers us to compare them with respect to intertemporal poverty.

To illustrate the formula in (5.3), we now calculate its values for the examples considered earlier. The values of person i's intertemporal poverty, as determined by P_i^{BCD}, for these profiles are given as follows:

$$P_i^{BCD}\left(\frac{1}{2}, \frac{1}{4}, 0, \frac{1}{8}, 0, \frac{1}{2}\right) = \frac{1}{6}\left(\frac{1}{2}.2 + \frac{1}{4}.2 + 0.1 + \frac{1}{8}.1 + 0.1 + \frac{1}{2}.1\right) = \frac{21}{48},$$

$$P_i^{BCD}\left(\frac{1}{2}, \frac{1}{4}, 0, 0, \frac{1}{8}, 0, \frac{1}{2}\right) = \frac{1}{7}\left(\frac{1}{2}.2 + \frac{1}{4}.2 + 0.2 + 0.2 + \frac{1}{8}.1 + 0.1 + \frac{1}{2}.1\right) = \frac{17}{56},$$

$$P_i^{BCD}\left(\frac{1}{2}, \frac{1}{4}, \frac{1}{8}, 0, \frac{1}{2}\right) = \frac{1}{5}\left(\frac{1}{2}.3 + \frac{1}{4}.3 + \frac{1}{8}.3 + 0.1 + \frac{1}{2}.1\right) = \frac{25}{40},$$

$$P_i^{BCD}\left(\frac{1}{2}, \frac{1}{4}, \frac{1}{8}, \frac{1}{2}, 0\right) = \frac{1}{5}\left(\frac{1}{2}.4 + \frac{1}{4}.4 + \frac{1}{8}.4 + \frac{1}{2}.4 + 0.1\right) = \frac{44}{40}.$$

The first two calculations clearly indicate that individual intertemporal poverty decreases as the breaks between poverty blocks become longer, and the other two calculations show that it increases whenever the lengths of poverty blocks increase.

In the property that reflects sensitivity of P_i^{BCD} to the length of a poverty block, we assumed an arbitrary number of poverty periods. We will now state a related property of a general individual intertemporal poverty index involving the lengths of poverty blocks in profiles with only two poverty periods. This postulate will be stated as a necessary and sufficient requirement. To illustrate the idea, consider the profile $p_i = \left(0, \frac{1}{4}, 0, 0, \frac{1}{2}\right)$. The common length of each of the two poverty blocks in this profile is 1, and they are separated by a nonpoverty block of length 2. Now, if we swap the poverty experiences of periods 3 and 5 in this profile, the resulting profile turns out to be $\left(0, \frac{1}{4}, \frac{1}{2}, 0, 0\right)$. The value of the index P_i^{BCD} for this postswitch intertemporal profile is 6/20. But $P_i^{BCD}(p_i) = 3/20$. This means that contiguous locations of poverty occurrence increase intertemporal poverty. In other words, contiguous poverty periods in an intertemporal poverty profile generate higher impact on P_i^{BCD}. Conversely, we can derive the profile $p_i = \left(0, \frac{1}{4}, 0, 0, \frac{1}{2}\right)$ from the profile $\left(0, \frac{1}{4}, \frac{1}{2}, 0, 0\right)$ by moving two contiguous periods of poverty further apart. This movement decreases the value of P_i^{BCD}. Loosely speaking, this example shows that, in this particular case, switch of atemporal poverty locations in an intertemporal profile increases intertemporal poverty if and only if their postswitch positions are contiguous. We can state this property of P_i^{BCD} for a general intertemporal poverty index P_i^{INT} as follows:

Block Monotonicity: Suppose that there are only two distinct and nonadjacent poverty periods $s, t \in \{1, 2, \ldots, T\}$ in the intertemporal poverty profile $p_i \in \Re_+^T$, where $s < t$ and $T \geq 2$. Now, if $\tilde{p}_i \in \Re_+^T$ is obtained from $p_i \in \Re_+^T$ by trading temporal positions of these two poverty incidents to $\tilde{s}$ and $\tilde{t}$, where $\tilde{s} < \tilde{t}$, then $P_i^{INT}(p_i) < P_i^{INT}(\tilde{p}_i)$ holds if and only if $\tilde{s} = \tilde{t} - 1$.

Since contiguous sites of poverty experiences increase the length of a poverty block, which in turn intensifies intertemporal poverty, we refer to this axiom as block monotonicity axiom. Hoy and Zheng (2015) defined intertemporal poverty on the space of lifetime income distributions and called it strong chronic poverty axiom.

Of the four properties we introduce next, for a general index P_i^{INT}, the first three were suggested by Bossert et al. (2012), and the fourth one is by Calvo and Dercon (2009). The first postulate claims that if there is only one period, then one-period poverty is the same as individual intertemporal poverty. Formally,

One-Period Equivalence: For all $p_i \in \Re_+^1$,

$$P_i^{INT}(p_i) = p_i. \tag{5.4}$$

The next property says that when the individual is in poverty for all the periods, then for any subperiod $t \in \{1,2, \ldots, T-1\}$, $T \geq 2$, intertemporal poverty can be calculated as the sum of the intertemporal poverties of the profiles $(p_i^1, p_i^2, \ldots, p_i^t)$ and $(p_i^{t+1}, p_i^{t+2}, \cdots, p_i^T)$. More precisely,

Single-Block Additive Decomposability: For all $T \geq 2$, all $p_i = (p_i^1, p_i^2, \ldots, p_i^T) \in D^T$ and all $t \in \{1,2,\ldots,T-1\}$,

$$P_i^{INT}(p_i) = P_i^{INT}(p_i^1, p_i^2, \ldots, p_i^t) + P_i^{INT}(p_i^{t+1}, p_i^{t+2}, \ldots, p_i^T), \tag{5.5}$$

where D^T is the strictly positive part of the T dimensional Euclidean space.

Repeated application of this postulate shows that

$$P_i^{INT}(p_i) = \sum_{t=1}^{T} p_i^t, \tag{5.6}$$

given that $p_i^t > 0$ for all $t \in \{1, 2, \ldots, T\}$. That is, an individual's intertemporal poverty is simply the sum of periodwise poverty levels. This decomposition becomes quite useful from antipoverty policy perspective; it enables us to identify those periods that are more poverty stricken. In consequence, if $p_i = \left(\frac{1}{2}, \frac{1}{4}, \frac{1}{8}\frac{1}{2}\right)$, we can partition the set of periods $\{1, 2, 3, 4\}$ into nonoverlapping subsets, say, $\{1, 2\}$ and $\{3, 4\}$, and intertemporal poverty $P_i^{INT}\left(\frac{1}{2}, \frac{1}{4}, \frac{1}{8}\frac{1}{2}\right)$ equals $P_i^{INT}\left(\frac{1}{2}, \frac{1}{4}\right) + P_i^{INT}\left(\frac{1}{8}, \frac{1}{2}\right)$.

According to the third property, for all nonnegative poverty profiles, if two subgroups of periods are separated by at least one zero-poverty period, then the total intertemporal poverty can be expressed as the weighted average of subgroup intertemporal poverty values, where the weights are the proportional lengths of the subgroups. Analytically,

Across-Blocks Average Decomposability: For all $T \geq 2$, all $t \in \{1,2,\ldots, T-1\}$, all $p_i = (p_i^1, p_i^2, \ldots, p_i^T) \in \Re_+^T$ if p_i^t or $p_i^{t+1} = 0$, then

$$P_i^{INT}(p_i) = \frac{t}{T} P_i^{INT}(p_i^1, p_i^2, \ldots, p_i^t) + \frac{T-t}{T} P_i^{INT}(p_i^{t+1}, p_i^{t+2}, \ldots, p_i^T). \tag{5.7}$$

This axiom shows significance of the lengths of poverty blocks and lengths of blocks out of poverty. The length of a block becomes an important characteristic for evaluation of intertemporal poverty. Accordingly, if $p_i = \left(\frac{1}{2}, \frac{1}{4}, \frac{1}{8}, 0, \frac{1}{2}\right)$, then $P_i^{INT}\left(\frac{1}{2}, \frac{1}{4}, \frac{1}{8}, 0, \frac{1}{2}\right)$ equals $\frac{3}{5} P_i^{INT}\left(\frac{1}{2}, \frac{1}{4}, \frac{1}{8}\right) + \frac{2}{5} P_i^{INT}\left(0, \frac{1}{2}\right)$.

However, across-blocks average decomposability does not apply to any arbitrary poverty profile, rather to some restricted profiles. A stronger decomposability condition, presented by Calvo and Dercon (2009), applies to any arbitrary profile of poverty. This stronger form, the subperiod decomposability postulate, does not require the separating spell t or $(t + 1)$ to be a zero-poverty spell, where $1 < t < T$ is arbitrary. More concretely,

Subperiod Decomposability: For all $T \geq 2$, all $t \in \{1,2,..,T-1\}$, all $p_i = (p_i^1, p_i^2, \cdots, p_i^T) \in \Re_+^T$,

$$P_i^{INT}(p_i) = \frac{t}{T} P_i^{INT}(p_i^1, p_i^2, \ldots, p_i^t) + \frac{T-t}{T} P_i^{INT}(p_i^{t+1}, p_i^{t+2}, \ldots, p_i^T). \tag{5.8}$$

This is a direct counterpart of the population subgroup decomposability axiom considered in the poverty measurement literature. Repeated application of the postulate shows that $P_i^{INT}(p_i) = \frac{1}{T}\sum_{t=1}^{T} p_i^t$ (see also Hoy and Zheng, 2015).

The following axiom also specifies a reasonable requirement.

Intertemporal Continuity: For all $T \geq 1, i \in \{1, 2, \dots, n\}$, P_i^{INT} is a continuous function of each period's poverty level provided that the person's poverty status remains unchanged in all periods.

The poverty statistic P_i^{BCD} is a violator of subperiod decomposability. However, it fulfills the other three postulates of the set of the aforementioned four postulates. In the example taken earlier, $P_i^{BCD}\left(\frac{1}{2}, \frac{1}{4}, \frac{1}{8}, 0, \frac{1}{2}\right) = \frac{25}{40}$, $\frac{3}{5}P_i^{BCD}\left(\frac{1}{2}, \frac{1}{4}, \frac{1}{8}\right) = \frac{21}{40}$, and $\frac{2}{5}P_i^{BCD}\left(0, \frac{1}{2}\right) = \frac{4}{40}$. Then the percentage contribution made by the subgroup $\{1, 2, 3\}$ of the periods to total intertemporal poverty of the person is $84\% = \left(\frac{\frac{21}{40}}{\frac{25}{40}}\right).100$. Hence from antiperiod policy perspective, the subgroup $\{1, 2, 3\}$ of periods requires more attention. This illustration demonstrates an appropriate policy relevance of the axiom across-blocks average decomposability.

We now employ the periodwise Bourguignon–Chakravarty poverty function for individual i in (5.3). The resulting individual intertemporal poverty index becomes a positive weighted function of individual temporal poverty levels p_i^ts, where p_i^t, person i's poverty in period t, is evaluated using his achievements in the period by the individual function F associated with P_{BC}.

$$P_i^{BCD}(p_i) = \frac{1}{T}\sum_{t=1}^{T} l_i^t \left[\sum_{j=1}^{d} \frac{1}{d}\left(1 - \frac{\hat{x}_{ij}^t}{z_j}\right)^{\alpha}\right]^{\frac{\beta}{\alpha}}. \tag{5.9}$$

If $\left(1 - \frac{\hat{x}_{ij}^t}{z_j}\right) > 0$ for at least one $j \in Q$, then for a given value of $\beta > 0$, an increase in the value of $\alpha > 1$ increases the intertemporal continuous poverty index P_i^{BCD} in (5.9). Since for any $p_i^t \geq 0$, l_i^t is positive, this index unambiguously verifies the period-restricted monotonicity axioms for any $\beta > 0$ and $\alpha > 1$.

Another desirable postulate is formulated in terms of a transfer of a bundle of achievements from one period to another, where the dimensions that are affected by the transfer are more deprived in the former than in the latter. To state this property formally, let $S_{t_1 t_2}^i(x_{i.}^{INT})$ be the identical set of dimensions in which person i is deprived in periods t_1 and t_2 in $x_{i.}^{INT}$, where $t_1, t_2 \in \{1, 2, \dots, T\}$ are arbitrary and $T \geq 2$. Formally, $S_{t_1 t_2}^i(x_{i.}^{INT}) = \{j \in Q | x_{ij}^{t_1} < z_j\} = \{j \in Q | x_{ij}^{t_2} < z_j\}$. Assume further that the person's deprivations in different dimensions in period t_2 are lower than his corresponding deprivations in period t_1. More precisely, for all $j \in S_{t_1 t_2}^i(x_{i.}^{INT})$, $x_{ij}^{t_1} < x_{ij}^{t_2} < z_j$.

Definition 5.3 For any $T, n \in N$, $T \geq 2$, consider arbitrary $t_1, t_2 \in \{1, 2, \ldots, T\}$. Then for $x_{i.}^{INT} = (x_{i.}^1, x_{i.}^2, \ldots, x_{i.}^T)$, suppose that the set $S_{t_1 t_2}^i(x_{i.}^{INT})$ is nonempty, where $i \in \{1, 2, \ldots, n\}$ is arbitrary. Let $y_{i.}^{t_1} = x_{i.}^{t_1} - \delta$ and $y_{i.}^{t_2} = x_{i.}^{t_2} + \delta$, $\delta = (\delta_1, \delta_2, \ldots, \delta_d)$, where $\delta_j \geq 0$ for $j \in S_{t_1 t_2}^i(x_{i.}^{INT})$, with $>$ for at least one j; $y_{ij}^{t_2} < z_j$ for all $j \in S_{t_1 t_2}^i$; and $\delta_j = 0$ for all $j \in Q \backslash S_{t_1 t_2}^i(x_{i.}^{INT})$. In addition, let $y_{i.}^t = x_{i.}^t$ for all $t \neq t_1, t_2$. Then we say that the intertemporal profile $(y_{i.}^1, y_{i.}^2, \ldots, y_{i.}^T)$ of achievements is obtained from the profile $(x_{i.}^1, x_{i.}^2, \ldots, x_{i.}^T)$ by an across-periods Pigou–Dalton bundle of regressive transfers.

Since $\delta_j \geq 0$ can at most be $x_{ij}^{t_1}$, it is ensured that for any $j \in S_{t_1 t_2}^i(x_{i.}^{INT})$, $y_{ij}^{t_1} \geq 0$. The inequality $y_{ij}^{t_2} < z_j$ guarantees that the regressive transfer in any dimension from the bequest period t_1 to the beneficiary period t_2 does not permit the person to be nondeprived in the dimension in the beneficiary period.

In the example we have taken earlier to illustrate the monotonicity axioms, let $t_1 = 1$ and $t_2 = 2$. Then $S_{12}^i(x_{i.}^{INT}) = \{\text{life expectancy}, \text{income}\}$. Choose $\delta = (0, 0, 5)$. As a result, $y_{i.}^1 = x_{i.}^1 - \delta = (2700, 59.4, 440) - (0, 0, 5) = (2700, 59.4, 435)$ and $y_{i.}^2 = x_{i.}^2 + \delta = (2700, 59.5, 490) + (0, 0, 5) = (2700, 59.5, 495)$. Then we say that the intertemporal profile $(y_{i.}^1, y_{i.}^2, y_{i.}^3) = ((2700, 59.4, 435), (2700, 59.5, 495), (2500, 62, 600))$ is obtained from the profile $(x_{i.}^1, x_{i.}^2, x_{i.}^3) = ((2700, 59.4, 440), (2700, 59.5, 490), (2500, 62, 600))$ by an across-periods Pigou–Dalton bundle of regressive transfers. (Strictly speaking, since income is the only affected dimension, it is one-dimensional regressive transfer considered by Bourguignon and Chakravarty (2003).)

The following axiom, which can be viewed as a multidimensional companion of the one-dimensional intertemporal regressive transfer axiom advocated by Gradin et al. (2012), can now be stated:

Across-Periods Transfer: For all $T, n \in N$, $P_i^{INT}(p_i^1, p_i^2, \ldots, p_i^T) < P_i^{INT}(\tilde{p}_i^1, \tilde{p}_i^2, \ldots, \tilde{p}_i^T)$, given that for all $t \in \{1, 2, \ldots, T\}$, $p_i^t = F(x_{i.}^t; \underline{z})$ and $\tilde{p}_i^t = F(y_{i.}^t; \underline{z})$, where F is an individual poverty function and $y_{i.}^{INT} = (y_{i.}^1, y_{i.}^2, \ldots, y_{i.}^T)$ is obtained from $x_{i.}^{INT} = (x_{i.}^1, x_{i.}^2, \ldots, x_{i.}^T)$ by an across-periods Pigou–Dalton bundle of regressive transfers.

The across-periods transfer axiom requires that individual intertemporal poverty should rise under an across-periods Pigou–Dalton bundle of regressive transfers. Similarly, intertemporal poverty should decrease if a bundle of progressive transfers takes place. The two time locations t_1 and t_2 we have chosen in the period profile are arbitrary. Therefore, one sufficient condition that ensures satisfaction of the transfer axiom is that all poverty spells in (5.9) are assigned the same weight in the aggregation. For unequally weighted spells, some restrictions may be required for fulfillment of the axiom. Given $\beta > 0$ and $\alpha > 1$, a sufficient condition that ensures its verification of the axiom of across-periods Pigou–Dalton bundle of regressive transfers by P_i^{BCD} in (5.9) is that $l_i^{t_1} > l_i^{t_2}$. An intertemporal poverty index will be called transfer sensitive if it fulfills the across-periods transfer postulate.

5.3.2 Aggregate Multidimensional Intertemporal Poverty Index

We assume that the society intertemporal poverty index P_A^{INT} is a nonnegative real-valued function of individual intertemporal poverty components. Since under this assumption, the index relies only on individualistic intertemporal poverty features, we name it as independence of irrelevant information.

For the reason that a typical element of the set $\mathfrak{R}_+^n$ of all intertemporal poverty profiles of an n person society is $(P_1, P_2, \ldots, P_n)$, the set of all possible intertemporal poverty profiles at the society level is $\mathfrak{R}_+ = U_{n\in N}\mathfrak{R}_+^n$. Following Bossert et al. (2012), we define the average intertemporal poverty index for the society as $P_A^{BCD} : \mathfrak{R}_+ \to \mathfrak{R}_+^1$, where for all $n \in N$, $(P_1, P_2, \ldots, P_n) \in \mathfrak{R}_+^n$,

$$P_A^{BCD}(P_1, P_2, \ldots, P_n) = \frac{1}{n}\sum_{i=1}^{n} P_i = \frac{1}{nT}\sum_{i=1}^{n}\sum_{t=1}^{T} p_i^t l_i^t. \tag{5.10}$$

For any $(P_1, P_2, \ldots, P_n) \in \mathfrak{R}_+^n$, $P_A^{BCD}(P_1, P_2, \ldots, P_n)$ gives the level of overall intertemporal poverty associated with the intertemporal poverty profile $(P_1, P_2, \ldots, P_n)$ across persons. That is, the overall intertemporal poverty level is the simple arithmetic average of individual intertemporal poverty values. We allow variability of the population size to broaden the framework sufficiently so that across-populations collation of overall intertemporal poverty becomes possible.

For P_i of the form given by (5.9), the resulting index turns out to be

$$P_A^{BCD}(P_1, P_2, \ldots, P_n) = \frac{1}{nT}\sum_{i=1}^{n}\sum_{t=1}^{T} l_i^t \left[\sum_{j=1}^{d} \frac{1}{d}\left(1 - \frac{\hat{x}_{ij}^t}{z_j}\right)^{\alpha}\right]^{\frac{\beta}{\alpha}}. \tag{5.11}$$

This population replication invariant overall intertemporal poverty index enables us to perform cross-population comparisons of intertemporal poverty allowing variability of the sampling period. It can as well be employed to compare intertemporal poverty extents of the same population for different sampling periods. The population replication invariance principle views global intertemporal poverty as a per-capita concept. Its subgroup decomposability property facilitates us to button down those persons in the society who are beset more by intertemporal poverty and hence to design antipoverty policy. This policy is about lifetime elude or lack of elude from poverty. It is definitely about a future situation, not just involving one future period distress.

The per-capita notion of global poverty is also reflected by the average critical levels postulate, which necessitates that if a person with average poverty level migrates to the society, then global poverty remains unchanged (see Blackorby et al., 2005). This property is captured by the index P_A^{BCD}.

Average Critical Levels: For all $n \in N$, for all $(P_1, P_2, \ldots, P_n) \in \Re^n_+$, $P_A^{BCD}((P_1, P_2, \ldots, P_n)) = P_A^{BCD}\left((P_1, P_2, \ldots, P_n), \frac{1}{n}\sum_{i=1}^{n} P_i\right)$.

Observe that the average of intertemporal poverty levels across persons takes into account all information on periodwise poverty thresholds. In consequence, the choice of the average intertemporal poverty as the critical level does not lead to any loss of information.

If any two individuals trade their positions in (5.10), then this exchange has no effect on P_A^{BCD} because of its anonymity property. It also gladdens an impartiality principle with respect to an increment or a decrement in individual poverty. If a single person's intertemporal poverty changes by a certain amount, then it is immaterial whose poverty changes. For the postulate to be well defined, it is necessary to assume that the change in poverty is the same across persons. In order to state this postulate rigorously, let $1_j^n = (w_1, w_2, \ldots, w_n) \in \Re^n_+$, where $w_i = 0$ for all $i \neq j$ and $w_j = 1$.

Incremental Equity: For all $n \in N$, $n \geq 2$, for all $(P_1, P_2, \ldots, P_n) \in \Re^n_+$, for all $c \in \Re^1$ and for all $j, k \in \{1, 2, \ldots, n\}, j \neq k$, such that $(P_1, P_2, \ldots, P_n) + c1_j^n, (P_1, P_2, \ldots, P_n) + c1_k^n \in \Re^n_+$, $P_A^{BCD}((P_1, P_2, \ldots, P_n) + c1_j^n) = P_A^{BCD}((P_1, P_2, \ldots, P_n) + c1_k^n)$.

Thus, incremental equity needs that the impact on global poverty of a change in any person j's poverty has the effect of a similar change in a different person k's poverty. Consequently, the persons j and k are treated anonymously from this perspective.

The index takes on the value 0 if $P_i = 0$ for all i. More generally, if $P_i = c \geq 0$ for all i, then $P_A^{BCD} = c$. For any $(P_1, P_2, \ldots, P_n) \in \Re^n_+$, P_A^{BCD} is bounded between the minimal and maximal values of individualwise intertemporal poverty levels. More precisely, $\min_i P_i \leq P_A^{BCD} \leq \max_i P_i$.

If for some pair (j, t), there is an increase in $P_i^{BCD}(p_i) = \frac{1}{T}\sum_{t=1}^{T} l_i^t \left[\sum_{j=1}^{d} \frac{1}{d}\left(1 - \frac{\hat{x}_{ij}^t}{z_j}\right)^{\alpha}\right]^{\frac{\beta}{\alpha}}$, say, following a reduction in $\hat{x}_{ij}^t$, then P_A^{BCD} increases unambiguously. Formally,

Strong Monotonicity: For all $n \in N$, and for all $(P_1, P_2, \ldots, P_n), (P_1', P_2', \ldots, P_n') \in \Re^n_+$, $P_A^{BCD}(P_1, P_2, \ldots, P_n) < P_A^{BCD}(P_1', P_2', \ldots, P_n')$, where $P_i < P_i'$ for some i and $P_j = P_j'$ for all $j \neq i$.

This strong monotonicity property of P_A^{BCD} demands that society's intertemporal poverty increases under an upsurge of any individual's intertemporal poverty. It implies its weak sister, which says that overall intertemporal increases when all the individuals' intertemporal poverty levels get augmented. More precisely,

Weak Monotonicity: For all $n \in N$, and for all $(P_1, P_2, \dots, P_n), (P'_1, P'_2, \dots, P'_n) \in \Re^n_+$, $P_A^{BCD}(P_1, P_2, \dots, P_n) < P_A^{BCD}(P'_1, P'_2, \dots, P'_n)$, where $P_i < P'_i$ for all i.

Among the other notions of monotonicity that are captured by P_A^{BCD} are (i) ratio-scale improvement, (ii) translation-scale improvement, and (iii) minimal increasingness. According to the ratio-scale improvement postulate, an equiproportionate contraction in individualwise intertemporal poverty values leads to a shrinkage of global intertemporal poverty (Shorrocks, 1983). More concretely,

Ratio-Scale Improvement: For all $n \in N$, for all $(P_1, P_2, \dots, P_n) \in \Re^n_+$,where $(P_1, P_2, \dots, P_n) \neq 0.1^n$, and for all scalars c, $0 < c < 1$, $P_A^{BCD}(P_1, P_2, \dots, P_n) > P_A^{BCD}(cP_1, cP_2, \dots, cP_n)$.

The translation-scale improvement condition claims that an equal absolute diminution of amounts of all persons' intertermporal poverties generates a lessening of society's intertemporal poverty value (Shorrocks, 1983).

Translation-Scale Improvement: For all $n \in N$, for all $(P_1, P_2, \dots, P_n) \in \Re^n_+$, $(P_1, P_2, \dots, P_n) \neq 0.1^n$, and for all scalars $c < 0$ such that $P_i + c \geq 0$ for all i, $P_A^{BCD}(P_1, P_2, \dots, P_n) > P_A^{BCD}(P_1 + c, P_2 + c, \dots, P_n + c)$.

Finally, minimal increasingness appeals that if intertemporal poverty is equal across individuals, then lower poverty is preferred to higher poverty (Blackorby and Donaldson, 1984). More explicitly,

Minimal Increasingness: For all $n \in N$,and for all $a, b \in \Re^1_+$, where $a > b$, $P_A^{BCD}(a.1^n) > P_A^{BCD}(b.1^n)$.

This axiom, formulated in terms of an equal intertemporal poverty across persons, is very weak and appealing.

5.3.3 A Review of Some Related One-Dimensional Proposals

The literature contains several recommendations for measuring individual intertemporal poverty in the univariate case. A comparative analysis of the proposals that bear similarity with our block-approach-based endorsement explored earlier, when it is adapted to the single-variable situation, will be a useful exercise. This is the objective of this subsection.

We denote individual i's income in period t by u_i^t, $i = 1,2, \dots, n$, and $t = 1,2, \dots, T$. Denote the time-invariant income poverty line by $z > 0$. The censored income level associated with u_i^t is symbolized by $\hat{u}_i^t$, that is, $\hat{u}_i^t = \min(u_i^t, z)$. We write $g_i^t = \left(1 - \frac{\hat{u}_i^t}{z}\right)$ for the income deprivation indicator for the person in period t.

The three steps that were employed in the Calvo–Dercon formulation for developing lifetime individual statistic of poverty are as follows: focus (truncation of above-threshold incomes in different periods), transformation (all atemporal deprivations are transformed by some increasing and strictly convex function so that unidimensional monotonicity and monotonicity sensitivity axioms are fulfilled), and aggregation of transformed deprivations into an overall index of individual lifetime poverty. We denote these three steps by F, T, and A, respectively. The six possible orderings of the steps are FTA, FAT, TFA, TAF, AFT, and ATF. Since the orderings FTA and AFT draw out all the insights in TFA and ATF, respectively, the latter two can be ignored.

Under the sequence FTA, after focus, identical increasing and strictly convex transformation is imposed on the atemporal deprivations to preserve the monotonicity axioms, before aggregation. The resulting indices resemble "the well-known Chakravarty and Foster–Greer–Thorbecke measures of aggregate poverty" (Calvo and Dercon, 2009, p. 40). Formally, they are given respectively by

$$P_{i,e}^{CD}\left(u_i^1, u_i^2, \ldots, u_i^T; z\right) = \sum_{t=1}^{T} \gamma^{T-t}\left[1-\left(\frac{\hat{u}_i^t}{z}\right)^e\right], \tag{5.12}$$

where $0 < e < 1, \gamma > 0$, and

$$P_{i,\alpha}^{CD}\left(u_i^1, u_i^2, \ldots, u_i^T; z\right) = \sum_{t=1}^{T} \gamma^{T-t}\left(1-\frac{\hat{u}_i^t}{z}\right)^\alpha, \tag{5.13}$$

where $\alpha > 1$ and $\gamma > 0$. The common parameter γ in the aforementioned two indices is a discounting parameter. Consequently, γ ascertains the rate of time discounting. It gives us the weights assigned to transformed deprivations in different periods over the profile $(1, 2, \ldots, T)$. If the weights are chosen in decreasing order of time, then distant future-period spells are paid lower attention in the aggregation. A necessary condition that guarantees this is that $\gamma > 1$. Thus, while in P_i^{BCD}, equal weight is assigned to the spells in a block, and as the size of the block increases, the constant weight across the spells in the block increases, for the Calvo–Dercon indices, the weight unambiguously decreases as the period becomes more distant. If $\gamma = 1$, each spell is allotted the same weight (=1), and this happens irrespective of its location in the profile $(1, 2, \ldots, T)$. In other words, these indices remain invariant under any rearrangement of the periods in the profile $(1, 2, \ldots, T)$. As a result, there is no discounting of the periods. In this case, a progressive transfer of income from a less deprived period to a more deprived one decreases individual intertemporal poverty. In other words, of two deprived periods, the higher one can be subsidized by the lower one.

The two subperiod decomposable Calvo–Dercon indices comply with the one-dimensional versions of the monotonicity and monotonicity sensitivity axioms. For $\alpha = 0$ and $\gamma = 1$, $P_{i,\alpha}^{CD}$ becomes the number of periods in which the person stays below the poverty line. This is the individual intertemporal period count index for income poverty.

When the sequences AFT and TAF are adopted, the variants of the pair of indices ((5.11), (5.12)) are given respectively by the pairs

$$\left(1-\left\{\min\left[1,\frac{\sum_{t=1}^{T}\gamma^{T-t}u_i^t}{\sum_{t=1}^{T}\gamma^{T-t}z}\right]\right\}^e,\left\{1-\min\left[1,\frac{\sum_{t=1}^{T}\gamma^{T-t}u_i^t}{\sum_{t=1}^{T}\gamma^{T-t}z}\right]\right\}^\alpha\right) \quad \text{and}$$

$$\left(\text{Max}\left[\sum_{t=1}^{T}\gamma^{T-t}\left[\left(1-\left(\frac{u_i^t}{z}\right)\right)^e,0\right]\right],\text{Max}\left[\sum_{t=1}^{T}\gamma^{T-t}\left(1-\frac{u_i^t}{z}\right)^\alpha,0\right]\right),$$

where the parameters α, e, and γ obey the same restrictions as in (5.12) and (5.13). Each component of the two pairs is a violator of subperiod decomposability. While each constituent of the first pair fails to meet monotonicity sensitivity, monotonicity is risked for any constituent of the second pair. The set of violators of subperiod decomposability and monotonicity sensitivity also include indices derived under the sequence FAT. In view of these problems identified with the indices underlying these three sequences, we do not analyze them further.

Dutta et al. (2013) proposed a deviant of the Bossert–Chakravarty–D'Ambrosio quantifier of individual intertemporal poverty. They noted that in the Bossert–Chakravarty–D'Ambrosio formulation, the distribution of nonpoverty spells does not play any role in the determination of individual intertemporal poverty. Their alternative approach relies on the assumption that the longer nonpoverty spells experienced by an individual prior to becoming poor make him more capable of dealing with poverty. However, preceding poverty periods cannot be made milder by nonpoverty spells. In other words, affluence cannot weaken a previous poverty spell but can help one to be better equipped to fight poverty in future. They also characterized a family of individual intertemporal poverty indices.

The explicit form of their alternative recommendation is given by

$$P_i^{DRZ}(p_i)=\frac{1}{T}\sum_{t=1}^{T}\frac{[1+c_1(g_i^t)]^{\alpha_1}}{[1+c_2(g_i^t)]^{\alpha_2}}(g_i^t)^{\alpha_3}, \tag{5.14}$$

where g_i^t is income deprivation indicator in period t, $c_1(g_i^t)$ is the number of consecutive poverty periods prior to period t, $c_2(g_i^t)$ is the number of nonpoverty periods immediately prior to period t, and α_i's, $i=1,2,3$, are positive parameters. The parameter α_3 represents sensitivity of period-by-period deprivation indicators to intertemporal poverty in the sense that given g_i^t values, how a change in α_3 changes P_i^{DRZ}, and α_1 and α_2 determine, respectively, sensitivity of the poverty block size prior to period t and the number of nonpoverty periods just prior to period t. Evidently, under ceteris paribus assumptions, P_i^{DRZ} increases as $c_1(g_i^t)$ increases (i.e., as poverty periods cluster) and P_i^{DRZ} decreases as $c_2(g_i^t)$ increases (i.e., as nonpoverty periods cluster just before a poverty period). The approach has a clear merit – in the aggregation, it incorporates the characteristic of appeasing in terms of preceding nonpoverty spells and increasing impact of bunching of poverty spells. This nonnegative individual intertemporal index that upholds the block monotonicity and one-period equivalence axioms is a normalized index in the sense that it takes on the value 0 if $g_i^t = 0$ for all t. Dutta et al. (2013) suggested a modification of (5.14) by replacing $c_2(g_i^t)$ by $\tilde{c}_2(g_i^t) = \sum k_t$ and $k_t = k > 1$, if income is above certain threshold limit υ, and 1 otherwise. Under this modification, the index verifies a weak poverty mitigation axiom, which claims that there is some particular level of income, υ, exceeding the poverty line, such that income in a nonpoverty period can lighten the effect of poverty episodes in other periods but only up to the specified limit υ. To understand this, let $u^{INT} = (26, 11, 9, 10)$ and $\tilde{u}^{INT} = (20, 11, 9, 10)$ be two lifetime income profiles, the poverty line $z = 12$ and $\upsilon = 22$. Then u^{INT} should have less lifetime poverty than $\tilde{u}^{INT}$ because mitigation effect happens to exist up to the limit $\upsilon = 22$. Further, the profile $v^{INT} = (30, 11, 9, 10)$ has the same intertemporal poverty as u^{INT}, although period 1 income in u^{INT} is lower than that in v^{INT}. The reason behind this is that an increase in income beyond υ has no further mitigation effect. However, it fails to verify the strong poverty mitigation axiom, which requires continuity of the mitigation operation and impact to be increasing with income (see Hoy and Zheng, 2015).

Another one-dimensional variant of the Bossert–Chakravarty–D'Ambrosio proposal was suggested by Gradin et al. (2012). According to these authors, a regressive transfer of income from one period to another, where the size of the poverty block to which the bequest period belongs is at least as high as that of the poverty block to which the beneficiary period is attached, should increase individual intertemporal poverty under ceteris paribus assumptions. (See the across-periods transfer axiom presented in the Section 5.3.1.) To perceive this in greater detail, let $u_{i.}^{INT} = (10, 2, 1, 4, 9, 3, 4)$ be person i's intertemporal income profile and $z = 5$ be the income poverty line. The person is poor in periods 2,3,4,6, and 7. Now, consider a regressive income transfer of size 1 from period 3 to period 6 generating the profile $v_{i.}^{INT} = (10, 2, 0, 4, 9, 4, 4)$. The size of the block to which the bequest period pertains is 3 (with poverty periods being 2, 3, and 4). In contrast, the size of the block to which the beneficiary period is attached is 2 (with poverty periods being 6 and 7). Hence, this regressive transfer should increase person i's intertemporal poverty.

The alternative functional form for person i's intertemporal poverty index suggested by these authors is

$$P_i^{GdC}(p_i) = \frac{1}{T}\sum_{t=1}^{T}\left(\frac{l_i^t}{T}\right)^{\rho} p_i^t, \qquad (5.15)$$

where p_i^t is the individual income poverty function in period t and l_i^t is the same as in equation (5.3). Standard examples of p_i^t can be $\left(1-\frac{\hat{u}_i^t}{z_j}\right)^{\alpha}$ and $\left[1-\left(\frac{\hat{u}_i^t}{z_j}\right)^{e}\right]$, where $\alpha > 1$ and $0 < e < 1$ are parameters. These two functions correspond respectively to the Foster et al. (1984) and Chakravarty (1983) poverty indices. The parameter ρ attaches higher weight to longer poverty spells reflecting the idea that continuous enlargement of the size of a poverty block intensifies a person's intertemporal poverty experience. However, P_i^{GdC} is a violator of the time replication invariance axiom. The authors argued that for looking at poverty differences between two intertemporal distributions with sizes T_1 and T_2, where $T_1 < T_2$, one can choose a subsample of T_1 periods of the second distribution and make the necessary comparison. Their index fails to take into account the act of poverty mitigation. The authors also suggested an aggregate index of intertemporal poverty by considering an average of an increasing strictly convex transformation of P_i^{GdC} values over the entire population.

The key factor underlying the Mendola–Busetta path of measuring intertemporal poverty is the "cumulative hardship" property, which requires intensification of intertemporal poverty as periodwise poverty situations become closer even if the postswitch stations of poverty periods are not contiguous. It is weaker than the block monotonicity axiom, which requires augmentation of intertemporal poverty only when postrotated locations of poverty periods are contiguous.

The cumulative hardship postulate is consistent with the Hoy and Zheng (2011, 2015) chronic poverty axiom, which we state next on the space of intertemporal poverty profiles:

Chronic Poverty: Suppose that there are only two distinct and nonadjacent poverty periods $s, t \in \{1, 2, \dots, T\}$ in the intertemporal poverty profile $p_i \in \Re_+^T$, where $s < t$ and $T \geq 2$. Now, if $\tilde{p}_i \in \Re_+^T$ is obtained from $p_i \in \Re_+^T$ by exchanging temporal locations of these two poverty situations to $\tilde{s}$ and $\tilde{t}$, where $\tilde{s} = s - k < t + k = \tilde{t}$ for some $k \geq 1$, then $P_i(p_i) < P_i(\tilde{p}_i)$.

This statement of the axiom has a minor difference with the Hoy–Zheng formulation since we replace their weak inequality $P_i(p_i) \leq P_i(\tilde{p}_i)$ by the strict inequality $P_i(p_i) < P_i(\tilde{p}_i)$. All indices that verify this axiom are members of the class that can be identified under the category "the closeness approach." The proposals P_i^{BCD}, P_i^{DRZ}, and P_i^{GdC} are violators of this axiom since in this axiom, it is not unambiguously required that the postswitch locations are contiguous.

The Mendola and Busetta (2012) index of individual intertemporal poverty for determining the extent of poverty in a profile spanning T periods is defined as

$$P_i^{MB}(p_i) = b(T) \sum_{p_s>0, p_t>0, s>t} \frac{(p_i^t + p_i^s)}{2(s-t)} c, \tag{5.16}$$

where $b(T) > 0$ is a normalization coefficient and $c > 0$ is a decay factor discounting the individual's early period poverty happenings. Although it satisfies the chronic poverty axiom, it is a violator of the decomposability axioms analyzed earlier and the two poverty mitigation axioms.

Essential to the Hoy and Zheng (2011) closeness-reliant proposal is the chronic poverty axiom. According to these authors, each period of poverty and an individual's entire lifetime are important ingredients of an individual's lifetime poverty. They characterized the following functional form of individual intertemporal poverty index using an axiomatic framework:

$$P_i^{HZ}(p_i) = \chi(T)\left\{\sum_{t=1}^{T} a(t,T)p_i^t\right\} + (1-\chi(T))\overline{p}_i, \tag{5.17}$$

where $\overline{p}_i = F\left(\frac{1}{T}\sum_{t=1}^{T} u_i^t; z\right)$, with F being the one-dimensional poverty index; $0 \leq \chi(T) \leq 1$ and $a(t,T) > 0$. The term $\sum_{t=1}^{T} a(t,T)p_i^t$ is a weighted average of periodwise poverty experiences of the person, and $\overline{p}_i$ is the extent of poverty associated with the person's lifetime average income. In the polar case $\chi(T) = 0$, intertemporal poverty is represented by the person's deprivation arising from the shortfall of his lifetime average income from the threshold limit. Consequently, poverty situations of different periods do not play any role here. In other words, knowledge of period-by-period poverty extents is not necessary. In contrast, when $\chi(T) = 1$, a recollection period-by-period poverty experience is required to determine the overall intertemporal poverty of the person. Hence, the parameter $\chi(T)$ may be interpreted as representing a "memory factor" in the sense that the extreme cases $\chi(T) = 1$ and $\chi(T) = 0$ correspond, respectively, to "perfect recall" and "no recall" of poverty episodes. A value of $\chi(T)$ lying between 0 and 1 shows that each term of the across-periods poverty sequence $\{p_i^t\}_{t==1}^{T}$ and lifetime poverty value $\overline{p}_i$ are decisive factors in the evaluation of individual intertemporal poverty. In this intermediate case, the index upholds the strong poverty mitigation axiom.

Hoy and Zheng (2011) showed that satisfaction of the early poverty axiom by P_i^{HZ} requires that $a(t,T)$ is a decreasing function of t. The early poverty axiom demands that poverty episodes in early phases of life have more harmful effects on life. Poverty in childhood periods is likely to have detrimental effects on physical and mental conditions of a person later in life. Similarly, verification of the chronic poverty axiom by P_i^{HZ} necessitates that $a(t,T)$ is strictly concave in t. Examples of the function $a(t,T)$ that meet these requirements are $1-\left(\frac{t}{1+T}\right)^{c_1}$ and $\left(1-\frac{t}{1+T}\right)^{c_2}$, where $c_1 > 1$ and $0 < c_2 < 1$ are constants.

As noted by Zheng (2012), the additive structure of P_i^{HZ} does not enable us to take into account across-periods poverty interactions. To overcome this,

Zheng (2012) developed an axiomatic characterization of the following class of gravitational indices of intertemporal poverty

$$P_i^Z(p_i) = \sum_{s \leq t} G_{st}(p_i^s, p_i^t, v_{st}), \tag{5.18}$$

where G_{st} is continuous in its arguments, increasing in the first two arguments, decreasing in the third argument, $v_{st} = t - s + 1$, and $G_{st}(0, 0, v_{st}) = 0$. Zheng (2012) refers to this class as gravitational class since its formulation relies on Newton's Universal Law of Gravitation – "the force is proportional to the product of two masses and inversely proportional to the square of distance between the point masses."

Two illustrative examples of the family (5.18) are

$$P_i^{Z1}(p_i) = \sum_{s \leq t} \frac{(p_i^s)^{\alpha_1}(p_i^t)^{\beta_1}}{(v_{st})^{\gamma_1}}, \tag{5.19}$$

$$P_i^{Z2}(p_i) = \sum_{s \leq t} (p_i^s)^{\alpha_1}(p_i^t)^{\beta_1}\left(1 - \frac{v_{st}}{T}\right)^{\gamma_1}, \tag{5.20}$$

where α_1, β_1, and γ_1 are positive constants. As these two examples indicate, P_i^Z is increasing in each pair of poverty experiences, and as the gap between any two poverty spells reduces so that $v_{st} = t - s + 1$ decreases, P_i^Z increases.

5.4 An Exploration of the Counting Approaches to Multidimensional Intertemporal Deprivations

While in the preceding subsection, our scrutiny was restricted to unidimensional variants of the block-approach-contingent multidimensional enquiry, in this section, we scrutinize some alternative proposals for analyzing multidimensional intertemporal deprivations using the counting approach.

The Nicholas and Ray (2011) suggestion for quantifying multidimensional intertemporal deprivation combines the Chakravarty and D'Ambrosio (2006); Bossert et al. (2012), and Gradin et al. (2012) approaches. Essential to this counting-dependent generalization is the number of periods in which a person becomes deprived in different dimensions. In terms of the notation we have introduced in the chapter, this proposal can formally be defined as

$$E_A^{NR}(X; \underline{z}) = \frac{1}{n}\sum_{i=1}^{n}\left[\frac{1}{dT}\sum_{j=1}^{d}\left(\sum_{t=1}^{T}(g_{ij}^t)^0 s_{ij}^t\right)\right]^{\alpha}, \tag{5.21}$$

where $s_{ij}^t \in [0, 1]$, desired to capture the impact of the spread of the deprivation spells, is a nonnegative increasing function of c_{ij}^t, the length of the deprivation spell to which individual i's deprivation occurrence in dimension j in period t

corresponds, and $\alpha \geq 0$ is a parameter. For $\alpha = 0$, E_A^{NR} becomes the proportion of persons that are deprived in at least one dimension for at least one period. Clearly, E_A^{NR} upholds the multidimensional version of the block monotonicity axiom, stated in terms of number of dimensionwise deprivations of a person across periods. The index may or may not satisfy the time replication invariance principle, although it is population replication invariant. Its transgression of the time replication invariance is evident if we choose $s_{ij}^t = \left(\frac{c_{ij}^t}{T+1}\right)^r$, where $r > 0$ is a constant. Consequently, it is not suitable for comparison of intertemporal deprivations across profiles with different lengths of time profiles.

The concern of Bossert et al. (2014) counting approach is the intertemporal deprivation in material living conditions. Assume that there are $m \geq 2$ dimensions of materials living conditions. Let us consider a binary variable $b_{ij}^t \in \{0, 1\}$, where a value of 1 indicates that person i is deprived with respect to dimension j in period t, whereas a value of 0 identifies him as nondeprived in the dimension–period pair $(j, t) \in \{1, 2, \ldots, m\} \times \{1, 2, \ldots, T\}$. Then person i's material deprivation in period t is given by $\sum_{j=1}^{m} b_{ij}^t w_j$, where w_j is a positive weight assigned to dimension j. A simple index of material deprivation for the person, when we follow the Foster (2009)-type aggregation rule, is given by E_i^F, the average value of periodwise deprivations. Formally,

$$E_i^F(b^i) = \frac{1}{T}\sum_{t=1}^{T}\sum_{j=1}^{m} b_{ij}^t w_j, \tag{5.22}$$

for all $b_i \in (\{0, 1\}^m)^T$. The corresponding aggregate intertemporal material deprivation E_A^F is the average of intertemporal material deprivation values across persons. More precisely, for all $b \in ((\{0, 1\}^m)^T)^n$,

$$E_A^F(b) = \frac{1}{n}\sum_{i=1}^{n}\frac{1}{T}\sum_{t=1}^{T}\sum_{j=1}^{m} b_{ij}^t w_j. \tag{5.23}$$

In order to discuss adaption of the Bossert et al. (2012) approach to the current setting, we say that person i is deprived in period t if and only if he is deprived with respect to at least one dimension in the period. This is the same as the requirement that $\sum_{j=1}^{m} b_{ij}^t \geq 1$. The sum $\sum_{j=1}^{m} b_{ij}^t$ is the deprivation score of person i in period t. In order to be identified as deprived in a period, the concerned person's deprivation score in the period must be at least 1. Equivalently, we are following here the union method of identification of deprivation. Given that person i is deprived in period t in b_i, let l_i^t be the maximal number of consecutive periods including t in which person is deprived, where $b_i \in (\{0, 1\}^m)^T$ is arbitrary. Similarly, if person i is nondeprived in period t in b_i, let l_i^t stand for the maximal number of consecutive periods including

t in which person is nondeprived (see Bossert et al., 2014). Thus, if $T = 5$ and the person is deprived only in periods 2 and 3, then $l_i^1 = 1$, $l_i^2 = l_i^3 = 2$ and $l_i^4 = l_i^5 = 1$. Bossert et al. (2014) suggested the use of the following as a numerical representation of individual material deprivation

$$E_i^{BCCD}(b_i) = \frac{1}{T}\sum_{t=1}^{T} l_i^t \sum_{j=1}^{m} b_{ij}^t w_j, \tag{5.24}$$

where $b_i \in (\{0,1\}^m)^T$ is arbitrary. According to these authors, the aggregate intertemporal material deprivation can be ascertained, for any arbitrary $b \in ((\{0,1\}^m)^T)^n$, by

$$E_A^{BCCD}(b) = \frac{1}{nT}\sum_{i=1}^{n}\sum_{t=1}^{T} l_i^t \sum_{j=1}^{m} b_{ij}^t w_j. \tag{5.25}$$

This population replication invariant aggregate intertemporal deprivation measure endorses the time replication invariance principle as well.

Finally, we describe how the Hojman and Kast (2009) recommendation can be redesigned in the context of material deprivation. At the individual level, intertemporal deprivation has two constituents; the first indicates the quantity of individual intertemporal material deprivation, as determined by (5.22), and the second represents changes in individual intertemporal material deprivation over time, measured by weighted sum of upward and downward shifts of individual deprivation over time. To understand this, consider two situations b_i and $\tilde{b}_i$ with $T = 3$, where in the former, the person is deprived in periods 2 and 3, whereas in the latter, he is deprived in periods 1 and 3. The Hojman–Kast approach demands that b_i should be regarded as more intertemporally deprived than $\tilde{b}_i$. The individual material deprivation levels are the same in the two situations. In the former, there is only one poverty production in the movement from period 1 to period 2. In the latter, there is one poverty ruination in the step from period 1 to period 2, which is then followed by a single poverty formation in the move from period 2 to period 3. This expresses the view that poverty formation (destruction) takes place under an increase (a reduction) in deprivation.

To formalize the aforementioned discussion analytically, for any arbitrary $i \in \{1, 2, \ldots, n\}$ and $t \in \{1,2, \ldots, T-1\}$, we introduce two indicator functions, formally defined as

$$\Gamma_i^t(b_i^t) = \begin{cases} 1 & \text{if} \sum_{j=1}^{m} b_{ij}^t w_j > \sum_{j=1}^{m} b_{ij}^{(t+1)} w_j \\ 0 & \text{otherwise} \end{cases}, \tag{5.26}$$

and

$$\tilde{\Gamma}_i^t(b_i^t) = \begin{cases} 1 & \text{if} \sum_{j=1}^{m} b_{ij}^t w_j < \sum_{j=1}^{m} b_{ij}^{(t+1)} w_j \\ 0 & \text{otherwise} \end{cases}, \tag{5.27}$$

for all $b_i^t \in \{0, 1\}^m$. They are desired to seize, respectively, the gains (reductions in individual material deprivation) and losses (enhancement of individual material deprivation).

Then for any individual i, intertemporal material deprivation, in the Hojman–Kast framework, is given by

$$E_i^{HK}(b_i) = \frac{1}{T}\sum_{t=1}^{T}\sum_{j=1}^{m} b_{ij}^t w_j + \frac{1}{T}\sum_{t=1}^{T}\sum_{j=1}^{m}(a_1^t \tilde{\Gamma}_i^t(b_i^t) - a_2^t \Gamma_i^t(b_i^t)), \tag{5.28}$$

where $b_i \in (\{0, 1\}^m)^T$ is arbitrary, and a_1^t and a_2^t are positive constants such that $a_1^t \geq a_2^t$ for all $t \in \{1,2, \dots , T - 1\}$. If the inequality $a_1^t > a_2^t$ holds, then losses are assigned higher weights than gains in the aggregation. If $a_1^t = a_2^t$, then they get equal importance; an increase in deprivation can be exactly matched by a reduction of the same amount.

Aggregate intertemporal deprivation in the Hojman–Kast framework is determined by E_A^{HK}. Formally, for all $b \in ((\{0, 1\}^m)^T)^n$,

$$E_A^{HK}(b) = \frac{1}{nT}\sum_{i=1}^{n}\sum_{t=1}^{T}\sum_{j=1}^{m} b_{ij}^t w_j + \frac{1}{nT}\sum_{i=1}^{n}\sum_{t=1}^{T}\sum_{j=1}^{m}(a_1^t \tilde{\Gamma}_i^t(b_i^t) - a_2^t \Gamma_i^t(b_i^t)). \tag{5.29}$$

One common feature of the counting-dependent proposals investigated in this section is that they apply to both ratio-scale and ordinal dimensions of well-being.

5.5 The Multidimensional Duration Approach

Because of close connection between one- and multidimensional duration propositions for poverty measurement, it will be rewarding to analyze some one-dimensional submissions briefly. In view of this, our organization of this section is divided into several subsections.

5.5.1 A Review of One-Dimensional Duration-Reliant Offers

Recall the notation we have introduced in Section 5.3.3. We denote individual i's censored income in period t by $\hat{u}_i^t$ and the time-invariant income poverty line by $z > 0$, where $i = 1,2, \dots , n$ and $t = 1,2, \dots , T$. The income deprivation indicator of person i in period t is $g_i^t = \frac{z-\hat{u}_i^t}{z}$. The duration approach identifies a person as chronically income poor (chronically poor, for short), if he remains in income poverty for at least a certain fraction of time periods τ, $0 < \tau \leq 1$. Equivalently, the person is chronically poor, by this method of identification, if he becomes income deprived in at least t_0 periods, where $t_0 = \min\left\{t \,\middle|\, 1 \leq t \leq T, \frac{t}{T} \geq \tau\right\}$, that is, t_0 is the minimum number of periods for which $\frac{t_0}{T} \geq \tau$ holds. It should be clear that the value of t_0 is unique. For instance, if we have observations on achievements for 11 periods and $\tau = \frac{1}{2}$, then $t_0 = 6$.

We refer to t_0 as the duration threshold. Several suggestions have been made in the literature concerning the choice of t_0. For instance, according to Gaiha and Deolikar (1993), those families with incomes below the poverty line in at least five out of nine periods of observations can be taken as chronically poor. Hulme and Shepherd (2003) argued that the necessary condition for a person to be identified as suffering from chronic capability deprivation is poverty experience for at least five successive years (see Hoy and Zheng, 2015, for further discussion). However, our definition of chronic poverty does not require poverty experiences in consecutive periods. Unless specified, we will assume that t_0 is given.

Let $u_{n\times T}$ be a panel of income distributions of n persons over T periods. The tth column of the panel gives the distribution of income among n persons in period t. Similarly, the ith row of the panel shows person i's incomes in T periods. Let $S_C(u_{n\times T}; z; t_0)$ be the set of chronically poor persons in $u_{n\times T}$. In other words, $S_C(u_{n\times T}; z; t_0)$ is the set of all the persons who remain in poverty for at least t_0 periods of time. Then $|S_C(u_{n\times T}; z; t_0)|$, the cardinality of the set $S_C(u_{n\times T}; z; t_0)$, gives the number of chronically poor persons in $u_{n\times T}$. The fraction $\frac{|S_C(u_{n\times T};z;t_0)|}{n}$ is the chronic head-count ratio, the proportion of persons that are chronically poor in $u_{n\times T}$.

The chronic income poverty index suggested by Foster (2009) is defined as

$$P_F^C(u_{n\times T}; z; t_0) = \frac{1}{nT} \sum_{i\in S_C(u_{n\times T};z;t_0)} \sum_{t=1}^{T} \left(1 - \frac{\hat{u}_i^t}{z}\right)^{\alpha}, \tag{5.30}$$

where $\alpha \geq 0$ is a parameter. We can rewrite (5.30) as $P_F^C(u_{n\times T}; z, t_0) = \frac{|S_C(u_{n\times T};z;t_0)|}{n} \frac{1}{|S_C(u_{n\times T};z;t_0)|T} \sum_{i\in S_C(u_{n\times T};z;t_0)} \sum_{t=1}^{T} \left(1 - \frac{\hat{u}_i^t}{z}\right)^{\alpha}$, the product of the chronic head-count ratio and the average of the transformed deprivations $\left(1 - \frac{\hat{u}_i^t}{z}\right)^{\alpha}$ of the chronically poor across all periods. As Foster (2009) mentioned, P_F^C satisfies several useful properties. For $\alpha = 0$, the index becomes the duration-adjusted head-count ratio $\frac{|S_C(u_{n\times T};z;t_0)|}{n} D^C(u_{n\times T}; z; t_0)$, where $D^C(u_{n\times T}; z; t_0)$ is the average duration of poverty among the chronically poor, given by $\frac{1}{|S_C(u_{n\times T};z;t_0)|T} \sum_{i\in S_C(u_{n\times T};z;t_0)} \sum_{t=1}^{T} \left(1 - \frac{\hat{u}_i^t}{z}\right)^{0}$.

According to Jalan and Ravallion (1998), a person is regarded as chronically poor if the mean of his periodwise incomes falls below the poverty line. Let $\overline{u}_{n\times T}$ be the panel of income distributions in which for any $i \in \{1, 2, \ldots, n\}$,

u_i^t is replaced by $\overline{u}_i$ for all $t = 1,2,\ldots,T$, where $\overline{u}_i = \frac{1}{T}\sum_{t=1}^{T} u_i^t$ is the average income of person i across T periods. In other words, $\overline{u}_{n\times T}$ is obtained from $u_{n\times T}$ by replacing the entries in the ith row by the common number $\overline{u}_i$, for all $i = 1,2,\ldots,n$.

The Jalan–Ravallion index of chronic income poverty, P_{JR}^C, can then be obtained by aggregating the squared deprivations $\left(1 - \frac{\hat{u}_i^t}{z}\right)^2$ of all chronically poor persons in the smoothed panel $\overline{u}_{n\times T}$. Formally,

$$P_{JR}^C(\overline{u}_{n\times T}; z) = \frac{1}{nT}\sum_{i\in S_C(\overline{u}_{n\times T};z)}\sum_{t=1}^{T}\left(1 - \frac{\overline{u}_i}{z}\right)^2, \tag{5.31}$$

where the set $S_C(\overline{u}_{n\times T}; z)$ of chronically poor persons now consists of all those persons whose average incomes over the entire length of the period profile $(1,2,\ldots,T)$ fall below the poverty line. Evidently, in this case, the chronic poverty identification problem is a one-period issue: if the mean income of a person over all the periods is below the poverty threshold, then he is chronically poor, otherwise not. This analysis clearly shows that, given the one-period notion of identification of the chronically poor, the Jalan–Ravallion index can be calculated using the type of aggregation invoked in Foster (2009), under the additional assumption that $\alpha = 2$.

The Foster (2009) approach can, in fact, be extended to the entire family of subgroup-decomposable income poverty indices. The general ditto of P_F^C can be defined as

$$P_\psi^C(u_{n\times T}; z; t_0) = \frac{1}{nT}\sum_{i\in S_C(u_{n\times T};z;t_0)}\sum_{t=1}^{T}\psi\left(\frac{\hat{u}_i^t}{z}\right), \tag{5.32}$$

where ψ is continuous, decreasing, and strictly convex. For $\psi(t) = t^\alpha, \alpha \geq 0, P_\psi^C$ becomes Foster's (2009) proposal. Alternatively, if we choose $\psi(t) = 1 - t^e, 0 < e < 1$, then P_ψ^C becomes a chronic poverty translation of the Chakravarty (1983) income poverty index (see Chakravarty, 2009). We can also apply the Jalan–Ravallion identification criterion to P_ψ^C to get variants of P_{JR}^C.

5.5.2 Axioms for a Chronic Multidimensional Poverty Quantifier

Throughout this and the next two subsections, we follow the notation adopted in Section 5.2. Given a well-defined method of identification of the multidimensionally poor in each period, the duration approach identifies a person as chronic multidimensionally poor if he remains in poverty for some exogenously given t_0 periods of time. As before, we adopt the union method of identification of poor.

This duration-dependent approach involves a two-step identification problem. The first step requires identification of the multidimensionally poor persons in each period. The exercise at the second step is to identify the chronically poor among these multidimensionally poor persons in different periods. Recall our notation that M^{nT} stands for the set of all $nT \times d$ dimensional intertemporal distribution matrices when the population size is n, and M denotes the set of such matrices for all possible population sizes (assuming that T and d are given).

For all $n \in N$, $\underline{z} \in Z$, let $\prod^C(X; \underline{z}, t_0)$ be the set of all persons who are chronically poor in $X \in M^{nT}$, that is, the set of all persons who are counted as multidimensionally poor for at least t_0 periods in the intertemporal distribution matrix X. Formally, $\prod^C(X; \underline{z}; t_0) = \{i \in \{1, 2, \dots, n\} \,|\, i$ is multidimensionally poor in X for at least t_0 periods$\}$. We denote the number of chronically poor persons in X by $\left|\prod^C(X; \underline{z}; t_0)\right|$. A multidimensional chronic poverty index in this framework can be written as a function $P^C(X; \underline{z}; t_0)$, where $X \in M$.

As an illustrative example assume that $d = 2, n = 3$ and $T = 4$. The social matrices for the four periods are $X^1 = \begin{bmatrix} 3 & 3 \\ 2 & 2 \\ 8 & 4 \end{bmatrix}$, $X^2 = \begin{bmatrix} 7 & 10 \\ 4 & 8 \\ 5 & 9 \end{bmatrix}$, $X^3 = \begin{bmatrix} 9 & 4 \\ 8 & 3 \\ 8 & 8 \end{bmatrix}$, $X^4 = \begin{bmatrix} 2 & 5 \\ 2 & 9 \\ 3 & 6 \end{bmatrix}$, and the vector of common poverty cutoffs is $\underline{z} = (5, 4)$. The entries in the first row of matrix X^i indicate person 1's achievements in period i, where $i =$ 1,2,3,4. Similarly, figures in the other rows of the four matrices can be explained. By the union method of identification of the poor, while person 2 is poor in all the four periods, person 3 is poor only in period 4. On the other hand, person 1 is poor in periods 1 and 4. Assume that the duration threshold $t_0 = 2$. Then although persons 1 and 2 are chronically poor, person 3 is not so. It may be worthy to note that by the intersection identification procedure, persons 1 and 2 are poor in period 1. However, nobody is chronically poor by this notion of identification.

The corresponding intertemporal social matrix with 12 rows and 2 columns, denoted by $\overline{X}_{12\times 2}$, is now obtained by placing the rows of X^i, where $i = 1,2,3,4$, contiguously as rows of $\overline{X}_{12\times 2}$ from above to below. In consequence, the entries in rows 1, 4, 7, and 10 of $\overline{X}_{12\times 2}$ quantify person 1's achievements in periods 1, 2, 3, and 4, respectively, in the two dimensions. Other rows of $\overline{X}_{12\times 2}$ can be explained analogously. The number $\left|\prod^C(\overline{X}_{12\times 2}); (5, 4); 2\right|$ here is 2 and the corresponding set consists of persons 1 and 2. We will use the matrix $\overline{X}_{12\times 2}$ to illustrate the axioms defined for a general index.

The explicit representation of the intertemporal social matrix $\overline{X}_{12\times2}$, associated with our example, is given by

$$\overline{X}_{12\times2} = \begin{bmatrix} 3 & 3 \\ 2 & 2 \\ 8 & 4 \\ 7 & 10 \\ 4 & 8 \\ 5 & 9 \\ 9 & 4 \\ 8 & 3 \\ 8 & 8 \\ 2 & 5 \\ 2 & 9 \\ 3 & 6 \end{bmatrix}.$$

The following axioms can now be stated for a general multidimensional chronic poverty index P^C. Of these, the first two axioms parallel the Bourguignon–Chakravarty focus axioms. The four axioms that follow these are directly adapted to the chronic poverty setup from the literature. Each of the next five axioms is a multidimensional version of Foster's (2009) corresponding unidimensional postulate. They are followed by a chronic twin of the Alkire and Foster (2011) dimensional monotonicity axiom. The remaining postulates are chronic reproductions of the corresponding properties proposed in Chapter 3.

Chronic Weak Focus: For all $n \in N$, $\underline{z} \in Z$, $X \in M^{nT}$, suppose that person i is not chronically poor in X, and $Y \in M^{nT}$ is obtained from X as follows: $y^t_{ij} = x^t_{ij} + \delta$ for a triplet $(t, i, j) \in \{1, 2, \dots, T\} \times \{1, 2, \dots, n\} \times \{1, 2, \dots, d\}$, where $\delta > 0$ and $y^l_{sq} = x^l_{sq}$ for all triplets $(l, s, q) \neq (t, i, j)$. Then $P^C(X; \underline{z}; t_0) = P^C(Y; \underline{z}; t_0)$.

According to this axiom, an increase in the achievement in a dimension of a chronically nonpoor person in any period does not change the value of the poverty index. That is, the poverty index is independent of the achievements of all persons who are chronically nonpoor. In the matrix $\overline{X}_{12\times2}$, person 3 is chronically nonpoor. An increase in his achievement in dimension 1 in period 4 from 3 to 4 reduces his poverty level in the period but does not affect his chronic poverty status.

Chronic Strong Focus: For all $n \in N$, $\underline{z} \in Z$, $X \in M^{nT}$, suppose that $Y \in M^{nT}$ is obtained from X as follows: $y^t_{ij} = x^t_{ij} + \delta$ for a triplet $(t, i, j) \in \{1, 2, \dots, T\} \times \{1, 2, \dots, n\} \times \{1, 2, \dots, d\}$, where $x^t_{ij} \geq z_j$, $\delta \neq 0$ is such that $y^t_{ij} \geq z_j$ and $y^l_{sq} = x^l_{sq}$ for all triplets $(l, s, q) \neq (t, i, j)$. Then $P^C(X; \underline{z}; t_0) = P^C(Y; \underline{z}; t_0)$.

In this case, person i may or may not be chronically poor. In either case, if his achievement in a nondeprived dimension j in some period t increases, the poverty index remains unaffected. If person i is chronically nonpoor, then the strong focus axiom reduces to its weak version. In $\overline{X}_{12\times2}$ person 1, who is chronically poor, is nondeprived in dimension 1 in period 3. His chronic poverty position remains unaltered, if this achievement increases from 9 to any higher level.

Period-Restricted Anonymity: For all $n \in N$, $\underline{z} \in Z$, $X \in M^{nT}$, suppose that $Y \in M^{nT}$ is obtained from X as follows: $Y^t = BX^t$, where B is any $n \times n$ permutation matrix, $t \in \{1, 2, \ldots, T\}$ is arbitrary, and $Y^l = X^l$ for all $l \in \{1, 2, \ldots, T\}/\{t\}$. Then $P^C(X; \underline{z}; t_0) = P^C(Y; \underline{z}; t_0)$.

This postulate demands that a rearrangement of the rows of the distribution matrix in any period, keeping the distribution matrices in all other periods unchanged, does not affect chronic poverty. Thus, in our social matrix $\overline{X}_{12\times2}$, if we exchange only the first two rows, that is, the first row now becomes (2,2), whereas the second row is given by (3,3) and all other rows remain unaltered, then the chronic poverty levels of the new intertemporal matrix and the original matrix $\overline{X}_{12\times2}$ are the same.

The next axiom becomes helpful in cross-population comparisons of chronic poverty.

Chronic Population Replication Invariance: For all $n \in N$, $\underline{z} \in Z$, $X \in M^{nT}$, $P^C(X; \underline{z}; t_0) = P^C(Y; \underline{z}; t_0)$,where $Y \in M^{nqT}$ is the q-fold replication of $X \in M^{nT}$, $q \geq 2$ being a positive integer, that is, in Y each row of X appears q times.

This axiom ensures that chronic poverty is measured in per-capita terms. Consequently, comparison of chronic poverty levels of two societies whose population sizes are different becomes possible. If the intertemporal matrix $\overline{X}_{12\times2}$ is replicated twice, in the resulting matrix $\overline{Y}_{24\times2}$, each row of $\overline{X}_{12\times2}$ appears twice and the postulate requires that $P^C(\overline{X}_{12\times2}; \underline{z}; t_0) = P^C(\overline{Y}_{24\times2}; \underline{z}; t_0)$.

Chronic Strong Ratio-Scale Invariance: For all $n \in N$, $\underline{z} \in Z$, $X \in M^{nT}$, suppose that $Y \in M^{nT}$ is obtained from X as follows: for all $t \in \{1, 2, \ldots, T\}$, $Y^t = X^t\Omega$, where Ω is any $d \times d$ positive diagonal matrix. Then $P^C(X; \underline{z}\,; t_0) = P^C(Y; \underline{z}\Omega\,; t_0)$.

According to this axiom, if all the achievements in any dimension in all the periods and the corresponding threshold limit are subjected to the same equiproportionate change, then chronic poverty remains unchanged. A weaker form of this axiom, chronic ratio-scale invariance, demands that the proportionality factor is the same across the dimensions in all the periods. For four X^i matrices associated with $\overline{X}_{12\times2}$, define Y^i by $X^i\Omega$ and let the corresponding intertemporal matrix be $\overline{Y}_{12\times2}$, where $\Omega = \text{diag}(2, 3)$. Then the strong invariance postulate demands that $P^C(\overline{X}_{12\times2}; (5, 4)\,; t_0) = P^C(\overline{Y}_{12\times2}; (10, 12)\,; t_0)$.

The postulate, subgroup decomposability, establishes consistency between local and global evaluations of chronic poverty in a specific way.

Chronic Subgroup Decomposability: For all $n_i \in N$, $\underline{z} \in Z$, $X^i \in M^{n_iT}$,

$$P^C(X;\underline{z};t_0) = \sum_{i=1}^{m} \frac{n_i}{n} P^C(X^i;\underline{z};t_0),$$

where $\sum_{i=1}^{m} n_i = n$ and $X \in M^{nT}$ is obtained by placing the matrices $X^i \in M^{n_iT}$ from above to below for $i = 1,2,\ldots,m$, where $m \geq 2$.

The formulation of the axiom indicates that for any division of the population into two or more nonoverlapping subgroups, aggregate chronic poverty is the population share weighted average of its subgroup brothers. Since the numbering of the matrices $X^i \in M^{n_iT}$ is arbitrary, the arrangement of the rows of $X \in M^{nT}$ is also arbitrary. Under an alternative numbering of the matrices, the positioning of the rows of $X \in M^{nT}$ will be in the manner consistent with the numbering. Suppose that a reduction in chronic poverty in one subgroup, say, as a result of implementation of some targeted poverty alleviation policy, takes place. Then, under the ceteris paribus condition that poverty extents remain fixed in all other subgroups, this shrinkage in the particular subgroup's poverty must lead to a reduction in overall chronic poverty.

To illustrate this axiom, suppose that the three individuals we have considered in our example have been partitioned into two subgroups S_1 and S_2, with respect to their regions of residence, say, where S_1 consists of person 1 and the other subgroup consists of persons 2 and 3. Then the axiom claims that $P^C(\overline{X}_{12\times2};\underline{z};t_0) = \frac{1}{3}P^C(\overline{X}^{S_1}_{4\times2};\underline{z};t_0) + \frac{2}{3}P^C(\overline{X}^{S_2}_{8\times2};\underline{z};t_0)$,where $\overline{X}^{S_1}_{4\times2}$ and $\overline{X}^{S_2}_{8\times2}$ denote the intertemporal social matrices associated with the subgroups S_1 and S_2, respectively.[3]

Time Anonymity: For all $n \in N$, $\underline{z} \in Z$, $X \in M^{nT}$, if the sequence of matrices $(Y^1, Y^2, \ldots, Y^T)$ is obtained by a reordering of the sequence of period-by-period matrices $(X^1, X^2, \ldots, X^T)$ under X, then $P^C(X;\underline{z};t_0) = P^C(Y;\underline{z};t_0)$.

This desideratum claims that an interchange of positions two periodwise distribution matrices in the sequence of timings $(1, 2, \ldots, T)$ does not affect chronic poverty. Consequently, if the distribution matrix that appears in period t (respectively, t') under X appears in period t' (respectively, t) under

3 Given the availability of panel data on multidimensional achievements, a time variant of this postulate was employed by Alkire et al. (2015, Ch. 9) to identify different subgroups of population depending on how poverty statuses of the individuals belonging to these subgroups change over the panel. See also Hulme et al. (2001), Hulme and Shepherd (2003), and Narayan and Petesch (2007).

Y, and for the remaining periods the distribution matrices under X and Y are the same, then chronic poverty in X will be equal to that in Y. In the illustrative matrix $\overline{X}_{12\times2}$, suppose that the positions of X^2 and X^4 are interchanged, and the positions of X^1 and X^3 are kept unchanged. If we denote the resulting intertemporal distribution matrix by $\overline{Y}_{12\times2}$, then the time anonymity axiom asserts that $P^C(\overline{X}_{12\times2}; \underline{z}; t_0) = P^C(\overline{Y}_{12\times2}; \underline{z}; t_0)$.

Clearly, an intertemporal poverty index that verifies the block monotonicity axiom so that higher weights are assigned to poverty blocks with larger sizes is a violator of this postulate. Evidently, the time anonymity axiom does not make any distinction between two situations with the same number of poverty spells where in the former, the poverty spells appear consecutively, but in the latter, they are separated by at least one zero-poverty spell. It treats the profiles $p_i = \left(\frac{1}{2}, \frac{1}{4}, \frac{1}{8}, 0, \frac{1}{2}\right)$ and $p_j = \left(\frac{1}{2}, \frac{1}{4}, \frac{1}{8}, \frac{1}{2}, 0\right)$ as identically intertemporally poor. But the block approach regards the latter as poorer than the former because in the former, the lengths of the two poverty blocks are 3 and 1, respectively, whereas in the latter, the single poverty block has a length of 4. The time anonymity axiom brings out a major distinguishing feature between the two approaches. An index that agrees with this axiom also fails to meet the Hoy–Zheng chronic poverty axiom.

Chronic Monotonicity: For all $n \in N$, $\underline{z} \in Z$, $X \in M^{nT}$, suppose that the matrix $Y \in M^{nT}$ is obtained from X as follows: $y_{ij}^t = x_{ij}^t - \delta$ for a triplet $(t, i, j) \in \{1, 2, \dots, T\} \times \{1, 2, \dots, n\} \times \{1, 2, \dots, d\}$, where person i is chronically poor, $0 < x_{ij}^t < z_j$, $\delta > 0$, and $y_{sq}^l = x_{sq}^l$ for all triplets $(l, s, q) \neq (t, i, j)$. Then $P^C(X; \underline{z}; t_0) < P^C(Y; \underline{z}; t_0)$.

If achievement in a deprived dimension of a chronically poor person reduces, then a natural requirement is that poverty should go up. This is what the chronic monotonicity axiom demands. In $\overline{X}_{12\times2}$, if achievement in dimension 2 in period 1 of person 2, a chronically poor person, goes down from 2 to 1, then poverty should indicate an upward trend.

Time Monotonicity: For all $n \in N$, $\underline{z} \in Z$, $X \in M^{nT}$, suppose that person i is chronically poor in X and $Y \in M^{nT}$ is related to X as follows: $x_{ij}^t < z_j \leq y_{ij}^t$ for a triplet $(t, i, j) \in \{1, 2, \dots, T\} \times \{1, 2, \dots, n\} \times \{1, 2, \dots, d\}$, and $y_{sq}^l = x_{sq}^l$ for all triplets $(l, s, q) \neq (t, i, j)$. Then $P^C(Y; \underline{z}; t_0) < P^C(X; \underline{z}; t_0)$.

Poverty should go up under an increase in the number of periods of deprivation suffered by a chronically poor person in some dimension. Our time monotonicity axiom states this necessity. In the matrix $\overline{X}_{12\times2}$, person 1 is chronically poor but nondeprived in dimension 1 in period 2. If this achievement gets slashed from 7 to 4, then his duration of deprivation in the dimension increases from 2 to 3. Hence, chronic poverty should go up.

Duration Monotonicity: For all $n \in N$, $\underline{z} \in Z$, $X \in M^{nT}$, given the duration threshold $t_0 > 1$, if $\bar{t}_0 = t_0 - k$, where $k \geq 1$ is an integer such that $t_0 - k \geq 1$, then $P^C(X; \underline{z}; t_0) \leq P^C(X; \underline{z}; \bar{t}_0)$.

If the duration threshold goes down, then there is a possibility that some newer persons who were not chronically poor originally become chronic poverty stricken now. Hence, we are adding some new chronically poor persons without changing the statuses of the existing poor. Consequently, chronic poverty should not go down under a reduction in the duration threshold. In our social matrix $\overline{X}_{12\times 2}$, suppose that t_0 reduces from 2 to 1, then all the three persons become chronically poor, whereas for $t_0 = 2$, only two persons are chronically poor. Accordingly, $P^C(\overline{X}_{12\times 2}; \underline{z}; 2) < P^C(\overline{X}_{12\times 2}; \underline{z}; 1)$.

None of the axioms stated so far was concerned with the inequality among the chronically poor. In the case of cross-sectional multidimensional poverty, if there is a Pigou–Dalton bundle of transfers of achievements, in deprived dimensions, from a poorer poor to a richer poor that do not change their statuses, then the posttransfer social distribution should have higher multidimensional poverty than the pretransfer one.

Given $n \in N$, n > 1, $X \in M^{nT}$, $\underline{z} \in Z$, and t_0, suppose that in all the dimensions of $S^t_{hi}(X; \underline{z}; t_0)$, the common set of deprived dimensions of the chronically poor persons h and i in period t, the former has higher deprivations than the latter. More precisely, for all $j \in S^t_{hi}(X; \underline{z}; t_0)$, $x^t_{hj} < x^t_{ij} < z_j$, where $S^t_{hi}(X; \underline{z}; t_0) = \{j \in Q | x^t_{hj} < z_j\} = \{j \in Q | x^t_{ij} < z_j\}$,with $i, h \in \{1, 2, \ldots, n\}$ and $t \in \{1, 2, \ldots, T\}$ being arbitrary. Assume that $S^t_{hi}(X; \underline{z}; t_0)$ is nonempty.

Definition 5.4 For all $n \in N$, $\underline{z} \in Z$, $X \in M^{nT}$, $n > 1$, $Y \in M^{nT}$ is said to be obtained from $X_{nT\times d}$ by a Pigou–Dalton bundle of regressive transfers from chronically poor person h to chronically poor person i if (i) $y^t_{p.} = x^t_{p.}$ for all $p \in \{1, 2, \ldots, n\}/\{h, i\}$; (ii) $y^t_{h.} = x^t_{h.} - \delta$, $y^t_{i.} = x^t_{i.} + \delta$, where $\delta = (\delta_1, \delta_2, \ldots, \delta_d)$; $(a)\ \delta_j = 0$ for all $j \in Q \backslash S^t_{hi}(X; \underline{z}; t_0)$; $(b)\ \delta_j \geq 0$ for any $j \in S^t_{hi}(X)$, with > for at least one j, and $y^t_{ij} < z_j$ for all $j \in S^t_{hi}(X; \underline{z}; t_0)$; (iii) $X^l = Y^l$ for all $l \neq t \in \{1, 2, \ldots, T\}$.

We have assumed at the outset that the same set of deprived dimensions of the chronically poor persons h and i in period t, with the additional characteristic that h has higher deprivations than i, is nonempty. Condition (i) of Definition 5.4 demands that all individuals except persons h and i have identical achievements in all the dimensions in both X^t and Y^t. Part (a) of condition (ii) says that each of persons h and i has identical achievements in all nondeprived dimensions in period t. According to part (b) of condition (ii), we get $y_{h.}$ and $y_{i.}$ by dimensionwise regressive transfers of achievements from person h to person i in their common set of deprived dimensions, where the size of the transfer is nonnegative for any dimension in the set, and for at least one deprived dimension, the transfer has a positive size. In part (b) of condition (ii), it is ensured that the size of the transfer in any dimension does not allow the recipient to be nondeprived in the dimension. Finally, condition (iii) of the definition requires that in all the periods other than t, social matrices in both X and Y are the same. Since for any $j \in S^t_{hi}(X; \underline{z}; t_0)$, $\delta_j \geq 0$ cannot exceed x_{hj}, it is confirmed that $0 \leq y^t_{hj} < y^t_{ij}$.

This bundle of regressive transfers increases inequality in the achievement distributions among the poor. The following may be regarded as the chronic poverty ditto of this property:

Chronic Transfer: For all $n \in N, \underline{z} \in Z, X \in M^{nT}, n > 1$, if $Y \in M^{nT}$ is obtained from X by a Pigou–Dalton bundle of regressive transfers between two chronically poor persons, then $P^C(X; \underline{z}; t_0) < P^C(Y; \underline{z}; t_0)$.

In the matrix $\overline{X}_{12\times 2}$, persons 1 and 2 are chronically poor, and person 2 has higher deprivations than person 1 in both the dimensions in period 1. Then a Pigou–Dalton bundle of regressive transfers consisting of sizes of 1 and 0.5 units of achievements in dimensions 1 and 2, respectively, from person 2 to person 1 will raise chronic poverty.

Chronic Dimensional Monotonicity: For all $n \in N, \underline{z} \in Z, X \in M^{nT}$, suppose that person i is chronically poor in X, and $Y \in M^{nT}$ is related to X as follows: $x^t_{ij} \geq z_j$, $y^t_{ij} = x^t_{ij} - \delta < z_j$ for a triplet $(t, i, j) \in \{1, 2, \ldots, T\} \times \{1, 2, \ldots, n\} \times \{1, 2, \ldots, d\}$, and $y^l_{sq} = x^l_{sq}$ for all triplets $(l, s, q) \neq (t, i, j)$, where $\delta > 0$. Then $P^C(X; \underline{z}; t_0) < P^C(Y; \underline{z}; t_0)$.

This property insists that chronic poverty goes up when a chronically poor person who is nondeprived in a dimension in some period becomes deprived in the dimension in that period. In the distribution matrix $\overline{X}_{12\times 2}$, person 1 is chronically poor but nondeprived in dimension 2 in period 4. If this achievement falls down to a level below the threshold limit, say from 5 to 3, then the person becomes deprived in dimension 2 in period 4. This expansion in the number of deprived dimensions of the chronically poor, person 1, should augment chronic poverty.

The next axiom is concerning association between dimensions of well-being. Consequently, it represents a unique feature of multidimensional chronic poverty analysis.

Definition: Suppose that persons i and h are chronically poor in the intertemporal social matrix $X \in M^{nT}$. Assume also that they are deprived in dimensions j and q in some period $t \in \{1, 2, \ldots, T\}$ and (i) $x^t_{ij} < x^t_{hj} < z_j$, (ii) $x^t_{hq} < x^t_{iq} < z_q$, (iii) $x^t_{ik} \leq x^t_{hk}$ for all $k \in Q/\{j, q\}$. Next, suppose that Y^t is obtained from X^t as follows: (iv) $y^t_{hj} = x^t_{hj}, y^t_{ij} = x^t_{ij}$, (v) $y^t_{hq} = x^t_{iq}, y^t_{iq} = x^t_{hq}$, (vi) $y^t_{hk} = x^t_{hk}, y^t_{ik} = x^t_{ik}$ for all $k \in Q/\{j, q\}$, and (vii) $y^t_{l.} = x^t_{l.}$ for all $l \neq i, h$, where $y^t_{l.}(x^t_{l.})$ is the lth row of $Y^t(X^t)$. If $Y^l = X^l$ for all $l \neq t \in \{1, 2, \ldots, T\}$, then we say that $Y \in M^{nT}$ is obtained from X by a correlation-increasing switch between two chronically poor persons. Conversely, it can be said that $X \in M^{nT}$ is derived from $Y \in M^{nT}$ by a correlation-decreasing switch between two persons who are chronically poor.

Conditions (i) and (ii) of the aforementioned definition state that in X^t, person i has lower achievement than person h in dimension j, and the reverse inequality holds in dimension q. According to condition (iii), in all other dimensions, achievements of person h are at least as large as those of person i. Condition (iv) formally states that in period t, a switch between achievements of persons i and h in dimension j has been performed. Conditions (iv) and (v) jointly ensure that in the postswitch situation, person h has higher achievements than person i in both the dimensions j and q in the period. This swap of achievements between persons i and h increases the correlation between the dimensional achievements. Note that in Y^t in no dimension, person i has higher achievement than person h.

Increasing Chronic Poverty under Correlation-Increasing Switch: For all $n \in N$, $\underline{z} \in Z$, $X \in M^{nT}$, $n > 1$, if $Y \in M^{nT}$ is obtained from X by a correlation-increasing switch between two chronically poor persons, then $P^C(X; \underline{z}; t_0) < P^C(Y; \underline{z}; t_0)$ given that the two dimensions affected by the switch are substitutes.

Similarly, when the underlying dimensions are complements, the reverse inequality $P^C(X; \underline{z}; t_0) > P^C(Y; \underline{z}; t_0)$ holds. If the dimensions are independents, the perfect equality $P^C(X; \underline{z}; t_0) = P^C(Y; \underline{z}; t_0)$ is achieved.

Suppose that the matrix $\tilde{Y}_{12\times 2}$ is derived from $\overline{X}_{12\times 2}$ by a switch of achievements in dimension 2 of persons 1 and 2 in period 1. Assume that all other entries in the two matrices are the same. We can then say that $\tilde{Y}_{12\times 2}$ is obtained from $\overline{X}_{12\times 2}$ by a correlation-decreasing switch.

Chronic Monotonicity in Threshold Limits: For all $n \in N$, $\underline{z} \in Z$, $X \in M^{nT}$, suppose that person i, who is chronically poor in X, is deprived in dimension j in period t so that $x^t_{ij} < z_j$. Then $P^C(X; \underline{z}; t_0) < P^C(X; \underline{\tilde{z}}; t_0)$, where $\tilde{z}_l = z_l + \beta$, for $l = j$, $\tilde{z}_l = z_l$ for $l \in Q/\{j\}$, and $\beta > 0$ is constant.

This postulate asserts that chronic poverty increases under an increase in the threshold limit of a dimension in which a chronically poor person is deprived in some period. In the social matrix $\overline{X}_{12\times 2}$, person 1 is chronically poor and deprived in dimension 2 in period 1. If the threshold limit of the dimension increases from 4 to 5, say, then the person's deprivation in the dimension in period 2 also goes up. This increased deprivation of person 1 leads to a higher chronic poverty. More precisely, $P^C(\overline{X}_{12\times 2}; (5, 4); t_0) < P^C(\overline{X}_{12\times 2}; (5, 5); t_0)$.

The following axioms also seem appropriate for a duration-based index.

Chronic Boundedness: For all $n \in N$, $\underline{z} \in Z$, $X \in M^{nT}$, $0 \leq P^C(X;\underline{z};t_0) \leq 1$, where (a) $P^C(X;\underline{z};t_0) = 0$ if $\left|\prod^C(X;\underline{z};t_0)\right| = 0$, and (b) $P^C(X;\underline{z};t_0) = 1$ if $x_{ij}^t = 0$ for all triplets $(t, i, j) \in \{1, 2, \dots, T\} \times \{1, 2, \dots, n\} \times \{1, 2, \dots, d\}$.

This axiom claims that the chronic poverty index is bounded between 0 and 1, where the lower bound, showing minimal poverty (0), is achieved if there is no chronically poor person in the society. In contrast, the index attains its upper bound, representing maximum poverty (1), when everybody in the society is maximally deprived in all the dimensions in all periods.

The next axiom is self-explanatory.

Chronic Continuity: Given $\underline{z} \in Z$, for any arbitrary population size $n \in N$, P^C varies continuously with changes in achievements in each period provided that individuals' poverty statuses remain unchanged in all the periods.

5.5.3 The Bourguignon–Chakravarty Approach to Chronic Multidimensional Poverty Measurement

This subsection proposes a scalar representation of multidimensional chronic poverty in a society and evaluates it with respect to the axioms introduced earlier. It follows the Bourguignon and Chakravarty (2003) aggregation rule and, in consequence, can be regarded as the chronic twin of the Bourguignon–Chakravarty multidimensional poverty index.

The numerical representation of multidimensional chronic poverty, we suggest, is given by

$$P_{BC}^C(X;\underline{z};t_0) = \frac{1}{n} \sum_{i \in \prod^C(X;\underline{z};t_o)} \frac{1}{T} \sum_{t=1}^{T} \left[\sum_{j=1}^{d} \frac{1}{d} \left(1 - \frac{\hat{x}_{ij}^t}{z_j}\right)^{\alpha} \right]^{\frac{\beta}{\alpha}}, \tag{5.33}$$

where $\alpha > 1$, $\beta > 0$ are sensitivity parameters along the Bourguignon–Chakravarty lines of multidimensional poverty measurement; with $X \in M^{nT}$, $n \in N$, and $\underline{z} \in Z$ being arbitrary. As we will see, adoption of this functional form will capacitate us to identify any pair of dimensions in terms of a well-defined notion of association between them. This chronic poverty metric is time replication invariant as well.

Person i's deprivation indicator in dimension j in the tth period is given by $g_{ij}^t = \left(1 - \frac{\hat{x}_{ij}^t}{z_j}\right)$. The third bracketed term in (5.33) is the simple unweighted average of transformed values of such indicators over all dimensions in the period for the chronically poor person i, where the transformed values are generated by applying the nonnegative increasing, strictly convex transformation $(g_{it}^t)^{\alpha}$, $\alpha > 1$. These periodic dimensional averages are then aggregated across periods to arrive at $\frac{1}{T}\sum_{t=1}^{T}\left[\sum_{j=1}^{d}\frac{1}{d}(g_{ij}^{t})^{\alpha}\right]^{\frac{\beta}{\alpha}}$, where $\beta > 0$. These quantities have been calculated for any arbitrary chronically poor person i in the population. If we sum these values over all chronically poor persons in the society and divide the resulting expression by the population size n, then we arrive at the summary standard in (5.33).

Now, person i is fully deprived in any dimension j in a year t, if $g_{ij}^{t} = 1$. If this situation of maximum deprivation occurs for all periods in all the dimensions for a chronically poor person i, then the sum $\sum_{t=1}^{T}\left[\sum_{j=1}^{d}\left(1-\frac{\hat{x}_{ij}^{t}}{z_j}\right)^{\alpha}\right]^{\frac{\beta}{\alpha}}$ becomes Td for all $\alpha > 1$ and $\beta > 0$. If all the persons in the society are chronically poor and are characterized by maximum deprivation for all (period, dimension) combinations, then the value of the expression $\sum_{i\in\prod^{C}(X;z;t_0)}\sum_{t=1}^{T}\left[\sum_{j=1}^{d}\left(1-\frac{\hat{x}_{ij}^{t}}{z_j}\right)^{\alpha}\right]^{\frac{\beta}{\alpha}}$ is nTd. This in turn establishes that P_{BC}^{C} is bounded above by 1. It attains the lower bound 0 if nobody is chronically poor.

The following proposition, which is easy to demonstrate, describes some properties of P_{BC}^{C}.

Proposition 5.1 The multidimensional index given by (5.33) verifies the following chronic poverty axioms: weak focus, strong focus, population replication invariance, ratio-scale invariance, subgroup decomposability, monotonicity, dimensional monotonicity, transfer, monotonicity in threshold limits, boundedness, and continuity. It also fulfills period-restricted anonymity, time anonymity, time monotonicity, and duration monotonicity. It increases under a correlation-increasing switch if $\beta > \alpha > 1$. The opposite happens if $\alpha > 1$ and $\beta < \alpha$. The switch keeps the index unchanged if $\beta = \alpha$.

The index can be expressed as the sum of dimensionwise indices when $\beta = \alpha$. Using this breakdown, we can calculate contribution of each dimension to the chronic poverty of the society (see Chapter 3). One can search for the factors that are likely to relegate people into poverty. Given a positive α, as $\beta \to 0$, P_{BC}^{C} approaches $H^{C}(X;\underline{z};t_0)\frac{\mu^{C}(X;\underline{z};t_0)}{|\prod^{C}(X;\underline{z};t_0)|}$, where $H^{C}(X;\underline{z};t_0) = \left(\frac{|\prod^{C}(X;\underline{z};t_0)|}{n}\right)$ is the chronic head-count ratio, the proportion of persons that are chronically poor in X, and $\mu^{C}(X;\underline{z};t_0)$ is the average number of (period, dimension) combinations in which the chronically poor persons are deprived, that is, $\sum_{i\in\prod^{C}(X;\underline{z};t_0)}\sum_{t=1}^{T}\left[\sum_{j=1}^{d}\left(1-\frac{\hat{x}_{ij}^{t}}{z_j}\right)^{0}\right]$, expressed as a fraction of dT. The normalized quantity $\frac{\mu^{C}(X;\underline{z};t_0)}{|\prod^{C}(X;\underline{z};t_0)|}$ is the average duration of poverty among all chronic multidimensionally poor persons. Then the fraction $H^C(X;\underline{z};t_0)\frac{\mu^C(X;\underline{z};t_0)}{|\prod^C(X;\underline{z};t_0)|}$ is the multidimensional twin of the duration-adjusted head-count ratio. On the other hand, for $\alpha = \beta = 1$, the index becomes $\frac{1}{ndT}\sum_{i\in\prod^C(X;\underline{z};t_0)}\sum_{t=1}^{T}\left[\sum_{j=1}^{d}\left(1-\frac{\hat{x}_{ij}^t}{z_j}\right)\right]$, the sum of deprivations experienced by the chronically poor persons across all dimensions and periods, divided by ndT, the maximum possible value that this number can assume. We can write it alternatively as

$$H^C(X;\underline{z};t_0).\left(\frac{1}{\left|\prod^C(X;\underline{z};t_0)\right|Td}\sum_{i\in\prod^C(X;\underline{z};t_0)}\sum_{t=1}^{T}\left[\sum_{j=1}^{d}\left(1-\frac{\hat{x}_{ij}^t}{z_j}\right)\right]\right). \tag{5.34}$$

The component $\frac{1}{|\prod^C(X;\underline{z};t_0)|Td}\sum_{i\in\prod^C(X;\underline{z};t_0)}\sum_{t=1}^{T}\left[\sum_{j=1}^{d}\left(1-\frac{\hat{x}_{ij}^t}{z_j}\right)\right]$ of this multiplicative decomposition is the average deprivation of the chronically poor persons in the poverty spells across all dimensions and periods. Each of the two terms of this simple multiplicative decomposition conveys significant information on different aspects of chronic poverty, confronted by the society. The first term tells us the extent of poverty arising from the fraction of population affected by chronic poverty. When this term divides the overall chronic poverty value $\frac{1}{nTd}\left(\sum_{i\in\prod^C(X;\underline{z};t_0)}\sum_{t=1}^{T}\left[\sum_{j=1}^{d}\left(1-\frac{\hat{x}_{ij}^t}{z_j}\right)\right]\right)$, we are left with the third bracketed term of the decomposition, which indicates the average depth of deprivation felt by the chronically poor persons in all d dimensions throughout the period profile $(1, 2, \ldots, T)$. Evidently, while the former simply counts the proportion of persons affected by chronic multidimensional poverty, the latter represents its intensity. Each of these factors is quite important from policy perspective.

In order to illustrate the calculation of P_{BC}^C, let us consider again the social matrix $\overline{X}_{12\times 2}$. Assume, as before, that $\underline{z} = (5, 4)$ and $t_0 = 2$. Recall that under these specifications, only persons 1 and 2 are chronically poor. Then the corresponding 8×2 dimensional deprivation matrix whose entries represent deprivations of the chronically poor persons is given by

$$\Delta_{8\times 2} = .\begin{bmatrix} 0.4 & 0.25 \\ 0.6 & 0.5 \\ 0 & 0 \\ 0.2 & 0 \\ 0 & 0 \\ 0 & 0.25 \\ 0.6 & 0 \\ 0.6 & 0 \end{bmatrix}.$$

The entries in the 1st, 3rd, 5th, and 7th rows of $\Delta_{8\times2}$ indicate deprivations of person 1 in the two dimensions in periods 1, 2, 3, and 4, respectively. Entries in the 2nd, 4th, 6th, and 8th rows register similar figures for person 2. Since person 3 is chronically nonpoor, we do not include his deprivations in the matrix. The sum 3.4 of all possible entries in $\Delta_{8\times2}$ divided by $ndT(= 24)$ is the value of P_{BC}^{C} when $\beta = \alpha = 1$. This value then becomes $\frac{3.4}{24}$. The head count ratio is $\frac{2}{3}$. As a result, the average deprivation of the chronically poor person is $\left(\frac{3.4}{24}\right) / \left(\frac{2}{3}\right) = \frac{3.4}{16}$. We can similarly calculate P_{BC}^{C} for other choices of β and α.

In our analysis in the earlier subsection, if we assume that the duration threshold $t_0 = 0$, then the resulting situation should include deprivations of all the poor persons for the determination of overall poverty. For any $n \in N$, $\underline{z} \in Z$, and $X \in M^{nT}$, we denote this by $P_{BC}(X; \underline{z}; 0)$. In contrast, for arbitrary $n \in N$, $\underline{z} \in Z$, and $X \in M^{nT}$, any restriction imposing a given positive value of t_0 means that $P_{BC}^{C}(X; \underline{z}; t_0)$ takes into account only deprivations of the chronically poor persons. In consequence, it is reasonable to regard the difference

$$P_{BC}^{Tr}(X; \underline{z}) = P_{BC}(X; \underline{z}; 0) - P_{BC}^{C}(X; \underline{z}; t_0), \tag{5.35}$$

as a transient multidimensional poverty standard, where $n \in N$, $\underline{z} \in Z$, and $X \in M^{nT}$ are chosen arbitrarily. The decomposition (5.35) capacitates us to judge the contributions of both transient and chronic poverty, which may be helpful in analyzing the lifetime poverty.

Recall that in $\overline{X}_{12\times2}$, person 3 is deprived only in the dimension 1 in period 4 and the value of the corresponding deprivation indicator is 0.4. This deprivation of person 3, in addition to those that are relevant to $P_{BC}^{C}(\overline{X}_{12\times2}; (5,4); 2)$, should be included for the calculation of the overall poverty $P_{BC}(\overline{X}_{12\times2}; (5,4); 0)$. For $\alpha = \beta = 1$, the aggregate poverty $P_{BC}(\overline{X}_{12\times2}; (5,4); 0)$ is $\frac{3.8}{24}$. Consequently, the level of the related transient poverty is $\frac{0.4}{24}$. The head-count ratio also increases from $\frac{2}{3}$ to 1, which shows that the transient head-count ratio here is $\frac{1}{3}$.

5.6 Intertemporal Poverty Orderings

An important issue of investigation in intertemporal poverty analysis is to rank lifetime poverty profiles of different persons or of a society by members of some class of poverty indices. Duclos, Sahn, and Younger developed intertemporal poverty orderings that parallel the Bresson and Duclos (2015) bidimensional poverty dominances. (See Chapter 3.) In this section, we provide a discussion on this.

The authors considered a bidimensional individual well-being standard $\Lambda(x_1, x_2)$, where $x_1 \geq 0$ may be taken as a person's income during his working life and $x_2 \geq 0$ may be regarded as his retired income. This standard is assumed to be continuous and nondecreasing in its arguments. Intertemporal poverty is defined by the situations (x_1, x_2) in which $\Lambda(x_1, x_2) \leq 0$. Consequently, the set of points $(x_1, x_2) \in \Re^2_+$, satisfying the constraint $\Lambda(x_1, x_2) \leq 0$, represents the intertemporal poverty domain. A person with achievement vector (x_1, x_2) that fulfills the inequality $\Lambda(x_1, x_2) < 0$ is treated as poor in this setup. The poverty frontier, which separates the poor from the nonpoor, is represented by a locus $\Lambda(x_1, x_2) = 0$.

Exchange between two periods' incomes is permitted. In consequence, a person's poverty remains unchanged if instead of enjoying incomes x_1 and x_2 in periods 1 and 2, respectively, he enjoys x_1 in period 2 and x_2 in period 1. This is equivalent to the requirement poverty intertemporal poverty spells are equally valued (Calvo and Dercon, 2009). In other words, the rate of time discounting parameter takes on the value 1. The poverty frontier is then defined by a locus $\Lambda(x_1, x_2) = \Lambda(x_2, x_1) = 0$. In other words, the frontier is symmetric with respect to its arguments. Hence, if for any $(x_1, x_2) \in \Re^2_+$, $\Lambda(x_1, x_2) = 0$ holds, then it must be the case that $\Lambda(x_2, x_1) = 0$.

Bresson and Duclos (2015) demonstrated that under perfect substitutability, of two intertemporal profiles, one is regarded as more intertemporally poverty stricken than the other by all subgroup-decomposable poverty indices that are continuous along the poverty frontier and nonincreasing in incomes if and only if the sum of proportions of intertemporal income profiles whose incomes fall within two rectangles with common breadth *OA* and length *OB* along two axes is higher for the former than for the latter. Each of these rectangles corresponds to those persons who have low incomes in one period. The common breadth *OA* is the length of a side of a square, which represents the two-dimensional poverty space here. Since the choice of the common length *OB* and breadth *OA* can be arbitrary, this condition should be checked for all possible breadths and lengths of the rectangles below the frontier (see Figure 5.1). Evidently, all those persons who are deprived in both the periods, that is, whose incomes are in the two-dimensional poverty space, are counted twice.

We can define z^* as the minimum permanent income as that level of income, which if enjoyed in each period, empowers a person to get away from poverty. More precisely, $\Lambda(z^*, z^*) = 0$. In this two-period setup, suppose that a person is identified as chronically poor if his income in each period falls below z^* (Hulme and Shepherd, 2003). Then all those persons who are not chronically poor but whose incomes are below the frontier are transiently poor. More precisely, transiently poor are those whose incomes are below the frontier but not in the two-dimensional space.[4]

4 They also developed ordering results when the symmetry assumption between the arguments of the well-being function is dropped. This is ensured by the condition that the rate of time discounting is not 1. Some of their results take into account intertemporal inequality. For further details, see Bresson and Duclos (2015).

Figure 5.1 Intertemporal poverty ordering.

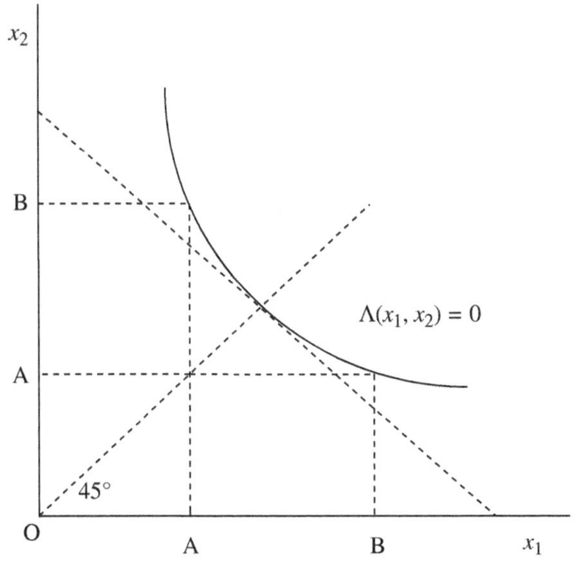

5.7 Concluding Remarks

The significance of time in assessing a person's poverty position in a society has received considerable attention from both researchers and policy-makers. The concern with intertemporal poverty is, in fact, long established (see, e.g., Godley, 1847). Since for many people in the world, poverty is a situation from which it is difficult to escape over time, it becomes important to look at poverty over multiple periods. Long disclosure to poverty has highly significant implications on future planning of individuals. Investigation of poverty from a dynamic perspective standpoint is highly likely to provide helpful insights for poverty reduction policies (World Bank, 2000). This of course requires information on panel data on different dimensions of well-being of the population. It may be justifiable to mention that duration-contingent approaches have been employed to measure other economic indices, such as unemployment rates. (See, e.g., Sengupta, 2009 and Shorrocks, 2009b.)

Research on axiomatic formulations of intertemporal poverty in multidimensional frameworks has started very recently. In this chapter, we made an attempt to discuss how different episodes of poverty and nonpoverty of an individual should be taken into consideration in evaluating his lifetime poverty. Throughout the chapter, it has been assumed implicitly that all the individuals live for the entire period of analysis. This is a limitation. Demises of some people at early ages may affect the analysis significantly (Kanbur and Mukherjee, 2007).

Since the history of axiomatic foundations of this literature is not old, there are weighty future tasks for the literature. A concrete line of investigation can be the contention of extending the results when threshold limits are not the same across periods. Appropriate reformulations of the axioms and investigations of their implications will be a worthy exercise.

References

Addison, T., D. Hulme, and R. Kanbur (eds.). 2009. *Poverty Dynamics: Interdisciplinary Perspectives*. Oxford: Oxford University Press.

Alkire, S., M. Apablaza, S.R. Chakravarty, and G. Yalonetzky. 2017. Measuring Chronic Multidimensional Poverty. *Journal of Policy Modelling*. In Press.

Alkire, S. and J.E. Foster. 2011. Counting and Multidimensional Poverty Measurement. *Journal of Public Economics* 95: 476–487.

Alkire, S., J.E. Foster, S. Seth, M.E. Santos, J.M. Roche, and P. Ballon. 2015. *Multidimensional Poverty Measurement and Analysis*. New York: Oxford University Press.

Arranz, J.M. and O. Cantó. 2012. Measuring the Effect of Spell Recurrence on Poverty Dynamics - Evidence from Spain. *Journal of Economic Inequality* 10: 191–217.

Baluch, B. and J. Hoddinott (eds.) 2000. Special Issue on Economic Mobility and Poverty Dynamics in Developing Countries. *Journal of Development Studies* 36: 1–200.

Baluch B. and E. Masset 2003. Do Monetary and Non-monetary Indicators Tell the Same Story about Chronic Poverty? A Study of Vietnam in the 1990s. *World Development* 31: 441–53.

Bane M. and D. Ellwood. 1986. Slipping into and out of Poverty. *Journal of Human Resources* 21: 1–23.

Betti, G. and A. Lemmi (eds.). 2014. *Poverty and Social Exclusion: New Methods of Analysis*. London: Routledge.

Blackorby, C., W. Bossert, and D. Donaldson. 2005. *Population Issues in Social Choice Theory, Welfare Economics and Ethics*. Cambridge: Cambridge University Press.

Blackorby, C. and D. Donaldson. 1984. Social Criteria for Evaluating Population Change. *Journal of Public Economics* 25: 13–33.

Bossert, W., L. Ceriani, S.R. Chakravarty, and C. D'Ambrosio. 2014. Inter-temporal Material Deprivation. In G. Betti and A. Lemmi (eds.)128–142.

Bossert, W., S.R. Chakravarty, and C. D'Ambrosio. 2012. Poverty and Time. *Journal of Economic Inequality* 10: 145–162.

Bourguignon, F. and S.R. Chakravarty. 2003. The Measurement of Multidimensional Poverty. *Journal of Economic Inequality* 1: 25 – 49.

Bourguignon, F. and C. Morrison (2002). Inequality among World Citizens: 1820–1992. *American Economic Review* 92: 727–744.

Bresson, F. and J.-Y. Duclos. 2015. Intertemporal Poverty Comparisons. *Social Choice and Welfare* 44: 567–616.

Calvo S. and S. Dercon. 2009. Chronic Poverty and All That: The Measurement of Poverty over Time. T. Addison, D. Hulme, and R. Kanbur (eds.), 29–58.

Cappellari, L. and S.P. Jenkins. 2004. Modeling Low Income Transitions. *Journal of Applied Econometrics* 19: 593–610.

Carter, M.R. and C.B. Barrett. 2006. The Economics of Poverty Traps and Persistent Poverty: An Asset-based Approach. *Journal of Development Studies* 42: 178–199.

Chakravarty, S.R. 1983. A New Index of Poverty. *Mathematical Social Sciences* 6: 307 –313.

Chakravarty, S.R. 2009. *Inequality, Polarization and Poverty: Advances in Distributional Analysis*. New York: Springer.

Chakravarty, S.R. and C. D'Ambrosio. 2006. The Measurement of Social Exclusion. *Review of Income and Wealth* 52: 377–398.

Chronic Poverty Research Center. 2005. *The Chronic Poverty Report 2004-5*. Manchester: University of Manchester.

Decancq, K., A. Decoster, and E. Schokkaert. 2006. The Evolution of World Inequality in Well-Being. *World Development* 37: 11–25.

Duclos, J.-Y., A. Araar, and J. Giles. 2010. Chronic and Transient Poverty: Measurement and Estimation. *Journal of Development Economics* 91: 266–277.

Duncan, G.J. and W. Rodgers. 1991. Has Children Poverty Become More Persistent? *American Sociological Review* 56: 538–550.

Dutta, I., L. Roope, and H. Zank. 2013. On Inter-temporal Poverty Measures: The Role of Affluence and Want. *Social Choice and Welfare* 41: 741–62.

Foster J.E. 2009. A Class of Chronic Poverty Measures. In T. Addison, D. Hulme, and R. Kanbur (eds.), 59–76.

Foster, J.E., J. Greer, and E. Thorbecke. 1984. A Class of Decomposable Poverty Measures. *Econometrica* 52: 761–766.

Foster, J.E. and M.E. Santos. 2014. Measuring Chronic Poverty. In G. Betti and A. Lemmi (eds.), 143–165.

Gaiha, R. 1989. Are the Chronically Poor also the Poorest in Rural India? *Development and Change* 20: 295–322.

Gaiha, R. and A.B. Deolikar. 1993. Persistent, Expected and Innate Poverty: Estimates for Semi -arid Rural South India 1975-1984. *Cambridge Journal of Economics* 17: 409–21.

Godley, J.R. 1847. *Observations on an Irish Poor Law (Addressed to the Committee of Landed Properties, Assembled in Dublin)*. Dublin: Grant and Bolton.

Gradin, C., C. del Rio, and O. Cantó. 2012. Measuring Poverty Accounting for Time. *Review of Income and Wealth* 58: 330–54.

Green, M. and D. Hulme. 2005. From Correlates and Characteristics to Causes: Thinking about Poverty from a Chronic Poverty Perspective. *World Development* 33: 867–879.

Hojman, D. and F. Kast. 2009. On the Measurement of Poverty Dynamics. *Faculty Research Working Paper 09-035*. Harvard Kennedy School.

Hoy, M., B.S. Thompson, and B. Zheng (2012). Empirical Issues in Lifetime Poverty Measurement. *Journal of Economic Inequality* 10: 163–189.

Hoy, M. and B. Zheng. 2011. Measuring Lifetime Poverty. *Journal of Economic Theory* 146: 2544–2562.

Hoy, M. and B. Zheng. 2015. Measuring Lifetime/Inter-temporal Poverty. *Research on Economic Inequality*. Forthcoming.

Hulme, D., K. Moore, and A. Shepherd. 2001. Chronic Poverty: Meanings and Analytical Frameworks. *CPRC Working Paper* 2.

Hulme, D. and A. Shepherd. 2003. Conceptualizing Chronic Poverty. *World Development* 31: 403–423.

Jalan J. and M. Ravallion. 1998. Transient Poverty in Post-reform Rural China. *Journal of Comparative Economics* 26: 338–357.

Jenkins, S.P. 2000. Modeling Household Income Dynamics. *Journal of Population Economics* 13: 529–567.

Kanbur, R. and D. Mukherjee. 2007. Premature Mortality and Poverty Measurement. *Bulletin of Economic Research* 59: 339–359.

Kurosaki, T. 2006. The Measurement of Transient Poverty: Theory and Application to Pakistan. *Journal of Economic Inequality* 4: 325–346.

Levy, F. 1997. How big is the American underclass? *Working Paper*. Washington D.C.: Urban Institute.

Lillard, L. and R. Willis. 1978. Dynamic Aspects of Earnings Mobility. *Econometrica* 46: 985–1012.

Lybbert, T.J., C.B. Barrett, S. Desta, and D.L. Coppock. 2004. Stochastic Wealth Dynamics and Risk Management among a Poor Population. *Economic Journal* 114: 750–77.

McKay, A., and D. Lawson. 2003. Assessing the Extent and Nature of Chronic Poverty in Low Income Countries: Issues and Evidence. *World Development* 31: 425–439.

Mehta, A.K. and A.K. Shah. 2003. Chronic Poverty in India: Incidence, Causes and Policies. *World Development* 31: 473–490.

Mendola, D. and A. Busetta. 2012. The Importance of Consecutive Spells of Poverty: A Path-dependent Index of Longitudinal Poverty. *Review of Income and Wealth* 58: 355–74.

Morduch, J. 1994. Poverty and Vulnerability. *American Economic Review Papers and Proceedings* 84: 221–225.

Narayan, D. and P. Petesch (eds.) 2007. *Moving Out of Poverty: Cross-Disciplinary Perspectives on Mobility*. Washington, DC: World Bank.

Nicholas, A. and R. Ray. 2011. Duration and Persistence in Multidimensional Deprivation: Methodology and Australian Application. *Economic Record* 88: 106–126.

Porter C. and N.N. Quinn. 2008. Inter-temporal Poverty Measurement: Tradeoffs and Policy Options. *CSAE Working Paper* 2008-21.

Porter C. and N.N. Quinn. 2014. Measuring Inter-temporal Poverty: Policy Options for the Poverty Analyst. In G. Betti and A. Lemmi (eds.) (2014), 166–193.

Ravallion, M. 1988. Expected Poverty under Risk-induced Welfare Variability. *Economic Journal* 98: 1171–1182.

Ravallion, M., D. van de Walle, and M. Gautam. (1995). Testing a Social Safety Net. *Journal of Public Economics* 57: 175–199.

Rodgers, J.R. and J.L. Rodgers. 2003. Chronic Poverty in the United States. *Journal of Human Resources* 28: 25–54.

Sen, A.K. 1992. *Inequality Re-examined*. Cambridge, MA: Harvard University Press.

Sengupta, M. 2009. Unemployment Duration and the Measurement of Unemployment. *Journal of Economic Inequality* 7: 273–294.

Shorrocks, A.F. 1983. Ranking Income Distributions. *Economica* 50: 3–17.

Shorrocks, A.F. 2009a. Spell Incidence, Spell Duration and the Measurement of Unemployment. *Journal of Economic Inequality* 7: 295–310.

Shorrocks, A.F. 2009b. On the Measurement of Unemployment. *Journal of Economic Inequality* 7: 311–327.

Walker, R. 1995. The Dynamics of Poverty and Social Exclusion. In G. Room (ed.) *Beyond the Threshold*. Bristol: Policy Press, 102–128.

World Bank. 2000. *World Development Report 2000/2001: Attacking Poverty*. New York: Oxford University Press.

Yaqub, S. 2000a. Inter-temporal Welfare Dynamics: Extent and Causes. Paper presented at the *Globalization, New Opportunities, New Vulnerabilities Workshop*. Washington, DC: Brookings Institution.

Yaqub, S. 2000b. Chronic Poverty: Scrutinizing Estimates, Patterns, Correlates and Explanations. *Chronic Poverty Research Centre Working Paper No. 21*. Manchester: University of Manchester.

Zheng, B. 2012. Measuring Chronic Poverty: A Gravitational Approach. *Working Paper, Department of Economics*. Colorado Denver: University of Colorado.

6

Vulnerability to Poverty: A Multidimensional Evaluation

6.1 Introduction

Vulnerability is concerned with security risks. We can broadly define it in terms of a system's exposure and capacity to deal adequately with distress. For instance, a situation of economic vulnerability arises when a country faces an economic shock. Similarly, an ecosystem's exposure to climatic shocks may be regarded as a case of environmental vulnerability. A farmer with a low income from agriculture may be nonpoor currently. But since his agricultural output depends on the weather conditions, he may become poor in the future if the weather badly affects production. In the dimension of health, vulnerability may be regarded as a situation where a person with a reasonably good health condition currently will undergo an incident of health problem so that he becomes health-poor over time. (See Dercon and Krishnan, 2000, for an illustration). A person with a contractual nature of employment may be vulnerable to unemployment in the future (see, for example, Basu and Nolen, 2005).

From the aforementioned illustrations, it is clear that the notion of vulnerability is forward-looking. In the study of vulnerability, our concern should be not only with current conditions, such as income and health status, but also with the risks a person faces and his ability to avert, bring down, and conquer these. On the other hand, in the standard poverty analysis, both intertemporal and cross section, the analysis is based on observable information, more precisely, on the assumption of complete certainty. As a result, the analysis of vulnerability requires a separate treatment.

The study of vulnerability is quite important because of its highly significant implications for economic efficiency and long-term individual welfare. Many individuals face adversity in terms of continued illness, natural calamities, and other risks. These people can fall into poverty in the wake of adverse shocks. In consequence, the removal of vulnerability should be a concern of high priority from policy perspective. In the words of Sen (1999, p. 1): "The challenge of development includes not only the elimination of persistent

Analyzing Multidimensional Well-Being: A Quantitative Approach, First Edition. Satya R. Chakravarty.

and endemic deprivation, but also the removal of vulnerability to sudden and severe destitution." Protection of "vulnerable groups during episodes of macroeconomic contraction is vital to poverty reductions in developing countries" (World Bank, 1997, p. 1).

Klasen and Povel (2013) argued that vulnerability at the individual level can be broadly classified into the following four broad categories: (i) vulnerability representing uninsured exposure to risk; (ii) vulnerability as a quantifier of low expected utility; (iii) vulnerability indicating expected poverty; and (iv) vulnerability to poverty. Discussions on the first three categories of vulnerability were made, among others, by Hoddinott and Quisumbing (2003); Ligon and Schechter (2003), and Gaiha and Imai (2009) (see also Hoogeveen et al., 2004). Vulnerability to poverty was introduced and analyzed by Calvo and Dercon (2013). (See Chakravarty et al., 2016; Fujii, 2016, for recent discussions.) In order to discuss these four divisions of vulnerability in greater detail, we assume that income is the only dimension of well-being.

Vulnerability indicating uninsured exposure to risk determines the extent to which income shocks yield changes in consumption (see Townsend, 1994; Amin et al., 2003; Skoufias and Quisumbing, 2005). The concerns of this concept of vulnerability are changes in the current magnitudes of consumption and not current sizes of consumption. This approach ignores a person's temperament about risks.

Vulnerability manifesting low expected utility identifies vulnerability with variability in a positive monotonic way in the sense that an increase in variability is regarded as a higher level of vulnerability. In the theory of statistical decision-making, there has been a long tradition of employing the variance as a measure of risk (Rothschild and Stiglitz, 1970). A sophisticated formulation of this was developed by Ligon and Schechter (2003). To get an insight of the underlying central idea, we consider two individuals, each of whom has the same expected consumption, not below some exogenously given norm, in some future period. It is also true that while for the first person there is a positive probability of destitution in the future, for the second person no such risk exists. It is quite likely that positive probability of adversity in the future period will relegate the first person to a situation of vulnerability. Since vulnerability is a forward-looking concept, it is evident that the two individuals should not be treated identically in terms of vulnerability. According to Ligon and Schechter (2003), vulnerability in a setting of this type can be interpreted as low expected utility.

The Ligon–Schechter index of vulnerability is given by the difference between the utility received from a threshold income, income poverty line, and the individual's expected utility obtained from income in a vulnerable situation. A higher (positive) difference between the two utility values indicates a greater level of vulnerability. This notion of vulnerability regards a person as nonvulnerable if his income is not below the poverty line (see also Glewwe and Hall, 1998; Dercon, 2002; Coudouel and Hentschel, 2000). Since the formulation depends directly on the von Neumann–Morgenstern utility function, an important characteristic of this approach is that it takes into account an individual's attitudes toward risks in an explicit manner. The harshness and possibility of disturbance on individual welfare are incorporated directly into the framework because of nonconstancy of the utility function and probabilistic formulation. Since all the individuals are assumed to possess the same utility function, levels of vulnerability are comparable across persons. Elbers and Gunning (2003) extended the Ligon–Schechter framework over an infinite time horizon. In Morduch (1994), vulnerability was expressed in terms of deviations from the permanent income poverty line.

Vulnerability as expected poverty deals with the risk of an individual's income falling below the income poverty line. This notion of vulnerability was introduced by Ravallion (1988) and advanced and discussed further by Holzmann and Jorgensen (1999). An analysis of this approach was developed in a more formalistic manner by Chaudhuri et al. (2002), which expresses the probability that an individual's income will fall below an exogenous income poverty line. (See also Christiaensen and Boisvert, 2000; Chaudhuri, 2003). However, it does not incorporate the awareness about risks. An individual's status in terms of vulnerability relies simply on some expected income. Hoddinott and Quisumbing (2003) made an attempt to address this shortcoming by considering vulnerability as expected poverty using the Foster et al. (1984) poverty index. When the negative of poverty is interpreted as utility, the Arrow (1965)–Pratt (1964) absolute risk aversion measure, an index of the extent to which a person is risk-averse, for the underlying utility function, increases as the value of the associated parameter increases. However, empirical findings did not support such a risk preference unambiguously (see Hoddinott and Quisumbing, 2003 and Binswanger, 1981). Additional empirical applications of this approach can be found in Suryahadi and Sumarto (2003); Kamanou and Morduch (2004); Christiaensen and Subbarao (2005), and Günther and Harttgen (2009). In Pritchett et al. (2000), vulnerability has been defined in terms of the probability of tumbling into poverty in three consecutive periods.

The concept of vulnerability to poverty was initiated by Calvo and Dercon (2013). They established an axiomatic characterization of an index of vulnerability as a weighted average of future state-contingent deprivations, where the weights are the probabilities of state-contingent returns in the future. "Ligon and Schechter's measure is the expected poverty gap, whereas Calvo and Dercon's measure is the expected Chakravarty index and Kamanou and Morduch (2004) employs the expected Foster–Greer–Thorbecke (FGT) index" (Dutta et al., 2011, p. 645). More generally, these indices are essentially expected poverty indices. In a different contribution, Calvo and Dercon (2009) showed how their index, "which in itself was based on the Chakravarty measure of poverty" (op.cit., p. 46), can be amended as a dynamic and forward-looking index of vulnerability. Dutta et al. (2011) developed an axiomatic characterization of an index of vulnerability that relies explicitly on the current and future incomes. Therefore, while in the Calvo–Dercon approach, deprivations depend on future incomes, the Dutta–Foster–Mishra framework allows us to look at relative changes under vulnerability.

In a recent contribution, López-Calva and Ortiz-Juarez (2014) suggested a view of the middle class that relies on vulnerability to poverty. They employed panel data for income to determine the level of comparable income corresponding to a low probability of falling into poverty. This in turn defines the lower bound of the middle class income. The countries they have considered in their analysis are Chile, Mexico, and Peru.

The examples provided at the beginning of this section clearly show that, similar to poverty, vulnerability is a multidimensional phenomenon (see Calvo, 2008). The objective of this chapter is to study vulnerability to poverty from a multidimensional perspective. This notion of vulnerability represents the strains laid down by the threat of multidimensional poverty. As a background material, we present a brief review of one-dimensional measurement of vulnerability to poverty in the next section. Section 6.3 deals with an axiomatic analysis of multidimensional vulnerability to poverty. Finally, Section 6.4 winds up the chapter. A brief analysis of the Calvo and Dercon (2009) amended index is also presented in this section.

6.2 A Review of One-Dimensional Measurement

Since the one-dimensional approach to vulnerability to poverty measurement is closely related to the multidimensional analysis of the issue, we begin this section with a rigorous discussion on the former. For expositional ease, we assume that income is the only dimension of human well-being. In addition, initially the analysis is carried out at the individual level.

The indices of vulnerability we scrutinize here are based on anticipated changes, that is, they are ex-ante measures in the sense that they incorporate future uncertainty with reference to income. Thus, income is regarded as an uncertain prospect. An absolutely necessary characteristic of these indices is that the underlying risks are downside risks, that is, in the future, there is possibility of downward trend of income. Individual vulnerability here is developed in terms of shortfall of income from the exogenously given income poverty line resulting from economic and other shocks.

Since income is considered as an uncertain prospect, there are different levels of returns on the prospect. These returns are state-contingent or state-dependent outcomes. A state of nature is a situation for the prospect that can arise in the future. Accordingly, by a state-contingent return we mean a return whenever a particular state materializes. In order to illustrate this, consider a farmer for whom there is a high impact of weather conditions (rainfall) on crop production. Relevant states of nature are the rainfall conditions, say: (i) drought, (ii) less than barely sufficient but not drought, (iii) barely sufficient, (iv) optimum, and (v) more than optimum (flood). There is a return associated with each state. These are state-contingent returns.

Assume that the society under consideration consists of n individuals and k states, where $n \in N$ is arbitrary and $k \geq 2$ is an integer. We denote the set of states by $\omega = \{1, 2, \ldots, k\}$. In order to compare individual vulnerabilities across persons, we will assume throughout the section that the set of states remain the same for all individuals in the society. For individual i, the associated state-contingent returns are represented by a vector $\underline{u}^i = (u_1^i, u_2^i, \ldots, u_k^i)$, that is, u_j^i is the unique income that individual i receives if state j emerges; $1 \leq i \leq n, 1 \leq j \leq k$. As a consequence, when production of a crop gets affected by variations in rainfall, different levels of rainfall describe the states, and the level of production, when a particular state comes into perceptible existence, is the state-contingent return.

Individual i assumes that the probability of appearance of state j is $\ell_j^i; 1 \leq i \leq n, 1 \leq j \leq k$. We denote the vector of probabilities $(\ell_1^i, \ell_2^i, \ldots, \ell_k^i)$ by $\underline{l}^i$. Evidently, $0 \leq \ell_j^i \leq 1$ for all $1 \leq i \leq n$, $1 \leq j \leq k$ and $\sum_{j=1}^{k} \ell_j^i = 1, 1 \leq i \leq n$. Since the return u_j^i is uniquely associated with state j, we can as well say that u_j^i comes into existence with probability ℓ_j^i. For any given state j, these probabilities are likely to vary across persons. That is, for any two persons i and h, and for any state j, ℓ_j^i need not be the same as ℓ_j^h, where $1 \leq i \neq h \leq n$ and $1 \leq j \leq k$. To illustrate this, we consider two farmers, one of whom has easy access to deep tube well for pumping out underground water if the rainfall is inadequate for crop production. However, for the other person, such a facility does not exist. Therefore, if the rainfall for crop production is not at the requisite level, while it is highly unlikely that the former person's crop production will be badly affected by drought, for the latter individual, this chance is quite high. In other words, the probability of appearance of "drought" is quite low for the first person, whereas for the second person, the probability is quite high. In general, such differences arise because the probabilities may be affected by some external factors, which cannot be ignored. Hence, these probabilities are subjective probabilities – they are based on personal feelings.

Denote the exogenously given threshold limit, the income poverty line, by $z > 0$, and assume, as in Chapter 3, that $z \in [z_-, z_+]$, where $0 < z_- < z_+ < \infty$, that is, z takes on values in a finite nondegenerate positive interval of $\mathfrak{R}^1_+$, the nonnegative part of the real line $\mathfrak{R}^1$. We say that individual i is poor in state j, equivalently, state j is meager for i, if $u_j^i < z$. Otherwise, that is, if $u_j^i \geq z$, the person is nonpoor in the state, equivalently, the state is nonmeager for him. Person i is identified as vulnerable if there is at least one state j such that $u_j^i < z$ and $\ell_j^i > 0$. This can be regarded as the vulnerable analog to the contention of identification of a poor person arising in an income poverty situation. A one-dimensional vulnerable situation involving the state-contingent returns $\underline{u}^i = (u_1^i, u_2^i, \ldots, u_k^i) \in \Re_+^k$, the corresponding probability vector $\underline{l}^i = (\ell_1^i, \ell_2^i, \ldots, \ell_k^i) \in \Delta_+^k$ and the poverty line $z \in [z_-, z_+]$ may be expressed more compactly as $(\underline{u}^i, \underline{\ell}^i, z)$, say, where $\Re_+^k$ is the nonnegative orthant of the k-dimensional Euclidean space $\Re^k$, and Δ_+^k is nonnegative k-dimensional unit simplex, the set of all k-coordinated vectors whose coordinates are nonnegative real numbers that add up to 1. Let S_V^i denote the set of all one-dimensional vulnerable situations for person i, that is, $S_V^i = \{(\underline{u}^i, \underline{\ell}^i, z) | \underline{u}^i \in \Re_+^k, \underline{\ell}^i \in \Delta_+^k, z \in [z_-, z_+]\}$. The censored state-contingent return vector associated with $\underline{u}^i = (u_1^i, u_2^i, \ldots, u_k^i)$ is denoted by $\underline{\hat{u}}^i = (\hat{u}_1^i, \hat{u}_2^i, \ldots, \hat{u}_k^i)$, where $\hat{u}_j^i = \min(u_j^i, z)$.

Since we focus on the downside risk, that is, given that each u_j^i has a chance of being less than z, the possibility of future poverty occurrence is considered in the framework. In order to determine vulnerability at the individual level, it may be worthwhile to consider the shortfalls of the state-contingent returns from the poverty line in different states of nature. For any person i, these shortfalls, when expressed in relative or proportionate terms, are given by $g_j^i = \frac{z-\hat{u}_j^i}{z}$; $1 \le j \le k$, $1 \le i \le n$. By definition, each of them is homogeneous of degree 0, that is, invariant under equiproportionate changes in the corresponding state-contingent return and the threshold limit. We refer to them as vulnerability deprivation indicators, which, for a given threshold limit, are decreasing in state-level returns. They are positive if and only if state-dependent returns are below the threshold limit. The issue of considering a vulnerable person's deprivations parallels the idea of looking into the poverty shortfall of an income-poor person.

For any person i, the situations of the type $(\underline{u}^i, \underline{\ell}^i, z)$ are transformed into vulnerability levels experienced by person i using a function $V^i : S_V^i \to \Re_+^1$. In more explicit terms, $V^i : \Re_+^k \times \Delta_+^k \times [z_-, z_+] \to \Re_+^1$; $1 \le i \le n$. The function V^i can be designated as the individual vulnerability index. The presence of superscript i in V^i explicitly recognizes that V^i determines the extent of poverty suffered by person i under probable realization of different states. For any $(\underline{u}^i, \underline{\ell}^i, z) \in \Re_+^k \times \Delta_+^k \times [z_-, z_+]$, $V^i(\underline{u}^i, \underline{\ell}^i, z)$ determines the extent of vulnerability that the person undergoes.

We now suggest the following axioms for the individual vulnerability index. Variants of some of these axioms were discussed by Calvo and Dercon (2013), Chakravarty and Chattopadhyay (2015), and Chakravarty et al. (2015).

State-Restricted Focus: For any $(\underline{u}^i, \underline{\ell}^i, z) \in \Re_+^k \times \Delta_+^k \times [z_-, z_+]$, if for some $j \in \omega$, $u_j^i \ge z$, then $V^i(\underline{u}^i, \underline{\ell}^i, z) = V^i(\underline{\tilde{u}}^i, \underline{\ell}^i, z)$, where $\tilde{u}_j^i = u_j^i + c$, $\tilde{u}_q^i = u_q^i$ for all $q \in \omega / \{j\}$ and $c > 0$.

State-Restricted Monotonicity: For any $(\underline{u}^i, \underline{\ell}^i, z) \in \Re^k_+ \times \Delta^k_+ \times [z_-, z_+]$, if for some $j \in \omega$, $0 < u^i_j < z$, $\ell^i_j > 0$, then $V^i(\underline{u}^i, \underline{\ell}^i, z) < V^i(\underline{\tilde{u}}^i, \underline{\ell}^i, z)$, where $\tilde{u}^i_j = u^i_j - c \geq 0, \tilde{u}^i_q = u^i_q$ for all $q \in \omega/\{j\}$ and $c > 0$.

Across-States Transfer: For any $(\underline{u}^i, \underline{\ell}^i, z) \in \Re^k_+ \times \Delta^k_+ \times [z_-, z_+]$ if for some $j, q \in \omega, z > u^i_j > u^i_q > 0, 0 < \ell^i_j \leq \ell^i_q < 1$, then $V^i(\underline{u}^i, \underline{\ell}^i, z) < V^i(\underline{\tilde{u}}^i, \underline{l}^i, z)$, where $\tilde{u}^i_j = u^i_j + c < z, \tilde{u}^i_q = u^i_q - c \geq 0, \tilde{u}^i_t = u^i_t$ for all $t \in \omega/\{j, q\}$ and $c > 0$.

State-Restricted Monotonicity in Threshold Limit: For any $(\underline{u}^i, \underline{\ell}^i, z) \in \Re^k_+ \times \Delta^k_+ \times [z_-, z_+]$, if for at least one state $j \in \omega$, $u^i_j < z$ and $\ell^i_j > 0$, then $V^i(\underline{u}^i, \underline{\ell}^i, z) < V^i(\underline{u}^i, \underline{\ell}^i, \tilde{z})$, where $\tilde{z} > z$ and $\tilde{z} \in [z_-, z_+]$.

Severity of Downside Risks: For any $(\underline{u}^i, \underline{\ell}^i, z) \in \Re^k_+ \times \Delta^k_+ \times [z_-, z_+]$, if for some $j, q \in \omega$, $z > u^i_j > u^i_q, \ell^i_q > \ell^i_j > 0$, then $V^i(\underline{u}^i, \underline{\ell}^i, z) < V^i(\underline{u}^i, \underline{\tilde{\ell}}^i, z)$, where $\tilde{\ell}^i_j = \ell^i_j - c \geq 0$, $1 > \tilde{\ell}^i_q = \ell^i_q + c$, $\tilde{\ell}^i_t = \ell^i_t$ for all $t \in \omega/\{j, q\}$ and $c > 0$.

State-Restricted Boundedness: The index V^i is bounded between 0 and 1, where the lower bound is achieved if for any $(\underline{\ell}^i, z) \in \Delta^k_+ \times [z_-, z_+]$, $\underline{u}^i \in \Re^k_+$ is such that $u^i_j \geq z$ for all $j \in \omega$. V^i reaches its upper bound if for any $(\underline{\ell}^i, z) \in \Delta^k_+ \times [z_-, z_+]$, $u^i_j = 0$ for all $j \in \omega$.

State-Restricted Replication Principle: For any $(\underline{u}^i, \underline{\ell}^i, z) \in \Re^k_+ \times \Delta^k_+ \times [z_-, z_+]$, suppose that for each $j \in \omega$, the state-contingent return u^i_j is replicated m times and the corresponding probability value ℓ^i_j is split equally among the replicated figures of u^i_j, then $V^i(\underline{u}^i, \underline{\ell}^i, z) = V^i(\underline{\tilde{u}}^i, \underline{\tilde{\ell}}^i, z)$, where $\underline{\tilde{u}}^i$ is the mk-coordinated vector of replicated returns and $\underline{\tilde{\ell}}^i$ is the mk-coordinated vector of split probabilities, $m \geq 2$ being any integer.

Continuity in State-Contingent Returns: For given $(\underline{\ell}^i, z) \in \Delta_+{}^k \times [z_-, z_+]$, V^i varies continuously with respect to variations in returns such that the vulnerability status of the person remains unchanged.

One common feature of these state-restricted properties is that they can be termed as individualistic axioms in the sense that the underlying operations involve only one person's vulnerability. The focus axiom here demands that an increase in the return from a nondeprived state does not change the vulnerability index. Since vulnerability is concerned with downside risk, this axiom is quite plausible. If the low return from a state with a positive probability of being deprived reduces further, then the extent of vulnerability increases. The current version of the monotonicity axiom makes this sensible claim. To illustrate this axiom, suppose that person i foresees that because of economic shocks, his current income 620 may reduce to 610, 590, and 580, respectively, with probabilities $\frac{1}{6}, \frac{1}{3}$, and $\frac{1}{2}$. Assume that the threshold income $z = 600$. Then $\underline{u}^i = (610, 590, 580)$ and $\underline{\ell}^i = \left(\frac{1}{6}, \frac{1}{3}, \frac{1}{2}\right)$. Suppose that the person revises his prediction under some apprehension that the lowest anticipated income 580 will actually be 570. Now, given that the probabilities and the other anticipated incomes remain unchanged, we have $\underline{\tilde{u}}^i = (610, 590, 570)$ and the monotonicity axiom demands that $V^i(\underline{u}^i, \underline{\ell}^i, z) < V^i(\underline{\tilde{u}}^i, \underline{\ell}^i, z)$.

According to the present form of the transfer axiom, vulnerability goes up under a transfer of return from a state with low positive return and high downside risk to another state possessing a higher return but not higher risk. The intuitive reasoning behind this postulate is that downside risk is not lower in state q than in state j, and the transfer decreases the lower return in q further and increases that in j, which already had higher return. Hence, vulnerability should increase. Undoubtedly, such a transfer may be regarded as an across-states regressive transfer. Suppose in the aforementioned example, $\underline{\tilde{u}}^i = (610, 592, 578)$ is generated from $\underline{u}^i = (610, 590, 580)$ by a regressive transfer of income from state 3 to state 2. Since state 3 has a lower return but higher probability than state 2, according to the across-states transfer axiom, $V^i(\underline{u}^i, \underline{\ell}^i, z) < V^i(\underline{\tilde{u}}^i, \underline{\ell}^i, z)$. We note the similarity and dissimilarity between the income poverty transfer axiom and the transfer axiom proposed here. While for a notion of transfer to be valid in the income poverty case, there should be at least two persons; here we need existence of at least two states for the prospect, and it concerns only one person.

If in a deprived state, which has a positive probability of appearance, the person becomes more deprived resulting from an increase in the threshold limit, then vulnerability should increase unambiguously. The variant of the axiom of monotonicity in poverty line suggested in the current section asserts this. Since vulnerability is concerned with downside risk, if this type of risk of return from a state with low return goes up and the corresponding risk from a state with high return goes down, then evidently vulnerability should demonstrate an upward trend. This legitimate requirement is affirmed by the axiom of severity of downside risk. This postulate is a unique characteristic of the vulnerability index and does not parallel any standard poverty property. Given that $\underline{u}^i = (610, 590, 580)$ and $\underline{\ell}^i = \left(\frac{1}{6}, \frac{1}{3}, \frac{1}{2}\right)$, suppose that person i increases his subjective probability of falling his current income from 620 to 580 by $\frac{1}{12}$ and reduces that of falling to 590 by $\frac{1}{12}$. Hence, $\underline{\ell}^i = \left(\frac{1}{6}, \frac{1}{3}, \frac{1}{2}\right)$ changes to $\underline{\tilde{\ell}}^i = \left(\frac{1}{6}, \frac{1}{4}, \frac{7}{12}\right)$. Of states 2 and 3, originally the latter had a lower return accompanied by a higher probability. Hence, the conditions laid down in the severity of downside risk axiom are satisfied. As a result, $V^i(\underline{u}^i, \underline{\ell}^i, z) < V^i(\underline{u}^i, \underline{\tilde{\ell}}^i, z)$.

The boundedness axiom related to the one-dimensional vulnerability of a person insists that vulnerability index takes on a finite value lying between 0 and 1, where the minimum value 0 is attained if none of the returns falls below the threshold limit so that the person has a nonvulnerable status. It obtains its upper bound 1 if the return from each state is 0 so that the person is maximally deprived. Since there is no possibility of further reduction of the return from any state, this maximum value is achieved irrespective of the probability distribution. To understand the state-restricted replication principle, let $\underline{u}^i = (610, 590, 580)$ and $\underline{\ell}^i = \left(\frac{1}{6}, \frac{1}{3}, \frac{1}{2}\right)$. Assume that each state-contingent return is replicated twice. Then $\underline{\tilde{u}}^i = (610, 610, 590, 590, 580, 580)$ and $\underline{\tilde{\ell}}^i = \left(\frac{1}{12}, \frac{1}{12}, \frac{1}{6}, \frac{1}{6}, \frac{1}{4}, \frac{1}{4}\right)$. The individual vulnerability levels of the two situations are the same. The final axiom, continuity in state-specific returns ensures smooth behavior of the vulnerability index with respect to variations in returns under ceteris paribus conditions. Note that change in one probability will require a change in at least one different probability, so the sum of all probabilities equals 1.

As an illustrative example, we consider the Calvo and Dercon (2013) individual vulnerability index defined as

$$V^i_{CD}(\underline{u}^i, \underline{\ell}^i, z) = \sum_{j=1}^{k} \ell^i_j \left(1 - \left(\frac{\hat{u}^i_j}{z}\right)^e\right), \tag{6.1}$$

where the constant $0 < e < 1$ controls risk awareness. As Dutta et al. (2011) noted, this is the expected Chakravarty (1983) poverty index. The restriction $0 < e < 1$ ensures that the focused, normalized, and continuous index V^i_{CD} satisfies the monotonicity (in returns), transfer, and downside risk severity axioms. It increases if the poverty threshold increases under the minor restriction considered. For $e = 1$, it is the proportionate gap between the poverty line and the expected state-dependent return. This is the situation of risk neutrality. On the other hand, as $e \to 0$, $V^i_{CD} \to 0$. This index is a member of a family of expected poverty or deprivation indices given by $\sum_{j=1}^{k} \ell^i_j \psi(g^i_j)$, where $\psi : [0,1] \to \Re^1_+$ satisfying $\psi(0) = 0$ is a transformed deprivation indicator. It is also assumed to be decreasing, continuous, and strictly convex in state-contingent return. Decreasingness and strict convexity ensure satisfaction of the monotonicity and the transfer axioms, respectively. The normalization condition $\psi(0) = 0$ guarantees attainability of the lower bound of $\sum_{j=1}^{k} \ell^i_j \psi(g^i_j)$. Depending on the forms of ψ chosen, we have different vulnerability indicators. In the Calvo–Dercon case, $\psi(g^i_j) = 1 - (1 - g^i_j)^e$.

If the transformed deprivation indicator is given by $\psi(g^i_j) = \left(1 - \frac{\hat{u}^i_j}{z}\right)^\alpha$, where $\alpha > 1$ is a parameter, then the expected poverty index $\sum_{j=1}^{k} \ell^i_j \psi(g^i_j)$ turns out to be the expected Foster et al. (1984) poverty index (see Kamanou and Morduch, 2002):

$$V^i_{FGT}(\underline{u}^i, \underline{\ell}^i, z) = \sum_{j=1}^{k} \ell^i_j \left(1 - \frac{\hat{u}^i_j}{z}\right)^\alpha. \tag{6.2}$$

Under the parametric restriction $\alpha > 1$, all the vulnerability axioms are abided by V^i_{FGT}. For $\alpha = 1$, V^i_{FGT} coincides with V^i_{CD} if $e = 1$. For a given $(\underline{u}^i, \underline{\ell}^i, z) \in \Re^k_+ \times \Delta^k_+ \times [z_-, z_+]$, as the value of α increases, more weight is assigned to higher proportionate gaps. In addition, given $(\underline{u}^i, \underline{\ell}^i, z) \in \Re^k_+ \times \Delta^k_+ \times [z_-, z_+]$, an increase in the value of α does not increase the value of the index.

Assuming that all the state-contingent returns are positive, we may use $\psi(g^i_j) = \log\left(\frac{z}{u^i_j}\right)$ as a transformed deprivation indicator. The resulting vulnerability index becomes the expected Watts (1968) individual poverty function, defined as

$$V^i_W(\underline{u}^i, \underline{\ell}^i, z) = \sum_{j=1}^{k} \ell^i_j \log\left(\frac{z}{\hat{u}^i_j}\right). \tag{6.3}$$

Because of positivity restriction of the state-contingent returns, $V^i_W(\underline{u}^i, \underline{\ell}^i, z)$ is not bounded above. However, it meets all other axioms.

As the final illustrative example, we consider the Bourguignon and Chakravarty (2003) individual vulnerability index defined as

$$V^i_{BC}(\underline{u}^i, \underline{\ell}^i, z) = \left(\sum_{j=1}^{k} \ell^i_j \left(1 - \frac{\hat{u}^i_j}{z}\right)^{\alpha}\right)^{\frac{\beta}{\alpha}}, \tag{6.4}$$

where $\alpha > 1$ and $\beta > 0$ are parameters. This index agrees with all the vulnerability postulates we have analyzed. It, however, does not fit in the structure $\sum_{j=1}^{d} \ell^i_j \psi(g^i_j)$ unless $\alpha = \beta$, in which case it coincides with V^i_{FGT}.

We define the one-dimensional global or overall vulnerability index V^O as a nonnegative real-valued function of all one-dimensional vulnerable situations of different persons. As we have assumed, the set of states is the same for all persons, and the threshold income is exogenous. For a set of population $\{1, 2, \ldots, n\}$ consisting of n individuals, where $n \in N$ is arbitrary, let S^O_V denote the set of all one-dimensional vulnerable situations, when all the individuals are taken together, that is, $S^O_V = \{((\underline{u}^1, \underline{\ell}^1, z), (\underline{u}^2, \underline{\ell}^2, z), \ldots, (\underline{u}^n, , \underline{\ell}^n, z)) | \text{for any } i \in \{1, 2, \ldots, n\}, (\underline{u}^i, \underline{\ell}^i, z) \in \Re^k_+ \times \Delta^k_+ \times [z_-, z_+]\}$. Let $v^O(\underline{u}, \underline{\ell}, z)$, or, v^O (for short) stand for any arbitrarily chosen $((\underline{u}^1, \underline{\ell}^1, z), (\underline{u}^2, \underline{\ell}^2, z), \ldots, (\underline{u}^n, \underline{\ell}^n, z)) \in S^O_V$. By definition, $v^O \in S^O_V$. The set S^O_V is the domain of our global vulnerability index V^O. Formally, $V^O : S^O_V \to \Re^1_+$.

As an illustrative example, we regard V^O as the arithmetic average of individual vulnerability indices (see also Calvo and Dercon, 2013). Then our global vulnerability index V^O_A is defined as

$$V^O_A(v^O) = \frac{1}{n}\sum_{i=1}^{n} V^i(\underline{u}^i, \underline{\ell}^i, z), \tag{6.5}$$

where $v^O \in S_V^O$ is arbitrary. The idea of defining the aggregate vulnerability index as a function of individual indices may be regarded as representing a property, which we can refer to as independence of irrelevant information. This is because all individualistic nonvulnerability features are ignored in this definition.

By construction, the vulnerability index V_A^O in (6.5) obeys subgroup decomposability. Thus, it has nice policy relevance in the sense that it becomes helpful in identifying higher vulnerability affected subgroups that may become a policy adviser's targeted subgroups for reducing social vulnerability.

It possesses several interesting properties, assuming that V^i unambiguously meets all the axioms proposed earlier.

i) It is bounded between 0 and 1, where the lower bound is achieved if everybody in the society has a nonvulnerable status. The upper bound is attained if all the individuals are subject to maximum deprivation in all states. (For the index associated with (6.3), the upper bound is not attained.)
ii) It varies continuously for changes in meager achievement levels, under certain ceteris paribus conditions.
iii) It meets a strong monotonicity property in the sense that an increase in an individual's income vulnerability increases its value. This property parallels the strong Pareto principle analyzed in Chapter 1.
iv) Discussion on the next postulate relies on the following definition.

Definition 6.1 Let there be two persons $i, h \in \{1, 2, \ldots, n\}$ and two states $j, q \in \{1, 2, \ldots, k\}$ such that in the one-dimensional global vulnerable situation $v^O = (v^1, v^2, \ldots, v^n)$, where for all $r \in \{1, 2, \ldots, n\}$, $v^r = (\underline{u}^r, \underline{\ell}^r, z) \in \Re_+^k \times \Delta_+^k \times [z_-, z_+]$, $z > u_j^h > u_q^i > 0$, $0 < \ell_j^h \leq \ell_q^i < 1$. Then we say that a regressive transfer generates $\tilde{v}^O = (\tilde{v}^1, \tilde{v}^2, \ldots, \tilde{v}^n)$ from $v^O = (v^1, v^2, \ldots, v^n)$, if for any $r \in \{1, 2, \ldots, n\}$, $\tilde{v}^r = (\underline{\tilde{u}}^r, \underline{\ell}^r, z)$, where $\underline{\tilde{u}}^r = \underline{u}^r$ for $r \in \{1, 2, \ldots, n\}/\{i, h\}$, $\tilde{u}_j^h = u_j^h + c < z, \tilde{u}_q^i = u_q^i - c \geq 0$, $\tilde{u}_t^h = u_t^h$ for $t \in \omega/\{j\}$, $\tilde{u}_t^i = u_t^i$, for $t \in \omega/\{q\}, c > 0$.

In state q, person i has higher deprivation than person h in state j, and the corresponding probability for i's deprivation is not lower than that for h's. The regressive transfer (of size $c > 0$) takes place from person i's return in state q to the return for person h in state j. Since the probability vectors in the two situations and the threshold limit remain the same, the regressive transfer should increase global vulnerability. Further, given that the regressive transfer occurs between two persons, we can refer to it as a one-dimensional nonindividualistic transfer. In addition, it involves two states. We can present the following axiom for our one-dimensional overall vulnerability index $V_A^O : S_V^O \to \Re_+^1$.

Across-States One-Dimensional Nonindividualistic Regressive Transfer: If the one-dimensional global vulnerable situation $\tilde{v}^O = (\tilde{v}^1, \tilde{v}^2, \ldots, \tilde{v}^n)$ is obtained from the situation $v^O = (v^1, v^2, \ldots, v^n)$ by a nonindividualistic regressive transfer, $V_A^O(v^O) < V_A^O(\tilde{v}^O)$.

v) Any reordering of individual vulnerability levels does not change the value of V_A^O. Hence, the individuals are separated only by vulnerability levels.
vi) Any m-fold replication of the population leaves global vulnerability unchanged, where $m \geq 2$ is an integer. In consequence, this characteristic enables us to compare vulnerabilities of two societies with different population sizes. This population replication principle is stated under the supposition that the vectors of state-contingent returns and probabilities remain unchanged.

Although properties stated in (i)–(vi) are examined for the global index V_A^O that meets subgroup decomposability, they may as well be regarded as desirable postulates for a general global vulnerability index $V^O : S_V^O \to \Re^1_+$, which may not be subgroup decomposable. One such possible example is $\left(\frac{1}{n}\sum_{i=1}^{n}(V^i(\underline{u}^i; \underline{\ell}^i; z))^{\xi}\right)^{\frac{1}{\xi}}$, where $\xi > 1$.

We conclude this section by providing one illustration of V^A using V_{BC}^i as the individual index. The resulting global index turns out to be

$$V_{BC}^O(v^O) = \frac{1}{n}\sum_{i=1}^{n}\left(\sum_{j=1}^{k}\ell_j^i\left(1-\frac{\hat{u}_j^i}{z}\right)^{\alpha}\right)^{\frac{\beta}{\alpha}}, \tag{6.6}$$

where, as before, $\alpha > 1$ and $\beta > 0$ are parameters. The major difference between this index and the overall Foster–Greer–Thorbecke index, which arises when $\alpha = \beta$, and the Calvo–Dercon expected Chakravarty index $\frac{1}{n}\sum_{i=1}^{n}\sum_{j=1}^{k}\ell_j^i\left(1-\left(\frac{\hat{u}_j^i}{z}\right)^e\right)$ is that, while in the former the individual expected income poverty levels are aggregated nonlinearly across persons, the latter two employ a simple linear aggregation.

6.3 Multidimensional Representation of Vulnerability to Poverty: An Axiomatic Investigation

As we have argued in several chapters earlier, the well-being of a population is a multidimensional issue. Hence, to get a complete picture of individual and social vulnerabilities in a population, it is necessary to investigate the problem from a multidimensional perspective. Since in the capability-functioning approach, capability failure captures the notion of deprivation that people experience in day-to-day living conditions, it is a multidimensional phenomenon. Consequently, multidimensional vulnerability to poverty is a problem of expected capability deprivation.

As in Chapter 3, we denote the number of dimensions of well-being in a society consisting of n individuals by d, where $n \in N$ is arbitrary. We denote the set of all dimensions $\{1, 2, \dots, d\}$ by Q. The d-dimensional row vector of poverty thresholds or threshold limits in different dimensions is the vector $\underline{z} = (z_1, z_2, \dots, z_d) \in Z$. The notion of vulnerability we consider, in this section, is a multidimensional distress in the sense that the affected person faces descending trend of dimensional achievements. More precisely, there are downside risks that the individual's achievements in different dimensions drop down to levels lower than the corresponding thresholds.

For any dimension j, there are $k_j \geq 2$ states of nature, and the set of such states is designated by $\omega(j)$, $j \in Q$. Since different dimensions reflect different aspects of well-being, it is unlikely that the types and numbers of states will be the same across dimensions. Let $x^i_{js} \geq 0$ and ℓ^i_{js} stand, respectively, for person i's achievement in state s of dimension j and the probability of appearance of x^i_{js}; $1 \leq i \leq n$, $1 \leq j \leq d$. Evidently, $0 \leq \ell^i_{js} \leq 1$ and $\sum_{s \in \omega(j)} \ell^i_{js} = 1$ for all $j \in Q$ and $i \in \{1, 2, \dots, n\}$.

The k_j dimensional row vector of returns for person i from dimension j and the corresponding probability vector are given, respectively, by $\underline{x}^i_j = (x^i_{j1}, x^i_{j2}, \dots, x^i_{jk_j})$ and $\underline{\ell}^i_j = (\ell^i_{j1}, \ell^i_{j2} \dots, \ell^i_{jk_j})$. For any $j \in Q$, each triplet $(\underline{x}^i_j, \underline{\ell}^i_j, z_j)$ is an element of $\Re^{k_j}_+ \times \Delta^{k_j}_+ \times Z_j$, where Z_j is that subset of the positive part of the real line in which z_j can vary. More precisely, for any $j \in Q$, $(\underline{x}^i_j, \underline{\ell}^i_j, z_j) \in \Re^{k_j}_+ \times \Delta^{k_j}_+ \times Z_j$, where $i \in \{1, 2, \dots, n\}$ and $n \in N$ are arbitrary. Given that there are d dimensions of well-being, for any $i \in \{1, 2, \dots, n\}$, a multidimensional vulnerable situation is of the form $((\underline{x}^i_1, \underline{\ell}^i_1, z_1), (\underline{x}^i_2, \underline{\ell}^i_2, z_2), \dots, (\underline{x}^i_d, \underline{\ell}^i_d, z_d))$. Let $S^{i,d}_V$ stand for the set of all multidimensional vulnerable situations for person i, that is, $S^{i,d}_V = \{((\underline{x}^i_1, \underline{\ell}^i_1, z_1), (\underline{x}^i_2, \underline{\ell}^i_2, z_2), \dots, (\underline{x}^i_d, \underline{\ell}^i_d, z_d)) |$ for any $j \in Q, (\underline{x}^i_j, \underline{\ell}^i_j, z_j) \in \Re^{k_j}_+ \times \Delta^{k_j}_+ \times Z_j\}$.

We follow the union method of identification in this multidimensional framework, that is, person i is called multidimensionally vulnerable if there is at least one dimension j and one state $s \in \omega(j)$ such that $x^i_{js} < z_j$ and $\ell^i_{js} > 0$. Let $\underline{\hat{x}}^i_j = (\hat{x}^i_{j1}, \hat{x}^i_{j2}, \dots, \hat{x}^i_{jk_j})$ be the vector of censored returns for person i from different states in dimension j, where $\hat{x}^i_{js} = \min(x^i_{js}, z_j)$, with $s \in \omega(j)$ and $j \in Q$ being arbitrary. We similarly symbolize $(\underline{\hat{x}}^i_1, \underline{\hat{x}}^i_2, \dots, \underline{\hat{x}}^i_d)$ by $\underline{\hat{x}}^{i,d}$.

The extent of destitution felt by person i in state $s \in \omega(j)$ is measured by the deprivation indicator $g^i_{js}(x^i_{js}) = \frac{z_j - \hat{x}^i_{js}}{z_j}$, which we designate by g^i_{js}, for short; $j \in Q$, $i \in \{1, 2, \ldots, n\}$. The vector $g^i_j(\underline{x}^i_j) = (g^i_{j1}(x^i_{j1}), g^i_{j2}(x^i_{j2}), \ldots, g^i_{jk_j}(x^i_{jk_j}))$ stands for the vector of such indicators associated with $\underline{x}^i_j = (x^i_{j1}, x^i_{j2}, \ldots, x^i_{jk_j})$. For any person $i \in \{1, 2, \ldots, n\}$, the expected poverty in dimension j corresponding to $\underline{x}^i_j = (x^i_{j1}, x^i_{j2}, \ldots, x^i_{jk_j})$ is $P^i_j(\psi^i_j(\underline{x}^i_j)) = \sum\limits_{s \in \omega(j)} p^i_{js} \psi(g^i_{js})$, where the transformed deprivation indicator $\psi : [0, 1] \rightarrow \Re^1_+$ satisfying $\psi(0) = 0$ is continuous, decreasing, and strictly convex in state-contingent returns. For any $j \in Q$ and $i \in \{1, 2, \ldots, n\}$, $P^i_j(\psi^i_j(\underline{x}^i_j))$ is based on the returns censored at z_j.

The task of a multidimensional vulnerability index $V^{i,d}$ for person i is to summarize the information contained in the multidimensional vulnerable situation of the type $((\underline{x}^i_1, \underline{\ell}^i_1, z_1), (\underline{x}^i_2, \underline{\ell}^i_2, z_2), \ldots, (\underline{x}^i_d, \underline{\ell}^i_d, z_d))$ for the person in terms of a nonnegative real number. Hence, the domain of the nonnegative real-valued function $V^{i,d}$ is $S^{i,d}_V$. More precisely, $V^{i,d} : S^{i,d}_v \rightarrow \Re^1_+$.

Most of the individualistic axioms suggested in the earlier section, for a one-dimensional individual vulnerability index, can be adapted in the multidimensional system under certain alterations in the statements. For the sake of completeness, next we state these axioms analytically.

State-Restricted Weak Focus: For any $((\underline{x}^i_1, \underline{\ell}^i_1, z_1), (\underline{x}^i_2, \underline{\ell}^i_2, z_2), \ldots, (\underline{x}^i_d, \underline{\ell}^i_d, z_d)) \in S^{i,d}_v$, if for all $j \in Q$, $s \in \omega(j)$, $x^i_{js} \geq z_j$, then $V^{i,d}((\underline{x}^i_1, \underline{\ell}^i_1, z_1), (\underline{x}^i_2, \underline{\ell}^i_2, z_2), \ldots, (\underline{x}^i_d, \underline{\ell}^i_d, z_d)) = V^{i,d}((\underline{\tilde{x}}^i_1, \underline{\ell}^i_1, z_1), (\underline{\tilde{x}}^i_2, \underline{\ell}^i_2, z_2), \ldots, (\underline{\tilde{x}}^i_d, \underline{\ell}^i_d, z_d))$, where $\tilde{x}^i_{js} = x^i_{js} + c$, $c > 0$, $\tilde{x}^i_{js'} = x^i_{js'}$ for all $s' \in \omega(j)/\{s\}$; $\tilde{x}^i_{qs} = x^i_{qs}$ for all $s \in \omega(q)$, $q \in Q/\{j\}$; and for any $j \in Q$, $\underline{\tilde{x}}^i_j = (\tilde{x}^i_{j1}, \tilde{x}^i_{j2}, \ldots, \tilde{x}^i_{jk_j})$.

State-Restricted Strong Focus: For any $((\underline{x}^i_1, \underline{\ell}^i_1, z_1), (\underline{x}^i_2, \underline{\ell}^i_2, z_2), \ldots, (\underline{x}^i_d, \underline{\ell}^i_d, z_d)) \in S^{i,d}_v$, if for some $j \in Q$, $s \in \omega(j)$, $x^i_{js} \geq z_j$, then $V^{i,d}((\underline{x}^i_1, \underline{\ell}^i_1, z_1), (\underline{x}^i_2, \underline{\ell}^i_2, z_2), \ldots, (\underline{x}^i_d, \underline{\ell}^i_d, z_d)) = V^{i,d}((\underline{\tilde{x}}^i_1, \underline{\ell}^i_1, z_1), (\underline{\tilde{x}}^i_2, \underline{\ell}^i_2, z_2), \ldots, (\underline{\tilde{x}}^i_d, \underline{\ell}^i_d, z_d))$, where $\tilde{x}^i_{js} = x^i_{js} + c$, $c > 0$, $\tilde{x}^i_{js'} = x^i_{js'}$ for all $s' \in \omega(j)/\{s\}$; $\tilde{x}^i_{qs} = x^i_{qs}$ for all $s \in \omega(q)$, $q \in Q/\{j\}$; and for any $j \in Q$, $\underline{\tilde{x}}^i_j = (\tilde{x}^i_{j1}, \tilde{x}^i_{j2}, \ldots, \tilde{x}^i_{jk_j})$.

State-Restricted Monotonicity: For any $((\underline{x}^i_1, \underline{\ell}^i_1, z_1), (\underline{x}^i_2, \underline{\ell}^i_2, z_2), \ldots, (\underline{x}^i_d, \underline{\ell}^i_d, z_d)) \in S^{i,d}_v$ if for some $j \in Q$, $s \in \omega(j)$, $0 < x^i_{js} < z_j$, $\ell^i_{js} > 0$, then $V^{i,d}((\underline{x}^i_1, \underline{\ell}^i_1, z_1), (\underline{x}^i_2, \underline{\ell}^i_2, z_2), \ldots, (\underline{x}^i_d, \underline{\ell}^i_d, z_d)) < V^{i,d}((\underline{\tilde{x}}^i_1, \underline{\ell}^i_1, z_1), (\underline{\tilde{x}}^i_2, \underline{\ell}^i_2, z_2), \ldots, (\underline{\tilde{x}}^i_d, \underline{\ell}^i_d, z_d))$, where $\tilde{x}^i_{js} = x^i_{js} - c \geq 0$, $c > 0$, $\tilde{x}^i_{js'} = x^i_{js'}$ for all $s' \in \omega(j)/\{s\}$; $\tilde{x}^i_{qs} = x^i_{qs}$ for all $s \in \omega(q)$, $q \in Q/\{j\}$; and for any $j \in Q$, $\underline{\tilde{x}}^i_j = (\tilde{x}^i_{j1}, \tilde{x}^i_{j2}, \ldots, \tilde{x}^i_{jk_j})$.

Across-States Transfer: For any $((\underline{x}^i_1, \underline{\ell}^i_1, z_1), (\underline{x}^i_2, \underline{\ell}^i_2, z_2), \ldots, (\underline{x}^i_d, \underline{\ell}^i_d, z_d)) \in S^{i,d}_v$ if for some $j \in Q$; $s, s' \in \omega(j), s \neq s', z_j > x^i_{js} > x^i_{js'} > 0, 0 < \ell^i_{js} \leq \ell^i_{js'} < 1$, then $V^{i,d}((\underline{x}^i_1, \underline{\ell}^i_1, z_1), (\underline{x}^i_2, \underline{\ell}^i_2, z_2), \ldots, (\underline{x}^i_d, \underline{\ell}^i_d, z_d)) < V^{i,d}((\underline{\tilde{x}}^i_1, \underline{\ell}^i_1, z_1), (\underline{\tilde{x}}^i_2, \underline{\ell}^i_2, z_2), \ldots, (\underline{\tilde{x}}^i_d, \underline{\ell}^i_d, z_d))$, where $\tilde{x}^i_{js} = x^i_{js} + c < z_j$, $\tilde{x}^i_{js'} = x^i_{js'} - c \geq 0$, $\tilde{x}^i_{j\bar{s}} = x^i_{j\bar{s}}$, where $\bar{s} \in \omega(j)/\{s, s'\}$; $\tilde{x}^i_{qs} = x^i_{qs}$ for all $q \in Q/\{j\}$, $s \in \omega(q)$; and for any $j \in Q$, $\underline{\tilde{x}}^i_j = (\tilde{x}^i_{j1}, \tilde{x}^i_{j2}, \ldots, \tilde{x}^i_{jk_j})$.

State-Restricted Monotonicity in Threshold Limits: For any $((\underline{x}^i_1, \underline{\ell}^i_1, z_1), (\underline{x}^i_2, \underline{\ell}^i_2, z_2), \ldots, (\underline{x}^i_d, \underline{\ell}^i_d, z_d)) \in S^{i,d}_v$, if for at least one $j \in Q, x^i_{js} < z_j$ and $\ell^i_{js} > 0$, then $V^{i,d}((\underline{x}^i_1, \underline{\ell}^i_1, z_1), (\underline{x}^i_2, \underline{\ell}^i_2, z_2), \ldots, (\underline{x}^i_d, \underline{\ell}^i_d, z_d)) < V^{i,d}((\underline{x}^i_1, \underline{\ell}^i_1, \tilde{z}_1), (\underline{x}^i_2, \underline{\ell}^i_2, \tilde{z}_2), \ldots, (\underline{x}^i_d, \underline{\ell}^i_d, \tilde{z}_d))$, where, $\tilde{z}_j > z_j$, $\tilde{z}_q = z_q$, for all $q \in Q/\{j\}$ and $\tilde{z}_j \in Z_j$.

Severity of Downside Risks: For any $((\underline{x}^i_1, \underline{\ell}^i_1, z_1), (\underline{x}^i_2, \underline{\ell}^i_2, z_2), \ldots, (\underline{x}^i_d, \underline{\ell}^i_d, z_d)) \in S^{i,d}_v$ if for some $j \in Q$, $z_j > x^i_{js} > x^i_{js'}, 0 < \ell^i_{js} < \ell^i_{js'} < 1$, then $V^{i,d}((\underline{x}^i_1, \underline{\ell}^i_1, z_1), (\underline{x}^i_2, \underline{\ell}^i_2, z_2), \ldots, (\underline{x}^i_d, \underline{\ell}^i_d, z_d)) < V^{i,d}((\underline{x}^i_1, \underline{\tilde{\ell}}^i_1, z_1), (\underline{x}^i_2, \underline{\tilde{\ell}}^i_2, z_2), \ldots, (\underline{x}^i_d, \underline{\tilde{\ell}}^i_d, z_d))$, where $1 > \tilde{\ell}^i_{js'} = \ell^i_{js'} + c$, $\tilde{\ell}^i_{js} = \ell^i_{js} - c \geq 0$, $c > 0$; $\tilde{\ell}^i_{js''} = \ell^i_{js''}$ for all $s'' \in \omega(j)/\{s, s'\}$; $\tilde{\ell}^i_{qs} = \ell^i_{qs}$ for all $s \in \omega(q)$, $q \in Q/\{j\}$; and for any $j \in Q$, $\underline{\tilde{\ell}}^i_j = (\tilde{\ell}^i_{j1}, \tilde{\ell}^i_{j2}, \ldots, \tilde{\ell}^i_{jk_j})$.

State-Restricted Boundedness: The index $V^{i,d}$ is bounded between 0 and 1, where the lower bound is achieved if for $((\underline{x}^i_1, \underline{\ell}^i_1, z_1), (\underline{x}^i_2, \underline{\ell}^i_2, z_2), \ldots, (\underline{x}^i_d, \underline{\ell}^i_d, z_d)) \in S^{i,d}_v$, $x^i_{js} \geq z_j$ for all $i \in \{1, 2, \ldots, n\}$, $s \in \omega(j)$ and $j \in Q$. $V^{i,d}$ reaches its upper bound if for $((\underline{x}^i_1, \underline{\ell}^i_1, z_1), (\underline{x}^i_2, \underline{\ell}^i_2, z_2), \ldots, (\underline{x}^i_d, \underline{\ell}^i_d, z_d)) \in S^{i,d}_v$, $x^i_{js} = 0$ for all $i \in \{1, 2, \ldots, n\}$, $s \in \omega(j)$ and $j \in Q$, assuming that this case of maximal deprivation is well defined.

Continuity in State-Contingent Returns: For given probability vectors and threshold limits, $V^{i,d}$ varies continuously in state-contingent returns, assuming that the vulnerability status of the person remains unchanged.

For a given profile of probability vectors and vector of threshold limits, if a person is not deprived in any state of any dimension, then giving him more return in some state of some arbitrary dimension should not have any impact on his vulnerability. The state-restricted weak focus axiom demands this. The remaining axioms stated in the section are simple multivariate translations, involving states of nature in different dimensions, of univariate vulnerability axioms specified in Section 6.2. Our discussion on postulates for the one-dimensional indices applies equally well here under obvious modifications.

An example of an individual vulnerability index in this multidimensional framework can be

$$V_{BC}^{i,d}\left(\left(\underline{x}_1^i, \underline{\ell}_1^i, z_1\right), \dots, \left(\underline{x}_d^i, \underline{\ell}_d^i, z_d\right)\right) = \left(\frac{1}{d}\sum_{j=1}^{d} P_j^{i,\alpha}\left(g_j^i\left(\underline{x}_j^i\right)\right)\right)^{\frac{\beta}{\alpha}}$$

$$= \left(\frac{1}{d}\sum_{j=1}^{d}\sum_{s\in\omega(j)} \ell_{js}^i\left(\psi_\alpha\left(g_j^i\left(x_{js}^i\right)\right)\right)\right)^{\frac{\beta}{\alpha}}, \tag{6.7}$$

where $((\underline{x}_1^i, \underline{\ell}_1^i, z_1), (\underline{x}_2^i, \underline{\ell}_2^i, z_2), \dots, (\underline{x}_d^i, \underline{\ell}_d^i, z_d)) \in S_V^{i,d}$ is arbitrary and $\psi_\alpha(g_j^i(x_{js}^i)) = \left(\frac{z_j - \hat{x}_{js}^i}{z_j}\right)^\alpha$. Here the expression $P_j^{i,\alpha}(g_j^i(\underline{x}_j^i)) = \sum_{s\in\omega(j)} \ell_{js}^i(\psi_\alpha(g_j^i(x_{js}^i))) = \sum_{s\in\omega(j)} \ell_{js}^i\left(\frac{z_j - \hat{x}_{js}^i}{z_j}\right)^\alpha$ can be regarded as expected poverty from dimension j ascertained by the Bourguignon–Chakravarty multidimensional vulnerability index for person i. The parametric restrictions $\alpha > 1$ and $\beta > 0$ are sufficient to guarantee that $V_{BC}^{i,d}$ agrees with all the axioms laid down for an arbitrary $V^{i,d}$.

For defining an aggregate multidimensional vulnerability index for a given set of population $\{1, 2, \dots, n\}$ with n individuals, we denote the arbitrary vulnerable situation $((\underline{x}_1^i, \underline{\ell}_1^i, z_1), (\underline{x}_2^i, \underline{\ell}_2^i, z_2), \dots, (\underline{x}_d^i, \underline{\ell}_d^i, z_d)) \in S_V^{i,d}$ by $v^{i,d}(\underline{x}^{i,d}, \underline{\ell}^{i,d}, \underline{z})$, or, by $v^{i,d}$ (for short), where $\underline{x}^{i,d} = (\underline{x}_1^i, \underline{x}_2^i, \dots, \underline{x}_d^i)$ and $\underline{\ell}^{i,d} = (\underline{\ell}_1^i, \underline{\ell}_2^i, \dots, \underline{\ell}_d^i)$. Further, let $v^{A,d}$ stand for a multidimensional global vulnerable situation $(v^{1,d}, v^{2,d}, \dots, v^{n,d})$. The set of all multidimensional global vulnerable situations is $S_V^{A,d} = \{(v^{1,d}, v^{2,d}, \dots, v^{n,d}) | \text{for any } i \in \{1, 2, \dots, n\}, v^{i,d} \in S_V^{i,d}\}$. Let $\underline{P}^i$ stand for the d dimensional vector $(P_1^i, P_2^i, \dots, P_d^i)$ corresponding to $v^{i,d}$, where P_j^i is person i's expected poverty in dimension j.

The arithmetic average of individual multidimensional vulnerability indices can now be taken as an index of the aggregate multidimensional vulnerability index. Accordingly, for any arbitrary population size of $n \in N$, this global index $V^{A,d}$ is defined as

$$V^{A,d}(v^{A,d}) = \frac{1}{n}\sum_{i=1}^{n} V^{i,d}(v^{i,d}), \tag{6.8}$$

where $v^{i,d} = ((\underline{x}_1^i, \underline{\ell}_1^i, z_1), (\underline{x}_2^i, \underline{\ell}_2^i, z_2), \dots, (\underline{x}_d^i, \underline{\ell}_d^i, z_d)) \in S_V^{i,d}$ is arbitrary for each i and $V^{i,d}$ fulfills the axioms stated in the section.

A clear distinction exists between the aggregation rule employed in (6.8) and the dashboard and composite index approaches. As we have observed, different dimensional indices of deprivation (or well-being) can be assembled in a set, framing the dashboard approach. On the other hand, when the dimensional indices are united, using some aggregator, we have a composite index. It may be recalled here that one common problem with dashboards and composite indices is that they ignore joint distributions of deprivations or well-beings.

Observe that in (6.7) statewise deprivations of person i in a dimension are aggregated initially. The aggregated dimension level figures are clubbed together to arrive at $V^{i,d}$. Then in (6.8), we have a vector of individual multidimensional indices $(V^{1,d}, V^{2,d}, \dots, V^{n,d})$ that are combined using the unweighted arithmetic averaging criterion. By construction, joint distribution of deprivations across the dimensions is explicitly taken into account.

In view of satisfaction of population subgroup decomposability by $V^{A,d}$, its policy applicability for pinpointing population subgroups that are distressed more by multidimensional vulnerability is evident. Several attractive features of this aggregate vulnerability index $V^{A,d}$ are analyzed next.

i) It reaches the lower bound 0 when everybody is nondeprived in all states of different dimensions. In contrast, it arrives at the upper bound 1 if all the persons are maximally deprived in all the dimensions.
ii) It is continuous in achievement quantities under certain mild conditions.
iii) Because of increasingness in individual arguments $V^{i,d}$, where $i = 1,2, \dots, n$, it is strongly monotonic. Therefore, any change in an individual index, as desired by the axioms, specified earlier, is taken into account by the index properly.
iv) It also fulfills a multidimensional regressive transfer principle, which we define next.

Definition 6.2 Let there be two persons $i, h \in \{1, 2, \dots, n\}$ and at least one dimension j, with at least one vulnerable state $s \in \omega(j)$, such that in the multidimensional global vulnerable situation $(v^{1,d}, v^{2,d}, \dots, v^{n,d})$, where for all $r \in \{1, 2, \dots, n\}$, $v^{r,d} = ((\underline{x}^r_1, \underline{\ell}^r_1, z_1), (\underline{x}^r_2, \underline{\ell}^r_2, z_2), \dots, (\underline{x}^r_d, \underline{\ell}^r_d, z_d)) \in S^{r,d}_V$, the following conditions hold: (i)$z_j > x^i_{js} > x^h_{js} > 0$, (ii) $0 < \ell^i_{js} \le \ell^h_{js} < 1$. Then we say that a regressive transfer generates $\tilde{v}^{A,d} = (\tilde{v}^{1,d}, \tilde{v}^{2,d}, \dots, \tilde{v}^{n,d})$ from $v^{A,d} = (v^{1,d}, v^{2,d}, \dots, v^{n,d})$, if for any $r \in \{1, 2, \dots, n\}$, $\tilde{v}^{r,d} = ((\underline{y}^r_1, \underline{\ell}^r_1, z_1), (\underline{y}^r_2, \underline{\ell}^r_2, z_2), \dots, (\underline{y}^r_d, \underline{\ell}^r_d, z_d)) \in S^{r,d}_V$, where $y^r_{js} = x^r_{js}$ for all $r \in \{1, 2, \dots, n\}/\{i, h\}$, $s \in \omega(r)$; $y^h_{js} = x^h_{js} - c_{js} \ge 0$, $y^i_{js} = x^i_{js} + c_{js} < z_j$, $y^i_{js'} = x^i_{js'}$, $y^h_{js'} = x^h_{js'}$ for all $s' \in \omega(j)/\{s\}$,; $c_{js} > 0$ for all $s \in \omega(j)$, $j \in \{1, 2, \dots, d\}$, such that both (i) and (ii) hold and $c_{js} = 0$, otherwise.

In the aforementioned definition, given that all the probability distributions and the threshold limits are the same across the profiles $v^{A,d} = (v^{1,d}, v^{2,d}, \dots, v^{n,d})$ and $\tilde{v}^{A,d} = (\tilde{v}^{1,d}, \tilde{v}^{2,d}, \dots, \tilde{v}^{n,d})$, we can say that $\tilde{v}^{A,d} = (\tilde{v}^{1,d}, \tilde{v}^{2,d}, \dots, \tilde{v}^{n,d})$ is obtained from $v^{A,d} = (v^{1,d}, v^{2,d}, \dots, v^{n,d})$ by a regressive transfer of achievement in state $s \in \omega(j)$ from person h to person i. In $v^{A,d}$, person h, the donor of the transfer, has higher deprivation than person i, the transfer recipient, in state s of dimension j, and the corresponding positive downside risk is also not lower for the donor. This regressive transfer of achievement in state s of dimension j makes the donor more deprived in the state, where $j \in Q$, $s \in \omega(j)$ and $i, h \in \{1, 2, \ldots, n\}$ are arbitrary. Both the numbers of dimensions and the corresponding states for which (i) and (ii) hold can be more than 1. Accordingly, it is a multidimensional phenomenon. Given that the donor has at least a high positive downside risk than the recipient in the state under consideration, the regressive transfer that generates $\tilde{v}^{A,d}$ from $v^{A,d}$ should increase vulnerability.

To get more insights into this definition, let $n = d = 2$, $k_1 = k_2 = 3$, $z_1 = 600$, and $z_2 = 2000$. Assume that $\underline{x_1^1} = (620, 590, 580)$, $\underline{\ell_1^1} = \left(\frac{1}{6}, \frac{1}{3}, \frac{1}{2}\right)$, $\underline{x_2^1} = (1800, 2100, 1900)$, $\underline{\ell_2^1} = \left(\frac{1}{3}, \frac{1}{3}, \frac{1}{3}\right)$; $\underline{x_1^2} = (610, 590, 575)$, $\underline{\ell_1^2} = \left(\frac{1}{6}, \frac{1}{4}, \frac{7}{12}\right)$, $\underline{x_2^2} = (1800, 1900, 1800)$, and $\underline{\ell_2^2} = \left(\frac{1}{3}, \frac{5}{12}, \frac{1}{4}\right)$. In state 3 of dimension 2, person 2 has a higher deprivation but lower probability than person 1. Therefore, a regressive transfer between the two persons in state 3 of dimension 2 is ruled out. Since in state 1 of the dimension, the two persons are equally deprived, a regressive transfer is not possible here as well. Finally, in state 2 of the dimension, person 1 is not deprived but person 2 is deprived. In consequence, this state does not come under the purview of a transfer. Continuing this way, we can identify that only in state 3 of dimension 1, a regressive transfer from person 2 to person 1 is permissible.

The following axiom can now be stated formally:

Multidimensional Vulnerability Regressive Transfer: If the multidimensional global vulnerable situation $\tilde{v}^{A,d}$ is obtained from the situation $v^{A,d}$ by a multidimensional regressive transfer, $V^{A,d}(v^{A,d}) < V^{A,d}(\tilde{v}^{A,d})$.

v) Given that the index is simple unweighted average of individual multidimensional vulnerability indices, it is a symmetric function of individual indices. In other words, this postulate states that any permutation of individual vulnerability extents keeps its value unchanged.
vi) Since the index is defined as the average of individual multidimensional vulnerability indices, it remains unaltered under replications of the population.

Even though properties scrutinized in (i)–(vi) are specified for the subgroup decomposable index $V^{A,d}$, they can be taken as intuitively reasonable postulates for a general multidimensional vulnerability index $\overline{V}^{A,d} : S^{A,d} \rightarrow \Re^1_+$, which may not be subgroup decomposable.

As an example of a multidimensional vulnerability index at the society level, we may suggest the use of the following:

$$V_{BC}^{A,d}(v^{1,d}, v^{2,d}, \dots, v^{n,d}) = \frac{1}{n}\sum_{i=1}^{n}\left(\frac{1}{d}\sum_{j=1}^{d}\sum_{s\in\omega(j)} \ell_{js}^{i}\left(\frac{z_j - \hat{x}_{js}^{i}}{z_j}\right)^{\alpha}\right)^{\frac{\beta}{\alpha}}, \tag{6.9}$$

where for any $r \in \{1, 2, \dots, n\}$, $v^{r,d} = ((\underline{x}_1^r; \underline{\ell}_1^r; \underline{z}), (\underline{x}_2^r; \underline{\ell}_2^r; \underline{z}), \dots, (\underline{x}_d^r; \underline{\ell}_d^r; \underline{z})) \in S_V^{r,d}$; $\alpha > 1$ and $\beta > 0$. Equation (6.9) can be rewritten in terms of individual expected poverties $P_j^{i,\alpha}(g_j^i(\underline{x}_j^i)) = \sum_{s\in\omega(j)} \ell_{js}^{i}\left(\frac{z_j - \hat{x}_j^i}{z_j}\right)^{\alpha}$ for different dimensions as

$$V_{BC}^{A,d}(v^{1,d}, v^{2,d}, \dots, v^{n,d}) = \frac{1}{n}\sum_{i=1}^{n}\left(\frac{1}{d}\sum_{j=1}^{d} P_j^{i,\alpha}(d_j^i(\underline{x}_j^i))\right)^{\frac{\beta}{\alpha}}. \tag{6.10}$$

The subgroup decomposable Bourguignon–Chakravarty multidimensional vulnerability to poverty index $V_{BC}^{A,d}(v^{1,d}, v^{2,d}, \dots, v^{n,d})$, encompassing the whole population, is bounded between 0 and 1, strongly monotonic, symmetric, population replication invariant, and correctly responsive to the multidimensional vulnerability regressive transfer principle for all $\alpha > 1$ and $\beta > 0$. (See properties stated in (i)–(vi) earlier.)

6.4 Concluding Remarks

In this chapter, we have only addressed the problem of representing a vulnerable situation, formulated in a particular way, numerically. In a recent paper, Chakravarty et al. (2015) developed a vulnerability ordering that regards one situation (e.g., agriculture) as not less vulnerable than another (say, fisheries) if and only if the former does not have lower level of vulnerability than the latter for a family of expected poverty indices, assuming that income is the only dimension of well-being. The family includes expected poverty indices, where the underlying transformed deprivation indicators are continuous, normalized, and convex. While such indicators we have discussed in Section 6.2 are homogeneous of degree 0 in the state-level returns and the threshold limit, the ordering does not require this property. Expected poverty indices with translation invariant transformed deprivation indicators that remain unchanged under equal absolute changes in such returns and the threshold limit can as well be included in this family. An example of such a function is the Zheng (2000) transformed deprivation function defined by $e^{\theta(z-\hat{u}_j^i)} - 1$, where $\theta > 0$ is a constant. This function is decreasing, continuous, and strictly convex in state-dependent returns below the threshold limit. The main result developed by Chakravarty et al. (2015) does not require equality of the number of states across the situations. It banks explicitly on Blackwell's (1951, 1953) well-known results for comparisons of experiments (see also Cremer, 1982 and Leshno and Spector, 1992). A novelty of this ordering is that it can be regarded as vulnerability analog to the Hardy et al. (1934) classical result on the measurement of inequality. Hardeweg et al. (2013) considered a stochastic dominance-based partial ordering in this context. The multidimensional extension of these orderings is an issue of a natural investigation here. We have also not incorporated ordinally measurable dimensions into our analysis. Research on axiomatic approach to vulnerability has just begun. Many more relevant aspects are yet to be explored.

In a recent contribution, Chakravarty et al. (2016) investigated the implications of vulnerability on the income poverty line. More accurately, the problem of adapting the income poverty threshold under vulnerability so that the adjusted poverty line also represents the subsistence standard of living in a situation of vulnerability has been addressed. The central idea underlying this process of modification is that the individual utility derived from the existing poverty line and the expected utility generated by the new poverty line affected by a random error (noise) indicating vulnerability are the same. Consequently, the formulation relies on the implicit assumption that the vulnerability is treated as a low expected utility situation. Under certain sensible assumptions about the noise, in an additive model, the harmonized poverty line is shown to exceed the existing poverty line by a constant amount if the utility function possesses constant Arrow–Pratt absolute risk aversion. Likewise, in a multiplicative model, the adjusted poverty line becomes a scale transformation of the existing poverty line, where the underlying scalar is greater than unity, if the utility function exhibits constant Arrow–Pratt relative risk aversion. (The relative risk aversion measure is obtained by multiplying its absolute counterpart by income.) An empirical illustration of the developed methodology has been provided using data from the Asia-Pacific region. Clearly, an extension of this approach to the multidimensional setup will require consideration of joint distribution of the noise term representing vulnerability.

In an earlier contribution, Dang and Lanjouw (2014) developed two formal approaches to the determination of the vulnerability line. According to the first approach, for a population subgroup that is clearly not vulnerable, the vulnerability line has been defined as the lower-bound income of subgroup. In contrast, in the second approach, a subgroup that is not poor currently but faces a real risk of falling into poverty is considered. The upper-bound income for this subgroup has been taken as the vulnerability line. While essential to the Chakravarty et al. (2016) approach is the Arrow–Pratt theory of risk aversion, the Dang–Lanjouw approach relies on a probabilistic formulation.

In Chapter 5, we have assumed perfect foresight of period-by-period achievements on different dimensions for all the individuals. In their highly interesting contribution, Calvo and Dercon (2009) suggested one-dimensional statistic of vulnerability in a dynamic world in which the assumption of realization of incomes in the future periods with certainty is relaxed. Let u^t_{ij} stand for person i's income when state $j \in \omega(t)$ materializes in period t, where $\omega(t)$ denotes the set of states of nature in period $t \in \{1, 2, \dots, T\}$ and $i \in \{1, 2, \dots, n\}$. We write $\hat{u}^t_{ij}$ for the corresponding censored income. Let $0 \leq \ell^t_{ij} \leq 1$ be the probability that state $j \in \omega(t)$ in period t emerges. Evidently, for all $i \in \{1, 2, \dots, n\}$ and $t \in \{1, 2, \dots, T\}$, $\sum_{j \in \omega(t)} \ell^t_{ij} = 1$. The expected value of transformed normalized (censored) incomes in period t is $E\left(\frac{\hat{u}^t_i}{z}\right)^e = \sum_{j \in \omega(t)} \left(\frac{\hat{u}^t_{ij}}{z}\right)^e \ell^t_{ij}$, where $0 < e < 1$ is a constant (see Eq. (6.1)), E denotes the expected value operator, and z is the income poverty line.

The authors proposed the use of the following modified version of (5.12)

$$\tilde{V}^i_{CD}(\underline{u^i_T}, \underline{\ell^i_T}, z) = \sum_{t=1}^{T} \gamma^{T-t} \left[1 - E\left(\frac{\hat{u}^t_i}{z}\right)^e\right] \tag{6.11}$$

as a forward-looking and dynamic metric of poverty, where $\underline{u^i_T}$ is the profile of the vectors of person i's incomes associated with different sates of nature in all T periods, $\underline{\ell^i_T}$ is the corresponding profile of probability vectors, and $\gamma > 0$ is the rate of time discounting. This index can be regarded as a representation of upcoming intertemporal individual poverty because it is not based on evaluation of poverty for a single period; instead, it takes into account poverty assessments for a sequence of forthcoming periods in a world of uncertainty. According to the authors, "one of the contributions of this paper is to identify the Chakravarty poverty index as the best choice if the poverty analysis moves from static poverty on to vulnerability" (Calvo and Dercon, 2009, p. 57). Clearly, this index can be employed for arriving at a complete ordering of different possible paths of standard of living, judged by utilizing future uncertain incomes. A natural generalization of this nice proposal with many innovative features is to develop analogous quantifiers in the multidimensional setup.

References

Amin, S., A.S. Rai, and G. Topa. 2003. Does Microcredit Reach the Poor and Vulnerable? Evidence from Northern Bangladesh. *Journal of Development Economics* 70: 59–82.

Arrow, K.J. 1965. *Aspects of the Theory of Risk Bearing*. Helsinki: Yrjo Jahnssonin Saatio.

Basu, K. and P. Nolen. 2005. Vulnerability, Unemployment and Poverty: A New Class of Measures, its Axiomatic Properties and Applications. *BREAD Working Paper* 38.

Binswanger, H.P. 1981. Attitudes Toward Risk: Theoretical Implications of an Experiment in Rural India. *Economic Journal* 91: 867–890.

Blackwell, D. 1951. Comparison of Experiments. *Proceedings of the Second Berkeley Symposium on Mathematical Statistics and Probability*. Berkeley: University of California Press, 93–102.

Blackwell, D. 1953. Equivalent Comparisons of Experiments. *Annals of Mathematical Statistics* 24: 265–272.

Bourguignon, F. and S.R. Chakravarty.2003. The Measurement of Multidimensional Poverty. *Journal of Economic Inequality* 1: 25–49.

Calvo, C. 2008. Vulnerability to Multidimensional Poverty: Peru, 1998–2002. *World Development* 36: 1011–1020.

Calvo S. and S. Dercon. 2009. Chronic Poverty and All that: The Measurement of Poverty over Time. In T. Addison, D. Hulme, and R. Kanbur (eds.) *Poverty Dynamics: Interdisciplinary Perspectives*. Oxford: Oxford University Press, 29–58.

Calvo, C. and S. Dercon. 2013. Vulnerability of Individual and Aggregate Poverty. *Social Choice and Welfare* 41: 721–740.

Chakravarty, S.R. 1983. A New Index of Poverty. *Mathematical Social Sciences* 6: 307–313.

Chakravarty, S.R. and N. Chattopadhyay.2015. Measuring Vulnerability to Poverty: An Expected Poverty Approach. In S. Guha, R.P. Kundu, and S. Subramanian (eds.) *Contributions to Economic Analysis: Essays in Honor of Satish Jain*. London: Routledge, 313–323.

Chakravarty, S.R., N. Chattopadhyay, and L. Qingbin. 2015. Vulnerability Orderings for Expected Poverty Indices. *Japanese Economic Review* 66: 300–310.

Chakravarty, S.R., N. Chattopadhyay, J. Silber, and G. Wan. 2016. Measuring the Impact of Vulnerability on the Number of Poor: A New Methodology with Empirical Illustration. In J. Silber and G. Wan, 84–117.

Chaudhuri, S. 2003. *Assessing Vulnerability to Poverty: Concepts, Empirical Methods and Illustrative Examples. Mimeographed*, Columbia University.

Chaudhuri, S., J. Jalan, and A. Suryahadi. 2002. Assessing Household Vulnerability to Poverty from Cross-section Data: A Methodology and Estimates from Indonesia. *Discussion Paper Series* 0102-52, Department of Economics, Columbia University.

Christiaensen, L. and R. Boisvert. 2000. On Measuring Household Food Vulnerability: Case Evidence from Northern Mali. *Working Paper 2000-5*. Department of Agricultural, Resource and Managerial Economics, Cornell University.

Christiaensen, L. and K. Subbarao. 2005. Towards an Understanding of Household Vulnerability in Rural Kenya. *Journal of African Economies* 14: 520–558.

Coudouel, A. and J. Hentschel. 2000. *Poverty Data and Measurement. Preliminary Draft for a Sourcebook on Poverty Reduction Strategies.* Washington DC: The World Bank.

Cremer, J. 1982. A Simple Proof of Blackwell's "Comparison of Experiments' Theorem". *Journal of Economic Theory* 27: 439–444.

Dang, H.H. and P.F. Lanjouw. 2014. Two Definitions of a Vulnerability Line and their Empirical Application. *Policy Research Working Paper* No. 6944. Washington, DC: World Bank.

Dercon, S. 2002. Income Risk, Coping Strategies and Safety Nets. *World Bank Research Observer* 17: 141–166.

Dercon, S. and P. Krishnan.2000. Vulnerability, Seasonality and Poverty in Ethiopia. *Journal of Development Studies* 36: 25–53.

Dutta, I., J.E. Foster, and A. Mishra. 2011. On Measuring Vulnerability to Poverty. *Social Choice and Welfare* 37: 743–761.

Elbers, C. and J.W. Gunning. 2003. *Vulnerability in a Stochastic Dynamic Model. Mimeographed*, Tinbergen Institute.

Foster, J.E., J. Greer, and E. Thorbecke. 1984. A Class of Decomposable Poverty Measures. *Econometrica* 52: 761–766.

Fujii, T. 2016. Vulnerability: A Review of Literature. In J. Silber and G. Wan, 53–83.

Gaiha, R. and K. Imai. 2009. Measuring Vulnerability and Poverty: Estimates for Rural India. In I.W. Naudé, A. Santos-Paulino, and M. McGillivray (eds.) *Vulnerability in Developing Countries.* Tokyo: United Nations University Press, 13–54.

Glewwe, P. and G. Hall. 1998. Are Some Groups More Vulnerable to Macroeconomic Shocks than Others? Hypothesis Tests Based on Panel Data from Peru. *Journal of Development Economics* 56: 181–206.

Günther, I. and K. Harttgen. 2009. Estimating Household Vulnerability to Idiosyncratic and Covariance Shocks: A Novel Method Applied in Madagascar. *World Development* 37: 1222–1234.

Hardeweg, B., A. Wagner, and H. Waibel. 2013. A Distributional Approach Comparing Vulnerability applied to Rural Provinces in Thailand and Vietnam. *Journal of Asian Economics* 25: 53–65.

Hardy, G.H., J.E. Littlewood, and G. Polya. 1934. *Inequalities.* New York: Cambridge University Press.

Hoddinott, J. and A. Quisumbing. 2003. Methods for Micro-Econometric Risk and Vulnerability Assessments. *Social Protection Discussion Paper* 0324. Washington, DC: World Bank.

Holzmann R. and S. Jorgensen. 1999. Social Protection as Social Risk Management: Conceptual Underpinnings for the Social Protection Sector Strategy Paper. *Social Protection Discussion Paper* 9904. Washington, DC: World Bank.

Hoogeveen, J., E. Tesliuc, R. Vakis, and S. Dercon. 2004. A Guide to Analysis of Risk, Vulnerability and Vulnerable Groups. *Policy Research Working Paper*. Washington, DC: World Bank.

Kamanou, G. and J. Morduch. 2002. Measuring Vulnerability to Poverty. *WIDER Discussion Paper*, 2002/58.

Kamanou, G. and J. Morduch. 2004. Measuring Vulnerability to Poverty. In S. Dercon (ed.) *Insurance Against Poverty*. New York: Oxford University Press, 155–175.

Klasen, S. and F. Povel. 2013. Defining and Measuring Vulnerability: State of the Art and New Proposals. In S. Klasen and H. Waibel (eds.) *Vulnerability to Poverty: Theory, Measurement and Determinants*. London: Palgrave–Macmillan, 17–47.

Leshno, M. and Y. Spector. 1992. An Elementary Proof of Blackwell's Theorem. *Mathematical Social Sciences* 25: 95–98.

Ligon, E. and L. Schechter. 2003. Measuring Vulnerability. *Economic Journal* 113: C95–C102.

López-Calva, L.F. and E. Ortiz-Juarez.2014. A Vulnerability Approach to the Definition of the Middle Class. *Journal of Economic Inequality* 12: 23–47.

Morduch, J. 1994. Poverty and Vulnerability. *American Economic Review: Papers and Proceedings* 84: 221–225.

Pratt, J.W. 1964. Risk Aversion in the Small and the Large. *Econometrica* 32: 122–136.

Pritchett, L., A. Suryahadi, and S. Sumarto. 2000. Quantifying Vulnerability to Poverty: A Proposed Measure, with Application to Indonesia. *Social Monitoring and Early Response Unit Working Paper*. Washington, DC: World Bank.

Ravallion, M. 1988. Expected Poverty under Risk-'Induced Welfare Variability. *Economic Journal* 98: 1171–1182.

Rothschild, M. and J.E. Stiglitz. 1970. Increasing Risk: I. A Definition. *Journal of Economic Theory* 2: 225–243.

Sen, A.K. 1999. A Plan for Asia's Growth: Build on Much that is Good in the 'Eastern Strategy'. *Asia Week*, October 8, 25(40). Available at: http://edition.cnn.com/ASIANOW/asiaweek/magazine/99/1008/viewpoint.html.

Silber, J. and G. Wan. (eds.) 2016. *The Asian Poverty Miracle: Impressive Accomplishments or Incomplete Achievements?* Northampton: Edward Elgar, Forthcoming.

Skoufias, E. and A.R. Quisumbing. 2005. Consumption Insurance and Vulnerability to Poverty: A Synthesis of Evidence from Bangladesh, Ethiopia, Mali, Mexico and Russia. *European Journal of Development Research* 17: 24–58.

Suryahadi, A. and S. Sumarto. 2003. Poverty and Vulnerability in Indonesia Before and After the Economic Crisis. *Asian Economic Journal* 17: 45–64.

Townsend, R. 1994. Risk and Insurance in Village India. *Econometrica* 62: 539–591.

Watts, H.W. 1968. An Economic Definition of Poverty. In D.P. Moynihan (ed.) On Understanding of Poverty. New York: Basic Books, 316–319.

World Bank. 1997. *Identifying the Vulnerable: New Evidence* from *Peru, Poverty Lines*, A Joint Publication by the Policy Research and Social Policy Departments. Washington, DC: World Bank. Available at: http://web.worldbank.org/archive/website00002/WEB/PDF/PL_N06.PDF.

Zheng, B. 2000. Minimum Distribution Sensitivity, Poverty Aversion, and Poverty Orderings. *Journal of Economic Theory* 95: 116–137.

7

An Exploration of Some Composite and Individualistic Indices

7.1 Introduction

A composite index is a summary statistic giving a comprehensive picture of dimensional indices associated with a dashboard, a portfolio of dimension-by-dimension metrics, constructed for a multidimensional evaluation task. In other words, it is a real-valued representation of dimensional indices. In some situations, dashboards corresponding to two social matrices may possess the ability of ranking the underlying matrices to judge whether one of them performs better than the other with respect to the purpose for which the dashboards have been designed. However, the ranking is possible only when the dimensionwise changes are unidirectional. In contrast, the composite indices can rank the matrices unambiguously since each of them is a real number, which clusters the information available in a social matrix in terms of a real number by employing some given aggregation principles. Hence, a composite index has this comparative advantage over a dashboard (see (Stiglitz et al., 2009).[1] While a composite index employs aggregation, first at the level of individuals in a dimension and then across the dimensions, in an individualistic index, the process of aggregation is reversed (Kolm, 1977).

A prominent example of a composite index is the human development index (HDI), proposed by the United Nations Development Program (UNDP) in (UNDP, 1990) and is computed and made available annually since then in the Human Development Reports. It is a combined measure of three country-level indicators of functionings: health, education, and income. It provides a capability-based view of development from a multidimensional perspective.

While the HDI measures average achievement, in 1997, UNDP proposed a composite index, the human poverty index (HPI), for measuring the multidimensional poverty. The HPI measures deprivations in the same aspects as the HDI from a deprivational perspective (UNDP, 1997). UNDP's gender inequality index, an individualistic measure, determines the loss of human

1 On issues related to ranking by such indices, see Høyland et al. (2012).

Analyzing Multidimensional Well-Being: A Quantitative Approach, First Edition. Satya R. Chakravarty.

well-being arising from existence of intersex (male–female) inequality in the distributions of attainments in the following three dimensions: reproductive health, empowerment, and labor market. The next three sections are devoted to the analysis of HDI, HPI, and gender inequality index, respectively.

The better life index proposed by the Organization for Economic Co-operation and Development (OECD) was designed with the objective of visualizing a comprehensive picture of well-being using 11 materialistic and quality of life indicators. The active citizenship composite index, evolved in European situation, is a summary measure of value-based participation of citizens, defined in a quite general way. These two measures are surveyed in Sections 7.5 and 7.6, respectively.

The concern of a human opportunity index is the distribution of accesses of individuals in a society to different available opportunities. (See Section 2.6 for a list of references.) Section 7.7 of the chapter proposes and analyzes a counting-based individualistic measure of human opportunity.

Attempts have been made in the literature to determine the progress made by a society toward achievements of Millennium Development Goals, proposed by the United Nations (UN) in September 2000 (see (Bourguignon et al., 2008, 2010)). The subject of Section 7.8 is a brief analytical discussion on related issues.

Air pollution is an environmental problem of considerable importance. Monitoring of air quality requires observations of pollutant concentrations on a regular basis. Given large amount of data on concentrations of pollutants, it is desirable that information on air quality should be transmitted in a simple way. This is taken care of by an air quality index. In Section 7.9, we examine the issue from a general perspective.

In the concluding section, Section 7.10, we briefly analyze the indices of economic freedom, green economy progress, and environmental performance, each of which is a composite measure of the respective multidimensional situation.

7.2 Human Development Index

Human development can be defined as a procedure of enlargement of people's choices that empower them "to lead a long and healthy life, to acquire knowledge and to have access to resources needed for a decent standard of living" (UNDP, 1990, p. 10). More generally, human development stresses importance on positive freedom (Desai, 1991, p. 356). The HDI is a measuring device that aims to mark the capabilities of individuals in a society with respect to the three critical ingredients of human welfare, stated earlier. In the construction of the index, these three essential components are represented, respectively, by life expectancy, education, and income. Consequently, the HDI evaluates development from a broader perspective than that done by income alone.

The original HDI is the arithmetic mean of country-level standardized attainments in health, education, and income (UNDP, 1990). Attainments in health are indicated by life expectancy (*LE*), and attainments in education (*ED*) are represented by the weighted average of literacy rate and combined gross enrolment rate with respective weight of two-thirds and one-third. The log of the per capita GDP, at purchasing power parity, was chosen to signify income (*IN*). Let x_{LE}, x_{ED} and x_{IN} denote, respectively, the country-level attainments in these three dimensions. The respective spaces to which they belong are $\Omega_{LE} = [\boldsymbol{m}_{LE}, \boldsymbol{M}_{LE}]$, $\Omega_{ED} = [\boldsymbol{m}_{ED}, \boldsymbol{M}_{ED}]$, and $\Omega_{IN} = [\boldsymbol{m}_{IN}, \boldsymbol{M}_{IN}]$, where for each dimension $j \in Q_{HD} = \{LE, ED, IN\}$, $\boldsymbol{m}_j$ and $\boldsymbol{M}_j$ denote, respectively, the lower and upper bounds of attainment in j. The subscript "*H*" assigned to Q_{HD} indicates that it is the set of dimensions considered by the UNDP for defining the HDI. The attainable upper bound for a dimensional achievement is the maximum value that the society can obtain in the concerned dimension. Similarly, the lower bound is the lowest level of achievement below which materialization of achievement is ruled out.

Each of the three components of the HDI, W_{LE}, W_{ED}, and W_{IN}, the standardized attainments in the three dimensions, is a continuous function, defined on the respective space, and takes values in the interval [0, 1]. More precisely, $W_{LE} : \Omega_{LE} \to [0,1]$, $W_{ED} : \Omega_{ED} \to [0,1]$, and $W_{IN} : \Omega_{IN} \to [0,1]$. These three metrics are aspired to capture achievements in the three functionings: health, schooling, and income, for the purpose of enlargement of the capability set of the individuals in the society.

The specific forms of these three standards chosen by the UNDP are

$$W_{LE}(x_{LE}) = \frac{x_{LE} - m_{LE}}{M_{LE} - m_{LE}},\ W_{ED}(x_{ED}) = \frac{x_{ED} - m_{ED}}{M_{ED} - m_{ED}},\ \text{and}$$
$$W_{IN}(x_{IN}) = \frac{x_{IN} - m_{IN}}{M_{IN} - m_{IN}}.$$

These three welfare metrics, when taken in isolation, are normalized values of attainments in the corresponding dimensions. They are partial capability measurement functions. They are increasing in respective arguments. The common lower bound zero is achieved when the dimensional attainment x_j is at the minimum level $\boldsymbol{m}_j$. On the other hand, the upper bound one is reached if the attainment x_j is at the highest level $\boldsymbol{M}_j$, where $j \in Q_{HD}$.

The HDI is an equally weighted average of the standardized metrics W_{LIE}, W_{ED} and W_{IN} in the dimensions; health, schooling, and income, respectively. Formally,

$$HDI_{old} = \frac{1}{3} \sum_{j \in Q_{HD}} W_j. \tag{7.1}$$

Since its inception by the United Nations in 1990, it became a protocol to measure country-level degree of development. High expositional simplicity of this composite index made it quite appalling to many users. It came out to be the most successful multidimensional welfare metric in more than last two decades. It has been very influential. "So far only one measure has succeeded in challenging the hegemony of growth-centric thinking. This is known as the HDI, which turns 20 this year" (New York Times, 10 May, 2010). (A useful summary of the history of the HDI was provided by Klugman et al., 2011.)

Major critical issues of the HDI_{old} are concerning transformations of original variables, choice of dimensions, choice of weights assigned to dimensional welfare standards, and aggregation of these standards. Logged income ensures that the index demonstrates the sensible property of diminishing marginal gain from additional income. For the other dimensions, these gains are constant. The selection of dimensions and weights on corresponding welfare standards is an issue of value judgments (see Chapter 1). Aggregation of dimensional metrics means the choice of a specific composite index. Any aggregation implicitly defines the trade-off, the marginal social rate of substitution, between dimensional attainments. Because of additivity across dimensional standardized attainments, HDI_{old} treats any two dimensions as perfect substitutes. The HDI_{old} contour is a negatively sloped straight line.

The perfect substitutability assumption, which has been criticized substantially, can be avoided if we adopt "Chakravarty's aggregation formula" (Ravallion, 2011b, p. 476). Using Ravallion's (Ravallion, 2012) notation, the generalized form of the old HDI, characterized by Chakravarty (Chakravarty, 2003), can be written as

$$HDI^C = \frac{1}{3}\sum_{j\in Q_{HD}} f(W_j), \tag{7.2}$$

where $f : [0,1] \rightarrow [0,1]$ is increasing and strictly concave with $f(0) = 0$ and $f(1) = 1$. These restrictions on f can be deduced from primitive axioms (see (Chakravarty, 2003), Theorem 1). Strict concavity of f ensures imperfect substitutability. Given the assumptions about f, the three axioms that lead to the additive structure of HDI^C are normalization (when all the dimensionwise components $f(W_j)$ assume a constant value, then the HDI value will coincide with it), symmetry in the components $f(W_j)$ across dimensions, and consistency in aggregation (HDI for a sum of finite number of component-level indices equals the sum of component-level HDIs). Linearity of HDI^C in componentwise indices drops out as an implication of the consistency axiom. Strict concavity of f guarantees that HDI^C exhibits the plausible requirement of diminishing marginal gain from an extra unit of attainment in any dimension. (Note that log transformation of income is not necessary in HDI^C. The reason is that the transformation $f(W_j)$ of W_j itself is strictly concave in dimensional attainment x_j, where $j \in Q_{HD}$ is arbitrary.) The conditions $f(0) = 0$ and $f(1) = 1$ ensure that the attainable lower and upper bounds of HDI^C are, respectively, 0 and 1.

Given that f is differentiable, the trade-off, the marginal social rate of substitution, between attainments in any two dimensions $j, k \in Q_{HD}$, becomes $\frac{f'(W_j)}{f'(W_k)}\left(\frac{M_k - m_k}{M_j - m_j}\right)$, where f' stands for the first order derivative of f. This trade-off satisfies an independence principle: independence of the attainments in the remaining dimension of Q_H. The contours of the generalized HDI, HDI^C, involving the two dimensions are strictly convex to the origin. As we go down along a contour, the society has to give up more units of attainments in dimension k to get an additional unit of attainment in dimension j. This follows from strict concavity of f, equivalently, from decreasingness of f'.

It may be worthwhile to investigate the special case of HDI^C that corresponds to $f(W_j) = (W_j)^r$, where $0 < r < 1$ is a constant. This parametric restriction ensures strict concavity of f. The constant $(r - 1)$ is the elasticity of the marginal gain with respect to achievement standardized between 0 and 1 in any dimension. The corresponding special case of HDI^C becomes

$$HDI_r^C = \frac{1}{3}\sum_{j\in Q_{HD}} (W_j)^r. \tag{7.3}$$

The old HDI drops out as a polar case of this parametric form of HDI for $r = 1$. In HDI_r^C perfect substitutability between dimensions is possible if and only if $r = 1$. Since HDI_r^C is a composite measure, it is factor decomposable, a property that often becomes helpful in policy applications (see Chapters 1 and 2).

In 2010, the UNDP suggested the following new functional form for HDI:

$$HDI_{new} = \prod_{j\in Q_{HD}} (W_j)^{\frac{1}{3}}, \tag{7.4}$$

where all the three-dimensional welfare metrics are assumed to be positive, that is, $W_j \in (0, 1]$ for all $j \in Q_H$. In HDI_{new}, GDP was replaced by Gross National Income (GNI), still at purchasing power parity, and logged. In the dimension education, literacy and gross enrolment rate were substituted by the mean years of schooling and the expected years of schooling, the years of schooling that a child expects to have, given the current enrolment rates. Note that for any $j \in Q_H$, if attainment x_j is at the minimum level $\boldsymbol{m}_j$, then the Cobb–Douglas functional form $\prod_{j\in Q_{HD}} (W_j)^{\frac{1}{3}}$ becomes 0, and this happens irrespective of how large the other welfare metrics are. (For this reason, we assume at the outset that W_js are positive for all $j \in Q_{HD}$.) Further, logarithmic transformation of income was not necessary for satisfaction of decreasingness of marginal gains since the transformation $(W_j)^{\frac{1}{3}}$ itself is increasing and strictly concave (see also Ravallion, 2011b, 2012). One major objective behind adoption of this Cobb–Douglas specification was to avoid "perfect substitutability across dimensions" (UNDP, 2010, p. 15) in the HDI_{old}.

Following Ravallion (2011b, 2012), we now look at several implications of the switch to the multiplicative form HDI_{new} from the additive structure given in HDI_{old}. "The effect on the weights" of shifting to the new functional form, the old one can be evaluated using the ratio between two marginals $\frac{\partial HDI_{new}}{\partial x_j}$ and $\frac{\partial HDI_{old}}{\partial x_j}$, which can be written as $\frac{HDI_{new}}{W_j}$. One implication of this switch is lowering of weights on longevity for all but five countries. Further, because of adoption of the Cobb–Douglas form, in richer countries, an extra life is assigned much higher value than in poor ones (see also (Klugman et al., 2011)). In addition, much higher valuation is assigned to education than to income.

The imperfect substitutability requirement can be imposed initially as an axiom to deduce a functional form for HDI instead of suggesting an HDI formula and then checking whether the suggested formula verifies this requirement. Chakravarty (Chakravarty, 2011a) showed that the only functional form for the HDI that satisfies the independence principle, symmetry, linear homogeneity (an equiproportionate scaling up of all dimensional welfare metrics will scale up the HDI by the proportionality factor itself), and normalization is given by

$$HDI_r = \left(\frac{1}{3}\sum_{j\in Q_{HD}} (W_j)^r\right)^{\frac{1}{r}}, 0 < r < 1. \tag{7.5}$$

Evidently, $(HDI_r)^r$, an increasing transformation of HDI_r, becomes identical to HDI_r^C for all $0 < r < 1$. Consequently, the rankings of any two societies provided by HDI_r and HDI_r^C coincide.

Ravallion (Ravallion, 2012) refers to HDI_C as "an alternative HDI with less troubling tradeoffs" (p. 206).[2] "The less appealing properties of the new index could have been avoided to a large extent, while allowing imperfect substitutability, by using the alternative index proposed here, exploiting the aggregation function proposed by Chakravarty (Chakravarty, 2003) – in fact a straightforward generalization of the functional form used by the old HDI" (Ravallion, 2012, p. 208). According to Zambrano (Zambrano, 2016), "while the Chakravarty indices clearly exhibit more sensible trade-offs than the HDI, the HDI produces more sensible rankings than the Chakravarty indices" (p. 1).

The Cobb–Douglas procedure of aggregation considered in (7.4) was characterized in a recent contribution by Zambrano (Zambrano, 2014). The axioms invoked for this purpose are the weak Pareto principle (see Chapter 1), symmetry, a separability condition that says that of two societies, if welfare metrics of one are at least as large as those of the other in two dimensions, then their ranking by human development should hold for all common values of the metric in the third dimension, subsistence (no trade-off is possible when the sociality's performance in a dimension is the worst), normalization, and a condition

2 He also looks at implications of the implicit trade-offs in details.

allowing flexibility in the ways of contributions of higher values of dimensional welfare metrics toward enhancement of human development. A general multiplicative form of the HDI_{new} was also considered by Desai (1991) and Sagar and Najam (1998).

One common feature of the HDI_{old} and its alternatives and variants analyzed in this chapter is that they do not incorporate inequalities in the distributions of health, education, and income. The reason behind this is that they are based on macro-level attainments.[3] Hicks (Hicks, 1997) and Foster, López-Calva and Székely (Foster et al., 2005) suggested modified versions of the HDI by taking into account distributional sensitivity. Following a suggestion put forward by Anand and Sen (1994a), Hicks suggested the use of the arithmetic mean of the dimensional Gini welfare functions as an alternative index. Formally, $HDI_H = \frac{1}{3} \sum_{j \in Q_{HD}} W_G^j$, where W_G^j is the Gini welfare function, which is also termed as the Gini mean and the Sen mean, for standardized attainments in dimension j. Hence, HDI_H is the simple average of the components of the Gini welfare dashboard of well-being dimensions (see Chapter 1).

Foster, López-Calva and Székely (Foster et al., 2005) suggested a modified index using the Atkinson–Kolm–Sen aggregation principle (see Chapter 1). They first employed the symmetric mean of order $\theta < 1$ of normalized or standardized attainments in a dimension as the dimensional welfare metric (see Chapter 1). Then these dimensional welfare standards are aggregated once again by applying the Atkinson–Kolm–Sen criterion. Formally, for any $j \in Q_H$, $W_j = \left(\frac{1}{n} \sum_{k=1}^{n} (x_{jk})^\theta \right)^{\frac{1}{\theta}}$, where x_{jk} is the normalized attainment of individual k in dimension j. (For sources of these micro-level observations, see the Technical Notes, Human Development Report, 2015). For $\theta = 0$, this standard reduces to the geometric mean of the attainments. The modified index is then given by

$$HDI_{FLS} = \left(\frac{1}{3} \sum_{j \in Q_{HD}} (W_j)^\theta \right)^{\frac{1}{\theta}}, \theta < 1.$$

Herrero et al. (Herrero et al., 2010) characterized the geometric mean of dimensional egalitarian equivalents of standardized micro-level attainments as a social evaluation index. The egalitarian equivalent associated with a dimension is a positive-valued function of standardized attainments in it, which, if

3 On various related issues, including choice of dimensions, aggregation formula, absence of distributional judgments, and so on, see, among others, Hicks and Streeten (1979), Ram (1982), Osberg (1985), Hopkins (1991), Kelley (1991), McGillivray (1991), McGillivray and White (1993), Anand and Sen (1994a,b), Aturupane et al. (1994), Srinivasan (1994), Gormely (1995), Ravallion (1997, 2011a), Noorbakhsh (1998), Crafts (1997, 2002), Lal (2000), Philipson and Soares (2001), Alkire (2002), Booysen (2002), Osberg and Sharpe (2002), Chatterjee (2005), Becker et al. (2005), Ranis et al. (2006), Cherchye et al. (2008), Grimm et al. (2008), Seth (2009), Kovacevic (2010), Prados de la Escosura (2010), Chakravarty (2011b), Herrero et al. (2012), Pinar et al. (2013), and Foster et al. (2013).

replaces the similarly transformed attainments in the dimension, keeping all other similar converted attainments unchanged, makes the distributions of actual transformed attainments socially equivalent.

For a partitioning of the population into male and female subgroups, the ratio between the HDIs of the latter and the former subgroups is known as the gender development index. It is a scalar representation of the gender disparity with respect to achievements in the three dimensions incorporated in the HDI formulation. Similarly, the gender parity index is employed to assess the relative performance of females and males in a dimension of well-being. More precisely, it is defined as the ratio between the value of a summary measure of attainments in a dimension for females and that of males. For these indices to be well defined, we assume that for males, they assume positive values. As a result, they are bounded below by zero, which is achieved when the attainments of the females are at their respective lowest levels. When they take on the value 1, we can say that parity between the two sexes has been achieved in terms of the objective for which the index is designed. A value of each of them greater than unity means that females are better off than the males, whereas a value of less than 1 indicates that the males are better off. The less is the value of the measure than 1, the worse becomes the performance of the females.

In a recent contribution, Zheng and Zheng (2015) made an assessment of human development ranking using a truth value function, which indicates the probability whether a randomly drawn bundle of weights will assign a higher rank to a country than another in the human development profile. According to Streeten (Streeten, 1994, p. 235), in the measurement of human development, "not only are the weights of the three components arbitrary, but also what is excluded and what is included." Zheng and Zheng's (2015) evaluation regards this as a source of vagueness in human development measurement.

7.3 Human Poverty Index

It was noted that a high value of the HDI does not necessarily mean low level of poverty (UNDP, 1999). Consequently, keeping watch on poverty is important for policy formulation of a country, irrespective of the HD position obtained by the country. In 1997, the UNDP suggested the HPI, a composite index of multidimensional poverty, which becomes helpful for this purpose (see also Sen and Anand (1997)). The objective of this section is to scrutinize the HPI from different perspectives.

Let Q_{HP} stand for the set of dimensions that are relevant to the measurement of human poverty. Let p_j denote the proportion of persons suffering from deprivation in dimension $j \in Q_{HP}$. Then the general formula for HPI can be defined as

$$HPI = \left(\sum_{j \in Q_{HP}} w_j (p_j)^{\varepsilon} \right)^{\frac{1}{\varepsilon}}, \varepsilon \geq 1, \tag{7.6}$$

where $w_j > 0$ is the weighted assigned to dimension j $\left(\sum_{j \in Q_{HP}} w_j = 1\right)$. The identical values of w_j chosen by the UNDP are $\frac{1}{3}$ or $\frac{1}{4}$, depending on whether the evaluation is performed for the developing or developed countries. Under the strict inequality $\varepsilon > 1$, the poverty contours comes out to be strictly convex to the origin. As the value of ε rises, higher weight is assigned to the dimension with higher deprivation. The elasticity of substitution between any two dimensions is given by $\frac{1}{(\varepsilon - 1)}$. For $\varepsilon = 1$, we get a straight-line isopoverty curve, and the associated dimensions are perfect substitutes. On the other hand, if $\varepsilon \to \infty$, $HPI \to \max_{j \in Q_{HP}} \{p_j\}$. The poverty contours become rectangular, and the underlying dimensions are perfect complements. Initially, the three dimensions included in the formulation were longevity, knowledge, and decent standard of living, and later, a fourth dimension, social exclusion, was added for rich countries. In either case, the value of the parameter ε was set equal to 3 to assign "additional but not overwhelming weight to areas of more acute deprivation" (UNDP, 2005, p. 342). (For recent discussions, see also Aaberge and Brandolini, 2015; Duclos and Tiberti, 2016.)

For developing countries, Q_{HP} includes longevity, knowledge, and decent living standard. The deprived proportions of population in the first two dimensions are defined, respectively, by proportion of newborns not expected to survive up to 40 and proportion of illiterate adults. For the third dimension, it is defined as the unweighted average of the proportion of the population without access to drinking water, population proportion without access to health services, and the proportion of underweight children aged less than 5. For developed countries, the deprived proportions in the four dimensions are, respectively, proportion of persons whose life expectancy is below 60 years of age, proportion of illiterate adults, and proportion of the population living below the poverty line, the long-term unemployment rate.

Chakravarty and Majumder (2005) developed an axiomatic characterization of the following variant of HPI:

$$HPI^C = \sum_{j \in Q_{HP}} w_j (p_j)^{\varepsilon}, \varepsilon \geq 1. \tag{7.7}$$

Note that HPI^C and HPI are ordinally equivalent, that is, the former can be obtained from the latter by applying an increasing transformation. Formally, $HPI^C = (HPI)^{\varepsilon}$. In HPI^C, the overall HPI^C human poverty is determined by weighted average of the dimensional human poverty levels. Obviously, HPI^C is factor decomposable. This is an advantage of this summary measure of human poverty. For simplicity, assume that the dimensions in HPI^C are equally weighted, which may result either from "an 'agnostic' attitude …or from the lack of information about some kind of 'consensus' view" (Aaberge and Brandolini, 2015, p. 153). Then a direct application HPI^C enables us to determine the percentage contributions made by different dimensions to global poverty. Clearly, the high contributing dimensions deserve attention from policy point of view for reducing their contributions so that a lower position in human poverty profile is obtained. High contributing dimensions may be regarded as sources of accumulated poverty within a country. In consequence, the policy evaluators can judge why the country has more human poverty than another, formulate policies to reduce appropriate deficiencies, and redesign the priorities of the country.

Evidently, similarly to HDI, HPI is also distributionally insensitive. Because of their focus on dimension-by-dimension attainments/deprivations, "both of these measures are better understood as composite indicators of unidimensional indices" (Duclos and Tiberti, 2016, p. 695). UNDP recently started using the multidimensional poverty index (MPI) in its annual reports on human development. The MPI identifies multiple deprivation in the three principal dimensions of life, namely education, health, and standard of living (Alkire and Santos, 2010). It aggregates the deprivations of those for whom weighted proportion of deprived dimensions does not fall below a cutoff proportion of dimensions in which individuals are regarded as poor (see Chapter 3). By concentrating only on such individuals, MPI takes into account deprivations of individuals who are affected by multiple deprivations (see Chapter 3). This index is factor decomposable and hence has interesting policy appeals. (For further discussions on the MPI, see, among others, Alkire, 2016; Duclos and Tiberti, 2016; Klasen and Dotter, 2014; Pogge and Wisor, 2016; Silber, 2011; and Calderon and Kovacevic, 2014).

7.4 Gender Inequality Index

Gender inequality deals with inequality in the distributions of achievements of individuals belonging to the categories "male" and "female," which are denoted by MA and FE, respectively, in the following three dimensions: empowerment, labor market, and reproductive health. The construction of the UNDP gender inequality index involves a sequence of aggregations. At the outset, for each category, a well-being standard is deduced by aggregating the dimensional achievements of individuals belonging to both the sexes. These categorywise well-being indices are then combined to arrive at an overall measure of social well-being, from which the gender inequality index is deduced by taking proportionate shortfall of the global well-being standard from a reference measure of well-being. This is Kolm's (Kolm, 1977) individualistic approach, applied to the measurement of gender inequality. It reverses the procedure adopted by a composite index (see Chapter 1). In order to ensure positivity of dimensional attainments, it is assumed that a minimum value of 0.1% is chosen for all attainments.

In examining gender inequality in this section, we follow the UNDP definitions of the dimensions. However, the functional form of the index, we analyze, is more general than the one proposed by the UNDP. (See the technical notes provided by the Human Development Report 2015, UNDP (2015).) For each of the two sexes, empowerment is based on the share of parliament seats (PR_k) and attainment at secondary and higher education levels (SE_k), where $k = MA, FE$. For the dimension labor market, the indicator is taken as the labor market participation rate ($LFPR_k$), proportion of population that is either employed or actively searching for employment, where $k = MA, FE$. For women and girls, the reproductive health dimension is inversely related to the indicators, maternal mortality ratio (MMR), and adolescent fertility rate (AFR). Evidently, the two indicators in this dimension are unique to women and girls.

The first step toward the formation of the index is the construction of categorywise well-being functions. We follow the Atkinson–Kolm–Sen aggregation rule here. For women and girls, it is defined as

$$W_{FE}=\left(\frac{1}{3}\left[\left(\left(\frac{10}{MMR}\cdot\frac{1}{AFR}\right)^{\frac{1}{2}}\right)^{\theta}+\left((SE_{FE}.PR_{FE})^{\frac{1}{2}}\right)^{\theta}+(LFPR_{FE})^{\theta}\right]\right)^{\frac{1}{\theta}}, \quad (7.8)$$

and for men and boys, the definition is

$$W_{MA}=\left[\frac{1}{3}\left[1^{\theta}+\left((SE_{MA}.PR_{MA})^{\frac{1}{2}}\right)^{\theta}+(LFPR_{MA})^{\theta}\right]\right]^{\frac{1}{\theta}}, \quad (7.9)$$

where $\theta < 1$. For $\theta = 0$, they reduce respectively to $\sqrt[3]{\left(\frac{10}{MMR}\cdot\frac{1}{AFR}\right)^{\frac{1}{2}}\times(SE_{FE}.PR_{FE})^{\frac{1}{2}}\times LFPR_{FE}}$ and $\sqrt[3]{\left(1.(SE_{MA}.PR_{MA})^{\frac{1}{2}}\right)\times(LFPR_{MA})}$, the geometric means of the respective welfare metrics at the category levels. For each category, the attainment in the empowerment dimension is defined as the square root of the associated indicators. For women and girls, attainment in reproductive health is defined by taking well-defined monotone decreasing transformations of the reverse indicators. For men and boys, this attainment is taken as 1. The multiplicative factor of the inverse maternal mortality ratio ensures truncation of the maternal mortality at a minimum of 10. For $\theta = 0$, they coincide with the UNDP formulae.

In the UNDP report, the overall well-being is defined as the harmonic mean of the categorywise well-being levels. A more general way is to define it as the symmetric mean of order $\theta < 1$. More precisely, the global index may be defined as

$$W_{\theta}(W_{MA}, W_{FE}) = \begin{cases} \left(\frac{1}{2}[(W_{MA})^{\theta}+(W_{FE})^{\theta}]\right)^{\frac{1}{\theta}}, \theta < 1, \theta \neq 0, \\ (W_{MA}.W_{FE})^{\frac{1}{2}}, \theta = 0. \end{cases} \quad (7.10)$$

The UNDP index corresponds to the case $\theta = -1$. Higher weights are assigned to the minimum of the two quantities W_{MA} and W_{FE} as the value of θ decreases. As $\theta \to -\infty$, W_θ approaches $\min\{(W_{MA}, W_{FE})\}$. Adler (2012) argued in favor of using this welfare standard for situations that have highly relevant social implications.

Now, for each of the dimensions' empowerment and labor market, the norm is obtained by taking simple average of the respective category-level attainments. More precisely,

$$\overline{Empowerment} = \frac{(SE_{MA}.PR_{MA})^{\frac{1}{2}} + (SE_{FE}.PR_{FE})^{\frac{1}{2}}}{2} \text{ and } \overline{LFPR_{MA}} = \frac{LFPR_{MA} + LFPR_{FE}}{2}.$$

Finally, $\overline{Health} = \frac{\left(\frac{10}{MMR} \cdot \frac{1}{AFR}\right)^{\frac{1}{2}} + 1}{2}$. The reference standard is then deduced by aggregating the norm attainments defined earlier. Formally, $W_{MA,FE} = \left[\frac{1}{3}\left[\overline{(Empowerment)}^{\theta} + \overline{(LFPR)}^{\theta} + \overline{(Health)}^{\theta}\right]\right]^{\frac{1}{\theta}}$. The particular case $\sqrt[3]{\overline{Empowerment}.\overline{LFPR}.\overline{Health}}$ that corresponds to the case $\theta = -1$ was chosen by the UNDP for the required purpose.

The gender inequality can now be defined as

$$I_\theta(MA, FE) = 1 - \frac{W_\theta(W_{MA}, W_{FE})}{W_{MA,FE}}. \tag{7.11}$$

It determines the size of welfare loss resulting from inequality in the distributions of dimensional attainments across sexes. For $\theta = 1$, there is perfect substitutability between the sexwise welfare standards in the numerator. As the value of θ goes down, it becomes more concerned with lower of the two sexwise welfare standards. Consequently, the choice of the parameter θ will represent society's concern about gender inequality. For $\theta = -1$, it coincides with the UNDP index. It is bounded between 0 and 1, where the minimum value 0 is achieved when men and women are treated equally in terms of dimensional attainments.

7.5 Better Life Index

The better life index launched by the Organization for Economic Co-operation and Development (OECD) in May 2011 brings together information on 11 indicators related to material living conditions and quality of life to arrive at a summary measure of welfare. The dimensions reflecting material living conditions chosen are housing, income, and jobs. On the other hand, the dimensions selected providing evidence of quality of life are community, education, environment, governance, health, life satisfaction, safety, and work-life balance. Most of the dimensions consist of more than one indicator, so that as a whole 24 indicators were taken into account. Each of the indicators was normalized between 0 and 1. (See Boarini and Mira D'Ercole, 2013); and (Durand, 2015), for additional details). The index empowers us to compare well-being across countries.

To define the index formally, we write d for the number of dimensions considered. The corresponding vector of normalized macro-level indicators is denoted by $(m^1, m^2, \dots, m^d)$. This vector is assigned to each individual in an n person society. When assigned to individual i, it denotes the ith row of an $n \times d$ outcome matrix X. The jth column of this matrix gives the outcomes of all individuals in dimension j.

The vector of positive weights assigned to different dimensional indicators is given by $w = (w_1, w_2, \dots, w_d)$, where $\sum_{j=1}^{d} w_j = 1$. The choice of these weights is a matter of value judgment. Alternative weighting schemes have been suggested in the literature.[4] The OECD better life index can now be formally defined as

$$BIL_{OECD}(X; w) = \frac{1}{n}\sum_{i=1}^{n}\sum_{j=1}^{d} m^j w_j. \tag{7.12}$$

The better life index defined above is simply the mean across all individuals of a weighted average of macro-level indicators. A higher value of this composite index means that the extent of well-being is better. By construction, BIL_{OECD} includes a higher number of dimensions than the HDI. Furthermore, BIL_{OECD} allows flexibility in the choice of dimensional indicators, whereas the HDI attaches equal importance to its three indicators.

However, BIL_{OECD} is not distribution-sensitive. In a recent contribution, Decancq (Decancq, 2015) suggested a multidimensional distribution-sensitive better life index. It follows the sequential aggregation steps considered in Bosmans, Decancq and Ooghe (Bosmans et al., 2015). The construction of the index requires a micro-level data set on individual outcomes. Let x_{ij} stand for the outcome of individual i in dimension j. The $1 \times d$ vector $x_{i.}$ specifies the outcomes of individual i in different dimensions. It is the ith row of an $n \times d$ outcome matrix X whose jth column describes the distribution of outcomes in dimension j among n individuals of the society. The individual outcomes can now be aggregated to construct a measure of individual well-being using a

4 The weighting scheme proposed by Mizobuchi (2014) relies on data envelopment analysis. Markovic et al.'s (2015) suggestion for choosing weights is based on i-distance approach. A sensitivity analysis of the ranking of the countries based on the choice of weights was carried out by Kasparian and Rolland (2012).

CES-type aggregation. Formally,

$$W(x_{i.}; w) = WB(x_{i.}; w; \beta) = \left(\sum_{j=1}^{d} w_j x_{ij}^{\beta} \right)^{\frac{1}{\beta}}, \quad \beta < 1, \ \beta \neq 0, \tag{7.13}$$

where $w_j s$ are the same as in (7.12) and β is related to the complementarity between different dimensions of well-being. (See Equations (2.19a) and (2.19b) in Chapter 2 and the related discussion.)

The individual well-being functions are then averaged by applying once again a CES-type operator to achieve a social well-being function SW. Analytically,

$$SW(W(x_{i.}); \alpha) = \left(\frac{1}{n} \sum_{i=1}^{n} W(x_{i.}; w)^{\alpha} \right)^{\frac{1}{\alpha}}, \quad \alpha < 1, \ \alpha \neq 0. \tag{7.14}$$

The parameter α reflects different judgments on evaluation of social well-being involving individual well-beings. As its value goes down, $SW(X)$ becomes more concerned with the well-beings of the worse-off persons. By setting $\alpha = 1$, we deduce social well-being as an arithmetic of individual well-beings. As $\alpha \to -\infty$, social well-being coincides with the well-being of the worst-off person. (See Equations (2.20a) and (2.20b) of Chapter 2.)

By substituting the form of $W(x_{i.}; w)$ given by (7.13) into (7.14), we derive the following explicit form of the distribution-sensitive better life index:

$$BLI_D(X; \beta; \alpha) = \left(\frac{1}{n} \sum_{i=1}^{n} \left(\left(\sum_{j=1}^{d} w_j x_{ij}^{\beta} \right)^{\frac{1}{\beta}} \right)^{\alpha} \right)^{\frac{1}{\alpha}}. \tag{7.15}$$

The subscript D is used to signify that it was first analyzed by Decancq (Decancq, 2015). Two important differences between the OECD index and this distribution-sensitive index are worthy of analysis. While BLI_{OECD} uses a macro-level data set, construction of BLI_D requires a micro-level data set. Further, the latter involves two normative parameters α and β in order to take into account distributional sensitivity. But no such parameter appears in the former. For $\alpha < \beta$, a correlation-increasing switch between any two dimensions decreases BLI_D. (See the discussion on the multidimensional inequality index given by Equation (2.22). See also (Bourguignon, 1999).) For $\alpha = \beta$, BLI_D shows insensitivity to a correlation-increasing switch, a property possessed by BLI_{OECD} as well. (See also Foster et al., 2005, for a similar index suggested for human development.) However, there is no a priori reason for equality between the two parameters to hold.

Decancq (Decancq, 2015) defined a "potential BLI_D," the value of BLI_D when $\alpha = 1$, and the outcome matrix X is replaced by its smoothed counterpart X_{λ}. The smoothed matrix is obtained from X by replacing its entries in the jth column by the mean of outcomes in dimension j, where $j = 1, 2, \ldots, d$. The shortfall of the ratio between the actual BLI_D and the potential BLI_D, from unity, gives us the loss resulting from multidimensional inequality. As a result, BLI_D becomes the product of the gap between one and this loss and potential BLI_D. While the potential BLI_D depends on the average levels of outcomes, the loss resulting from inequality depends explicitly on the multidimensional distribution. Thus, the decomposition is a natural way of representation of trade-off between average outcomes and inequality (see Bosmans et al., 2015).

7.6 Active Citizenship Composite Index

The active citizenship composite indicator is a summary measure of value-based participation of the citizens, developed within a European context, with a view to reduce the gaps between citizens and governing bodies and increasing social attachment. Here our discussion on this composite index will be brief and analytical. Detailed discussions are available in Hoskins et al. (2006) and Mascherini and Hoskins (2008).

The construction of the indicator relies on 63 basic indicators, which were classified under four dimensions, and 19 European countries were covered. The data were drawn mainly from European Social Survey, 2002. Four dimensions of active citizenship considered are "participation in political life," "participation in civil society," "participation in community life," and "values." The indicators covered under the first dimension, participation in political life, may take the forms of association with a political party in terms of becoming its member, renewal of membership on a regular basis, donating money, working for the party, taking part in voting and delegation of women in the country's parliament, and so on. In total, 11 indicators were identified under this dimension.

The second dimension, participation in civil society, refers to association with political nongovernment organizations. Four subdimensions chosen under this dimension were involvement in protest, activities of human rights organizations, environmental organizations, and trade union organizations. Protest may take the forms of signing a petition, attendance in a demonstration, and so on. Participation in human rights organizations may be described by the provision of voluntary assistance in terms of donation, work, and so on. Cooperation with environmental and trade union organizations may be characterized with respect to donation, accepting membership, providing voluntary work, and so on.

The third dimension, participation in community life, is concerned with activities that are more inclined toward the community and less toward political actions. This dimension has been divided into seven subdimensions, and in total, 25 base indicators were considered. Examples of subdimensions are attachment with cultural organizations, religious organizations, sport organizations, social organizations, and so on.

The fourth dimension, values, is a mixture of human rights and democracy. The three subdimensions under which 11 base indicators were clustered are human rights, democracy, and intercultural competencies. The three base indicators identified under the first subdimension are concerned with the same rights of immigrants, law against discrimination in the place of work, and law against racial contempt. The five base indicators covered under the next subdimension represent different aspects of a citizen's awareness about democracy. Finally, the three indicators that fall under the last subdimension deal with intercultural understanding, which is regarded as one of the major competencies of active citizenship.

Let S^i denote the set of all subdimensions of dimension i. Denote the set of all base indicators in subdimension j of dimension i by S^i_j. Since the dimensions, subdimensions, and base indicators are the same for all counties, the sets S^i and S^i_j are common across the countries. We write $\{c_1, c_2, \ldots, c_{19}\}$ for the set of countries covered in the analysis. For any country, $c \in \{c_1, c_2, \ldots, c_{19}\}$, any dimension i, subdimension $j \in S^i$, any base indicator $h \in S^i_j$, we write x^c_{ijh} for country c's outcome in base indicator h of subdimension j of dimension i. (See Nardo et al., 2005, for a discussion on measurement scales of base indicators. See also Chapter 1 for a general discussion on scales of measurability.)

Since different scales of measurement have been followed to construct the base indicators, the value of any arbitrary base indicator $h \in S^i_j$ is standardized using the following HDI-type normalization for the purpose of aggregation:

$$C^c_{ijh} = \frac{x^c_{ijh} - \min_c(x^c_{ijh})}{\max_c(x^c_{ijh}) - \min_c(x^c_{ijh})}. \tag{7.16}$$

For any country, these standardized achievements are aggregated sequentially across base indicators in a subdimension, subdimensions in a dimension, and dimensions to deduce the country-level indicator, the active citizenship composite index for the country.

Since the standardized indicators are independent of units of measurement, for any country c, they can now be combined across indicators in a subdimension of a given dimension i in the following simple way

$$C^c_{ij.} = \sum_{h\in S^i_j} w^i_{hj} C^c_{ijh}, \tag{7.17}$$

where $0 \leq w^i_{jh} \leq 1$ and $\sum_{h\in S^i_j} w^i_{hj} = 1$. In other words, each subdimensional achievement statistic is a linear weighted average of standardized indicators in the subdimension. Note that the weights vary from subdimension to subdimension in a dimension. Each $C^c_{ij.}$ is bounded between 0 and 1, where the lower bound is achieved in the case of the worst performance; the achievement in the base indicator in the subdimension coincides with its minimum value across the countries. Similarly, the upper bound is attained when the performance is the best. It has a monotonicity property; an increase in x^c_{ijh} does not decrease the value of $C^c_{ij.}$.

At the third step, subdimensional indicators in a dimension are clubbed together using a linear weighting system to arrive at a dimensional metric:

$$C^c_{i.} = \sum_{j \in S^i} w^i_j C^c_{ij.}, \tag{7.18}$$

where $0 \le w^i_j \le 1$ and $\sum_{j \in S^i} w^i_j = 1$.

Finally, in order to get a country-level summary measure C^c, the active citizenship composite index for country c, we amalgamate the dimensional metrics of the country by employing the same aggregation criterion that was followed in $C^c_{i.}$ and $C^c_{ij.}$. Formally,

$$C^c = \sum_{i=1}^{4} w^i C^c_{i.}, \tag{7.19}$$

where $0 \le w^i \le 1$, $\sum_{i=1}^{4} w^i = 1$, and $c \in \{c_1, c_2, \dots, c_{19}\}$ is arbitrary. Since the subdimensional, dimensional, and country-level indicators follow the same type of aggregation, C^c and $C^c_{i.}$ retain the basic properties of $C^c_{ij.}$, namely boundedness and monotonicity. We can rewrite C^c more explicitly in terms of C^c_{ijh}s as follows:

$$C^c = \sum_{i=1}^{4} w^i \sum_{j \in S^i} w^i_j \sum_{h \in S^i_j} w^i_{hj} C^c_{ijh}. \tag{7.20}$$

The active citizenship composite indicator within a European context combines the four dimensions of protest and social change, community life, representative democracy, and democratic values using a very simple sequential aggregation process. It has been proved to be a very useful device for monitoring the extents of citizenship in Europe.

7.7 Measuring Human Opportunity: A Counting Approach

The human opportunity index we analyze here is concerned with the inequality in the distribution of a profile of basic noncircumstantial opportunities available to individuals in a society (see Chapter 2, Section 2.4). It provides a way of accounting for differences in accesses to these opportunities across individuals. It demonstrates how equally individuals have accesses to these basic services required to maintain a standard living condition. The basic profile may include opportunity to achieve a health condition described by the category "good" or higher (see Chapter 3); opportunity to have an education status of just ability to read and write or higher (see Chapter 4); scope to earn a monthly income of $1000 or more; access to metropolitan water supply, sanitation, electricity, and so on. Let d be the number of such basic opportunities or dimensions. This is the number of elements in the profile of basic advantages. (The term "basic opportunities" is taken from Ferreira and Peragine, 2016, p. 778.)

Let T stand for the total number of types or circumstances. Let S^t be the set of persons of a particular type t in an n-person society. We denote the number of persons in S^t by n^t, that is, $|S^t| = n^t$. To identify the persons who belong to this set and additionally who have access to the basic advantages, we define the following intersection-type identification function $\rho_i^t(b)$:

$$\rho_i^t(b) = \begin{cases} 1 \text{ if person } i \text{ of type } t \text{ has access to the basic opportunities,} \\ 0, \text{otherwise.} \end{cases}$$

Then the number of persons of type of t enjoying the basic advantages can be specified by $|S_b^t| = n_b^t = \sum_{i \in S^t} \rho_i^t(b)$, and $p_b^t = \frac{n_b^t}{n^t}$ denotes the corresponding proportion of persons, where S_b^t is the subset of S^t consisting of individuals who are equipped with the basic advantages.

Out of a total of n^t persons in the set S^t, n_b^t is the number of persons in S^t with comparative advantage over the remaining $(n^t - n_b^t)$ persons in the set in terms of possession of the basic facilities. Then $n_b = \sum_{t=1}^{T} n_b^t$ is the total number of persons who enjoy the basic advantages, and the corresponding population proportion is $p_b = \frac{n_b}{n} = \sum_{t=1}^{T} \frac{n_b^t}{n^t} . \frac{n^t}{n} = \sum_{t=1}^{T} p_b^t . \frac{n^t}{n}$. The proportion p_b of the population that has access to the given opportunities is known as the overall coverage in the literature. Similarly, p_b^t is known as the coverage of type t (Paes de Barros et al., 2009). Hence, we apply here a counting method for identifying the proportion of persons who are endowed with the particularized facilities.

The human opportunity index we propose here has the following simple specification:

$$HOI = p_b(1 - I_O), \tag{7.21}$$

where $I_O = \frac{1}{2p_b} \sum_{t=1}^{T} w^t |p_b^t - p_b|$ indicates inequality in access to basic opportunities and $w^t = \frac{n^t}{n}$, the share of type t in the total population. The inequality index I_O has a structure similar to that of the Kuznets ratio, which is also known as the "maximum equalization percentage." This is because it determines the percentage of the total income that has to be transferred from earners above the mean to those below the mean with the objective of establishing perfect equality of incomes.[5] The index I_O is a measure of the extent of inequality of basic advantages that is explained by types. It achieves its lower bound 0 if all the individuals enjoy the basic facilities. The difference $(1 - I_O)$ may be treated as a measure of opportunity equity.

By definition, *HOI* is expressed as a multiplicative function of two factors: the level of coverage and opportunity equity. It is unambiguously bounded above by 1, which is achieved when all the individuals enjoy the basic advantages; otherwise, its value falls below 1. A higher value of *HOI* is desirable, and the index can serve as a tool to recommend policy for improving overall access to basic advantages and ensuring its equitable distribution. This can be achieved by making the basic facilities accessible to an increased number of individuals of one or more types. As a result, there will be increase in both opportunity equity and overall coverage, which we refer to as equity and efficiency components of opportunity.

There is a minor difference between the *HOI* proposed here and that suggested by Paes de Barros et al. (2009). While the latter authors consider one particular opportunity for children, we consider a collection of opportunities so that human opportunity may be regarded as a multidimensional phenomenon. The aggregations put through in the two cases are the same. (Roemer and Trannoy (2015), provide further discussion on the Paes de Barros et al., 2009, formulation.)

Yalonetzky (2012) considers many opportunities and employed dissimilarity-type indices to study opportunity inequality. Hence, it is a multidimensional approach as well, although opportunity-by-opportunity aggregation has been executed. Consequently, Yalonetzky's approach generates a composite index, and the opportunity measure analyzed in this section is an individualistic index.

7.8 Assessment of Progress toward Achievements in Millennium Development Goals

The Millennium Development Goals (MDGs) are numerically specified targets, adopted at the United Nations Millennium Summit in September 2000. The objective was to achieve them for improving the well-being of a population in different contexts – reduction in income poverty, hunger, disease, inadequacy of sufficing shelter, exclusion and promotion of gender equality, health, education, and environmental sustainability. The deadline year set was 2015. Within each goal, certain targets have been set, and corresponding to each target, there are one or more indicators (see http://www.un.org/milleniumgoals). Each of

---

5 Formally, for any income distribution $u \in \Re^n_{++}$ with mean income λ, the Kuznets ratio is defined as $K(u) = \frac{1}{2n\lambda} \sum_{i=1}^{n} |u_i - \lambda|$. By multiplying $K(u)$ with 2, we get the relative mean deviation, another well-known measure of income inequality.

these goals can be regarded as a dimension of well-being. Since these goals are concrete and unambiguously stated, they can be treated as norms for progress toward a clear targeted perception of development. Hence, an analysis concerning progress toward the achievements of the MDGs is highly desirable, and this, obviously, is to be carried out in a multidimensional phenomenon. As the MDGs have been designed for the purpose of reducing the constraints on people's ability to maintain a good living condition, inability to reach the targets may be termed as capability failure to achieve the goals.

In Millennium Development Goals Report, 2015, published by the UN, it was noted that the MDGs helped people across the world to improve living conditions. But it was also noted that progress is still necessary to form a world of honor for all.[6]

Despite the fact that the MDGs have been devised by the UN, country-level drives are necessary for their achievement. "The emerging post-2015 development agenda, including the set of Sustainable Development Goals, strives to reflect these lessons, build on our successes and put all countries, together, firmly on track towards a more prosperous, sustainable and equitable world" (Ki-Moon, 2015, p. 3). As a result from policy point of view, every poor country needs to assess its performance toward reaching the goals through sound monitoring.

Formulation of appropriate national efforts for monitoring progression for attainments of goals becomes an issue of major policy concern. Recognition of new actions and their implementation, including creation of additional resources and removal of barriers toward headway, may be necessary. An index of perceived progress at the level of each indicator, which specifies the level of reduction in deprivation desired, may be useful for this purpose. A simple average of such indictorwise measures, a composite index, which gives us a comprehensive picture of growth to be realized, can be employed to judge the performance of the economy.

To present this analytically, let $x_j \in [\boldsymbol{m}_j, \boldsymbol{M}_j]$ denote the macro-level outcome of indicator j, where $\boldsymbol{m}_j$ and $\boldsymbol{M}_j$ are, respectively, the minimum and maximum values that the indicator can assume. The upper and lower bounds can be interpreted from a general perspective (see Morris, 1979; Sen, 1981; Dasgupta and Weale, 1992; Dasgupta, 1993; Kakwani, 1993). For instance, if j is the per capita monthly income, then $\boldsymbol{m}_j$ and $\boldsymbol{M}_j$ can, respectively, be 0 and \$1000. The attainable upper bound $\boldsymbol{M}_j$ is the goal or targeted value of the indicator, and the lower bound $\boldsymbol{m}_j$ is attained when the economy has the worst performance with respect to the indicator. The deprivation function for this indicator is defined by $b_j = \frac{(M_j - x_j)}{(M_j - m_j)}$. It is simply the shortfall of the outcome of j divided by the maximum shortfall that may arise in the context. If outcome is minimal, $m_j = x_j$, then

6 Several studies have investigated countries' progression in different MDGs (see, e.g., Sahn and Stifel, 2003 and Esterly, 2009). See also Bourguignon et al. (2008, 2010).

deprivation is maximized, and it is minimized if outcome reaches the targeted value. A positive value of b_j signifies economy's failure with respect to achievement of the goal. The progression of the indicator toward its targeted value increases if and only if the level of associated deprivation reduces.

Let $b_j^o > 0$ be the deprivation of indicator $j \in Q$ in the base year t_0, where $Q = \{1, 2, \dots, d\}$ is the set of indicators. A value of 0 for deprivation means that the economy has already achieved its target in the indicator, and in such a case, the indicator does not come under the purview of our analysis. Similarly, $b_j^T \geq 0$ stands for the deprivation in the indicator in the target period t_T. More precisely, $b_j^0 = \frac{(M_j - x_j^o)}{(M_j - m_j)}$ and $b_j^T = \frac{(M_j - x_j^T)}{(M_j - m_j)}$, where x_j^o and x_j^T are, respectively, the macro-level outcomes of the indicator in the initial and target periods. Chakravarty and Majumder (2008) characterized the normalized difference $\frac{(b_j^o - b_j^T)}{b_j^0}$ as a measure of the size of desired progress toward arriving at a specified objective in deprivation in the target period in comparison with the base period. In other words, it can be termed as a quantifier of the size of reduction in deprivation desired for arriving at x_j^T from x_j^o. If x_j^T equals the target M_j, then the reduction sought is maximized. Since we have excluded $b_j^o = 0$ from our analysis, the measure is well defined.

Often from policy point of view, it may be necessary to monitor how much reduction in deprivation has been achieved over one or more subperiods of the global period $[t_0, t_T]$. Suppose that the global period $[t_0, t_T]$ has been partitioned into l subperiods $[t_0, t_1], [t_1, t_2], \dots, [t_{l-2}, t_{l-1}]$ and $[t_{l-1}, t_T]$, where $l \geq 2$ is arbitrary. Assume further that deprivations in the indicator have been observed for the periods $t_0, t_1, \dots, t_{l-1}$, which we denote by b_j^i, $i = 0, 1, 2, \dots, l-1$, respectively. Then $a_j^i = \frac{(b_j^i - b_j^{i+1})}{b_j^0}$ is the curtailment in deprivation realized, standardized as a proportion of the base year deprivation, over the periods $[t_i, t_{i+1}]$, $i = 0, 1, 2, \dots, l-2$. Evidently, the perceived progress index $\frac{(b_j^o - b_j^T)}{b_j^o}$ can be broken down as

$$\frac{(b_j^0 - b_j^T)}{b_j^o} = \sum_{i=0}^{l-2} a_j^i + \frac{b_j^{l-1} - b_j^T}{b_j^0}. \tag{7.22}$$

This decomposition, which Chakravarty and Majumder (2008) refer to as period consistency, enables a policy-maker to determine how much progress has already been made over the periods $[t_i, t_{i+1}]$, $i = 0, 1, 2, \dots, l-2$, and how much more progress needs to be made over the remaining period $[t_{l-1}, t_T]$. The second term on the right-hand side of the aforementioned equation, $\frac{b_j^{l-1} - b_j^T}{b_j^0}$, is the extent of failure that the society needs to reduce over the subperiod $[t_{l-1}, t_T]$ in order to arrive at targeted level of deprivation.

The global targeted progress index J can be defined as the arithmetic average of dimensionwise indices:

$$J = \frac{1}{d}\sum_{j=1}^{d} \frac{(b_j^o - b_j^T)}{b_j^o}. \tag{7.23}$$

The measure J determines the extent of reduction in deprivation sought globally to achieve global targeted deprivation quantity. The factor decomposability property enables us to calculate the contribution of each indicator to the global progress desired. These indicatorwise quantitative evaluations are of immense help in pinpointing the indicators whose contributions are higher. Such indicators require more attention from policy perspective for increasing the corresponding levels of desired deprivation reductions. Mobilization of resources from other sectors of the economy may be necessary in this context. Once we split up the global index by the period consistency property, the policy may be implemented at micro levels.

Tsui (Tsui, 1996) axiomatically characterized a multidimensional progress function, PR_T, with the objective of measuring a country's progress with respect to d indicators between the time periods, say, 1 and 2, which we refer to as initial and final periods, respectively. It can formally be defined as

$$PR_T(y_1, y_2, \dots, y_d; x_1, x_2, \dots, x_d) = \frac{\prod_{j=1}^{d}(M_j - y_j)^{r_j} - \prod_{j=1}^{d}(M_j - x_j)^{r_j}}{\prod_{j=1}^{d}(M_j - m_j)^{r_j}}, \tag{7.24}$$

where $0 < r_j < 1$ are constants for all $j \in Q$, and $y_j, x_j \in [\boldsymbol{m}_j, \boldsymbol{M}_j]$ denote the actual or observed macro-level outcomes of indicator j in periods 1 and 2, respectively. The numerator of (7.24) is simply the difference between aggregate measures of shortfalls of indicator outcomes in the initial and final periods from respective attainable upper bounds. The denominator is the maximum value that this aggregated shortfall can assume in any period. The restrictions $0 < r_j < 1$ follow from the requirements that PR_T is monotonic and verifies increasing difficulty of improvement. Monotonicity means that an increase in the outcome level reduces the value of PR_T. To understand the latter postulate, we follow Sen (1981), who argued that for some indicators such as life expectancy, improvement becomes harder as the outcome of the indicator becomes higher (see also Sen, 1992 and Dasgupta, 1993).

A reduction in the value of the aggregated shortfall in the final period increases the progress function, and the reverse trend in progress is observed if it goes down in the initial period. This measure summarizes improvement in overall well-being, measured in terms of indicatorwise absolute deprivations or shortfalls, between the two periods.[7] This is a multidimensional extension of a one-dimensional progress measure proposed by Kakwani (1993), which has been characterized and analyzed further by Chakravarty and Majumder (1996).

Chakravarty and Mukherjee (1999) proposed a unified approach for quantifying amelioration in the living standard between the considered periods in a multidimensional framework. Their index may be defined as

$$PR_{CM}(y_1, y_2, \dots, y_d; x_1, x_2, \dots, x_d) = \frac{1}{d}\sum_{j=1}^{d}(f(b_j^1) - f(b_j^2)), \tag{7.25}$$

where $b_j^1 = \frac{(M_j - y_j)}{(M_j - m_j)}$, $b_j^2 = \frac{(M_j - x_j)}{(M_j - m_j)}$, $j \in Q$; $f : [0,1] \to \mathfrak{R}_+^1$ is increasing, continuous, and strictly concave on the subdomain $(0,1]$ and $f(1) - f(0) = 1$. Increasingness and strict concavity of f are necessitated by satisfaction of monotonicity and increasing difficulty of improvement. The condition $f(1) - f(0) = 1$ ensures that PR_{CM} takes on the value 1 when $b_j^2 = 0$ and $b_j^1 = 1$ for all $j \in Q$, that is, when improvement is maximized. (Evidently, this stipulation holds also when deprivations in terms of absolute shortfalls are considered, as we do in PR_T.) Examples of the function f that fulfill the aforementioned conditions are $f_1(t) = t^r$, $0 < r < 1$ and $f_2(t) = \frac{2t}{(t+1)}$. The factor-decomposable measure PR_{CM} can isolate indicators with lower improvements and hence formulate appropriate policies for placing the society on a better position in terms of its well-being.

Permanyer (2013) introduced a multidimensional success function with the objective of comparing changes in outcomes with the changes that should be achieved to reach the targets in the final period, given the outcomes in the initial period. In other words, a success function verifies whether the outcome changes are sufficient to ensure arrival at the a priori given targets. In contrast, a progress function relies on indicatorwise deprivations between the two periods.

To present the success function formally, as before, let $y_j, x_j, \in [\boldsymbol{m}_j, \boldsymbol{M}_j]$ denote indicator j's outcomes in the initial and final periods, respectively. Permanyer (Permanyer, 2013) characterized the following success function for

7 In a recent paper, Permanyer (2016) analyzed the issue of ranking of societies using well-being improvement indices and shortfall improvement indices that rely on macro-based outcomes of indicators in a consistent way. The consistency condition requires that ranking of two societies with respect to respective well-being improvement functions should be identical to that generated by the shortfall improvement functions.

a specific indicator

$$s_j = s(x_j - y_j, \chi - y_j, y_j - \boldsymbol{m}_j)$$

$$= \begin{cases} 1 \; if \; x_j \geq \chi, \; if \; (y_j, x_j) \notin \{(\boldsymbol{m}_j, \boldsymbol{m}_j), (\boldsymbol{M}_j, \boldsymbol{M}_j)\}, \\ \dfrac{x_j - y_j}{\chi - y_j}, y_j \leq x_j < \chi, (y_j, x_j) \notin \{(\boldsymbol{m}_j, \boldsymbol{m}_j), (\boldsymbol{M}_j, \boldsymbol{M}_j)\}, \\ \dfrac{x_j - y_j}{y_j - \boldsymbol{m}_j}, x_j < y_j, (y_j, x_j) \notin \{(\boldsymbol{m}_j, \boldsymbol{m}_j), (\boldsymbol{M}_j, \boldsymbol{M}_j)\}, \\ 0, (y_j, x_j) \in \{(\boldsymbol{m}_j, \boldsymbol{m}_j), (\boldsymbol{M}_j, \boldsymbol{M}_j)\}. \end{cases}, \tag{7.26}$$

where χ is a function of the actual outcome y_j and the upper bound $\boldsymbol{M}_j$; $\chi = \chi(y_j, \boldsymbol{M}_j)$. For instance, χ can be a convex combination of y_j and $\boldsymbol{M}_j$ so that $\chi = c\boldsymbol{M}_j + (1 - c)y_j$, where $0 < c < 1$ is a constant. In other words, the target value lies in between the initial outcome and the upper bound. The value of c will depend on the specific indicator. As an illustrative example, if we think that targeted maternal mortality should be one-fourth of its current level, then $c = \frac{3}{4}$. Similarly, if current income poverty should go down by 50%, then $c = \frac{1}{2}$.

In the aforementioned specification for s_j, the second expression simply compares the progress $(x_j - y_j)$ experienced by the society with the targeted gap $(\chi - y_j)$ to be filled in for improvement. The third expression compares the progress with the declined situation $(y_j - \boldsymbol{m}_j)$. The first expression represents the situation when the society has fully achieved the goals. Finally, if there is no progress, then s_j will assume the value 0. The function s_j is bounded between −1 and 1, where the lower bound is attained if $x_j = \boldsymbol{m}_j$ (given that $(y_j - \boldsymbol{m}_j) > 0$).

The overall success function considered by Permanyer (2013) can now be defined as

$$S_{PE}(y_1, y_2, \ldots, x_d; x_1, x_2, \ldots, x_d) = 1 - \left(\sum_{j=1}^{d} w_j (1 - s_j)^{\varepsilon}\right)^{\frac{1}{\varepsilon}}. \tag{7.27}$$

where $\varepsilon \geq 1$ is a parameter, and w_js are positive weights adding up to 1. Clearly, S_{PE} is monotonic; an increase in each s_j increases its value. For $\varepsilon = 1$, it becomes the weighted average of indicatorwise successes. As $\varepsilon \to \infty$, $S_{PE} \to \min_{j \in Q}\{s_j\}$, the Rawlsian maximin success function. Given the weights, an increased value of the parameters assigns more importance to lower successes. The aggregated function S_{PE} gives us a comprehensive picture of success toward achievement of all targets. It is bounded between 0 and 1, where the upper bound arises when there is complete success for all indicators ($s_j = 1$ for all $j \in Q$). The lower bound arises if there is the lowest possible success for each indicator ($s_j = -1$ for all $j \in Q$). It satisfies a strict separability condition; for any partitioning of the indicators into two or more subgroups, the overall success of each subgroup can be calculated independently of the indicators of the other subgroups, and the global success can be determined by averaging the subgroup-level averages. One common feature of all the indices examined in this section is that they are composite indices, although they have been proposed for different purposes.

7.9 Air Quality Index

Since air quality is quite critical to our health and many other living conditions, management of air quality is a vital policy issue in the context of reduction of environmental risks. For this purpose, regular overseeing of pollutant concentrations is necessary so that necessary steps can be taken to ensure maintenance of air quality at the desired level. Consequently, monitoring schedules have been framed in different parts of the world for collection of data on gathering of major substances that pollute such as carbon monoxide (CO), nitrogen dioxide (NO_2), ozone (O_3), sulfur dioxide (SO_2), and particulate matter ($PM_{2.5}$, PM_{10}). Observation of each of them is necessary to administer the air quality properly.

Nevertheless, separate observations of the clustering levels of pollutants do not give us a comprehensive idea about air quality. In view of this, an aggregated measure that gives us an overall picture of air pollution, determined using observations of contaminantwise collection, becomes essential. A device that serves this purpose properly is an air quality index (AQI). It determines the effects of pollutants on air quality.

Each of the pollutants may be claimed to represent a dimension, and there is a level of concentration corresponding to the dimension. Each of these concentration levels becomes helpful in defining the respective one-dimensional indices of air quality, which can then be aggregated to construct a composite index. Hence, formation of an overall air quality index is multidimensional exercise.

In this section, we consider a composite index of air quality that relies on the methodology composed by the US Environmental Protection Agency (EPA) (2013). The EPA methodology is utilized for the evaluation of daily air quality. As per the EPA methodology, each dimensionwise concentration is converted into a one-dimensional index.

At the outset, the range of 1-hour and 8-hour concentrations for each pollutant is split up into the nonoverlapping subsets [0, 50], [51, 100], [101, 105], [151, 200], [201, 300], and 301 and above. (Any fractional value lying between any two subintervals is rounded to the nearest integer.) These subintervals correspond respectively to the categories good, moderate, unhealthy for sensitive groups, unhealthy, very unhealthy, and hazardous. (See Table 1 in The Technical Assistance Document for the Reporting of Daily Air Quality, released by the US Environmental Protection Agency in December 2013. EPA suggested the following truncations on the concentration figures of different pollutants:

CO – truncate to one decimal place; NO_2 – truncate to integer; O_3 – truncate to three decimal places; SO_2 – truncate to integer; $PM_{2.5}$ – truncate to one decimal place; and PM_{10} – truncate to integer.)

For any concentration level associated with a pollutant in a subinterval, a subinterval of values for the corresponding AQI subindex of the pollutant is specified. The lower and upper bounds of this subinterval are known as breakpoints that are respectively less than or equal to and greater than or equal to the concentration transmitted (see Table 2 of the report).

The index for dimension j is then defined as follows:

$$I_j = \frac{I_{HI} - I_{Lo}}{BP_{HI} - BP_{LO}}(C_j - BP_{LO}) + I_{Lo}, \tag{7.28}$$

where I_j = the (one-dimensional) index for dimension/pollutant j, C_j = the level of concentration of pollutant j, BP_{HI} = the breakpoint that is greater than or equal to C_j, BP_{LO} = the breakpoint that is less than or equal to C_j, I_{HI} = the AQI value corresponding to BP_{HI}, and I_{Lo} = the AQI value corresponding to BP_{LO}.

To illustrate the EPA methodology, we consider the following example taken from the EPA technical report. Given an 8-hour ozone value of 0.087, we note from Table 2 that it is contained in the interval [0.076, 0.095]. The lower and upper limits 0.076 and 0.095 are the respective breakpoints associated with this level of concentration. Note further that the value 0.087 corresponds to the subinterval [101, 150] of the grand interval [0, 500] showing the entire range of index values. Consequently, the value of AQI index corresponding to this level of ozone concentration becomes $\frac{(150-101)}{(0.095-0.076)}(0.087 - 0.076) + 101 = 129$. If both 1-hour and 8-hour concentrations are available for a pollutant, it is desirable to calculate AQI for each, and the higher AQI value is to be reported.

If AQI values for more than one pollutant are available, then the responsible pollutant is the one bearing the highest AQI value. This implicitly defines the overall AQI as the maximum value of AQIs across dimensions. EPA used this as a global measure. However, by concentrating on the maximum value of dimensionwise AQIs, AQIs corresponding to other pollutants whose health impacts may not also be good are ignored. For instance, suppose that in a society, a pollutant representing the category "hazardous" indicates the highest AQI. But the society is also affected by some pollutants whose categories are "very unhealthy" and "unhealthy." In such a case, effects of such pollutants should also be incorporated in the calculation of global AQI.

We may consider a general framework to suggest such a global index. Let S_p be the set of all pollutants/dimensions to be considered. Let $\overline{S}_p$ be that subset of S_p whose elements correspond to the categories "unhealthy for sensitive groups," "unhealthy," "very unhealthy," and "hazardous." Our objective is to aggregate one-dimensional AQIs that correspond to these categories. Assume that there are k dimensions in $\overline{S}_p$. Assume also that AQIs for dimensions in $\overline{S}_p$, which we denote by $AQI_1, AQI_2, \dots, AQI_k$, are nondecreasingly ordered, that is, $AQI_1 \leq AQI_2 \leq \cdots \leq AQI_k$. Then we suggest the use of

$$AQI_O = \frac{1}{k^\rho}\sum_{j=1}^{k}[j^\rho - (j-1)^\rho]AQI_j, \tag{7.29}$$

as a global air quality index, where $\rho > 1$ is a parameter. By construction, it is a composite index of air quality. Its value increases as the value of any one-dimensional AQI increases. Given the one-dimensional AQIs, as the parameter ρ increases more weights are assigned to higher AQIs in AQI_O. For $\rho = 1$, AQI_O becomes the arithmetic mean of dimensional AQIs. As $\rho \to \infty$, $AQI_O \to \max_{j \in \bar{S}_p}\{AQI_j\}$, the maximax index of air pollution. Since AQI_O employs an S-Gini type aggregation, we refer to it as the S-Gini global index of air quality (Donaldson and Weymark, 1980).

7.10 Concluding Remarks

Our deliberation on composite indices, conferred in Sections 7.2–7.9, is certainly not exhaustive. In this section, we provide some additional examples of such indices, which are also of high relevance.

The Index of Economic Freedom (IEF) is a device that summarizes the liberty of the individuals in a society to perform economic activities (Heritage Foundation, 2008). It relies on indices on outcomes in 10 dimensions that are related to economic freedom. All these dimensional indices are normalized between 0 and 100. Each of the 10 dimensional indices is calculated using a number of indicators in the dimension. The 10 dimensions taken into consideration are government size, property rights, freedom from corruption, and freedoms in terms of business, trade, fiscal, monetary, investment, financial, and labor (see heritage.org/index/book/methodology). The composite index, IEF, is calculated as the simple arithmetic average of dimensional indices. The IEF for 2016 ranks 157 countries with respect to its values, where a high value means a better performance in terms of economic freedom.

The Environmental Performance Index (EPI) is a summary statistic indicating the performance of a society with respect to its environmental conditions. Several versions of EPI exist (see (Esty et al., 2008)). The difference arises with respect to aggregation of the components. The construction of the 2016 version depends on nine dimensions representing health impacts, air pollution, impact of water and sanitation, water resources, agriculture, forests, fisheries, biodiversity and habitat, and climate and energy. Each of these dimensions contains one or more indicators. Consequently, aggregations at the levels of indicators and dimensions are necessary to arrive at a composite index that gives us an overall picture of environmental performance.

The green economy progress index, formulated by the United Nations Environmental Program (UNEP), focuses on a society's progress toward realizing a green economy. It has similarity with the indices designed for evaluation of progress toward achievements in Millennium Development Goals. The central idea underlying the index is to judge society's improvement with respect to well-being, social equity, environmental risks, and ecological scarcities. As a consequence, betterment of economic opportunities and growth accomplished by green economy policies, social equity generated by policies that lead to reduction in inequality and poverty, and polices aiming at reduced levels of environmental risks and ecological scarcities become a policy-maker's primary concerns in this context. (The detailed list of indicators can be found in Mueller, 2015).

References

Aaberge, R. and A. Brandolini. 2015. Multidimensional Poverty and Inequality. In A.B. Atkinson and F. Bourguignon (eds.), Vol. 2A, 141–216.

Adler, M.D. 2012. *Well-Being and Fair Distribution: Beyond Cost-Benefit Analysis.* Oxford: Oxford University Press.

Adler, M.D. and M. Fleurbaey (eds.) 2016. *Oxford Handbook of Well-Being and Public Policy.* New York: Oxford University Press.

Alkire, S. 2002. *Valuing Freedoms. Sen's Capability Approach and Poverty Reduction.* New York: Oxford University Press.

Alkire, S. 2016. The Capability Approach and Well-Being Measurement for Public Policy. In M.D. Adler and M. Fleurbaey (eds.), 615–644.

Alkire, S. and M. Santos. 2010. Acute Multidimensional Poverty: A New Index for Developing Countries. Human Development Research Paper 2010/11. New York: UNDP-HDRO.

Anand, S. and A.K. Sen. 1994a. Human Development Index: Methodology and Measurement. *Human Development Report Office Occasional Paper* 12, New York: United Nations Development Program.

Anand, S. and A.K. Sen. 1994b. The Income Component of the Human Development Index *Journal of Human Development* 1: 83–106.

Atkinson, A.B. and F. Bourguignon (eds.). 2015. *Handbook of Income Distribution,* Vol. 2A. Amsterdam: North Holland.

Aturupane, H., P. Glewwe, and P. Isenman. 1994. Poverty, Human Development and Growth: An Emerging Consensus? *American Economic Review* 84: 244–249.

Becker, G.S., T.J. Philipson, and R.R. Soares. 2005. The Quantity and Quality of Life and the Evolution of World Inequality. *American Economic Review* 95: 277–291.

Boarini, R. and M. Mira D'Ercole. 2013. Going beyond GDP: An OECD Perspective, *Fiscal Studies* 34: 289–314.

Booysen, F. 2002. An Overview and Evaluation of Composite Indices of Development. *Social Indicators Research* 59: 115–151.

Bosmans, K., K. Decancq, and E. Ooghe. 2015. What do Normative Indices of Multidimensional Inequality Really Measure? *Journal of Public Economics* 130: 94–104.

Bourguignon, F. 1999. Comment on Multidimensional Approaches to Welfare Analysis by E. Maasoumi. In J. Silber (ed.) *Handbook of Income Inequality Measurement*. London: Kluwer Academic, 477–484.

Bourguignon, F., A. Bénassy-Quéré, S. Dercon, A. Estache, J.W. Gunning, R. Kanbur, S. Klasen, S. Maxwell, J.-P. Platteau, and A. Spadaro. 2008. *Millennium Development Goals at Midpoint: Where do We Stand and Where do We need to go?* European Report on Development.

Bourguignon, F., A. Bénassy-Quéré, S. Dercon, A. Estache, J.W. Gunning, R. Kanbur, S. Klasen, S. Maxwell, J.-P. Platteau, and A. Spadaro. 2010. Millennium Development Goals: An Assessment. In R. Kanbur and M. Spence (eds.) *Equity and Growth in a Globalizing World*. Washington, DC: World Bank, Chapter 2.

Calderon, M.C. and M. Kovacevic. 2014. The 2014 Multidimensional Poverty Index: New Specification. Human Development Research Paper. New York: UNDP-HDRO.

Chakravarty, S.R. 2003. A Generalized Human Development Index. *Review of Development Economics*, 7: 99–114.

Chakravarty, S.R. 2011a. A Reconsideration of the Tradeoffs in the New Human Development Index. *Journal of Economic Inequality* 9: 471–474.

Chakravarty, S.R. 2011b. On Tradeoffs in the Human Development Indices. *Indian Journal of Human Development* 6: 1–25.

Chakravarty, S.R., Majumder, A. 1996. Achievement and Improvement in Living Standards. *Journal of Development Economics* 50: 189–195.

Chakravarty, S.R., Majumder, A. 2005. Measuring Human Poverty: A Generalized Index and an Application Using Basic Dimensions of Life and Some Anthropometric Indicators, *Journal of Human Development*, 6: 275–299.

Chakravarty, S.R. and A. Majumder. 2008. Millennium Development Goals: Measuring Progress towards their Achievement. *Journal of Human Development* 9: 109–129.

Chakravarty, S. and D. Mukherjee. 1999. Measuring Improvement in Well-being. *Keio Economic Studies* 36: 65–79.

Chatterjee, S.K. 2005. Measurement of Human Development: An Alternative Approach. *Journal of Human Development* 6: 31–44.

Cherchye, L., E. Ooghe, and T. van Puyenbroeck. 2008. Robust Human Development Rankings. *Journal of Economic Inequality* 6: 287–321.

Crafts, N. 1997. The Human Development Index and Changes in Standards of Living: Some Historical Comparisons. *European Review of Economic History* 1: 299–322.

Crafts, N. 2002. The Human Development Index, 1870-1999: Some Revised Estimates. *European Review of Economic History* 6: 395–405.

Dasgupta, P. 1993. *An Inquiry into Wellbeing and Destitution*. Oxford: Clarendon.

Dasgupta, P. and M. Weale. 1992. On Measuring the Quality of Life. *World Development*, 20: 119–131.

Decancq, K. 2015. Measuring Multidimensional Inequality in the OECD Member Countries with a Distribution-sensitive Better Life Index, ECINEQ WP 2015 – 386.

Desai, M. 1991. Human Development: Concept and Measurement. *European Economic Review* 35: 350–357.

Donaldson D. and J.A. Weymark.1980. A Single Parameter Generalization of the Gini indices of inequality. *Journal of Economic Theory* 22: 67–86.

Duclos, J.-Y. and L. Tiberti. 2016. Multidimensional Poverty Indices: A Critical Assessment. In M.D. Adler and M. Fleurbaey (eds.) (2016), 677–708.

Durand, M. 2015. The OECD Better Life Initiative: How's Life? and the Measurement of Well-Being. *Review of Income and Wealth* 61: 4–17.

Easterly, W. 2009. How the Millennium Development Goals are unfair to Africa. *World Development* 37: 26–35.

Esty, D.C., C. Kim, T. Srebotnjak, M.A. Levy, A. de Sherbinin, and V. Mara. 2008. *Environmental Performance Index. Yale Center for Environmental Law and Policy*. New Haven, CT: Yale University.

Ferreira, F.H.G. and V. Peragine. 2016. Individual Responsibility and Equality of Opportunity. In M.D. Adler and M. Fleurbaey (eds.), 746–784.

Foster, J.E., L.F. López-Calva, and M. Székely. 2005. Measuring the Distribution of Human Development: Methodology and an Application to Mexico. *Journal of Human Development and Capabilities* 6: 5–29.

Foster, J.E., M. McGillivray, and S. Seth. 2013. Composite Indices: Rank Robustness, Statistical Association and Redundancy. *Econometric Reviews* 22: 35–56.

Gormely, P.J. 1995. The Human Development Index in 1994: Impact of Income on Country Rank. *Journal of Economic and Social Measurement* 21: 253–267.

Grimm, M., K. Harttgen, S. Klasen, and M. Misseklhorn. 2008. A Human Development Index by Income Groups. *World Development* 36: 2527–2546.

Heritage Foundation. 2008. *Index of Economic Freedom*. Washington, D.C.: The Heritage Foundation.

Herrero, C., R. Martínez, and A. Villar. 2010. Multidimensional Social Evaluation. An Application to the Measurement of Human Development. *Review of Income and Wealth* 56: 483–497.

Herrero, C., R. Martínez, and A. Villar. 2012. A Newer Human Development Index. *Journal of Human Development and Capabilities* 13: 247–268.
Hicks, D.A. 1997. The Inequality-Adjusted Human Development Index: A Constructive Proposal. *World Development* 28: 1283–1298.
Hicks, D.A. and P. Streeten. 1979. Indicators of Development: The Search for a Basic Needs Yardstick. *World Development* 7: 567–580.
Hopkins, M. 1991. Human Development Revisited: A New UNDP Report. *World Development* 14: 1469–1473.
Hoskins, B., J. Jesinghaus, M. Mascherini, G. Munda, M. Nardo, M. Saisana, D. Van Nijlen, D. Vidoni, E. Villalba. 2006. *Measuring Active Citizenship in Europe* – EUR 22530 EN – Joint Research Center of the European Commission.
Høyland, B., K. Moene, and F. Willumsen. 2012. The Tranny of International Index Ranking. *Journal of Development Economics* 97: 1–14.
Kakwani, N.C. 1993. Performance in Living Standards: An International Comparison. *Journal of Development Economics* 41: 307–336.
Kasparian, J. and A. Rolland. 2012. OECD's 'Better Life Index': Can any Country be Well Ranked? *Journal of Applied Statistics* 393: 2223–2230.
Kelley, A.C. 1991. The Human Development Index: Handle with Care. *Population and Development Review* 17: 315–324.
Ki-Moon, Ban.2015. *The Millennium Development Goals Report*. New York: United Nations.
Klasen, S. and C. Dotter. 2014. The Multidimensional Poverty Index: Achievements, Conceptual, and Empirical Issues. *Human Development Research Paper*. New York: UNDP-HDRO, http://hdr.undp.org.
Klugman, J., F. Rodríguez, and H.-J. Choi. 2011. The HDI 2010: New Controversies, Old Critiques. *Journal of Economic Inequality* 9: 249–288.
Kolm, S.C. 1977. Multidimensional Egalitarianism. *Quarterly Journal of Economics* 91: 1–13.
Kovacevic, M. 2010. Measurement of Inequality in Human Development—A Review. Human Development Research Paper. New York: UNDP-HDRO, http://hdr.undp.org/en/content.
Lal, D. 2000. Temporal Analysis of Human Development Indicators: Principal Component Approach. *Social Indicators Research* 51: 331–366.
Markovic, M., S. Zdravkovic, M. Mitrovic, and A. Radojicic. 2015. An Iterative Multivariate Post Hoc I-Distance Approach in Evaluating OECD Better Life Index. *Social Indicators Research* 119: 1–19.
Mascherini, M. and B. Hoskins. 2008. *Retrieving the Expert Opinion on Weights for the Active Citizenship Composite Indicator*. European Commission.
McGillivray, M. 1991. The Human Development Index: Yet another Redundant Development Composite Indicator? *World Development* 19: 1461–1468.
McGillivray, M. and H. White. 1993. Measuring Development? The UNDP's Human Development Index. *Journal of International Development* 5: 183–192.

Mizobuchi, H. 2014. Measuring World Better Life Frontier: A Composite Indicator for OECD Better Life Index. *Social Indicators Research* 118: 987–1007.

Morris, D. 1979. *Measuring the Condition of the World Poor: The Physical Quality of Life Index*. New York: Pergamon.

Mueller, G. 2015. *The Green Economy Progress Index*. Brussels: UNEP.

Nardo, M., M. Saisana, A .Saltelli, S. Tarantola, A. Hoffman and E. Giovannini. 2005. *Handbook on Constructing Composite Indicators: Methodology and User Guide*. Paris: OECD Statistics.

Noorbakhsh, F. 1998, A Modified Human Development Index. *World Development* 26: 517–528.

Osberg, L. 1985. *The Measurement of Economic Well-being*. In D. Laidler (coordinator), *Approaches to Economic Well-Being*. Toronto: University of Toronto Press.

Osberg, L. and A. Sharpe. 2002. An Index of Economic Well-Being for Selected OECD Countries. *Review of Income and Wealth* 48: 291–316.

Paes de Barros, R., F.H.G. Ferreira, J.R. Vega Molinas, and J.S. Chanduvi. 2009. *Measuring Inequality of Opportunities in Latin America and Caribbean*. Washington, DC: World Bank.

Permanyer, I. 2013. The Measurement of Success in Achieving the Millennium Development Goals. *Journal of Economic Inequality* 11: 393–415.

Permanyer, I. 2016. Measuring Achievement and Shortfall Improvements in a Consistent Way. *Review of Income and Wealth* 62: 758–774.

Philipson, T. and R. Soares. 2001. *Human Capital, Longevity, and Economic Growth: A Quantitative Assessment of Full Income Measures*. University of Chicago.

Pinar, M., T. Stengos, and N. Topaloglou. 2013. Measuring Human Development: A Stochastic Dominance Approach. *Journal of Economic Growth* 18: 69–108.

Pogge, T. and S. Wisor. 2016. Measuring Poverty: A Proposal. In M.D. Adler and M. Fleurbaey (eds.), 645–676.

Prados de la Escosura, L. 2010. Improving Human Development: A Long-run View. *Journal of Economic Surveys* 24: 841–894.

Ram, R.M. 1982. Composite Indices of Physical Quality of Life, Basic Needs Fulfilment, and Income. A Principal Component Representation. *Journal of Development Economics* 11: 227–247.

Ranis, G., F. Stewart, and E. Samman. 2006. Human Development: Beyond the Human Development Index. *Journal of Human Development* 7: 323–358.

Ravallion, M. 1997. Good and Bad Growth: The Human Development Reports. *World Development* 25: 631–638.

Ravallion, M. 2011a. On Multidimensional Indices of Poverty', *Journal of Economic Inequality* 9: 235–248.

Ravallion, M. 2011b. The Human Development Index: A Response to Klugman, Rodriguez and Choi. *Journal of Economic Inequality* 9: 475–478.

Ravallion, M. 2012. Troubling Tradeoffs in the Human Development Index. *Journal of Development Economics* 99: 201–209.

Roemer, J.E. and A. Trannoy. 2015. Equality of Opportunity. In A.B. Atkinson and F. Bourguignon (eds.), Vol. 2A: 217–300.

Sagar, A. and A. Najam. 1998. The Human Development Index: A Critical Review. *Ecological Economics* 25: 249–264.

Sahn, D. and D. Stifel. 2003. Progress toward the Millennium Development Goals in Africa. *World Development* 31: 23–52.

Sen A.K. 1981. Public Action and the Quality of Life in Developing Countries. *Oxford Bulletin of Economics and Statistics* 43: 287–319.

Sen, A.K. 1992. *Inequality Reexamined*. New York: Clarendon Press.

Sen A.K. and S. Anand. 1997. Concepts of Human Development and Poverty: A Multidimensional Perspective. In: *Poverty and Human Development: Human Development Papers* 1997. New York: UNDP, 1-20. Reprinted in S. Fukuda-Parr and A.K. Shiva Kumar, (eds.) *Readings in Human Development* 2003. New Delhi: Oxford University Press.

Seth, R. 2009. Inequality, Interactions, and Human Development. *Journal of Human Development and Capabilities* 10: 375–396.

Silber, J. 2011. A Comment on the MPI Index. *Journal of Economic Inequality* 9: 479–481.

Srinivasan, T.N. 1994. Human Development : A New Paradigm or Reinvention of the Wheel? *American Economic Review Papers and Proceedings* 84: 238–243.

Stiglitz, J.E., A. Sen, and J.-P. Fitoussi. 2009. *Report by the Commission on the Measurement of Economic Performance and Social Progress*, www.stiglitz-sen-fitoussi.fr.

Streeten, P. 1994. Human Development: Means and Ends. *American Economic Review Papers and Proceedings* 84: 232–237.

Tsui, K.-Y. 1996. Improvement Indices of Well-being. *Social Choice and Welfare* 13: 291–303.

UNDP. 1990. *Human Development Report. United Nations Development Program*, New York: Oxford University Press.

UNDP. 1997. *Human Development Report. United Nations Development Program*, New York: Oxford University Press.

UNDP. 1999. *Human Development Report. United Nations Development Program*, New York: Oxford University Press.

UNDP. 2005. *Human Development Report 2005*. New York: UNDP.

UNDP. 2010. *Human Development Report. United Nations Development Program*, New York: Oxford University Press.

UNDP. 2015. *Human Development Report. United Nations Development Program*, New York: Oxford University Press.

US Environmental Protection Agency. 2013. *Technical Assistance Document for the Reporting of Daily Air Quality—the Air Quality Index*. North Carolina: U.S. Environmental Protection Agency Research Triangle Park.

Yalonetzky, G. 2012. A Dissimilarity Index of Multidimensional Index of Opportunity. *Journal of Economic Inequality* 10: 343–373.
Zambrano, E. 2014. An Axiomatization of the Human Development Index. *Social Choice and Welfare* 42: 853–872.
Zambrano, E. 2016. The Troubling Tradeoffs Paradox and a Resolution. *Review of Income and Wealth*. DOI: 10.1111/roiw.12235.
Zheng, B. and C. Zheng. 2015. Fuzzy Ranking of Human Development: A Proposal. *Mathematical Social Sciences* 78: 39–47.

Index

Analyzing Multidimensional Well-Being: A Quantitative Approach, First Edition. Satya R. Chakravarty.

g

h

i